matrix methods in urban and regional analysis

matrix methods in urban and regional analysis

ANDREI ROGERS
NORTHWESTERN UNIVERSITY

HOLDEN-DAY
SAN FRANCISCO

500 Sansome Street, San Francisco, California 94111

Library of Congress Catalog Card Number: 79-170636
ISBN: 0-8162-7275-1

Printed in the United States of America

2 3 4 5 6 7 8 9 0   MP   7 9 8 7 6 5 4 3

to maria

preface

In recent years, public policy has become increasingly concerned with the problems created by the changing character of the growth and development of our subnational areas. That mathematics is becoming an indispensable tool in the study of such problems is no longer a very controversial proposition. We have learned that mathematical methods are necessary both at the theoretical and at the applied levels. Theoretical models enable us to formulate problems more precisely and to gain insight into the inner workings of complex interdependent urban and regional systems. Applied models allow us to estimate the parameters and to obtain quantitative forecasts of the future performance of such systems.

The enthusiasm with which the growth of the mathematical approach has been received by planners, geographers, demographers, engineers, economists, sociologists, and others concerned with urban and regional problems is reflected in the wide range of opportunities available for persons trained in this specialty. The need for urban and regional researchers who have a competence in mathematical methods has led to the development of courses that focus on the mathematical analysis of urban and regional phenomena. This, in turn, has generated a need for texts and teaching materials that this book will help fulfill.

The incentive to write this book arose from my experience in teaching courses in urban and regional analysis at the University of California. In order to cover the field adequately, a wide range of topics had to be covered and students were referred of necessity to a variety of sources. These differed considerably in approach, in degree of difficulty, and in notation and terminology. Often the references were to unpublished materials, and occasionally the published references involved entries in more than a dozen books. Hence, the need for a single text with a unified presentation became apparent.

As I taught these courses, I realized that the topics in them did not just constitute a miscellaneous collection of unrelated techniques, but that they could be tied together in a logical way by means of matrix algebra. Moreover, I found that one could introduce applications in urban and regional analysis all along the way, and, by expressing a number of seemingly unrelated problems in matrix form, prove them to be structurally identical. Thus one could use simple matrix multiplication to develop a model of interregional or intraregional population growth and use the concept of the inverse matrix in interindustry analysis to solve the input-output model. Regression analysis could then be introduced in a succinct manner by drawing on the compact presentation afforded by matrix notation. Next, the inverse matrix could be generalized to include singular and rectangular matrices, and the corresponding solution method for rectangular linear equation systems could be used to introduce linear statistical models and linear programming. And linear programming could be used to introduce the theory of games and network flow theory, with its applications in traffic assignment and PERT. The analysis of stable states in demographic and economic models could proceed as an application of characteristic roots and characteristic vectors, and factor analysis could be presented as axis rotation in multidimensional space. Finally, because I have found that the material in this text cannot be satisfactorily taught without relying on the services of a digital computer, I have included a very brief appendix on FORTRAN programming of simple matrix operations. When complemented by any one of the myriad of texts on the FORTRAN language and supplemented by various "canned" matrix routines available at most computer centers, the material in the Appendix provides the student with a capability that is sufficient for the execution of the exercises. For those without access to a computer, I have also included problems that can be carried out with the aid of a desk calculator.

The basic prerequisite for comprehending most of the topics discussed in this book is high-school algebra. Computations are emphasized rather than formal proofs, and I have attempted, where possible, to maintain the mathematical presentation on a relatively informal level. Differential calculus is used only on a few pages, and these can be omitted without sacrificing a general understanding of the subject matter. In every chapter, the theoretical discussion is illustrated both with elementary numerical examples and with applications taken from urban and regional analysis. The computations in the numerical examples use fractions in order to avoid discrepancies arising from round-off errors. Those in sections describing applications, however, were carried out on a computer to twelve significant digits and then separately rounded to the number of digits shown in the text. I have tried to develop the applications using real data from different parts of the world whenever possible and to avoid hypothetical illustrations. All of the data used to carry out the computations are included in the text in order to allow the reader to test his own computer programs. Finally, exercises and references are included at the end of each chapter for further study. These are designed to test the student's comprehension of the material covered in each chapter and also to suggest extensions and generalizations of the arguments presented there.

The influences of many different people are reflected in this book. Among those to whom I am indebted are Robert M. Oliver of the University of California, whose course on network flows led to the development of Chapter 6 of this book, and to George Nicholson and F. Stuart Chapin, Jr., of the University of North Carolina, who pushed me into mathematical statistics early in my student days. I also have been stimulated by the work of Nathan Keyfitz in mathematical demography and by S. R. Searle's text on matrix methods in the biological sciences [Searle (1966)]. Finally, in writing this book I have benefited from the questions, criticisms, and general assistance of my students. In particular, Ronald Choy, Michael Fajans, Caj Falcke, and Pieter van den Steenhoven, in their roles as teaching assistants for my courses, at various times have computed solutions to numerical examples, identified errors, and provided suggestions for improving the quality of the exposition.

Many institutions have contributed, financially and otherwise, to the development of this text. I am indebted to the Institute of Transportation and Traffic Engineering at the University of California for financial support in 1966, during which time Chapter 6 was developed and subsequently published as a monograph. Parts of Chapters 1, 2, 4, and 7 were drafted during a sabbatical spent with the American-Yugoslav Project in Ljubljana, Yugoslavia, in 1967. I am grateful for the support provided by that project and to the Town Planning Institute of Slovenia for assembling the Yugoslavian population data that appear in different parts of this book. The demographic sections of this text also have benefited from the experience I gained while developing a population forecasting system for Brazil's Federal Department for Urbanism in Rio de Janeiro, where I spent six months as a member of a consulting team organized by the Planning and Development Collaborative International (PADCO) and supported by the U. S. Agency for International Development (USAID). Finally, I wish to thank the staffs of the Department of City and Regional Planning and the Center for Planning and Development Research at the University of California for their efforts to expedite the completion of the early drafts of this book, and to Laverne Marts for typing and retyping the final manuscript cheerfully and accurately.

Andrei Rogers
June 1970

contents

matrix methods in urban and regional analysis

one introduction to matrix analysis

Whenever it has seemed useful to do so, mathematicians have invented new kinds of numbers. They began with the set of *positive integers:* 1, 2, 3, ... Next, in order to define subtraction, this number system was extended to include zero and the *negative integers:* $-1, -2, -3, \ldots$. Then, in order to allow any number to be divided by any other nonzero number, mathematicians invented *rational numbers,* such as $\frac{1}{3}$, $-\frac{2}{5}$, and $\frac{127}{375}$. Subsequently, in order to be able to associate with every positive number a square root, a cube root, and so on, the number system was expanded to include indefinite decimals, or *irrational numbers,* such as $\pi = 3.14159\ldots$ and $e = 2.71828\ldots$. Finally, in order to define solutions for quadratic equations, such as

$$x^2 + 1 = 0$$

mathematicians invented *complex numbers,* such as $2 + i$, $-5 + 3i$, and $1 + 0i$.

In this text we shall be concerned with the algebra of one of the most recent and most successful new kinds of numbers: *matrices.* Matrices are currently being used in such diverse fields as statistics, economics, sociology, engineering, and atomic physics. In particular, matrix algebra provides a compact and elegant method for treating a wide array of important problems in urban and regional analysis. Formulating such problems in matrix form confers both a notational and an analytical advantage: (1) economy in notation often leads to insights that otherwise may have been obscured by a more complicated expression, and (2) a matrix formulation of a problem places at our disposal a large collection of theorems that have been proved about matrices. Occasionally, these two advantages interact to suggest important conclusions that otherwise might be very difficult to establish.

1.1 DEFINITIONS AND NOTATION

A *matrix* is a rectangular array of numbers arranged in rows and columns, as in

$$\mathbf{A} = \begin{bmatrix} a_{11} & a_{12} & \cdots & a_{1n} \\ a_{21} & a_{22} & \cdots & a_{2n} \\ \vdots & \vdots & \ddots & \vdots \\ a_{m1} & a_{m2} & \cdots & a_{mn} \end{bmatrix} \tag{1.1}$$

A matrix does not have a numerical value; it is simply a convenient way to represent tabular arrangements of numbers. These numbers are called the *elements* of the matrix and are represented by double-subscripted lower case letters. The two subscripts denote, respectively, the row and column position of the element in the rectangular arrangement. For example, a_{21} denotes the number that occupies the position in the second row and first column in the matrix **A**.

The matrix in (1.1) has m rows and n columns. It therefore may be said to be of order m by n (generally written as $m \times n$). Thus we may adopt the more compact form

$$\underset{m\times n}{\mathbf{A}} = [a_{ij}]_{m\times n} \tag{1.2}$$

Two matrices are equal if, and only if, they are of the same order and if their corresponding elements are equal. That is, $\mathbf{A}_{m\times n} = \mathbf{B}_{m\times n}$ if, and only if, $a_{ij} = b_{ij} (i = 1, 2, \ldots, m; j = 1, 2, \ldots, n)$.

The matrix

$$\underset{n\times m}{\mathbf{A}'} = \begin{bmatrix} a_{11} & a_{21} & \cdots & a_{m1} \\ a_{12} & a_{22} & \cdots & a_{m2} \\ \vdots & \vdots & \ddots & \vdots \\ a_{1n} & a_{2n} & \cdots & a_{mn} \end{bmatrix} \tag{1.3}$$

obtained by interchanging the rows and columns of **A**, is defined to be the *transpose* of **A**. Thus, if **A** is an $m \times n$ matrix, then the transpose of **A**, **A′**, say, is the $n \times m$ matrix **B** with $b_{ji} = a_{ij}$ for $i = 1, 2, \ldots, m$, and $j = 1, 2, \ldots, n$.

Examples. The transpose of the matrix

$$\underset{2\times 4}{\mathbf{A}} = \begin{bmatrix} 1 & 2 & 3 & 4 \\ 8 & 7 & 6 & 5 \end{bmatrix} \quad \text{is} \quad \underset{4\times 2}{\mathbf{A}'} = \begin{bmatrix} 1 & 8 \\ 2 & 7 \\ 3 & 6 \\ 4 & 5 \end{bmatrix}$$

and the transpose of the matrix

$$\underset{3\times 3}{\mathbf{B}} = \begin{bmatrix} \sqrt{2} & 0 & 2 \\ 1 & \sqrt{3} & \frac{1}{2} \\ 0 & 2 & \sqrt{4} \end{bmatrix} \quad \text{is} \quad \underset{3\times 3}{\mathbf{B}'} = \begin{bmatrix} \sqrt{2} & 1 & 0 \\ 0 & \sqrt{3} & 2 \\ 2 & \frac{1}{2} & \sqrt{4} \end{bmatrix}$$

A matrix with only a single column is called a *column vector* and will be denoted as

$$\underset{m\times 1}{\mathbf{a}} = \begin{bmatrix} a_1 \\ a_2 \\ \vdots \\ a_m \end{bmatrix} \tag{1.4}$$

Similarly, a matrix with only a single row is called a *row vector.* In consonance with the notation for a transposed matrix, these will be denoted by

$$\underset{1\times n}{\mathbf{a}'} = [a_1 \quad a_2 \quad \cdots \quad a_n] \tag{1.5}$$

A matrix with only a single row and a single column contains only one element and is simply a number or *scalar.*

Using the definition of column and row vectors, we may rewrite the matrix $\mathbf{A}$ as a set of n column vectors:

$$\underset{m\times n}{\mathbf{A}} = [\mathbf{a}_1 \quad \mathbf{a}_2 \quad \cdots \quad \mathbf{a}_n] \tag{1.6}$$

or, alternatively, as a set of m row vectors:

$$\underset{m\times n}{\mathbf{A}} = \begin{bmatrix} \mathbf{a}_1' \\ \mathbf{a}_2' \\ \vdots \\ \mathbf{a}_m' \end{bmatrix} \tag{1.7}$$

Examples. The two matrices in the above numerical examples may be expressed, respectively, as

$$\mathbf{A} = \begin{bmatrix} \mathbf{a}_1' \\ \mathbf{a}_2' \end{bmatrix} \quad \text{and} \quad \mathbf{B} = [\mathbf{b}_1 \quad \mathbf{b}_2 \quad \mathbf{b}_3]$$

where

$$\mathbf{a}_1' = [1 \quad 2 \quad 3 \quad 4] \qquad \mathbf{a}_2' = [8 \quad 7 \quad 6 \quad 5]$$

and

$$\mathbf{b}_1 = \begin{bmatrix} \sqrt{2} \\ 1 \\ 0 \end{bmatrix} \qquad \mathbf{b}_2 = \begin{bmatrix} 0 \\ \sqrt{3} \\ 2 \end{bmatrix} \qquad \mathbf{b}_3 = \begin{bmatrix} 2 \\ \frac{1}{2} \\ \sqrt{4} \end{bmatrix}$$

1.2 SIMPLE MATRIX OPERATIONS

The operations of addition, subtraction, and multiplication of ordinary algebra may be carried over to matrices with slight modification. The matrix analogue of division, however, is considerably more complicated. Its description, therefore, will be postponed until the next chapter.

1.2.1 MATRIX ADDITION

Matrix addition is only defined for matrices that are of the same order. Such matrices are said to be *conformable for addition.* Each element of their sum is formed by adding the elements in the corresponding positions in the matrices to be summed. Thus if

$$\underset{m\times n}{\mathbf{A}} = \begin{bmatrix} a_{11} & a_{12} & \cdots & a_{1n} \\ a_{21} & a_{22} & \cdots & a_{2n} \\ \vdots & \vdots & \ddots & \vdots \\ a_{m1} & a_{m2} & \cdots & a_{mn} \end{bmatrix}$$

and

$$\underset{m\times n}{\mathbf{B}} = \begin{bmatrix} b_{11} & b_{12} & \cdots & b_{1n} \\ b_{21} & b_{22} & \cdots & b_{2n} \\ \vdots & \vdots & \ddots & \vdots \\ b_{m1} & b_{m2} & \cdots & b_{mn} \end{bmatrix}$$

then

$$\underset{m\times n}{\mathbf{C}} = \underset{m\times n}{\mathbf{A}} + \underset{m\times n}{\mathbf{B}} = \begin{bmatrix} a_{11} + b_{11} & a_{12} + b_{12} & \cdots & a_{1n} + b_{1n} \\ a_{21} + b_{21} & a_{22} + b_{22} & \cdots & a_{2n} + b_{2n} \\ \vdots & \vdots & \ddots & \vdots \\ a_{m1} + b_{m1} & a_{m2} + b_{m2} & \cdots & a_{mn} + b_{mn} \end{bmatrix} \tag{1.8}$$

or, more compactly,

$$\underset{m\times n}{\mathbf{C}} = [c_{ij}]_{m\times n} = [a_{ij} + b_{ij}]_{m\times n} \tag{1.9}$$

It is evident from the above definition that matrix addition is *commutative* and *associative*, that is,

$$\mathbf{A} + \mathbf{B} = \mathbf{B} + \mathbf{A}$$

and

$$(\mathbf{A} + \mathbf{B}) + \mathbf{D} = \mathbf{A} + (\mathbf{B} + \mathbf{D})$$

Also, it is easily demonstrated that the transpose of a sum is the sum of the individual transposes:

$$(\mathbf{A} + \mathbf{B})' = \mathbf{A}' + \mathbf{B}'$$

1.2.2 MATRIX SUBTRACTION

Matrix subtraction is defined in a manner exactly analogous to that of matrix addition. We first designate by $-\mathbf{A}$ the matrix in which every element is the negative of the corresponding element in $\mathbf{A}$ and then proceed as in addition. Thus if

$$\mathbf{A} = [a_{ij}]_{m\times n} \qquad \text{and} \qquad \mathbf{B} = [b_{ij}]_{m\times n}$$

then $-\mathbf{B} = [-b_{ij}]_{m\times n}$, and

$$\mathbf{D} = [d_{ij}]_{m\times n} = \mathbf{A} - \mathbf{B} = [a_{ij} - b_{ij}]_{m\times n} \tag{1.10}$$

1.2.3 SCALAR MULTIPLICATION

As in ordinary algebra, multiplication by a number or *scalar* may be viewed as the addition or subtraction of several identical quantities. For example, the sum of two equal matrices may be obtained by multiplying every element of one of the matrices by two. Generalizing this, we may define the multiplication of a matrix $\mathbf{A}$ by a scalar c to be

$$\underset{m\times n}{c\mathbf{A}} = [ca_{ij}]_{m\times n} \tag{1.11}$$

Since scalar multiplication may be expressed in terms of addition and subtraction of matrices, it also must possess their commutative and distributive properties. Thus

$$c\mathbf{A} = \mathbf{A}c$$

and

$$c(\mathbf{A} + \mathbf{B}) = c\mathbf{A} + c\mathbf{B}$$

Examples. The two matrices

$$\mathbf{A} = \begin{bmatrix} 2 & 0 & 7 \\ 4 & 1 & 3 \end{bmatrix} \qquad \mathbf{B} = \begin{bmatrix} 4 & 3 & 5 \\ 0 & 0 & 4 \end{bmatrix}$$

may be added to form the sum

$$\mathbf{C} = \mathbf{A} + \mathbf{B} = \begin{bmatrix} 6 & 3 & 12 \\ 4 & 1 & 7 \end{bmatrix}$$

Their difference is

$$\mathbf{D} = \mathbf{A} - \mathbf{B} = \begin{bmatrix} -2 & -3 & 2 \\ 4 & 1 & -1 \end{bmatrix}$$

and the difference of a particular weighted combination of **A** and **B** is, for example,

$$\begin{aligned} \mathbf{E} &= 3\mathbf{A} - 2\mathbf{B} \\ &= \begin{bmatrix} 6 & 0 & 21 \\ 12 & 3 & 9 \end{bmatrix} - \begin{bmatrix} 8 & 6 & 10 \\ 0 & 0 & 8 \end{bmatrix} = \begin{bmatrix} -2 & -6 & 11 \\ 12 & 3 & 1 \end{bmatrix} \end{aligned}$$

1.2.4 MATRIX MULTIPLICATION

One might choose to define the multiplication of two matrices in a number of different ways, such as simply multiplying the corresponding elements of the two matrices. It turns out, however, that such a definition does not lead to practically useful results. Matrices have been used a great deal in problems involving simultaneous linear equations and linear transformations. As a result, matrix multiplication has been defined so as to facilitate such operations. Consider, for example, the two simultaneous equations

$$\begin{aligned} 3x_1 + 5x_2 &= 15 \\ 2x_1 + 4x_2 &= 8 \end{aligned} \tag{1.12}$$

We may express these two equations more compactly in matrix form, as follows:

$$\begin{bmatrix} 3 & 5 \\ 2 & 4 \end{bmatrix} \begin{bmatrix} x_1 \\ x_2 \end{bmatrix} = \begin{bmatrix} 15 \\ 8 \end{bmatrix} \tag{1.13}$$

The economy of notation, of course, increases with the order of the matrix. However, for (1.12) and (1.13) to be equivalent expressions, we need to adopt a definition of matrix multiplication that equates the left-hand sides of both equations. The following definition satisfies this requirement. If

$$\underset{m \times n}{\mathbf{A}} = \begin{bmatrix} a_{11} & a_{12} & \cdots & a_{1n} \\ a_{21} & a_{22} & \cdots & a_{2n} \\ \vdots & \vdots & \ddots & \vdots \\ a_{m1} & a_{m2} & \cdots & a_{mn} \end{bmatrix}$$

and

$$\underset{n \times p}{\mathbf{B}} = \begin{bmatrix} b_{11} & b_{12} & \cdots & b_{1p} \\ b_{21} & b_{22} & \cdots & b_{2p} \\ \vdots & \vdots & \ddots & \vdots \\ b_{n1} & b_{n2} & \cdots & b_{np} \end{bmatrix}$$

then

$$\underset{m \times p}{\mathbf{C}} = \underset{m \times n}{\mathbf{A}}\ \underset{n \times p}{\mathbf{B}} = \begin{bmatrix} c_{11} & c_{12} & \cdots & c_{1p} \\ c_{21} & c_{22} & \cdots & c_{2p} \\ \vdots & \vdots & \ddots & \vdots \\ c_{m1} & c_{m2} & \cdots & c_{mp} \end{bmatrix} \tag{1.14}$$

where

$$c_{ij} = \sum_{k=1}^{n} a_{ik}b_{kj} = a_{i1}b_{1j} + a_{i2}b_{2j} + \cdots + a_{in}b_{nj}$$

The element in the ith row and jth column of the matrix product of **A** and **B**, that is, c_{ij}, is formed by multiplying the elements of the ith row of **A** (the *premultiplier*) by the corresponding elements in the jth column of **B** (the *postmultiplier*), and adding. This leads to the following two important observations:

(i) Matrix multiplication is defined only for matrices that are *conformable for multiplication.* Two matrices are said to be conformable for multiplication if the number of columns in the first is equal to the number of rows in the second.

(ii) The matrix product of two matrices that are conformable for multiplication will always have as many rows as the first and as many columns as the second.

Both of the above observations may be represented schematically as

$$[m \times n][n \times p] = [m \times p]$$

↑ ↑ (i)

↖ ↗ (ii)

Unlike multiplication in ordinary algebra, matrix multiplication is not commutative in most instances. That is,

$$\mathbf{AB} \neq \mathbf{BA}$$

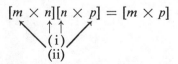

Indeed, frequently the reverse multiplication is undefined. This may be seen by reversing the matrices in (1.14). Thus

$$[n \times p][m \times n]$$

and the multiplication cannot be performed since the two matrices are not conformable for multiplication. If $p = m$, the multiplication is defined; however, the matrix product has a dimension of $n \times n$ instead of the previous $m \times m$. And if $m = n$, then we satisfy a necessary condition for two matrices to be commutative, but we do not have a sufficient condition. This will be illustrated in the examples that follow.

It may be readily determined that the associative and distributive laws hold for matrix multiplication. That is,

$$(\mathbf{AB})\mathbf{C} = \mathbf{A}(\mathbf{BC})$$

$$\mathbf{A}(\mathbf{B} + \mathbf{C}) = \mathbf{AB} + \mathbf{AC}$$

and

$$(\mathbf{A} + \mathbf{B})\mathbf{C} = \mathbf{AC} + \mathbf{BC}$$

Finally, the following not intuitively obvious result may be established for the transpose of a matrix product:

$$(\mathbf{AB})' = \mathbf{B}'\mathbf{A}'$$

Examples.

(i) $$\begin{bmatrix} 3 & 5 \\ 2 & 4 \end{bmatrix} \begin{bmatrix} 10 \\ -3 \end{bmatrix} = \begin{bmatrix} 3(10) + 5(-3) \\ 2(10) + 4(-3) \end{bmatrix} = \begin{bmatrix} 15 \\ 8 \end{bmatrix}$$

(ii) $$\begin{bmatrix} 1 & 3 & 2 \\ 0 & 1 & 4 \end{bmatrix} \begin{bmatrix} 2 & 3 \\ 5 & 0 \\ 0 & 1 \end{bmatrix}$$

$$= \begin{bmatrix} 1(2) + 3(5) + 2(0) & 1(3) + 3(0) + 2(1) \\ 0(2) + 1(5) + 4(0) & 0(3) + 1(0) + 4(1) \end{bmatrix} = \begin{bmatrix} 17 & 5 \\ 5 & 4 \end{bmatrix}$$

(iii) $$\begin{bmatrix} 2 & 5 \\ 3 & 4 \end{bmatrix} \begin{bmatrix} 1 & 6 \\ 0 & 3 \end{bmatrix}$$

$$= \begin{bmatrix} 2(1) + 5(0) & 2(6) + 5(3) \\ 3(1) + 4(0) & 3(6) + 4(3) \end{bmatrix} = \begin{bmatrix} 2 & 27 \\ 3 & 30 \end{bmatrix}$$

(iv) $$\begin{bmatrix} 1 & 6 \\ 0 & 3 \end{bmatrix} \begin{bmatrix} 2 & 5 \\ 3 & 4 \end{bmatrix}$$

$$= \begin{bmatrix} 1(2) + 6(3) & 1(5) + 6(4) \\ 0(2) + 3(3) & 0(5) + 3(4) \end{bmatrix} = \begin{bmatrix} 20 & 29 \\ 9 & 12 \end{bmatrix}$$

(v) $$\begin{bmatrix} 1 & 3 \\ 2 & 6 \end{bmatrix} \begin{bmatrix} 3 & 6 \\ -1 & -2 \end{bmatrix}$$

$$= \begin{bmatrix} 1(3) + 3(-1) & 1(6) + 3(-2) \\ 2(3) + 6(-1) & 2(6) + 6(-2) \end{bmatrix} = \begin{bmatrix} 0 & 0 \\ 0 & 0 \end{bmatrix}$$

(vi) $$[2 \quad 1 \quad 3] \begin{bmatrix} 2 \\ 1 \\ 3 \end{bmatrix} = [2^2 + 1^2 + 3^2] = 14$$

(vii) $$\begin{bmatrix} 2 \\ 1 \\ 3 \end{bmatrix} [2 \quad 1 \quad 3] = \begin{bmatrix} 2(2) & 2(1) & 2(3) \\ 1(2) & 1(1) & 1(3) \\ 3(2) & 3(1) & 3(3) \end{bmatrix} = \begin{bmatrix} 4 & 2 & 6 \\ 2 & 1 & 3 \\ 6 & 3 & 9 \end{bmatrix}$$

1.3 SPECIAL MATRICES

Many special types of matrices occur repeatedly in matrix analysis and accordingly have received special names. A *square* matrix is one in which the number of rows equals the number of columns. Such a matrix is called an "mth-order" matrix, and the elements beginning from the upper left corner and proceeding in a diagonal direction to the lower right corner (that is, $a_{11}, a_{22}, \ldots, a_{mm}$) constitute its *principal diagonal.* Those immediately below the principal diagonal are said to be in the *principal subdiagonal.* The sum of the elements along the principal diagonal of a square matrix is called the *trace* of that matrix.

A *symmetric* matrix is a square matrix that is equal to its transpose, as, for example,

$$\begin{bmatrix} 3 & 1 & 2 \\ 1 & 5 & 4 \\ 2 & 4 & 6 \end{bmatrix}$$

A *triangular* matrix is a square matrix with all of its elements below or above the principal diagonal equal to zero. If the zero elements are below the principal diagonal, the matrix is said to be in *upper triangular form*; if all elements above the principal diagonal are zero, the matrix is in *lower triangular form,* for example,

$$\mathbf{A} = \begin{bmatrix} a_{11} & a_{12} & \cdots & a_{1m} \\ 0 & a_{22} & \cdots & a_{2m} \\ \vdots & \vdots & \ddots & \vdots \\ 0 & \cdots & 0 & a_{mm} \end{bmatrix} \qquad \mathbf{B} = \begin{bmatrix} b_{11} & 0 & \cdots & 0 \\ b_{21} & b_{22} & \cdots & \vdots \\ \vdots & \vdots & \ddots & 0 \\ b_{m1} & b_{m2} & \cdots & b_{mm} \end{bmatrix}$$

A *zero* or *null* matrix is one in which all elements are zero. It fulfills a purpose in matrix algebra analogous to that served by zero in ordinary algebra and is denoted by **0**.

A *diagonal* matrix is a square matrix with all elements, except those on the principal diagonal, equal to zero. A *scalar* matrix is a diagonal matrix with all elements on the principal diagonal equal to the same scalar quantity. If this scalar is unity, the matrix is called the *identity* matrix and is denoted by **I**. It serves a purpose in matrix algebra analogous to that of the number one in scalar algebra. Examples of diagonal, scalar, and identity matrices, respectively, are

$$\begin{bmatrix} 3 & 0 & 0 \\ 0 & 4 & 0 \\ 0 & 0 & 2 \end{bmatrix} \qquad \begin{bmatrix} 5 & 0 & 0 \\ 0 & 5 & 0 \\ 0 & 0 & 5 \end{bmatrix} \qquad \begin{bmatrix} 1 & 0 & 0 \\ 0 & 1 & 0 \\ 0 & 0 & 1 \end{bmatrix}$$

From the above definitions, it may be observed that premultiplication by a diagonal matrix is equivalent to multiplying the elements of each row of the premultiplied matrix by the scalar in that row of the diagonal matrix. Postmultiplication by a diagonal matrix, on the other hand, results in the multiplication of the elements of each column in the postmultiplied matrix by the scalar in that column of the diagonal matrix. It should be clear that multiplication by the identity matrix does not alter the matrix that is multiplied:

$$\underset{m\times m}{\mathbf{A}}\;\underset{m\times m}{\mathbf{I}} = \underset{m\times m}{\mathbf{I}}\;\underset{m\times m}{\mathbf{A}} = \underset{m\times m}{\mathbf{A}}$$

Frequently it is necessary or expedient to deal with submatrices of a large matrix. In such situations, the large matrix may be *partitioned* into several smaller matrices, and dashed lines may be introduced to indicate the particular partitioning scheme that is adopted. For example,

$$\underset{4\times 5}{\mathbf{A}} = \left[\begin{array}{ccc:cc} a_{11} & a_{12} & a_{13} & a_{14} & a_{15} \\ a_{21} & a_{22} & a_{23} & a_{24} & a_{25} \\ \hdashline a_{31} & a_{32} & a_{33} & a_{34} & a_{35} \\ a_{41} & a_{42} & a_{43} & a_{44} & a_{45} \end{array}\right] = \left[\begin{array}{c:c} \underset{2\times 3}{\mathbf{A}_{11}} & \underset{2\times 2}{\mathbf{A}_{12}} \\ \hdashline \underset{2\times 3}{\mathbf{A}_{21}} & \underset{2\times 2}{\mathbf{A}_{22}} \end{array}\right]$$

Partitioning lines always run across the entire matrix, and partitioned matrices may be added, subtracted, or multiplied, provided they are appropriately partitioned, that is, conformably. Thus, for example, we may postmultiply the above partitioned matrix **A** by the partitioned matrix

$$\underset{5\times3}{\mathbf{B}} = \left[\begin{array}{cc:c} b_{11} & b_{12} & b_{13} \\ b_{21} & b_{22} & b_{23} \\ b_{31} & b_{32} & b_{33} \\ \hdashline b_{41} & b_{42} & b_{43} \\ b_{51} & b_{52} & b_{53} \end{array}\right] = \left[\begin{array}{c:c} \underset{3\times2}{\mathbf{B}_{11}} & \underset{3\times1}{\mathbf{B}_{12}} \\ \hdashline \underset{2\times2}{\mathbf{B}_{21}} & \underset{2\times1}{\mathbf{B}_{22}} \end{array}\right]$$

to form the partitioned matrix

$$\underset{4\times3}{\mathbf{C}} = \underset{4\times5}{\mathbf{A}}\ \underset{5\times3}{\mathbf{B}} = \left[\begin{array}{c:c} \underset{2\times3}{\mathbf{A}_{11}} & \underset{2\times2}{\mathbf{A}_{12}} \\ \hdashline \underset{2\times3}{\mathbf{A}_{21}} & \underset{2\times2}{\mathbf{A}_{22}} \end{array}\right] \left[\begin{array}{c:c} \underset{3\times2}{\mathbf{B}_{11}} & \underset{3\times1}{\mathbf{B}_{12}} \\ \hdashline \underset{2\times2}{\mathbf{B}_{21}} & \underset{2\times1}{\mathbf{B}_{22}} \end{array}\right]$$

$$= \left[\begin{array}{c:c} \underset{2\times3}{\mathbf{A}_{11}}\underset{3\times2}{\mathbf{B}_{11}} + \underset{2\times2}{\mathbf{A}_{12}}\underset{2\times2}{\mathbf{B}_{21}} & \underset{2\times3}{\mathbf{A}_{11}}\underset{3\times1}{\mathbf{B}_{12}} + \underset{2\times2}{\mathbf{A}_{12}}\underset{2\times1}{\mathbf{B}_{22}} \\ \hdashline \underset{2\times3}{\mathbf{A}_{21}}\underset{3\times2}{\mathbf{B}_{11}} + \underset{2\times2}{\mathbf{A}_{22}}\underset{2\times2}{\mathbf{B}_{21}} & \underset{2\times3}{\mathbf{A}_{21}}\underset{3\times1}{\mathbf{B}_{12}} + \underset{2\times2}{\mathbf{A}_{22}}\underset{2\times1}{\mathbf{B}_{22}} \end{array}\right] = \left[\begin{array}{c:c} \underset{2\times2}{\mathbf{C}_{11}} & \underset{2\times1}{\mathbf{C}_{12}} \\ \hdashline \underset{2\times2}{\mathbf{C}_{21}} & \underset{2\times1}{\mathbf{C}_{22}} \end{array}\right]$$

Example. Consider the two matrices

$$\mathbf{A} = \begin{bmatrix} 1 & 3 & 2 & 0 & 3 \\ 4 & 2 & 5 & 1 & 7 \\ 6 & 0 & 7 & 3 & 2 \\ 2 & 1 & 5 & 1 & 8 \end{bmatrix} \quad \text{and} \quad \mathbf{B} = \begin{bmatrix} 1 & 4 & 2 \\ 6 & 5 & 3 \\ 5 & 1 & 0 \\ 0 & 1 & 3 \\ 3 & 4 & 7 \end{bmatrix}$$

On defining

$$\mathbf{A}_{11} = \begin{bmatrix} 1 & 3 & 2 \\ 4 & 2 & 5 \end{bmatrix} \qquad \mathbf{A}_{12} = \begin{bmatrix} 0 & 3 \\ 1 & 7 \end{bmatrix}$$

$$\mathbf{A}_{21} = \begin{bmatrix} 6 & 0 & 7 \\ 2 & 1 & 5 \end{bmatrix} \qquad \mathbf{A}_{22} = \begin{bmatrix} 3 & 2 \\ 1 & 8 \end{bmatrix}$$

and

$$\mathbf{B}_{11} = \begin{bmatrix} 1 & 4 \\ 6 & 5 \\ 5 & 1 \end{bmatrix} \qquad \mathbf{B}_{12} = \begin{bmatrix} 2 \\ 3 \\ 0 \end{bmatrix}$$

$$\mathbf{B}_{21} = \begin{bmatrix} 0 & 1 \\ 3 & 4 \end{bmatrix} \qquad \mathbf{B}_{22} = \begin{bmatrix} 3 \\ 7 \end{bmatrix}$$

we may express the product matrix $\mathbf{C} = \mathbf{AB}$ in partitioned form and compute its numerical value. Thus

$$\mathbf{C} = \left[\begin{array}{c:c} \mathbf{A}_{11}\mathbf{B}_{11} + \mathbf{A}_{12}\mathbf{B}_{21} & \mathbf{A}_{11}\mathbf{B}_{12} + \mathbf{A}_{12}\mathbf{B}_{22} \\ \hdashline \mathbf{A}_{21}\mathbf{B}_{11} + \mathbf{A}_{22}\mathbf{B}_{21} & \mathbf{A}_{21}\mathbf{B}_{12} + \mathbf{A}_{22}\mathbf{B}_{22} \end{array}\right] = \left[\begin{array}{c:c} \mathbf{C}_{11} & \mathbf{C}_{12} \\ \hdashline \mathbf{C}_{21} & \mathbf{C}_{22} \end{array}\right]$$

$$= \left[\begin{array}{c:c} \begin{bmatrix} 29 & 21 \\ 41 & 31 \end{bmatrix} + \begin{bmatrix} 9 & 12 \\ 21 & 29 \end{bmatrix} & \begin{bmatrix} 11 \\ 14 \end{bmatrix} + \begin{bmatrix} 21 \\ 52 \end{bmatrix} \\ \hdashline \begin{bmatrix} 41 & 31 \\ 33 & 18 \end{bmatrix} + \begin{bmatrix} 6 & 11 \\ 24 & 33 \end{bmatrix} & \begin{bmatrix} 12 \\ 7 \end{bmatrix} + \begin{bmatrix} 23 \\ 59 \end{bmatrix} \end{array}\right] = \left[\begin{array}{cc:c} 38 & 33 & 32 \\ 62 & 60 & 66 \\ \hdashline 47 & 42 & 35 \\ 57 & 51 & 66 \end{array}\right]$$

1.4 ELEMENTARY TRANSFORMATIONS

Consider, once again, the following system of two linear equations in two unknowns:

$$3x_1 + 5x_2 = 15$$
$$2x_1 + 4x_2 = 8$$

To solve this system using elementary scalar algebra, we may begin by dividing the second equation by two:

$$3x_1 + 5x_2 = 15$$
$$x_1 + 2x_2 = 4$$

and then, by interchanging the two equations, obtain

$$x_1 + 2x_2 = 4$$
$$3x_1 + 5x_2 = 15$$

Next, we may subtract the first equation three times (or three times the first equation) from the second equation,

$$x_1 + 2x_2 = 4$$
$$0 - x_2 = 3$$

and add two times the second equation to the first:

$$x_1 + 0 = 10$$
$$0 - x_2 = 3$$

Finally, we may multiply the second equation by minus one to find the solution

$$x_1 + 0 = 10$$
$$0 + x_2 = -3$$

or

$$x_1 = 10$$
$$x_2 = -3$$

Three fundamental operations were used in the above computations:

1. multiplication of an equation by a nonzero number (division may be viewed as multiplication by a fraction);
2. interchange of two equations; and
3. addition of a multiple of an equation to another equation (subtraction may be expressed as negative addition).

Since linear equation systems may be expressed in matrix form, it is not surprising that the foregoing operations can also be carried out by means of matrix algebra, using analogous matrix operations called *elementary row transformations*:

1. multiplication of all elements of a row of a matrix by a nonzero number;
2. interchange of any two rows of a matrix; and
3. addition of a multiple of any row of a matrix to any other row of the same matrix.

Elementary row transformations may be performed by means of matrix multiplication. They are carried out by multiplying the matrix to be transformed by a suitably constructed *elementary matrix*. An elementary matrix is any square matrix formed by performing a single elementary transformation on the identity matrix. Thus the multiplication, or *scaling*, of the elements of any row of a matrix is accomplished by premultiplying the matrix to be scaled with the elementary matrix that is obtained by scaling the same row in the identity matrix. For example,

$$\begin{bmatrix} 1 & 0 \\ 0 & \frac{1}{2} \end{bmatrix} \begin{bmatrix} 3 & 5 \\ 2 & 4 \end{bmatrix} = \begin{bmatrix} 3 & 5 \\ 1 & 2 \end{bmatrix}$$

Similarly, the interchange of two rows of a matrix may be effected by premultiplying the matrix to be transformed with the elementary matrix that is obtained by the interchange of the same two rows in the identity matrix. Thus,

$$\begin{bmatrix} 0 & 1 \\ 1 & 0 \end{bmatrix} \begin{bmatrix} 3 & 5 \\ 1 & 2 \end{bmatrix} = \begin{bmatrix} 1 & 2 \\ 3 & 5 \end{bmatrix}$$

Finally, the addition of a multiple of any row of a matrix to any other row of the same matrix may be carried out by premultiplying the matrix with the elementary matrix that is obtained by the addition of the identical multiple of the same row in the identity matrix. For example,

$$\begin{bmatrix} 1 & 0 \\ -3 & 1 \end{bmatrix} \begin{bmatrix} 1 & 2 \\ 3 & 5 \end{bmatrix} = \begin{bmatrix} 1 & 2 \\ 0 & -1 \end{bmatrix}$$

Observe that *elementary column transformations* may be carried out by postmultiplication with elementary matrices formed in an analogous manner, that is, by transforming the identity matrix in the same way as we wish to transform the original matrix. Also note that several elementary transformations can be carried out in a single multiplication by the application of a *transformation matrix* that is equal to the product, in the correct sequence, of the appropriate individual elementary matrices. Thus,

$$\begin{bmatrix} 1 & 0 \\ -3 & 1 \end{bmatrix} \begin{bmatrix} 0 & 1 \\ 1 & 0 \end{bmatrix} \begin{bmatrix} 1 & 0 \\ 0 & \frac{1}{2} \end{bmatrix} = \begin{bmatrix} 0 & \frac{1}{2} \\ 1 & -\frac{3}{2} \end{bmatrix}$$

and

$$\begin{bmatrix} 0 & \frac{1}{2} \\ 1 & -\frac{3}{2} \end{bmatrix} \begin{bmatrix} 3 & 5 \\ 2 & 4 \end{bmatrix} = \begin{bmatrix} 1 & 2 \\ 0 & -1 \end{bmatrix}$$

Elementary transformations carried out by elementary matrices may be reversed, or "undone," by the application of elementary matrices that are reciprocals, or *inverses*, of the original elementary matrices. These inverse matrices are formed in exactly analogous ways as the original elementary matrices, but now the modification of the identity matrix is exactly opposite to the original modification. For example, the inverse of the elementary matrix

$$\begin{bmatrix} 1 & 0 \\ 0 & \frac{1}{2} \end{bmatrix}$$

is the elementary matrix

$$\begin{bmatrix} 1 & 0 \\ 0 & 2 \end{bmatrix}$$

Notice that it restores the earlier transformed matrix back to its untransformed state:

$$\begin{bmatrix} 1 & 0 \\ 0 & 2 \end{bmatrix} \begin{bmatrix} 3 & 5 \\ 1 & 2 \end{bmatrix} = \begin{bmatrix} 3 & 5 \\ 2 & 4 \end{bmatrix}$$

Consequently, the product of an elementary matrix and its inverse always is the identity matrix. For example,

$$\begin{bmatrix} 1 & 0 \\ 0 & \frac{1}{2} \end{bmatrix} \begin{bmatrix} 1 & 0 \\ 0 & 2 \end{bmatrix} = \begin{bmatrix} 1 & 0 \\ 0 & 1 \end{bmatrix}$$

In conclusion, let us outline the complete sequence of elementary transformations that will reduce, to an identity matrix, the coefficient matrix of the linear system

$$\begin{bmatrix} 3 & 5 \\ 2 & 4 \end{bmatrix} \begin{bmatrix} x_1 \\ x_2 \end{bmatrix} = \begin{bmatrix} 15 \\ 8 \end{bmatrix} \tag{1.15}$$

Along with each elementary transformation, we also include its inverse.

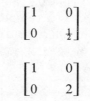

Elementary Transformation	Inverse Transformation
$\begin{bmatrix} 1 & 0 \\ 0 & \frac{1}{2} \end{bmatrix}\begin{bmatrix} 3 & 5 \\ 2 & 4 \end{bmatrix}=\begin{bmatrix} 3 & 5 \\ 1 & 2 \end{bmatrix}$	$\begin{bmatrix} 1 & 0 \\ 0 & 2 \end{bmatrix}\begin{bmatrix} 3 & 5 \\ 1 & 2 \end{bmatrix}=\begin{bmatrix} 3 & 5 \\ 2 & 4 \end{bmatrix}$
$\begin{bmatrix} 0 & 1 \\ 1 & 0 \end{bmatrix}\begin{bmatrix} 3 & 5 \\ 1 & 2 \end{bmatrix}=\begin{bmatrix} 1 & 2 \\ 3 & 5 \end{bmatrix}$	$\begin{bmatrix} 0 & 1 \\ 1 & 0 \end{bmatrix}\begin{bmatrix} 1 & 2 \\ 3 & 5 \end{bmatrix}=\begin{bmatrix} 3 & 5 \\ 1 & 2 \end{bmatrix}$
$\begin{bmatrix} 1 & 0 \\ -3 & 1 \end{bmatrix}\begin{bmatrix} 1 & 2 \\ 3 & 5 \end{bmatrix}=\begin{bmatrix} 1 & 2 \\ 0 & -1 \end{bmatrix}$	$\begin{bmatrix} 1 & 0 \\ 3 & 1 \end{bmatrix}\begin{bmatrix} 1 & 2 \\ 0 & -1 \end{bmatrix}=\begin{bmatrix} 1 & 2 \\ 3 & 5 \end{bmatrix}$
$\begin{bmatrix} 1 & 2 \\ 0 & 1 \end{bmatrix}\begin{bmatrix} 1 & 2 \\ 0 & -1 \end{bmatrix}=\begin{bmatrix} 1 & 0 \\ 0 & -1 \end{bmatrix}$	$\begin{bmatrix} 1 & -2 \\ 0 & 1 \end{bmatrix}\begin{bmatrix} 1 & 0 \\ 0 & -1 \end{bmatrix}=\begin{bmatrix} 1 & 2 \\ 0 & -1 \end{bmatrix}$
$\begin{bmatrix} 1 & 0 \\ 0 & -1 \end{bmatrix}\begin{bmatrix} 1 & 0 \\ 0 & -1 \end{bmatrix}=\begin{bmatrix} 1 & 0 \\ 0 & 1 \end{bmatrix}$	$\begin{bmatrix} 1 & 0 \\ 0 & -1 \end{bmatrix}\begin{bmatrix} 1 & 0 \\ 0 & 1 \end{bmatrix}=\begin{bmatrix} 1 & 0 \\ 0 & -1 \end{bmatrix}$

Applying the above sequence of elementary transformations to both sides of the linear equation system in (1.15), we have

$$\begin{bmatrix} 1 & 0 \\ 0 & \frac{1}{2} \end{bmatrix}\begin{bmatrix} 3 & 5 \\ 2 & 4 \end{bmatrix}\begin{bmatrix} x_1 \\ x_2 \end{bmatrix}=\begin{bmatrix} 1 & 0 \\ 0 & \frac{1}{2} \end{bmatrix}\begin{bmatrix} 15 \\ 8 \end{bmatrix}$$

$$\Longrightarrow \begin{bmatrix} 3 & 5 \\ 1 & 2 \end{bmatrix}\begin{bmatrix} x_1 \\ x_2 \end{bmatrix}=\begin{bmatrix} 15 \\ 4 \end{bmatrix}$$

$$\begin{bmatrix} 0 & 1 \\ 1 & 0 \end{bmatrix}\begin{bmatrix} 3 & 5 \\ 1 & 2 \end{bmatrix}\begin{bmatrix} x_1 \\ x_2 \end{bmatrix}=\begin{bmatrix} 0 & 1 \\ 1 & 0 \end{bmatrix}\begin{bmatrix} 15 \\ 4 \end{bmatrix}$$

$$\Longrightarrow \begin{bmatrix} 1 & 2 \\ 3 & 5 \end{bmatrix}\begin{bmatrix} x_1 \\ x_2 \end{bmatrix}=\begin{bmatrix} 4 \\ 15 \end{bmatrix}$$

$$\begin{bmatrix} 1 & 0 \\ -3 & 1 \end{bmatrix}\begin{bmatrix} 1 & 2 \\ 3 & 5 \end{bmatrix}\begin{bmatrix} x_1 \\ x_2 \end{bmatrix}=\begin{bmatrix} 1 & 0 \\ -3 & 1 \end{bmatrix}\begin{bmatrix} 4 \\ 15 \end{bmatrix}$$

$$\Longrightarrow \begin{bmatrix} 1 & 2 \\ 0 & -1 \end{bmatrix}\begin{bmatrix} x_1 \\ x_2 \end{bmatrix}=\begin{bmatrix} 4 \\ 3 \end{bmatrix}$$

$$\begin{bmatrix} 1 & 2 \\ 0 & 1 \end{bmatrix}\begin{bmatrix} 1 & 2 \\ 0 & -1 \end{bmatrix}\begin{bmatrix} x_1 \\ x_2 \end{bmatrix}=\begin{bmatrix} 1 & 2 \\ 0 & 1 \end{bmatrix}\begin{bmatrix} 4 \\ 3 \end{bmatrix}$$

$$\Longrightarrow \begin{bmatrix} 1 & 0 \\ 0 & -1 \end{bmatrix}\begin{bmatrix} x_1 \\ x_2 \end{bmatrix}=\begin{bmatrix} 10 \\ 3 \end{bmatrix}$$

$$\begin{bmatrix} 1 & 0 \\ 0 & -1 \end{bmatrix}\begin{bmatrix} 1 & 0 \\ 0 & -1 \end{bmatrix}\begin{bmatrix} x_1 \\ x_2 \end{bmatrix}=\begin{bmatrix} 1 & 0 \\ 0 & -1 \end{bmatrix}\begin{bmatrix} 10 \\ 3 \end{bmatrix}$$

$$\Longrightarrow \begin{bmatrix} 1 & 0 \\ 0 & 1 \end{bmatrix}\begin{bmatrix} x_1 \\ x_2 \end{bmatrix}=\begin{bmatrix} 10 \\ -3 \end{bmatrix}$$

or

$$\begin{bmatrix} x_1 \\ x_2 \end{bmatrix} = \begin{bmatrix} 10 \\ -3 \end{bmatrix}$$

The reader should verify for himself that by applying the sequence of *inverse* transformations in the appropriate order to

$$\begin{bmatrix} 1 & 0 \\ 0 & 1 \end{bmatrix} \begin{bmatrix} x_1 \\ x_2 \end{bmatrix} = \begin{bmatrix} 10 \\ -3 \end{bmatrix}$$

one obtains the original equation system once again.

Let us now derive the transformation matrix **T**, say, which will accomplish the same result with only a single multiplication:

$$\mathbf{T} = \begin{bmatrix} 1 & 0 \\ 0 & -1 \end{bmatrix} \begin{bmatrix} 1 & 2 \\ 0 & 1 \end{bmatrix} \begin{bmatrix} 1 & 0 \\ -3 & 1 \end{bmatrix} \begin{bmatrix} 0 & 1 \\ 1 & 0 \end{bmatrix} \begin{bmatrix} 1 & 0 \\ 0 & \frac{1}{2} \end{bmatrix}$$
$$= \begin{bmatrix} 2 & -\frac{5}{2} \\ -1 & \frac{3}{2} \end{bmatrix} \tag{1.16}$$

and

$$\begin{bmatrix} 2 & -\frac{5}{2} \\ -1 & \frac{3}{2} \end{bmatrix} \begin{bmatrix} 3 & 5 \\ 2 & 4 \end{bmatrix} = \begin{bmatrix} 1 & 0 \\ 0 & 1 \end{bmatrix}$$

Thus we observe that the transformation matrix **T** is a matrix which, when applied to the coefficient matrix of the equation system (1.15), yields the identity matrix. Hence, if both sides are premultiplied by the same matrix, we have that

$$\begin{bmatrix} 2 & -\frac{5}{2} \\ -1 & \frac{3}{2} \end{bmatrix} \begin{bmatrix} 3 & 5 \\ 2 & 4 \end{bmatrix} \begin{bmatrix} x_1 \\ x_2 \end{bmatrix} = \begin{bmatrix} 2 & -\frac{5}{2} \\ -1 & \frac{3}{2} \end{bmatrix} \begin{bmatrix} 15 \\ 8 \end{bmatrix}$$
$$\begin{bmatrix} 1 & 0 \\ 0 & 1 \end{bmatrix} \begin{bmatrix} x_1 \\ x_2 \end{bmatrix} = \begin{bmatrix} 10 \\ -3 \end{bmatrix}$$

or

$$\begin{bmatrix} x_1 \\ x_2 \end{bmatrix} = \begin{bmatrix} 10 \\ -3 \end{bmatrix}$$

We shall see in a later section that such transformation matrices, called *inverses*, perform the role of division in matrix algebra. Notice that the inverse of the above transformation matrix may be found by multiplying, *in the correct sequence*, the inverses of the individual elementary matrices.

Thus, if we denote the inverse of the transformation matrix by $\mathbf{T}^{-1}$, we have that

$$\mathbf{T}^{-1} = \begin{bmatrix} 1 & 0 \\ 0 & 2 \end{bmatrix} \begin{bmatrix} 0 & 1 \\ 1 & 0 \end{bmatrix} \begin{bmatrix} 1 & 0 \\ 3 & 1 \end{bmatrix} \begin{bmatrix} 1 & -2 \\ 0 & 1 \end{bmatrix} \begin{bmatrix} 1 & 0 \\ 0 & -1 \end{bmatrix}$$

$$= \begin{bmatrix} 3 & 5 \\ 2 & 4 \end{bmatrix}$$

Observe that $\mathbf{TT}^{-1} = \mathbf{T}^{-1}\mathbf{T} = \mathbf{I}$.

1.5 APPLICATION: MATRIX ANALYSIS OF INTERREGIONAL POPULATION GROWTH AND DISTRIBUTION

Population projections generally are executed by applying a set of birth, death, and migration rates to an initial population in order to carry it forward over the number of years for which projections are desired. Mathematical demographers have shown that this process of surviving a population forward through time may be expressed by matrix multiplication. In addition to the economies generated by such a compact expression of the growth process, the matrix model of population growth and change yields theoretical results that cannot be derived by more conventional demographic forecasting procedures. In this section, we summarize a few of the more important features of the demographer's matrix model of population growth and distribution. In subsequent chapters, we shall consider several theoretical results that may be derived with this model.

1.5.1 THE INTERREGIONAL COMPONENTS-OF-CHANGE MODEL

Imagine an interregional demographic system consisting of only two regions, i and j, say, and, to simplify the analysis further, let us focus only on the total population of these two regions. After a unit time interval, the new population is equal to the old population plus the increase attributable to births and in-migration, minus the decrease resulting from deaths and out-migration. Thus the growth of such a population system may be expressed by the following two equations, which describe the interaction of the above three components of change:

$$\begin{aligned} w_i(t+1) &= w_i(t) + b_i(t) - d_i(t) - m_{ij}(t) + m_{ji}(t) \\ w_j(t+1) &= w_j(t) + b_j(t) - d_j(t) - m_{ji}(t) + m_{ij}(t) \end{aligned} \qquad (1.17)$$

where

$w_i(t), w_j(t)$ = the total populations of the ith and jth regions, respectively, at time t;

$b_i(t), b_j(t)$ = the total number of births in the ith and jth regions, respectively, during the time interval $(t, t + 1)$, that survive to the end of the time interval;

$d_i(t), d_j(t)$ = the total number of deaths in the ith and jth regions, respectively, during the time interval $(t, t + 1)$; and

$m_{ij}(t), m_{ji}(t)$ = the total number of migrants from the ith region to the jth region and from the jth region to the ith region, respectively, during the time interval $(t, t + 1)$, that survive to the end of the time interval.

Expressing (1.17) in matrix form, we have that

$$\begin{bmatrix} w_i(t+1) \\ w_j(t+1) \end{bmatrix}$$

$$= \begin{bmatrix} \dfrac{w_i(t)+b_i(t)-d_i(t)-m_{ij}(t)}{w_i(t)} & \dfrac{m_{ji}(t)}{w_j(t)} \\ \dfrac{m_{ij}(t)}{w_i(t)} & \dfrac{w_j(t)+b_j(t)-d_j(t)-m_{ji}(t)}{w_j(t)} \end{bmatrix} \begin{bmatrix} w_i(t) \\ w_j(t) \end{bmatrix}$$

$$= \begin{bmatrix} g_{ii} & g_{ji} \\ g_{ij} & g_{jj} \end{bmatrix} \begin{bmatrix} w_i(t) \\ w_j(t) \end{bmatrix}$$

or, more compactly,[1]

$$\mathbf{w}(t + 1) = \mathbf{G}\mathbf{w}(t) \tag{1.18}$$

Note that the off-diagonal elements are migration rates, and that the diagonal elements denote each region's growth rate in the absence of in-migration. Further, observe that we have not specified the orders of the matrix and vectors in (1.18). This is because the matrix equation may be used to express the growth of any interregional population system with a

[1] Notice that we have reversed the conventional subscripting order in **G** so as to simplify the identification of the origin and destination of the migrants. Thus, for example, the element in the first row and second column is denoted by g_{ji} instead of g_{ij}. This is because it refers to the migration from region j to region i.

finite number of regions. And if we are willing to assume that the growth schedule, **G**, for this two-region system will remain constant over another unit time interval, we may project the interregional population distribution for 1970 either by applying **G** to **w**(1960) or by applying $\mathbf{G}^2$ to **w**(1950). That is,

$$\mathbf{w}(t+2) = \mathbf{G}\mathbf{w}(t+1) = \mathbf{G}[\mathbf{G}\mathbf{w}(t)] = \mathbf{G}^2\mathbf{w}(t)$$

and, in general,

$$\mathbf{w}(t+n) = \mathbf{G}^n\,\mathbf{w}(t) \tag{1.19}$$

Example. To illustrate the operation of the above matrix model of population growth and distribution, let us fit (1.18) to the hypothetical data presented in Table 1.1. To simplify matters, we have assumed that these data describe the population of an isolated hypothetical island, *Islandia*, which has been divided into three regions: Northern, Central, and Southern Islandia, respectively. It is assumed that Islandia has no contact with the rest of the world and that, therefore, it experiences no immigration or emigration.

In 1950, each of Islandia's three regions had the same number of people, and during the following unit time interval of 15 years, each of these regions experienced the same number of births and deaths. The level of migration into and out of each region was not the same for all three regions; consequently, over the next 15 years, Northern Islandia's population increased while that of the other two regions decreased.

To express the interregional growth process that occurred in Islandia during the 15 years between 1950 and 1965 in matrix form, we first compute the rates of out-migration from each region to every other region. This produces the following off-diagonal elements in the growth matrix **G**:

Table 1.1. Components of Population Change in Islandia: 1950–1965

Region	Population 1950	Births	Deaths	Out-Migrants to: Northern Islandia	Out-Migrants to: Central Islandia	Out-Migrants to: Southern Islandia	In-Migrants from: Northern Islandia	In-Migrants from: Central Islandia	In-Migrants from: Southern Islandia	Population 1965
1. Northern Islandia	288	132	108	—	36	36	—	72	72	384
2. Central Islandia	288	132	108	72	—	36	36	—	36	276
3. Southern Islandia	288	132	108	72	36	—	36	36	—	276
Total	864	396	324	—	—	—	—	—	—	936

Out-migration rate from:

$$\text{Northern to Central Islandia} = g_{12} = \frac{36}{288} = \frac{1}{8}$$

$$\text{Northern to Southern Islandia} = g_{13} = \frac{36}{288} = \frac{1}{8}$$

$$\text{Central to Northern Islandia} = g_{21} = \frac{72}{288} = \frac{1}{4}$$

$$\text{Central to Southern Islandia} = g_{23} = \frac{36}{288} = \frac{1}{8}$$

$$\text{Southern to Northern Islandia} = g_{31} = \frac{72}{288} = \frac{1}{4}$$

$$\text{Southern to Central Islandia} = g_{32} = \frac{36}{288} = \frac{1}{8}$$

Next, we compute the rates of growth due to natural increase in each region and subtract from them the appropriate set of out-migration rates. This produces the following diagonal elements of $\mathbf{G}$:

Rate of growth due to natural increase less out-migration for:

$$\text{Northern Islandia} = g_{11} = \left(\frac{288 + 132 - 108}{288}\right) - \left(\frac{36 + 36}{288}\right) = \frac{5}{6}$$

$$\text{Central Islandia} = g_{22} = \left(\frac{288 + 132 - 108}{288}\right) - \left(\frac{72 + 36}{288}\right) = \frac{17}{24}$$

$$\text{Southern Islandia} = g_{33} = \left(\frac{288 + 132 - 108}{288}\right) - \left(\frac{72 + 36}{288}\right) = \frac{17}{24}$$

Collecting the above diagonal and off-diagonal elements, we have the following interregional growth matrix:

$$\mathbf{G} = \begin{bmatrix} g_{11} & g_{21} & g_{31} \\ g_{12} & g_{22} & g_{32} \\ g_{13} & g_{23} & g_{33} \end{bmatrix} = \begin{bmatrix} \frac{5}{6} & \frac{1}{4} & \frac{1}{4} \\ \frac{1}{8} & \frac{17}{24} & \frac{1}{8} \\ \frac{1}{8} & \frac{1}{8} & \frac{17}{24} \end{bmatrix}$$

and, therefore, the growth process defined by (1.18):

$$\mathbf{w}(t + 1) = \mathbf{G}\mathbf{w}(t) = \begin{bmatrix} \frac{5}{6} & \frac{1}{4} & \frac{1}{4} \\ \frac{1}{8} & \frac{17}{24} & \frac{1}{8} \\ \frac{1}{8} & \frac{1}{8} & \frac{17}{24} \end{bmatrix} \begin{bmatrix} 288 \\ 288 \\ 288 \end{bmatrix} = \begin{bmatrix} 384 \\ 276 \\ 276 \end{bmatrix} \tag{1.20}$$

1.5.2 THE SINGLE-REGION COHORT SURVIVAL MODEL

Rates are more meaningful when they refer to homogeneous groups. A desirable step in this direction, in demographic analysis, is to disaggregate populations into different age groups for each sex and to derive and apply rates that are specific to each of these groups.

Let us now disaggregate our regional populations into age groups, say into five-year age groups, and focus only on the growth process of the total population in a single region, region i. Over a unit time interval, the population changes in each of the age groups, except the first, may be attributed to the effects of death and net migration. The population of the first age group is formed by births that occur during the unit time interval and survive long enough to be included in the population at the start of the next time interval. This growth process may be described by the following system of equations:

$$\begin{aligned} w_1(t+1) &= b_1 w_1(t) + b_2 w_2(t) + \cdots + b_n w_n(t) \\ w_2(t+1) &= s_1 w_1(t) + m_1 w_1(t) = (s_1 + m_1) w_1(t) \\ &\vdots \\ w_n(t+1) &= s_{n-1} w_{n-1}(t) + m_{n-1} w_{n-1}(t) = (s_{n-1} + m_{n-1}) w_{n-1}(t) \end{aligned} \tag{1.21}$$

where

$w_k(t)$ = the total population in the kth age group at time t;

b_k = the number of babies born during the unit time interval who survive to the end of the unit time interval, per person in the kth age group ($b_k = 0$ for nonchildbearing age groups);

s_k = the proportion of people in the kth age group who survive to the $k + 1$st age group after a unit time interval;

m_k = the number of net migrants, during the unit time interval, who survive to the end of the unit time interval, per person in the kth age group.

We may express (1.21) in matrix form, as follows:

$$\begin{bmatrix} w_1(t+1) \\ w_2(t+1) \\ \cdot \\ \cdot \\ \cdot \\ w_n(t+1) \end{bmatrix} = \begin{bmatrix} 0 & 0 \cdots b_u & b_{u+1} \cdots b_v \; 0 \cdots 0 & 0 \\ s_1 + m_1 & 0 \quad \cdot \quad \cdot \quad \cdot & 0 & 0 \\ 0 & s_2 + m_2 \quad \cdot \quad \cdot \quad \cdot & 0 & 0 \\ \vdots & \vdots & \vdots & \vdots \\ 0 & 0 \quad \cdot \quad \cdot \quad \cdot & s_{n-1} + m_{n-1} & 0 \end{bmatrix} \begin{bmatrix} w_1(t) \\ w_2(t) \\ \cdot \\ \cdot \\ \cdot \\ w_n(t) \end{bmatrix}$$

or, more compactly,

$$\mathbf{w}(t+1) = \mathbf{G}\mathbf{w}(t) \tag{1.22}$$

Note that (1.22) is identical to (1.18); only the definition of the elements of **G** and the order of the matrix are different. And observe that no members of the last age group survive the unit time interval. In practical applications of the matrix model, the impact of this restriction may be minimized by extending the age disaggregation far enough, say to ages beyond 90 years at last birthday. Or the last age interval may be defined to be open-ended, say 85 years and over, and the last diagonal element of the growth matrix, accordingly, may be converted into a positive number that will carry over some of the members of the last age group into the same open age group in the next time period.

Example. To fit the matrix model in (1.22) to Islandia's population, we need the age-specific birth and death data that appear in Table 1.2. Since the sexes will not be considered separately, sex breakdowns are not included, and because Islandia experiences no emigration or immigration, migration data are not presented. Finally, to simplify the exposition, we have limited our age breakdown to only the four age groups: 0–14, 15–29, 30–44, and 45–59. Consequently, we must assume that no one in Islandia lives to the ripe old age of 60 years.

According to the data in Table 1.2, 36 people in each of the first three age groups in 1950 died during the subsequent unit time interval of 15 years. Hence the survivorship rate associated with each of those age groups is

$$s_1 = s_2 = s_3 = \frac{216 - 36}{216} = \frac{180}{216} = \frac{5}{6}$$

Next, we note that women in the second age group gave birth to 162 babies who survived to their 15th birthday. Thus,

$$b_2 = \frac{162}{216} = \frac{3}{4}$$

In an analogous way, we obtain

$$b_3 = \frac{180}{216} = \frac{5}{6}$$

Table 1.2. Age-Specific Population Data for Islandia: 1950–1965

Age Group	Population 1950	Births by Age of Mother	Deaths	Population 1965
1. 0–14	216	0	36	396
2. 15–29	216	162	36	180
3. 30–44	216	180	36	180
4. 45–59	216	54	216	180
Total	864	396	324	936

and

$$b_4 = \frac{54}{216} = \frac{1}{4}$$

Finally, since the first age group is nonchildbearing,

$$b_1 = \frac{0}{216} = 0$$

Collecting the survivorship and birth rates derived above, we may define the following single-region growth matrix for Islandia's population:

$$\mathbf{G} = \begin{bmatrix} b_1 & b_2 & b_3 & b_4 \\ s_1 & 0 & 0 & 0 \\ 0 & s_2 & 0 & 0 \\ 0 & 0 & s_3 & 0 \end{bmatrix} = \begin{bmatrix} 0 & \frac{3}{4} & \frac{5}{6} & \frac{1}{4} \\ \frac{5}{6} & 0 & 0 & 0 \\ 0 & \frac{5}{6} & 0 & 0 \\ 0 & 0 & \frac{5}{6} & 0 \end{bmatrix}$$

and, therefore, the growth process:

$$\mathbf{w}(t+1) = \mathbf{Gw}(t) = \begin{bmatrix} 0 & \frac{3}{4} & \frac{5}{6} & \frac{1}{4} \\ \frac{5}{6} & 0 & 0 & 0 \\ 0 & \frac{5}{6} & 0 & 0 \\ 0 & 0 & \frac{5}{6} & 0 \end{bmatrix} \begin{bmatrix} 216 \\ 216 \\ 216 \\ 216 \end{bmatrix} = \begin{bmatrix} 396 \\ 180 \\ 180 \\ 180 \end{bmatrix} \tag{1.23}$$

1.5.3 THE MULTIREGIONAL COHORT SURVIVAL MODEL

Having defined the single-region cohort survival model, we may quite easily extend our results to include several regions. Let us return to our two-region demographic system, and consider how we might modify (1.21) to take into account in- and out-migration flows between the two regions and the changes in the age distribution of region j. To differentiate between the populations and rates of the two regions, we introduce an additional subscript to the equations in (1.21), and to separate in- and out-migration flows, we decompose each net migration rate into the corresponding in- and out-migration rates. Thus we have (1.24) (see p. 24) where $w(t)$, b, and s are defined as before, and where ${}_k g_{rs}$ denotes the proportion of people, in the kth age group in region r, who during the unit time period move into the $k+1$st age group in region s and survive to the end of the unit time interval.

We may express (1.24) in matrix form as shown below (1.24)

$$
\begin{aligned}
w_{i1}(t+1) &= b_{i1}w_{i1}(t) + b_{i2}w_{i2}(t) + \cdots + b_{in}w_{in}(t) \\
w_{i2}(t+1) &= s_{i1}w_{i1}(t) - {}_{1}g_{ij}w_{i1}(t) + {}_{1}g_{ji}w_{j1}(t) = (s_{i1} - {}_{1}g_{ij})w_{i1}(t) + {}_{1}g_{ji}w_{j1}(t) = {}_{1}g_{ii}w_{i1}(t) + {}_{1}g_{ji}w_{j1}(t) \\
&\ \vdots \\
w_{i(n-1)}(t+1) &= s_{i(n-1)}w_{i(n-1)}(t) - {}_{(n-1)}g_{ij}w_{i(n-1)}(t) + {}_{(n-1)}g_{ji}w_{j(n-1)}(t) = (s_{i(n-1)} - {}_{(n-1)}g_{ij})w_{i(n-1)}(t) + {}_{(n-1)}g_{ji}w_{j(n-1)}(t) \\
&= {}_{(n-1)}g_{ii}w_{i(n-1)}(t) + {}_{(n-1)}g_{ji}w_{j(n-1)}(t) \\
w_{j1}(t+1) &= b_{j1}w_{j1}(t) + b_{j2}w_{j2}(t) + \cdots + b_{jn}w_{jn}(t) \qquad (1.24) \\
w_{j2}(t+1) &= s_{j1}w_{j1}(t) - {}_{1}g_{ji}w_{j1}(t) + {}_{1}g_{ij}w_{i1}(t) = (s_{j1} - {}_{1}g_{ji})w_{j1}(t) + {}_{1}g_{ij}w_{i1}(t) = {}_{1}g_{jj}w_{j1}(t) + {}_{1}g_{ij}w_{i1}(t) \\
&\ \vdots \\
w_{j(n-1)}(t+1) &= s_{j(n-1)}w_{j(n-1)}(t) - {}_{(n-1)}g_{ji}w_{j(n-1)}(t) + {}_{(n-1)}g_{ij}w_{i(n-1)}(t) = (s_{j(n-1)} - {}_{(n-1)}g_{ji})w_{j(n-1)}(t) + {}_{(n-1)}g_{ij}w_{i(n-1)}(t) \\
&= {}_{(n-1)}g_{jj}w_{j(n-1)}(t) + {}_{(n-1)}g_{ij}w_{i(n-1)}(t)
\end{aligned}
$$

$$
\begin{bmatrix} w_{i1}(t+1) \\ w_{i2}(t+1) \\ \vdots \\ w_{in}(t+1) \\ \hdashline w_{j1}(t+1) \\ w_{j2}(t+1) \\ \vdots \\ w_{jn}(t+1) \end{bmatrix}
=
\left[\begin{array}{cccc:cccc}
0 & 0 \cdots b_{iu} \cdots b_{iv} \cdots & 0 & 0 & 0 & \cdot\ \cdot\ \cdot & 0 & 0 \\
{}_{1}g_{ii} & \cdot\ \cdot\ \cdot & 0 & 0 & {}_{1}g_{ji} & \cdot\ \cdot\ \cdot & 0 & 0 \\
\vdots & \cdot\ \cdot\ \cdot & \vdots & \vdots & \vdots & \cdot\ \cdot\ \cdot & \vdots & \vdots \\
0 & \cdot\ \cdot\ \cdot & {}_{(n-1)}g_{ii} & 0 & 0 & \cdot\ \cdot\ \cdot & {}_{(n-1)}g_{ji} & 0 \\
\hdashline
0 & \cdot\ \cdot\ \cdot & 0 & 0 & 0 & 0 \cdots b_{ju} \cdots b_{jv} \cdots & 0 & 0 \\
{}_{1}g_{ij} & \cdot\ \cdot\ \cdot & 0 & 0 & {}_{1}g_{jj} & \cdot\ \cdot\ \cdot & 0 & 0 \\
\vdots & \cdot\ \cdot\ \cdot & \vdots & \vdots & \vdots & \cdot\ \cdot\ \cdot & \vdots & \vdots \\
0 & \cdot\ \cdot\ \cdot & {}_{(n-1)}g_{ij} & 0 & 0 & \cdot\ \cdot\ \cdot & {}_{(n-1)}g_{jj} & 0
\end{array}\right]
\begin{bmatrix} w_{i1}(t) \\ w_{i2}(t) \\ \vdots \\ w_{in}(t) \\ \hdashline w_{j1}(t) \\ w_{j2}(t) \\ \vdots \\ w_{jn}(t) \end{bmatrix}
$$

or, more compactly,

$$\mathbf{w}(t+1) = \mathbf{G}\mathbf{w}(t) \tag{1.25}$$

Once again we observe that the fundamental matrix expression remains unchanged.

Migration data that are reported by a census typically are obtained by asking a resident population, aged x and over, where they resided x years ago. Thus migrants who have returned to their original place of residence within the time interval of x years are not identified, and no migration data are available for children under age x at the time of the census. Consequently, in the above formulation of the interregional growth process, we have assumed that repeated migration within the unit time interval is negligible and that the first age group is unaffected by migration processes. For a time interval longer than one year, the latter assumption can introduce significant errors into the projection process. In such instances, the contribution of migration to the first age group may be expressed by introducing additional positive elements into the growth matrix [Keyfitz (1968), p. 321].

Example. Turning to Islandia's three-region population system once again, consider the regionally disaggregated age-specific population data that appear in Table 1.3. By means of arguments such as were used in fitting the single-region model, we may obtain the following regional birth rates:

$$b_{11} = b_{21} = b_{31} = \frac{0}{72} = 0$$

$$b_{12} = b_{22} = b_{32} = \frac{54}{72} = \frac{3}{4}$$

$$b_{13} = b_{23} = b_{33} = \frac{60}{72} = \frac{5}{6}$$

$$b_{14} = b_{24} = b_{34} = \frac{18}{72} = \frac{1}{4}$$

Notice, however, that unlike the single-region model, the elements in the principal subdiagonal of the growth matrix in (1.25) now must be decreased to reflect out-migration. Out-migration rates are computed by dividing the number of out-migrants in each group by the number of people in the region of origin. Thus, we have that

$${}_kg_{12} = {}_kg_{13} = {}_kg_{23} = {}_kg_{32} = \frac{12}{72} = \frac{1}{6}$$

and

$${}_kg_{21} = {}_kg_{31} = \frac{24}{72} = \frac{1}{3}$$

Table 1.3. Age-Specific Population Data for Northern, Central, and Southern Islandia: 1950–1965

Region and Age Group	Population 1950	Births by Age of Mother	Deaths	Out-Migrants to: Northern Islandia	Out-Migrants to: Central Islandia	Out-Migrants to: Southern Islandia	In-Migrants from: Northern Islandia	In-Migrants from: Central Islandia	In-Migrants from: Southern Islandia	Population 1965	Region and Age Group
1. Northern Islandia:											1. Northern Islandia:
Age Group:											*Age Group:*
(1) 0–14	72	0	12	—	12	12	—	—	—	132	(1) 0–14
(2) 15–29	72	54	12	—	12	12	—	24	24	84	(2) 15–29
(3) 30–44	72	60	12	—	12	12	—	24	24	84	(3) 30–44
(4) 45+	72	18	72	—	—	—	—	24	24	84	(4) 45+
Subtotal	288	132	108	—	36	36	—	72	72	384	Subtotal
2. Central Islandia:											2. Central Islandia:
Age Group:											*Age Group:*
(1) 0–14	72	0	12	24	—	12	—	—	—	132	(1) 0–14
(2) 15–29	72	54	12	24	—	12	12	—	12	48	(2) 15–29
(3) 30–44	72	60	12	24	—	12	12	—	12	48	(3) 30–44
(4) 45+	72	18	72	—	—	—	12	—	12	48	(4) 45+
Subtotal	288	132	108	72	—	36	36	—	36	276	Subtotal
3. Southern Islandia:											3. Southern Islandia:
Age Group:											*Age Group:*
(1) 0–14	72	0	12	24	12	—	—	—	—	132	(1) 0–14
(2) 15–29	72	54	12	24	12	—	12	12	—	48	(2) 15–29
(3) 30–44	72	60	12	24	12	—	12	12	—	48	(3) 30–44
(4) 45+	72	18	72	—	—	—	12	12	—	48	(4) 45+
Subtotal	288	132	108	72	36	—	36	36	—	276	Subtotal
Total	864	396	324	—	—	—	—	—	—	936	Total

for all $k = 1, 2, 3$. Consequently, the elements in the principal diagonal are

$$
\begin{aligned}
{}_k g_{11} &= {}_k s_{11} - {}_k g_{12} - {}_k g_{13} = \frac{5}{6} - \frac{1}{6} - \frac{1}{6} = \frac{1}{2} \\
{}_k g_{22} &= {}_k s_{22} - {}_k g_{21} - {}_k g_{23} = \frac{5}{6} - \frac{1}{3} - \frac{1}{6} = \frac{1}{3} \\
{}_k g_{33} &= {}_k s_{33} - {}_k g_{31} - {}_k g_{32} = \frac{5}{6} - \frac{1}{3} - \frac{1}{6} = \frac{1}{3}
\end{aligned}
$$

for all $k = 1, 2, 3$.

Collecting the various birth, death, and out-migration rates, we obtain the following multiregional growth matrix:

$$
\mathbf{G} = \left[\begin{array}{cccc|cccc|cccc}
0 & b_{12} & b_{13} & b_{14} & 0 & 0 & 0 & 0 & 0 & 0 & 0 & 0 \\
{}_1g_{11} & 0 & 0 & 0 & {}_1g_{21} & 0 & 0 & 0 & {}_1g_{31} & 0 & 0 & 0 \\
0 & {}_2g_{11} & 0 & 0 & 0 & {}_2g_{21} & 0 & 0 & 0 & {}_2g_{31} & 0 & 0 \\
0 & 0 & {}_3g_{11} & 0 & 0 & 0 & {}_3g_{21} & 0 & 0 & 0 & {}_3g_{31} & 0 \\
\hline
0 & 0 & 0 & 0 & 0 & b_{22} & b_{23} & b_{24} & 0 & 0 & 0 & 0 \\
{}_1g_{12} & 0 & 0 & 0 & {}_1g_{22} & 0 & 0 & 0 & {}_1g_{32} & 0 & 0 & 0 \\
0 & {}_2g_{12} & 0 & 0 & 0 & {}_2g_{22} & 0 & 0 & 0 & {}_2g_{32} & 0 & 0 \\
0 & 0 & {}_3g_{12} & 0 & 0 & 0 & {}_3g_{22} & 0 & 0 & 0 & {}_3g_{32} & 0 \\
\hline
0 & 0 & 0 & 0 & 0 & 0 & 0 & 0 & 0 & b_{32} & b_{33} & b_{34} \\
{}_1g_{13} & 0 & 0 & 0 & {}_1g_{23} & 0 & 0 & 0 & {}_1g_{33} & 0 & 0 & 0 \\
0 & {}_2g_{13} & 0 & 0 & 0 & {}_2g_{23} & 0 & 0 & 0 & {}_2g_{33} & 0 & 0 \\
0 & 0 & {}_3g_{13} & 0 & 0 & 0 & {}_3g_{23} & 0 & 0 & 0 & {}_3g_{33} & 0
\end{array}\right]
$$

$$
= \left[\begin{array}{cccc|cccc|cccc}
0 & \frac{3}{4} & \frac{5}{6} & \frac{1}{4} & 0 & 0 & 0 & 0 & 0 & 0 & 0 & 0 \\
\frac{1}{2} & 0 & 0 & 0 & \frac{1}{3} & 0 & 0 & 0 & \frac{1}{3} & 0 & 0 & 0 \\
0 & \frac{1}{2} & 0 & 0 & 0 & \frac{1}{3} & 0 & 0 & 0 & \frac{1}{3} & 0 & 0 \\
0 & 0 & \frac{1}{2} & 0 & 0 & 0 & \frac{1}{3} & 0 & 0 & 0 & \frac{1}{3} & 0 \\
\hline
0 & 0 & 0 & 0 & 0 & \frac{3}{4} & \frac{5}{6} & \frac{1}{4} & 0 & 0 & 0 & 0 \\
\frac{1}{6} & 0 & 0 & 0 & \frac{1}{3} & 0 & 0 & 0 & \frac{1}{6} & 0 & 0 & 0 \\
0 & \frac{1}{6} & 0 & 0 & 0 & \frac{1}{3} & 0 & 0 & 0 & \frac{1}{6} & 0 & 0 \\
0 & 0 & \frac{1}{6} & 0 & 0 & 0 & \frac{1}{3} & 0 & 0 & 0 & \frac{1}{6} & 0 \\
\hline
0 & 0 & 0 & 0 & 0 & 0 & 0 & 0 & 0 & \frac{3}{4} & \frac{5}{6} & \frac{1}{4} \\
\frac{1}{6} & 0 & 0 & 0 & \frac{1}{6} & 0 & 0 & 0 & \frac{1}{3} & 0 & 0 & 0 \\
0 & \frac{1}{6} & 0 & 0 & 0 & \frac{1}{6} & 0 & 0 & 0 & \frac{1}{3} & 0 & 0 \\
0 & 0 & \frac{1}{6} & 0 & 0 & 0 & \frac{1}{6} & 0 & 0 & 0 & \frac{1}{3} & 0
\end{array}\right]
$$

and the interregional growth process

$$\mathbf{w}(t+1) = \mathbf{G}\mathbf{w}(t) = \left[\begin{array}{cccc:cccc:cccc} 0 & \frac{3}{4} & \frac{5}{6} & \frac{1}{4} & 0 & 0 & 0 & 0 & 0 & 0 & 0 & 0 \\ \frac{1}{2} & 0 & 0 & 0 & \frac{1}{3} & 0 & 0 & 0 & \frac{1}{3} & 0 & 0 & 0 \\ 0 & \frac{1}{2} & 0 & 0 & 0 & \frac{1}{3} & 0 & 0 & 0 & \frac{1}{3} & 0 & 0 \\ 0 & 0 & \frac{1}{2} & 0 & 0 & 0 & \frac{1}{3} & 0 & 0 & 0 & \frac{1}{3} & 0 \\ \hdashline 0 & 0 & 0 & 0 & 0 & \frac{3}{4} & \frac{5}{6} & \frac{1}{4} & 0 & 0 & 0 & 0 \\ \frac{1}{6} & 0 & 0 & 0 & \frac{1}{3} & 0 & 0 & 0 & \frac{1}{6} & 0 & 0 & 0 \\ 0 & \frac{1}{6} & 0 & 0 & 0 & \frac{1}{3} & 0 & 0 & 0 & \frac{1}{6} & 0 & 0 \\ 0 & 0 & \frac{1}{6} & 0 & 0 & 0 & \frac{1}{3} & 0 & 0 & 0 & \frac{1}{6} & 0 \\ \hdashline 0 & 0 & 0 & 0 & 0 & 0 & 0 & 0 & 0 & \frac{3}{4} & \frac{5}{6} & \frac{1}{4} \\ \frac{1}{6} & 0 & 0 & 0 & \frac{1}{6} & 0 & 0 & 0 & \frac{1}{3} & 0 & 0 & 0 \\ 0 & \frac{1}{6} & 0 & 0 & 0 & \frac{1}{6} & 0 & 0 & 0 & \frac{1}{3} & 0 & 0 \\ 0 & 0 & \frac{1}{6} & 0 & 0 & 0 & \frac{1}{6} & 0 & 0 & 0 & \frac{1}{3} & 0 \end{array}\right] \left[\begin{array}{c} 72 \\ 72 \\ 72 \\ 72 \\ \hdashline 72 \\ 72 \\ 72 \\ 72 \\ \hdashline 72 \\ 72 \\ 72 \\ 72 \end{array}\right]$$

$$= \left[\begin{array}{c} 132 \\ 84 \\ 84 \\ 84 \\ \hdashline 132 \\ 48 \\ 48 \\ 48 \\ \hdashline 132 \\ 48 \\ 48 \\ 48 \end{array}\right] \qquad (1.26)$$

1.5.4 CONSOLIDATION OF POPULATION GROWTH MATRICES

The growth matrices in (1.20), (1.23), and (1.26) all have been fitted to data describing population growth and change in Islandia during the time period 1950 to 1965. In (1.20), Islandia's population was disaggregated into three regions: Northern, Central, and Southern Islandia, respectively, whereas in (1.23), it was disaggregated into four age groups: 0–14, 15–29,

30–44, and 45–59. In (1.26), Islandia's population was disaggregated both into the three regions *and* the four age groups. Since all three disaggregations came from the same data base, we would expect the first two to be special cases of the last and, therefore, derivable from it. That is, it would seem that having fitted the **G** in (1.26), one should not need to return to the original data in order to fit the **G** in (1.20) and the **G** in (1.23), but one should be able to derive these matrices by some transformation of the **G** in (1.26). It turns out that this indeed is the case, and we shall now outline how one can carry out such consolidations.

First, let us consider how consolidation operations may be carried out on matrices and vectors. To consolidate a three-dimensional vector $\mathbf{w}$, say, into a two-dimensional vector $\hat{\mathbf{w}}$, say, with a first element that is the sum of the first two elements of $\mathbf{w}$, we define the *consolidation matrix*

$$\mathbf{C} = \begin{bmatrix} 1 & 1 & 0 \\ 0 & 0 & 1 \end{bmatrix}$$

which, when applied to $\mathbf{w}$, will produce $\hat{\mathbf{w}}$. That is,

$$\hat{\mathbf{w}} = \mathbf{C}\mathbf{w} = \begin{bmatrix} 1 & 1 & 0 \\ \\ 0 & 0 & 1 \end{bmatrix} \begin{bmatrix} w_1 \\ w_2 \\ w_3 \end{bmatrix} = \begin{bmatrix} w_1 + w_2 \\ w_3 \end{bmatrix}$$

We may reverse this consolidation with the *deconsolidation matrix*

$$\mathbf{D} = \begin{bmatrix} d_1 & 0 \\ d_2 & 0 \\ 0 & 1 \end{bmatrix}$$

where $d_1 = w_1/(w_1 + w_2)$ and $d_2 = 1 - d_1$. Thus

$$\mathbf{w} = \mathbf{D}\hat{\mathbf{w}} = \begin{bmatrix} \dfrac{w_1}{w_1 + w_2} & 0 \\ \dfrac{w_2}{w_1 + w_2} & 0 \\ 0 & 1 \end{bmatrix} \begin{bmatrix} w_1 + w_2 \\ w_3 \end{bmatrix} = \begin{bmatrix} w_1 \\ w_2 \\ w_3 \end{bmatrix}$$

Consider now how these two matrices enter into our basic matrix population model

$$\mathbf{w}(t + 1) = \mathbf{G}\mathbf{w}(t)$$

Observe that

$$\hat{\mathbf{w}}(t + 1) = \mathbf{C}\mathbf{w}(t + 1)$$

and

$$\mathbf{w}(t) = \mathbf{D}(t)\hat{\mathbf{w}}(t)$$

where **D** now receives the temporal index of the vector to which it is applied, in order to reflect the time at which the proportional weights are computed. Hence, by simple substitution, we have that

$$\hat{\mathbf{w}}(t+1) = \mathbf{C}\mathbf{w}(t+1) = \mathbf{C}\mathbf{G}\mathbf{w}(t) = \mathbf{C}\mathbf{G}\mathbf{D}(t)\hat{\mathbf{w}}(t)$$

or

$$\hat{\mathbf{w}}(t+1) = \hat{\mathbf{G}}\hat{\mathbf{w}}(t) \tag{1.27}$$

where $\hat{\mathbf{G}} = \mathbf{C}\mathbf{G}\mathbf{D}(t)$.

Example. Equation (1.27) is the basic consolidation process which, with appropriately defined consolidation and deconsolidation matrices, enables us to "collapse" age groups and regions in the matrix model of interregional population growth and distribution. For example, to derive the **G** in (1.20) from the **G** in (1.26), we first define a **C** such that

$$\underset{3\times1}{\hat{\mathbf{w}}(1950)} = \underset{3\times12}{\mathbf{C}}\ \underset{12\times1}{\mathbf{w}(1950)}$$

where

$$\underset{3\times1}{\hat{\mathbf{w}}(1950)} = \begin{bmatrix} 288 \\ 288 \\ 288 \end{bmatrix}$$

and

$$\underset{12\times1}{\mathbf{w}(1950)} = \begin{bmatrix} 72 \\ 72 \\ 72 \\ 72 \\ \hdashline 72 \\ 72 \\ 72 \\ 72 \\ \hdashline 72 \\ 72 \\ 72 \\ 72 \end{bmatrix}$$

Thus, we have

$$\underset{3\times12}{\mathbf{C}} = \left[\begin{array}{cccc:cccc:cccc} 1 & 1 & 1 & 1 & 0 & 0 & 0 & 0 & 0 & 0 & 0 & 0 \\ 0 & 0 & 0 & 0 & 1 & 1 & 1 & 1 & 0 & 0 & 0 & 0 \\ 0 & 0 & 0 & 0 & 0 & 0 & 0 & 0 & 1 & 1 & 1 & 1 \end{array}\right] \tag{1.28}$$

Next, we transpose **C** and replace the unities in it by proportional weights to define **D**(1950). Thus,

$$\underset{12\times 3}{\mathbf{D}(1950)} = \left[\begin{array}{ccc} \frac{1}{4} & 0 & 0 \\ \frac{1}{4} & 0 & 0 \\ \frac{1}{4} & 0 & 0 \\ \frac{1}{4} & 0 & 0 \\ \hdashline 0 & \frac{1}{4} & 0 \\ 0 & \frac{1}{4} & 0 \\ 0 & \frac{1}{4} & 0 \\ 0 & \frac{1}{4} & 0 \\ \hdashline 0 & 0 & \frac{1}{4} \\ 0 & 0 & \frac{1}{4} \\ 0 & 0 & \frac{1}{4} \\ 0 & 0 & \frac{1}{4} \end{array}\right] \qquad (1.29)$$

and

$$\underset{12\times 1}{\mathbf{w}(1950)} = \underset{12\times 3}{\mathbf{D}(1950)}\ \underset{3\times 1}{\hat{\mathbf{w}}(1950)}$$

Finally, we apply (1.27) to the **G** in (1.26), with **C** and **D**(1950) as defined by (1.28) and (1.29), respectively, to obtain the **G** in (1.20). That is,

$$\underset{3\times 3}{\hat{\mathbf{G}}} = \underset{3\times 12}{\mathbf{C}} \cdot \underset{12\times 12}{\mathbf{G}} \cdot \underset{12\times 3}{\mathbf{D}(1950)} = \begin{bmatrix} \frac{5}{6} & \frac{1}{4} & \frac{1}{4} \\ \frac{1}{8} & \frac{17}{24} & \frac{1}{8} \\ \frac{1}{8} & \frac{1}{8} & \frac{17}{24} \end{bmatrix}$$

To derive the **G** in (1.23) from the **G** in (1.26), we proceed in an analogous manner. First, we define **C**:

$$\underset{4\times 12}{\mathbf{C}} = \left[\begin{array}{c:c:c} \underset{4\times 4}{\mathbf{I}} & \underset{4\times 4}{\mathbf{I}} & \underset{4\times 4}{\mathbf{I}} \end{array}\right] \qquad (1.30)$$

where **I** is a four-by-four identity matrix. Thus

$$\underset{4\times 1}{\hat{\mathbf{w}}(1950)} = \underset{4\times 12}{\mathbf{C}}\ \underset{12\times 1}{\mathbf{w}(1950)}$$

Next, we define $\mathbf{D}(1950)$:

$$\underset{12\times 4}{\mathbf{D}(1950)} = \begin{bmatrix} \frac{1}{3} & 0 & 0 & 0 \\ 0 & \frac{1}{3} & 0 & 0 \\ 0 & 0 & \frac{1}{3} & 0 \\ 0 & 0 & 0 & \frac{1}{3} \\ \hline \frac{1}{3} & 0 & 0 & 0 \\ 0 & \frac{1}{3} & 0 & 0 \\ 0 & 0 & \frac{1}{3} & 0 \\ 0 & 0 & 0 & \frac{1}{3} \\ \hline \frac{1}{3} & 0 & 0 & 0 \\ 0 & \frac{1}{3} & 0 & 0 \\ 0 & 0 & \frac{1}{3} & 0 \\ 0 & 0 & 0 & \frac{1}{3} \end{bmatrix} \tag{1.31}$$

and compute

$$\underset{4\times 4}{\hat{\mathbf{G}}} = \underset{4\times 12}{\mathbf{C}} \cdot \underset{12\times 12}{\mathbf{G}} \cdot \underset{12\times 4}{\mathbf{D}(1950)} = \begin{bmatrix} 0 & \frac{3}{4} & \frac{5}{6} & \frac{1}{4} \\ \frac{5}{6} & 0 & 0 & 0 \\ 0 & \frac{5}{6} & 0 & 0 \\ 0 & 0 & \frac{5}{6} & 0 \end{bmatrix}$$

where the matrices **C**, **G**, and $\mathbf{D}(1950)$ are those defined by (1.30), (1.26), and (1.31), respectively.

1.5.5 PERFECT AGGREGATION

The consolidation procedures described in the preceding section may be used to show that the results of a demographic analysis always depend on the particular consolidation scheme that is used to combine people, regions, and time [Rogers (1969)]. We begin by considering the circumstances under which it is possible to consolidate a multiregional cohort survival model and yet obtain with it results that are consistent with those that would have been derived with the original unconsolidated model. Consolidated models that satisfy this requirement may be said to have been *perfectly aggregated.*

To identify consolidation schemes that produce perfect aggregation, we first observe that both

$$\hat{\mathbf{w}}(t+n) = \mathbf{C}\mathbf{w}(t+n) = \mathbf{C}\mathbf{G}^n\mathbf{w}(t) \tag{1.32}$$

and

$$\mathbf{w}(t+n) = \mathbf{G}^n\mathbf{w}(t) = \mathbf{G}^n\mathbf{D}(t)\hat{\mathbf{w}}(t) \tag{1.33}$$

are products of the unconsolidated model, and therefore may be said to be the *errorless* consolidated and unconsolidated projections of the vector $\mathbf{w}$ at time $t + n$. Corresponding to each of these errorless results, we also have the *potentially erroneous* projections of the consolidated model:

$$\hat{\mathbf{w}}(t + n) = \hat{\mathbf{G}}^n\hat{\mathbf{w}}(t) = \hat{\mathbf{G}}^n\mathbf{C}\mathbf{w}(t) \tag{1.34}$$

and

$$\mathbf{w}(t + n) = \mathbf{D}(t + n)\hat{\mathbf{w}}(t + n) = \mathbf{D}(t + n)\hat{\mathbf{G}}^n\hat{\mathbf{w}}(t) \tag{1.35}$$

Denoting the difference between the errorless and potentially erroneous projections by the vector $\boldsymbol{\phi}$, we use (1.32) and (1.34) to define

$$\begin{aligned}\boldsymbol{\phi}_1 &= \mathbf{C}\mathbf{G}^n\mathbf{w}(t) - \hat{\mathbf{G}}^n\mathbf{C}\mathbf{w}(t) \\ &= (\mathbf{C}\mathbf{G}^n - \hat{\mathbf{G}}^n\mathbf{C})\mathbf{w}(t)\end{aligned} \tag{1.36}$$

and (1.33) and (1.35) to define

$$\begin{aligned}\boldsymbol{\phi}_2 &= \mathbf{G}^n\mathbf{D}(t)\hat{\mathbf{w}}(t) - \mathbf{D}(t + n)\hat{\mathbf{G}}^n\hat{\mathbf{w}}(t) \\ &= [\mathbf{G}^n\mathbf{D}(t) - \mathbf{D}(t + n)\hat{\mathbf{G}}^n]\hat{\mathbf{w}}(t)\end{aligned} \tag{1.37}$$

It follows, therefore, that *perfect aggregation* occurs when $\boldsymbol{\phi}_1$ or $\boldsymbol{\phi}_2$ are null vectors, and this will happen if

$$\mathbf{C}\mathbf{G}^n = \hat{\mathbf{G}}^n\mathbf{C} \quad \text{[Consolidation Rule I]} \tag{1.38}$$

or

$$\mathbf{G}^n\mathbf{D}(t) = \mathbf{D}(t + n)\hat{\mathbf{G}}^n \quad \text{[Consolidation Rule II]} \tag{1.39}$$

We shall refer to (1.38) and (1.39) as the *sufficient conditions for perfect aggregation* in multiregional cohort survival models. To test his comprehension of the above arguments, the reader should try to interpret the meaning of the consolidation rules defined in (1.38) and (1.39) and try to establish whether either one of them is not only *sufficient*, but also *necessary* for perfect aggregation to be possible [Exercise 3(a)]. Another useful exercise is the extension of the above results to temporal consolidations [Exercise 3(b)].

Example. Recall Islandia's demographic growth processes as defined by (1.20), (1.23), and (1.26), and consider the population that is projected for $t + 2$, that is, for 1980, if $\mathbf{G}$ is assumed to remain constant over another unit time interval. If we define the growth process in (1.26) to be the errorless projection of Islandia's population, then one may easily demonstrate that (1.23) is a perfect aggregation and (1.20) is not. For (1.20) projects a total population of 1,014 persons for Islandia in 1980, whereas both (1.23) and (1.26) project a total population of 960 persons for the same date. The reader should confirm that the consolidation of (1.26) into (1.23) satisfies the first consolidation rule and, therefore, is an example of perfect aggregation, while the consolidation of (1.26) into (1.20) meets neither of the two consolidation rules and introduces an error into the projection process. For an illustration of a consolidation that satisfies the second consolidation rule, the reader should consolidate the regions of Northern and Central Islandia in (1.20), and assume that the initial population distribution of the three-region system is in the proportions $\frac{1}{2}:\frac{1}{4}:\frac{1}{4}$. That is,

$$\mathbf{w}(t) = \begin{bmatrix} 432 \\ 216 \\ 216 \end{bmatrix}$$

1.5.6 APPLICATION: MATRIX MODELS OF POPULATION GROWTH AND DISTRIBUTION IN CALIFORNIA AND THE REST OF THE UNITED STATES

To illustrate the use of the above described models with empirical data, let us first fit the matrix equation in (1.18) to the data presented in Table 1.4:[2]

$$\begin{bmatrix} w_i(1960) \\ w_j(1960) \end{bmatrix} = \begin{bmatrix} \dfrac{10586+3346-933-1461}{10586} & \dfrac{4180}{140111} \\ \dfrac{1461}{10586} & \dfrac{140111+35667-11157-4180}{140111} \end{bmatrix} \begin{bmatrix} 10586 \\ 140111 \end{bmatrix}$$

$$= \begin{bmatrix} 1.0899 & 0.0298 \\ 0.1380 & 1.1451 \end{bmatrix} \begin{bmatrix} 10586 \\ 140111 \end{bmatrix} = \begin{bmatrix} 15718 \\ 161902 \end{bmatrix} \tag{1.40}$$

Table 1.4. Components of Population Change in California and the Rest of the United States: 1950–1960 (Population Data in Thousands)

Region	Population 1950	Births 1950–60	Deaths 1950–60	Out-Migrants 1950–60	In-Migrants 1950–60	Population 1960
California	10,586	3,346	933	1,461	4,180	15,718
Rest of the United States	140,111	35,667	11,157	4,180	1,461	161,902
Total	150,697	39,013	12,090	—	—	177,620

Source: Estimated by author using data from the U.S. Census.

[2] To simplify matters, we assume zero net immigration and use data that are neither strictly hypothetical nor strictly accurate. Where published data are lacking, crude estimates have been used. Discrepancies are due to rounding errors.

Next, in Figure 1.1, we illustrate the application of (1.22) to the same data. The first age group contains the population between the ages 0 and 9, and the last age group is an open-ended one, containing all people aged 80 and over. Instead of defining the last diagonal element to be a positive number, in order to carry over some of the members of the last age group to the next time period, we have inflated the last survivorship rate to obtain the same result. And because net immigration was assumed to be zero, all $m_k = 0$.

$$\underset{\mathbf{w}(1960)}{\begin{bmatrix} 39013 \\ 29182 \\ 21671 \\ 23532 \\ 22481 \\ 18037 \\ 13400 \\ 8048 \\ 2255 \end{bmatrix}} = \underset{\mathbf{G}}{\begin{bmatrix} 0 & 0.2238 & 1.0142 & 0.4119 & 0.0369 & 0 & 0 & 0 & 0 \\ 0.9938 & 0 & 0 & 0 & 0 & 0 & 0 & 0 & 0 \\ 0 & 0.9970 & 0 & 0 & 0 & 0 & 0 & 0 & 0 \\ 0 & 0 & 0.9919 & 0 & 0 & 0 & 0 & 0 & 0 \\ 0 & 0 & 0 & 0.9876 & 0 & 0 & 0 & 0 & 0 \\ 0 & 0 & 0 & 0 & 0.9358 & 0 & 0 & 0 & 0 \\ 0 & 0 & 0 & 0 & 0 & 0.8641 & 0 & 0 & 0 \\ 0 & 0 & 0 & 0 & 0 & 0 & 0.7275 & 0 & 0 \\ 0 & 0 & 0 & 0 & 0 & 0 & 0 & 0.4052 & 0 \end{bmatrix}} \underset{\mathbf{w}(1950)}{\begin{bmatrix} 29364 \\ 21736 \\ 23724 \\ 22763 \\ 19274 \\ 15507 \\ 11062 \\ 5564 \\ 1703 \end{bmatrix}}$$

Source: Estimated by author using data from the U.S. Census.

Figure 1.1. The Single-Region Cohort Survival Process for the United States: 1950–1960 (Population Data in Thousands)

Finally, Figure 1.2 illustrates the fit of (1.25) to the same data, now disaggregated by age and region.

Consolidated versions of the growth matrix in Figure 1.2 may be derived using the procedures described in Section 1.5.4. For example, to derive the **G** in (1.40) from the **G** in Figure 1.2, we first define **C** as follows:

$$\underset{2\times 18}{\mathbf{C}} = \left[\begin{array}{ccccccccc|ccccccccc} 1 & 1 & 1 & 1 & 1 & 1 & 1 & 1 & 1 & 0 & 0 & 0 & 0 & 0 & 0 & 0 & 0 & 0 \\ 0 & 0 & 0 & 0 & 0 & 0 & 0 & 0 & 0 & 1 & 1 & 1 & 1 & 1 & 1 & 1 & 1 & 1 \end{array}\right] \tag{1.41}$$

w(1960)									G										w(1950)
3346	=	0	0.3251	1.1794	0.4873	0.0512	0	0	0	0	0	0	0	0	0	0	0	0	1947
2514		0.8474	0	0	0	0	0	0	0	0	0.0315	0	0	0	0	0	0	0	1283
2000		0	0.8369	0	0	0	0	0	0	0	0	0.0453	0	0	0	0	0	0	1698
2319		0	0	0.7498	0	0	0	0	0	0	0	0	0.0475	0	0	0	0	0	1750
2045		0	0	0	0.8110	0	0	0	0	0	0	0	0	0.0298	0	0	0	0	1438
1528		0	0	0	0	0.8272	0	0	0	0	0	0	0	0	0.0190	0	0	0	1125
1102		0	0	0	0	0	0.8027	0	0	0	0	0	0	0	0	0.0138	0	0	819
655		0	0	0	0	0	0	0.6514	0	0	0	0	0	0	0	0	0.0119	0	404
208		0	0	0	0	0	0	0	0.3703	0	0	0	0	0	0	0	0	0.0113	122
35667		0	0	0	0	0	0	0	0	0	0	0.2175	1.0015	0.4056	0.0357	0	0	0	27417
26667		0.1473	0	0	0	0	0	0	0	0	0.9622	0	0	0	0	0	0	0	20453
19670		0	0.1532	0	0	0	0	0	0	0	0	0.9521	0	0	0	0	0	0	22026
21211		0	0	0.2350	0	0	0	0	0	0	0	0	0.9449	0	0	0	0	0	21013
20434		0	0	0	0.1640	0	0	0	0	0	0	0	0	0.9588	0	0	0	0	17836
16508		0	0	0	0	0.1082	0	0	0	0	0	0	0	0	0.9168	0	0	0	14382
12298		0	0	0	0	0	0.0617	0	0	0	0	0	0	0	0	0.8503	0	0	10243
7393		0	0	0	0	0	0	0.0578	0	0	0	0	0	0	0	0	0.7171	0	5160
2046		0	0	0	0	0	0	0	0.0470	0	0	0	0	0	0	0	0	0.3929	1581

Source: Estimated by author using data from the U.S. Census.

Figure 1.2. The Multiregional Cohort Survival Process for California and the Rest of the United States: 1950–1960 (Population Data in Thousands)

Next, we define $\mathbf{D}(1950)$:

$$\underset{18\times 2}{\mathbf{D}(1950)} = \left[\begin{array}{cc} 0.1839 & 0 \\ 0.1212 & 0 \\ 0.1604 & 0 \\ 0.1653 & 0 \\ 0.1358 & 0 \\ 0.1063 & 0 \\ 0.0774 & 0 \\ 0.0382 & 0 \\ 0.0115 & 0 \\ \hdashline 0 & 0.1957 \\ 0 & 0.1460 \\ 0 & 0.1572 \\ 0 & 0.1500 \\ 0 & 0.1273 \\ 0 & 0.1026 \\ 0 & 0.0731 \\ 0 & 0.0368 \\ 0 & 0.0113 \end{array}\right] \tag{1.42}$$

and observe that

$$\underset{18\times 1}{\mathbf{w}(1950)} = \underset{18\times 2}{\mathbf{D}(1950)}\,\underset{2\times 1}{\hat{\mathbf{w}}(1950)}$$

Finally, we apply (1.27) to the **G** in Figure 1.2, with **C** and $\mathbf{D}(1950)$ as defined by (1.41) and (1.42), respectively, to find the **G** in (1.40). That is,

$$\underset{2\times 2}{\hat{\mathbf{G}}} = \underset{2\times 18}{\mathbf{C}} \cdot \underset{18\times 18}{\mathbf{G}} \cdot \underset{18\times 2}{\mathbf{D}(1950)} = \begin{bmatrix} 1.0899 & 0.0298 \\ 0.1380 & 1.1451 \end{bmatrix}$$

To derive the **G** in Figure 1.1 from the **G** in Figure 1.2, we proceed in an analogous manner. First, we define **C**:

$$\underset{9\times 18}{\mathbf{C}} = \left[\begin{array}{c:c} \underset{9\times 9}{\mathbf{I}} & \underset{9\times 9}{\mathbf{I}} \end{array}\right] \tag{1.43}$$

where **I** is a 9×9 identity matrix. Thus,

$$\underset{9\times 1}{\hat{\mathbf{w}}(1950)} = \underset{9\times 18}{\mathbf{C}}\ \underset{18\times 1}{\mathbf{w}(1950)}$$

Next, we define $\mathbf{D}(1950)$:

$$\underset{18\times 9}{\mathbf{D}(1950)} = \begin{bmatrix} \underset{9\times 9}{\mathbf{D}_1(1950)} \\ \hdashline \underset{9\times 9}{\mathbf{D}_2(1950)} \end{bmatrix} \tag{1.44}$$

where $\mathbf{D}_1(1950)$ and $\mathbf{D}_2(1950)$ are diagonal matrices with diagonal elements

$$d_{ij} = \frac{w_{ij}(1950)}{\sum_{i=1}^{2} w_{ij}(1950)}$$

For example,

$$d_{11}(1950) = \frac{1{,}947}{1{,}947 + 27{,}417} = 0.0663$$

and

$$d_{21}(1950) = \frac{27{,}417}{1{,}947 + 27{,}417} = 0.9337$$

The growth matrix in Figure 1.1 then follows from

$$\underset{9\times 9}{\hat{\mathbf{G}}} = \underset{9\times 18}{\mathbf{C}} \cdot \underset{18\times 18}{\mathbf{G}} \cdot \underset{18\times 9}{\mathbf{D}(1950)}$$

1.5.7 A SHORT DIGRESSION ON THE LIFE TABLE AND AN IMPROVED METHOD FOR OBTAINING THE POPULATION GROWTH MATRIX

The matrix models of population growth and distribution that have been described in the preceding sections all have been expressed in terms of rates: birth rates, survivorship rates, and migration rates. Most of the more interesting questions in demographic analysis, however, are phrased in terms of probabilities and not rates, questions such as: what is the probability that a woman who is 65–69 years old today will die during the next five years, if the current female death rate for this age group remains unchanged? We therefore need to consider how one might infer probabilities from rates. For example, how can one infer an age-specific probability of dying, q_k, say, from an observed age-specific annual death rate, M_k, say.

According to Table 1.5, the female population of Yugoslavia, aged 65–69 at last birthday in 1961, suffered a loss of 7,170 women during that calendar year. If we are willing to assume that this population in mid-1961 adequately approximates the average number of women (or, more accurately, the total number of years lived by that female population during the calendar year 1961) who were exposed to the possibility of dying, then

Table 1.5. Population by Age and Sex, Births by Sex and Age of Mother, and Deaths by Age and Sex: Yugoslavia, 1961

Age at Last Birthday	Population on July 1 (in Thousands)			Births by Age of Mother			Deaths		
Age	Total	Males	Females	Total	Males	Females	Total	Males	Females
0– 4	1,883.5	967.8	915.7				41,341	21,873	19,468
5– 9	2,012.7	1,033.4	979.3				1,432	794	638
10–14	1,798.0	919.2	878.8	124	65	59	981	574	407
15–19	1,384.0	706.5	677.5	35,447	18,159	17,288	1,336	771	565
20–24	1,603.7	815.3	788.4	140,348	72,076	68,272	2,084	1,152	932
25–29	1,706.7	866.2	840.5	127,248	65,567	61,681	2,735	1,463	1,272
30–34	1,579.2	783.7	795.5	71,892	36,873	35,019	2,943	1,599	1,344
35–39	1,269.3	573.1	696.2	33,466	17,125	16,341	2,802	1,412	1,390
40–44	789.2	357.3	431.9	10,475	5,438	5,037	2,502	1,299	1,203
45–49	894.0	409.0	485.0	2,077	1,103	974	4,149	2,278	1,871
50–54	980.4	475.3	505.1	663	324	339	7,425	4,261	3,164
55–59	839.8	404.4	435.4				10,138	6,026	4,112
60–64	673.4	308.0	365.4				13,494	7,489	6,005
65–69	449.3	189.2	260.1				14,450	7,280	7,170
70–74	336.7	135.0	201.7				17,696	8,008	9,688
75–79	224.7	89.4	135.3				17,545	7,742	9,803
80–84	113.4	45.1	68.3				13,611	5,727	7,884
85+	68.4	25.5	42.9				10,697	4,325	6,372
Total	18,606.4	9,103.4	9,503.0	421,740	216,730	205,010	167,361	84,073	83,288

Source: Rogers and McDougall (1968).

$$_5M_{65} = \frac{_5D_{65}}{_5w_{65}} = \frac{7{,}170}{260{,}100} = 0.027566$$

or, more generally,

$$_xM_k = \frac{_xD_k}{_xw_k} \tag{1.45}$$

where

$_xM_k =$ the *annual* death rate of people aged k to $k + x$ at last birthday;

$_xD_k =$ the number of deaths registered during a calendar year among people aged k to $k + x$ at last birthday;

$_xw_k =$ the number of people aged k to $k + x$ at last birthday at mid-year.

Since, henceforth, we frequently shall be dealing with five-year age groups in cases except the first year of age, the subscript x, when omitted, will be understood to be equal to five. Also, to maintain a consistent notation, we shall adopt the same system of subscripts for identifying the various age groups in the population, instead of referring to them as the first, second, . . . , and nth age groups as before.

To derive a set of $_xq_k$ from a corresponding set of $_xM_k$, we must first specify how the deaths were distributed over time. It is often assumed that deaths were evenly distributed over time and over the ages within the age group interval. In such instances, we may say that people in the age interval $(k, k + x)$ died at the rate of $_xD_k$ per year, so that $_xD_k$ times $x/2$ represents the number of people who were alive at the beginning of the unit time interval of x years and died by the time the unit interval was half over. Thus if $_xw_k$ denotes the population at the mid-point of the interval of x years, then

$$_xq_k = \frac{x\,_xD_k}{_xw_k + (x/2)\,_xD_k}$$

and, dividing both the numerator and denominator by $_xw_k$, we find that

$$_xq_k = \frac{x\,_xM_k}{1 + (x/2)\,_xM_k} \tag{1.46}$$

or, for $x = 5$,

$$q_k = \frac{5M_k}{1 + (5/2)M_k} \tag{1.47}$$

For Yugoslavian women aged 65–69 in 1961, therefore, the probability of dying during the next five years, if the death rate for that age group during 1961 remained unchanged, was

$$q_{65} = \frac{5M_{65}}{1 + (5/2)M_{65}} = \frac{5(0.027566)}{1 + (5/2)(0.027566)} = 0.128945$$

The assumption that allowed us to express q_k as a function of M_k is generally acceptable for short intervals such as a year. Deaths in the older age groups, however, tend to rise from age to age, and to attribute a half of them to the first half of the age interval may introduce significant errors into the analysis when the age interval is as wide as five or ten years. In such instances, one may adopt an iterative method, developed by Keyfitz (1968, pp. 19–23), that leads to more precise estimates of q_k.

Using the estimated probabilities of dying at each age or age interval, we can obtain several other useful measures of mortality by exposing a hypothetical population, born on the same day and of fixed initial size, to these probabilities and observing the consequences of this particular pattern of age-specific mortality. Such calculations usually are carried out in the process of creating what demographers and actuaries call a *life table.*

A life table describes the life history of an artificial population, called a *cohort,* as it gradually decreases in size over time until all of its members have died. It is assumed that the observed cross-sectionally collected mortality experience to which this cohort is exposed remains constant and that the cohort is undisturbed by migration. Thus changes in the cohort's membership occur only as a consequence of losses due to death.

All of the columns in a life table originate from a set of probabilities of dying at each age or in each age group (q_k). Life tables that deal with age intervals longer than a year are called *abridged* life tables. However, they too separate out the first year of age in order to permit a more accurate assessment of the effects of infant mortality.

By applying, in sequence, a particular set of probabilities of dying to a cohort of a given *radix,* that is, of an initial size of 100,000 or some such standard number, we can describe how this cohort is diminished over time by calculating the number of survivors to each age, l_{k+x}:

$$l_{k+x} = (1 - q_k)l_k \tag{1.48}$$

For example, in Table 1.6 we find that the probability of dying during the first year of age, for females in Yugoslavia in 1961, was 0.081570. Therefore of an inital cohort of 100,000 female births, exposed to this probability of death, only

$$l_1 = (1 - q_0)l_0 = (1 - 0.081570)100{,}000 = 91{,}843$$

would survive to age one. This implies that

$$d_0 = l_0 - l_1 = 100{,}000 - 91{,}843 = 8{,}157$$

female babies would die during the first year of age. Generalizing, we conclude that the number of deaths between one age and another, ${}_xd_k$, is simply the number of survivors at that age less the number at the next age, that is,

$${}_xd_k = l_k - l_{k+x} \tag{1.49}$$

Table 1.6. Abridged Life Table: Yugoslavian Females, 1961

Age Group	(1) q_k	(2) l_k	(3) d_k	(4) L_k	(5) m_k	(6) s_k	(7) T_k	(8) e_k
0	0.081570*	100,000	8,157	95,921	0.085039	—**	6,653,237	66.53
1– 4	0.021039*	91,843	1,932	363,507	0.005316	0.976914	6,557,315	71.40
5– 9	0.003252	89,911	292	448,822	0.000651	0.997217	6,193,808	68.89
10–14	0.002313	89,618	207	447,573	0.000463	0.996764	5,744,986	64.11
15–19	0.004161	89,411	372	446,125	0.000834	0.994975	5,297,412	59.25
20–24	0.005893	89,039	525	443,883	0.001182	0.993287	4,851,287	54.48
25–29	0.007538	88,514	667	440,903	0.001513	0.992026	4,407,404	49.79
30–34	0.008412	87,847	739	437,387	0.001690	0.990831	3,966,501	45.15
35–39	0.009933	87,108	865	433,377	0.001997	0.988128	3,529,114	40.51
40–44	0.013831	86,243	1,193	428,232	0.002785	0.983551	3,095,737	35.90
45–49	0.019104	85,050	1,625	421,188	0.003858	0.975086	2,667,505	31.36
50–54	0.030838	83,425	2,573	410,694	0.006264	0.961635	2,246,318	26.93
55–59	0.046132	80,853	3,730	394,938	0.009444	0.937858	1,835,623	22.70
60–64	0.078927	77,123	6,087	370,395	0.016434	0.897091	1,440,686	18.68
65–69	0.128945	71,036	9,160	332,278	0.027566	0.831266	1,070,290	15.07
70–74	0.214412	61,876	13,267	276,212	0.048032	0.744979	738,012	11.93
75–79	0.306713	48,609	14,909	205,772	0.072454	0.635479	461,800	9.50
80–84	0.447904	33,700	15,094	130,764	0.115432	0.957939	256,028	7.60
85+	1.000000	18,606	18,606	125,264	0.148531	—	125,264	6.73

* To calculate this probability we have assumed that the first year of age contributes $\frac{1}{5}$ of the population and $\frac{4}{5}$ of the deaths to the 0–4 age group totals.
** Age groups 0 and 1–4 have been added together to calculate s_0.
Source: Calculated using the data in Table 1.5. Programmed by Ervin Bell.

The number of years lived by the life table cohort at each age, or in each age group, is denoted by ${}_xL_k$. This statistic cannot be calculated exactly, but must be approximated on the basis of an assumption regarding the distribution of deaths over the age interval used in the life table. The simplest such assumption is that deaths are evenly distributed over the interval, and, therefore, that the curve of survivors (l_k) declines linearly over the x years from k to $k + x$. For example, in Column 2 of Table 1.6, we see that 61,876 of 71,036 women, aged 65–69 at last birthday, survived to age 70–74. If the 71,036 − 61,876 = 9,160 deaths were distributed evenly over the five-year interval, then the 9,160 women who died lived an average of two and a half years each, or $(\frac{5}{2})(9{,}160) = 22{,}900$ person-years. The 61,876 who survived lived a full five years each, or $5(61{,}876) = 309{,}380$ person-years. Hence the total number of person-years lived by the cohort, during the five-year interval, was[3]

$$\begin{aligned} L_{65} &= \frac{5}{2}(9{,}160) + 5(61{,}876) \\ &= 22{,}900 + 309{,}380 \\ &= 332{,}280 \end{aligned}$$

[3] The slight discrepancy from the number 332,278 in Table 1.6 is due to rounding.

or, more generally,

$$
\begin{aligned}
{}_xL_k &= \frac{x}{2}\,{}_xd_k + xl_{k+x} \\
&= \frac{x}{2}\,(l_k - l_{k+x}) + xl_{k+x} \\
&= \frac{x}{2}\,(l_k + l_{k+x})
\end{aligned} \tag{1.50}
$$

Another life table statistic is the age-specific life table death rate, ${}_xm_k$, which is defined to be the ratio of deaths per person-year lived at any age interval:

$$
{}_xm_k = \frac{{}_xd_k}{{}_xL_k} \tag{1.51}
$$

This rate cannot be computed until ${}_xL_k$ is found. However, it is often assumed that ${}_xm_k$ is equal to ${}_xM_k$, the corresponding observed age-specific death rate. In such instances,

$$
{}_xm_k = {}_xM_k = \frac{{}_xd_k}{{}_xL_k}
$$

or

$$
{}_xL_k = \frac{{}_xd_k}{{}_xM_k} \tag{1.52}
$$

The impact of mortality on the life table population may be expressed in terms of a survival probability or proportion, ${}_xs_k$, where

$$
{}_xs_k = \frac{L_{k+x}}{L_k} \tag{1.53}
$$

These age-specific survival probabilities are more precise estimates of the subdiagonal elements of the population growth matrix **G** in (1.22) than are the survival rates defined earlier. Thus they should be used whenever accuracy and precision are at a premium.[4]

[4] Two alternative interpretations of the set of l_k in a life table are possible. We may continue to think of the l_k as the expected number of survivors of a *cohort* of l_0 babies born at the same moment and exposed to the same age-specific pattern of mortality, with ${}_xL_k$ representing the total number of person-years lived by that cohort between the ages k and $k + x$. Or we may interpret the l_k as a *stationary population* that is constant in size as well as in age distribution, which includes ${}_xL_k$ persons between the ages k and $k + x$. This latter interpretation is particularly useful in understanding (1.53), for in a stationary population persons alive between the ages $k + x$ and $k + 2x$ at time $t + 1$ (${}_xL_{k+x}$) are the survivors of persons alive between the ages k and $k + x$ at time t (${}_xL_k$). Hence (1.53) defines the probability that an individual between the ages k and $k + x$ at time t will survive the subsequent interval of x years to become a member of the next age group at time $t + 1$.

In Table 1.6 we note that

$$s_{65} = \frac{L_{70}}{L_{65}} = \frac{276{,}212}{332{,}278} = 0.831266$$

Thus we would expect that of the 260,100 Yugoslavian women aged 65–69 at last birthday,

$$w_{65}s_{65} = 260{,}100(0.831266) = 216{,}212$$

would survive to the 70–74-year age group if exposed to the pattern of mortality described by the life table, and if Yugoslavia experienced no immigration or emigration during that period.

The last two columns of the life table in Table 1.6 describe the total number of person-years lived after each age by the members of the cohort (T_k) and the mean expectation of life at each age (e_k). The former statistic is simply the sum of the number of years lived by the cohort after some particular age; the latter is the average number of years lived by each member in the cohort after each age. Hence we conclude that

$$T_k = \sum_{i=k}^{\infty} {}_xL_i \tag{1.54}$$

where the summation begins with age k and continues, in x-year increments, to the end of life in the cohort, and

$$e_k = \frac{T_k}{l_k} \tag{1.55}$$

The value e_0 is commonly referred to as the *expectation of life at birth,* and for Yugoslavian females in 1961 it was:

$$e_0 = \frac{T_0}{l_0} = \frac{6{,}653{,}237}{100{,}000} = 66.53 \quad \text{years}$$

The terminal age interval in a life table is a half-open interval: z years and over. For this interval q_z is set to unity, and the statistics D_z, M_z, l_z, d_z, T_z, and e_z all refer to the interval age z and over. Because the length of this interval is infinite, a slight modification of (1.50) is necessary in order to determine L_z. Setting $k = z$ in (1.52), we have

$$L_z = \frac{d_z}{M_z}$$

and, since each of the l_z people aged z and over ultimately will die, $l_z = d_z$, and

$$L_z = \frac{l_z}{M_z} \tag{1.56}$$

By definition,

$$T_z = L_z \tag{1.57}$$

Consequently,

$$e_z = \frac{T_z}{l_z} = \frac{L_z}{l_z} \tag{1.58}$$

Equation (1.22) may be used to project the Yugoslavian female population, alive in 1961, five years forward to 1966. However, to do this we first must obtain estimates of the expected number of births, during the five years, *that survive to the end of the interval.* The life table provides the necessary survivorship factor [Keyfitz (1968), p. 30]:

$$\frac{L_0}{5l_0} \tag{1.59}$$

For example, we note in Table 1.5 that 68,272 live female births were registered to Yugoslavian women 20–24 years of age at last birthday in 1961. Thus the corresponding age-specific birth rate was

$$F_{20} = \frac{68{,}272}{788{,}400} = 0.0865956$$

or, in general, for $x = 5$,

$$F_k = \frac{B_k}{w_k} \tag{1.60}$$

where

F_k = the *annual* age-specific birth rate of women aged k to $k + 5$ at last birthday;

B_k = the number of live female births registered during a calendar year to women aged k to $k + 5$ at last birthday;

w_k = the number of women aged k to $k + 5$ at last birthday at midyear.

Usually, the annual birth rate, F_k, is applied to the arithmetic mean of the initial and final populations in the k to $k + 5$ age group:

$$\frac{w_k(t) + w_k(t+1)}{2} = \frac{1}{2}\left[w_k(t) + \frac{L_k}{L_{k-5}} w_{k-5}(t)\right] \tag{1.61}$$

and, since this population is exposed to the fertility schedule for five years, we multiply (1.61) by five. This age group's contribution to the total number of births during the five-year time interval $(t, t + 1)$, therefore, is

$$\frac{5}{2}\left[w_k(t) + \frac{L_k}{L_{k-5}} w_{k-5}(t)\right] F_k$$

0	0.00015	0.05858	0.25654	0.36637	0.26889	0.15455	0.08039	0.03133	0.00612	0.00154	0	0	0	0	0	0	0
0.97691	0	0	0	0	0	0	0	0	0	0	0	0	0	0	0	0	0
0	0.99722	0	0	0	0	0	0	0	0	0	0	0	0	0	0	0	0
0	0	0.99676	0	0	0	0	0	0	0	0	0	0	0	0	0	0	0
0	0	0	0.99498	0	0	0	0	0	0	0	0	0	0	0	0	0	0
0	0	0	0	0.99329	0	0	0	0	0	0	0	0	0	0	0	0	0
0	0	0	0	0	0.99203	0	0	0	0	0	0	0	0	0	0	0	0
0	0	0	0	0	0	0.99083	0	0	0	0	0	0	0	0	0	0	0
0	0	0	0	0	0	0	0.98813	0	0	0	0	0	0	0	0	0	0
0	0	0	0	0	0	0	0	0.98355	0	0	0	0	0	0	0	0	0
0	0	0	0	0	0	0	0	0	0.97509	0	0	0	0	0	0	0	0
0	0	0	0	0	0	0	0	0	0	0.96164	0	0	0	0	0	0	0
0	0	0	0	0	0	0	0	0	0	0	0.93786	0	0	0	0	0	0
0	0	0	0	0	0	0	0	0	0	0	0	0.89709	0	0	0	0	0
0	0	0	0	0	0	0	0	0	0	0	0	0	0.83127	0	0	0	0
0	0	0	0	0	0	0	0	0	0	0	0	0	0	0.74498	0	0	0
0	0	0	0	0	0	0	0	0	0	0	0	0	0	0	0.63548	0	0
0	0	0	0	0	0	0	0	0	0	0	0	0	0	0	0	0.95794	0

Source: Table 1.6 and calculations using the data in Table 1.5.

Figure 1.3. The Single-Region Population Growth Matrix for Yugoslavian Females: 1961

Table 1.7. Population by Age and Sex, Births by Sex and Age of Mother, and Deaths by Age and Sex: Slovenia, 1961

Age at Last Birthday	Population on July 1 (in Thousands)			Births by Age of Mother			Deaths		
Age	Total	Males	Females	Total	Males	Females	Total	Males	Females
0– 4	138.8	71.0	67.8				995	578	417
5– 9	151.9	77.8	74.1				76	44	32
10–14	143.3	72.6	70.7	7	2	5	62	41	21
15–19	121.5	61.4	60.1	1,971	1,018	953	124	93	31
20–24	127.1	64.2	62.9	8,994	4,550	4,444	159	112	47
25–29	133.2	66.7	66.5	8,720	4,516	4,204	164	119	45
30–34	130.9	63.8	67.1	5,539	2,781	2,758	236	169	67
35–39	110.5	47.6	62.9	2,951	1,513	1,438	187	110	77
40–44	70.0	30.5	39.5	672	364	308	185	109	76
45–49	88.0	40.1	47.9	68	34	34	420	249	171
50–54	95.9	44.6	51.3	27	12	15	656	388	268
55–59	85.0	38.9	46.1				1,022	653	369
60–64	70.2	30.6	39.6				1,321	808	513
65–69	49.3	19.8	29.5				1,546	783	763
70–74	35.3	13.6	21.7				1,928	892	1,036
75–79	23.3	8.9	14.4				1,931	843	1,088
80–84	11.4	4.3	7.1				1,778	737	1,041
85+	6.0	2.4	3.6				1,223	490	733
Total	1,591.6	758.8	832.8	28,949	14,790	14,159	14,013	7,218	6,795

Source: Rogers and McDougall (1968).

and adding this quantity over all of the childbearing age groups, beginning with age α and ending with β, yields [Keyfitz (1968), p. 30]:

$$\frac{5}{2}\sum_{\alpha}^{\beta-5}\left[w_k(t) + \frac{L_k}{L_{k-5}}\, w_{k-5}(t)\right] F_k$$

$$= \frac{5}{2}\sum_{\alpha-5}^{\beta-5}\left(F_k + \frac{L_{k+5}}{L_k}\, F_{k+5}\right) w_k(t) \qquad (1.62)$$

Equation (1.62) describes the total number of births that are expected during the five-year time interval. But what we want is the total number of babies that survive to the beginning of the next time interval. Hence, we multiply (1.62) by the survivorship factor in (1.59) and, assuming that $\alpha = 15$ and $\beta = 50$, obtain the following improved estimate of the growth matrix **G** in (1.22):

$$
\mathbf{G} = \begin{bmatrix}
0 & 0 & \frac{L_0}{2l_0}\left(\frac{L_{15}}{L_{10}}F_{15}\right) & \frac{L_0}{2l_0}\left(F_{15} + \frac{L_{20}}{L_{15}}F_{20}\right) & \cdots & 0 \\
\frac{L_5}{L_0} & 0 & 0 & 0 & \cdots & 0 \\
0 & \frac{L_{10}}{L_5} & 0 & 0 & \cdots & 0 \\
0 & 0 & \cdot & & & \cdot \\
\cdot & & & \cdot & & \cdot \\
\cdot & & & & \cdot & \cdot \\
0 & 0 & 0 & & & 0
\end{bmatrix} \qquad (1.63)
$$

Figure 1.3 illustrates the growth matrix that results from the application of (1.63) to the data on Yugoslavian females contained in Tables 1.5 and 1.6. The reader should test his understanding of the life table by constructing such a table for females in Slovenia, Yugoslavia, and another one for females in the rest of Yugoslavia, using the data in Tables 1.5 and 1.7 (Exercise 4). Next, he should attempt to extend the definition of **G** in (1.63) to the interregional case by treating out-migration as another category of "death" (Exercise 5). Table 1.8 presents the necessary data for such an extension.

Table 1.8. Interregional Migration by Age and Sex: Yugoslavia, 1961

Age at Last Birthday	Slovenia to Rest of Yugoslavia			Rest of Yugoslavia to Slovenia		
Age	Total	Males	Females	Total	Males	Females
0– 4	368	176	192	472	241	231
5– 9	378	208	170	352	202	150
10–14	212	107	105	241	114	127
15–19	472	162	310	760	341	419
20–24	824	373	451	1,566	886	680
25–29	795	427	368	1,156	764	392
30–34	554	302	252	635	380	255
35–39	342	231	111	367	224	143
40–44	109	69	40	170	98	72
45–49	60	34	26	105	64	41
50–54	61	27	34	121	62	59
55–59	50	21	29	123	43	80
60–64	48	13	35	104	38	66
65–69	36	8	28	52	16	36
70–74	30	11	19	24	10	14
75–79	24	8	16	22	10	12
80–84	5	0	5	16	4	12
85+	7	3	4	5	2	3
Total	4,375	2,180	2,195	6,291	3,499	2,792

Source: Rogers and McDougall (1968).

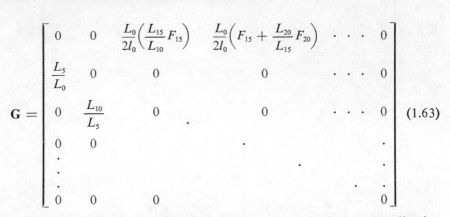

1.6 APPLICATION: A SPATIAL ACTIVITY ALLOCATION MODEL

Spatial activity allocation models are concerned with the geographical distribution of human activities in urban and regional areas. Their principal purpose is to assign activities to the subareas of a region in a way that reflects the locational interdependencies of such activities. Properly used, they are potentially powerful tools for projecting future urban environments and for testing the probable developmental consequences of alternative policies in areas such as transportation investment, land use controls, and urban renewal. In this section, we shall describe a very simplified matrix version of such a model: the Lowry model.[5]

1.6.1 THE JOURNEY FROM WORK TO HOME AND RESIDENTIAL LOCATION

Consider an urban region that has been divided into m zones, and assume that the population of this region locates with respect to its place of employment. In short, assume that people, in striving to reduce the costs of their journey to work, tend to live clustered in a regular manner around their places of employment.

If all employees had to live in the zone in which they worked, then the population of each zone could be found by applying a population-per-employee ratio to the number of employees in each zone:

$$w_i(t) = a_i e_i(t) \tag{1.64}$$

where

$w_i(t)$ = the total population in zone i at time t;
$e_i(t)$ = the total employment in zone i at time t; and
a_i = the population-per-employee ratio of zone i (that is, the reciprocal of the zonal labor force participation rate).

However, employees do not always live in the zone in which they work; consequently, the total number of employees who live in zone i may be represented as the sum of those who work in zone 1, zone 2, and so on. We conclude, therefore, that

$$w_i(t) = a_i[p_{i1}e_1(t) + p_{i2}e_2(t) + \cdots + p_{im}e_m(t)]$$

where p_{ij} denotes the proportion of employees who work in zone j and live in zone i. Thus in matrix form:

$$\begin{bmatrix} w_1(t) \\ w_2(t) \\ \vdots \\ w_m(t) \end{bmatrix} = \begin{bmatrix} a_1 & 0 & 0 \cdots 0 \\ 0 & a_2 & 0 \cdots 0 \\ \vdots & \vdots & \ddots \quad \vdots \\ 0 & 0 & \cdots \quad a_m \end{bmatrix} \begin{bmatrix} p_{11} & p_{12} \cdots & p_{1m} \\ p_{21} & p_{22} \cdots & p_{2m} \\ \vdots & \vdots \ddots & \vdots \\ p_{m1} & p_{m2} & p_{mm} \end{bmatrix} \begin{bmatrix} e_1(t) \\ e_2(t) \\ \vdots \\ e_m(t) \end{bmatrix}$$

$$= \mathbf{APe}(t)$$

[5] Lowry (1964).

or

$$\mathbf{w}(t) = \mathbf{Me}(t) \tag{1.65}$$

where $\mathbf{M} = \mathbf{AP}$. We shall call $\mathbf{P}$ the *journey-from-work-to-home matrix.*

Example. To illustrate the operation of the spatial activity allocation model defined in (1.65), let us return to our hypothetical island, Islandia, and its three regions, each of which had, in 1950, a total population of 288 people. Assume that, in 1950, 96 employees lived in each region and that an equal number worked in each region. Then the population-per-employee ratio in each region would be three, and, if all employees lived in the region in which they worked,

$$w_i(1950) = a_i e_i(1950) = 3(96) = 288$$

for $i = 1, 2,$ and 3, or, in matrix form,

$$\begin{bmatrix} w_1(1950) \\ w_2(1950) \\ w_3(1950) \end{bmatrix} = \begin{bmatrix} 3 & 0 & 0 \\ 0 & 3 & 0 \\ 0 & 0 & 3 \end{bmatrix} \begin{bmatrix} 1 & 0 & 0 \\ 0 & 1 & 0 \\ 0 & 0 & 1 \end{bmatrix} \begin{bmatrix} 96 \\ 96 \\ 96 \end{bmatrix} = \begin{bmatrix} 288 \\ 288 \\ 288 \end{bmatrix} \tag{1.66}$$

If we assume that only a half of the employees working in each region also live there, and that the other half live, in equal proportions, in the other two regions, then we have the data in Table 1.9. Consequently, the identity matrix in (1.66) must be replaced by

$$\mathbf{P} = \begin{bmatrix} \frac{1}{2} & \frac{1}{4} & \frac{1}{4} \\ \frac{1}{4} & \frac{1}{2} & \frac{1}{4} \\ \frac{1}{4} & \frac{1}{4} & \frac{1}{2} \end{bmatrix}$$

whence

$$\mathbf{M} = \begin{bmatrix} 3 & 0 & 0 \\ 0 & 3 & 0 \\ 0 & 0 & 3 \end{bmatrix} \begin{bmatrix} \frac{1}{2} & \frac{1}{4} & \frac{1}{4} \\ \frac{1}{4} & \frac{1}{2} & \frac{1}{4} \\ \frac{1}{4} & \frac{1}{4} & \frac{1}{2} \end{bmatrix} = \begin{bmatrix} \frac{3}{2} & \frac{3}{4} & \frac{3}{4} \\ \frac{3}{4} & \frac{3}{2} & \frac{3}{4} \\ \frac{3}{4} & \frac{3}{4} & \frac{3}{2} \end{bmatrix}$$

Table 1.9. The Journey to Work in Islandia: 1950

Region of Residence \ Region of Employment	Northern Islandia	Central Islandia	Southern Islandia	Total Number of Employees by Region of Residence
Northern Islandia	48	24	24	96
Central Islandia	24	48	24	96
Southern Islandia	24	24	48	96
Total Number of Employees by Region of Employment	96	96	96	288

and

$$\begin{bmatrix} w_1(1950) \\ w_2(1950) \\ w_3(1950) \end{bmatrix} = \begin{bmatrix} \frac{3}{2} & \frac{3}{4} & \frac{3}{4} \\ \frac{3}{4} & \frac{3}{2} & \frac{3}{4} \\ \frac{3}{4} & \frac{3}{4} & \frac{3}{2} \end{bmatrix} \begin{bmatrix} 96 \\ 96 \\ 96 \end{bmatrix} = \begin{bmatrix} 288 \\ 288 \\ 288 \end{bmatrix}$$

1.6.2 EMPLOYMENT GROWTH AND POPULATION GROWTH

Equation (1.65) relates a region's interzonal employment distribution, at time t, to its interzonal population distribution at the same point in time. The model, therefore, is static and may be fitted to cross-sectional data. In order to introduce a dynamic dimension to the model, we may adopt a model of employment growth and then trace through the implications of this growth on the region's population.

Assume that the growth and distribution of employment in the study area may be expressed by an employment growth model that is analogous to the components-of-change population growth model defined in (1.18):

$$\mathbf{e}(t + 1) = \mathbf{S}\mathbf{e}(t) \tag{1.67}$$

where

s_{ij} = the proportion of employees, working in zone i at time t, who are working in zone j at time $t + 1$;

s_{ii} = the sum of two proportions: (1) the proportion of employees, working in zone i at time t, who are working in zone i at time $t+1$, and (2) the region's "new" employees (that is, "employee births" and "employee migrants" into the urban area) that are allocated to zone i, during the time interval $(t, t+1)$, as a proportion of total employees working in zone i at time t.

Then, combining (1.65) and (1.67), we have that

$$\mathbf{w}(t+1) = \mathbf{Me}(t+1) = \mathbf{MSe}(t) \tag{1.68}$$

and the model now has a time dimension.

Example. Table 1.10 describes the components of employment change, in the three regions of Islandia, during the 15 years between 1950 and 1965. Using an estimation procedure that is directly analogous to the one described in Section 1.5.1, we obtain the employment growth matrix

$$\mathbf{S} = \begin{bmatrix} \frac{5}{3} & \frac{1}{4} & \frac{1}{6} \\ \frac{1}{12} & \frac{1}{3} & \frac{1}{6} \\ \frac{1}{12} & \frac{1}{4} & \frac{1}{4} \end{bmatrix}$$

and with it find $\mathbf{e}(t+1)$:

$$\mathbf{e}(1965) = \mathbf{Se}(1950) = \begin{bmatrix} \frac{5}{3} & \frac{1}{4} & \frac{1}{6} \\ \frac{1}{12} & \frac{1}{3} & \frac{1}{6} \\ \frac{1}{12} & \frac{1}{4} & \frac{1}{4} \end{bmatrix} \begin{bmatrix} 96 \\ 96 \\ 96 \end{bmatrix} = \begin{bmatrix} 200 \\ 56 \\ 56 \end{bmatrix}$$

Having found $\mathbf{e}(1965)$, we now may obtain $\mathbf{w}(1965)$, by using the relation defined in (1.68):

$$\mathbf{w}(1965) = \mathbf{Me}(1965) = \begin{bmatrix} \frac{3}{2} & \frac{3}{4} & \frac{3}{4} \\ \frac{3}{4} & \frac{3}{2} & \frac{3}{4} \\ \frac{3}{4} & \frac{3}{4} & \frac{3}{2} \end{bmatrix} \begin{bmatrix} 200 \\ 56 \\ 56 \end{bmatrix} = \begin{bmatrix} 384 \\ 276 \\ 276 \end{bmatrix}$$

Table 1.10. Components of Employment Change in Islandia: 1950–1965

	Total Employment 1950	Employee Births	Employee Deaths	Employee Out-Migrants to: Northern Islandia	Central Islandia	Southern Islandia	Employee In-Migrants from: Northern Islandia	Central Islandia	Southern Islandia	Total Employment 1965
Northern Islandia	96	120	40	—	8	8	—	24	16	200
Central Islandia	96	20	36	24	—	24	8	—	16	56
Southern Islandia	96	8	48	16	16	—	8	24	—	56
Total	288	148	124	—	—	—	—	—	—	312

Alternatively,

$$\mathbf{w}(1965) = \mathbf{Me}(1965) = \mathbf{MSe}(1950)$$

$$= \begin{bmatrix} \frac{3}{2} & \frac{3}{4} & \frac{3}{4} \\ \frac{3}{4} & \frac{3}{2} & \frac{3}{4} \\ \frac{3}{4} & \frac{3}{4} & \frac{3}{2} \end{bmatrix} \begin{bmatrix} \frac{5}{3} & \frac{1}{4} & \frac{1}{6} \\ \frac{1}{12} & \frac{1}{3} & \frac{1}{6} \\ \frac{1}{12} & \frac{1}{4} & \frac{1}{6} \end{bmatrix} \begin{bmatrix} 96 \\ 96 \\ 96 \end{bmatrix}$$

$$= \begin{bmatrix} \frac{21}{8} & \frac{13}{16} & \frac{9}{16} \\ \frac{23}{16} & \frac{7}{8} & \frac{9}{16} \\ \frac{23}{16} & \frac{13}{16} & \frac{5}{8} \end{bmatrix} \begin{bmatrix} 96 \\ 96 \\ 96 \end{bmatrix} = \begin{bmatrix} 384 \\ 276 \\ 276 \end{bmatrix}$$

Notice that these projections of $\mathbf{w}(1965)$ are identical to those obtained by the components-of-change population growth model in (1.20).

The above matrix formulation of intraregional employment and population growth leads to a very simple and compact expression of an empirically verifiable relationship between the spatial patterns of population and employment in an urban area. It can be used to assess the spatial implications of changes in the sizes of the labor force and labor force participation rates, and changes in accessibilities to employment centers. The model also relates employment growth to population growth and, more importantly, it readily accepts refinements in the hypothesized population-employment

Table 1.11. The Journey to Work of Industrial Workers in the Ljubljana

Commune of Residence	Commune of Employment							
	1. Kranj	2. Skofja Loka	3. Trzic	4. Cerknica	5. Domzale	6. Grosuplje	7. Kamnik	8. Litija
1. Kranj	10,006	65	97		5		35	
2. Skofja Loka	284	3,173	1		1			
3. Trzic	213	2	3,217					
4. Cerknica				1,975				
5. Domzale	1				5,273		263	18
6. Grosuplje						904		
7. Kamnik	12				249		3,655	
8. Litija					1	4		1,449
9. Ljubljana-Bezigrad	12	4			65	1	1	6
10. Ljubljana-Center	25	3		1	13	5	6	9
11. Ljubljana-Moste-Polje	16	1			16	2		11
12. Ljubljana-Siska	344	41	2		117	1	19	5
13. Ljubljana-Vic-Rudnik	31	3	1	21	17	2	2	9
14. Logatec		7		3	1			
15. Vrhnika				6		1	1	1
16. Rest of Slovenia	292	3	7	62	2	46		16
Total Number of Industrial Employees by Commune of Employment	11,236	3,302	3,325	2,068	5,760	966	3,982	1,524

Source: Town Planning Institute of Slovenia, Ljubljana, Yugoslavia. We assume that

linkages. For example, employment may be disaggregated into *basic* and *nonbasic* components and the model generalized to assume the form of the Garin-Lowry model.[6] Such an extension is discussed in the next chapter.

[6] Garin (1966).

Metropolitan Region and the Rest of Slovenia: 1963

Commune of Employment								
9. Ljubljana-Bezigrad	10. Ljubljana-Center	11. Ljubljana-Moste-Polje	12. Ljubljana-Siska	13. Ljubljana-Vic-Rudnik	14. Logatec	15. Vrhnika	16. Rest of Slovenia	Total No. Industrial Employees by Commune of Residence
	21	3	198	3		1	316	10,750
37	58	8	148	3	13		8	3,734
	1		5				9	3,447
	4				6	1	7	1,993
367	76	71	32	9			42	6,152
8	240	10	19	49			2	1,232
54	31	3	16	3			4	4,027
6	91	160	32				60	1,803
2,939	868	109	319	34	1	5	5	4,369
201	1,243	210	303	58	1	3	8	2,089
170	1,188	3,860	123	24		10	3	5,424
497	1,725	71	8,258	24		5	3	11,112
141	1,751	208	225	3,538	2	59	6	6,016
3	8		5	3	1,642	8		1,680
6	113	3	46	73	15	1,726		1,991
	149	30	38	15	86	2	110,133	110,881
4,429	7,567	4,746	9,767	3,836	1,766	1,820	110,606	176,700

all Slovenian workers live and work in Slovenia.

1.6.3 APPLICATION: A SPATIAL ACTIVITY ALLOCATION MODEL FOR THE LJUBLJANA METROPOLITAN REGION IN NORTHERN YUGOSLAVIA

Table 1.11 presents data on the journey to work of industrial workers in the Ljubljana Metropolitan Region of Slovenia, Yugoslavia, in 1963. This region contains 15 communes and the capital of the Slovenian Republic,

$$
\mathbf{P} = \begin{bmatrix}
0.8905 & 0.0197 & 0.0292 & 0 & 0.0009 & 0 & 0.0088 & 0 & 0 & 0.0028 & 0.0006 & 0.0203 & 0.0008 & 0 & 0.0005 & 0.0029 \\
0.0253 & 0.9609 & 0.0003 & 0 & 0.0002 & 0 & 0 & 0 & 0.0084 & 0.0077 & 0.0017 & 0.0152 & 0.0008 & 0.0074 & 0 & 0.0001 \\
0.0190 & 0.0006 & 0.9675 & 0 & 0 & 0 & 0 & 0 & 0 & 0.0001 & 0 & 0.0005 & 0 & 0 & 0 & 0.0001 \\
0 & 0 & 0 & 0.9550 & 0 & 0 & 0 & 0 & 0 & 0.0005 & 0 & 0 & 0 & 0.0034 & 0.0005 & 0.0001 \\
0.0001 & 0 & 0 & 0 & 0.9155 & 0 & 0.0660 & 0.0118 & 0.0829 & 0.0100 & 0.0150 & 0.0033 & 0.0023 & 0 & 0 & 0.0004 \\
0 & 0 & 0 & 0 & 0 & 0.9358 & 0 & 0 & 0.0018 & 0.0317 & 0.0021 & 0.0019 & 0.0128 & 0 & 0 & 0.0000 \\
0.0011 & 0 & 0 & 0 & 0.0432 & 0 & 0.9179 & 0 & 0.0122 & 0.0041 & 0.0006 & 0.0016 & 0.0008 & 0 & 0 & 0.0000 \\
0 & 0 & 0 & 0 & 0.0002 & 0.0041 & 0 & 0.9508 & 0.0014 & 0.0120 & 0.0337 & 0.0033 & 0 & 0 & 0 & 0.0005 \\
0.0011 & 0.0012 & 0 & 0 & 0.0113 & 0.0010 & 0.0003 & 0.0039 & 0.6636 & 0.1147 & 0.0230 & 0.0327 & 0.0089 & 0.0006 & 0.0027 & 0.0000 \\
0.0022 & 0.0009 & 0 & 0.0005 & 0.0023 & 0.0052 & 0.0015 & 0.0059 & 0.0454 & 0.1643 & 0.0442 & 0.0310 & 0.0151 & 0.0006 & 0.0016 & 0.0001 \\
0.0014 & 0.0003 & 0 & 0 & 0.0028 & 0.0021 & 0 & 0.0072 & 0.0384 & 0.1570 & 0.8133 & 0.0126 & 0.0063 & 0 & 0.0055 & 0.0000 \\
0.0306 & 0.0124 & 0.0006 & 0 & 0.0203 & 0.0010 & 0.0048 & 0.0033 & 0.1122 & 0.2280 & 0.0150 & 0.8455 & 0.0063 & 0 & 0.0027 & 0.0000 \\
0.0028 & 0.0009 & 0.0003 & 0.0102 & 0.0030 & 0.0021 & 0.0005 & 0.0059 & 0.0318 & 0.2314 & 0.0438 & 0.0230 & 0.9223 & 0.0011 & 0.0324 & 0.0001 \\
0 & 0.0021 & 0 & 0.0015 & 0.0002 & 0 & 0 & 0 & 0.0007 & 0.0011 & 0 & 0.0005 & 0.0008 & 0.9298 & 0.0044 & 0 \\
0 & 0 & 0 & 0.0029 & 0 & 0.0010 & 0.0003 & 0.0007 & 0.0014 & 0.0149 & 0.0006 & 0.0047 & 0.0190 & 0.0085 & 0.9484 & 0 \\
0.0260 & 0.0009 & 0.0021 & 0.0300 & 0.0003 & 0.0476 & 0 & 0.0105 & 0 & 0.0197 & 0.0063 & 0.0039 & 0.0039 & 0.0487 & 0.0011 & 0.9957
\end{bmatrix}
$$

Source: Calculated using the data in Table 1.11. Programmed by William Stock.

Figure 1.4. The Journey-from-Work-to-Home Matrix: The Ljubljana Metropolitan Region and the Rest of Slovenia, 1963

Table 1.12. Employment and Population in the Ljubljana Metropolitan Region and the Rest or Slovenia: 1963 and Projected to 1968

Commune	1. Industrial Employment by Commune of Employment 1963	2. Industrial Employment by Commune of Residence 1963	3. Communal Population 1963	4. Population per-Industrial-Employee Ratio	5. Industrial Employment by Commune of Employment 1968	6. Communal Population 1968	7. Communal Population 1968
	e(1963)	**Pe(1963)**	**Me(1963)**	a_i	**e(1968)**	**Me(1968)**	**Gw(1963)**
1. Kranj	11,236	10,750	48,922	4.5509	12,018	52,231	54,769
2. Skofja Loka	3,302	3,734	24,773	6.6344	3,529	26,446	26,311
3. Trzic	3,325	3,447	11,320	3.2840	3,386	11,564	12,010
4. Cerknica	2,068	1,993	13,908	6.9784	2,051	13,795	14,083
5. Domzale	5,760	6,152	28,147	4.5753	6,063	29,985	30,646
6. Grosuplje	966	1,232	22,453	18.2248	1,075	24,231	21,896
7. Kamnik	3,982	4,027	20,246	5.0276	4,112	20,987	21,424
8. Litija	1,524	1,803	16,517	9.1608	1,547	17,073	16,438
9. Lj.-Bezigrad	4,429	4,369	33,900	7.7592	5,618	39,742	42,319
10. Lj.-Center	7,567	2,089	42,391	20.2925	6,730	42,571	42,556
11. Lj.-Moste-Polje	4,746	5,424	34,596	6.3783	5,996	40,637	44,033
12. Lj.-Siska	9,767	11,112	47,223	4.2497	10,203	48,804	54,891
13. Lj.-Vic-Rudnik	3,836	6,016	55,197	9.1750	5,126	65,338	60,410
14. Logatec	1,766	1,680	10,812	6.4357	1,835	11,241	11,422
15. Vrhnika	1,820	1,991	12,610	6.3335	1,914	13,284	13,473
Subtotal (L.M.R.)	66,093	65,819	423,016	—	71,203	457,929	466,681
16. Rest of Slovenia	110,606	110,881	1,186,418	10.6999	115,750	1,241,514	1,229,765
Total (Slovenia)	176,700	176,700	1,609,434	—	186,953	1,699,443	1,696,446

Source: Rogers and McDougall (1968) and calculations using the data in Table 1.11 and Figure 1.5. Programmed by William Stock.

1.00566	0.02638	0.03480	0.00404	0.00389	0.00318	0.00749	0.00457	0.00209	0.00454	0.00148	0.00769	0.00253	0.00854	0.00133	0.00264
0.00766	0.97814	0.00187	0.00182	0.00183	0.00053	0.00129	0.00097	0.00224	0.00145	0.00247	0.00353	0.00159	0.01552	0.00051	0.00076
0.00378	0.00104	0.98252	0.00246	0.00037	0.00066	0.00051	0.00032	0.00046	0.00085	0.00005	0.00055	0.00021	0.00003	0.00002	0.00043
0.00042	0.00061	0.00045	0.94005	0.00020	0.00150	0.00002	0.00033	0.00049	0.00119	0.00087	0.00056	0.00114	0.00182	0.00042	0.00060
0.00079	0.00087	0.00006	0.00149	0.98837	0.00164	0.02367	0.00422	0.00325	0.00441	0.00438	0.00474	0.00232	0.00191	0.00167	0.00111
0.00112	0.00063	0.00005	0.00275	0.00109	0.89261	0.00053	0.00540	0.00221	0.00250	0.00282	0.00239	0.00382	0.00094	0.00046	0.00084
0.00166	0.00005	0.00135	0.00040	0.01265	0.00029	0.97522	0.00210	0.00179	0.00241	0.00165	0.00114	0.00115	0.00005	0.00083	0.00070
0.00053	0.00004	0.00003	0.00072	0.00227	0.00295	0.00100	0.91250	0.00200	0.00115	0.00313	0.00128	0.00095	0.00224	0.00081	0.00068
0.00615	0.00529	0.00882	0.00570	0.01488	0.01449	0.00570	0.00827	0.80858	0.08109	0.04639	0.03873	0.03407	0.00373	0.00759	0.00372
0.00407	0.00577	0.00313	0.00797	0.00619	0.01703	0.00665	0.00999	0.06549	0.65072	0.05463	0.04324	0.04756	0.00840	0.01231	0.00388
0.00439	0.00425	0.00217	0.00935	0.00974	0.01836	0.00622	0.01917	0.06022	0.08395	0.86064	0.03092	0.03123	0.00336	0.00954	0.00313
0.00830	0.01321	0.00260	0.00640	0.00937	0.01350	0.00596	0.01292	0.05220	0.06354	0.03600	0.86836	0.03188	0.00976	0.00767	0.00376
0.00328	0.00530	0.00327	0.01124	0.00662	0.01854	0.00544	0.01288	0.03432	0.07003	0.03995	0.03457	0.85590	0.00714	0.01886	0.00362
0.00094	0.00340	0.00003	0.00316	0.00038	0.00088	0.00027	0.00033	0.00048	0.00097	0.00021	0.00104	0.00041	0.97943	0.00894	0.00031
0.00074	0.00024	0.00176	0.00178	0.00197	0.00071	0.00270	0.00265	0.00123	0.00172	0.00109	0.00073	0.00361	0.00682	0.96644	0.00048
0.03692	0.02589	0.02746	0.04559	0.03715	0.04729	0.03193	0.05974	0.03833	0.08038	0.03914	0.03731	0.03353	0.03214	0.03833	1.02167

Source: Rogers and McDougall (1968).

Figure 1.5. Five-Year Components-of-Change Population Growth Matrix: Ljubljana Metropolitan Region and the Rest of Slovenia, 1963

Ljubljana, a city of approximately 200,000 people.[7]

Dividing each of the elements of the journey-to-work matrix in Table 1.11 by its column sum, we obtain the journey-from-work-to-home matrix that appears in Figure 1.4. And applying this matrix to the vector **e**(1963) that appears in Column 1 of Table 1.12, we find, as a check on our arithmetic, the elements of **Pe**(1963) that appear in Column 2. Finally, dividing the elements of Column 3 by the corresponding elements of Column 2, we obtain the 15 communal population-per-employee ratios that appear in Column 4.

In order to project the Ljubljana Metropolitan Region's industrial employment and population into the future, we need an estimate of the employment growth matrix **S** in (1.67). Such data are not available. Therefore, we shall assume that the components-of-change population growth matrix for this region, that appears in Figure 1.5, is a close enough approximation to the components-of-change employment growth matrix **S** and use (1.68) to project the 1963 industrial employment forward one unit time interval to 1968. The results of this projection appear in Column 5 of Table 1.12. Applying the journey-from-work-to-home matrix and the population-per-employee ratios to this vector we find the elements of Column 6. In Column 7 we include, for purposes of comparison, the population projection that results when the components-of-change population growth matrix in Figure 1.5 is applied directly to the communal population vector in Column 3.

1.7 APPLICATION: INPUT-OUTPUT ANALYSIS

Input-output analysis is concerned with the empirical study of the quantitative interdependence of producing and consuming units in a modern economy. Originally developed as a tool for analyzing and measuring the productive processes of a national economy, it also has been successfully applied in studies of smaller economic regions such as states and metropolitan areas. In all applications, however, the approach is essentially the same. An economy is viewed as a collection of industrial sectors with levels of output that are assumed to be dependent on the output levels of some or all of the other sectors. This dependence is defined by a set of m linear equations in m unknowns, and the specific structural characteristics of the economy are reflected in the numerical magnitudes of the coefficients in these equations. Such coefficients are empirically determined from an interindustry accounting matrix called the input-output table.

[7] A *commune* is the smallest fundamental socioeconomic territorial unit in the Yugoslavian political system. The capital city of the Republic of Slovenia, Ljubljana, contains five communes (numbered 9 through 13 in Table 1.11).

1.7.1 THE INPUT-OUTPUT TABLE

The formal properties of an input-output table may be set out in matrix form, as in Table 1.13. The principal features of such tables are the separation of intermediate, or *interindustry*, demands from *final* demands, and the differentiation between *produced* inputs and nonproduced, or *primary*, inputs. This cross classification divides the input-output table into four quadrants.

Quadrant I, the interindustry flow submatrix, sets out in considerable detail the origins, destinations, and levels of product flows between industrial sectors in an economy. Each sector appears twice in the accounting system: as a producer and as a purchaser of commodity inputs. The entries in each row describe the disposition of a sector's output; the elements of each column define the inputs that were used to produce that sector's output. Thus each entry, x_{ij}, denotes the amount of the output of sector i that was used by sector j, typically measured in constant prices.

Quadrant II, the final demand submatrix, describes the final use of the commodities and services produced by the economic system, disaggregated by major types of use. The sum of these entries is approximately equal to the economy's gross national product. Thus I_i, C_i, G_i, and E_i denote, respectively, the amounts of the output of sector i that were allocated to the investment, consumption, government, and foreign trade sectors.[8]

*Table 1.13. The Input-Output Table**

To / From		Purchasing Sector: Interindustry Demand $1, 2 \cdots j \cdots m$	Purchasing Sector: Final Demand $I \quad C \quad G \quad E$	Total Production X
Producing Sector	1	$x_{11} \cdots x_{1j} \cdots x_{1m}$	$I_1 \quad C_1 \quad G_1 \quad E_1$	X_1
	2	$\cdot \quad \cdot \quad \cdot$	$\cdot \quad \cdot \quad \cdot \quad \cdot$	$\vdots$
	$\vdots$	(Quadrant I)	(Quadrant II)	
	i	$x_{i1} \cdots x_{ij} \cdots x_{im}$	$I_i \quad C_i \quad G_i \quad E_i$	X_i
	$\vdots$	$\vdots \quad \vdots \quad \vdots$	$\vdots \quad \vdots \quad \vdots \quad \vdots$	$\vdots$
	m	$x_{m1} \cdots x_{mj} \cdots x_{mm}$	$I_m \quad C_m \quad G_m \quad E_m$	X_m
Primary Inputs (Value Added)		$V_1 \cdots V_j \cdots V_m$ (Quadrant III)	$V_I \quad V_C \quad V_G \quad V_E$ (Quadrant IV)	V
Total Production		$X_1 \cdots X_j \cdots X_m$	$I \quad C \quad G \quad E$	X

* Entries generally are values expressed in constant prices.

[8] Imports may be treated as negative exports or may be added to primary inputs. In the latter case, however, the column sums no longer represent total domestic production.

Quadrant III, the primary input submatrix, defines the distribution of inputs that are not produced within the interindustry system, such as labor, capital (in the static model), and natural resources. The total payment for the use of these inputs approximately measures the value added in production. Thus, V_j denotes the total value added by the jth sector.

Quadrant IV contains transactions that typically do not enter into input-output analysis and is included in the table for accounting purposes only. The entries in it describe the direct use of primary factors by different classes of final demand. Government employment and domestic services are prime examples of such transaction flows.

The formal structure of the accounts described in an input-output table can be expressed by the following pair of accounting identities:

$$\begin{aligned} X_i &= \sum_{j=1}^{m} x_{ij} + I_i + C_i + G_i + E_i \\ &= W_i + Y_i \qquad (i = 1, 2, \ldots, m) \end{aligned} \tag{1.69}$$

and

$$\begin{aligned} X_j &= \sum_{i=1}^{m} x_{ij} + V_j \\ &= U_j + V_j \qquad (j = 1, 2, \ldots, m) \end{aligned} \tag{1.70}$$

The first equation states that total production in each sector is equal to interindustry demand plus final demand. The second equation states that total production in each sector is equal to the value of inputs purchased from all other industrial sectors plus value added in that sector.

Example. At this point, a numerical example may be instructive. Table 1.14 provides a simplified picture of flows in a three-sector economy over a period of time, say one year, for our hypothetical island, Islandia. The three sectors are Agriculture, with a total output valued at 200 units; Manufacturing, which produced an output valued at 300 units; and Households,

Table 1.14. A Simplified Two-Industry Input-Output Table: Islandia, 1950 (in Arbitrary Units of Value)

From \ To	Ag.	Mfg.	Ho.	Total
Agriculture	40	60	100	200
Manufacturing	80	180	40	300
Households	80	60	60	200
Total Production	200	300	200	700

which supplied labor valued at 200 units. The first row of the table shows that of Agriculture's total output, a half was directly consumed by Households, and the remaining 100 units of output were used by the Agricultural sector itself (40 units) and by the Manufacturing sector (60 units). The first column of the input-output table records the levels of inputs used by Agriculture to produce its total output. Thus, 40 units of its own product, 80 units of the output of the Manufacturing sector, and 80 units of the primary input, labor, were used by the Agricultural sector to produce 200 units of output.

1.7.2 THE STATIC INPUT-OUTPUT MODEL

To convert the accounting system that is expressed by an input-output table into the analytical tool that is called the input-output model requires the adoption of several strong assumptions. The most important of these are: (1) a given commodity is produced by only one sector; (2) there are no joint products; and (3) the inputs used by any sector are in every case proportional to the level of output of that sector. These assumptions allow us to define a *structural* relationship to complement the purely *definitional* relationships specified by (1.69) and (1.70). In particular, using the third assumption, we may express the demand of each sector for each commodity as a function of that sector's level of output. That is,

$$x_{ij} = a_{ij} X_j \tag{1.71}$$

or

$$a_{ij} = \frac{x_{ij}}{X_j} \tag{1.72}$$

The parameter a_{ij} is called an *input coefficient*, and the matrix $\mathbf{A}$ of such coefficients describes the technological structure of the economy. It is commonly referred to as the *structural* or *technical coefficient matrix* of the economy.

Recalling the definitional relationship described by (1.69), and substituting into it the structural relationship specified by (1.71), we have the static input-output model:

$$X_i = \sum_{j=1}^{m} a_{ij} X_j + Y_i \tag{1.73}$$

and

$$Y_i = X_i - \sum_{j=1}^{m} a_{ij} X_j \qquad (i = 1, 2, \ldots, m) \tag{1.74}$$

If the final demand for all commodities is known, and if the structural matrix $\mathbf{A}$ has been estimated, we may solve the above system of m equations in m unknowns for the levels of total output $X_1, X_2, \ldots, X_m$. We may express (1.73) and (1.74) in matrix form, as follows:

$$\mathbf{x} = \mathbf{A}\mathbf{x} + \mathbf{y} \tag{1.75}$$

$$\mathbf{y} = (\mathbf{I} - \mathbf{A})\mathbf{x} \tag{1.76}$$

The static input-output model defined by (1.75) is said to be "open" in that final demand is assumed to be given and is not generated by the model itself, that is, it is exogenously specified. It is possible, however, to "close" the model by assuming that final demands may be determined in the same manner as interindustry demands. For example, we may assume that certain fixed proportions of the economy's total output vector are needed to "produce" the labor of households. In such instances, (1.75) simplifies to

$$\mathbf{x} = \mathbf{A}\mathbf{x} + \mathbf{i} \tag{1.77}$$

where now only net investment, $\mathbf{i}$, remains in final demand. A static system cannot be completely closed since investment or disinvestment must be accounted for by the model. This aspect will be taken up in the next section when we consider the dynamic input-output model.

Examples.

(i) To illustrate the solution of an input-output model, let us turn to the simple numerical example described in Table 1.14 involving the economy of Islandia. We first estimate the structural matrix $\mathbf{A}$:

$$\mathbf{A} = \begin{bmatrix} \frac{1}{5} & \frac{1}{5} \\ \frac{2}{5} & \frac{3}{5} \end{bmatrix} \tag{1.78}$$

and then solve the open model for the final demand vector

$$\mathbf{y} = \begin{bmatrix} 100 \\ 40 \end{bmatrix}$$

To satisfy this final demand, the economy must produce at least 100 units of Agricultural output and 40 units of Manufacturing output. In addition, it must supply the Agricultural sector with $\frac{1}{5}(100)$ units of its own product and $\frac{2}{5}(100)$ units of the product of the Manufacturing sector, as input needed to produce the 100 units for final demand. Also, Manufacturing requires $\frac{3}{5}(40)$ of its own output and $\frac{1}{5}(40)$ units of Agriculture's output in order to supply the final demand for its product. Thus, in order to satisfy *direct* demands, Agricultural production must be $100 + 20 + 8 = 128$ units and Manufacturing production must be $40 + 24 + 40 = 104$ units. More generally, in order to satisfy a final demand of Y_1 and Y_2 units, respectively, the economy must produce additional "first-round" inputs of $a_{11}Y_1 + a_{12}Y_2$ of the first commodity and $a_{21}Y_1 + a_{22}Y_2$ units of the second commodity, respectively. However, this is not all that is required of the economy. We also must take into account the input requirements generated by the first-round inputs themselves. To supply the inputs needed for the production of first-round inputs, the economy must supply the Agricultural sector with $\frac{1}{5}(28)$ units of its own product and $\frac{2}{5}(28)$ units of the Manufacturing sector's product. Moreover, it must supply the Manufacturing sector with $\frac{3}{5}(64)$ units of its own product and $\frac{1}{5}(64)$ units of Agriculture's product. That is, the economy must provide additional "second-round" inputs of $a_{11}(a_{11}Y_1 + a_{12}Y_2) + a_{12}(a_{21}Y_1 + a_{22}Y_2)$ units of Agricultural output and $a_{21}(a_{11}Y_1 + a_{12}Y_2) + a_{22}(a_{21}Y_1 + a_{22}Y_2)$ units of Manufacturing output. These second-round input requirements fall into the category of *indirect* demands. Continuing, in this manner, to determine the successive "*n*th-round" demands, we observe that the total outputs which are needed to sustain a final demand of Y_1 and Y_2 may be expressed as the sums of two infinite series, namely,

$$\begin{aligned} X_1 &= Y_1 + (a_{11}Y_1 + a_{12}Y_2) + [a_{11}(a_{11}Y_1 + a_{12}Y_2) + a_{12}(a_{21}Y_1 + a_{22}Y_2)] + \cdots \\ &= (1 + a_{11} + a_{12}a_{21} + a_{11}^2 + \cdots)Y_1 + (a_{12} + a_{11}a_{12} + a_{12}a_{22} + \cdots)Y_2 \\ &= A_{11}Y_1 + A_{12}Y_2 \end{aligned} \tag{1.79}$$

and

$$\begin{aligned} X_2 &= Y_2 + (a_{21}Y_1 + a_{22}Y_2) + [a_{21}(a_{11}Y_1 + a_{12}Y_2) + a_{22}(a_{21}Y_1 + a_{22}Y_2)] + \cdots \\ &= (a_{21} + a_{21}a_{11} + a_{22}a_{21} + \cdots)Y_1 + (1 + a_{22} + a_{21}a_{12} + a_{22}^2 + \cdots)Y_2 \\ &= A_{21}Y_1 + A_{22}Y_2 \end{aligned} \tag{1.80}$$

In both (1.79) and (1.80), A_{ij} is the total *direct* and *indirect* input of commodity i that is needed to sustain a unit of final demand for commodity j. Thus $A_{11}Y_1$ is the total amount of X_1 that is needed to support Y_1, and $A_{12}Y_2$ is the total amount needed to support Y_2.

Rewriting the infinite series of (1.79) and (1.80) in matrix form, we have

$$\begin{aligned} \mathbf{x} &= \mathbf{Iy} + \mathbf{Ay} + \mathbf{A}^2\mathbf{y} + \cdots \\ &= (\mathbf{I} + \mathbf{A} + \mathbf{A}^2 + \cdots)\mathbf{y} \end{aligned} \tag{1.81}$$

The iterative solution of the simple numerical example in Table 1.14 appears in Table 1.15 below. The last column presents the limiting values of total output to which the iterative process is converging. These limits may by derived directly by methods which will be described in the next chapter.

The derivation of the total output necessary to serve a final demand of 100 units of Agricultural products and 40 units of Manufacturing products

Table 1.15. Iterative Solution of the Two-Industry Input-Output Model: Islandia, 1950

Industrial Sector	Final Demand	Total Output after:				Total Output
		1st Round	3rd Round	5th Round		
Agriculture	100	128	160.0	177.7	...	200
Manufacturing	40	104	190.7	239.1	...	300
Total	140	232	350.7	416.8	...	500

Table 1.16. A Simplified Four-Sector Input-Output Table with a Savings-Investment Sector: Islandia, 1950 (in Arbitrary Units of Value)

From \ To	Ag.	Mfg.	Ho.	Inv.	Total
Agriculture	40	60	30	70	200
Manufacturing	80	180	10	30	300
Households	80	60	40	20	200
Savings			120		
Total Production	200	300	200		700

was unnecessary, of course, since we already have that information in the input-output table presented in Table 1.14. Its inclusion here merely serves as a check on our arithmetic.

(ii) To illustrate the general solution of the closed input-output model defined by (1.77), we must remove net investment from the Household sector in Table 1.14. If we assume that saving only occurs in the Household sector, and that this total saving of 120 units is allocated among Agriculture, Manufacturing, and Households in the proportions $(\frac{7}{12}, \frac{3}{12}, \frac{2}{12})$, respectively, we obtain Table 1.16.

Using the data in Table 1.16, we estimate the following structural matrix for the closed model:

$$\mathbf{A} = \begin{bmatrix} \frac{1}{5} & \frac{1}{5} & \frac{3}{20} \\ \frac{2}{5} & \frac{3}{5} & \frac{1}{20} \\ \frac{2}{5} & \frac{1}{5} & \frac{1}{5} \end{bmatrix} \tag{1.82}$$

and then solve the model with the net investment vector

$$\mathbf{i} = \begin{bmatrix} 70 \\ 30 \\ 20 \end{bmatrix}$$

The reader should check his understanding of the iterative solution method by working out the solution on his own. As with the open model, the answer is useful only as a check on the computations, since it merely confirms the information on total output that is provided by Table 1.16.

1.7.3 THE DYNAMIC INPUT-OUTPUT MODEL

The dynamic input-output model is a straightforward generalization of the static model described above. In addition to removing capital formation, or *investment,* from the final demand vector, we attach a time dimension to every variable, and introduce a lagged intersectoral dependence between stocks and flows. This dependence arises out of the assumption that normal additions to capital stocks depend on the rates at which outputs are changing. In particular, a simple accelerator model is adopted in which a capital coefficient, b_{ij}, defines the amount of stock produced by sector i which sector j must maintain *per unit* of its full capacity output. The matrix $\mathbf{B}$ of such coefficients may be said to define the capital structure of the economy.

Let us denote the total output of the ith industry in period t by $X_i(t)$ and total final demand for the ith commodity during the same period by $Y_i(t)$. [Recall that $Y_i(t)$ no longer includes investment, I_i.] Then we may express the dynamic counterpart of (1.69) as

$$X_i(t) = \sum_{j=1}^{m} a_{ij} X_j(t) + I_i(t) + Y_i(t) \qquad (i = 1, 2, \ldots, m)$$

or, more compactly, as

$$\mathbf{x}(t) = \mathbf{A}\mathbf{x}(t) + \mathbf{i}(t) + \mathbf{y}(t) \tag{1.83}$$

That is, total current output can be used for three purposes: (1) as input into current production; (2) as net addition to capital stocks; or (3) as current consumption. If we denote the current stock of capital good i by $S_i(t)$, we may express $I_i(t)$ as

$$I_i(t) = S_i(t + 1) - S_i(t)$$

Hence

$$\mathbf{i}(t) = \mathbf{s}(t + 1) - \mathbf{s}(t)$$

and

$$\mathbf{x}(t) = \mathbf{A}\mathbf{x}(t) + [\mathbf{s}(t + 1) - \mathbf{s}(t)] + \mathbf{y}(t) \tag{1.84}$$

Finally, expressing the simple accelerator model which relates stocks to flows as

$$\mathbf{s}(t) = \mathbf{B}\mathbf{x}(t) \tag{1.85}$$

we obtain the fundamental dynamic input-output model:

$$\mathbf{x}(t) = \mathbf{A}\mathbf{x}(t) + \mathbf{B}[\mathbf{x}(t+1) - \mathbf{x}(t)] + \mathbf{y}(t) \tag{1.86}$$

Let us review the structural assumptions that are implied by the dynamic input-output model of (1.86). First, it is assumed that a *fixed* amount, a_{ij}, of $x_{ij}(t)$ is required in order to produce a single unit of $X_j(t)$. Second, a *fixed* amount, b_{ij}, of $s_{ij}(t)$ is required in order to be able to produce a single unit of $X_j(t)$. The a_{ij} define flow input requirements per unit of flow output. The b_{ij} define the stock input requirements per unit of flow output. (It should be noted that the latter coefficients, unlike the former, depend on the length of the time interval that is used in the analysis.)

Examples.

(i) To introduce dynamics into our simple numerical example of Table 1.14, let us supplement the structural matrix **A** with the following capital coefficient matrix for Islandia during the 15-year unit interval of time:

$$\mathbf{B} = \begin{bmatrix} \frac{1}{10} & \frac{3}{50} \\ \frac{3}{100} & \frac{2}{25} \end{bmatrix} \tag{1.87}$$

The entries in the first column show that $\frac{1}{10}$ of a unit of Agricultural goods and $\frac{3}{100}$ of a unit of Manufactured goods are required in order to increase the productive capacity of the Agricultural sector by one unit, over a time interval of 15 years. The second column provides analogous information for the Manufacturing sector.

Drawing on (1.86), we express the total output of this hypothetical economy:

$$\mathbf{x}(1950) = \begin{bmatrix} \frac{1}{5} & \frac{1}{5} \\ \frac{2}{5} & \frac{3}{5} \end{bmatrix} \mathbf{x}(1950) + \begin{bmatrix} \frac{1}{10} & \frac{3}{50} \\ \frac{3}{100} & \frac{2}{25} \end{bmatrix} [\mathbf{x}(1965) - \mathbf{x}(1950)] + \mathbf{y}(1950) \tag{1.88}$$

We have two equations in six unknowns. Therefore, to obtain a solution we must specify the values of four unknowns. In particular, if we assume that

$$\mathbf{x}(1950) = \begin{bmatrix} 200 \\ 300 \end{bmatrix} \quad \text{and} \quad \mathbf{y}(1950) = \begin{bmatrix} 100 \\ 40 \end{bmatrix}$$

then

$$\mathbf{x}(1965) = \begin{bmatrix} 200 \\ 300 \end{bmatrix}$$

This result provides us with a simple check of the internal consistency of our solution. We have already seen from the static model that to support the final demand we have specified, the economy must produce exactly the total output of 200 units of Agricultural commodities and 300 units of Manufactured goods. Hence our net addition to capital stock must be zero and, therefore, the total output for the next time period remains unchanged. That is, the economy in this particular case maintains itself without expansion or contraction of any kind.

(ii) So far we have only considered the open dynamic input-output model. The introduction of the temporal dimension into the closed model is straightforward. We simply introduce a temporal index in (1.77) and obtain the closed dynamic input-output model

$$\mathbf{x}(t) = \mathbf{A}\mathbf{x}(t) + \mathbf{i}(t) = \mathbf{A}\mathbf{x}(t) + \mathbf{B}[\mathbf{x}(t+1) - \mathbf{x}(t)] \tag{1.89}$$

Expanding the capital coefficient matrix $\mathbf{B}$ in our numerical example to include the Household sector:

$$\mathbf{B} = \begin{bmatrix} \frac{1}{10} & \frac{3}{50} & \frac{4}{25} \\ \frac{3}{100} & \frac{2}{25} & 0 \\ \frac{1}{10} & 0 & 0 \end{bmatrix} \tag{1.90}$$

we have, from (1.89), that

$$\mathbf{x}(1950) = \begin{bmatrix} \frac{1}{5} & \frac{1}{5} & \frac{3}{20} \\ \frac{2}{5} & \frac{3}{5} & \frac{1}{20} \\ \frac{2}{5} & \frac{1}{5} & \frac{1}{5} \end{bmatrix} \mathbf{x}(1950) + \begin{bmatrix} \frac{1}{10} & \frac{3}{50} & \frac{4}{25} \\ \frac{3}{100} & \frac{2}{25} & 0 \\ \frac{1}{10} & 0 & 0 \end{bmatrix} [\mathbf{x}(1965) - \mathbf{x}(1950)] \tag{1.91}$$

Table 1.17. Input-Output Table for the Yugoslavian Economy: 1962 (in Millions of Dinars)

Origin \ Destination	Manu-facturing	Agri-culture	Forestry	Con-struction	Transport and Communi-cations	Trade	Services and Crafts	Others	Subtotal (1–8)
	1	2	3	4	5	6	7	8	9
1. Manufacturing	1,848,873	81,378	4,584	253,527	118,369	37,904	43,704	9,326	2,397,665
2. Agriculture	230,180	523,069	3,566		78	3,897	44		760,834
3. Forestry	79,122	466	550	6,656	220	1,299	370	76	88,759
4. Construction	16,086	1,322	1,235	137,391	26,189	3,113	408	703	186,447
5. Transport and Communications	106,351	11,314	2,453	39,900	32,946	12,299	1,253	859	207,375
6. Trade	71,643	14,292	746	20,508	6,407	5,579	10,714	894	130,783
7. Services and Crafts	31,624	9,028	958	8,939	8,561	7,069	1,613	614	68,406
8. Others	39,256	237	130	2,100	1,063	2,849	378	277	46,290
9. Subtotal (1–8)	2,423,135	641,106	14,222	469,021	193,833	74,009	58,484	12,749	3,886,559
10. Depreciation	149,666	42,677	11,458	21,300	54,785	16,112	2,096	2,106	300,200
11. Personal Income	402,748	525,599	60,257	173,067	94,313	120,266	38,621	16,090	1,430,961
12. Accumulation (savings)	1,060,709	203,281	30,673	202,960	134,187	340,735	34,764	37,870	2,045,179
13. Subtotal (9–12)	4,036,258	1,412,663	116,610	866,348	477,118	551,122	133,965	68,815	7,662,899
14. Decrease in Stocks	11,983	37,598	2,090						51,671
15. Imports	668,171	146,133	1,122		20,247			9,588	845,261
16. Total (13–15)	4,716,412	1,596,394	119,822	866,348	497,365	551,122	133,965	78,403	8,559,831

Table 1.17. Input-Output Table for the Yugoslavian Economy: 1962 (Continued)

Destination / Origin	Increase in Stocks	Gross Investment	Exports	Consumption			Subtotal (10–14)	Total Output (9+16)
				Personal Con-sumption	General Con-sumption	Total Con-sumption (13–14)		
	10	11	12	13	14	15	16	17
1. Manufacturing	178,952	463,623	552,553	960,817	162,802	1,123,619	2,318,747	4,716,412
2. Agriculture	6,918		72,637	731,979	24,026	756,005	835,560	1,596,394
3. Forestry		681	8,835	20,423	1,124	21,547	31,063	119,822
4. Construction		655,773	380		23,748	23,748	679,901	866,348
5. Transport and Communications	3,501	6,733	109,758	150,851	19,147	169,998	289,990	497,365
6. Trade	6,106	39,485	51,571	306,870	16,307	323,177	420,339	551,122
7. Services and Crafts	1,204	2,645		50,684	11,026	61,710	65,559	133,965
8. Others	264		1,008	10,190	20,651	30,841	32,113	78,403
9. Subtotal (1–8)	196,945	1,168,940	796,742	2,231,814	278,831	2,510,645	4,673,272	8,559,831

Source: *Savezni Zavod za Statistiku* (1966). "Medusobni Odnosi Privrednih Delatnosti Jugoslavije u 1962 Godini" ("Interindustry Relations of the Yugoslav Economy in 1962"). Beograd.

In (1.91), we have three equations in six unknowns. Thus, to obtain a solution, we must specify the values of three unknowns. In particular, if we assume that

$$\mathbf{x}(1950) = \begin{bmatrix} 200 \\ 300 \\ 200 \end{bmatrix}$$

then

$$\mathbf{x}(1965) = \begin{bmatrix} 400 \\ 600 \\ 400 \end{bmatrix}$$

We conclude, therefore, that this particular closed economy is capable of doubling the total output of every sector over a unit time interval. Why is this result different from the one we derived for the open dynamic model?

1.7.4 APPLICATION: AN INPUT-OUTPUT MODEL OF THE YUGOSLAVIAN ECONOMY

Table 1.17 presents a 1962 input-output table for Yugoslavia, which contains an eight-by-eight interindustry flow submatrix. Total output was found to be slightly over eight and a half billion dinars. Almost one half of this total consisted of interindustry demands. The various subtotals associated with the different categories of final demand appear in Columns 10 through 15 of the table.

Adopting the structural relationship defined by (1.71), we may obtain the technical coefficients that appear in Figure 1.6, form the infinite series described in (1.81),

$$\mathbf{x} = (\mathbf{I} + \mathbf{A} + \mathbf{A}^2 + \cdots)\mathbf{y}$$

and compute the total output that is necessary to satisfy the final demand

$$\mathbf{A} = \begin{bmatrix} 0.3920 & 0.0510 & 0.0383 & 0.2926 & 0.2380 & 0.0688 & 0.3262 & 0.1190 \\ 0.0488 & 0.3277 & 0.0298 & 0 & 0.0002 & 0.0071 & 0.0003 & 0 \\ 0.0168 & 0.0003 & 0.0046 & 0.0077 & 0.0004 & 0.0024 & 0.0028 & 0.0010 \\ 0.0034 & 0.0008 & 0.0103 & 0.1586 & 0.0527 & 0.0056 & 0.0030 & 0.0090 \\ 0.0225 & 0.0071 & 0.0205 & 0.0461 & 0.0662 & 0.0223 & 0.0094 & 0.0110 \\ 0.0152 & 0.0090 & 0.0062 & 0.0237 & 0.0129 & 0.0101 & 0.0800 & 0.0114 \\ 0.0067 & 0.0057 & 0.0080 & 0.0103 & 0.0172 & 0.0128 & 0.0120 & 0.0078 \\ 0.0083 & 0.0001 & 0.0011 & 0.0024 & 0.0021 & 0.0052 & 0.0028 & 0.0035 \end{bmatrix}$$

Source: Calculated using the data in Table 1.17. Programmed by Ervin Bell.

Figure 1.6. Technical Coefficient Matrix for the Yugoslavian Economy: 1962

Table 1.18. Iterative Solution of the Input-Output Model: Yugoslavia, 1962

Industrial Sector	Final Demand	Total Output after:				Total Output 20th Round
		1st Round	2nd Round	3rd Round	10th Round	
1. Manufacturing	2,318,747	3,593,595	4,203,567	4,483,704	4,715,489	4,716,412
2. Agriculture	835,560	1,226,465	1,418,674	1,512,349	1,596,030	1,596,394
3. Forestry	31,063	76,903	100,006	110,812	119,786	119,822
4. Construction	679,901	814,776	848,359	859,071	866,321	866,348
5. Transport and Communications	289,990	409,701	458,548	479,915	497,296	497,365
6. Trade	420,339	492,930	524,941	539,248	551,074	551,122
7. Services and Crafts	65,559	104,519	120,686	127,933	133,941	133,965
8. Others	32,113	56,310	68,182	73,751	78,385	78,403
Total	4,673,272	6,775,199	7,742,963	8,186,783	8,558,322	8,559,831

Source: Calculated using the data in Table 1.17 and Figure 1.6. Programmed by Ervin Bell.

Table 1.19. Input-Output Table for the Yugoslavian Economy: 1958 (in Millions of Dinars)

Destination / Origin	Manu-facturing	Agri-culture	Forestry	Con-struction	Transport and Communi-cations	Trade	Services and Crafts	Others	Subtotal (1–8)
	1	2	3	4	5	6	7	8	9
1. Manufacturing	1,081,250	49,133	1,485	104,452	85,882	21,919	86,083	5,166	1,435,370
2. Agriculture	123,354	268,853	5,377		50	2,316	868	10	400,828
3. Forestry	50,030	1,019	15,462	4,222	195	1,227	1,320	6	73,481
4. Construction	4,922	199	299		10,437	73		498	16,428
5. Transport and Communications	47,216	3,654	1,393	15,685	14,843	8,208	2,635	301	93,935
6. Trade	33,143	7,680	79	10,845	1,158	397	9,738		63,040
7. Services and Crafts	12,992	7,102	88	56,352	2,829	4,912			84,275
8. Others	26,496			414	370	1,849	662	40	29,831
9. Subtotal (1–8)	1,379,403	337,640	24,183	191,970	115,764	40,901	101,306	6,021	2,197,188
10. Depreciation	73,362	20,789	1,971	7,933	34,500	7,249	4,391	1,249	151,444
11. Personal Income	156,018	388,407	45,332	55,435	41,358	54,695	56,380	8,446	806,071
12. Accumulation (savings)	630,132	77,250	28,967	52,622	50,085	139,197	45,267	22,676	1,046,196
13. Subtotal (9–12)	2,238,915	824,086	100,453	307,960	241,707	242,042	207,344	38,392	4,200,899
14. Decrease in Stocks	1,851								1,851
15. Imports	443,691	91,566	683	30	8,086			2,558	546,614
16. Total (13–15)	2,684,457	915,652	101,136	307,990	249,793	242,042	207,344	40,950	4,749,364

Table 1.19. Input-Output Table for the Yugoslavian Economy: 1958 (Continued)

Destination / Origin	Increase in Stocks	Gross Investment	Exports	Consumption: Personal Con-sumption	Consumption: General Con-sumption	Consumption: Total Con-sumption (13–14)	Subtotal (10–14)	Total Output (9+16)
	10	11	12	13	14	15	16	17
1. Manufacturing	119,406	281,797	276,257	438,903	132,724	571,627	1,249,087	2,684,457
2. Agriculture	10,549	5,953	70,250	419,447	8,625	428,072	514,824	915,652
3. Forestry		1,113	7,544	17,830	1,168	18,998	27,655	101,136
4. Construction		272,000	426		19,136	19,136	291,562	307,990
5. Transport and Communications	1,010	4,946	58,688	74,599	16,615	91,214	155,858	249,793
6. Trade	1,986	18,959	25,628	120,135	12,294	132,429	179,002	242,042
7. Services and Crafts	2,301		2,584	102,374	15,810	118,184	123,069	207,344
8. Others	480		242	4,159	6,238	10,397	11,119	40,950
9. Subtotal (1–8)	135,732	584,768	441,619	1,177,447	212,610	1,390,057	2,552,176	4,749,364

Source: *Savezni Zavod za Statistiku* (1962). "Medusobni Odnosi Privrednih Delatnosti Jugoslavije u 1958 Godini" ("Interindustry Relations of the Yugoslav Economy in 1958"). Beograd.

that appears in Column 16 of Table 1.17. The sequence of "round-by-round" iterations produces the results set out in Table 1.18.

To test his understanding of input-output analysis and, in particular, the iterative solution method, the reader should repeat the calculations described above using the data of the 1958 input-output table for Yugoslavia that is presented in Table 1.19 (Exercise 10).

EXERCISES

1. Solve the following equation system using only elementary row transformations:

$$\begin{bmatrix} 2 & 4 \\ 1 & 3 \end{bmatrix} \begin{bmatrix} x_1 \\ x_2 \end{bmatrix} = \begin{bmatrix} 6 \\ 1 \end{bmatrix}$$

2. Given the population model of (1.18) with

$$\mathbf{G} = \begin{bmatrix} \frac{1}{3} & \frac{1}{4} & \frac{1}{3} \\ \frac{1}{3} & \frac{1}{2} & \frac{1}{3} \\ \frac{1}{3} & \frac{1}{4} & \frac{1}{3} \end{bmatrix} \quad \text{and} \quad \mathbf{w}(t) = \begin{bmatrix} 1600 \\ 1100 \\ 900 \end{bmatrix}$$

find $\mathbf{w}(t+5)$. Consolidate the first and third regions and find $\hat{\mathbf{w}}(t+5)$. Are the two projections of the total population in the three-region system identical? Why or why not? Now modify the model, as follows:

$$\mathbf{w}(t+1) = \mathbf{G}\mathbf{w}(t) + \mathbf{f}$$

where

$$\mathbf{f} = \begin{bmatrix} 100 \\ -200 \\ 100 \end{bmatrix}$$

Find $\mathbf{w}(t+5)$ and interpret the process and the result.

3. (a) Interpret the two conditions for perfect aggregation that are defined by (1.38) and (1.39). Determine whether in addition to being *sufficient*, they also are *necessary*. That is, establish whether perfect aggregation can ever occur when neither of the two conditions for perfect aggregation is met.

(b) Extend the arguments on consolidation that appear in Subsection 1.5.4 to include *temporal* consolidation, that is, the consolidation of adjacent age groups and the corresponding expansion of the length of the unit time interval. Derive the conditions for perfect temporal aggregation. Illustrate your results by consolidating Islandia's four 15-year age groups into two 30-year age groups, and obtain both the consolidated and unconsolidated projections of Islandia's population in 1980.

(c) Consolidate the single-region population growth matrix in Figure 1.3 into one that will project 10-year age groups over a 10-year unit time interval, and obtain both the temporally consolidated and unconsolidated projections of Yugoslavian females in 1971.

4. Construct separate life tables for males and females in Slovenia and the rest of Yugoslavia using the data in 1961. Contrast the mortality patterns that are described by the four life tables thus obtained.

5. Extend the definition of **G** in (1.63) to the interregional case by interpreting out-migration as another form of death. Next, develop an interregional age and sex disaggregated matrix model of population growth and distribution for Yugoslavia, using the data in Tables 1.5 through 1.8. Illustrate the performance of your model by using it to obtain 1981 population projections for Slovenia and the rest of Yugoslavia. Finally, consolidate the two regions and repeat the projection. Compare the error that is introduced by this regional consolidation with the one that results from the consolidation of the two sexes.

6. Using the matrix spatial activity allocation model described in Section 1.6, test the respective consequences, over the next 30 years, of the following changes in Islandia:

(a) a sudden decline in total employment, which produces a corresponding decline in the labor force participation rate $(1/a)$ from $\frac{1}{3}$ to $\frac{1}{4}$, for all three regions;

(b) the construction of a new highway, which doubles the accessibility of Southern Islandia with respect to the other two regions and thereby doubles the number of commuters who journey to that region to work; and

(c) the implementation of a new zoning ordinance, which imposes land use controls that restrict the residential capacity of each region to 120 percent of its 1950 population.

Finally, find the population and employment distributions that would exist in Islandia if present patterns of locational behavior and growth (as defined by the values taken on by p, **S**, and a) remained unchanged over a period of 100 years, 150 years, and 200 years, respectively. Does the proportional distribution of population and employment among the three regions ultimately converge to a stable set of values? What is the 15-year growth rate of population and employment at that point?

7. Write a FORTRAN program that will carry out the computations of the spatial activity allocation model described in Section 1.6. Test this program by verifying the results presented in the text, and then find the population and employment distributions that ultimately would exist in the Ljubljana Metropolitan Region if current patterns of locational behavior and growth remained constant forever. Repeat this exercise with the components-of-change population growth model for the same region. Discuss your findings.

8. The following input-output table depicts transactions for a hypothetical economy. For simplicity, arbitrary value units are assumed.

(a) Find the technical coefficient matrix **A**.

(b) Consolidate the four industrial sectors into the following two sectors: Services + Agriculture (1 + 2), and Basic Industry and Finished Goods (3 + 4). Use the matrix approach outlined in Subsection 1.5.4. What are

Producing Sector \ Purchasing Sector	1. S.	2. A.	3. B.	4. F.	Final Demand	Total Output
1. Services	20	25	25	80	50	200
2. Agriculture		25		120	105	250
3. Basic Industry		25	45	40	40	150
4. Finished Goods				100	300	400
Primary Inputs	180	175	80	60	495	
Total Output	200	250	150	400		1,000

the appropriate consolidation and deconsolidation matrices?

(c) Obtain the technical coefficient matrix $\hat{\mathbf{A}}$ for the consolidated input-output model, and use the iterative solution method to derive the total output that is necessary to support the final demand vector

$$\hat{\mathbf{y}} = \begin{bmatrix} 200 \\ 400 \end{bmatrix}$$

9. Develop a static interregional input-output model and illustrate its use with a numerical example.

10. Using the input-output data in Table 1.19:

(a) Find the 1958 eight-by-eight technical coefficient matrix for the Yugoslavian economy.

(b) Carry out the sequence of "round-by-round" iterations on the 1958 data, and construct a table such as Table 1.18 to show the rate of convergence of this particular iterative solution. Is the convergence more or less rapid than in Table 1.18? Why?

(c) Repeat (b) using the 1962 technical coefficient matrix with the 1958 final demand vector and the 1958 technical coefficient matrix with the 1962 final demand vector. Discuss your findings.

REFERENCES AND SELECTED READINGS

THEORY

Almon, C., Jr. *Matrix Methods in Economics*. Reading, Mass.: Addison-Wesley, 1967.

Gantmacher, F. R. *The Theory of Matrices*, I and II. New York: Chelsea, 1959.

Gere, J. M. and W. Weaver, Jr. *Matrix Algebra for Engineers*. Princeton, N. J.: D. van Nostrand, 1965.

Hadley, G. *Linear Algebra*. Reading, Mass.: Addison-Wesley, 1961.

Noble, B. *Applied Linear Algebra*. Englewood Cliffs, N. J.: Prentice-Hall, 1969

Schneider, H. and G. P. Barker. *Matrices and Linear Algebra.* New York: Holt, Rinehart & Winston, 1968.

Searle, S. R. *Matrix Algebra for the Biological Sciences.* New York: John Wiley & Sons, 1966.

APPLICATION: POPULATION ANALYSIS

Chiang, C. L. *Introduction to Stochastic Processes in Biostatistics.* New York: John Wiley & Sons, 1968.

Keyfitz, N. *Introduction to the Mathematics of Population.* Reading, Mass.: Addison-Wesley, 1968.

Rogers, A. *Matrix Analysis of Interregional Population Growth and Distribution.* Berkeley, Calif.: University of California Press, 1968.

——— "On Perfect Aggregation in the Matrix Cohort-Survival Model of Interregional Population Growth," *Journal of Regional Science*, **IX**: 3, 1969, 417–424.

——— and S. McDougall. *An Analysis of Population Growth and Change in Slovenia and the Rest of Yugoslavia*, Working Paper No. 81, Center for Planning and Development Research, University of California, Berkeley, 1968.

APPLICATION: ACTIVITY ALLOCATION ANALYSIS

Garin, R. "A Matrix Formulation of the Lowry Model for Intrametropolitan Activity Allocation," *Journal of the American Institute of Planners*, **XXXII**: 6, 1966, 361–364.

Lowry, I. S. *A Model of Metropolis.* Santa Monica, Calif.: RAND Corporation, 1964.

Cripps, E. L. and D. H. S. Foot. "The Empirical Development of an Elementary Residential Location Model for Use in Sub-Regional Planning," *Environment and Planning*, **I**: 1, 1969, 81–90.

APPLICATION: INPUT-OUTPUT ANALYSIS

Artle, R. *Studies in the Structure of the Stockholm Economy*, 2d ed. Ithaca, N.Y.: Cornell University Press, 1965.

Chenery, H. B. and P. G. Clark. *Interindustry Economics.* New York: John Wiley & Sons, 1959.

Fisher, W. D. *Clustering and Aggregation in Economics.* Baltimore, Md.: Johns Hopkins Press, 1969.

Isard, W., *et al. Methods of Regional Analysis: An Introduction to Regional Science* (Ch. 8, 309–374). New York: M.I.T. Press and John Wiley & Sons, 1960.

Leontief, W. W. *The Structure of the American Economy, 1919–1939*, 2d. ed. New York: Oxford University Press, 1951.

two the inverse of a square matrix

The reciprocal of a number, a, say, in ordinary scalar algebra, is defined to be the number, b, say, which when multiplied by a produces unity. Thus

$$ab = ba = 1$$

and

$$b = 1/a = a^{-1}$$

Analogously, in matrix algebra, we define the reciprocal of a square matrix, $\mathbf{A}$, say, to be the square matrix, $\mathbf{B}$, say, which when multiplied by $\mathbf{A}$ produces the identity matrix. That is,

$$\mathbf{AB} = \mathbf{BA} = \mathbf{I}$$

and

$$\mathbf{B} = \mathbf{A}^{-1}$$

The reciprocal matrix is commonly referred to as the *inverse* matrix, and its use in matrix algebra is analogous to division in ordinary scalar algebra.

To illustrate the use of the inverse matrix in the solution of simultaneous equations, consider a set of equations of the form

$$\underset{m\times m}{\mathbf{A}}\ \underset{m\times 1}{\mathbf{x}} = \underset{m\times 1}{\mathbf{b}} \tag{2.1}$$

If $\mathbf{A}^{-1}$ exists, we may premultiply both sides of (2.1) by it to find

$$\mathbf{A}^{-1}\mathbf{Ax} = \mathbf{A}^{-1}\mathbf{b}$$

$$\mathbf{Ix} = \mathbf{A}^{-1}\mathbf{b}$$

or

$$\mathbf{x} = \mathbf{A}^{-1}\mathbf{b} \tag{2.2}$$

For example, recalling the numerical equation system and inverse matrix described in (1.15) and (1.16), we have that

$$\begin{bmatrix} 3 & 5 \\ 2 & 4 \end{bmatrix} \begin{bmatrix} x_1 \\ x_2 \end{bmatrix} = \begin{bmatrix} 15 \\ 8 \end{bmatrix}$$

$$\begin{bmatrix} 2 & -\frac{5}{2} \\ -1 & \frac{3}{2} \end{bmatrix} \begin{bmatrix} 3 & 5 \\ 2 & 4 \end{bmatrix} \begin{bmatrix} x_1 \\ x_2 \end{bmatrix} = \begin{bmatrix} 2 & -\frac{5}{2} \\ -1 & \frac{3}{2} \end{bmatrix} \begin{bmatrix} 15 \\ 8 \end{bmatrix}$$

$$\begin{bmatrix} 1 & 0 \\ 0 & 1 \end{bmatrix} \begin{bmatrix} x_1 \\ x_2 \end{bmatrix} = \begin{bmatrix} 10 \\ -3 \end{bmatrix}$$

or

$$\begin{bmatrix} x_1 \\ x_2 \end{bmatrix} = \begin{bmatrix} 10 \\ -3 \end{bmatrix}$$

2.1 DETERMINANTS

Our development of a formal method for obtaining the inverse of a matrix makes use of numbers called *determinants*. Hence, we interrupt our exposition of matrix analysis at this point, in order to define what a determinant is and to list some of its properties.

2.1.1 DEFINITIONS AND NOTATION

Associated with every square matrix, **A**, say, is a unique number, denoted by $|\mathbf{A}|$, called its *determinant*. This number is formally defined as the sum of the products of all possible permutations of the elements in the matrix, such that each product contains an element from each row and from every column. Each product in the sum receives a positive sign if the number of inversions, v, say, necessary to transform the particular permutation of the second subscripts $i, j, \ldots, p$ to the natural order $1, 2, \ldots, m$ is even, and a negative sign if it is odd. That is,

$$\left| \underset{m \times m}{\mathbf{A}} \right| = \sum^{m!} (-1)^v a_{1i} a_{2j} \cdots a_{mp} \tag{2.3}$$

where the second subscripts take on all possible $[m! = m \cdot (m-1) \cdots (2) \cdot (1)]$ permutations of the numbers $1, 2, \ldots, m$. An inversion is carried out simply by interchanging the positions of two adjacent numbers. Thus, for example, the sequence 3, 2, 1 may be transformed into the natural order by three inversions (that is, $v = 3$):

$$\begin{array}{ccc} 3 & 2 & 1 \\ 2 & 3 & 1 \\ 2 & 1 & 3 \\ 1 & 2 & 3 \end{array}$$

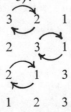

Examples.

(i) $|a_{11}| = a_{11}$.

(ii) $$\begin{vmatrix} a_{11} & a_{12} \\ a_{21} & a_{22} \end{vmatrix} = a_{11}a_{22} - a_{12}a_{21}$$

(iii) $$\begin{vmatrix} a_{11} & a_{12} & a_{13} \\ a_{21} & a_{22} & a_{23} \\ a_{31} & a_{32} & a_{33} \end{vmatrix} = a_{11}a_{22}a_{33} + a_{12}a_{23}a_{31} + a_{13}a_{21}a_{32} - a_{13}a_{22}a_{31}$$
$$- a_{11}a_{23}a_{32} - a_{12}a_{21}a_{33}$$

(iv) $$\begin{vmatrix} 3 & 5 \\ 2 & 4 \end{vmatrix} = 3(4) - 5(2) = 2$$

The *order* of a determinant refers to the order of the square matrix with which that determinant is associated. A *minor* is the determinant of a submatrix formed by removing an equal number of rows and columns from a given square matrix. The *cofactor* of the element a_{ij} in a square matrix **A** is defined as the product of $(-1)^{i+j}$ and the minor of the submatrix formed by deleting the ith row and jth column of **A**. The cofactor of a_{ij} will be denoted by $\mathbf{A}^c_{ij}$.

It can be shown that the determinant of the square matrix **A** can be evaluated in terms of the cofactors of the elements of any row or column, as follows:

$$\left|\underset{m\times m}{\mathbf{A}}\right| = a_{i1}\mathbf{A}^c_{i1} + \cdots + a_{im}\mathbf{A}^c_{im} \qquad (i = 1, 2, \ldots, m) \tag{2.4}$$

$$= a_{1j}\mathbf{A}^c_{1j} + \cdots + a_{mj}\mathbf{A}^c_{mj} \qquad (j = 1, 2, \ldots, m) \tag{2.5}$$

This method is called *expansion by cofactors,* and its application may be illustrated with a third-order determinant. Expanding such a determinant in terms of the cofactors of the first row,

$$\begin{vmatrix} a_{11} & a_{12} & a_{13} \\ a_{21} & a_{22} & a_{23} \\ a_{31} & a_{32} & a_{33} \end{vmatrix} = a_{11}\begin{vmatrix} a_{22} & a_{23} \\ a_{32} & a_{33} \end{vmatrix} - a_{12}\begin{vmatrix} a_{21} & a_{23} \\ a_{31} & a_{33} \end{vmatrix} + a_{13}\begin{vmatrix} a_{21} & a_{22} \\ a_{31} & a_{32} \end{vmatrix}$$

$$= a_{11}(a_{22}a_{33} - a_{23}a_{32}) - a_{12}(a_{21}a_{33} - a_{23}a_{31}) + a_{13}(a_{21}a_{32} - a_{22}a_{31})$$

$$= a_{11}a_{22}a_{33} + a_{12}a_{23}a_{31} + a_{13}a_{21}a_{32} - a_{13}a_{22}a_{31} - a_{12}a_{21}a_{33} - a_{11}a_{23}a_{32}$$

$$= \sum^{3!} (-1)^v a_{1i}a_{2j}a_{3k}$$

Expressions (2.4) and (2.5) are quite long and difficult to remember. For second- and third-order determinants, the following schematic diagrams serve as useful substitutes:

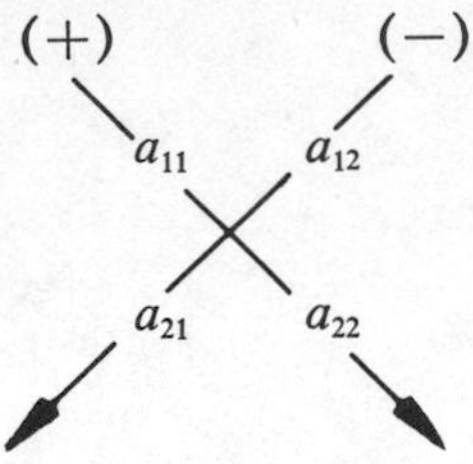

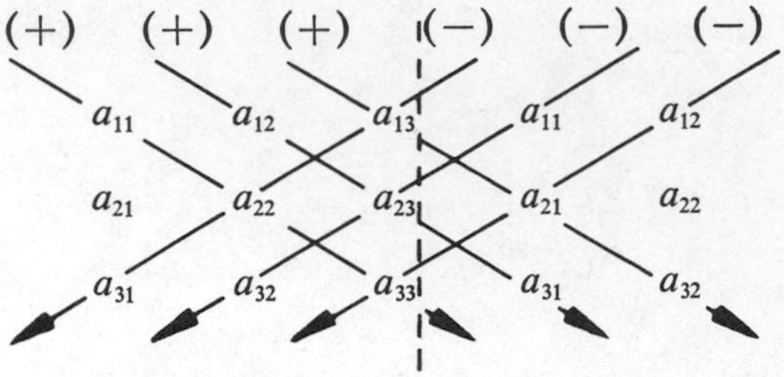

In the diagram on the right, the first two columns of the matrix are repeated and then triple products are computed along the arrows. Products formed along arrows from left to right are assigned positive signs; those formed along arrows from right to left are assigned negative signs. The evaluation procedure for the second-order determinant is analogous.

Example. The determinant of the matrix

$$\begin{bmatrix} 3 & 2 & 5 \\ 4 & 1 & 0 \\ 0 & 2 & 2 \end{bmatrix}$$

may be found using expansion by cofactors, for example, as follows:

$$\begin{vmatrix} 3 & 2 & 5 \\ 4 & 1 & 0 \\ 0 & 2 & 2 \end{vmatrix} = 3\begin{vmatrix} 1 & 0 \\ 2 & 2 \end{vmatrix} - 4\begin{vmatrix} 2 & 5 \\ 2 & 2 \end{vmatrix} + 0\begin{vmatrix} 2 & 5 \\ 1 & 0 \end{vmatrix}$$

$$= 3(2 - 0) - 4(4 - 10) + 0(0 - 5)$$

$$= 6 + 24 + 0 = 30$$

Alternatively, we may obtain the same result using the above schematic diagram:

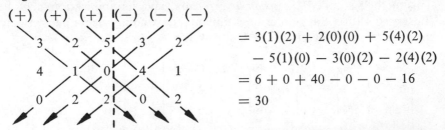

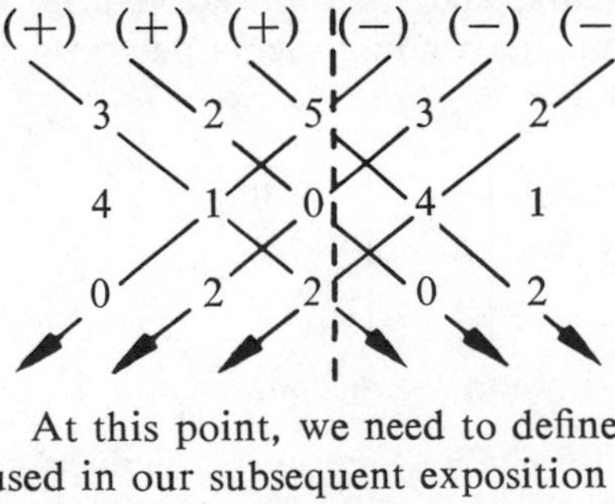

$$= 3(1)(2) + 2(0)(0) + 5(4)(2)$$
$$- 5(1)(0) - 3(0)(2) - 2(4)(2)$$
$$= 6 + 0 + 40 - 0 - 0 - 16$$
$$= 30$$

At this point, we need to define the two kinds of matrices which will be used in our subsequent exposition of matrix inversion by the method of determinants: *cofactor* matrices and *adjoint* matrices. The cofactor matrix of a square matrix **A** is formed by replacing each a_{ij} in **A** by its cofactor $\mathbf{A}^c_{ij}$. We denote this cofactor matrix $\mathbf{A}^c$. For example, the cofactor matrix

$\mathbf{A}^c$ of a third-order matrix $\mathbf{A}$ is

$$\mathbf{A}^c = \begin{bmatrix} A_{11}^c & A_{12}^c & A_{13}^c \\ A_{21}^c & A_{22}^c & A_{23}^c \\ A_{31}^c & A_{32}^c & A_{33}^c \end{bmatrix} \tag{2.6}$$

where, for example,

$$A_{21}^c = \begin{vmatrix} a_{12} & a_{13} \\ a_{32} & a_{33} \end{vmatrix} = -(a_{12}a_{33} - a_{13}a_{32})$$

The adjoint matrix of a matrix $\mathbf{A}$ is simply the transpose of its cofactor matrix and may be denoted by $\mathbf{A}^a$. Thus, for the above third-order matrix $\mathbf{A}$, we have

$$\mathbf{A}^a = (\mathbf{A}^c)' = \begin{bmatrix} A_{11}^c & A_{21}^c & A_{31}^c \\ A_{12}^c & A_{22}^c & A_{32}^c \\ A_{13}^c & A_{23}^c & A_{33}^c \end{bmatrix} \tag{2.7}$$

Examples.

(i) $\mathbf{A} = \begin{bmatrix} 3 & 5 \\ 2 & 4 \end{bmatrix} \qquad \mathbf{A}^c = \begin{bmatrix} 4 & -2 \\ -5 & 3 \end{bmatrix} \qquad \mathbf{A}^a = \begin{bmatrix} 4 & -5 \\ -2 & 3 \end{bmatrix}$

(ii) $\mathbf{B} = \begin{bmatrix} 3 & 1 & 0 \\ 2 & 4 & 1 \\ 0 & 1 & 3 \end{bmatrix} \qquad \mathbf{B}^c = \begin{bmatrix} 11 & -6 & 2 \\ -3 & 9 & -3 \\ 1 & -3 & 10 \end{bmatrix}$

$$\mathbf{B}^a = \begin{bmatrix} 11 & -3 & 1 \\ -6 & 9 & -3 \\ 2 & -3 & 10 \end{bmatrix}$$

2.1.2 PROPERTIES OF DETERMINANTS

The method of expansion by cofactors allows us to establish quickly several properties of determinants which are especially useful as computational aids. A few of the more important ones are listed below and are illustrated with a third-order determinant.

1. *If all the elements of a row (or column) in a square matrix are zero, its determinant is zero.*

$$\begin{vmatrix} 0 & 0 & 0 \\ a_{21} & a_{22} & a_{23} \\ a_{31} & a_{32} & a_{33} \end{vmatrix} = 0\begin{vmatrix} a_{22} & a_{23} \\ a_{32} & a_{33} \end{vmatrix} - 0\begin{vmatrix} a_{21} & a_{23} \\ a_{31} & a_{33} \end{vmatrix} + 0\begin{vmatrix} a_{21} & a_{22} \\ a_{31} & a_{32} \end{vmatrix} = 0$$

2. *The determinant of a triangular or diagonal square matrix is equal to the product of the elements in the principal diagonal.*

$$\begin{vmatrix} a_{11} & a_{12} & a_{13} \\ 0 & a_{22} & a_{23} \\ 0 & 0 & a_{33} \end{vmatrix} = a_{11}\begin{vmatrix} a_{22} & a_{23} \\ 0 & a_{33} \end{vmatrix} - 0\begin{vmatrix} a_{12} & a_{13} \\ 0 & a_{33} \end{vmatrix} + 0\begin{vmatrix} a_{12} & a_{13} \\ a_{22} & a_{23} \end{vmatrix} = a_{11}a_{22}a_{33}$$

3. *If two rows (or columns) of a square matrix are interchanged, the sign of its determinant will be reversed.*

$$\begin{vmatrix} a_{11} & a_{12} & a_{13} \\ a_{21} & a_{22} & a_{23} \\ a_{31} & a_{32} & a_{33} \end{vmatrix} = a_{11}\begin{vmatrix} a_{22} & a_{23} \\ a_{32} & a_{33} \end{vmatrix} - a_{12}\begin{vmatrix} a_{21} & a_{23} \\ a_{31} & a_{33} \end{vmatrix} + a_{13}\begin{vmatrix} a_{21} & a_{22} \\ a_{31} & a_{32} \end{vmatrix}$$

$$= -\left\{-a_{11}\begin{vmatrix} a_{22} & a_{23} \\ a_{32} & a_{33} \end{vmatrix} + a_{12}\begin{vmatrix} a_{21} & a_{23} \\ a_{31} & a_{33} \end{vmatrix} - a_{13}\begin{vmatrix} a_{21} & a_{22} \\ a_{31} & a_{32} \end{vmatrix}\right\}$$

$$= -\begin{vmatrix} a_{21} & a_{22} & a_{23} \\ a_{11} & a_{12} & a_{13} \\ a_{31} & a_{32} & a_{33} \end{vmatrix}$$

4. *If the elements of a row (or column) of an mth-order square matrix are multiplied by a scalar, c, say, the value of its determinant increases c times. If every element of the matrix is multiplied by c, the value of the determinant increases c^m times.*

$$\begin{vmatrix} ca_{11} & ca_{12} & ca_{13} \\ a_{21} & a_{22} & a_{23} \\ a_{31} & a_{32} & a_{33} \end{vmatrix} = ca_{11}\begin{vmatrix} a_{22} & a_{23} \\ a_{32} & a_{33} \end{vmatrix} - ca_{12}\begin{vmatrix} a_{21} & a_{23} \\ a_{31} & a_{33} \end{vmatrix} + ca_{13}\begin{vmatrix} a_{21} & a_{22} \\ a_{31} & a_{32} \end{vmatrix}$$

$$= c\left\{a_{11}\begin{vmatrix} a_{22} & a_{23} \\ a_{32} & a_{33} \end{vmatrix} - a_{12}\begin{vmatrix} a_{21} & a_{23} \\ a_{31} & a_{33} \end{vmatrix} + a_{13}\begin{vmatrix} a_{21} & a_{22} \\ a_{31} & a_{32} \end{vmatrix}\right\}$$

$$\begin{vmatrix} ca_{11} & ca_{12} & ca_{13} \\ ca_{21} & ca_{22} & ca_{23} \\ ca_{31} & ca_{32} & ca_{33} \end{vmatrix} = c\begin{vmatrix} a_{11} & a_{12} & a_{13} \\ ca_{21} & ca_{22} & ca_{23} \\ ca_{31} & ca_{32} & ca_{33} \end{vmatrix} = c^2\begin{vmatrix} a_{11} & a_{12} & a_{13} \\ a_{21} & a_{22} & a_{23} \\ ca_{31} & ca_{32} & ca_{33} \end{vmatrix}$$

$$= c^3\begin{vmatrix} a_{11} & a_{12} & a_{13} \\ a_{21} & a_{22} & a_{23} \\ a_{31} & a_{32} & a_{33} \end{vmatrix}$$

5. *If two rows or columns of a square matrix are equal, its determinant is zero. The determinant of a square matrix with proportional rows or columns is also zero.*

$$\begin{vmatrix} a_{11} & a_{12} & a_{13} \\ a_{11} & a_{12} & a_{13} \\ a_{31} & a_{32} & a_{33} \end{vmatrix} = a_{31}\begin{vmatrix} a_{12} & a_{13} \\ a_{12} & a_{13} \end{vmatrix} - a_{32}\begin{vmatrix} a_{11} & a_{13} \\ a_{11} & a_{13} \end{vmatrix} + a_{33}\begin{vmatrix} a_{11} & a_{12} \\ a_{11} & a_{12} \end{vmatrix}$$

$$= a_{31}(0) - a_{32}(0) + a_{33}(0) = 0$$

$$\begin{vmatrix} a_{11} & a_{12} & a_{13} \\ ca_{11} & ca_{12} & ca_{13} \\ a_{31} & a_{32} & a_{33} \end{vmatrix} = c\begin{vmatrix} a_{11} & a_{12} & a_{13} \\ a_{11} & a_{12} & a_{13} \\ a_{31} & a_{32} & a_{33} \end{vmatrix} = c(0) = 0$$

6. *The determinant of a square matrix is unchanged if a scalar multiple of a row (or column) is added to another row (or column).*

$$\begin{vmatrix} a_{11} + ca_{21} & a_{12} + ca_{22} & a_{13} + ca_{23} \\ a_{21} & a_{22} & a_{23} \\ a_{31} & a_{32} & a_{33} \end{vmatrix}$$

$$= (a_{11} + ca_{21})\begin{vmatrix} a_{22} & a_{23} \\ a_{32} & a_{33} \end{vmatrix} - (a_{12} + ca_{22})\begin{vmatrix} a_{21} & a_{23} \\ a_{31} & a_{33} \end{vmatrix}$$

$$+ (a_{13} + ca_{23})\begin{vmatrix} a_{21} & a_{22} \\ a_{31} & a_{32} \end{vmatrix}$$

$$= \begin{vmatrix} a_{11} & a_{12} & a_{13} \\ a_{21} & a_{22} & a_{23} \\ a_{31} & a_{32} & a_{33} \end{vmatrix} + \begin{vmatrix} ca_{21} & ca_{22} & ca_{23} \\ a_{21} & a_{22} & a_{23} \\ a_{31} & a_{32} & a_{33} \end{vmatrix}$$

$$= \begin{vmatrix} a_{11} & a_{12} & a_{13} \\ a_{21} & a_{22} & a_{23} \\ a_{31} & a_{32} & a_{33} \end{vmatrix} + 0 = \begin{vmatrix} a_{11} & a_{12} & a_{13} \\ a_{21} & a_{22} & a_{23} \\ a_{31} & a_{32} & a_{33} \end{vmatrix}$$

7. *If the elements of a given row (or column) in a square matrix are multiplied by the cofactors of another row (or column) and then added, the result is equal to zero.* Such an operation is commonly referred to as expansion by *alien* cofactors.

$$\begin{vmatrix} a_{11} & a_{12} & a_{13} \\ a_{21} & a_{22} & a_{23} \\ a_{31} & a_{32} & a_{33} \end{vmatrix} = a_{11}\begin{vmatrix} a_{22} & a_{23} \\ a_{32} & a_{33} \end{vmatrix} - a_{12}\begin{vmatrix} a_{21} & a_{23} \\ a_{31} & a_{33} \end{vmatrix} + a_{13}\begin{vmatrix} a_{21} & a_{22} \\ a_{31} & a_{32} \end{vmatrix}$$

$$= a_{31}\begin{vmatrix} a_{12} & a_{13} \\ a_{22} & a_{23} \end{vmatrix} - a_{32}\begin{vmatrix} a_{11} & a_{13} \\ a_{21} & a_{23} \end{vmatrix} + a_{33}\begin{vmatrix} a_{11} & a_{12} \\ a_{21} & a_{22} \end{vmatrix}$$

$$a_{11}\begin{vmatrix} a_{12} & a_{13} \\ a_{22} & a_{23} \end{vmatrix} - a_{12}\begin{vmatrix} a_{11} & a_{13} \\ a_{21} & a_{23} \end{vmatrix} + a_{13}\begin{vmatrix} a_{11} & a_{12} \\ a_{21} & a_{22} \end{vmatrix} = a_{11}(a_{12}a_{23} - a_{13}a_{22})$$
$$- a_{12}(a_{11}a_{23} - a_{13}a_{21}) + a_{13}(a_{11}a_{22} - a_{12}a_{21}) = 0$$

2.2 APPLICATION: INTERPOLATION[1]

Interpolations are required frequently in urban and regional analysis, and determinants provide a single general procedure for carrying out such operations. In this section, we introduce the method using the example of simple linear interpolation, generalize it to include polynomial interpolation, and conclude with an application in demographic analysis. Other extensions appear as exercises at the end of this chapter [Exercises 1(a), 1(b), and 1(c)].

2.2.1 LINEAR INTERPOLATION

Imagine that we are given two points, $y_1 = f(x_1)$ and $y_2 = f(x_2)$, say, and assume that we wish to interpolate linearly between these two points to find the value of a third, $y_0 = f(x_0)$, say, where

$$y = f(x) = a + bx \tag{2.8}$$

Since y_0, y_1, and y_2 all lie on the straight line defined by (2.8),

$$a + bx_0 - y_0 = 0$$
$$a + bx_1 - y_1 = 0$$
$$a + bx_2 - y_2 = 0$$

or, in matrix form,

$$\begin{bmatrix} 1 & x_0 & -y_0 \\ 1 & x_1 & -y_1 \\ 1 & x_2 & -y_2 \end{bmatrix} \begin{bmatrix} a \\ b \\ 1 \end{bmatrix} = \begin{bmatrix} 0 \\ 0 \\ 0 \end{bmatrix} \tag{2.9}$$

For these equations to be *consistent* with one another, the determinant of the square matrix on the left-hand side of (2.9) must be equal to zero[2]:

$$\begin{vmatrix} 1 & x_0 & -y_0 \\ 1 & x_1 & -y_1 \\ 1 & x_2 & -y_2 \end{vmatrix} = 0 \tag{2.10}$$

[1] This section draws liberally from the exposition provided by Keyfitz (1968). For an extensive discussion of the use of determinants in interpolation and graduation, the reader should consult Chapter 11 of that text and the references cited there.

[2] Consistency in linear equation systems is not discussed until Chapter 4. Hence, at this point, the reader is asked to accept this statement on faith.

Expanding (2.10) by the cofactors of the third column, we observe that

$$-y_0\begin{vmatrix}1 & x_1\\ 1 & x_2\end{vmatrix} + y_1\begin{vmatrix}1 & x_0\\ 1 & x_2\end{vmatrix} - y_2\begin{vmatrix}1 & x_0\\ 1 & x_1\end{vmatrix} = 0$$

or,

$$y_0 = f(x_0) = \frac{y_1\begin{vmatrix}1 & x_0\\ 1 & x_2\end{vmatrix} - y_2\begin{vmatrix}1 & x_0\\ 1 & x_1\end{vmatrix}}{\begin{vmatrix}1 & x_1\\ 1 & x_2\end{vmatrix}}$$

$$= \frac{\begin{vmatrix}1 & x_0 & 0\\ 1 & x_1 & -y_1\\ 1 & x_2 & -y_2\end{vmatrix}}{\begin{vmatrix}1 & x_1\\ 1 & x_2\end{vmatrix}} \tag{2.11}$$

Example. To illustrate the use of (2.11), let us set $x_1 = 2$, $y_1 = 3$, $x_2 = 6$, and $y_2 = 5$ and obtain, by linear interpolation, the value of y_0 for $x_0 = 4$:

$$y_0 = f(x_0) = \frac{\begin{vmatrix}1 & x_0 & 0\\ 1 & x_1 & -y_1\\ 1 & x_2 & -y_2\end{vmatrix}}{\begin{vmatrix}1 & x_1\\ 1 & x_2\end{vmatrix}} = \frac{\begin{vmatrix}1 & 4 & 0\\ 1 & 2 & -3\\ 1 & 6 & -5\end{vmatrix}}{\begin{vmatrix}1 & 2\\ 1 & 6\end{vmatrix}} = \frac{16}{4} = 4$$

2.2.2 POLYNOMIAL INTERPOLATION

The advantage of using determinants to express interpolation operations becomes apparent when nonlinear interpolations are desired. For example, to interpolate between the three points $y_1 = f(x_1)$, $y_2 = f(x_2)$, and $y_3 = f(x_3)$, with the quadratic equation

$$y = f(x) = a + bx + cx^2 \tag{2.12}$$

we observe that for any point, x_0, say, to lie on the quadratic, the following equations must be consistent:

$$\begin{aligned} a + bx_0 + cx_0^2 - y_0 &= 0\\ a + bx_1 + cx_1^2 - y_1 &= 0\\ a + bx_2 + cx_2^2 - y_2 &= 0\\ a + bx_3 + cx_3^2 - y_3 &= 0 \end{aligned}$$

which means that

$$\begin{vmatrix} 1 & x_0 & x_0^2 & -y_0 \\ 1 & x_1 & x_1^2 & -y_1 \\ 1 & x_2 & x_2^2 & -y_2 \\ 1 & x_3 & x_3^2 & -y_3 \end{vmatrix} = 0$$

and, expanding by the cofactors of the fourth column, we conclude that

$$y_0 = f(x_0) = \frac{\begin{vmatrix} 1 & x_0 & x_0^2 & 0 \\ 1 & x_1 & x_1^2 & y_1 \\ 1 & x_2 & x_2^2 & y_2 \\ 1 & x_3 & x_3^2 & y_3 \end{vmatrix}}{\begin{vmatrix} 1 & x_1 & x_1^2 \\ 1 & x_2 & x_2^2 \\ 1 & x_3 & x_3^2 \end{vmatrix}} \tag{2.13}$$

Notice that we used three points to carry out the quadratic interpolation, whereas our linear interpolation required only two points. This is always the case and, in general, $n + 1$ points are necessary to interpolate with a polynomial of degree n. Also note that the y's no longer have a minus sign in front of them.

Example. Assume that we are given the three points ($x_1 = 0$, $y_1 = 1$), ($x_2 = 2$, $y_2 = 4$), ($x_3 = 6$, $y_3 = 4$) and wish to interpolate between them with the quadratic in (2.12) to find the y_0 that corresponds to $x_0 = 4$. According to (2.13),

$$y_0 = f(x_0) = \frac{\begin{vmatrix} 1 & 4 & 16 & 0 \\ 1 & 0 & 0 & 1 \\ 1 & 2 & 4 & 4 \\ 1 & 6 & 36 & 4 \end{vmatrix}}{\begin{vmatrix} 1 & 0 & 0 \\ 1 & 2 & 4 \\ 1 & 6 & 36 \end{vmatrix}} = \frac{240}{48} = 5$$

2.2.3 APPLICATION: DECONSOLIDATION BY INTERPOLATION

Although our discussion of interpolation so far has been limited to interpolation among points, we can apply the method to data given as areas under a curve by cumulating the data, finding the part of the distribution that lies below x and below $x + 1$, and then obtaining the part that lies between x and $x + 1$ by subtraction. We may illustrate this procedure with an application drawn from demographic analysis.

Recall the 1950 and 1960 age distributions of the United States given in Figure 1.1, and assume that we wish to obtain a crude estimate of the proportion of people in the 35–36-year age group in 1950 who survived to the 45–46-year age group in 1960. We begin by cumulating the two population distributions, as shown in Table 2.1 and Figure 2.1. Next we interpolate linearly to find the number of people who were below age 35 and age 36 in 1950. These two interpolations yield

$$f(35) = \frac{\begin{vmatrix} 1 & 35 & 0 \\ 1 & 30 & -74824 \\ 1 & 40 & -97587 \end{vmatrix}}{\begin{vmatrix} 1 & 30 \\ 1 & 40 \end{vmatrix}} = 86{,}205.5$$

and

$$f(36) = \frac{\begin{vmatrix} 1 & 36 & 0 \\ 1 & 30 & -74824 \\ 1 & 40 & -97587 \end{vmatrix}}{\begin{vmatrix} 1 & 30 \\ 1 & 40 \end{vmatrix}} = 88{,}481.8$$

Table 2.1. Population by Age and Cumulated Population Totals: United States, 1950 and 1960 (Population Data in Thousands)

Age Group x to $x + 9$	Population 1950	Population under Age x 1950	Population 1960	Population under Age x 1960
0– 9	29, 364	0	39, 013	0
10–19	21, 736	29, 364	29, 182	39, 013
20–29	23, 724	51, 100	21, 671	68, 195
30–39	22, 763	74, 824	23, 532	89, 866
40–49	19, 274	97, 587	22, 481	113, 398
50–59	15, 507	116, 861	18, 037	135, 879
60–69	11, 062	132, 368	13, 400	153, 916
70–79	5, 564	143, 430	8, 048	167, 316
80+	1, 703	148, 994	2, 255	175, 364
Total	150, 697	150, 697	177, 619	177, 619

Source: Figure 1.1.

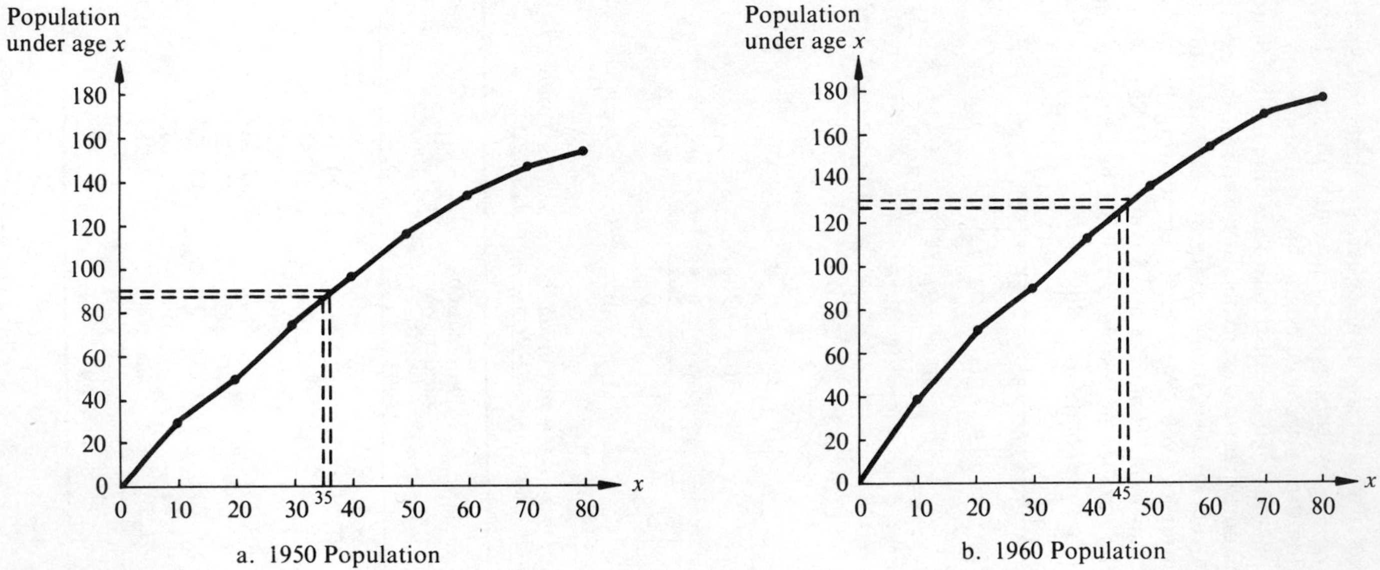

Source: Table 2.1

Figure 2.1. Population of the United States in 1950 and in 1960, Cumulated by Ten-year Age Groups

Subtracting $f(35)$ from $f(36)$, we obtain 88,481.8 − 86,205.5 = 2,276 as our crude estimate of the number of people in the 35–36-year age group in 1950.

Repeating the above calculations with the cumulated 1960 population, we estimate the number of people in the 45–46-year age group in 1960 to be 2,248. Hence our estimate of the ten-year survivorship rate of the 35–36-year age group is

$$s_{35} = \frac{2{,}248}{2{,}276} = 0.9877$$

2.3 MATRIX INVERSION BY THE METHOD OF DETERMINANTS

To develop a formal method for inverting matrices using the concepts of cofactors, adjoints, and determinants, we first consider the result of multiplying a matrix by its adjoint. Although we shall focus only on a third-order matrix, the same results may be derived for matrices of order m. We define the following product matrix:

$$\mathbf{AA}^a = \begin{bmatrix} a_{11} & a_{12} & a_{13} \\ a_{21} & a_{22} & a_{23} \\ a_{31} & a_{32} & a_{33} \end{bmatrix} \begin{bmatrix} A_{11}^c & A_{21}^c & A_{31}^c \\ A_{12}^c & A_{22}^c & A_{32}^c \\ A_{13}^c & A_{23}^c & A_{33}^c \end{bmatrix}$$

Observe that the diagonal elements of the product matrix $\mathbf{AA}^a$ are formed by summing the products of the row elements of $\mathbf{A}$ and their respective cofactors. Thus each diagonal element of $\mathbf{AA}^a$ is equal to $|\mathbf{A}|$. All off-diagonal elements, however, are constructed by summing the products of the row elements of $\mathbf{A}$ and *alien* cofactors. Therefore, by Property 7 in Subsection 2.1.2, all off-diagonal elements of $\mathbf{AA}^a$ are zero. Thus,

$$\mathbf{AA}^a = \begin{bmatrix} |\mathbf{A}| & 0 & 0 \\ 0 & |\mathbf{A}| & 0 \\ 0 & 0 & |\mathbf{A}| \end{bmatrix} = |\mathbf{A}|\mathbf{I} \tag{2.14}$$

Since the determinant of $\mathbf{A}$ is a scalar, we may divide both sides of (2.14) by $|\mathbf{A}|$ to find

$$\mathbf{A}\frac{\mathbf{A}^a}{|\mathbf{A}|} = \mathbf{I}$$

But by definition,

$$\mathbf{AA}^{-1} = \mathbf{I}$$

Hence,

$$\mathbf{A}^{-1} = \frac{\mathbf{A}^a}{|\mathbf{A}|} \tag{2.15}$$

Equation (2.15) provides us with a formal method for obtaining the inverse of a matrix, **A**. We simply divide the adjoint of **A** by the determinant of **A**, and the result is the inverse of **A**. Notice that the inverse exists only if $|\mathbf{A}| \neq 0$. If no inverse exists, the matrix is said to be *singular.*

Examples.

(i) $\mathbf{A} = \begin{bmatrix} 3 & 5 \\ 2 & 4 \end{bmatrix} \qquad \mathbf{A}^{-1} = \frac{1}{2}\begin{bmatrix} 4 & -5 \\ -2 & 3 \end{bmatrix} = \begin{bmatrix} 2 & -\frac{5}{2} \\ -1 & \frac{3}{2} \end{bmatrix}$

(ii) $\mathbf{B} = \begin{bmatrix} 3 & 1 & 0 \\ 2 & 4 & 1 \\ 0 & 1 & 3 \end{bmatrix}$

$$\mathbf{B}^{-1} = \frac{1}{27}\begin{bmatrix} 11 & -3 & 1 \\ -6 & 9 & -3 \\ 2 & -3 & 10 \end{bmatrix} = \begin{bmatrix} \frac{11}{27} & -\frac{1}{9} & \frac{1}{27} \\ -\frac{2}{9} & \frac{1}{3} & -\frac{1}{9} \\ \frac{2}{27} & -\frac{1}{9} & \frac{10}{27} \end{bmatrix}$$

2.4 MATRIX INVERSION BY THE METHOD OF SUCCESSIVE TRANSFORMATIONS

The method of determinants is not a practical means for inverting large matrices, because it requires so many time-consuming multiplications. Most computer programs for matrix inversion, therefore, adopt variations of the more efficient method of successive transformations. This is a procedure which, by elementary transformations alone, reduces a square matrix to an identity matrix and, at the same time, builds up an identity matrix into the inverse of the matrix it has so reduced. We may illustrate this technique by considering, once again, the linear system of equations

$$\mathbf{A}\mathbf{x} = \mathbf{b} \tag{2.16}$$

and its solution,

$$\mathbf{x} = \mathbf{A}^{-1}\mathbf{b} \tag{2.17}$$

In Subsection 1.1.4, we observed that a sequence of appropriate elementary transformations carried out on a nonsingular matrix **A** would reduce it to the identity matrix. In particular, we illustrated how the premultiplication of **A** by suitably constructed elementary matrices would transform **A** into **I**. Symbolically, we may express this as

$$\mathbf{E}_k \cdots \mathbf{E}_2\mathbf{E}_1\mathbf{A} = \mathbf{I} \tag{2.18}$$

where the $\mathbf{E}_i$ denote elementary matrices.

Recall also that the same sequence of elementary matrices, when applied to the vector **b** in (2.16), produced the solution vector **x** in (2.17). That is,

$$\mathbf{E}_k \cdots \mathbf{E}_2\mathbf{E}_1\mathbf{b} = \mathbf{x} = \mathbf{A}^{-1}\mathbf{b} \tag{2.19}$$

Now, rewriting (2.16) as

$$\mathbf{Ax} = \mathbf{Ib} \tag{2.20}$$

and applying the elementary matrices $\mathbf{E}_i$ ($i = 1, 2, \ldots, k$) to both sides of the equation, we obtain

$$\mathbf{E}_k \cdots \mathbf{E}_2\mathbf{E}_1\mathbf{Ax} = \mathbf{E}_k \cdots \mathbf{E}_2\mathbf{E}_1\mathbf{Ib} \tag{2.21}$$

whence, by (2.18) and (2.19),

$$\mathbf{Ix} = \mathbf{A}^{-1}\mathbf{b} \tag{2.22}$$

Equations (2.21) and (2.22) describe the reduction of the matrix **A** to the identity matrix and the corresponding transformation of the identity matrix into the inverse of **A**. We also observe that by applying the elementary matrices $\mathbf{E}_i$ to the partitioned matrix

$$[\mathbf{A} \mid \mathbf{I}]$$

we obtain the partitioned matrix

$$[\mathbf{I} \mid \mathbf{A}^{-1}]$$

and thereby may derive the inverse of any *nonsingular* square matrix.

Example. For a formal illustration of the method of successive transformations, let us recall the numerical example of Subsection 1.1.4 and apply the elementary matrices defined there on the partitioned matrix

$$[\mathbf{A} \mid \mathbf{I}] = \left[\begin{array}{cc|cc} 3 & 5 & 1 & 0 \\ 2 & 4 & 0 & 1 \end{array}\right] \tag{2.23}$$

We carry out the following sequence of transformations:

$$\begin{gathered}
\begin{bmatrix} 1 & 0 \\ 0 & \frac{1}{2} \end{bmatrix} \left[\begin{array}{cc|cc} 3 & 5 & 1 & 0 \\ 2 & 4 & 0 & 1 \end{array}\right] = \left[\begin{array}{cc|cc} 3 & 5 & 1 & 0 \\ 1 & 2 & 0 & \frac{1}{2} \end{array}\right] \\
\begin{bmatrix} 0 & 1 \\ 1 & 0 \end{bmatrix} \left[\begin{array}{cc|cc} 3 & 5 & 1 & 0 \\ 1 & 2 & 0 & \frac{1}{2} \end{array}\right] = \left[\begin{array}{cc|cc} 1 & 2 & 0 & \frac{1}{2} \\ 3 & 5 & 1 & 0 \end{array}\right] \\
\begin{bmatrix} 1 & 0 \\ -3 & 1 \end{bmatrix} \left[\begin{array}{cc|cc} 1 & 2 & 0 & \frac{1}{2} \\ 3 & 5 & 1 & 0 \end{array}\right] = \left[\begin{array}{cc|cc} 1 & 2 & 0 & \frac{1}{2} \\ 0 & -1 & 1 & -\frac{3}{2} \end{array}\right] \\
\begin{bmatrix} 1 & 2 \\ 0 & 1 \end{bmatrix} \left[\begin{array}{cc|cc} 1 & 2 & 0 & \frac{1}{2} \\ 0 & -1 & 1 & -\frac{3}{2} \end{array}\right] = \left[\begin{array}{cc|cc} 1 & 0 & 2 & -\frac{5}{2} \\ 0 & -1 & 1 & -\frac{3}{2} \end{array}\right] \\
\begin{bmatrix} 1 & 0 \\ 0 & -1 \end{bmatrix} \left[\begin{array}{cc|cc} 1 & 0 & 2 & -\frac{5}{2} \\ 0 & -1 & 1 & -\frac{3}{2} \end{array}\right] = \left[\begin{array}{cc|cc} 1 & 0 & 2 & -\frac{5}{2} \\ 0 & 1 & -1 & \frac{3}{2} \end{array}\right]
\end{gathered} \tag{2.24}$$

Note that (2.23) has been transformed to

$$[\mathbf{I} \mid \mathbf{A}^{-1}] = \left[\begin{array}{cc|cc} 1 & 0 & 2 & -\frac{5}{2} \\ 0 & 1 & -1 & \frac{3}{2} \end{array}\right]$$

and observe that

$$\mathbf{A}^{-1}\mathbf{A} = \mathbf{I} = \begin{bmatrix} 2 & -\frac{5}{2} \\ -1 & \frac{3}{2} \end{bmatrix} \begin{bmatrix} 3 & 5 \\ 2 & 4 \end{bmatrix} = \begin{bmatrix} 1 & 0 \\ 0 & 1 \end{bmatrix}$$

and

$$\mathbf{A}\mathbf{A}^{-1} = \mathbf{I} = \begin{bmatrix} 3 & 5 \\ 2 & 4 \end{bmatrix} \begin{bmatrix} 2 & -\frac{5}{2} \\ -1 & \frac{3}{2} \end{bmatrix} = \begin{bmatrix} 1 & 0 \\ 0 & 1 \end{bmatrix}$$

The sequence of elementary transformations used in the above numerical example was an arbitrary one. For large matrices, more systematic and efficient procedures are available. One of these is the technique of *pivotal condensation.* The essential feature of this method is the way in which the elementary transformations are determined. The sequence is as follows. First, the matrix **A** is systematically reduced to upper triangular form with unities along the principal diagonal. We begin by transforming the first column of **A** into the first column of the identity matrix by dividing the first row of **A** by a_{11}, the *first pivot.* Then, adding (or subtracting) appropriate multiples of the first row to other rows, we reduce their first column elements to zero. (If a_{11} is zero, we interchange two rows or two columns in order to obtain a nonzero pivot element.) Proceeding in an analogous manner with the second, third, . . . , and mth columns, we obtain our upper triangular transformation of **A**. At this point, we begin with the last row of **A** and by an appropriate elementary transformation reduce the (m — 1st) row into the (m — 1st) row of the identity matrix. Proceeding in this manner, we ultimately transform the first row of the triangular matrix into the first row of the identity matrix. The original square matrix **A** now has been reduced to an identity matrix. And if the same elementary transformations are carried out on an identity matrix appended to **A**, we will have $\mathbf{A}^{-1}$ in that position. The entire process may be illustrated with a two-by-two matrix, as follows:

$$\begin{bmatrix} \dfrac{1}{a_{11}} & 0 \\ 0 & 1 \end{bmatrix} \left[\begin{array}{cc|cc} a_{11} & a_{12} & 1 & 0 \\ a_{21} & a_{22} & 0 & 1 \end{array}\right] = \left[\begin{array}{cc|cc} 1 & \dfrac{a_{12}}{a_{11}} & \dfrac{1}{a_{11}} & 0 \\ a_{21} & a_{22} & 0 & 1 \end{array}\right]$$

$$\begin{bmatrix} 1 & 0 \\ -a_{21} & 1 \end{bmatrix} \left[\begin{array}{cc|cc} 1 & \dfrac{a_{12}}{a_{11}} & \dfrac{1}{a_{11}} & 0 \\ a_{21} & a_{22} & 0 & 1 \end{array}\right] = \left[\begin{array}{cc|cc} 1 & \dfrac{a_{12}}{a_{11}} & \dfrac{1}{a_{11}} & 0 \\ 0 & \dfrac{a_{11}a_{22} - a_{21}a_{12}}{a_{11}} & -\dfrac{a_{21}}{a_{11}} & 1 \end{array}\right]$$

$$\begin{bmatrix} 1 & 0 \\ 0 & \dfrac{a_{11}}{|\mathbf{A}|} \end{bmatrix} \left[\begin{array}{cc:cc} 1 & \dfrac{a_{12}}{a_{11}} & \dfrac{1}{a_{11}} & 0 \\ 0 & \dfrac{|\mathbf{A}|}{a_{11}} & -\dfrac{a_{21}}{a_{11}} & 1 \end{array}\right] = \left[\begin{array}{cc:cc} 1 & \dfrac{a_{12}}{a_{11}} & \dfrac{1}{a_{11}} & 0 \\ 0 & 1 & -\dfrac{a_{21}}{|\mathbf{A}|} & \dfrac{a_{11}}{|\mathbf{A}|} \end{array}\right]$$

$$\begin{bmatrix} 1 & -\dfrac{a_{12}}{a_{11}} \\ 0 & 1 \end{bmatrix} \left[\begin{array}{cc:cc} 1 & \dfrac{a_{12}}{a_{11}} & \dfrac{1}{a_{11}} & 0 \\ 0 & 1 & -\dfrac{a_{21}}{|\mathbf{A}|} & \dfrac{a_{11}}{|\mathbf{A}|} \end{array}\right] = \left[\begin{array}{cc:cc} 1 & 0 & \dfrac{1}{a_{11}} + \dfrac{a_{12}a_{21}}{a_{11}|\mathbf{A}|} & -\dfrac{a_{12}a_{11}}{a_{11}|\mathbf{A}|} \\ 0 & 1 & -\dfrac{a_{21}}{|\mathbf{A}|} & \dfrac{a_{11}}{|\mathbf{A}|} \end{array}\right]$$

But

$$\frac{1}{a_{11}} + \frac{a_{12}a_{21}}{a_{11}|\mathbf{A}|} = \frac{|\mathbf{A}| + a_{12}a_{21}}{a_{11}|\mathbf{A}|} = \frac{a_{11}a_{22} - a_{21}a_{12} + a_{21}a_{12}}{a_{11}|\mathbf{A}|}$$

$$= \frac{a_{11}a_{22}}{a_{11}|\mathbf{A}|} = \frac{a_{22}}{|\mathbf{A}|}$$

Therefore,

$$\begin{bmatrix} \dfrac{1}{a_{11}} + \dfrac{a_{12}a_{21}}{a_{11}|\mathbf{A}|} & -\dfrac{a_{12}a_{11}}{a_{11}|\mathbf{A}|} \\ -\dfrac{a_{21}}{|\mathbf{A}|} & \dfrac{a_{11}}{|\mathbf{A}|} \end{bmatrix} = \begin{bmatrix} \dfrac{a_{22}}{|\mathbf{A}|} & -\dfrac{a_{12}}{|\mathbf{A}|} \\ -\dfrac{a_{21}}{|\mathbf{A}|} & \dfrac{a_{11}}{|\mathbf{A}|} \end{bmatrix} = \frac{\mathbf{A}^a}{|\mathbf{A}|} \equiv \mathbf{A}^{-1}$$

Example. The application of pivotal condensation to the partitioned matrix in (2.23) yields the following sequence of transformations:

$$\begin{aligned}
\begin{bmatrix} \frac{1}{3} & 0 \\ 0 & 1 \end{bmatrix} \left[\begin{array}{cc:cc} 3 & 5 & 1 & 0 \\ 2 & 4 & 0 & 1 \end{array}\right] &= \left[\begin{array}{cc:cc} 1 & \frac{5}{3} & \frac{1}{3} & 0 \\ 2 & 4 & 0 & 1 \end{array}\right] \\
\begin{bmatrix} 1 & 0 \\ -2 & 1 \end{bmatrix} \left[\begin{array}{cc:cc} 1 & \frac{5}{3} & \frac{1}{3} & 0 \\ 2 & 4 & 0 & 1 \end{array}\right] &= \left[\begin{array}{cc:cc} 1 & \frac{5}{3} & \frac{1}{3} & 0 \\ 0 & \frac{2}{3} & -\frac{2}{3} & 1 \end{array}\right] \\
\begin{bmatrix} 1 & 0 \\ 0 & \frac{3}{2} \end{bmatrix} \left[\begin{array}{cc:cc} 1 & \frac{5}{3} & \frac{1}{3} & 0 \\ 0 & \frac{2}{3} & -\frac{2}{3} & 1 \end{array}\right] &= \left[\begin{array}{cc:cc} 1 & \frac{5}{3} & \frac{1}{3} & 0 \\ 0 & 1 & -1 & \frac{3}{2} \end{array}\right] \\
\begin{bmatrix} 1 & -\frac{5}{3} \\ 0 & 1 \end{bmatrix} \left[\begin{array}{cc:cc} 1 & \frac{5}{3} & \frac{1}{3} & 0 \\ 0 & 1 & -1 & \frac{3}{2} \end{array}\right] &= \left[\begin{array}{cc:cc} 1 & 0 & 2 & -\frac{5}{2} \\ 0 & 1 & -1 & \frac{3}{2} \end{array}\right]
\end{aligned} \tag{2.25}$$

Observe that the result is identical to that derived in (2.24), and note that one less transformation was required than before.

In this section and the preceding one, we have described two alternative methods for formally deriving the inverse of a square matrix. The first method is important because it establishes the sole necessary and sufficient condition for a square matrix to have an inverse. This condition is that the determinant of the matrix must be nonzero, a condition we defined as *nonsingularity*. The second method derives its importance from the efficiency with which it may be used to obtain the inverse of any nonsingular square matrix. Together the methods provide us with both a theoretically and a practically useful formal means for defining the inverse matrix.

2.5 PROPERTIES OF THE INVERSE MATRIX

In this section, we shall develop a few of the more useful properties of inverse matrices:

1. $\mathbf{AA}^{-1} = \mathbf{A}^{-1}\mathbf{A} = \mathbf{I}$.

(In our definition of the inverse matrix we assumed this identity. Now we prove it.) Since $\mathbf{AA}^a = \mathbf{A}^a\mathbf{A}$, the inverse $\mathbf{A}^{-1}$ as defined by (2.15) satisfies both $\mathbf{AA}^{-1} = \mathbf{I}$ and $\mathbf{A}^{-1}\mathbf{A} = \mathbf{I}$.

2. $\mathbf{I}^{-1} = \mathbf{I}$.

Since $\mathbf{I} \cdot \mathbf{I} = \mathbf{I}$, postmultiplication of both sides of the equation by $\mathbf{I}^{-1}$ yields $\mathbf{I} = \mathbf{I}^{-1}$.

3. *If* $\mathbf{D} = [d_{ij}]$ *with* $d_{ij} = 0$ *for* $i \neq j$, *then* $\mathbf{D}^{-1} = [1/d_{ij}]$.

This property may be verified by observing that $\mathbf{DD}^{-1} = \mathbf{I}$.

4. *The inverse matrix is unique.*

Assume that both $\mathbf{A}^{-1}$ and $\mathbf{B}$ are inverses of $\mathbf{A}$. Then

$$\mathbf{BA} = \mathbf{I}$$

and postmultiplying both sides of the equation by $\mathbf{A}^{-1}$, we have

$$\mathbf{BAA}^{-1} = \mathbf{IA}^{-1}$$

$$\mathbf{BI} = \mathbf{IA}^{-1}$$

or

$$\mathbf{B} = \mathbf{A}^{-1}$$

5. $(\mathbf{A}^{-1})^{-1} = \mathbf{A}$.

By definition,

$$(\mathbf{A}^{-1})^{-1}\mathbf{A}^{-1} = \mathbf{I}$$

Hence, postmultiplying both sides of the equation by $\mathbf{A}$, we have

$$(\mathbf{A}^{-1})^{-1}\mathbf{A}^{-1}\mathbf{A} = \mathbf{IA}$$

$$(\mathbf{A}^{-1})^{-1}\mathbf{I} = \mathbf{IA}$$

or

$$(\mathbf{A}^{-1})^{-1} = \mathbf{A}$$

6. $(\mathbf{A}')^{-1} = (\mathbf{A}^{-1})'$.

By definition,

$$\mathbf{AA}^{-1} = \mathbf{I}$$

Transposing, we obtain

$$(\mathbf{A}^{-1})'\mathbf{A}' = \mathbf{I}' = \mathbf{I}$$

and postmultiplying both sides of the equation by $(\mathbf{A}')^{-1}$ yields

$$(\mathbf{A}^{-1})'\mathbf{A}'(\mathbf{A}')^{-1} = \mathbf{I}(\mathbf{A}')^{-1}$$

or

$$(\mathbf{A}^{-1})' = (\mathbf{A}')^{-1}$$

7. $(\mathbf{AB})^{-1} = \mathbf{B}^{-1}\mathbf{A}^{-1}$.

Since

$$\mathbf{B}^{-1}\mathbf{A}^{-1} \cdot \mathbf{AB} = \mathbf{B}^{-1}\mathbf{IB} = \mathbf{B}^{-1}\mathbf{B} = \mathbf{I}$$

we may postmultiply both sides of the equation by $(\mathbf{AB})^{-1}$ to find

$$\mathbf{B}^{-1}\mathbf{A}^{-1} \cdot \mathbf{AB} \cdot (\mathbf{AB})^{-1} = \mathbf{I}(\mathbf{AB})^{-1}$$

or

$$\mathbf{B}^{-1}\mathbf{A}^{-1} = (\mathbf{AB})^{-1}$$

2.6 POWER SERIES EXPANSION OF THE INVERSE MATRIX

For a certain class of nonnegative square matrices, $\mathbf{A}$, say, we may establish the following useful power series expansion:

$$(\mathbf{I} - \mathbf{A})^{-1} = \mathbf{I} + \mathbf{A} + \mathbf{A}^2 + \cdots = \sum_{k=0}^{\infty} \mathbf{A}^k \tag{2.26}$$

This result is widely used and is the matrix analogue of the ordinary scalar geometric series in which

$$\sum_{k=0}^{\infty} a^k = 1 + a + a^2 + \cdots = \frac{1}{1-a} = (1-a)^{-1}$$

provided $-1 < a < 1$.

To derive (2.26), we begin by observing that

$$(\mathbf{I} - \mathbf{A})(\mathbf{I} + \mathbf{A} + \mathbf{A}^2 + \cdots + \mathbf{A}^n) = \mathbf{I} - \mathbf{A}^{n+1} \tag{2.27}$$

Here $\mathbf{A}^n$ denotes the nth power of $\mathbf{A}$ and may be obtained by multiplying $\mathbf{A}$ by itself n times. Now let n become very large, that is, let $n \to \infty$, and suppose that every element of $\mathbf{A}^{n+1}$ tends to zero. Then, in the limit, the right-hand side of (2.27) tends to $\mathbf{I}$ and, therefore,

$$\lim_{n\to\infty} (\mathbf{I} + \mathbf{A} + \mathbf{A}^2 + \cdots + \mathbf{A}^n) = (\mathbf{I} - \mathbf{A})^{-1}$$

In the above derivation we assumed that every element of $\mathbf{A}^{n+1}$ tended to zero. It can be shown that this will occur if the sum of the elements in each column of $\mathbf{A}$ is less than unity.[3]

[3] This condition can be weakened if the matrix is *indecomposable* (indecomposability is defined in Chapter 7). If a nonnegative matrix $\mathbf{A}$ is indecomposable, then $\lim_{n\to\infty} \mathbf{A}^n = 0$ if the sum of the elements in each column of $\mathbf{A}$ is less than or equal to unity and if at least one such column sum is less than unity.

Example. To illustrate the power series expansion of $(\mathbf{I} - \mathbf{A})^{-1}$, consider the following matrix:

$$\mathbf{A} = \begin{bmatrix} 0 & 0 & 0 \\ 1 & 0 & 0 \\ 0 & 1 & 0 \end{bmatrix}$$

This matrix meets the necessary and sufficient conditions for $\mathbf{A}^{n+1}$ to tend to zero. Indeed, all of the elements of $\mathbf{A}^3$ are zero.

Hence, by (2.26),

$$(\mathbf{I} - \mathbf{A})^{-1} = \mathbf{I} + \mathbf{A} + \mathbf{A}^2$$

2.7 APPLICATION: MATRIX ANALYSIS OF INTERREGIONAL POPULATION GROWTH AND DISTRIBUTION (CONTINUED)

Inventories and projections of human populations are a necessary component of most planning activities. Populations are the clients whose welfare the planning efforts are supposed to improve; they also are a primary resource used in the production of goods and services which lead to higher levels of welfare; and they consume resources that might be more profitably used elsewhere.

If one accepts the proposition that an increase in real per capita income reflects an increase in welfare, then clearly one can induce such an increase either by increasing the numerator (income) or by decreasing the denominator (population). The numerical impact of population policies that attempt to do the latter may be expressed and studied with the aid of the matrix models of interregional population growth that were described in the last chapter.

2.7.1 MATRIX ANALYSIS OF POPULATION CONTROL POLICIES

Population control in an interregional demographic system may be exercised through one or more of the three fundamental components of population growth and change: deaths, births, and migration. However, as Lowry (1968) points out, it is much easier and more appropriate for the planner to advocate a reduction in the size of a population through the regulation of the birth rate or migration rate, rather than through an increase in the death rate. A program to increase mortality is not only likely to be politically infeasible, but it also might introduce undesirable side effects; for example, such effects might include a lowering of the productivity of the labor force and a shift in the age distribution toward a younger age structure, with its correspondingly higher demands for expenses on childcare and education.

The effects of a birth or migration control policy on an interregional population whose growth is defined by the fundamental relationship

$$\mathbf{w}(t+1) = \mathbf{G}\mathbf{w}(t)$$

may be expressed by a constant intervention vector, **f**, say, which is added to the population in each time period, as follows:

$$\mathbf{w}(t+1) = \mathbf{G}\mathbf{w}(t) + \mathbf{f} \tag{2.28}$$

The vector **f** may have both positive and negative components. A positive f_i indicates the number of people that must be added to a region's population during each unit interval of time; a negative f_i denotes the population that has to be periodically withdrawn from region i. In analyses of alternative birth control policies, a negative f_i may be interpreted as the number of births that must be prevented from occurring during each unit interval of time.

Beginning with an initial population at some point in time, say, $t = 0$, we may trace through the effects of a particular policy control measure over time by repeatedly applying (2.28). Then, if **G** remains constant,

$$\begin{aligned} \mathbf{w}(1) &= \mathbf{G}\mathbf{w}(0) + \mathbf{f} \\ \mathbf{w}(2) &= \mathbf{G}\mathbf{w}(1) + \mathbf{f} = \mathbf{G}^2\mathbf{w}(0) + \mathbf{G}\mathbf{f} + \mathbf{f} \\ &\vdots \\ \mathbf{w}(t) &= \mathbf{G}^t\mathbf{w}(0) + (\mathbf{G}^{t-1} + \mathbf{G}^{t-2} + \cdots + \mathbf{I})\mathbf{f} \end{aligned} \tag{2.29}$$

and

$$\mathbf{w}(t) - \mathbf{G}^t\mathbf{w}(0) = (\mathbf{G}^{t-1} + \mathbf{G}^{t-2} + \cdots + \mathbf{I})\mathbf{f} \tag{2.30}$$

Premultiplying both sides of (2.30) by **G**, we obtain

$$\mathbf{G}[\mathbf{w}(t) - \mathbf{G}^t\mathbf{w}(0)] = (\mathbf{G}^t + \mathbf{G}^{t-1} + \cdots + \mathbf{G})\mathbf{f} \tag{2.31}$$

and, subtracting (2.31) from (2.30), we find

$$(\mathbf{I} - \mathbf{G})[\mathbf{w}(t) - \mathbf{G}^t\mathbf{w}(0)] = (\mathbf{I} - \mathbf{G}^t)\mathbf{f} \tag{2.32}$$

We conclude, therefore, that

$$\mathbf{f} = (\mathbf{I} - \mathbf{G}^t)^{-1}\{(\mathbf{I} - \mathbf{G})[\mathbf{w}(t) - \mathbf{G}^t\mathbf{w}(0)]\} \tag{2.33}$$

and

$$\mathbf{w}(t) = \mathbf{G}^t\mathbf{w}(0) + (\mathbf{I} - \mathbf{G})^{-1}(\mathbf{I} - \mathbf{G}^t)\mathbf{f} \tag{2.34}$$

In applying the population control model defined in (2.28) to empirical data, it is important to ensure that the interpretation of the intervention vector makes sense. This is less of a problem in the simple components-of-change model, since the intervention vector in such models typically will refer either to a control policy in which fertility and migration are confounded or to a "pure" birth control policy. Pure migration policies also may be studied, but care must be taken to recognize in such models that, because an in-migrant with respect to one region is an out-migrant with respect to another, the target populations are interrelated and one cannot, therefore, specify the target populations of all of the regions in an interregional system.

The application of the population control model to cohort survival models is a much more complex problem. For example, one cannot specify an arbitrary target age distribution for all of the regions, because control over the population beyond the first age group can only be effected through a pure migration policy, and we already have noted the kinds of restrictions that this places on the selection of target populations for the entire interregional system.

An interesting extension of the above arguments may be made by assuming that the degree or level of a population control policy may decline over time, so that the vector **f** is added at the beginning, but only $c\mathbf{f}$ is added during the next time period $(0 < c < 1)$, and, in general, only $c^k\mathbf{f}$ is added to the system during period k. Then

$$\begin{aligned}
\mathbf{w}(1) &= \mathbf{G}\mathbf{w}(0) + \mathbf{f} \\
\mathbf{w}(2) &= \mathbf{G}\mathbf{w}(1) + c\mathbf{f} = \mathbf{G}^2\mathbf{w}(0) + \mathbf{G}\mathbf{f} + c\mathbf{f} \\
&\vdots \\
\mathbf{w}(t) &= \mathbf{G}^t\mathbf{w}(0) + (\mathbf{G}^{t-1} + c\mathbf{G}^{t-2} + c^2\mathbf{G}^{t-3} + \cdots + c^{t-1}\mathbf{I})\mathbf{f}
\end{aligned} \tag{2.35}$$

and

$$\mathbf{w}(t) - \mathbf{G}^t\mathbf{w}(0) = (\mathbf{G}^{t-1} + c\mathbf{G}^{t-2} + c^2\mathbf{G}^{t-3} + \cdots + c^{t-1}\mathbf{I})\mathbf{f}$$

Premultiplying both sides by $(c\mathbf{I} - \mathbf{G})$, we obtain[4]

$$\begin{aligned}
(c\mathbf{I} - \mathbf{G})[\mathbf{w}(t) - \mathbf{G}^t\mathbf{w}(0)] &= (c\mathbf{I} - \mathbf{G})(\mathbf{G}^{t-1} + c\mathbf{G}^{t-2} + \cdots + c^{t-1}\mathbf{I})\mathbf{f} \\
&= (c^t\mathbf{I} - \mathbf{G}^t)\mathbf{f}
\end{aligned}$$

Whence

$$\mathbf{f} = (c^t\mathbf{I} - \mathbf{G}^t)^{-1}\{(c\mathbf{I} - \mathbf{G})[\mathbf{w}(t) - \mathbf{G}^t\mathbf{w}(0)]\} \tag{2.36}$$

or

$$\mathbf{w}(t) = \mathbf{G}^t\mathbf{w}(0) + (c\mathbf{I} - \mathbf{G})^{-1}(c^t\mathbf{I} - \mathbf{G}^t)\mathbf{f} \tag{2.37}$$

Another useful modification of (2.33) and (2.34) may be made in analyses of birth control policies. Denote by **S** any population growth matrix **G** which lacks a fertility schedule, and introduce the contribution of new births through the vector **f**. Then $\mathbf{S}^t$ will tend to the zero or *null* matrix as t increases; consequently,

$$\lim_{t\to\infty} \mathbf{w}(t) = (\mathbf{I} - \mathbf{S})^{-1}\mathbf{f} = \mathbf{y} \tag{2.38}$$

[4] The author is grateful to a former student of his, Christian Averous, for pointing out the error in an earlier formulation and suggesting the above argument.

say, and

$$\mathbf{f} = (\mathbf{I} - \mathbf{S})\mathbf{y} \tag{2.39}$$

It should be noted, however, that not all such target distributions are feasible goals once a particular growth regime has been defined. The binding constraint is that negative populations are not possible; consequently, **w** must never have negative elements as it moves from its initial distribution $\mathbf{w}(0)$ to its ultimate stationary distribution **y**. Hence

$$\mathbf{S}^t\mathbf{w}(0) + \sum_{k=0}^{t-1} \mathbf{S}^k(\mathbf{I} - \mathbf{S})\mathbf{y} \geqq 0$$

and, because $(\mathbf{I} + \mathbf{S} + \mathbf{S}^2 + \cdots + \mathbf{S}^{t-1})(\mathbf{I} - \mathbf{S}) = (\mathbf{I} - \mathbf{S}^t)$, we may reduce the above constraint to

$$\mathbf{S}^t\mathbf{w}(0) + (\mathbf{I} - \mathbf{S}^t)\mathbf{y} \geqq 0$$

or, equivalently,

$$\mathbf{S}^t[\mathbf{y} - \mathbf{w}(0)] \leqq \mathbf{y} \qquad \text{for all } t \geqq 0 \tag{2.40}$$

This constraint may appear, at first glance, to be impossible to impose, since an infinite number of conditions are specified. However, a theorem by Kemeny and Snell (1962, p. 68) provides a procedure for establishing feasibility in a finite number of steps (Exercise 5).

Examples. Recall the numerical example in Chapter 1 that describes population growth in Islandia. To simplify matters, let us consolidate Central and Southern Islandia into a single region. Then our two-region components-of-change population growth model has the following form:

$$\begin{aligned}\mathbf{w}(1965) &= \mathbf{G}\mathbf{w}(1950)\\ &= \begin{bmatrix} \frac{5}{6} & \frac{1}{4} \\ \frac{1}{4} & \frac{5}{6} \end{bmatrix} \begin{bmatrix} 288 \\ 576 \end{bmatrix} = \begin{bmatrix} 384 \\ 552 \end{bmatrix}\end{aligned} \tag{2.41}$$

(i) Consider the growth of this population over two consecutive time intervals:

$$\begin{aligned}\mathbf{w}(1980) &= \mathbf{G}^2\mathbf{w}(1950)\\ &= \begin{bmatrix} \frac{109}{144} & \frac{5}{12} \\ \frac{5}{12} & \frac{109}{144} \end{bmatrix} \begin{bmatrix} 288 \\ 576 \end{bmatrix} = \begin{bmatrix} 458 \\ 556 \end{bmatrix}\end{aligned}$$

and assume that it is desirable to achieve a redistribution of this population, such that by 1980 the total population of Islandia is equally divided among the two regions. What intervention vector **f** will achieve such a goal? First, we compute

$$(\mathbf{I} - \mathbf{G}^2)^{-1} = \begin{bmatrix} \frac{35}{144} & -\frac{5}{12} \\ -\frac{5}{12} & \frac{35}{144} \end{bmatrix}^{-1} = \begin{bmatrix} -\frac{1008}{475} & -\frac{1728}{475} \\ -\frac{1728}{475} & -\frac{1008}{475} \end{bmatrix}$$

Our target distribution is

$$\mathbf{w}(1980) = \begin{bmatrix} 507 \\ 507 \end{bmatrix}$$

hence we find

$$(\mathbf{I} - \mathbf{G})[\mathbf{w}(1980) - \mathbf{G}^2\mathbf{w}(1950)] = \begin{bmatrix} \frac{1}{6} & -\frac{1}{4} \\ -\frac{1}{4} & \frac{1}{6} \end{bmatrix} \begin{bmatrix} 49 \\ -49 \end{bmatrix} = \begin{bmatrix} \frac{245}{12} \\ -\frac{245}{12} \end{bmatrix}$$

and use (2.33) to derive

$$\begin{aligned} \mathbf{f} &= (\mathbf{I} - \mathbf{G}^2)^{-1}\{(\mathbf{I} - \mathbf{G})[\mathbf{w}(1980) - \mathbf{G}^2\mathbf{w}(1950)]\} \\ &= \begin{bmatrix} -\frac{1008}{475} & -\frac{1728}{475} \\ -\frac{1728}{475} & -\frac{1008}{475} \end{bmatrix} \begin{bmatrix} \frac{245}{12} \\ -\frac{245}{12} \end{bmatrix} \\ &= \begin{bmatrix} \frac{588}{19} \\ -\frac{588}{19} \end{bmatrix} \end{aligned}$$

As a check, observe that

$$\begin{aligned} \mathbf{w}(1965) &= \mathbf{G}\mathbf{w}(1950) + \mathbf{f} \\ &= \begin{bmatrix} \frac{5}{6} & \frac{1}{4} \\ \frac{1}{4} & \frac{5}{6} \end{bmatrix} \begin{bmatrix} 288 \\ 576 \end{bmatrix} + \begin{bmatrix} \frac{588}{19} \\ -\frac{588}{19} \end{bmatrix} = \begin{bmatrix} \frac{7884}{19} \\ \frac{9900}{19} \end{bmatrix} \end{aligned}$$

and

$$\begin{aligned} \mathbf{w}(1980) &= \mathbf{G}\mathbf{w}(1965) + \mathbf{f} \\ &= \begin{bmatrix} \frac{5}{6} & \frac{1}{4} \\ \frac{1}{4} & \frac{5}{6} \end{bmatrix} \begin{bmatrix} \frac{7884}{19} \\ \frac{9900}{19} \end{bmatrix} + \begin{bmatrix} \frac{588}{19} \\ -\frac{588}{19} \end{bmatrix} = \begin{bmatrix} 507 \\ 507 \end{bmatrix} \end{aligned}$$

(ii) Can the above target distribution be obtained with an intervention vector that declines exponentially over time, say $c^k\mathbf{f}$ where $c = \frac{1}{2}$? Recalling (2.36), we observe that for $t + 2 = 1980$,

$$\mathbf{f} = \left(\frac{1}{4}\mathbf{I} - \mathbf{G}^2\right)^{-1}\left(\frac{1}{2}\mathbf{I} - \mathbf{G}\right)[\mathbf{w}(1980) - \mathbf{G}^2\mathbf{w}(1950)]$$

$$= \begin{bmatrix} -\frac{10512}{1729} & \frac{8640}{1729} \\ \frac{8640}{1729} & -\frac{10512}{1729} \end{bmatrix} \begin{bmatrix} -\frac{1}{3} & -\frac{1}{4} \\ -\frac{1}{4} & -\frac{1}{3} \end{bmatrix} \begin{bmatrix} 49 \\ -49 \end{bmatrix}$$

$$= \begin{bmatrix} \frac{588}{13} \\ -\frac{588}{13} \end{bmatrix}$$

and

$$\mathbf{w}(1965) = \mathbf{G}\mathbf{w}(1950) + \mathbf{f}$$

$$= \begin{bmatrix} \frac{5}{6} & \frac{1}{4} \\ \frac{1}{4} & \frac{5}{6} \end{bmatrix} \begin{bmatrix} 288 \\ 576 \end{bmatrix} + \begin{bmatrix} \frac{588}{13} \\ -\frac{588}{13} \end{bmatrix} = \begin{bmatrix} \frac{5580}{13} \\ \frac{6588}{13} \end{bmatrix}$$

$$\mathbf{w}(1980) = \mathbf{G}\mathbf{w}(1965) + \frac{1}{2}\mathbf{f}$$

$$= \begin{bmatrix} \frac{5}{6} & \frac{1}{4} \\ \frac{1}{4} & \frac{5}{6} \end{bmatrix} \begin{bmatrix} \frac{5580}{13} \\ \frac{6588}{13} \end{bmatrix} + \begin{bmatrix} \frac{294}{13} \\ -\frac{294}{13} \end{bmatrix} = \begin{bmatrix} 507 \\ 507 \end{bmatrix}$$

(iii) Finally, let us illustrate the operation of the birth control model, defined in (2.39), by removing the contribution of new births from the two-region population growth matrix in (2.41) and introducing the component of change as an intervention vector:

$$\mathbf{w}(1965) = \mathbf{S}\mathbf{w}(1950) + \mathbf{f}$$

$$= \begin{bmatrix} \frac{3}{8} & \frac{1}{4} \\ \frac{1}{4} & \frac{3}{8} \end{bmatrix} \begin{bmatrix} 288 \\ 576 \end{bmatrix} + \begin{bmatrix} 132 \\ 264 \end{bmatrix} = \begin{bmatrix} 384 \\ 552 \end{bmatrix}$$

Thus, to obtain an ultimate population of 507 people in each of the two regions, we need the intervention vector

$$\mathbf{f} = (\mathbf{I} - \mathbf{S})\mathbf{y}$$

$$= \begin{bmatrix} \frac{5}{8} & -\frac{1}{4} \\ -\frac{1}{4} & \frac{5}{8} \end{bmatrix} \begin{bmatrix} 507 \\ 507 \end{bmatrix} = \begin{bmatrix} \frac{1521}{8} \\ \frac{1521}{8} \end{bmatrix}$$

Hence, we have the following population growth sequence:

$$\mathbf{w}(1965) = \begin{bmatrix} \frac{3}{8} & \frac{1}{4} \\ \frac{1}{4} & \frac{3}{8} \end{bmatrix} \begin{bmatrix} 288 \\ 576 \end{bmatrix} + \begin{bmatrix} \frac{1521}{8} \\ \frac{1521}{8} \end{bmatrix} = \begin{bmatrix} \frac{3537}{8} \\ \frac{3825}{8} \end{bmatrix}$$

$$\mathbf{w}(1980) = \begin{bmatrix} \frac{3}{8} & \frac{1}{4} \\ \frac{1}{4} & \frac{3}{8} \end{bmatrix} \begin{bmatrix} \frac{3537}{8} \\ \frac{3825}{8} \end{bmatrix} + \begin{bmatrix} \frac{1521}{8} \\ \frac{1521}{8} \end{bmatrix} = \begin{bmatrix} \frac{30429}{64} \\ \frac{30717}{64} \end{bmatrix}$$

$$\vdots$$

$$\mathbf{y} = \begin{bmatrix} \frac{3}{8} & \frac{1}{4} \\ \frac{1}{4} & \frac{3}{8} \end{bmatrix} \begin{bmatrix} 507 \\ 507 \end{bmatrix} + \begin{bmatrix} \frac{1521}{8} \\ \frac{1521}{8} \end{bmatrix} = \begin{bmatrix} 507 \\ 507 \end{bmatrix}$$

2.7.2 APPLICATION: ALTERNATIVE POPULATION CONTROL POLICIES AND THEIR IMPLICATIONS FOR THE FUTURE POPULATIONS OF CALIFORNIA AND THE REST OF THE UNITED STATES[5]

The population control models described above may be applied to the populations of California and the rest of the United States to assess the probable consequences of alternative population control policies. For example, consider the simple two-region components-of-change model that appears in (1.40). In the absence of any intervention, and assuming that **G** remains constant, the 1980 population vector will be

$$\mathbf{w}(1980) = \mathbf{G}^3\mathbf{w}(1950)$$

$$= \begin{bmatrix} 1.3083 & 0.1118 \\ 0.5177 & 1.5154 \end{bmatrix} \begin{bmatrix} 10586 \\ 140111 \end{bmatrix} = \begin{bmatrix} 29531 \\ 217782 \end{bmatrix}$$

[5] The numerical illustrations in this section were carried out by three of the author's former students: Christian Averous, Chyi Kang Lu, and Oscar Yujnovsky.

If we now adopt, for 1980, the target population vector

$$\mathbf{w}(1980) = \begin{bmatrix} 20000 \\ 200000 \end{bmatrix} \tag{2.42}$$

then, by (2.33),

$$\begin{aligned}
\mathbf{f} &= (\mathbf{I} - \mathbf{G}^3)^{-1}\{(\mathbf{I} - \mathbf{G})[\mathbf{w}(1980) - \mathbf{G}^3\mathbf{w}(1950)]\} \\
&= \begin{bmatrix} -5.1003 & 1.1062 \\ 5.1227 & -3.0512 \end{bmatrix} \begin{bmatrix} -0.0899 & -0.0298 \\ -0.1380 & -0.1451 \end{bmatrix} \begin{bmatrix} -9531 \\ -17782 \end{bmatrix} \\
&= \begin{bmatrix} -2758 \\ -4790 \end{bmatrix}
\end{aligned}$$

Thus, to redirect the growth of this two-region system toward the target population specified in (2.42), we must withdraw, every ten years, approximately 2,760,000 people from California's population and approximately 4,790,000 people from the population in the rest of the United States. These withdrawals may be in the form of births foregone or in-migrants kept out, or some combination of these two policies.

In order to derive the pure birth control policy that will direct the 1950 population toward the target population specified in (2.42), we must remove the regional birth rates from the growth matrix in (1.40), and introduce total births in the intervention vector:[6]

$$\begin{aligned}
\mathbf{w}(1960) &= \mathbf{S}\mathbf{w}(1950) + \mathbf{f} \\
&= \begin{bmatrix} 0.7739 & 0.0298 \\ 0.1380 & 0.8905 \end{bmatrix} \begin{bmatrix} 10586 \\ 140111 \end{bmatrix} + \begin{bmatrix} 3346 \\ 35667 \end{bmatrix} \\
&= \begin{bmatrix} 15714 \\ 161897 \end{bmatrix}
\end{aligned}$$

Then, entering the growth matrix **S** into (2.33), we obtain

$$\mathbf{f} = \begin{bmatrix} 1449 \\ 35723 \end{bmatrix}$$

Hence, to achieve the target population in (2.42) with a pure birth control policy, we must decrease the number of children born in California to 1,449,000 per decade and increase the corresponding number in the rest of the United States to 35,723,000 per decade.

[6] The small discrepancies between totals presented in this and the next equation and the totals presented in Chapter 1 are due to errors introduced by rounding the growth matrix to four decimal places before reading it into the computer.

The target distribution of 20,000,000 for California also may be obtained by means of a pure migration policy. However, we have noted earlier that in such models one cannot specify the target populations for all of the regions. This is because an in-migrant prevented from entering California, for example, must remain in the rest of the United States. Consequently, the target population of the latter region depends on that of the former and cannot be arbitrarily specified. Hence we proceed as follows. First, we set the appropriate migration rate in the growth matrix to zero (that is, the fraction of the population in the rest of the United States that migrates to California), and introduce the migration flow from the rest of the United States to California in the intervention vector:

$$\mathbf{w}(1960) = \begin{bmatrix} 1.0899 & 0 \\ 0.1380 & 1.1749 \end{bmatrix} \begin{bmatrix} 10586 \\ 140111 \end{bmatrix} + \begin{bmatrix} 4180 \\ -4180 \end{bmatrix}$$

$$= \begin{bmatrix} 15718 \\ 161897 \end{bmatrix}$$

Next, we enter this revised growth matrix, the target population for California, and an arbitrary target population for the rest of the United States, into (2.33) to find the appropriate level of intervention with regard to

Table 2.2. Alternative Intervention Vectors: California and the Rest of the United States (Population Data in Thousands)

Age Group	Policy 1	Policy 2
0- 9	100	5, 000
10-19	100	0
20-29	200	0
30-39	100	0
40-49	0	0
50-59	0	0
60-69	0	0
70-79	0	0
80+	0	0
0- 9	−100	30, 000
10-19	−100	0
20-29	−200	0
30-39	−100	0
40-49	0	0
50-59	0	0
60-69	0	0
70-79	0	0
80+	0	0

migration into California: $f_{cal} = 1{,}920$. Since these in-migrants will be coming from the rest of the United States, we have the intervention vector

$$\mathbf{f} = \begin{bmatrix} 1920 \\ -1920 \end{bmatrix}$$

and entering this intervention vector into (2.34), we obtain the revised target population

$$\mathbf{w}(1980) = \begin{bmatrix} 20000 \\ 226895 \end{bmatrix}$$

Table 2.3. Population Projections for Various Alternative Population Control Policies: California and the Rest of the United States (Population Data in Thousands)

Region	Age Group	1980 Population Totals				Stationary Population Totals	
		No Intervention	Policy la $c=1$	Policy lb $c=\frac{3}{4}$	Policy lc $c=\frac{1}{2}$	No Intervention	Policy 2
California	0– 9	6,508	7,117	6,994	6,884	3,346	5,000
	10–19	4,835	5,277	5,213	5,162	3,959	5,182
	20–29	4,890	5,234	5,127	5,045	4,890	5,678
	30–39	3,707	4,003	3,925	3,858	5,270	5,634
	40–49	2,542	2,730	2,710	2,691	5,258	5,425
	50–59	2,473	2,536	2,536	2,536	4,968	5,028
	60–69	1,931	1,931	1,931	1,931	4,407	4,404
	70–79	1,116	1,116	1,116	1,116	3,182	3,142
	80+	420	420	420	420	1,393	1,353
Total Population of California		28,422	30,364	29,972	29,643	36,673	40,846
Rest of U.S.	0– 9	41,854	41,334	41,443	41,540	35,667	30,000
	10–19	34,165	33,779	33,843	33,895	34,812	29,602
	20–29	33,751	33,408	33,515	33,598	33,751	28,978
	30–39	25,133	24,834	24,914	24,980	33,040	28,716
	40–49	18,670	18,478	18,497	18,517	32,543	28,457
	50–59	19,266	19,203	19,203	19,203	30,405	26,676
	60–69	16,246	16,246	16,246	16,246	26,160	22,993
	70–79	10,217	10,217	10,217	10,217	19,014	16,743
	80+	3,531	3,531	3,531	3,531	7,620	6,726
Total Population of the Rest of the U.S.		202,833	201,030	201,409	201,727	253,012	218,891
Total Population of the United States.		231,255	231,394	231,381	231,370	289,685	259,737

Source: Calculated using the data in Figure 1.2.

in which the revised target value for the rest of the United States now is consistent with the level of migration that will be permitted into California.

Finally, although the application of (2.33) to interregional cohort survival models is too complicated to be presented here, we may readily apply (2.34), (2.37), and (2.38) to measure the probable consequences of a set of prespecified alternative intervention policies. Table 2.2 presents two alternative intervention vectors that could be applied to the population growth process defined in Figure 1.2. Table 2.3 summarizes their impact on the populations of California and the rest of the United States. Policy 1 deals with the projected 1980 population, and Policy 2 is analyzed with respect to its impact on the stationary population. Notice that Policy 1 includes three options regarding the level of intervention during succeeding time intervals, that is, the parameter c in (2.37) is set equal to unity in Policy 1a, to $\frac{3}{4}$ in Policy 1b, and to $\frac{1}{2}$ in Policy 1c.

2.8 APPLICATION: A SPATIAL ACTIVITY ALLOCATION MODEL (CONTINUED)

Studies of an urban community's economic base generally divide the local economy into an exogenous or *basic* sector and an endogenous or *nonbasic* sector [Lane (1966)]. The levels of output, employment, and income in the basic sector depend on events over which the local community has no control—for example, exports to the rest of the world. Such events cause income to flow into the community, and a part of this income is spent within the community, thereby creating a local demand for goods and services that are produced by the local nonbasic sector—for example, haircuts. Since the level of activity in the nonbasic sector depends on the level of demand generated by the basic sector, it is reasonable to conclude that, at least in the short run, the basic sector is the principal driving force behind a community's economic growth and development.

In a recent study Lowry (1964) borrowed the basic and nonbasic dichotomy of urban economic base theory to develop a model of spatial activity allocation that reflects the economic base rationale in a spatial context. According to Lowry's model, employment in establishments that have specialized locational requirements is *basic* employment, whereas employment in those establishments that locate so as to best serve the local population is *nonbasic* or *population-serving* employment.

Given the spatial pattern of basic employment, the Lowry model distributes these employees to their place of residence by means of a journey-from-work-to-home function and then expands the resulting pattern of employment into a basic residential population by using the reciprocal of the labor force participation rate that is associated with each residential zone. Next, the model generates a population-serving employment total for each zone by means of a ratio of population-serving employment to total population. This nonbasic employment then is spatially distributed with a *journey-to-shop* function, and the resulting nonbasic employment, by place of work, is distributed to places of residence by the same journey-from-work-to-home function used earlier. This nonbasic employment, by place of residence, is expanded into a nonbasic residential population, and the first cycle of the process is concluded. The nonbasic population too requires nonbasic employees to serve it, hence another cycle in the locational process is initiated. This locational process is continued until an equilibrium is reached. The resulting final pattern of residential population, therefore, depends ultimately on the spatial distribution of basic employment, and the spatial pattern of nonbasic employment depends on the geographical arrangement of the residential population that it serves.

2.8.1 THE GARIN-LOWRY MODEL

The matrix model of intraregional employment and population growth developed in Section 1.6 led to a very simple and compact expression of a hypothesized relationship between the spatial patterns of population and employment in an urban area. In this section we shall disaggregate employment into *basic* and *nonbasic* components and illustrate how this model may be generalized to assume the form of Garin's (1966) matrix version of the Lowry model.

Let us denote the spatial distribution of basic employment in a region by the vector $\mathbf{e}_b(t)$, and assume that the residential population generated by these basic employees may be found by applying (1.65). That is, let

$$\mathbf{w}_b(t) = \mathbf{M}\mathbf{e}_b(t) \tag{2.43}$$

Now consider the spatial distribution of the nonbasic employees who serve this basic residential population. Assume that the number of such employees, needed to serve the population in each zone i, may be found by applying a nonbasic employee-per-person ratio, b_i, say, to the population of that zone. Further, assume that the spatial disposition of these employees may be found by means of a *journey-to-shop function* which distributes these nonbasic employees over all zones according to some observed inverse relationship with distance or travel time. Thus, we may define q_{ij} as the proportion of nonbasic employees who serve the population in zone j but work in zone i.

If all nonbasic employees had to work in the same zone as the population which they served, then the nonbasic employment in each zone could be found by applying a nonbasic employee-per-person ratio to the total population of that zone:

$$e_{nb_i}(t) = b_i w_i(t) \tag{2.44}$$

where

$e_{nb_i}(t) =$ the nonbasic employment in zone i at time t; and
$b_i =$ the nonbasic employee-per-person ratio in zone i.

But some nonbasic employees may serve the population of zone i at some other location. Thus, we may distribute the nonbasic employees that are needed to serve the population in zone i according to the journey-to-shop relationship that is defined by a particular set of q_{ij}'s:

$$e_{nb_i}(t) = q_{i1}b_1w_1(t) + q_{i2}b_2w_2(t) + \cdots + q_{im}b_mw_m(t)$$

where q_{ij} denotes the proportion of nonbasic employees who serve the population in zone j but work in zone i. Thus, in matrix form,

$$\begin{bmatrix} e_{nb_1}(t) \\ e_{nb_2}(t) \\ \vdots \\ e_{nb_m}(t) \end{bmatrix} = \begin{bmatrix} q_{11} & q_{12} & \cdots & q_{1m} \\ q_{21} & q_{22} & \cdots & q_{2m} \\ \vdots & \vdots & & \vdots \\ q_{m1} & q_{m2} & \cdots & q_{mm} \end{bmatrix} \begin{bmatrix} b_1 & 0 & \cdots & 0 \\ 0 & b_2 & \cdots & 0 \\ \vdots & \vdots & \ddots & \vdots \\ 0 & 0 & \cdots & b_m \end{bmatrix} \begin{bmatrix} w_1(t) \\ w_2(t) \\ \vdots \\ w_m(t) \end{bmatrix}$$
$$= \mathbf{QBw}(t)$$

or

$$\mathbf{e}_{nb}(t) = \mathbf{Nw}(t) \tag{2.45}$$

where $\mathbf{N} = \mathbf{QB}$. We shall call $\mathbf{Q}$ the *journey-to-shop matrix*.

But in (2.43) we have considered only the total *basic* population, $\mathbf{w}_b(t)$! Hence to find the nonbasic employment that is needed to serve this basic population, we simply apply (2.45) to $\mathbf{w}_b(t)$ instead of $\mathbf{w}(t)$ to find

$$\mathbf{e}_{nb}(t:1) = \mathbf{Nw}_b(t) \tag{2.46}$$

where $\mathbf{e}_{nb}(t:1)$ denotes the nonbasic employment vector that is needed to support the basic population vector at time t.

The index of unity in $\mathbf{e}_{nb}(t:1)$ is an iteration number, reflecting the fact that the newly located nonbasic employees will themselves generate a nonbasic population and, consequently, a demand for more nonbasic employees to serve this nonbasic population. That is,

$$\mathbf{w}_{nb}(t:1) = \mathbf{Me}_{nb}(t:1) = \mathbf{MNw}_b(t) = \mathbf{MNMe}_b(t) \tag{2.47}$$

hence,

$$\mathbf{e}_{nb}(t:2) = \mathbf{Nw}_{nb}(t:1) = \mathbf{NMNMe}_b(t)$$

or

$$\mathbf{e}_{nb}(t:2) = (\mathbf{NM})^2\mathbf{e}_b(t) \tag{2.48}$$

and, in general,

$$\mathbf{e}_{nb}(t:n) = (\mathbf{NM})^n\mathbf{e}_b(t) \tag{2.49}$$

It is apparent that with each new increment of nonbasic employment, we have an associated increment of residential population:

$$\begin{aligned}
\mathbf{e}_{nb}(t:1) &= (\mathbf{NM})\mathbf{e}_b(t) & \mathbf{w}_{nb}(t:1) &= \mathbf{M}(\mathbf{NM})\mathbf{e}_b(t)\\
\mathbf{e}_{nb}(t:2) &= (\mathbf{NM})^2\mathbf{e}_b(t) & \mathbf{w}_{nb}(t:2) &= \mathbf{M}(\mathbf{NM})^2\mathbf{e}_b(t)\\
&\vdots & &\vdots\\
\mathbf{e}_{nb}(t:n) &= (\mathbf{NM})^n\mathbf{e}_b(t) & \mathbf{w}_{nb}(t:n) &= \mathbf{M}(\mathbf{NM})^n\mathbf{e}_b(t)
\end{aligned}$$

Thus, total employment, $\mathbf{e}(t)$, and total population, $\mathbf{w}(t)$, will be equal to the following sums:

$$\begin{aligned}
\mathbf{e}(t) &= \mathbf{e}_b(t) + \mathbf{e}_{nb}(t:1) + \mathbf{e}_{nb}(t:2) + \cdots + \mathbf{e}_{nb}(t:n) + \cdots\\
&= [\mathbf{I} + (\mathbf{NM}) + (\mathbf{NM})^2 + \cdots + (\mathbf{NM})^n + \cdots]\mathbf{e}_b(t) \qquad (2.50)
\end{aligned}$$

and

$$\begin{aligned}
\mathbf{w}(t) &= \mathbf{w}_b(t) + \mathbf{w}_{nb}(t:1) + \mathbf{w}_{nb}(t:2) + \cdots + \mathbf{w}_{nb}(t:n) + \cdots\\
&= \mathbf{M}[\mathbf{I} + (\mathbf{NM}) + (\mathbf{NM})^2 + \cdots + (\mathbf{NM})^n + \cdots]\mathbf{e}_b(t) \qquad (2.51)
\end{aligned}$$

It can be shown that under very general conditions on the product matrix **NM** (which are met in practical applications of the model), the series[7]

$$\mathbf{I} + (\mathbf{NM}) + (\mathbf{NM})^2 + \cdots + (\mathbf{NM})^n + \cdots$$

converges to the inverse of the matrix $(\mathbf{I} - \mathbf{NM})$. Hence we may rewrite (2.50) and (2.51) as follows:

$$\mathbf{e}(t) = (\mathbf{I} - \mathbf{NM})^{-1}\mathbf{e}_b(t) \qquad (2.52)$$

and

$$\mathbf{w}(t) = \mathbf{M}(\mathbf{I} - \mathbf{NM})^{-1}\mathbf{e}_b(t) \qquad (2.53)$$

Notice that by substituting (2.52) into (2.53) we obtain the expression for the generalized matrix model presented in (1.65):

$$\mathbf{w}(t) = \mathbf{Me}(t)$$

and, therefore, we may continue as before to develop a dynamic dimension for this model.

Example. To illustrate the operation of the Garin-Lowry model, consider once again our numerical example involving the three regions of Islandia in Section 1.7. For simplicity, assume that $\mathbf{Q} = \mathbf{P}$, $b = \frac{1}{6}$, and $a = 3$ as before. We have, then, the following results:

[7] If $(\mathbf{NM})^n$ did not tend to the zero matrix as n increased, then an infinite amount of population-serving employment would be generated by a finite amount of basic employment, a most unrealistic event in practical applications of the model.

$$\mathbf{e}_{nb}(t:1) = \mathbf{N}\mathbf{w}_b(t) = \mathbf{QBM}\mathbf{e}_b(t)$$

$$= \begin{bmatrix} \frac{1}{2} & \frac{1}{4} & \frac{1}{4} \\ \frac{1}{4} & \frac{1}{2} & \frac{1}{4} \\ \frac{1}{4} & \frac{1}{4} & \frac{1}{2} \end{bmatrix} \begin{bmatrix} \frac{1}{6} & 0 & 0 \\ 0 & \frac{1}{6} & 0 \\ 0 & 0 & \frac{1}{6} \end{bmatrix} \begin{bmatrix} \frac{3}{2} & \frac{3}{4} & \frac{3}{4} \\ \frac{3}{4} & \frac{3}{2} & \frac{3}{4} \\ \frac{3}{4} & \frac{3}{4} & \frac{3}{2} \end{bmatrix} \begin{bmatrix} 48 \\ 48 \\ 48 \end{bmatrix}$$

$$= \begin{bmatrix} \frac{1}{12} & \frac{1}{24} & \frac{1}{24} \\ \frac{1}{24} & \frac{1}{12} & \frac{1}{24} \\ \frac{1}{24} & \frac{1}{24} & \frac{1}{12} \end{bmatrix} \begin{bmatrix} 144 \\ 144 \\ 144 \end{bmatrix}$$

$$= \begin{bmatrix} 24 \\ 24 \\ 24 \end{bmatrix}$$

$$\mathbf{w}_{nb}(t:1) = \mathbf{M}\mathbf{e}_{nb}(t:1)$$

$$= \begin{bmatrix} \frac{3}{2} & \frac{3}{4} & \frac{3}{4} \\ \frac{3}{4} & \frac{3}{2} & \frac{3}{4} \\ \frac{3}{4} & \frac{3}{4} & \frac{3}{2} \end{bmatrix} \begin{bmatrix} 24 \\ 24 \\ 24 \end{bmatrix}$$

$$= \begin{bmatrix} 72 \\ 72 \\ 72 \end{bmatrix}$$

$$\mathbf{e}(t) = \mathbf{e}_b(t) + \mathbf{e}_{nb}(t:1) + \mathbf{e}_{nb}(t:2) + \cdots = (\mathbf{I} - \mathbf{NM})^{-1}\mathbf{e}_b(t)$$

$$= \begin{bmatrix} 48 \\ 48 \\ 48 \end{bmatrix} + \begin{bmatrix} 24 \\ 24 \\ 24 \end{bmatrix} + \begin{bmatrix} 12 \\ 12 \\ 12 \end{bmatrix} + \cdots = \begin{bmatrix} \frac{1302}{961} & \frac{310}{961} & \frac{310}{961} \\ \frac{310}{961} & \frac{1302}{961} & \frac{310}{961} \\ \frac{310}{961} & \frac{310}{961} & \frac{1302}{961} \end{bmatrix} \begin{bmatrix} 48 \\ 48 \\ 48 \end{bmatrix}$$

$$= \begin{bmatrix} 96 \\ 96 \\ 96 \end{bmatrix}$$

and

$$\mathbf{w}(t) = \mathbf{w}_b(t) + \mathbf{w}_{nb}(t:1) + \mathbf{w}_{nb}(t:2) + \cdots = \mathbf{M}(\mathbf{I} - \mathbf{N}\mathbf{M})^{-1}\mathbf{e}_b(t)$$

$$= \begin{bmatrix} 144 \\ 144 \\ 144 \end{bmatrix} + \begin{bmatrix} 72 \\ 72 \\ 72 \end{bmatrix} + \begin{bmatrix} 36 \\ 36 \\ 36 \end{bmatrix} + \cdots$$

$$= \begin{bmatrix} \frac{3}{2} & \frac{3}{4} & \frac{3}{4} \\ \frac{3}{4} & \frac{3}{2} & \frac{3}{4} \\ \frac{3}{4} & \frac{3}{4} & \frac{3}{2} \end{bmatrix} \begin{bmatrix} \frac{1302}{961} & \frac{310}{961} & \frac{310}{961} \\ \frac{310}{961} & \frac{1302}{961} & \frac{310}{961} \\ \frac{310}{961} & \frac{310}{961} & \frac{1302}{961} \end{bmatrix} \begin{bmatrix} 48 \\ 48 \\ 48 \end{bmatrix}$$

$$= \begin{bmatrix} 288 \\ 288 \\ 288 \end{bmatrix}$$

2.8.2 APPLICATION: A SPATIAL ACTIVITY ALLOCATION MODEL FOR THE LJUBLJANA METROPOLITAN REGION IN NORTHERN YUGOSLAVIA (CONTINUED)

In order to apply the Garin-Lowry model to the Ljubljana Metropolitan Region, we need a journey-to-shop matrix, $\mathbf{Q}$. The data for estimating such a matrix are unavailable, and we shall therefore assume that the journey-to-work matrix (not to be confused with the journey-from-work-to-home matrix, $\mathbf{P}$) provides an adequate approximation. Hence, we begin by dividing each element of the matrix in Table 1.11 by its respective row sum. This produces the $\mathbf{Q}$ matrix shown in Figure 2.2. Next, we assume that industrial workers constitute the basic employment in that region and, therefore, that the intercommunal distribution in Column 1 of Table 1.12 represents $\mathbf{e}_b(1963)$. Then we adopt the diagonal values of the $\mathbf{A}$ matrix that appear in Column 4 of Table 1.12, and assume that all of the diagonal elements of the $\mathbf{B}$ matrix are equal to 0.06. Recalling that $\mathbf{M} = \mathbf{AP}$ and $\mathbf{N} = \mathbf{QB}$, we calculate the matrices $\mathbf{NM}$ and $(\mathbf{I} - \mathbf{NM})$ and then derive the matrix $(\mathbf{I} - \mathbf{NM})^{-1}$ that appears in Figure 2.3. Finally, applying the following two equations, in sequence,

$$\mathbf{e}(1963) = (\mathbf{I} - \mathbf{NM})^{-1}\mathbf{e}_b(1963)$$

and

$$\mathbf{w}(1963) = \mathbf{Me}(1963)$$

we obtain the results set out in Columns 2 and 3 of Table 2.4. If we now assume that the growth matrix in Figure 1.5 refers to total employment growth instead of basic employment growth, then

$$\mathbf{Q} = \begin{bmatrix}
0.9308 & 0.0060 & 0.0090 & 0 & 0.0005 & 0 & 0.0033 & 0 & 0 & 0.0020 & 0.0003 & 0.0184 & 0.0003 & 0 & 0.0001 & 0.0294 \\
0.0761 & 0.8498 & 0.0003 & 0 & 0.0003 & 0 & 0 & 0 & 0.0099 & 0.0155 & 0.0021 & 0.0396 & 0.0008 & 0.0035 & 0 & 0.0021 \\
0.0618 & 0.0006 & 0.9333 & 0 & 0 & 0 & 0 & 0 & 0 & 0.0003 & 0 & 0.0015 & 0 & 0 & 0 & 0.0026 \\
0 & 0 & 0 & 0.9910 & 0 & 0 & 0 & 0 & 0 & 0.0020 & 0 & 0 & 0 & 0.0030 & 0.0005 & 0.0035 \\
0.0002 & 0 & 0 & 0 & 0.8571 & 0 & 0.0428 & 0.0029 & 0.0597 & 0.0124 & 0.0115 & 0.0052 & 0.0015 & 0 & 0 & 0.0068 \\
0 & 0 & 0 & 0 & 0 & 0.7338 & 0 & 0 & 0.0065 & 0.1948 & 0.0081 & 0.0154 & 0.0398 & 0 & 0 & 0.0016 \\
0.0030 & 0 & 0 & 0 & 0.0618 & 0 & 0.9076 & 0 & 0.0134 & 0.0077 & 0.0007 & 0.0040 & 0.0007 & 0 & 0 & 0.0010 \\
0 & 0 & 0 & 0 & 0.0006 & 0.0022 & 0 & 0.8037 & 0.0033 & 0.0505 & 0.0887 & 0.0177 & 0 & 0 & 0 & 0.0333 \\
0.0027 & 0.0009 & 0 & 0 & 0.0149 & 0.0002 & 0.0002 & 0.0014 & 0.6727 & 0.1987 & 0.0249 & 0.0730 & 0.0078 & 0.0002 & 0.0011 & 0.0011 \\
0.0120 & 0.0014 & 0 & 0.0005 & 0.0062 & 0.0024 & 0.0029 & 0.0043 & 0.0962 & 0.5950 & 0.1005 & 0.1450 & 0.0278 & 0.0005 & 0.0014 & 0.0038 \\
0.0029 & 0.0002 & 0 & 0 & 0.0029 & 0.0004 & 0 & 0.0020 & 0.0313 & 0.2190 & 0.7117 & 0.0227 & 0.0044 & 0 & 0.0018 & 0.0006 \\
0.0310 & 0.0037 & 0.0002 & 0 & 0.0105 & 0.0001 & 0.0017 & 0.0004 & 0.0447 & 0.1552 & 0.0064 & 0.7432 & 0.0022 & 0 & 0.0004 & 0.0003 \\
0.0052 & 0.0005 & 0.0002 & 0.0035 & 0.0028 & 0.0003 & 0.0003 & 0.0015 & 0.0234 & 0.2911 & 0.0346 & 0.0374 & 0.5881 & 0.0003 & 0.0098 & 0.0010 \\
0 & 0.0042 & 0 & 0.0018 & 0.0006 & 0 & 0 & 0 & 0.0018 & 0.0048 & 0 & 0.0030 & 0.0018 & 0.9774 & 0.0048 & 0 \\
0 & 0 & 0 & 0.0030 & 0 & 0.0005 & 0.0005 & 0.0005 & 0.0030 & 0.0568 & 0.0015 & 0.0231 & 0.0367 & 0.0075 & 0.8669 & 0 \\
0.0026 & 0.0000 & 0.0001 & 0.0006 & 0.0000 & 0.0004 & 0 & 0.0001 & 0 & 0.0013 & 0.0003 & 0.0003 & 0.0001 & 0.0008 & 0.0000 & 0.9932
\end{bmatrix}$$

Source: Calculated using the data in Table 1.11. Programmed by Guenter Herrmann.

Figure 2.2. The Journey-to-Shop Matrix: The Ljubljana Metropolitan Region and the Rest of Slovenia, 1963

$$
(\mathbf{I}-\mathbf{NM})^{-1} = \begin{bmatrix}
1.2966 & 0.0145 & 0.0146 & 0.0035 & 0.0013 & 0.0139 & 0.0056 & 0.0016 & 0.0037 & 0.0090 & 0.0031 & 0.0162 & 0.0025 & 0.0054 & 0.0007 & 0.0697 \\
0.0537 & 1.4837 & 0.0020 & 0.0006 & 0.0016 & 0.0035 & 0.0010 & 0.0012 & 0.0195 & 0.0221 & 0.0082 & 0.0298 & 0.0041 & 0.0093 & 0.0006 & 0.0091 \\
0.0295 & 0.0016 & 1.2175 & 0.0004 & 0.0001 & 0.0015 & 0.0004 & 0.0002 & 0.0004 & 0.0010 & 0.0003 & 0.0016 & 0.0002 & 0.0006 & 0.0001 & 0.0074 \\
0.0004 & 0.0001 & 0.0000 & 1.6569 & 0.0000 & 0.0022 & 0.0000 & 0.0003 & 0.0005 & 0.0019 & 0.0006 & 0.0004 & 0.0004 & 0.0072 & 0.0011 & 0.0104 \\
0.0016 & 0.0005 & 0.0001 & 0.0010 & 1.2788 & 0.0056 & 0.0471 & 0.0114 & 0.0691 & 0.0260 & 0.0204 & 0.0108 & 0.0062 & 0.0014 & 0.0009 & 0.0168 \\
0.0112 & 0.0043 & 0.0004 & 0.0055 & 0.0100 & 4.0548 & 0.0046 & 0.0209 & 0.1398 & 0.4113 & 0.1390 & 0.1068 & 0.2194 & 0.0033 & 0.0142 & 0.0177 \\
0.0022 & 0.0002 & 0.0001 & 0.0002 & 0.0473 & 0.0015 & 1.3395 & 0.0014 & 0.0202 & 0.0102 & 0.0047 & 0.0050 & 0.0026 & 0.0003 & 0.0003 & 0.0033 \\
0.0058 & 0.0011 & 0.0004 & 0.0055 & 0.0027 & 0.0548 & 0.0008 & 1.7302 & 0.0281 & 0.0702 & 0.1125 & 0.0259 & 0.0110 & 0.0081 & 0.0021 & 0.1032 \\
0.0065 & 0.0033 & 0.0002 & 0.0011 & 0.0156 & 0.0160 & 0.0028 & 0.0111 & 1.3065 & 0.1445 & 0.0610 & 0.0654 & 0.0276 & 0.0015 & 0.0052 & 0.0052 \\
0.0122 & 0.0044 & 0.0004 & 0.0025 & 0.0101 & 0.0368 & 0.0046 & 0.0179 & 0.1210 & 1.2103 & 0.1144 & 0.0916 & 0.0513 & 0.0023 & 0.0068 & 0.0109 \\
0.0057 & 0.0019 & 0.0002 & 0.0010 & 0.0063 & 0.0187 & 0.0018 & 0.0137 & 0.0745 & 0.1564 & 1.3247 & 0.0423 & 0.0241 & 0.0010 & 0.0067 & 0.0040 \\
0.0235 & 0.0082 & 0.0009 & 0.0007 & 0.0131 & 0.0117 & 0.0043 & 0.0072 & 0.0833 & 0.1258 & 0.0373 & 1.2144 & 0.0165 & 0.0008 & 0.0032 & 0.0038 \\
0.0104 & 0.0037 & 0.0005 & 0.0126 & 0.0090 & 0.0279 & 0.0033 & 0.0179 & 0.0996 & 0.2665 & 0.1075 & 0.0727 & 1.4534 & 0.0029 & 0.0331 & 0.0068 \\
0.0005 & 0.0056 & 0.0000 & 0.0033 & 0.0006 & 0.0005 & 0.0001 & 0.0003 & 0.0034 & 0.0051 & 0.0016 & 0.0029 & 0.0036 & 1.5408 & 0.0078 & 0.0002 \\
0.0020 & 0.0008 & 0.0001 & 0.0064 & 0.0017 & 0.0103 & 0.0011 & 0.0042 & 0.0209 & 0.0548 & 0.0185 & 0.0232 & 0.0578 & 0.0128 & 1.4578 & 0.0010 \\
0.0632 & 0.0043 & 0.0054 & 0.0890 & 0.0024 & 0.3458 & 0.0010 & 0.0350 & 0.0197 & 0.0845 & 0.0345 & 0.0236 & 0.0318 & 0.1335 & 0.0054 & 2.7471
\end{bmatrix}
$$

Source: Calculated using the data in Table 1.11. Programmed by Guenter Herrmann.

Figure 2.3. The Inverse of the Matrix **(I − NM)**

$$\mathbf{e}(1968) = \mathbf{Se}(1963) = \mathbf{S}(\mathbf{I} - \mathbf{NM})^{-1}\mathbf{e}_b(1963)$$

and, consequently,[8]

$$\mathbf{w}(1968) = \mathbf{Me}(1968) = \mathbf{MS}(\mathbf{I} - \mathbf{NM})^{-1}\mathbf{e}_b(1963)$$

Table 2.4. Basic Employment, Total Employment, and Total Population in the Ljubljana Metropolitan Region and the Rest of Slovenia: 1963 and Projected to 1968

Commune	1. Industrial Employment by Commune of Employment 1963	2. Total Employment by Commune of Employment 1963	3. Communal Population 1963	4. Total Employment by Commune of Employment 1968	5. Communal Population 1968
	$\mathbf{e}_b(1963)$	$\mathbf{e}(1963)$	$\mathbf{Me}(1963)$	$\mathbf{e}(1968)$	$\mathbf{w}(1968)$
1. Kranj	11,236	22,707	99,187	24,488	106,866
2. Skofja Loka	3,302	7,155	52,459	7,647	56,286
3. Trzic	3,325	5,235	18,173	5,426	18,898
4. Cerknica	2,068	4,622	31,068	4,625	31,099
5. Domzale	5,760	10,194	50,809	10,910	55,123
6. Grosuplje	966	12,439	223,215	11,657	210,515
7. Kamnik	3,982	6,253	32,233	6,618	34,274
8. Litija	1,524	15,710	143,554	14,724	135,971
9. Lj.-Bezigrad	4,429	8,718	64,176	11,338	78,599
10. Lj.-Center	7,567	12,842	76,655	12,446	82,462
11. Lj.-Moste-Polje	4,746	8,914	64,272	11,898	80,249
12. Lj.-Siska	9,767	14,257	73,374	16,343	82,306
13. Lj.-Vic-Rudnik	3,836	10,352	127,825	12,828	150,429
14. Logatec	1,766	2,890	17,782	3,081	18,963
15. Vrhnika	1,820	3,903	26,838	4,153	28,697
Subtotal (L.M.R.)	66,093	146,191	1,101,622	158,180	1,170,738
16. Rest of Slovenia	110,606	306,666	3,289,278	319,631	3,427,824
Total (Slovenia)	176,700	452,857	4,390,900	477,811	4,598,562

Source: Calculated using the data in Tables 1.11 and 1.12, and Figures 1.5 and 2.2. Programmed by Guenter Herrmann.

[8] The reader should confirm that if **S** refers to basic employment growth, then

$$\mathbf{e}(1968) = (\mathbf{I} - \mathbf{NM})^{-1}\mathbf{Se}_b(1963)$$

and

$$\mathbf{w}(1968) = \mathbf{M}(\mathbf{I} - \mathbf{NM})^{-1}\mathbf{Se}_b(1963)$$

The equations lead to the distributions presented in Columns 4 and 5 in Table 2.4. (Why are the 1963 and 1968 population totals higher in Table 2.4 than in Table 1.12 ?)

2.9 APPLICATION: INPUT-OUTPUT ANALYSIS (CONTINUED)

In Section 1.7, we found that an "open" input-output model for which (1) the final demand for all commodities is known and (2) the structural matrix **A** has been estimated can be solved by an iterative method. An alternative solution method is one which involves the computation of the inverse of the matrix $(\mathbf{I} - \mathbf{A})$. To see this, we recall (1.76):

$$\mathbf{y} = (\mathbf{I} - \mathbf{A})\mathbf{x}$$

and observe that, if $|\mathbf{I} - \mathbf{A}| \neq 0$, the vector of total output may be derived by premultiplying both sides of (1.76) by $(\mathbf{I} - \mathbf{A})^{-1}$ to find

$$\mathbf{x} = (\mathbf{I} - \mathbf{A})^{-1}\mathbf{y} \tag{2.54}$$

The inverse of $(\mathbf{I} - \mathbf{A})$ is often called the *matrix multiplier* in input-output analysis.

2.9.1 THE MATRIX MULTIPLIER

The concept of the multiplier is one of the cornerstones of modern economic theory. Economists frequently use multipliers to measure the total impact of a given change in one variable on another. In the Garin-Lowry model, for example, we traced the effects of changes in basic employment on nonbasic employment and on total population by means of a multiplier. More frequently, however, multipliers are used to analyze the relationships between such economic variables as consumption and income. For example, if a population's total income is increased by an extra dollar, and if a half of this marginal increase in income is then spent on the consumption of goods and services, then the *marginal propensity to consume* is said to be a half and, correspondingly, the *marginal propensity to save* is also equal to a half. That is, given an extra dollar, this population would spend a half of it and save the other half. Now, if the people who receive the spent half dollar in the form of income also spend a half of it and save the other half, and so on, then the ultimate total impact of the extra dollar of new income will not be merely a dollar, but will be $1 + \frac{1}{2} + \frac{1}{4} + \frac{1}{8} + \cdots = 2$ dollars. In other words, the multiplier in this case is two.

Generalizing the above argument, we may conclude that if a fraction, a, say, of an increase in income is spent on consumption, then this initial expenditure of a dollar will produce a total expenditure or income of $1 + a + a^2 + \cdots = 1/(1 - a) = (1 - a)^{-1}$ dollars. The multiplier, therefore, is equal to $(1 - a)^{-1}$ or, in other words, it is the reciprocal of the propensity to save.

Aggregative multipliers involving single sectors are useful analytical tools, but they do not show how multiplier effects are transmitted through an economy with many interdependent sectors. For example, what effects will a reduction in defense spending have on the construction industry or on the economy as a whole? Approximate answers to such questions may be found by generalizing the aggregative scalar multiplier $(1 - a)^{-1}$ into the disaggregative matrix multiplier $(\mathbf{I} - \mathbf{A})^{-1}$ of input-output analysis.

The matrix multiplier $(\mathbf{I} - \mathbf{A})^{-1}$ summarizes the *direct* and *indirect* effects of changes in final demand. Each element in this matrix, A_{ij}, say, is a special multiplier that shows the total expansion of the output of commodity i that results from the delivery of an additional unit of commodity j to the final demand sector. These multipliers may be aggregated in many useful ways to show the impact of a dollar spent on a particular commodity or to identify the relative importance of various basic income sources to a particular industry.

In (1.81) we expressed the infinite series of (1.79) and (1.80) in matrix form, as follows:

$$\begin{aligned} \mathbf{x} &= \mathbf{I}\mathbf{y} + \mathbf{A}\mathbf{y} + \mathbf{A}^2\mathbf{y} + \cdots \\ &= (\mathbf{I} + \mathbf{A} + \mathbf{A}^2 + \cdots)\mathbf{y} \\ &= \left[\sum_{k=0}^{\infty} \mathbf{A}^k\right]\mathbf{y} \\ &= (\mathbf{I} - \mathbf{A})^{-1}\mathbf{y} \qquad \text{by (2.26)} \end{aligned}$$

Thus we see that the iterative solution method, in the limit, produces the same result as the inverse method. The A_{ij} in (1.79) and (1.80), therefore, are equal to the elements of the inverse of the matrix $(\mathbf{I} - \mathbf{A})$, and the inverse matrix, $(\mathbf{I} - \mathbf{A})^{-1}$, may be interpreted as a multiplier that measures the impacts of unit changes in one set of variables, final demand, $\mathbf{y}$, on another, total output, $\mathbf{x}$.

In applications involving a very large number of sectors, for example, 100 or more, it becomes economically and computationally difficult to obtain the inverse of the matrix $(\mathbf{I} - \mathbf{A})$. Therefore, in such instances one usually solves an input-output model by resorting to the iterative solution method. Since the cost of the inverse solution method increases approximately as the cube of the order of the matrix, while that of the iterative solution method increases only with the square, the latter procedure offers considerable advantages in applications involving a large number of industrial sectors. Frequently, in such instances, one finds that several iterations will produce results that are sufficiently accurate for most purposes. The advantage of the general solution provided by the inverse method, however, is that, once the inverse has been computed, new solutions for different vectors of final demand may easily be found by matrix multiplication. And the impact of each element of the final demand vector, **y**, can be determined separately. The inverse matrix, therefore, is especially useful in analyses of the general properties of a particular input-output system, analyses that require that many calculations be made with the same set of data.

Examples.

(i) To illustrate this more general solution method, let us return to the simple numerical example described in Table 1.14 and consider the static open model that had the structural matrix

$$\mathbf{A} = \begin{bmatrix} \frac{1}{5} & \frac{1}{5} \\ \frac{2}{5} & \frac{3}{5} \end{bmatrix}$$

and the final demand vector

$$\mathbf{y} = \begin{bmatrix} 100 \\ 40 \end{bmatrix}$$

This level of final demand implies a total output of

$$\begin{aligned} \mathbf{x} &= (\mathbf{I} - \mathbf{A})^{-1}\mathbf{y} \\ &= \begin{bmatrix} \frac{4}{5} & -\frac{1}{5} \\ -\frac{2}{5} & \frac{2}{5} \end{bmatrix}^{-1} \begin{bmatrix} 100 \\ 40 \end{bmatrix} \\ &= \begin{bmatrix} \frac{5}{3} & \frac{5}{6} \\ \frac{5}{3} & \frac{10}{3} \end{bmatrix} \begin{bmatrix} 100 \\ 40 \end{bmatrix} \\ &= \begin{bmatrix} 200 \\ 300 \end{bmatrix} \end{aligned}$$

which is precisely the result that appears in Table 1.14.

Having computed the inverse of $(\mathbf{I} - \mathbf{A})$, we now may easily solve for the total output, **x**, that is needed to serve any final demand vector, **y**, since

$$X_1 = \frac{5}{3} Y_1 + \frac{5}{6} Y_2$$

and

$$X_2 = \frac{5}{3} Y_1 + \frac{10}{3} Y_2$$

For example, if final demand were increased to 150 units of Agricultural output and 60 units of Manufacturing output, total output would have to be

$$X_1 = \frac{5}{3}(150) + \frac{5}{6}(60) = 300$$

and

$$X_2 = \frac{5}{3}(150) + \frac{10}{3}(60) = 450$$

Thus, given a vector of final demand for some future year, we can estimate the production levels that would be needed to sustain it with the technological structure that is implied by the current input-output table. Such exercises in projection may show, for example, that target production levels cannot be satisfied with the currently available resources, and may suggest the kinds of changes that will have to be made in order to avoid some of the foreseeable difficulties that such targets will impose on the economy.

(ii) To illustrate the general solution of the static closed input-output model defined by (1.77), we recall the structural matrix for the closed model of Islandia's economy:

$$\mathbf{A} = \begin{bmatrix} \frac{1}{5} & \frac{1}{5} & \frac{3}{20} \\ \frac{2}{5} & \frac{3}{5} & \frac{1}{20} \\ \frac{2}{5} & \frac{1}{5} & \frac{1}{5} \end{bmatrix}$$

and then solve the model with the net investment vector

$$\mathbf{i} = \begin{bmatrix} 70 \\ 30 \\ 20 \end{bmatrix}$$

This yields a total output of

$$\begin{aligned} \mathbf{x} &= (\mathbf{I} - \mathbf{A})^{-1}\mathbf{i} \\ &= \begin{bmatrix} \frac{155}{72} & \frac{95}{72} & \frac{35}{72} \\ \frac{85}{36} & \frac{145}{36} & \frac{25}{36} \\ \frac{5}{3} & \frac{5}{3} & \frac{5}{3} \end{bmatrix} \begin{bmatrix} 70 \\ 30 \\ 20 \end{bmatrix} \\ &= \begin{bmatrix} 200 \\ 300 \\ 200 \end{bmatrix} \end{aligned}$$

(iii) The dynamic open input-output model of Islandia's economy, which was presented in (1.88), may be expressed as follows:

$$\mathbf{x}(t+1) = \mathbf{B}^{-1}(\mathbf{I} - \mathbf{A} + \mathbf{B})\mathbf{x}(t) - \mathbf{B}^{-1}\mathbf{y}(t) \tag{2.55}$$

or

$$\mathbf{x}(1965) = \begin{bmatrix} \frac{471}{31} & -\frac{200}{31} \\ -\frac{320}{31} & \frac{261}{31} \end{bmatrix} \begin{bmatrix} 200 \\ 300 \end{bmatrix} - \begin{bmatrix} \frac{400}{31} & -\frac{300}{31} \\ -\frac{150}{31} & \frac{500}{31} \end{bmatrix} \begin{bmatrix} 100 \\ 40 \end{bmatrix} = \begin{bmatrix} 200 \\ 300 \end{bmatrix}$$

Thus we have confirmed our earlier finding that to support the final demand we have specified for Islandia, the economy must produce a total output of 200 units of Agricultural commodities and 300 units of Manufactured goods. The net addition to capital stock is zero; therefore, the total output in the subsequent period remains unchanged.

(iv) In (1.91) we "closed" the input-output model of Islandia's economy by defining net investment to be the only exogenous element. We may easily confirm, once again, that the economy described by (1.91) is capable of doubling the total output of every sector during the unit time interval of 15 years by setting $\mathbf{y}(t) = \mathbf{0}$ in (2.55):

$$\mathbf{x}(t+1) = \mathbf{B}^{-1}(\mathbf{I} - \mathbf{A} + \mathbf{B})\mathbf{x}(t) \tag{2.56}$$

whence

$$\mathbf{x}(1965) = \begin{bmatrix} -3 & -2 & 8 \\ -\frac{7}{2} & \frac{27}{4} & -\frac{29}{8} \\ \frac{141}{16} & -\frac{69}{32} & -\frac{229}{64} \end{bmatrix} \begin{bmatrix} 200 \\ 300 \\ 200 \end{bmatrix} = \begin{bmatrix} 400 \\ 600 \\ 400 \end{bmatrix}$$

2.9.2 APPLICATION: AN INTERREGIONAL INPUT-OUTPUT MODEL OF THE AMERICAN ECONOMY

In Chapter 1 we saw how the demographer's single-region cohort survival model could be generalized to describe population growth and change in interregional systems. A similar generalization can be applied to the economist's single-region input-output model by interpreting a regional division of sectors as a refinement of the classification system. Thus production and consumption of the same commodity in different areas may be regarded as separate sectors, and multiregional economies with m industries in each of n regions may be viewed as a single economy with mn industries. However, while the balance equations of the single-region model express the equality of each industry's output to its sales to all industries and final demand sectors, those of the interregional model equate each industry's output *in each region,* to its sales to *all* industries and final demand sectors in *all* regions. Therefore, the mn-by-mn technical coefficient matrix of an interregional input-output model embodies both the structure of production and the structure of regional trade. The elements of such a matrix are assumed to be constant and express the condition that to produce a unit of a particular commodity in a given region, certain fixed quantities of various inputs must be purchased from the different regions in the multiregional system. This information, together with a specification of final demands on every industry in each region, enables one to determine all output levels in all regions.

Table 2.5 presents a consolidated version of an interregional input-output model of the United States developed by Moses (1955). In it economic activities have been classified into three regions and four industries.[9] Thus the matrix consists of nine submatrices, each of which contains 16 entries. The three blocks of rows in every column block define the regional input requirements (in dollars) of the indicated region from itself and from each of the other two regions, per dollar of output of each industry.

The technical coefficient matrix in Table 2.5 identifies several important interregional linkages that exist in the three-region U.S. economy. First, note that the Middle West is relatively self-contained and has essentially only one major import: commodities of the Manufacturing sector in the East. However, it is an exporter of Manufacturing and Agricultural commodities to the other two regions, and is a particularly heavy exporter of Agricultural commodities to the East. Next, observe that the last two sectors, Trade and Services and Others, are relatively immobile and therefore have little interlinkages with sectors in other regions. Finally, in Table 2.6, we see that although the pattern of interindustry inputs is very similar among regions, considerable differences exist between the sectors in each region. The largest user of interindustry inputs is Agriculture, and the largest user of primary inputs (in addition to the labor supplied by Households) is the "Others" sector.

[9] The three regions are aggregations of regions defined by the U.S. Census: Region I (East) consists of the New England, Middle Atlantic, and South Atlantic states; Region III (West) is composed of the Pacific and Mountain states; and Region II (Middle West) contains all of the remaining states. The four sectors are aggregations of the 11 defined by Moses: Manufacturing is composed of Manufacturing and Minerals; Agriculture, Animals and Products, and Forest Products comprise our Agriculture and Forestry sector; Trade and Services consists of the Trade and Finance and the Services sectors; and all other sectors in Moses' model (including Households) have been aggregated into the sector called "Others."

Table 2.5. Interregional Technological Matrix: United States, 1947

Producing Region and Industry	Consuming Region and Industry											
	Region I (East)				Region II (Middle West)				Region III (West)			
	Industry				Industry				Industry			
	1.	2.	3.	4.	1.	2.	3.	4.	1.	2.	3.	4.
Region I (East)												
1. Manufacturing	0.3027	0.0558	0.0727	0.1329	0.0829	0.0153	0.0197	0.0356	0.0331	0.0066	0.0080	0.0149
2. Agriculture and Forestry	0.0311	0.1733	0.0090	0.0331	0.0033	0.0244	0.0016	0.0059	0.0005	0.0033	0.0003	0.0012
3. Trade and Services	0.0393	0.0785	0.1264	0.3427	0.0007	0.0018	0.0027	0.0070	0	0	0	0
4. Others	0.3947	0.3938	0.6202	0.1177	0.0003	0	0.0001	0	0	0	0	0
Region II (Middle West)												
1. Manufacturing	0.0851	0.0157	0.0202	0.0378	0.3076	0.0570	0.0731	0.1324	0.0937	0.0186	0.0227	0.0421
2. Agriculture and Forestry	0.0233	0.1772	0.0111	0.0432	0.0537	0.3398	0.0182	0.0678	0.0101	0.0681	0.0067	0.0249
3. Trade and Services	0.0003	0.0005	0.0008	0.0023	0.0386	0.0789	0.1237	0.3222	0.0005	0.0007	0.0011	0.0031
4. Others	0.0170	0.0002	0.0051	0.0006	0.4165	0.3916	0.6279	0.1431	0.0003	0	0.0001	0
Region III (West)												
1. Manufacturing	0.0061	0.0011	0.0014	0.0027	0.0132	0.0024	0.0031	0.0057	0.2703	0.0535	0.0671	0.1163
2. Agriculture and Forestry	0.0042	0.0206	0.0009	0.0032	0.0070	0.0370	0.0020	0.0069	0.0518	0.2544	0.0154	0.0539
3. Trade and Services	0	0	0	0	0.0004	0.0010	0.0015	0.0038	0.0389	0.0849	0.1249	0.3336
4. Others	0.0006	0.0005	0.0004	0.0007	0.0006	0.0001	0.0002	0.0003	0.4118	0.4479	0.6218	0.1348

Source: Consolidation of Table IV in Moses (1955).

Table 2.6. Total Interindustry and Primary Inputs by Region and Industry: United States, 1947

Producing Region	Consuming Region and Industry											
	Region I (East)				Region II (Middle West)				Region III (West)			
	Industry				Industry				Industry			
	1.	2.	3.	4.	1.	2.	3.	4.	1.	2.	3.	4.
Region I (East)	0.7678	0.7014	0.8283	0.6264	0.0872	0.0415	0.0241	0.0485	0.0336	0.0099	0.0083	0.0161
Region II (Middle West)	0.1257	0.1936	0.0372	0.0839	0.8164	0.8673	0.8429	0.6655	0.1046	0.0874	0.0306	0.0701
Region III (West)	0.0109	0.0222	0.0027	0.0066	0.0212	0.0405	0.0068	0.0167	0.7728	0.8407	0.8292	0.6386
Subtotal	0.9044	0.9172	0.8682	0.7169	0.9248	0.9493	0.8738	0.7307	0.9110	0.9380	0.8681	0.7248
Primary Inputs	0.0956	0.0828	0.1318	0.2831	0.0752	0.0507	0.1262	0.2693	0.0890	0.0620	0.1319	0.2752
Total	1.0000	1.0000	1.0000	1.0000	1.0000	1.0000	1.0000	1.0000	1.0000	1.0000	1.0000	1.0000

Source: Table 2.5.

Table 2.7. Interregional Matrix Multiplier, $(\mathbf{I}-\mathbf{A})^{-1}$*: United States, 1947*

Producing Region and Industry	Consuming Region and Industry											
	Region I (East)				Region II (Middle West)				Region III (West)			
	Industry				Industry				Industry			
	1.	2.	3.	4.	1.	2.	3.	4.	1.	2.	3.	4.
Region I (East)												
1. Manufacturing	1.8981	0.5470	0.5903	0.5755	0.4700	0.3426	0.3166	0.3109	0.2895	0.2242	0.1988	0.1968
2. Agriculture and Forestry	0.1517	1.3163	0.1200	0.1274	0.0711	0.1016	0.0553	0.0569	0.0405	0.0431	0.0303	0.0308
3. Trade and Services	0.6441	0.6607	1.8121	0.8437	0.1959	0.1720	0.1476	0.1474	0.1123	0.0934	0.0786	0.0782
4. Others	1.3698	1.2968	1.5916	2.0409	0.3804	0.3199	0.2705	0.2684	0.2268	0.1854	0.1578	0.1570
Region II (Middle West)												
1. Manufacturing	0.5447	0.4501	0.3748	0.3710	2.0150	0.7014	0.6716	0.6572	0.5612	0.4354	0.3858	0.3820
2. Agriculture and Forestry	0.3452	0.6141	0.2862	0.3007	0.4477	1.8751	0.3604	0.3797	0.2654	0.3683	0.2175	0.2263
3. Trade and Services	0.3169	0.3700	0.2362	0.2377	0.7809	0.8833	1.8999	0.9277	0.2791	0.2774	0.2092	0.2117
4. Others	0.6972	0.7866	0.5097	0.5098	1.7670	1.8532	1.8907	2.3470	0.6058	0.5886	0.4451	0.4489
Region III (West)												
1. Manufacturing	0.0673	0.0674	0.0472	0.0472	0.0990	0.0945	0.0699	0.0697	1.6917	0.4491	0.4539	0.4394
2. Agriculture and Forestry	0.0647	0.1052	0.0486	0.0503	0.0857	0.1488	0.0661	0.0688	0.2605	1.5329	0.2078	0.2206
3. Trade and Services	0.0548	0.0722	0.0403	0.0410	0.0815	0.1075	0.0665	0.0679	0.6376	0.7668	1.8036	0.8372
4. Others	0.1085	0.1416	0.0797	0.0810	0.1531	0.2014	0.1174	0.1197	1.3994	1.5594	1.6206	2.0816

Source: Calculated using the data in Table 2.5. Programmed by Michael Fajans.

Table 2.8. Total Regional Multipliers by Consumer Region and Industry: United States, 1947

Producing Region	Consuming Region and Industry											
	Region I (East)				Region II (Middle West)				Region III (West)			
	Industry				Industry				Industry			
	1.	2.	3.	4.	1.	2.	3.	4.	1.	2.	3.	4.
Region I (East)	4.0637	3.8208	4.1140	3.5875	1.1174	0.9361	0.7900	0.7836	0.6691	0.5461	0.4655	0.4628
Region II (Middle West)	1.9040	2.2208	1.4069	1.4192	5.0106	5.3130	4.8226	4.3116	1.7115	1.6697	1.2576	1.2689
Region III (West)	0.2953	0.3864	0.2158	0.2195	0.4193	0.5522	0.3199	0.3261	3.9892	4.3082	4.0859	3.5788
Total	6.2630	6.4280	5.7367	5.2262	6.5473	6.8013	5.9325	5.4213	6.3698	6.5240	5.8090	5.3105

Source: Table 2.7.

Table 2.9. Total Regional Multipliers by Producing Region and Industry: United States, 1947

Producing Region and Industry		Consuming Region			Total
		Region I (East)	Region II (Middle West)	Region III (West)	
Region I (East)	1. Manufacturing	3.6109	1.4401	0.9093	5.9603
	2. Agriculture and Forestry	1.7154	0.2849	0.1447	2.1450
	3. Trade and Services	3.9606	0.6629	0.3625	4.9860
	4. Others	6.2991	1.2392	0.7270	8.2653
Region II (Middle West)	1. Manufacturing	1.7406	4.0452	1.7644	7.5502
	2. Agriculture and Forestry	1.5462	3.0629	1.0775	5.6866
	3. Trade and Services	1.1608	4.4918	0.9774	6.6300
	4. Others	2.5033	7.8579	2.0884	12.4496
Region III (West)	1. Manufacturing	0.2291	0.3331	3.0341	3.5963
	2. Agriculture and Forestry	0.2688	0.3694	2.2218	2.8600
	3. Trade and Services	0.2083	0.3234	4.0452	4.5769
	4. Others	0.4108	0.5916	6.6610	7.6634

Source: Table 2.7.

Structural analysis of the interregional economy described in Table 2.5 may proceed along another dimension. We may consider the interregional matrix multiplier $(\mathbf{I} - \mathbf{A})^{-1}$ that is associated with the technical coefficient matrix in Table 2.5. Such a multiplier appears in Table 2.7 and in different condensed forms in Tables 2.8 and 2.9. The elements of this matrix multiplier indicate the total direct and indirect demand for the output of industry r in region i that is generated by a unit of final demand for the output of industry s in region j. Thus, to analyze the ultimate interregional impact of a demand for a particular commodity, produced in a given region, on all industries in all regions, one would study the elements of the column in $(\mathbf{I} - \mathbf{A})^{-1}$ that is associated with the industry producing that commodity in the given region. On the other hand, to study the ultimate effect of a unit change in all final demands in a region (or in all regions) upon the sales of a particular industry in a given region, one would analyze the elements of the row in $(\mathbf{I} - \mathbf{A})^{-1}$ that is associated with that industry. The former are generally called *impact studies,* whereas the latter typically are referred to as *marketing studies.* For example, a study of the repercussions on all industries, in all regions, arising out of a dollar increase in the demand for the output of the Agriculture sector in the Middle Western region would be classed as an impact study, while a study that traced the ultimate impact on the output of the Manufacturing sector in the Eastern region of a unit change in all final demands in the Middle Western region would be called a marketing study. Using Tables 2.8 and 2.9, we conclude that the total impact of the former would be an increased output of 6.8013 dollars, whereas the total impact of the latter would be a change of 1.4401 dollars.

EXERCISES

1. (a) Repeat the interpolation that was carried out in the numerical example of Subsection 2.2.2, using the function $y = f(x) = a + be^x + cx^2$ instead of the quadratic function that was used there.

(b) Extend the arguments of Section 2.2 to functions of more than one variable. That is, find $z_0 = f(x_0, y_0)$, where $z_1 = f(x_1, y_1)$, $z_2 = f(x_2, y_2)$, and $z_3 = f(x_3, y_3)$ are given, and $z = f(x, y) = a + bx + cy$. Illustrate your findings with a numerical example.

(c) Repeat the interpolation that was carried out in Subsection 2.2.3, using the quadratic function $y = f(x) = a + bx + cx^2$ instead of the linear function that was used there.

2. Using the process of deconsolidation by interpolation that is described in Subsection 2.2.3, deconsolidate the 1950 and 1960 population vectors and the nine-by-nine population growth matrix, for ten-year age groups, in Figure 1.1 into the corresponding 1950 and 1960 population vectors and 18-by-18 population growth matrix for five-year age groups. Use the deconsolidated growth process to obtain a projection of the 1970 population by five-year age groups.

3. The process of obtaining the inverse of a large matrix often can be simplified by partitioning the large matrix into four smaller submatrices in a manner such that the submatrices on the diagonal are square. The net result is that the problem of inverting a large matrix may be reduced to one of inverting four smaller matrices.

Given the partitioned matrix

$$\mathbf{A} = \left[\begin{array}{c|c} \mathbf{A}_{11} & \mathbf{A}_{12} \\ \hline \mathbf{A}_{21} & \mathbf{A}_{22} \end{array}\right]$$

where $\mathbf{A}_{11}$ and $\mathbf{A}_{22}$ are square, denote the corresponding partitioned form of $\mathbf{A}^{-1}$ as

$$\mathbf{A}^{-1} = \left[\begin{array}{c|c} \mathbf{B}_{11} & \mathbf{B}_{12} \\ \hline \mathbf{B}_{21} & \mathbf{B}_{22} \end{array}\right]$$

and show that

$$\begin{aligned} \mathbf{B}_{11} &= (\mathbf{A}_{11} - \mathbf{A}_{12}\mathbf{A}_{22}^{-1}\mathbf{A}_{21})^{-1} \\ \mathbf{B}_{12} &= -\mathbf{A}_{11}^{-1}\mathbf{A}_{12}\mathbf{B}_{22} \\ \mathbf{B}_{21} &= -\mathbf{A}_{22}^{-1}\mathbf{A}_{21}\mathbf{B}_{11} \\ \mathbf{B}_{22} &= (\mathbf{A}_{22} - \mathbf{A}_{21}\mathbf{A}_{11}^{-1}\mathbf{A}_{12})^{-1} \end{aligned}$$

Illustrate this process of inversion by partitioning and inverting the matrix

$$\mathbf{A} = \begin{bmatrix} 1 & 4 & 3 & 0 \\ 2 & 5 & 2 & 1 \\ 4 & 6 & 0 & 2 \\ 7 & 0 & 1 & 3 \end{bmatrix}$$

4. Given the growth matrix and 1960 population vector in (1.40),

$$\mathbf{G} = \begin{bmatrix} 1.0899 & 0.0298 \\ 0.1380 & 1.1451 \end{bmatrix} \quad \text{and} \quad \mathbf{w}(1960) = \begin{bmatrix} 15718 \\ 161902 \end{bmatrix}$$

find $\mathbf{G}^{-1}$ by the *method of pivotal condensation*. Check your result by finding the same inverse using the *method of determinants*. Use $\mathbf{G}^{-1}$ and $\mathbf{w}(1960)$ to obtain the 1950 population vector, $\mathbf{w}(1950)$. Check your result by comparing it to the $\mathbf{w}(1950)$ in (1.40).

5. Prove the following theorem and illustrate its application to the two-region (California and the rest of the United States) population growth process discussed in Section 2.7.

The Kemeny-Snell Theorem

(i) *If for some k the sum of the absolute values of the components of* $\mathbf{S}^k[\mathbf{y} - \mathbf{w}(0)]$ *is no greater than the least entry of* $\mathbf{y}$, *then* (2.40) *holds for all* $t \geq k$; *and this must occur for some k.*

(ii) *If* $\mathbf{S}^{k+1}[\mathbf{y} - \mathbf{w}(0)] \leq \mathbf{S}^k[\mathbf{y} - \mathbf{w}(0)]$ *and* (2.40) *holds for k, then* (2.40) *holds for* $t \geq k$.

(iii) *If* $\mathbf{Sy} \leqq \mathbf{y}$, *then* (2.40) *holds for all t, for all* $\mathbf{w}$.
[Hint: Let $\mathbf{h} = \mathbf{S}^k[\mathbf{y} - \mathbf{w}(0)]$. Then $\mathbf{S}^t[\mathbf{y} - \mathbf{w}(0)] = \mathbf{S}^{t-k}\mathbf{h}$, and the components of $\mathbf{S}$ to any power never exceed unity. Hence a component of $\mathbf{S}^{t-k}\mathbf{h}$ is bounded by $\sum |h_i|$. Thus if $\sum_i |h_i| \leqq \min_i y_i$, then (2.40) holds for $t \geqq k$, and we only need to show that $\mathbf{h}$ converges to the null vector $\mathbf{0}$ in order to complete the proof of (i).]

6. Extend the arguments in Section 2.7 regarding population control to the Garin-Lowry model of Section 2.8, and illustrate your results with the data on the Ljubljana Metropolitan Region. In particular, discuss what policies might be used to reduce the growth of the city of Ljubljana (that is, of the five communes numbered 9, 10, 11, 12, and 13 in Table 1.11).

7. (a) Show that the Garin-Lowry model reduces to traditional economic base analysis if all employment and population are located into a single zone. Use the Islandia example to illustrate your argument.

(b) Extend the Garin-Lowry model described in this chapter by introducing a *journey-from-work-to-shop* matrix which takes into account shopping trips that originate at the place of work. Assume that employees $e_i(1)$, working in zone i, will demand $e_i(1) \times \gamma_i$ nonbasic employees who are allocated to their respective places of work j by means of a journey-from-work-to-shop function r_{ij}. Illustrate the application of this extended model with the Islandia example in the text. Assume that $\gamma_i = \frac{1}{12}$ for all i, and that $r_{ij} = \frac{1}{3}$ for all i, j.

8. Identify and interpret the conditions under which perfect aggregation of sectors is possible in a static open input-output model, that is, conditions under which the aggregation of sectors that we have made will not introduce an error into the derivation of total output. Express these conditions in matrix form, and illustrate them with a numerical example.

9. Compare and contrast the Yugoslavian economy in 1958 and 1962 with the United States economy in 1947, using the input-output data presented in Subsections 1.7.4 and 2.9.2, respectively. To make the data more comparable, consolidate the eight sectors in the Yugoslavian tables into the following four sectors:

	Yugoslavia
1. Manufacturing	1
2. Agriculture and Forestry	2 + 3
3. Trade and Services	6 + 7
4. Others	4 + 5 + 8

Also consolidate the three-region U.S. matrix into a single-region one, by using the following proportional distribution of total output:

$$\mathbf{x}' = [0.125 \quad 0.023 \quad 0.080 \quad 0.170 \;\vdots\; 0.125 \quad 0.064 \quad 0.090 \quad 0.184 \;\vdots\; 0.021 \quad 0.016 \quad 0.031 \quad 0.061]$$

10. We have seen that in linear economic models, such as input-output models, the inverse matrix has a particularly useful interpretation in that its elements measure the impacts of unit changes in one set of variables on another. This multiplier property of the inverse matrix may be illustrated with another linear economic model: the simplest theory of the national income. We define national income (Y) to consist of consumption (C) and investment (I):

$$Y = C + I$$

and adopt the following linear behavioral relationship to describe consumption as a function of income:

$$C = c + aY$$

where c and a are constants, which are called, respectively, *autonomous consumption* and the *marginal propensity to consume*. Thus, in matrix form

$$\begin{bmatrix} c \\ I \end{bmatrix} = \begin{bmatrix} -a & 1 \\ 1 & -1 \end{bmatrix} \begin{bmatrix} Y \\ C \end{bmatrix}$$

(a) Express the vector $\left[\begin{smallmatrix} Y \\ C \end{smallmatrix}\right]$ as a function of the vector $\left[\begin{smallmatrix} c \\ I \end{smallmatrix}\right]$ to show that if autonomous consumption, investment, and the marginal propensity to consume are given, then consumption and national income are uniquely determined. Show that the effect of a unit change in investment on national income is $1/(1 - a)$ and that its effect on consumption is $a/(1 - a)$.

(b) Let R be the rate of interest, and assume the following slightly more complex model of national income:

$$\begin{aligned} Y &= C + I \quad (\text{or } 0 = Y - C - I) \\ C &= c + aY + bR \\ I &= i + dR \\ R &= r_0 \end{aligned}$$

where i, b, d, and r_0 are constants. Describe this model in matrix form, expressing 0, c, i, and R as linear functions of Y, C, I, and r_0. Find the inverse matrix, and determine the impact of a unit change in the interest rate on national income, on consumption, and on investment.

REFERENCES AND SELECTED READINGS

THEORY

Almon, C., Jr. *Matrix Methods in Economics*. Reading, Mass.: Addison-Wesley, 1967.

Gantmacher, F. R. *The Theory of Matrices*, I and II. New York: Chelsea, 1959.

Gere, J. M. and W. Weaver, Jr. *Matrix Algebra for Engineers*. Princeton, N. J.: D. van Nostrand, 1965.

Hadley, G. *Linear Algebra*. Reading, Mass.: Addison-Wesley, 1961.

Noble, B. *Applied Linear Algebra*. Englewood Cliffs, N. J.: Prentice-Hall, 1969.

Schneider, H. and G. P. Barker. *Matrices and Linear Algebra*. New York: Holt, Rinehart & Winston, 1968.

Searle, S. R. *Matrix Algebra for the Biological Sciences*. New York: John Wiley & Sons, 1966.

APPLICATION: POPULATION ANALYSIS

Kemeny, J. G. and J. L. Snell. *Mathematical Models in the Social Sciences.* Boston, Mass.: Ginn, 1962.

Keyfitz, N. *Introduction to the Mathematics of Population.* Reading, Mass.: Addison-Wesley, 1968.

Lowry, I. S. *Population Policy, Welfare, and Regional Development*, P-3968, The RAND Corporation, Santa Monica, Calif., 1968.

Pollard, J. H. "On the Use of the Direct Matrix Product in Analyzing Certain Stochastic Population Models," *Biometrika*, **LIII**: 3, 1966, 397–415.

Rogers, A. *Matrix Analysis of Interregional Population Growth and Distribution.* Berkeley, Calif.: University of California Press, 1968.

APPLICATION: ACTIVITY ALLOCATION ANALYSIS

Batty, M. "Some Problems of Calibrating the Lowry Model," *Environment and Planning*, **II**: 1, 1970, 95–114.

Garin, R. "A Matrix Formulation of the Lowry Model for Intrametropolitan Activity Allocation," *Journal of the American Institute of Planners*, **XXXII**: 6, 1966, 361–364.

Lane, T. "The Urban Base Multiplier: An Evaluation of the State of the Art," *Land Economics*, **XLII**: 3, 1966, 339–347.

Lowry, I. S. *A Model of Metropolis.* Santa Monica, Calif.: The RAND Corporation, 1964.

APPLICATION: INPUT-OUTPUT ANALYSIS

Artle, R. *Studies in the Structure of the Stockholm Economy*, 2d. ed. Ithaca, N. Y.: Cornell University Press, 1965.

Chenery, H. B. and P. G. Clark. *Interindustry Economics.* New York: John Wiley & Sons, 1959.

Isard, W., *et al. Methods of Regional Analysis: An Introduction to Regional Science* (Ch. 8, 309–374). New York: The M.I.T. Press and John Wiley & Sons, 1960.

Leontief, W. W. *The Structure of the American Economy, 1919–1939*, 2d. ed. New York: Oxford University Press, 1951.

Moses, L. N. "The Stability of Interregional Trading Patterns and Input-Output Analysis," *American Economic Review*, **XLV**: 5, 1955, 803–832.

appendix programming matrix operations in FORTRAN

A.1 PROGRAMMING MATRIX ADDITION, SUBTRACTION, AND MULTIPLICATION

The *addition* of two variables, a and b, say, to form the sum c, may be expressed in FORTRAN by the arithmetic statement

$$C = A + B \tag{A.1}$$

Thus, to define this operation on a pair of corresponding elements in two matrices, **A** and **B**, say, we introduce row and column subscripts into (A.1):

$$C(I, J) = A(I, J) + B(I, J)$$

To carry out this operation on the n elements constituting the ith row of the two matrices, we may introduce a DO loop, as follows:

```
      DO 1  J = 1, N
      C(I, J) = A(I, J) + B(I, J)
    1 CONTINUE
```

Finally, to repeat this process for each of the m rows of **A** and **B**, we include another DO loop to obtain

```
      DO 2   I = 1, M
      DO 1   J = 1, N
      C(I, J) = A(I, J) + B(I, J)                    (A.2)
    1 CONTINUE
    2 CONTINUE
```

Expressing (A.2) in a flowchart diagram, we have

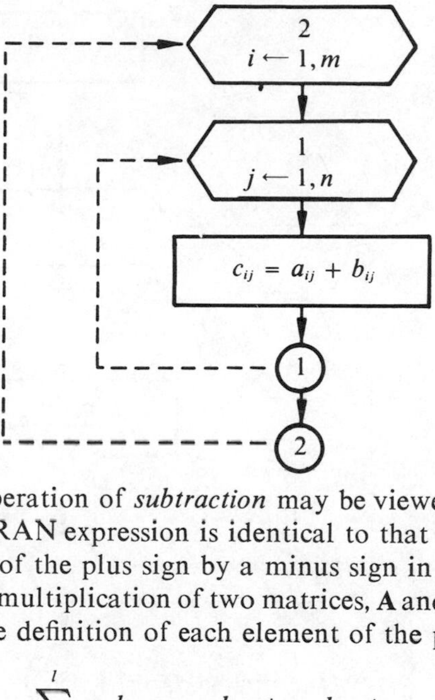

(A.3)

The matrix operation of *subtraction* may be viewed as negative addition. Hence its FORTRAN expression is identical to that of addition, except for the replacement of the plus sign by a minus sign in (A.2).

To express the multiplication of two matrices, **A** and **B**, say, in FORTRAN, we first recall the definition of each element of the product matrix **C**:

$$c_{ij} = \sum_{k=1}^{l} a_{ik}b_{kj} = a_{i1}b_{1j} + a_{i2}b_{2j} + \cdots + a_{il}b_{lj} \tag{A.4}$$

To carry out the above operation on a sequential machine, we need to create a looping process which accumulates, into a previously cleared storage register, the successive products in (A.4). That is, initially c_{ij} is set equal to zero, then after the first iteration through the looping process, c_{ij} is set equal to its previous value, plus the product $a_{i1}b_{1j}$. After the next iteration,

$$c_{ij} = 0 + a_{i1}b_{1j} + a_{i2}b_{2j}$$

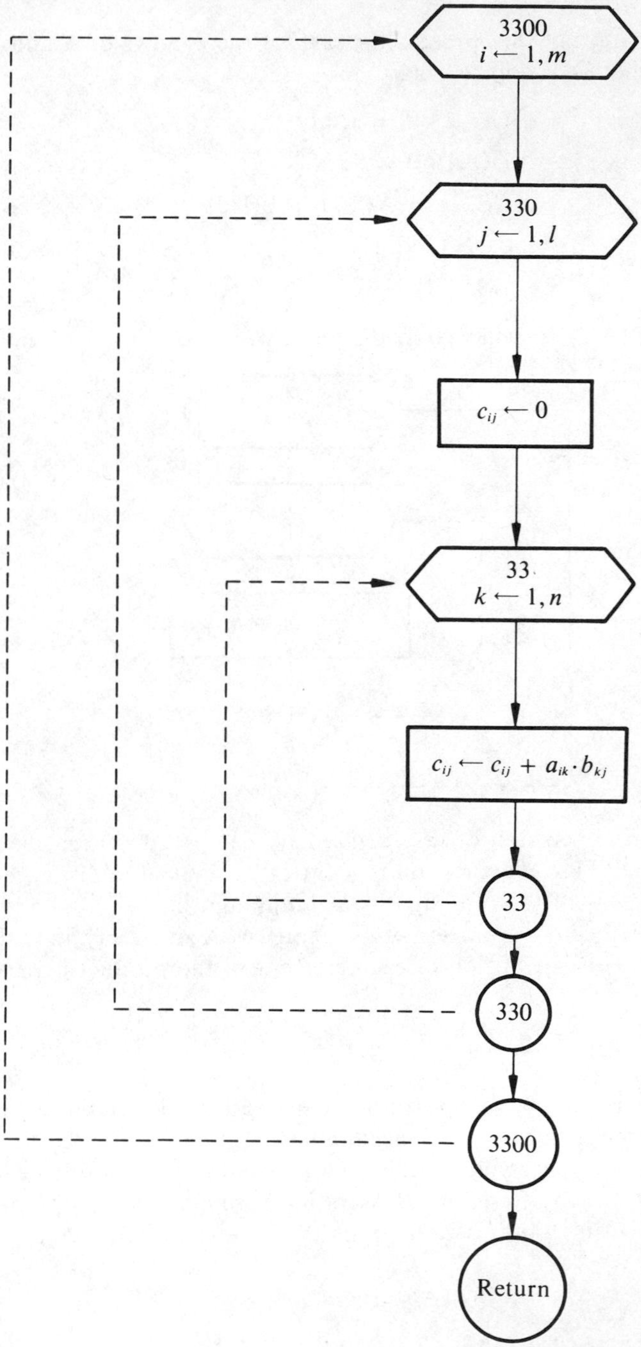

Figure A.1. Flowchart for Matrix Multiplication Subroutine

and after l iterations c_{ij} takes on the value defined for it by (A.4). Thus we have the FORTRAN routine:

```
      C(I, J) = 0.0
      DO 1  K = 1, L
      C(I, J) = C(I, J) + A(I, K)*B(K, J)                    (A.5)
 1    CONTINUE
```

To find all of the n elements in the ith row of the product matrix **C**, we repeat (A.5) for every $j = 1, 2, \ldots, n$, and to obtain each of the m rows of **C**, we repeat this process for every $i = 1, 2, \ldots, m$. Thus we have the FORTRAN routine:

```
      DO 3  I = 1, M
      DO 2  J = 1, N
      C(I, J) = 0.0
      DO 1  K = 1, L
      C(I, J) = C(I, J) + A(I, K)*B(K, J)                    (A.6)
 1    CONTINUE
 2    CONTINUE
 3    CONTINUE
```

Figure A.1 presents the flowchart equivalent of (A.6), and Figure A.2 illustrates how (A.6) may be incorporated into a subroutine for carrying out matrix multiplication. Figure A.3 presents a main program for matrix multiplication, which calls on "MLTPLY," the subroutine in Figure A.2, to perform the actual multiplication.

A.2 PROGRAMMING MATRIX INVERSION

In order to simplify the discussion that follows, it will be assumed, without loss of generality, that the "pivot" elements in successive matrix transformations lie on the principal diagonal of the square matrix to be inverted. The method of inversion is basically the method of successive transformations described in Section 2.4. To conserve storage space, however, a minor modification is introduced. This modification stems from the observation that, in the process of transforming **A** to the identity matrix, once an a_{ij} is reduced to zero or unity it remains unaffected by subsequent transformations. Therefore, the columns of the matrix to be inverted may be utilized, as they become available, for the storage of the corresponding columns of

```
C  MATRIX MULTIPLICATION SUBROUTINE "MLTPLY"
      SUBROUTINE MLTPLY
      COMMON A(20, 20), B(20, 20), C(20, 20), M, N, L
      DO 3300  I = 1, M
      DO  330  J = 1, L
      C(I, J) = 0.0
      DO 33  K = 1, N
      C(I, J) = C(I, J) + A(I, K)*B(K, J)
   33 CONTINUE
  330 CONTINUE
 3300 CONTINUE
      RETURN
      END
```

Figure A.2. FORTRAN Program for Matrix Multiplication Subroutine

the inverse matrix. That is, at the ith stage of the pivotal condensation process, the ith column of the **A** matrix is replaced by the ith column of the transformed identity matrix. For example, with an **A** matrix of order three, the first stage of the elimination would yield

$$a_{11\cdot 1} = \frac{1}{a_{11}}$$

$$a_{1j\cdot 1} = \frac{a_{1j}}{a_{11}} \qquad j = 2, 3$$

$$\left.\begin{aligned} a_{i1\cdot 1} &= -a_{i1}\frac{1}{a_{11}} \\ a_{ij} &= a_{ij} - a_{i1}\frac{a_{1j}}{a_{11}} \end{aligned}\right\} \qquad \begin{aligned} i &= 2, 3 \\ j &= 2, 3 \end{aligned}$$

"In-place" matrix inversion allows us to eliminate the storage space that otherwise would be required to store the appended identity matrix. To illustrate this, consider the reduction process of (2.25). There we had the sequence

$$\left[\begin{array}{cc|cc} 3 & 5 & 1 & 0 \\ 2 & 4 & 0 & 1 \end{array}\right]$$

```
C  MAIN PROGRAM TO MULTIPLY TWO MATRICES
      COMMON A(20, 20), B(20, 20), C(20, 20), M, N, L
      READ 1, M, N, L
    1 FORMAT (3I2)
      READ 2, ((A(I, J), J = 1, N), I = 1, M)
      READ 2, ((B(I, J), J = 1, L), I = 1, N)
    2 FORMAT (F10.0)
      PRINT 3
    3 FORMAT (1H114HINPUT MATRIX A)
      PRINT 4, ((A(I, J), J = 1, N), I = 1, M)
    4 FORMAT (1X, F12.4)
      PRINT 5
    5 FORMAT (1H114HINPUT MATRIX B)
      PRINT 4, ((B(I, J), J = 1, L), I = 1, N)
      CALL MLTPLY
      PRINT 6
    6 FORMAT (1H118HMATRIX PRODUCT A*B)
      PRINT 4, ((C(I, J), J = 1, L), I = 1, M)
      STOP
      END
```

Figure A.3. Main FORTRAN Program for Matrix Multiplication

$$\left[\begin{array}{cc|cc} 1 & \frac{5}{3} & \frac{1}{3} & 0 \\ 2 & 4 & 0 & 1 \end{array}\right]$$

$$\left[\begin{array}{cc|cc} 1 & \frac{5}{3} & \frac{1}{3} & 0 \\ 0 & \frac{2}{3} & -\frac{2}{3} & 1 \end{array}\right]$$

$$\left[\begin{array}{cc|cc} 1 & \frac{5}{3} & \frac{1}{3} & 0 \\ 0 & 1 & -1 & \frac{3}{2} \end{array}\right]$$

$$\left[\begin{array}{cc|cc} 1 & 0 & 2 & -\frac{5}{2} \\ 0 & 1 & -1 & \frac{3}{2} \end{array}\right]$$

Observe that, after each transformation, one may store the value of the transformed element of the appended matrix in the corresponding position

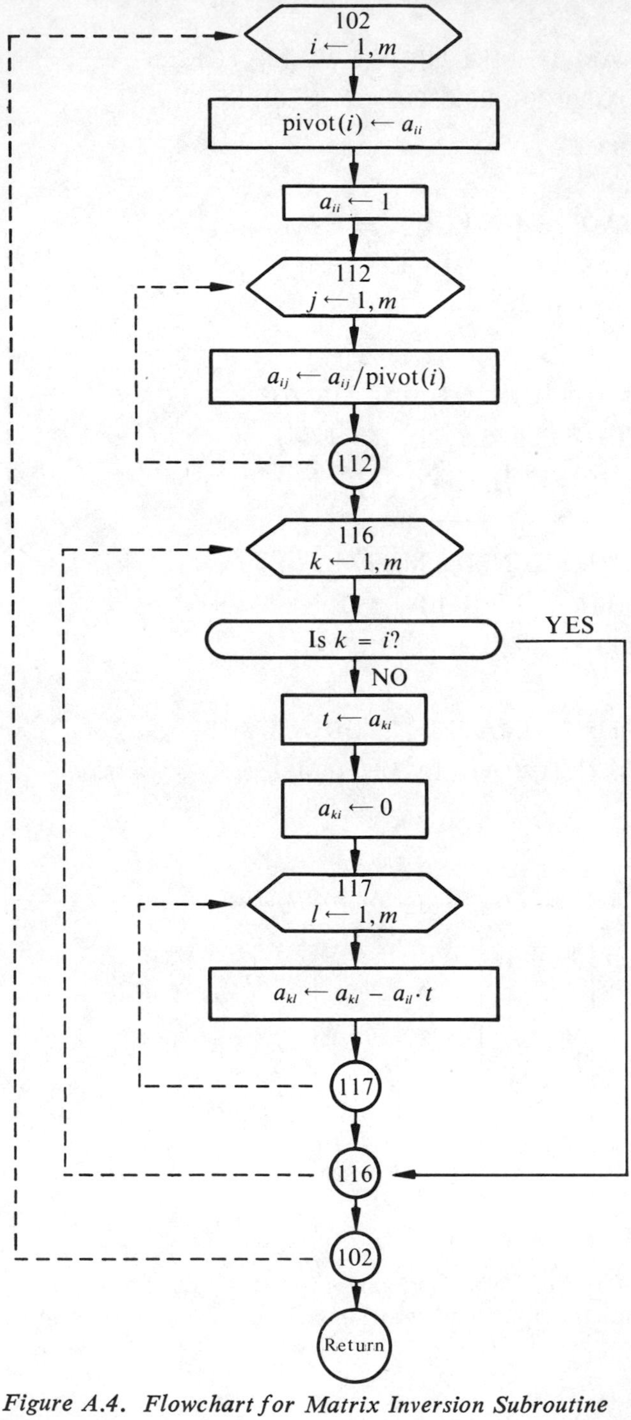

Figure A.4. Flowchart for Matrix Inversion Subroutine

of the **A** matrix. Thus $\frac{1}{3}$ may be stored in place of 1 after the first transformation, $-\frac{2}{3}$ in place of 0 after the second transformation, and so on. Therefore, we have the sequence

Matrix inversion with an appended identity matrix	Matrix inversion "in-place"
$\left[\begin{array}{cc:cc} 3 & 5 & 1 & 0 \\ 2 & 4 & 0 & 1 \end{array}\right]$	$\begin{bmatrix} 3 & 5 \\ 2 & 4 \end{bmatrix}$
$\left[\begin{array}{cc:cc} 1 & \frac{5}{3} & \frac{1}{3} & 0 \\ 2 & 4 & 0 & 1 \end{array}\right]$	$\begin{bmatrix} \frac{1}{3} & \frac{5}{3} \\ 2 & 4 \end{bmatrix}$
$\left[\begin{array}{cc:cc} 1 & \frac{5}{3} & \frac{1}{3} & 0 \\ 0 & \frac{2}{3} & -\frac{2}{3} & 1 \end{array}\right]$	$\begin{bmatrix} \frac{1}{3} & \frac{5}{3} \\ -\frac{2}{3} & \frac{2}{3} \end{bmatrix}$
$\left[\begin{array}{cc:cc} 1 & \frac{5}{3} & \frac{1}{3} & 0 \\ 0 & 1 & -1 & \frac{3}{2} \end{array}\right]$	$\begin{bmatrix} \frac{1}{3} & \frac{5}{3} \\ -1 & \frac{3}{2} \end{bmatrix}$
$\left[\begin{array}{cc:cc} 1 & 0 & 2 & \frac{5}{2} \\ 0 & 1 & -1 & \frac{3}{2} \end{array}\right]$	$\begin{bmatrix} 2 & \frac{5}{2} \\ -1 & \frac{3}{2} \end{bmatrix}$

Figure A.4 presents a flowchart for the "in-place" pivotal condensation, and Figure A.5 provides a FORTRAN subroutine that will carry out this procedure. Figure A.6 illustrates a main calling program for matrix inversion.

```
C   MATRIX INVERSION SUBROUTINE "INVERT"
      SUBROUTINE INVERT
      DIMENSION PIVOT(20)
      COMMON A(20, 20), M
C   DIVIDE PIVOT ROW BY PIVOT ELEMENT
      DO 102  I = 1, M
      PIVOT(I) = A(I, I)
      A(I, I) = 1.0
      DO 112  J = 1, M
      A(I, J) = A(I, J)/PIVOT(I)
  112 CONTINUE
```

Figure A.5. FORTRAN Program for Matrix Inversion Subroutine

```
C  REDUCE NONPIVOT ROWS
       DO 116   K = 1, M
       IF (K. EQ. I) GO TO 116
       T = A(K, I)
       A(K, I) = 0. 0
       DO 117   L = 1, M
       A(K, L) = A(K, L) - A(I, L)*T
   117 CONTINUE
   116 CONTINUE
   102 CONTINUE
       RETURN
       END
```

Figure A.5. FORTRAN Program for Matrix Inversion Subroutine (*Continued*)

```
C  MAIN PROGRAM TO INVERT A SQUARE MATRIX
       COMMON A(20, 20), M
       READ 1, M
     1 FORMAT (I2)
       READ 2, ((A(I, J), J = 1, M), I = 1, M)
     2 FORMAT (F10.0)
       PRINT 3
     3 FORMAT (1H114HINPUT MATRIX A)
       PRINT 4, ((A(I, J), J = 1, M), I = 1, M)
     4 FORMAT (1X, F12.4)
       CALL INVERT
       PRINT 5
     5 FORMAT (1H114MATRIX INVERSE)
       PRINT 4, ((A(I, J), J = 1, M), I = 1, M)
       STOP
       END
```

Figure A.6. Main FORTRAN Program for Matrix Inversion

A.3 A GENERAL PURPOSE MATRIX PROGRAM: GPMP

In this section we present a simple general matrix program that includes routines for matrix addition, subtraction, multiplication, and inversion. Input data to the program consist of two matrices, descriptions of their dimensions and formats, and a set of eight control digits which activate the particular routines that are to be carried out on the two matrices. A unit digit calls for the particular operation to be carried out. Any other digit indicates that the particular operation is not requested and turns over control of the program to the following control digit (except in Column 5, see below). The control digits appear in the first eight columns of the control card and have the following position and significance:

Column 1: A 1 in this column calls for the addition of the two matrices **A** and **B**, and stores their sum into **C**, that is, $\mathbf{C} \leftarrow \mathbf{A} + \mathbf{B}$.

Column 2: A 1 in this column calls for the subtraction of the two matrices **A** and **B**, and stores their difference into **C**, that is, $\mathbf{C} \leftarrow \mathbf{A} - \mathbf{B}$.

Column 3: A 1 in this column calls for the multiplication of the two matrices **A** and **B**, and stores their product into **C**, that is, $\mathbf{C} \leftarrow \mathbf{A} \cdot \mathbf{B}$.

Column 4: A 1 in this column calls for the formation of the identity matrix in **C**, that is, $\mathbf{C} \leftarrow \mathbf{I}$.

Column 5: A 1 in this column calls for the inversion of the matrix **A** and stores the inverse into **C**, that is, $\mathbf{C} \leftarrow \mathbf{A}^{-1}$. The matrix **A** is destroyed in the process. A 2 in this column calls for the same set of elementary transformations to be carried out on the matrix **B**. This allows us to solve linear equation systems of the form $\mathbf{Ax} = \mathbf{b}$.

Column 6: A 1 in this column calls for the division of the elements of **A** by their respective row sums and stores the resulting matrix into **C**, that is,

$$c_{ij} \leftarrow \frac{a_{ij}}{\sum_j a_{ij}}$$

Column 7: A 1 in this column calls for the division of the elements of **A** by their respective column sums and stores the resulting matrix into **C**, that is,

$$c_{ij} \leftarrow \frac{a_{ij}}{\sum_i a_{ij}}$$

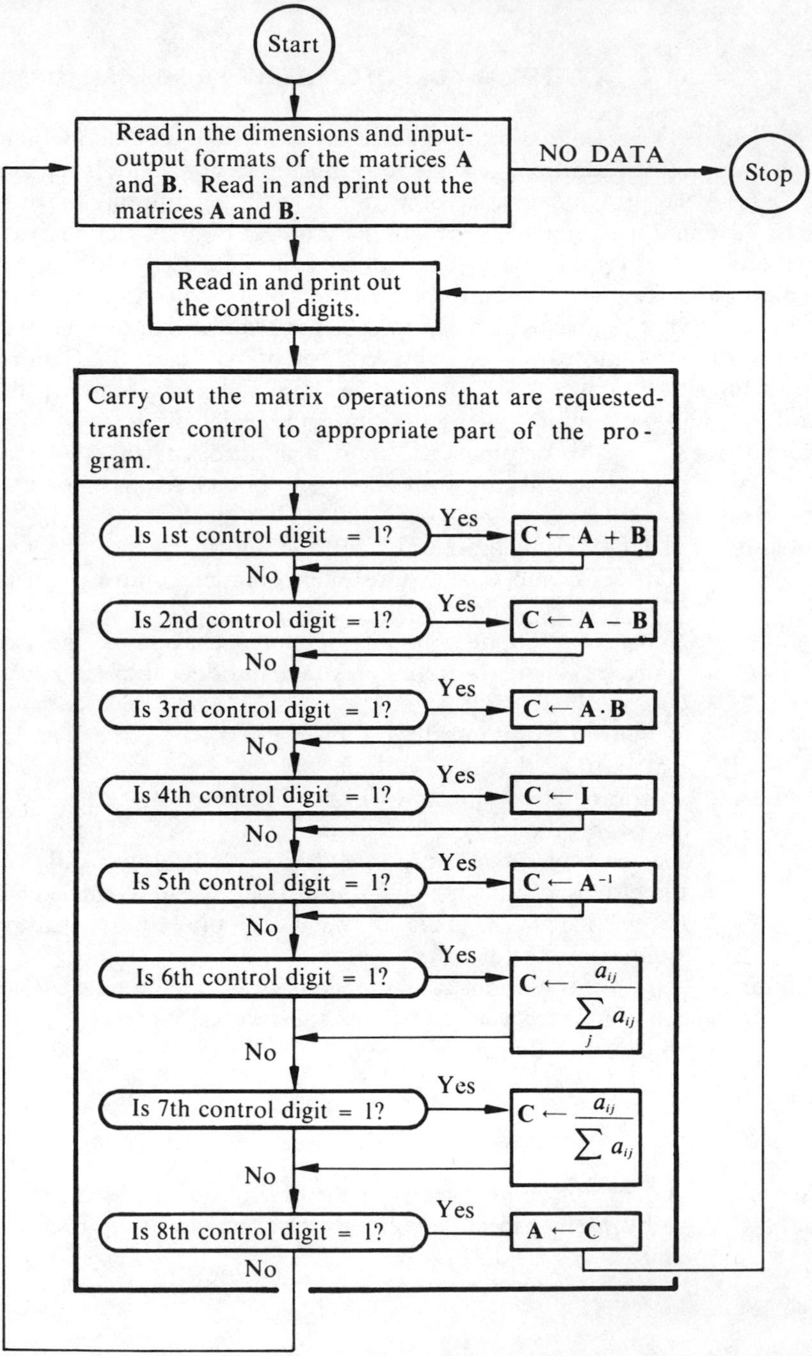

Figure A.7. Block Flowchart of General Purpose Matrix Program: GPMP

```
C   GENERAL PURPOSE MATRIX PROGRAM: GPMP
C   PROGRAM READS IN AN M BY N MATRIX A, AN MROW BY
C   NCOL MATRIX B, AND A SET OF CONTROL DIGITS WHICH
C   DEFINE THE APPROPRIATE SEQUENCE OF MATRIX OPERA-
C   TIONS THAT ARE TO BE PERFORMED ON THE TWO MA-
C   TRICES
C
C
      DIMENSION A(20, 20), B(20, 20), C(20, 20), IDIGIT(8),
     1 PIVOT(20), IPIVOT(20), ITEMP (20, 2), FMTA(12), FMTB(12),
     2 FMTPA(12), FMTPB(12)
C   READ IN THE DIMENSIONS OF THE A MATRIX AND READ
C   IN THE A MATRIX BY ROWS
  997 READ 1, M, N
    1 FORMAT (2I2)
      READ 2, (FMTA(I), I = 1, 12)
    2 FORMAT (12A6)
      READ 2, (FMTPA(I), I = 1, 12)
      READ FMTA, ((A(I, J), J = 1, N), I = 1, M)
C   READ IN THE DIMENSIONS OF THE B MATRIX AND READ
C   IN THE B MATRIX BY ROWS
      READ 1, MROWS, NCOLS
      READ 2, (FMTB(I), I = 1, 12)
      READ 2, (FMTPB(I), I = 1, 12)
      READ FMTB, ((B(I, J), J = 1, NCOLS), I = 1, MROWS)
C   PRINT OUT THE A AND B MATRICES BY ROWS
  996 PRINT 3
    3 FORMAT (1H114HINPUT MATRIX A)
      PRINT FMTPA, ((A(I, J), J = 1, N), I = 1, M)
      PRINT 4
    4 FORMAT (1H114HINPUT MATRIX B)
```

Figure A.8. General Purpose Matrix Program: GPMP

```
      PRINT FMTPB, ((B(I, J), J = 1, NCOLS), I = 1, MROWS)
C   READ IN AND PRINT OUT THE CONTROL DIGITS
      READ 5, (IDIGIT(I), I = 1, 8)
    5 FORMAT (8I1)
      PRINT 6, (IDIGIT(I), I = 1, 8)
    6 FORMAT (1H118HCONTROL DIGITS ARE//3X8I2)
      PRINT 7
    7 FORMAT (1H1)
C
C   PERFORM THE MATRIX OPERATIONS
      DO 999   INDEX = 1, 8
C   TRANSFER CONTROL TO THE APPROPRIATE SUBPROGRAM
      GO TO (10, 20, 30, 40, 50, 60, 70, 80), INDEX
C
C   DETERMINE IF MATRIX ADDITION IS REQUESTED
   10 IF (IDIGIT(INDEX)—1) 9, 11, 9
C   DETERMINE IF MATRICES ARE CONFORMABLE FOR ADDI-
C   TION
   11 IF (M. NE. MROWS. OR. N. NE. NCOLS) GO TO 12
C   CARRY OUT ADDITION AND PRINT OUT THE RESULT
      DO 130   I = 1, M
      DO 13   J = 1, N
      C(I, J) = A(I, J) + B(I, J)
   13 CONTINUE
  130 CONTINUE
      PRINT 14
   14 FORMAT (1H014HMATRIX SUM A + B)
      PRINT FMTPA, ((C(I, J), J = 1, N), I = 1, M)
      GO TO 999
    9 PRINT 15
```

Figure A.8. General Purpose Matrix Program: GPMP (Continued)

```
   15 FORMAT (1H029HMATRIX ADDITION NOT REQUESTED)
      GO TO 999
   12 PRINT 16
   16 FORMAT (1H041HMATRICES ARE NOT CONFORMABLE
     1FOR ADDITION)
      GO TO 999
C
C  DETERMINE IF MATRIX SUBTRACTION IS REQUESTED
   20 IF (IDIGIT(INDEX)—1) 19, 21, 19
C  DETERMINE IF MATRICES ARE CONFORMABLE FOR SUB-
C  TRACTION
   21 IF (M. NE. MROWS. OR. N. NE. NCOLS) GO TO 22
C  CARRY OUT SUBTRACTION AND PRINT OUT THE RESULT
      DO 230   I = 1, M
      DO 23   J = 1, N
      C(I, J) = A(I, J) - B(I, J)
   23 CONTINUE
  230 CONTINUE
      PRINT 24
   24 FORMAT (1H021HMATRIX DIFFERENCE A—B)
      PRINT FMTPA, ((C(I, J), J = 1, N), I = 1, M)
      GO TO 999
   19 PRINT 25
   25 FORMAT (1H032HMATRIX SUBTRACTION NOT RE-
     1QUESTED)
      GO TO 999
   22 PRINT 26
   26 FORMAT (1H044HMATRICES ARE NOT CONFORMABLE
     1FOR SUBTRACTION)
      GO TO 999
```

Figure A.8. General Purpose Matrix Program: GPMP (Continued)

```
C
C   DETERMINE IF MATRIX MULTIPLICATION IS REQUESTED
   30 IF (IDIGIT(INDEX)—1) 29, 31, 29
C   DETERMINE IF MATRICES ARE CONFORMABLE FOR MUL-
C   TIPLICATION
   31 IF (N. NE. MROWS) GO TO 32
C   CARRY OUT MULTIPLICATION AND PRINT OUT THE
C   RESULT
      DO 3300  I = 1, M
      DO 330   J = 1, NCOLS
      C(I, J) = 0. 0
      DO 33   K = 1, N
      C(I, J) = C(I, J) + A(I, K)*B(K, J)
   33 CONTINUE
  330 CONTINUE
 3300 CONTINUE
      PRINT 34
   34 FORMAT (1H018HMATRIX PRODUCT A*B)
      PRINT FMTPB, ((C(I, J), J = 1, NCOLS), I = 1, M)
      GO TO 999
   29 PRINT 35
   35 FORMAT  (1H035HMATRIX  MULTIPLICATION  NOT  RE-
     1QUESTED)
      GO TO 999
   32 PRINT 36
   36 FORMAT  (1H047HMATRICES  ARE  NOT  CONFORMABLE
     1FOR MULTIPLICATION)
      GO TO 999
C
C   DETERMINE IF IDENTITY MATRIX IN C IS REQUESTED
   40 IF (IDIGIT(INDEX)—1) 39, 41, 39
```

Figure A.8. General Purpose Matrix Program: GPMP (Continued)

```
C  FORM IDENTITY MATRIX IN C
   41 DO 43  I = 1, M
      DO 42  J = 1, M
      C(I, J) = 0. 0
      C(I, I) = 1. 0
   42 CONTINUE
   43 CONTINUE
      GO TO 999
   39 PRINT 44
   44 FORMAT (1H034HIDENTITY MATRIX IN C NOT REQUEST-
     1ED)
      GO TO 999
C
C  DETERMINE IF MATRIX INVERSION IS REQUESTED
   50 IF (IDIGIT(INDEX)—1) 49, 51, 51
C  DETERMINE IF MATRIX IS SQUARE
   51 IF (M. NE. N) GO TO 52
C  CARRY OUT INVERSION
C
C  INITIALIZATION
      DO 101  I = 1, M
      IPIVOT(I) = 0
  101 CONTINUE
      DO 102  I = 1, M
C
C  SEARCH FOR PIVOT ELEMENT
      T = 0. 0
      DO 103  J = 1, M
      IF (IPIVOT(J). EQ. 1) GO TO 103
      DO 104  K = 1, M
      IF (IPIVOT(K)—1) 105, 104, 999
```

Figure A.8. General Purpose Matrix Program: GPMP (Continued)

```
  105 IF (ABS(T). GE. ABS(A(J, K))) GO TO 104
      IR = J
      IC = K
      T = A(J, K)
  104 CONTINUE
  103 CONTINUE
      IPIVOT(IC) = IPIVOT(IC) + 1
C  INTERCHANGE ROWS TO PUT PIVOT ELEMENT ON DIAG-
C  ONAL
      IF (IR. EQ. IC) GO TO 106
      DO 107   L = 1, M
      T = A(IR, L)
      A(IR, L) = A(IC, L)
      A(IC, L) = T
  107 CONTINUE .
      IF (IDIGIT(INDEX)—1) 106, 106, 108
  108 DO 109   L = 1, M
      T = B(IR, L)
      B(IR, L) = B(IC, L)
      B(IC, L) = T
  109 CONTINUE
  106 ITEMP(I, 1) = IR
      ITEMP(I, 2) = IC
      PIVOT(I) = A(IC, IC)
C  CHECK FOR ZERO PIVOT
      IF (ABS (PIVOT(I))—.00001) 110, 110, 111
C  DIVIDE PIVOT ROW BY PIVOT ELEMENT
  111 A(IC, IC) = 1. 0
      DO 112   J = 1, M
      A(IC, J) = A(IC, J)/PIVOT(I)
  112 CONTINUE
```

Figure A.8. General Purpose Matrix Program: GPMP (Continued)

```
      IF (IDIGIT(INDEX)—1) 113, 113, 114
  114 DO 115  L = 1, M
      B(IC, L) = B(IC, L)/PIVOT(I)
  115 CONTINUE
C   REDUCE NONPIVOT ROWS
  113 DO 116  K = 1, M
      IF (K. EQ. IC) GO TO 116
      T = A(K, IC)
      A(K, IC) = 0. 0
      DO 117  L = 1, M
      A(K, L) = A(K, L) - A(IC, L)*T
  117 CONTINUE
      IF (IDIGIT(INDEX)—1) 116, 116, 118
  118 DO 119  L = 1, M
      B(K, L) = B(K, L) - B(IC, L)*T
  119 CONTINUE
  116 CONTINUE
  102 CONTINUE
C   INTERCHANGE COLUMNS
      DO 120  I = 1, M
      L = M - I + 1
      IF (ITEMP(L, 1). EQ. ITEMP(L, 2)) GO TO 120
      IR = ITEMP(L, 1)
      IC = ITEMP(L, 2)
      DO 121  K = 1, M
      T = A(K, IR)
      A(K, IR) = A(K, IC)
      A(K, IC) = T
  121 CONTINUE
  120 CONTINUE
C   STORE A INVERSE INTO C AND PRINT OUT THE RESULT
```

Figure A.8. General Purpose Matrix Program: GPMP (Continued)

```
      DO 1220  I = 1, M
      DO 122   J = 1, M
      C(I, J) = A(I, J)
  122 CONTINUE
 1220 CONTINUE
      PRINT 123
  123 FORMAT (1H019HINVERSE MATRIX OF A)
      PRINT FMTPA, ((C(I, J), J = 1, M), I = 1, M)
      GO TO 999
   49 PRINT 53
   53 FORMAT (1H030HMATRIX INVERSION NOT REQUESTED)
      GO TO 999
   52 PRINT 54
   54 FORMAT (1H017HMATRIX NOT SQUARE)
      GO TO 999
  110 PRINT 55
   55 FORMAT (1H018HMATRIX IS SINGULAR)
      GO TO 999
C
C  DETERMINE IF DIVISION OF MATRIX  A  BY  ROW  SUMS  IS
C  REQUESTED
   60 IF(IDIGIT (INDEX)—1) 59, 61, 59
C  FIND ROW SUMS OF THE MATRIX A
   61 DO 62   I = 1, M
      PIVOT(I) = 0. 0
      DO 63   J = 1, N
      PIVOT(I) = PIVOT(I) + A(I, J)
   63 CONTINUE
C  CHECK IF A ROW SUM IS ZERO
      IF (ABS(PIVOT(I))—.00001) 68, 68, 62
   62 CONTINUE
```

Figure A.8. General Purpose Matrix Program: GPMP (Continued)

```
C  DIVIDE ROW ELEMENTS BY ROW SUMS AND PRINT OUT
C  THE RESULT
      DO 640  I = 1, M
      DO 64  J = 1, N
      C(I, J) = A(I, J)/PIVOT(I)
   64 CONTINUE
  640 CONTINUE
      PRINT 65
   65 FORMAT (1H032HMATRIX A DIVIDED BY ITS ROW SUMS)
      PRINT FMTPA, ((C(I, J), J = 1, N), I = 1, M)
      GO TO 999
   59 PRINT 66
   66 FORMAT (1H034HDIVISION BY ROW SUMS NOT RE-
     1QUESTED)
      GO TO 999
   68 PRINT 67
   67 FORMAT (1H040HDIVISION REQUESTED BUT A ROW SUM
     1IS ZERO)
      GO TO 999
C
C  DETERMINE IF DIVISION OF MATRIX A BY COLUMN SUMS
C  IS REQUESTED
   70 IF(IDIGIT (INDEX)—1) 69, 71, 69
C  FIND COLUMN SUMS OF THE MATRIX A
   71 DO 72  J = 1, N
      PIVOT(J) = 0. 0
      DO 73  I = 1, M
      PIVOT(J) = PIVOT(J) + A(I, J)
   73 CONTINUE
C  CHECK IF A COLUMN SUM IS ZERO
      IF (ABS(PIVOT(J)—.00001)) 78, 78, 72
```

Figure A.8. General Purpose Matrix Program: GPMP (Continued)

```
   72 CONTINUE
C  DIVIDE COLUMN ELEMENTS BY COLUMN SUMS AND PRINT
C  OUT THE RESULT
      DO 740  J = 1, N
      DO 74  I = 1, M
      C(I, J) = A(I, J)/PIVOT(J)
   74 CONTINUE
  740 CONTINUE
      PRINT 75
   75 FORMAT (1H035HMATRIX A DIVIDED BY ITS COLUMN
     1SUMS)
      PRINT FMTPA, ((C(I, J), J = 1, N), I = 1, M)
      GO TO 999
   69 PRINT 76
   76 FORMAT (1H037HDIVISION BY COLUMN SUMS NOT RE-
     1QUESTED)
      GO TO 999
   78 PRINT 77
   77 FORMAT (1H043HDIVISION REQUESTED BUT A COLUMN
     1SUM IS ZERO)
      GO TO 999
C
C  DETERMINE IF THE MATRIX C IS TO BE STORED IN THE
C  MATRIX A AND ANOTHER CONTROL CARD IS TO BE READ
C  IN
   80 IF (IDIGIT(INDEX)—1) 999, 81, 999
C  STORE MATRIX C INTO MATRIX A, PRINT THE MATRICES
C  A AND B, AND READ IN ANOTHER CONTROL CARD
   81 IF (IDIGIT(3). EQ. 1) N = NCOLS
      IF (IDIGIT(4). EQ. 1) N = M
```

Figure A.8. General Purpose Matrix Program: GPMP (Continued)

```
      DO 820  I = 1, M
      DO 82  J = 1, N
      A(I, J) = C(I, J)
   82 CONTINUE
  820 CONTINUE
      GO TO 996
C
  999 CONTINUE
      GO TO 997
  998 STOP
      END
```

Figure A.8. General Purpose Matrix Program: GPMP (Continued)

Column 8: A 1 in this column calls for the transfer of the current contents of the matrix **C** into **A**, reads in another set of eight control digits, and activates another sequence of operations.

The overall structure of the program is outlined in Figure A.7. The program itself appears in Figure A.8.

Special features of the program should be noted:

1. The input and output formats of the two matrices, **A** and **B**, are read in at execution time. That is, instead of specifying their format with a FORMAT statement in the program itself, a procedure which would require changes in the program to reflect changes in the orders of the data matrices used, we allow the format to be read in as a data card. Thus, for example, the FORTRAN statements

```
      READ 2, (FMTA(I), I = 1, 12)
    2 FORMAT (12A6)
```

   input the data card which, in its first 72 columns, defines the format to be used in reading in the **A** matrix, and the statements

```
      READ 3, (FMTPA(I), I = 1, 12)
    3 FORMAT (12A6)
```

   input the data card which, in its first 72 columns, defines the format to be used in printing out the **A** matrix, after it has been read in.

2. The matrix inversion routine does not assume that the pivot element lies in the principal diagonal. Instead, it seeks the largest element of

the **A** matrix, permutes rows and columns in order to place it on the principal diagonal, carries out the elementary transformation, and then repeats the procedure with the remaining submatrix. After the inversion is completed, the program reorders the rows and columns of the inverse to correspond with the original form of the matrix **A**.

3. Checks for conformability and zero divisors appear throughout the program.

As an exercise to test his comprehension of the program, the reader should attempt to transform GPMP into a subroutine that is called into operation by a main program.

A.4 INPUT AND OUTPUT OF GPMP USING TEST DATA

The data cards for GPMP must follow the program in the order described below.

Card #1:	The dimensions of the **A** matrix are punched in the first and second pairs of columns of this card, respectively.
Card #2:	The input format of the **A** matrix.
Card #3:	The output format for the **A** matrix.
Card #4 to 4 + m:	The **A** matrix punched by rows.
Card #5 + m:	The dimensions of the **B** matrix are punched in the first and second pairs of columns of this card, respectively.
Card #6 + m:	The input format of the **B** matrix.
Card #7 + m:	The output format for the **B** matrix.
Card #8 + m to r:	The **B** matrix punched by rows.
Card #r + 1:	The eight control digits punched in the first eight columns of the card.
Card #r + 2:	(a) If the eighth control digit is unity, this card contains another set of eight control digits. (b) If the eighth control digit is not unity and another problem set is to be processed, this card contains the dimensions of the **A** matrix in the second problem set. (c) If the eighth control digit is not unity and only one problem set is to be run, this card is an "end of execution" card.

To illustrate the program's input and output formats, we present, in Figures A.9 and A.10, respectively, the input and output of GPMP using test data. Note that the matrix in the second problem set is singular.

```
 2 2
(2F8.0)
(2F12.4)
3.      5.
2.      4.
 2 1
(2F8.0)
(2F12.4)
15.     18.
11112111
00000003
 3 3
(9F8.0)
(3F12.4)
3.      5.      15.     2.      4.      8.      1.      2.      4.
 3 3
(9F8.0)
(3F12.4)
3.      5.      15.     2.      4.      8.      1.      2.      4.
11111000
$EOF
```

Figure A.9. Test Data Input to GPMP

```
INPUT MATRIX A
        3.0000      5.0000
        2.0000      4.0000

INPUT MATRIX B
       15.0000     18.0000

CONTROL DIGITS ARE
     1 1 1 1 2 1 1 1

MATRICES ARE NOT CONFORMABLE FOR ADDITION
```

Figure A.10 Test Data Output of GPMP

```
MATRICES ARE NOT CONFORMABLE FOR SUBTRACTION
MATRIX PRODUCT A*B
       135.0000     102.0000
INVERSE MATRIX OF A
         2.0000      -2.5000
        -1.0000       1.5000
MATRIX A DIVIDED BY ITS ROW SUMS
        -4.0000       5.0000
        -2.0000       3.0000
MATRIX A DIVIDED BY ITS COLUMN SUMS
         2.0000       2.5000
        -1.0000      -1.5000

INPUT MATRIX A
         2.0000       2.5000
        -1.0000      -1.5000

INPUT MATRIX B
       -15.0000      12.0000

CONTROL DIGITS ARE
       0 0 0 0 0 0 0 3

MATRIX ADDITION NOT REQUESTED
MATRIX SUBTRACTION NOT REQUESTED
MATRIX MULTIPLICATION NOT REQUESTED
IDENTITY MATRIX IN C NOT REQUESTED
MATRIX INVERSION NOT REQUESTED
DIVISION BY ROW SUMS NOT REQUESTED
DIVISION BY COLUMN SUMS NOT REQUESTED
```

Figure A.10. Test Data Output of GPMP (Continued)

INPUT MATRIX A

3.0000	5.0000	15.0000
2.0000	4.0000	8.0000
1.0000	2.0000	4.0000

INPUT MATRIX B

3.0000	5.0000	15.0000
2.0000	4.0000	8.0000
1.0000	2.0000	4.0000

CONTROL DIGITS ARE

1 1 1 1 1 0 0 0

MATRIX SUM A + B

6.0000	10.0000	30.0000
4.0000	8.0000	16.0000
2.0000	4.0000	8.0000

MATRIX DIFFERENCE A–B

0.	0.	0.
0.	0.	0.
0.	0.	0.

MATRIX PRODUCT A*B

34.0000	65.0000	145.0000
22.0000	42.0000	94.0000
11.0000	21.0000	47.0000

MATRIX IS SINGULAR

DIVISION BY ROW SUMS NOT REQUESTED

DIVISION BY COLUMN SUMS NOT REQUESTED

**** END OF INPUT DATA.

**** EXECUTION TERMINATED.

Figure A.10 Test Data Output of GPMP (Continued)

three regression analysis

Urban and regional analysis is usually concerned with relationships that exist, or appear to exist, between two or more variables. For example, residential density is a function of distance from the city center; interregional migration is a function of economic opportunities at origins and destinations and the distances separating them; the number of automobile trips originating in a traffic zone is a function of the number of households in that zone, their average annual incomes, and the accessibility of the zone to other zones. The task of regression analysis is to estimate the parameters of models describing such relationships and to ascertain whether the resulting fits are statistically significant. In the event the fit of the model is satisfactory, its use for prediction may be justified.

We begin our discussion of regression analysis in nonmatrix form and introduce matrix notation only after the fundamental ideas of simple linear regression have been fully developed. This allows readers who are familiar only with the more conventional introductory expositions of regression to follow our early arguments more easily and see how they lead to the more compact and more general matrix formulation.

3.1 THE SIMPLE LINEAR REGRESSION MODEL

The simplest definition of a relationship between variables is the linear model

$$Y = \beta_0 + \beta_1 X \tag{3.1}$$

Here we are dealing with a single relation in two variables. It is assumed that variations in the *dependent* variable, Y, are associated with variations in the *independent* variable, X. The precise dependence is specified by the

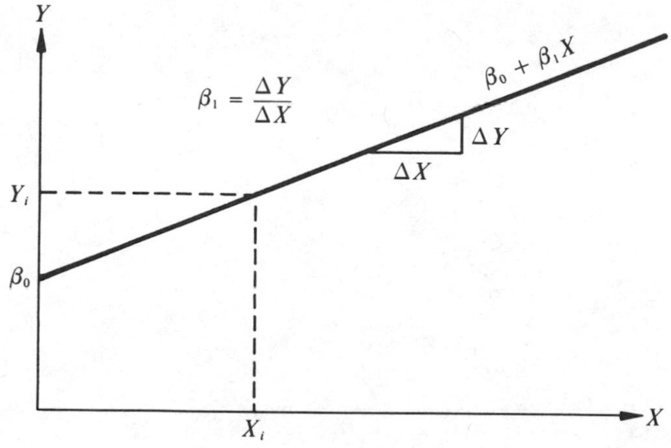

Figure 3.1. A Linear Relationship Between Two Variables

slope parameter, β_1, which defines the rate at which Y changes with respect to X. The parameter β_0 is the *intercept term* and denotes the value of Y when X is zero. A graphical expression of (3.1), with β_1 positive, appears in Figure 3.1.

Few phenomena exhibit the exact relationship defined by (3.1). An example is Ohm's law in physics, which defines an exact linear relationship between current and voltage in a simple circuit, if resistance is kept constant. More often, however, (3.1) approximates an association that is observed between two variables over a limited range of variation. For example, in an adult population, the weight of an individual member is directly related to his height and, in general, the relationship may be quite accurately approximated by a straight line.

Example. As an illustration of the association between two variables, Y and X, representing food store employees and total population, respectively, consider the following observed random sample drawn from a particular population of census tracts.

This same set of data may be presented graphically in the form of a *scatter* diagram such as the one in Figure 3.2.

Table 3.1. Employment-Population Data

Y (food empl.):	60	75	96	40	54	68	87	64	48	80
X (pop. in thousands):	4	6	8	2	4	6	8	4	2	6

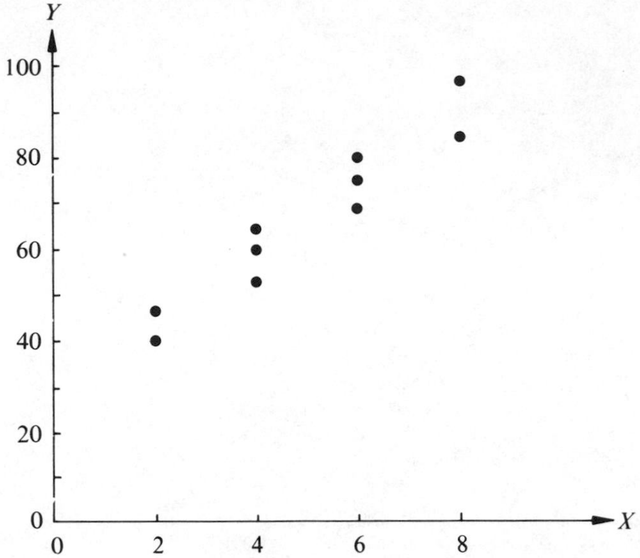

Figure 3.2. Scatter Diagram of Food Store Employment on Total Population

Note that, for any given population size, we have a range of observed employment totals. This variation in the dependent variable, Y, for each fixed value of the independent variable, X, may be attributed to errors in measuring Y, unpredictable random variation among individual observations, and variation in other important influencing factors that have not been taken into account, such as *total* employment.

In light of this variation, an exact relationship between food store employment and population is not a convincing hypothesis. A similar conclusion is generally reached in the analyses of most urban and regional phenomena. Thus it becomes more useful to adopt the slightly modified model defined as follows:

$$Y_i = \beta_0 + \beta_1 X_i + \varepsilon_i \qquad (i = 1, 2, \ldots, n) \tag{3.2}$$

Equation (3.2) retains the linear hypothesis expressed by (3.1), but includes a random error term, ε, which may take on either positive or negative values. Thus our new linear hypothesis depicts Y as a random variable and describes a distribution of Y values for each fixed value of X. The error term, ε_i, indicates the amount by which a particular ith observation deviates from the average Y value associated with its subgroup. Hence, in place of an exact relationship between food store employment and population, for example, we merely hypothesize a positive linear association between average observed food store employment and each of several prespecified average population totals. This relationship is called the *regression curve* of food store employment on population.

3.1.1 ASSUMPTIONS

To complete the specification of the simple linear model expressed by (3.2), we need to include some assumptions concerning the probability distribution of the error term. For purposes of estimating the parameters β_0 and β_1, assumptions need to be made regarding the mean, variance, and covariance of this distribution, and the nature of the X's.

The simplest and most common set of assumptions is that:

1. the mean, $E(\varepsilon_i)$, is zero;
2. the variance, $\text{Var}(\varepsilon_i)$ or $E(\varepsilon_i\varepsilon_i)$, is constant and independent of X;
3. the values of the error term occur independently of one another, that is, the covariance, $E(\varepsilon_i\varepsilon_j)$, is zero; and
4. the X_i are fixed numbers.

These four assumptions may be expressed symbolically by:

$$E(\varepsilon_i) = 0 \qquad \text{for} \quad i = 1, 2, \ldots, n \tag{3.3}$$

$$E(\varepsilon_i\varepsilon_j) = \begin{cases} 0 & \text{for} \quad i \neq j; \quad i, j = 1, 2, \ldots, n \\ \sigma^2 & \text{for} \quad i = j; \quad i, j = 1, 2, \ldots, n \end{cases} \tag{3.4}$$

$$E(X_i) = X_i \quad \text{and} \quad \text{Var}(X_i) = 0 \qquad \text{for} \quad i = 1, 2, \ldots, n \tag{3.5}$$

These assumptions are important. The first implies that positive and negative deviations are equally likely to occur around the straight line $\beta_0 + \beta_1 X$. The second asserts that the dispersion of error terms around their zero mean is of the same order irrespective of how large X is. This condition is called *homoscedasticity*. The third assumption requires that individual values of ε_i be independent of one another. Violation of this assumption occurs, for example, in instances of linear trends in time series data where the value of Y_{t+1} is likely to be strongly associated with the value of Y_t. Econometricians define this problem as *autocorrelation*. Finally, we need the additional assumption that the X's are a fixed set of numbers. This ensures that ε and X are independent, a condition necessary for the development of the estimation method to be discussed in the next section.

Since X is regarded as being fixed, we may easily derive the expected value of Y for each X,

$$\begin{aligned} E(Y|X_i) &= E(\beta_0 + \beta_1 X_i + \varepsilon_i) \\ &= \beta_0 + \beta_1 X_i + E(\varepsilon_i) \\ &= \beta_0 + \beta_1 X_i \end{aligned} \tag{3.6}$$

and the associated variance,

$$\begin{aligned} \text{Var}(Y|X_i) &= \text{Var}(\beta_0 + \beta_1 X_i + \varepsilon_i) \\ &= \text{Var}(\varepsilon_i) \\ &= \sigma^2 \end{aligned} \tag{3.7}$$

Thus we have the result that Y is a random variable, distributed according to some distribution, $f(Y|X_i)$, say, which has a mean equal to $\beta_0 + \beta_1 X_i$ and a variance equal to σ^2.

Equations (3.2), (3.3), (3.4), and (3.5) together define a linear model which may be expressed graphically by a three-dimensional diagram such as Figure 3.3. As in Figure 3.1, we illustrate a positive relationship between Y and X.

The fundamental problem of parameter estimation now presents itself. Our linear model is defined in terms of three unknown parameters: β_0, β_1, and σ^2. On the basis of a sample of n observations (X_i, Y_i), we wish to estimate the values of these parameters and thereby statistically summarize the observed association between Y and X. As we shall see later, this is but the first step. After estimating the parameters, we shall also wish to test hypotheses concerning the values of these parameters and to assess the adequacy of the fit of the model to the data.

Recalling the scatter diagram presented in Figure 3.2, we may express the parameter estimation problem, for this particular set of data, as follows: on the basis of the 10 employment-population observations, *estimate the intercept term* β_0, *the slope parameter* β_1, *and the variance of the error terms*

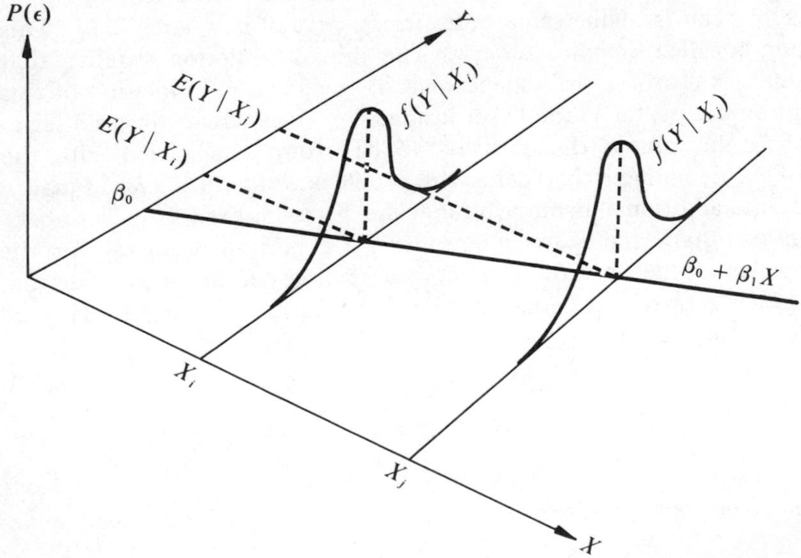

Figure 3.3. The Simple Linear Regression Model

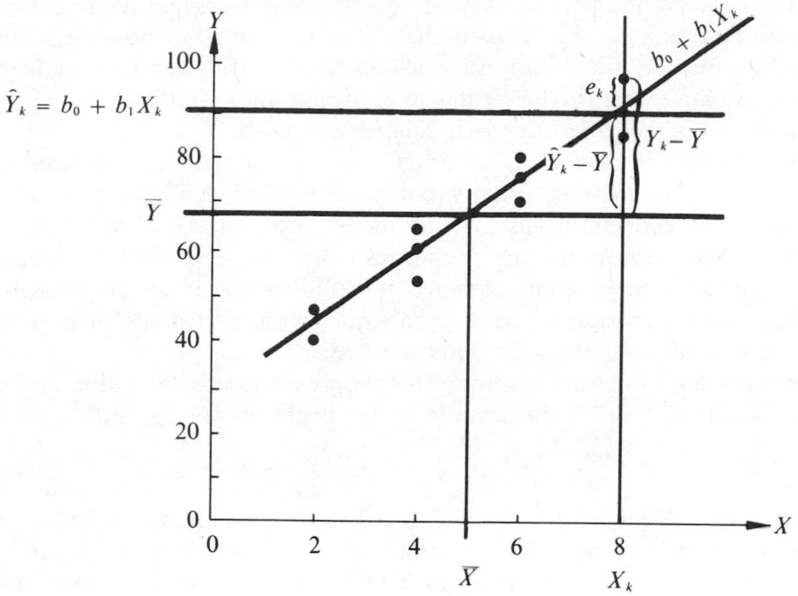

Figure 3.4. Least Squares Regression Line

around their respective means, σ^2. Denote these estimates by b_0, b_1, and s^2. Denote the estimated line by

$$\hat{Y} = b_0 + b_1X \tag{3.8}$$

and the deviation between observed and estimated values of Y by e, namely,

$$e_i = Y_i - \hat{Y}_i \tag{3.9}$$

Figure 3.4 illustrates a few of the relationships that result.

3.1.2 LEAST SQUARES PARAMETER ESTIMATORS

An infinite number of lines may be fitted to the points of a scatter diagram such as the one in Figure 3.4. The choice of a particular line depends only on the particular data set and the criterion used to locate the line. Intuitively, one recognizes that a desirable criterion for determining where to place the line amidst the point observations is one which somehow seeks to minimize deviations of observed and predicted values for Y, that is, $e = Y - \hat{Y}$. It turns out that a particularly desirable criterion is the *least squares principle.* Briefly, this principle defines estimates for β_0 and

β_1 in terms of the sum of the squared deviations of observed from predicted values for Y. More specifically, the least squares principle requires that estimates of β_0 and β_1 be so chosen that $\sum e_i^2$ is as small as possible. The method or formula for finding such values for b_0 and b_1 is called the *least squares estimator*, and the particular numerical values of b_0 and b_1 yielded by that formula are called the *least squares estimates*.

The use of the least squares criterion can be justified in a number of ways. First, it is computationally convenient. Second, if the conditions specified by the assumptions of the model are satisfied, least squares estimators have certain optimal properties (see Subsection 3.1.3). Finally, even when the assumed conditions are not fulfilled, estimates obtained by the method of least squares have certain properties that make them preferable to estimates obtained by other methods.

Having defined the least squares principle, we now may proceed to derive the estimators that fulfill this criterion. We begin by noting that

$$\sum e_i^2 = \sum (Y_i - \hat{Y}_i)^2 = \sum (Y_i - b_0 - b_1 X_i)^2 \qquad (3.10)$$

Thus the sum of squared deviations is a function of b_0 and b_1. A necessary condition for this quantity to be a minimum, therefore, is that the partial derivatives of the sum with respect to b_0 and b_1 should both be zero. Thus

$$\frac{\partial}{\partial b_0} \sum e_i^2 = -2 \sum (Y_i - b_0 - b_1 X_i) = 0$$

$$\frac{\partial}{\partial b_1} \sum e_i^2 = -2 \sum (Y_i - b_0 - b_1 X_i) X_i = 0$$

Simplifying these two equations, we have the so-called *normal equations* for a straight line fitted by the least squares principle:

$$\sum Y_i = nb_0 + b_1 \sum X_i \qquad (3.11)$$

$$\sum X_i Y_i = b_0 \sum X_i + b_1 \sum X_i^2 \qquad (3.12)$$

Solving these two equations for the two unknowns, b_0 and b_1, we have

$$b_0 = \frac{\sum X_i^2 \sum Y_i - \sum X_i \sum X_i Y_i}{n \sum X_i^2 - (\sum X_i)^2} \qquad (3.13)$$

$$b_1 = \frac{n \sum X_i Y_i - \sum X_i \sum Y_i}{n \sum X_i^2 - (\sum X_i)^2} \qquad (3.14)$$

Alternatively, if we divide both sides of (3.11) by n and solve for b_0,

$$b_0 = \bar{Y} - b_1 \bar{X} \qquad (3.15)$$

and since

$$\begin{aligned}\sum (X_i - \bar{X})(Y_i - \bar{Y}) &= \sum X_iY_i - \bar{X}\sum Y_i - \bar{Y}\sum X_i + n\bar{X}\bar{Y}\\ &= \sum X_iY_i - n\bar{X}\bar{Y}\\ &= \sum X_iY_i - (\sum X_i \sum Y_i)/n\end{aligned}$$

we may rewrite b_1 as

$$b_1 = \frac{n\sum X_iY_i - \sum X_i \sum Y_i}{n\sum X_i^2 - (\sum X_i)^2} = \frac{\sum (X_i - \bar{X})(Y_i - \bar{Y})}{\sum (X_i - \bar{X})^2} \qquad (3.16)$$

Substituting (3.15) into (3.8) yields the alternative expression for the estimated regression equation:

$$\hat{Y}_i = \bar{Y} + b_1 (X_i - \bar{X}) \qquad (3.17)$$

If we denote $(\hat{Y}_i - \bar{Y})$ by $\hat{y}_i$ and $(X_i - \bar{X})$ by x_i, we may rewrite (3.17) as

$$\hat{y}_i = b_1 x_i \qquad (3.18)$$

Similarly, if we denote $(y_i - \hat{y}_i)$ by e_i, we may rederive the least squares estimators as follows:

$$\sum e_i^2 = \sum (y_i - \hat{y}_i)^2 = \sum (y_i - b_1x_i)^2$$

and

$$\frac{\partial}{\partial b_1} \sum e_i^2 = -2 \sum (y_i - b_1x_i)x_i$$

hence

$$b_1 = \frac{\sum x_i y_i}{\sum x_i^2} \qquad (3.19)$$

which is the expression for b_1 in (3.16).

Example. To illustrate the computation of least squares estimates, consider the employment-population data in Table 3.1. We find the following quantities:

$$\begin{aligned} n &= 10\\ \sum Y_i &= 672\\ \bar{Y} &= 67.2\\ \sum X_i &= 50\\ \bar{X} &= 5.0\\ \sum X_iY_i &= 3{,}690\\ \sum X_i^2 &= 292\end{aligned}$$

$$b_0 = \frac{\sum X_i^2 \sum Y_i - \sum X_i \sum X_i Y_i}{n \sum X_i^2 - (\sum X_i)^2} = \frac{292(672) - 50(3{,}690)}{10(292) - (50)^2}$$

$$= \frac{11{,}724}{420} = 27.9143$$

$$b_1 = \frac{n \sum X_i Y_i - \sum X_i \sum Y_i}{n \sum X_i^2 - (\sum X_i)^2} = \frac{10(3{,}690) - 50(672)}{10(292) - (50)^2}$$

$$= \frac{3{,}300}{420} = 7.8571$$

and

$$\hat{Y}_i = 27.9143 + 7.8571 X_i$$

The fitted line is the one plotted in Figure 3.4. Table 3.2 presents, for each of the 10 observations, the observed Y, the fitted $\hat{Y}$, and the residual, e. The reader should confirm that the same regression line is produced by the formula in deviation form.

Table 3.2. Observed Values, Fitted Values, Residuals, and Squared Residuals

Observation	Y_i	$\hat{Y}_i$	$e_i = Y_i - \hat{Y}_i$	e_i^2
1	60	59.3399	0.6601	0.4357
2	75	75.0541	−0.0541	0.0029
3	96	90.7683	5.2317	27.3707
4	40	43.6257	−3.6257	13.1457
5	54	59.3399	−5.3399	28.5145
6	68	75.0541	−7.0541	49.7603
7	87	90.7683	−3.7683	14.2001
8	64	59.3399	4.6601	21.7165
9	48	43.6257	4.3743	19.1345
10	80	75.0541	4.9459	24.4619
Total	$\sum Y_i = 672$	$\sum \hat{Y}_i = 671.9200$	$\sum e_i = 0.0003$	$\sum e_i^2 = 198.7429$

3.1.3 PROPERTIES OF THE LEAST SQUARES ESTIMATORS

We now establish the properties of the least squares estimators. First, notice that they are *linear* functions of the observations on Y. Recalling (3.19), we have

$$b_1 = \frac{\sum x_i y_i}{\sum x_i^2} = \frac{\sum x_i (Y_i - \bar{Y})}{\sum x_i^2}$$

$$= \frac{\sum x_i Y_i}{\sum x_i^2} - \frac{\bar{Y} \sum x_i}{\sum x_i^2}$$

$$= \frac{\sum x_i Y_i}{\sum x_i^2} \qquad \text{since} \quad \sum x_i = 0$$

But we assumed the X_i to be a fixed set of numbers! Thus

$$c_1 = \frac{x_i}{\sum x_i^2} = \text{a constant} \tag{3.20}$$

and

$$b_1 = \sum c_i Y_i \tag{3.21}$$

Similarly, by substituting (3.21) for b_1 in (3.15), we may express b_0 as a linear function of the Y_i, namely,

$$b_0 = \bar{Y} - \bar{X} \sum c_i Y_i = \frac{1}{n} \sum Y_i - \bar{X} \sum c_i Y_i$$

$$= \sum \left(\frac{1}{n} - \bar{X} c_i \right) Y_i \tag{3.22}$$

Next, imagine holding the X_i fixed and drawing repeated samples of size n from some population. Applying the least squares estimators to each sample, we would derive a series of estimates for b_0 and b_1. These would vary from sample to sample, as a consequence of variations in the error term, and we would end up with a distribution of values for b_0 and b_1. Let us derive the mean and variance of each of these sampling distributions. We begin by establishing the following three properties of the c_i defined in (3.20):

$$\sum c_i = \frac{\sum x_i}{\sum x_i^2} = \frac{\sum (X_i - \bar{X})}{\sum x_i^2} = 0 \tag{3.23}$$

$$\sum c_i^2 = \frac{\sum x_i^2}{(\sum x_i^2)^2} = \frac{1}{\sum x_i^2} \tag{3.24}$$

and

$$\sum c_i x_i = \sum c_i X_i - \bar{X} \sum c_i = \sum c_i X_i$$

by (3.23); but

$$\sum c_i x_i = \frac{\sum x_i^2}{\sum x_i^2} = 1$$

hence

$$\sum c_i X_i = 1 \tag{3.25}$$

Consider now the expected value of b_1. From (3.21),

$$b_1 = \sum c_i Y_i$$

Substituting (3.2) for Y_i, we get

$$b_1 = \sum c_i(\beta_0 + \beta_1 X_i + \varepsilon_i)$$

$$= \beta_0 \sum c_i + \beta_1 \sum c_i X_i + \sum c_i \varepsilon_i$$

Using (3.23) and (3.25), this reduces to

$$b_1 = \beta_1 + \sum c_i \varepsilon_i \tag{3.26}$$

Hence

$$E(b_1) = \beta_1 + \sum c_i E(\varepsilon_i)$$
$$= \beta_1 \tag{3.27}$$

since by (3.3) the expectation of the error term is zero. Thus b_1 is an *unbiased linear* estimator of β_1. Similarly, b_0 is an unbiased linear estimator for β_0, since

$$b_0 = \sum \left(\frac{1}{n} - \bar{X}c_i\right) Y_i$$
$$= \sum \left(\frac{1}{n} - \bar{X}c_i\right)\left(\beta_0 + \beta_1 X_i + \varepsilon_i\right)$$
$$= \beta_0 - \beta_0 \bar{X} \sum c_i + \beta_1 X_i - \beta_1 \bar{X} \sum c_i X_i + \sum \left(\frac{1}{n} - \bar{X}c_i\right) \varepsilon_i$$

and, using (3.23) and (3.25),

$$b_0 = \beta_0 + \sum \left(\frac{1}{n} - \bar{X}c_i\right) \varepsilon_i \tag{3.28}$$

Hence, using (3.3),

$$E(b_0) = \beta_0 \tag{3.29}$$

Having established that b_0 and b_1 are unbiased, we now proceed to derive the variances of these estimates.

From (3.26) we have that

$$b_1 - \beta_1 = \sum c_i \varepsilon_i$$

hence

$$\text{Var}(b_1) = E[(b_1 - \beta_1)^2] = E[(\sum c_i \varepsilon_i)^2]$$
$$= E[\sum (c_i^2 \varepsilon_i^2)] + 2E\left[\sum_{i \neq j} (c_i c_j \varepsilon_i \varepsilon_j)\right]$$
$$= \sum c_i^2 E(\varepsilon_i^2) + 2 \sum_{i \neq j} c_i c_j E(\varepsilon_i \varepsilon_j)$$
$$= \sigma^2 \sum c_i^2$$

since $E(u_i u_j) = 0$ and $E(u_i^2) = \sigma^2$ from (3.4). Substituting for $\sum c_i^2$, we have, by (3.24),

$$\text{Var}(b_1) = \frac{\sigma^2}{\sum x_i^2} \tag{3.30}$$

In a similar fashion, we may derive the variance of b_0. From (3.28) we have that

$$b_0 - \beta_0 = \sum \left(\frac{1}{n} - \bar{X}c_i\right) \varepsilon_i$$

hence

$$\begin{aligned}\operatorname{Var}(b_0) &= E[(b_0 - \beta_0)^2] = E\left\{\left[\sum\left(\frac{1}{n} - \bar{X}c_i\right)\varepsilon_i\right]^2\right\} \\ &= \sigma^2 \sum\left(\frac{1}{n} - \bar{X}c_i\right)^2 \\ &= \sigma^2\left(\frac{1}{n} + \bar{X}^2 \sum c_i^2 - \frac{2\bar{X}\sum c_i}{n}\right) \\ &= \sigma^2\left(\frac{1}{n} + \frac{\bar{X}^2}{\sum x_i^2}\right)\end{aligned}$$

by (3.23) and (3.24). And, since $\sum (X_i - \bar{X})^2 = \sum X_i^2 - n\bar{X}^2$,

$$\operatorname{Var}(b_0) = \frac{\sum X_i^2}{n\sum x_i^2}\,\sigma^2 \tag{3.31}$$

The same procedure may be used to establish that the covariance of the two estimates is

$$\begin{aligned}\operatorname{Cov}(b_0, b_1) &= E[(b_0 - \beta_0)(b_1 - \beta_1)] \\ &= \frac{-\bar{X}}{\sum x_i^2}\,\sigma^2 \qquad (3.32)\end{aligned}$$

In addition to being *linear* and *unbiased*, the least squares estimators of β_0 and β_1 have two additional properties that make them more desirable than other estimators:

1. Least squares estimators are the *best* linear unbiased estimators. That is, of the class of all possible linear unbiased estimators, least squares estimators have the smallest variance.
2. If, in addition to the assumption concerning the error term made in (3.3) and (3.4), we assume that the ε_i are normally distributed, then the maximum likelihood estimators of β_0 and β_1 are identical to those derived by the least squares principle.[1]

The variances of b_0 an b_1, and their covariance, depend on σ^2 — the variance of the error term ε_i. This quantity cannot be observed and, therefore, must be estimated from the data. Consider the residuals

$$e_i = y_i - b_1 x_i \tag{3.33}$$

and average $Y_i = \beta_0 + \beta_1 X_i + \varepsilon_i$ over the n sample values to obtain

$$\bar{Y} = \beta_0 + \beta_1 \bar{X} + \bar{\varepsilon} \tag{3.34}$$

Now subtract (3.34) from (3.2) to find

$$y_i = \beta_1 x_i + (\varepsilon_i - \bar{\varepsilon}) \tag{3.35}$$

[1] A maximum likelihood estimator is one which selects those values for b_0 and b_1 that maximize the probability of obtaining the observed sample.

Substituting (3.35) for y_i in (3.33) yields

$$\begin{aligned} e_i &= \beta_1 x_i - b_1 x_i + (\varepsilon_i - \bar{\varepsilon}) \\ &= -(b_1 - \beta_1)x_i + (\varepsilon_i - \bar{\varepsilon}) \end{aligned} \tag{3.36}$$

Now it seems intuitively reasonable to estimate the variance of ε by beginning with the sample variance of the residuals about the fitted regression, namely,

$$\frac{\sum (e_i - \bar{e})^2}{n}$$

But

$$\bar{e} = \frac{\sum e_i}{n} = \frac{\sum (Y_i - b_0 - b_1 X_i)}{n} = \bar{Y} - b_0 - b_1 \bar{X} = 0$$

and we are left with only $\sum e_i^2/n$. However, as we shall see presently, this is a biased estimator of σ^2. To derive an unbiased estimator, we begin by considering the expected value of $\sum e_i^2$. Recalling (3.36), and squaring and summing both sides of the equation over the n sample values, we have

$$\sum e_i^2 = (b_1 - \beta_1)^2 \sum x_i^2 + \sum (\varepsilon_i - \bar{\varepsilon})^2 - 2(b_1 - \beta_1) \sum x_i(\varepsilon_i - \bar{\varepsilon})$$

Taking expected values of each term on the right-hand side, we have

$$E\left[(b_1 - \beta_1)^2 \sum x_i^2\right] = \sigma^2$$

from (3.30), and

$$E\left[\sum (\varepsilon_i - \bar{\varepsilon})^2\right] = E\left[\sum \varepsilon_i^2 - n\bar{\varepsilon}^2\right] = (n-1)\sigma^2$$

and, substituting for $(b_1 - \beta_1)$ from (3.26) in the third term,

$$\begin{aligned} E\left[(b_1 - \beta_1) \sum x_i(\varepsilon_i - \bar{\varepsilon})\right] &= E\left[\sum c_i \varepsilon_i x_i(\varepsilon_i - \bar{\varepsilon})\right] \\ &= E\left[\frac{\sum \varepsilon_i x_i}{\sum x_i^2}\left(\sum \varepsilon_i x_i - \bar{\varepsilon} \sum x_i\right)\right] \\ &= \sigma^2 \end{aligned}$$

since $\sum x_i = 0$. Thus

$$E\left(\sum e_i^2\right) = \sigma^2 + \sigma^2(n-1) - 2\sigma^2 = (n-2)\sigma^2$$

and an unbiased estimator of σ^2 may be defined by

$$s^2 = \frac{\sum e_i^2}{n-2} \tag{3.37}$$

where s is called the *standard error of the regression.*

3.1.4 SIGNIFICANCE TESTS AND CONFIDENCE INTERVALS

In the preceding paragraphs, least squares estimators and their properties were derived without making any assumptions about the probability distribution of the error terms, ε_i. If now we add the assumption that the ε_i are all identically distributed according to a normal distribution, with zero mean and variance σ^2, then we may perform a series of significance tests on hypotheses concerning the parameters of the linear regression model and assign confidence intervals around their values.

If ε_i is NORMAL $(0, \sigma^2)$, then, for a given X_i, Y is NORMAL$(\beta_0 + \beta_1 X_i, \sigma^2)$ by (3.6) and (3.7). The distributions $f(Y|X_i)$, in Figure 3.3, depict such normal distributions. Since b_0 and b_1 are linear combinations of independent normal variables, it follows that they themselves are normally distributed. Thus we have

$$b_0 \quad \text{is} \quad \text{NORMAL}\left(\beta_0, \frac{\sum X_i^2}{n \sum x_i^2} \sigma^2\right) \tag{3.38}$$

$$b_1 \quad \text{is} \quad \text{NORMAL}\left(\beta_1, \frac{1}{\sum x_i^2} \sigma^2\right) \tag{3.39}$$

To consider tests of significance about the parameters β_0 and β_1, we need the following well-known facts about normal sampling theory. Their proofs can be found in most standard texts on statistics.[2]

If a random sample of n observations, X_i, is drawn from a normal population with mean μ and variance σ^2, then

$$Z_i = \frac{X_i - \mu}{\sigma} \quad \text{is} \quad \text{NORMAL } (0, 1) \tag{3.40}$$

$$W^2 = \sum Z_i^2 = \frac{\sum (X_i - \mu)^2}{\sigma^2} \tag{3.41}$$

has a χ^2 distribution with n degrees of freedom; and if W^2 is distributed independently of Z, then

$$t = \frac{Z}{W/\sqrt{n}} \tag{3.42}$$

has a Student's t distribution with n degrees of freedom.

If W_1^2 and W_2^2 are independently distributed according to a χ^2 distribution, with n_1 and n_2 degrees of freedom, respectively, then

$$F = \frac{W_1^2/n_1}{W_2^2/n_2} \tag{3.43}$$

has an F distribution with (n_1, n_2) degrees of freedom.

[2] For example, Hoel (1963).

In order to make statistical inferences about b_i, we need to construct a statistic that is a function only of the variables X_i, Y_i, and the particular parameter β_1. In addition, we must derive the probability distribution of this statistic. Consider the statistic

$$t_{b_i} = \frac{b_i - \beta_i}{s_{b_i}} \tag{3.44}$$

where $s_{b_i}^2$ is an estimator of the variance of b_i, obtained by replacing σ^2, in (3.30) and (3.31), by its unbiased estimator s^2. We have that

$$s_{b_0}^2 = \frac{\sum X_i^2}{n \sum x_i^2} \frac{\sum e_i^2}{(n-2)} = \frac{\sum X_i^2 \sum e_i^2}{n(n-2)\,(\sum X_i^2 - n\bar{X}^2)} \tag{3.45}$$

and

$$s_{b_1}^2 = \frac{1}{\sum x_i^2} \frac{\sum e_i^2}{(n-2)} = \frac{\sum e_i^2}{(n-2)\,(\sum X_i^2 - n\bar{X}^2)} \tag{3.46}$$

Substituting the values for s_{b_i} defined in (3.45) and (3.46), into (3.44), we have

$$t_{b_0} = \frac{b_0 - \beta_0}{s_{b_0}} = \frac{b_0 - \beta_0}{\sqrt{\dfrac{\sum X_i^2 \sum e_i^2}{n(n-2)\,(\sum X_i^2 - n\bar{X}^2)}}} \tag{3.47}$$

and

$$t_{b_1} = \frac{b_1 - \beta_1}{s_{b_1}} = \frac{b_1 - \beta_1}{\sqrt{\dfrac{\sum e_i^2}{(n-2)\,(\sum X_i^2 - n\bar{X}^2)}}} \tag{3.48}$$

The values of the test statistics t_{b_0} and t_{b_1}, expressed by (3.47) and (3.48), depend only on the values of the sample statistics (X_1, Y_1) and on the parameters β_0 and β_1, respectively. No other unknown parameters are involved. Moreover, the test statistics are distributed according to a Student's t distribution. This can be seen by expressing t as the quotient of a normally distributed variable, Z, and the square root of a χ^2 distributed variable, W^2, divided by its degrees of freedom. Namely,

$$t_{b_0} = \frac{Z_{b_0}}{\sqrt{W^2 \dfrac{1}{(n-2)}}} = \frac{\dfrac{b_0 - \beta_0}{\sigma_{b_0}}}{\sqrt{\dfrac{\sum e_i^2}{\sigma^2} \dfrac{1}{(n-2)}}} = \frac{\dfrac{(b_0 - \beta_0)\sqrt{n(\sum X_i^2 - n\bar{X}^2)}}{\sigma \sqrt{\sum X_i^2}}}{\sqrt{\dfrac{(n-2)s^2}{\sigma^2(n-2)}}}$$

$$= \frac{(b_0 - \beta_0)\sqrt{n(\sum X_i^2 - n\bar{X}^2)}}{\sqrt{s^2 \sum X_i^2}} = \frac{b_0 - \beta_0}{\sqrt{\dfrac{\sum X_i^2 \sum e_i^2}{n(n-2)\,(\sum X_i^2 - n\bar{X}^2)}}}$$

and

$$t_{b_1} = \frac{Z_{b_1}}{\sqrt{W^2 \dfrac{1}{(n-2)}}} = \frac{\dfrac{b_1 - \beta_1}{\sigma_{b_1}}}{\sqrt{\dfrac{\sum e_i^2}{\sigma^2} \dfrac{1}{(n-2)}}} = \frac{\dfrac{(b_1 - \beta_1)\sqrt{\sum X_i^2 - n\bar{X}^2}}{\sigma}}{\sqrt{\dfrac{(n-2)s^2}{\sigma^2(n-2)}}}$$

$$= \frac{(b_1 - \beta_1)\sqrt{\sum X_i^2 - n\bar{X}^2}}{s} = \frac{b_1 - \beta_1}{\sqrt{\dfrac{\sum e_i^2}{(n-2)(\sum X_i^2 - n\bar{X}^2)}}}$$

It can be shown that W^2 has a χ^2 distribution with $n - 2$ degrees of freedom and is distributed independently of Z. Therefore, by (3.42), t_{b_0} and t_{b_1} each have a Student's t distribution with $n - 2$ degrees of freedom.

To test the hypothesis that $\beta_i = \beta$, where β is a specified value of the parameter β_i, we begin by establishing *critical regions* in the probability distribution of the test statistic t_{b_i} and proceed to compute the value of t_{b_i} with β_i set equal to β. If the computed value falls inside the predefined critical regions, we reject the hypothesis $\beta_i = \beta$ in favor of the alternative hypothesis, $\beta_i \neq \beta$. If the computed value falls outside the critical regions, we do not reject the hypothesis $\beta_i = \beta$. Notice that in the latter instance we do not *accept* the hypothesis, but merely fail to reject it.

Critical regions are set up in the following manner. We begin by establishing the *level of significance*, α, say, at which we wish to test our hypothesis. This is simply the probability that we shall incorrectly reject our hypothesis. That is, α, is the probability that we shall reject the hypothesis $\beta_i = \beta$ when, in fact, β_i *is equal* to β. Clearly, we wish to make this probability small. The particular value chosen depends on the nature of the experiment being tested. If it is particularly important not to commit such an error (for example, in testing the effects of a new drug), we choose for α an extremely low value, for example, $\alpha = 0.0001$. This ensures that we will, on the average, reject a " true " hypothesis only once in 10,000 experiments. If, however, the nature of the experiment is such that little harm would come out of the rejection of a true hypothesis, then larger values for α may be in order, for example, $\alpha = 0.05$.

Having established the appropriate α value for a particular test, we set off two regions in the range of values that the statistic t_{b_i} may take on. In particular, referring to Figure 3.5, we determine two boundary points t_1 and t_2 such that the probability of t_{b_i} having a value less than t_1 or greater than t_2 is α, that is, $P(t_1 < t_{b_i} < t_2) = 1 - \alpha$. The critical region is depicted by the two hatched areas in the figure.

We define $1 - \alpha$ to be the *confidence level* of the statement that t lies inside the range of values bounded by t_1 and t_2, and call this interval a

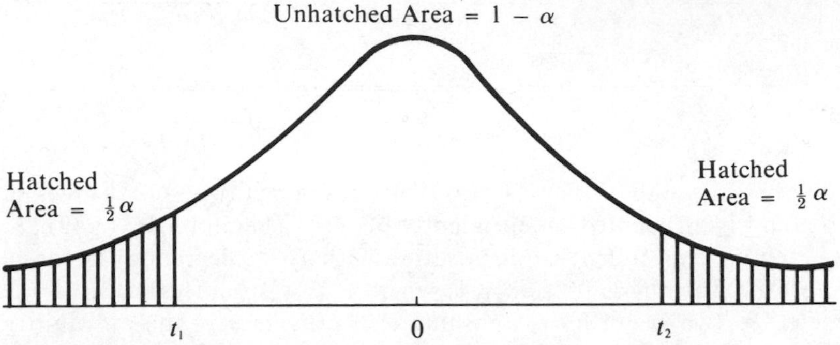

Figure 3.5. Distribution of the t Statistic

confidence interval. Thus, to find the 100(1 − α) percent confidence interval for β_i, we proceed as follows:

$$P(t_1 < t_{b_i} < t_2) = 1 - \alpha$$

$$P\left(t_1 < \frac{b_i - \beta_i}{s_{b_i}} < t_2\right) = 1 - \alpha$$

$$P(s_{b_i}t_1 < b_i - \beta_i < s_{b_i}t_2) = 1 - \alpha$$

$$P(-b_i + s_{b_i}t_1 < -\beta_i < -b_i + s_{b_i}t_2) = 1 - \alpha$$

$$P(b_i - s_{b_i}t_1 > \beta_i > b_i - s_{b_i}t_2) = 1 - \alpha \tag{3.49}$$

Example. Returning to the numerical example in Table 3.1, we may test the hypothesis that there is no relation between food store employment and population, in a randomly selected sample of census tracts. This is equivalent to testing whether $\beta_1 = 0$. We begin by selecting the significance level α and then use it to establish the critical region. For $\alpha = 0.05$, and a t distribution with eight degrees of freedom, we find the boundary points:

$$t_1 = -2.31$$

$$t_2 = 2.31$$

Thus, if the computed t_{b_1} is either less than −2.31 or greater than 2.31, we shall reject the hypothesis at the five percent level of significance. Otherwise, we shall fail to reject it. Substituting in the expression for t_{b_1}

in (3.45), we have

$$t_{b_1} = \frac{b_1 - \beta_1}{s_{b_1}} = \frac{b_1 - 0}{\sqrt{\dfrac{\sum e_i^2}{(n-2)\left(\sum X_i^2 - n\bar{X}^2\right)}}}$$

$$= \frac{7.8571}{\sqrt{\dfrac{198.7428}{8[292 - 10(5)^2]}}} = \frac{7.8571}{\sqrt{0.5915}}$$

$$= 10.22$$

Since the computed value of the test statistic lies in the critical region, we reject the hypothesis that no relation exists between food store employment and population. If the hypothesis were true, the probability of arriving at a value of $t_{b_1} = 10.22$ would be extremely small, occurring on the average only once in over a million experiments.

Alternatively, we may test whether food store employment is directly proportional to total population, that is, $Y = \beta_1 X + \varepsilon$, by testing whether $\beta_0 = 0$. Here we find

$$t_{b_0} = \frac{27.9143}{\sqrt{\dfrac{292\,(198.7429)}{10(8)\,[292 - 10(5)^2]}}} = \frac{27.9143}{\sqrt{17.2717}}$$

$$= 6.72$$

Once again we reject the hypothesis at the five percent level and conclude that food store employment is not simply proportional to total population; that is, the straight line does not go through the origin.

Finally, we may substitute into (3.49) and establish the following 95 percent confidence intervals for β_0 and β_1:

$$18.3474 < \beta_0 < 37.4742$$

and

$$6.0836 < \beta_1 < 9.6306$$

3.1.5 APPLICATION: THE DEMAND FOR HOUSING IN FINLAND

Many factors affect the demand for housing in urban areas and thus, indirectly, the pattern of urban residential land use. Among the most important of these factors is income. All of the studies of housing demand that have been carried out so far show that the consumption of housing is strongly related to income and that increases in housing expenditures accompany increases in income.

Quantitative studies of the demand for housing generally have approached the problem by estimating *consumption functions*, that is, equations that express housing expenditures as functions of personal income. The basic data that have been used in such studies are either time-series or cross-sectional data or, occasionally, both together. The former mainly describe short-run relationships between prices and quantities sold, whereas the latter generally are taken from household budget surveys and are used to describe long-run relationships between expenditures and a set of socio-economic variables, of which the most important is income. The simplest statistical models that have been used to analyze cross-sectional data typically are of the form

$$C = \beta_0 + \beta_1 Y + \varepsilon \tag{3.50}$$

where C denotes personal expenditure and Y personal disposable income.

For example, suppose that we are interested in studying the relationship between housing expenditures and disposable income that existed in Finland in 1955 and have available for such a study the sample data in Columns 2 and 3 of Tables 3.3 and 3.4, respectively. We may postulate the linear

Table 3.3. Housing Expenditures and Occupied Floor Area, Income, and Other Household Characteristics: Single Family Houses, Finland, 1955

Observation Number (1)	Housing Expenditures (in Fmks.) (2)	Disposable Income (in Fmks.) (3)	Permanent Income (in Fmks.) (4)	Household Size (5)	Location (6)	Socio-economic Status (7)	Occupied Housing Floor Area (Sq. Meters) (8)
1	1,220	5,690	4,845	5	2	4	65
2	580	7,470	7,223	2	2	4	24
3	2,090	9,700	7,911	4	2	4	60
4	990	6,490	2,838	4	4	4	50
5	720	4,330	3,490	3	4	1	72
6	930	5,440	4,215	3	4	3	30
7	630	7,000	5,350	3	4	1	32
8	630	7,050	3,087	5	4	3	65
9	480	3,850	3,174	3	4	4	24
10	910	4,910	3,794	5	4	4	50
11	870	5,210	4,267	5	4	4	82
12	540	5,440	4,162	6	4	3	48
13	860	6,330	6,059	3	4	4	70
14	1,490	7,130	5,916	5	4	4	72
15	1,110	6,840	5,581	2	4	4	42
16	660	6,910	5,967	5	4	4	36
17	650	5,590	3,897	4	4	4	40
18	1,480	5,790	5,079	5	4	4	55
19	1,470	7,840	5,750	5	4	2	85

Table 3.3. Housing Expenditures and Occupied Floor Area, Income, and Other Household Characteristics: Single Family Houses, Finland, 1955 (Continued)

Observation Number (1)	Housing Expenditures (in Fmks.) (2)	Disposable Income (in Fmks.) (4)	Permanent Income (in Fmks.) (4)	Household Size (5)	Location (6)	Socioeconomic Status (7)	Occupied Housing Floor Area (Sq. Meters) (8)
20	1,240	10,690	7,238	3	4	4	80
21	1,230	7,060	5,730	5	4	4	64
22	1,250	4,390	3,300	6	4	4	50
23	1,700	5,060	4,316	4	4	4	60
24	1,070	6,820	5,747	4	4	1	56
25	1,880	9,370	7,303	7	4	3	72
26	1,370	5,790	5,256	5	5	4	58
27	1,330	6,260	5,281	5	5	4	66
28	790	7,840	7,482	2	5	4	73
29	1,100	5,280	3,848	6	4	4	42
30	1,020	9,310	3,928	7	4	1	70
31	1,560	5,750	4,950	4	5	4	40
32	1,250	6,370	5,186	3	5	4	32
33	380	3,680	3,350	3	5	4	35
34	540	4,790	4,742	2	5	2	28
35	1,400	5,550	3,945	5	5	4	42
36	500	5,940	4,506	7	5	4	35
37	850	6,210	4,272	7	5	3	48
38	1,170	8,420	6,566	4	5	3	70
39	890	8,680	7,344	3	5	4	42
40	560	2,560	2,538	1	3	4	20
41	440	2,850	2,778	2	3	3	24
42	470	5,420	5,249	3	3	4	52
43	1,640	6,670	5,639	4	3	3	68
44	1,070	6,910	6,336	5	3	1	78
45	1,540	7,720	7,017	5	3	3	83
46	410	2,360	2,270	1	1	4	25
47	1,040	4,870	4,019	4	1	2	54
48	550	5,110	4,373	4	1	4	54
49	1,330	6,190	5,092	3	1	4	36
50	740	7,260	6,845	4	1	4	62
51	750	4,530	4,133	4	4	4	47
52	430	4,630	3,478	4	4	4	42
53	1,420	6,180	4,757	4	4	4	50
54	1,060	7,280	6,331	3	4	4	53
55	1,770	9,110	7,311	3	4	4	61

Source: A budget survey of urban wage and salary earning households in owner-occupied houses or apartments analyzed in Falcke (1969). Data provided by Falcke.

Table 3.4. Housing Expenditures and Occupied Floor Area, Income, and Other Household Characteristics: Apartments, Finland, 1955

Observation Number (1)	Housing Expenditures (in Fmks.) (2)	Disposable Income (in Fmks.) (3)	Permanent Income (in Fmks.) (4)	Household Size (5)	Location (6)	Socioeconomic Status (7)	Occupied Housing Floor Area (Sq. Meters.) (8)
56	450	2,040	1,758	1	2	4	18
57	1,090	3,770	3,493	1	2	2	55
58	1,380	5,580	5,115	4	2	4	48
59	950	5,940	5,894	2	2	3	45
60	790	6,360	5,525	1	2	1	21
61	570	7,220	5,740	3	2	4	33
62	1,420	7,950	7,275	3	2	4	39
63	2,870	9,110	7,368	5	2	1	86
64	2,400	10,120	9,191	4	2	1	72
65	2,720	10,170	8,226	4	2	1	82
66	1,700	11,920	11,255	2	2	1	45
67	2,230	13,340	12,302	2	2	1	75
68	370	2,510	2,482	1	2	2	27
69	710	2,690	2,141	1	2	4	30
70	490	4,620	4,321	2	2	3	25
71	490	5,130	4,097	2	2	4	20
72	500	7,240	6,858	2	2	4	33
73	1,400	9,310	8,936	3	2	4	47
74	720	7,170	7,097	2	2	3	46
75	1,960	8,990	7,616	4	2	1	64
76	350	4,400	4,173	4	4	4	25
77	1,850	6,030	5,009	2	4	4	56
78	1,470	7,680	6,757	3	4	1	36
79	760	4,320	3,882	3	5	4	34
80	2,110	8,720	8,516	3	5	4	80
81	2,250	9,390	8,646	6	5	2	70
82	980	6,670	6,204	2	4	4	26
83	2,090	7,230	6,158	5	4	1	79
84	1,990	9,620	9,558	4	4	1	79
85	1,810	7,990	6,973	2	4	4	54
86	500	6,680	6,467	2	5	4	21
87	1,470	6,050	5,272	4	5	4	30
88	1,810	6,390	5,830	4	5	3	47
89	960	6,870	6,542	3	5	4	12
90	1,110	8,040	7,603	4	5	3	50
91	660	5,210	4,194	3	3	4	24
92	1,380	5,600	4,883	2	3	4	42
93	1,480	7,330	6,867	4	3	4	44
94	1,240	7,450	6,699	3	3	4	36
95	1,290	7,990	6,000	4	3	4	44
96	390	2,510	2,469	1	1	2	27

Table 3.4. Housing Expenditures and Occupied Floor Area, Income, and Other Household Characteristics: Apartments, Finland, 1955 (Continued)

Observation Number	Housing Expenditures (in Fmks.)	Disposable Income (in Fmks.)	Permanent Income (in Fmks.)	Household Size	Location	Socioeconomic Status	Occupied Housing Floor Area (Sq. Meters.)
(1)	(2)	(3)	(4)	(5)	(6)	(7)	(8)
97	460	2,900	2,037	1	1	4	20
98	460	5,680	4,951	5	1	3	38
99	2,090	7,020	5,927	2	1	4	58
100	1,320	3,760	3,060	1	4	2	42
101	1,450	7,870	7,061	3	4	1	61

Source: Same as Table 3.3.

relationship that is defined in (3.50) and find the least squares estimate of that relationship:

$$C = -19.55 + 0.17926Y \tag{3.51}$$

Consider the meaning of (3.51). The intercept term $b_0 = -19.55$ is really quite meaningless, because it implies that if disposable personal income were zero, then housing expenditures would be negative. Since zero values of disposable income were not observed, and because one should not extrapolate beyond observed ranges of the independent variable, we shall ignore this particular parameter estimate and focus exclusively on the estimate of the slope of the straight line. The estimate $b_1 = 0.17926$ tells us that, all other things being equal (or, more exactly, remaining unchanged), we may expect a change of 1,000 Finnish marks in disposable income to be accompanied by a change in the same direction of about 179 marks in the average household's expenditure on housing, when both are measured in 1955 Finnish marks. Thus b_1 is, in the jargon of economists, an estimate of the *marginal propensity to consume* housing as a commodity.

The estimated standard error of b_1 is

$$s_{b_1} = 0.02049$$

and to see whether the slope parameter estimate differs significantly from zero, we may carry out a t test as described in (3.48):

$$t_{b_1} = \frac{0.17926 - 0}{0.02049} = 8.75$$

However, before formulating our null hypothesis and its alternatives, we should consider the economic meaning of the parameter β_1. We would expect that increases in disposable income would lead to increases and not decreases in housing expenditures. Thus, to make economic sense, b_1 should be significantly *greater* than zero and not merely *different* from zero. Hence, we shall test the null hypothesis

$$H_0 : \beta_1 \leq 0$$

against the alternative hypothesis

$$H_1 : \beta_1 > 0$$

Arbitrarily, we select the significance level to be equal to five percent (that is, $\alpha = 0.05$). And, since we have $101 - 2 = 99$ degrees of freedom, the "one-tailed" critical region is the region beyond $t = 1.65$. Since $t_{b_1} = 8.75$, we reject the null hypothesis H_0 in favor of H_1 and conclude that b_1 is significantly greater than zero.

Economists have found that the use of household budget data for the empirical study of consumer demand generally will lead to biased estimates if ordinary regression methods are used. Some of the causes of such biases are statistical in character, and a few of these are identified in Subsection 3.4.4. Others, however, stem from the particular form of the mathematical model that is adopted and the way its variables are measured.

For example, although economists agree that for a given set of prices, the income of a consumer is likely to be the most important single factor determining his demand for durable consumption goods, there is no such clear-cut agreement regarding which particular concept of income is the relevant one. One of the most popular, however, is the notion of *permanent income* proposed by Milton Friedman (1957). Here it is hypothesized that consumers plan their expenditures for durable goods, such as housing, with the recognition that such expenditures will commit them to periodically large outlays of money, and that therefore they will make such expenditure decisions not as a function of their current income, but as a function of what their expectations are regarding the income stream that they may expect in the future.

In Column 4 of Tables 3.3 and 3.4, we find estimates of permanent income, which include only earnings from sources of a permanent, non-transitory nature. Using this measure of income, we may reestimate (3.50) to find

$$C = 120.60 + 0.18608\, Y_p \tag{3.52}$$

Observe that the use of permanent income as the income measure has increased our estimate of the marginal propensity to consume housing. This supports the findings of other housing demand studies [for example, Lee (1968)].

Another finding of housing demand studies, one that is of particular interest to policy-making bodies, concerns the nature of the relationship between changes in personal income and corresponding changes in housing expenditures. The common measure of such relationships is called the *income elasticity of demand* and is defined to be the ratio of a small percentage change in expenditures and an equally small percentage change in personal income. Commodity groups for which the elasticity of demand is less than unity may be classified as "necessities" and are goods for which the demand is *inelastic*. Conversely, commodity groups for which the elasticity of demand is greater than unity may be classified as "luxuries" and are goods for which the demand is *elastic*. There appears to be some agreement among economists that the demand for housing is inelastic or, at most, has unit elasticity. The reader should confirm this finding using the data in Tables 3.3 and 3.4 [Exercise 2(a)]. To do this, he should first notice that a direct measure of elasticity may be found by estimating β_1 in a multiplicative formulation of the consumption function that is linearized by taking logarithms on both sides of the equation.

There is as yet little agreement about the way in which variables other than income contribute to the explanation of housing demand. The lack of accurate data is probably a major cause of this disagreement. The reader should use the additional data provided in Tables 3.3 and 3.4 to test the significance of the explanatory contribution of household size, location,[3] socioeconomic status, and occupied housing floor area [Exercise 2(b)].

3.2 THE ANALYSIS OF VARIANCE

In addition to hypothesis tests about the values of the individual parameters of the simple linear regression model, we also may wish to test the goodness of fit of the model to the data. To do this, we examine the proportion of the total variation of the dependent variable, Y, about its sample mean, $\bar{Y}$, that can be accounted for, or "explained," by the fitted regression equation, $b_0 + b_1 X$.

3.2.1 THE COEFFICIENT OF DETERMINATION

Recalling that the sample variance of Y, *the variance about the mean*, is $\sum(Y_i - \bar{Y})^2/n$ and that the variance of the residual from the regression line, *the variance about the regression*, is $\sum e_i^2/n$, we may construct the following ratio:

$$\frac{\text{"unexplained" variance}}{\text{total variance}} = \frac{\sum e_i^2/n}{\sum(Y_i - \bar{Y})^2/n} = \frac{\sum(Y_i - \hat{Y}_i)^2}{\sum(Y_i - \bar{Y})^2}$$

$$= \frac{\text{"unexplained" sum of squares}}{\text{total sum of squares}}$$

[3] The 101 observations were selected from 18 cities and towns in five major locations in Finland: (1) Turku; (2) Helsinki; (3) Tampere; (4) other small towns; and (5) other middle-sized cities.

Note that this ratio defines the proportion of the total variance that is *not* accounted for by the regression function. Hence,

$$1 - \frac{\text{“unexplained” sum of squares}}{\text{total sum of squares}} = 1 - \frac{\sum e_i^2}{\sum (Y_i - \bar{Y})^2}$$
$$= \frac{\sum (Y_i - \bar{Y})^2 - \sum (Y_i - \hat{Y}_i)^2}{\sum (Y_i - \bar{Y})^2}$$
$$= \frac{\text{“explained” sum of squares}}{\text{total sum of squares}}$$
$$= r^2 \tag{3.53}$$

denotes the proportion of total variance that *is* accounted for by the linear regression model. This proportion is commonly referred to as the *coefficient of determination* and is denoted by r^2, since it is equal to the square of the *coefficient of correlation, r.*

A computationally more convenient form of r^2 may be derived by partitioning the total sum of squares, $\sum (Y_i - \bar{Y})^2$, into “unexplained” and “explained” components, as follows:

$$\sum (Y_i - \bar{Y})^2 = \sum [Y_i - \hat{Y}_i - b_1(X_i - \bar{X})]^2 \qquad \text{by (3.17)}$$
$$= \sum (Y_i - \hat{Y}_i)^2 + b_1^2 \sum (X_i - \bar{X})^2$$
$$- 2b_1 \sum (Y_i - \hat{Y}_i)(X_i - \bar{X}) \tag{3.54}$$

Since

$$-2b_1 \sum (Y_i - \hat{Y}_i)(X_i - \bar{X})$$
$$= -2b_1 \sum [Y_i - \bar{Y} - b_1(X_i - \bar{X})](X_i - \bar{X}) \qquad \text{by (3.17)}$$
$$= -2b_1 \sum [(X_i - \bar{X})(Y_i - \bar{Y}) - b_1 (X_i - \bar{X})^2]$$
$$= -2b_1 \left[\sum (X_i - \bar{X})(Y_i - \bar{Y}) - b_1 \sum (X_i - \bar{X})^2\right]$$
$$= -2b_1 [b_1 \sum (X_i - \bar{X})^2 - b_1 \sum (X_i - \bar{X})^2] \qquad \text{by (3.16)}$$
$$= 0$$

we may then rewrite (3.54) as

$$\sum (Y_i - \bar{Y})^2 = \sum (Y_i - \hat{Y}_i)^2 + b_1^2 \sum (X_i - \bar{X})^2 \tag{3.55}$$
$$= \sum (Y_i - \hat{Y}_i)^2 + \sum (\hat{Y}_i - \bar{Y})^2 \tag{3.56}$$

by (3.17), or

$$\begin{pmatrix}\text{total sum}\\ \text{of squares}\end{pmatrix} = \begin{pmatrix}\text{“unexplained”}\\ \text{sum of squares}\end{pmatrix} + \begin{pmatrix}\text{“explained” sum}\\ \text{of squares}\end{pmatrix}$$

or, more accurately,

$$\begin{pmatrix}\text{total}\\ \text{sum of squares}\\ \text{about the mean:}\\ SS_T\end{pmatrix} = \begin{pmatrix}\text{error}\\ \text{sum of squares}\\ \text{about regression:}\\ SS_E\end{pmatrix} + \begin{pmatrix}\text{model}\\ \text{sum of squares}\\ \text{due to regression:}\\ SS_M\end{pmatrix}$$

Returning to our definition of r^2 in (3.53), and substituting in (3.55) for $\sum (Y_i - \bar{Y})^2$ in the numerator, we have the more common expression for the coefficient of determination:

$$r^2 = \frac{\sum (Y_i - \hat{Y}_i)^2 + b_1^2 \sum (X_i - \bar{X})^2 - \sum (Y_i - \hat{Y}_i)^2}{\sum (Y_i - \bar{Y})^2}$$

$$= \frac{b_1^2 \sum (X_i - \bar{X})^2}{\sum (Y_i - \bar{Y})^2} = \frac{\sum (\hat{Y}_i - \bar{Y})^2}{\sum (Y_i - \bar{Y})^2} \tag{3.57}$$

$$= \frac{\text{model sum of squares due to regression}}{\text{total sum of squares about the mean}} = \frac{SS_M}{SS_T} \tag{3.58}$$

or, alternatively,

$$r^2 = \frac{b_1 \sum (X_i - \bar{X})(Y_i - \bar{Y})}{\sum (Y_i - \bar{Y})^2} \tag{3.59}$$

$$= \frac{b_1 [\sum X_i Y_i - n\bar{X}\bar{Y}]}{\sum Y_i^2 - n\bar{Y}^2} \tag{3.60}$$

3.2.2 THE F STATISTIC

The partitioning of the total sum of squares, described in (3.55), may be used to establish an analysis of variance test for the goodness of fit of the regression model. We begin by recalling that

$$b_1 \text{ is NORMAL} \left[\beta_1, \frac{\sigma^2}{\sum (X_i - \bar{X})^2} \right]$$

Hence

$$\frac{(b_1 - \beta_1)\sqrt{\sum (X_i - \bar{X})^2}}{\sigma} \text{ is NORMAL (0,1)}$$

and, by (3.41),

$$\frac{(b_1 - \beta_1)^2 \sum (X_i - \bar{X})^2}{\sigma^2}$$

has a χ^2 distribution with one degree of freedom. Similarly, since

$$e_i \text{ is NORMAL } (0, \sigma^2),$$

$$\frac{e_i}{\sigma} \text{ is NORMAL (0, 1)}$$

and, by (3.41),

$$\frac{\sum e_i^2}{\sigma^2}$$

has a χ^2 distribution with $n - 2$ degrees of freedom. Since the latter distribution is independent of the former, we may use (3.43) to establish that

$$F = \frac{(b_1 - \beta_1)^2 \sum (X_i - \bar{X})^2 / 1}{\sum e_i^2 / (n - 2)} \tag{3.61}$$

has an F distribution with $(1, n-2)$ degrees of freedom. If $\beta_1 = 0$, then (3.61) reduces to

$$F = \frac{b_1^2 \sum (X_i - \bar{X})^2/1}{\sum (Y_i - \hat{Y}_i)^2/(n-2)} = \frac{SS_M/1}{SS_E/(n-2)} \tag{3.62}$$

and we may test the hypothesis of no relationship between Y and X (that is, $\beta_1 = 0$) by computing the F value using (3.62) and rejecting the hypothesis if the computed statistic lies in the critical region predefined by a specified level of significance, α.

The results of the computations may be set out in an analysis of variance table of the following form:

Source of Variation	Degrees of Freedom	Sum of Squares	Mean Square	F Ratio
Total (corrected for mean)	$n-1$	$SS_T = \Sigma(Y_i - \bar{Y})^2$ $= \Sigma Y_i^2 - n\bar{Y}^2$		
Model	1	$SS_M = b_1^2 \Sigma(X_i - \bar{X})^2$	$SS_M/1$	$\frac{SS_M/1}{SS_E/(n-2)}$
Error	$n-2$	$SS_E = \Sigma(Y_i - \hat{Y}_i)^2$ $= \Sigma e_i^2$	$SS_E/(n-2)$	

Alternative computational formulas for the model sum of squares due to regression are

$$\begin{aligned} SS_M = b_1^2 \sum (X_i - \bar{X})^2 &= b_1 \sum [(X_i - \bar{X})(Y_i - \bar{Y})] \\ &= b_1 \left[\sum X_i Y_i - n\bar{X}\bar{Y}\right] \qquad (3.63) \\ &= r^2 \sum (Y_i - \bar{Y})^2 \qquad (3.64) \end{aligned}$$

The error sum of squares is generally found by subtraction: $SS_E = SS_T - SS_M$.

A more general form of the analysis of variance table is one which incorporates the "correction for the mean" factor, $n\bar{Y}^2$, into the table and attributes it to the intercept term, b_0.

Source of Variation	Degrees of Freedom	Sum of Squares
Total (uncorrected for mean)	n	ΣY_i^2
Correction for the Mean (b_0)	1	$n\bar{Y}^2$
Total (corrected for mean)	$n-1$	$SS_T = \Sigma Y_i^2 - n\bar{Y}^2$
Model ($b_1 \mid b_0$)	1	$SS_M = b_1^2 \Sigma(X_i - \bar{X})^2$
Error	$n-2$	$SS_E = \Sigma e_i^2$

It should be noted that, in the particular case of fitting a straight line, the F statistic for testing the significance of the model is identical to the t statistic for testing the hypothesis that $\beta_1=0$. Recalling (3.48), we have that

$$F = \frac{b_1^2 \sum (X_i - \bar{X})^2}{\sum e_i^2/(n-2)} = \frac{b_1^2}{\sum e_i^2/(n-2)\,(\sum X_i^2 - n\bar{X}^2)} = t_{b_1}^2$$

Since the square of a t variable with n degrees of freedom is an F variable with $(1, n)$ degrees of freedom, the two tests are equivalent. This equivalence, however, exists only in simple linear regression. When more independent variables are introduced into the model, the F test of the significance of the model no longer corresponds to the t test of a coefficient.

Example. Returning once more to the numerical example of Table 3.1, we may derive the following analysis of variance table:

Source of Variation	Degrees of Freedom	Sum of Squares	Mean Square	F Ratio
Total (uncorrected for mean)	10	47,950.00		
Correction for the Mean (b_0)	1	45,158.40		
Total (corrected for mean)	9	2,791.60		
Model ($b_1 \mid b_0$)	1	2,592.86	2,592.86	104.37
Error	8	198.74	24.84	

In the above analysis of variance table, we see that the F statistic is 104.37, with (1,8) degrees of freedom. To test the significance of the model (in this case, whether $\beta_1 = 0$), we define a critical region in the probability distribution of the F statistic. If the computed F statistic falls inside this region, we reject the hypothesis; otherwise, we fail to reject the hypothesis. As in the case of the t test, failure to reject a hypothesis does not imply acceptance of the hypothesis.

If we look up the percentage points of the F distribution with one and eight degrees of freedom, we find that at the five percent level of significance (that is, $\alpha = 0.05$), the boundary point is 5.32. Since the calculated F ratio exceeds this value, we reject the hypothesis that no relation exists between the dependent and independent variables.

Notice that our computed value for the F ratio is the square of our earlier computed value for the t_{b_1} statistic:

$$F = 104.37 = (10.22)^2 = t_{b_1}{}^2$$

The computed values entered in the analysis of variance table also allow us to conveniently calculate the coefficient of determination, r^2. From (3.58), we have

$$r^2 = \frac{SS_M}{SS_T}$$

whence

$$r^2 = \frac{2{,}592.8571}{2{,}791.6000}$$
$$= 0.9288$$

Multiplying this value by 100, we are able to state that the regression model accounts for, or "explains," about 93 percent of the total variation in the dependent variable.

3.2.3 RELATIONSHIPS BETWEEN REGRESSION AND CORRELATION STATISTICS

Notice that the F test also tests the significance of r^2 (and of r), since the F statistic is readily transformed into a statistic involving only r^2 and the associated degrees of freedom. First, we establish from (3.53) that

$$r^2 \sum (Y_i - \bar{Y})^2 = \sum (Y_i - \bar{Y})^2 - \sum (Y_i - \hat{Y}_i)^2$$

and

$$\sum (Y_i - \hat{Y}_i)^2 = (1 - r^2) \sum (Y_i - \bar{Y})^2 \tag{3.65}$$

Next, recalling that

$$F = \frac{b_1^2 \sum (X_i - \bar{X})^2/1}{\sum (Y_i - \hat{Y}_i)^2/(n-2)}$$

we have, by (3.64) and (3.65),

$$F = \frac{r^2(\sum Y_i - \bar{Y})^2/1}{(1 - r^2) \sum (Y_i - \bar{Y})^2/(n-2)}$$

or

$$F = \frac{r^2/1}{(1 - r^2)/(n-2)} \tag{3.66}$$

This test is equivalent to the standard t test for the significance of an observed correlation between X and Y. The t test for the significance of r is performed by computing

$$t = \frac{r}{\sqrt{(1 - r^2)/(n-2)}} \tag{3.67}$$

but

$$F = \frac{r^2/1}{(1 - r^2)/(n-2)} = t^2$$

Another interesting linkage between correlation analysis and regression analysis may be established by recalling the definition of the coefficient of correlation, r. Reference to any standard text on statistical analysis will provide the following definition:

$$r = \frac{\sum (X_i - \bar{X})(Y_i - \bar{Y})}{\sqrt{[\sum (X_i - \bar{X})^2][\sum (Y_i - \bar{Y})^2]}} \tag{3.68}$$

From (3.16), we have that

$$b_1 = \frac{\sum (X_i - \bar{X})(Y_i - \bar{Y})}{\sum (X_i - \bar{X})^2}$$

and, by substitution into (3.68),

$$r = \frac{b_1 \sum (X_i - \bar{X})^2}{\sqrt{[\sum (X_i - \bar{X})^2][\sum (Y_i - \bar{Y})^2]}} = b_1 \frac{\sqrt{\sum (X_i - \bar{X})^2}}{\sqrt{\sum (Y_i - \bar{Y})^2}}$$

or

$$b_1 = \frac{\sqrt{\sum (Y_i - \bar{Y})^2}}{\sqrt{\sum (X_i - \bar{X})^2}}\, r \tag{3.69}$$

Notice that squaring both sides and multiplying both sides by $\sum (X_i - \bar{X})^2$ yields (3.64). Thus the square of the correlation coefficient is indeed equal to the coefficient of determination.

3.2.4 APPLICATION: MODEL LIFE TABLES

Demographic analyses carried out in most parts of the world are seriously impaired by the general lack of accurate data on mortality, fertility, and migration. Not only is the quality of available data frequently suspect, but its historic and geographic coverage generally is very limited. Thus, demographers have sought to use the regularities exhibited by such data to develop *model tables* that reflect the generalized experience in various parts of the world. Mortality data have been found to be particularly susceptible to this form of analysis, since in virtually every population for which mortality data are available, death rates fall regularly from birth to age five and rise after age 30.

A *model life table* is the result of an attempt to systematically approximate the mortality schedule of a region by resorting to the mortality experience in other regions with populations that may be presumed to be similar to the one being analyzed. The most common method for incorporating the mortality experience of more than one region, or more than one time period for the same region, is by means of regression, and several studies have used this method to develop model life tables for use in situations where accurate observed data are unavailable [Coale and Demeny (1966), United Nations (1955) and (1967)]. For example, consider the

Table 3.5. Probabilities of Dying by Age and Expectation of Life at Birth for Males in 12 Asian Countries

Age at Last Birthday	Indonesia 1961 $e_0=41.704$	China (Mainland) 1953 $e_0=43.554$	Pakistan 1961 $e_0=44.378$	India 1961 $e_0=46.024$	Korea 1960 $e_0=$ 54.799	Philippines 1960 $e_0=55.398$
0	0.174934	0.163286	0.156262	0.146107	0.095528	0.108383
1	0.095685	0.088979	0.083561	0.075798	0.041253	0.057026
5	0.025932	0.024072	0.023255	0.021466	0.013044	0.015392
10	0.019370	0.017932	0.017232	0.015872	0.009872	0.009433
15	0.027419	0.025362	0.024589	0.023029	0.015221	0.011836
20	0.038741	0.035909	0.034786	0.032631	0.021524	0.017342
25	0.042726	0.039601	0.038199	0.035872	0.023206	0.021608
30	0.049081	0.045493	0.043887	0.041043	0.026456	0.025625
35	0.058040	0.053765	0.052000	0.048738	0.031966	0.030093
40	0.071293	0.066016	0.064159	0.060285	0.040978	0.038796
45	0.086270	0.080000	0.078550	0.074269	0.053629	0.047719
50	0.112722	0.104472	0.103451	0.098266	0.074342	0.064916
55	0.144532	0.134401	0.134713	0.129096	0.103056	0.090195
60	0.199084	0.186125	0.187020	0.180122	0.148526	0.112367
65	0.268526	0.251736	0.254721	0.246828	0.210688	0.169623
70	0.366225	0.344846	0.350723	0.342019	0.300940	0.227115
75	0.494574	0.469097	0.477971	0.468195	0.423661	0.332206
80	0.638325	0.640840	0.641943	0.637523	0.621591	0.415464
85+	1.000000	1.000000	1.000000	1.000000	1.000000	1.000000
Age at Last Birthday	**Thailand 1960 $e_0=58.385$**	**Ceylon 1953 $e_0=58.993$**	**Japan 1950–52 $e_0=59.417$**	**China (Taiwan) 1956 $e_0=60.151$**	**Ceylon 1962 $e_0=$ 64.105**	**Japan 1963 $e_0=67.287$**
0	0.083387	0.090171	0.056760	0.033874	0.043942	0.025717
1	0.044219	0.062222	0.030005	0.036375	0.032360	0.007191
5	0.016956	0.014766	0.009962	0.007755	0.010213	0.003913
10	0.010787	0.006561	0.005143	0.005654	0.006227	0.002510
15	0.011079	0.008487	0.010175	0.007272	0.007414	0.004926
20	0.014491	0.010059	0.019184	0.014145	0.008002	0.008150
25	0.015913	0.012039	0.022151	0.012685	0.008879	0.009339
30	0.020140	0.014143	0.022352	0.016474	0.011388	0.010693
35	0.028214	0.019004	0.024458	0.022070	0.014928	0.013855
40	0.037263	0.023693	0.031107	0.030646	0.019898	0.019156
45	0.050563	0.034771	0.043426	0.046136	0.029477	0.028904
50	0.066114	0.045255	0.061995	0.072618	0.041506	0.045213
55	0.085284	0.070825	0.094364	0.111741	0.075965	0.074252
60	0.124183	0.103194	0.142914	0.173104	0.115000	0.117731
65	0.160892	0.153093	0.227709	0.253898	0.169096	0.183299
70	0.234381	0.233722	0.323984	0.390641	0.261686	0.281891
75	0.306091	0.329700	0.429797	0.513917	0.352703	0.417332
80	0.430516	0.477931	0.561531	0.744367	0.399438	0.571421
85+	1.000000	1.000000	1.000000	1.000000	1.000000	1.000000

Source: Keyfitz and Flieger (1968). By permission of the University of Chicago Press. Because Keyfitz and Flieger's method of life table construction differs slightly from ours, their expectations of life at birth also differ slightly from those that would be derived using the procedures set out in Subsection 1.5.7.

Table 3.6. Probabilities of Dying by Age and Expectation of Life at Birth for Females in 12 Asian Countries

Age at Last Birth-day	Indonesia 1961 e_0=42.093	China (Mainland) 1953 e_0=44.010	Pakistan 1961 e_0=42.447	India 1961 e_0=44.033	Korea 1960 e_0= 55.691	Philippines 1960 e_0=58.676
0	0.164496	0.153427	0.161895	0.152057	0.090641	0.086431
1	0.106870	0.099436	0.105174	0.097765	0.048308	0.053056
5	0.030021	0.027782	0.029938	0.027892	0.014815	0.012584
10	0.024158	0.022371	0.023816	0.022209	0.011785	0.006991
15	0.032194	0.029815	0.031826	0.029740	0.016867	0.008236
20	0.040570	0.037611	0.040086	0.037532	0.021964	0.012549
25	0.045715	0.042368	0.045117	0.042280	0.025092	0.017306
30	0.051720	0.047896	0.051002	0.047880	0.028482	0.023848
35	0.057294	0.053079	0.056510	0.053178	0.032340	0.029452
40	0.062777	0.058171	0.061911	0.058482	0.037027	0.033414
45	0.070326	0.065196	0.069409	0.065946	0.044358	0.040857
50	0.092470	0.085621	0.091109	0.087443	0.060201	0.053945
55	0.120010	0.111318	0.118496	0.113339	0.081622	0.080379
60	0.174007	0.162174	0.171879	0.164861	0.121702	0.103601
65	0.237347	0.221805	0.234559	0.228009	0.176895	0.143242
70	0.339074	0.318041	0.335172	0.325425	0.265926	0.223277
75	0.464498	0.438882	0.459906	0.449826	0.386228	0.306536
80	0.631123	0.618764	0.623709	0.632763	0.587595	0.411391
85+	1.000000	1.000000	1.000000	1.000000	1.000000	1.000000
Age at Last Birth-day	**Thailand 1960 e_0=63.756**	**Ceylon 1953 e_0=58.181**	**Japan 1950–52 e_0=62.747**	**China (Taiwan) 1956 e_0=64.781**	**Ceylon 1962 e_0= 64.425**	**Japan 1963 e_0=72.430**
0	0.062976	0.074249	0.050008	0.030689	0.036769	0.020855
1	0.040547	0.074670	0.029766	0.039245	0.037911	0.005604
5	0.015481	0.017373	0.008802	0.006362	0.011519	0.002502
10	0.008742	0.007098	0.005104	0.004111	0.006105	0.001537
15	0.009942	0.011487	0.009682	0.005997	0.008800	0.002655
20	0.014906	0.017751	0.017070	0.009219	0.011933	0.004746
25	0.017561	0.021630	0.020060	0.011456	0.013476	0.005894
30	0.021025	0.022088	0.020795	0.015094	0.017253	0.007039
35	0.027438	0.026560	0.022391	0.019164	0.020024	0.009306
40	0.032257	0.025677	0.026082	0.024895	0.019217	0.012866
45	0.034706	0.033480	0.034456	0.029552	0.027164	0.019352
50	0.043636	0.042252	0.046726	0.047562	0.036423	0.029014
55	0.054500	0.060596	0.066812	0.062632	0.059441	0.044350
60	0.080936	0.087384	0.100067	0.100968	0.092019	0.068371
65	0.110027	0.146208	0.161787	0.160841	0.150544	0.115458
70	0.170410	0.231617	0.245193	0.254209	0.236393	0.193704
75	0.228546	0.320457	0.351283	0.366360	0.311991	0.319824
80	0.340616	0.507813	0.503868	0.568678	0.421816	0.482689
85+	1.000000	1.000000	1.000000	1.000000	1.000000	1.000000

Source: Same as Table 3.5.

Table 3.7. Regressions of Probabilities of Dying by Age on Expectation of Life at Birth for 12 Asian Countries

Age at Last Birthday	Males				Females			
k	b_0	b_1	r^2	F	b_0	b_1	r^2	F
0	0.42208	−0.00594	0.9410	159.46	0.37767	−0.00512	0.9734	366.10
1	0.21868	−0.00301	0.8924	82.92	0.23882	−0.00316	0.9386	152.96
5	0.05782	−0.00078	0.8978	87.83	0.06720	−0.00089	0.9389	153.75
10	0.04594	−0.00065	0.9449	171.56	0.05701	−0.00080	0.9497	188.72
15	0.06572	−0.00094	0.9696	319.24	0.07530	−0.00105	0.9582	229.00
20	0.09178	−0.00129	0.9491	186.36	0.09138	−0.00123	0.9605	242.94
25	0.10116	−0.00142	0.9486	184.65	0.10169	−0.00136	0.9744	381.34
30	0.11527	−0.00161	0.9697	320.09	0.11347	−0.00150	0.9840	615.12
35	0.13320	−0.00184	0.9774	433.55	0.12266	−0.00158	0.9804	501.08
40	0.15983	−0.00216	0.9698	320.89	0.13152	−0.00167	0.9533	204.21
45	0.18138	−0.00233	0.9592	235.13	0.14136	−0.00173	0.9746	383.17
50	0.22627	−0.00279	0.9106	101.79	0.18115	−0.00216	0.9532	203.86
55	0.25708	−0.00281	0.8353	50.71	0.22583	−0.00258	0.9547	210.83
60	0.32844	−0.00329	0.6654	19.88	0.32008	−0.00358	0.9364	147.17
65	0.40546	−0.00354	0.4961	9.84	0.40393	−0.00410	0.8767	71.11
70	0.49397	−0.00347	0.2768*	3.83*	0.53724	−0.00491	0.8290	48.46
75	0.65562	−0.00436	0.2741*	3.78*	0.70196	−0.00597	0.7006	23.40
80	0.88328	−0.00584	0.2062*	2.60*	0.91786	−0.00696	0.5413	11.80

* Not significant at the five percent level.
Source: Calculated using the data in Tables 3.5 and 3.6. Computed by Ervin Bell and Guenter Herrmann.

Table 3.8. Probabilities of Dying by Age for Males in India and Japan: Observed and Predicted

Age at Last Birthday	India 1961 (e_0 = 46.024)			Japan 1963 (e_0 = 67.287)		
	Observed	Predicted	Deviation	Observed	Predicted	Deviation
0	0.1461	0.1486	−0.0025	0.0257	0.0223	0.0034
1	0.0758	0.0801	−0.0043	0.0072	0.0161	−0.0089
5	0.0215	0.0221	−0.0007	0.0039	0.0057	−0.0018
10	0.0159	0.0161	−0.0002	0.0025	0.0023	0.0003
15	0.0230	0.0227	0.0004	0.0049	0.0028	0.0021
20	0.0326	0.0322	0.0004	0.0082	0.0047	0.0034
25	0.0359	0.0356	0.0003	0.0093	0.0053	0.0040
30	0.0410	0.0409	0.0001	0.0107	0.0066	0.0041
35	0.0487	0.0487	0.0001	0.0139	0.0096	0.0042
40	0.0603	0.0603	0.0000	0.0192	0.0143	0.0048
45	0.0743	0.0742	0.0000	0.0289	0.0247	0.0042
50	0.0983	0.0979	0.0003	0.0452	0.0386	0.0066
55	0.1291	0.1279	0.0012	0.0743	0.0682	0.0061
60	0.1801	0.1771	0.0031	0.1177	0.1071	0.0106
65	0.2468	0.2426	0.0043	0.1833	0.1673	0.0160
70	0.3420	0.3343	0.0077	0.2819	0.2606	0.0213
75	0.4682	0.4550	0.0132	0.4173	0.3623	0.0551
80	0.6375	0.6146	0.0229	0.5714	0.4905	0.0809
Sum of Absolute Deviations			0.0616	Sum of Absolute Deviations		0.2378

Source: Same as Table 3.7.

mortality data for males and females in a dozen Asian countries that are presented in Tables 3.5 and 3.6. We may obtain a family of life tables by linearly regressing these observed probabilities of dying at each age, ${}_xq_k$, on the expectation of life at birth, e_0, and then using these estimated regression equations to derive a set of ${}_xq_k$ for any value of e_0. Thus, for ${}_1q_0$, we find

$$ {}_1q_0 = 0.42208 - 0.00594e_0 $$

for males and

$$ {}_1q_0 = 0.37767 - 0.00512e_0 $$

for females. The complete age- and sex-specific results are presented in Table 3.7. To test the quality of approximation that is afforded by these regression equations, we may refer to the coefficients of determination and the F statistics that appear alongside them and, for the two specific cases of Indian and Japanese males, may consider the matter further by comparing the predicted and observed values of ${}_xq_k$ that appear in Table 3.8.

A quick glance at Tables 3.7 and 3.8 reveals that the quality of fit is quite good for the early age groups, but declines with increasing age to the extent that the fit of the model to the last three male age groups is not significant at the five percent level. The reader should confirm that improved results for older age groups may be obtained by regressing the ${}_xq_k$ on the expectation of life at 10 years of age, rather than at birth [Exercise 3(a)], and also that more accurate fits may be obtained for the younger and older age groups by applying logarithmic transformations [Exercise 3(b)].

3.3 THE GENERAL MULTIPLE LINEAR REGRESSION MODEL

Having considered the simple linear regression model in which a dependent variable, Y, is expressed as a linear function of an independent variable, X, we now extend this model to include the general case where the dependent variable, Y, is expressed as a linear function of k independent variables, $X_1, X_2, \ldots, X_k$. We begin with the linear model

$$Y_i = \beta_0 + \beta_1 X_{1i} + \beta_2 X_{2i} + \cdots + \beta_k X_{ki} + \varepsilon_i \quad (i = 1, 2, \ldots, n) \tag{3.70}$$

The β coefficients and the parameters of the distribution of the error term, ε, are unknown. The problem is to obtain estimates of these unknowns and then to test the significance of the result. As in simple linear regression, hypotheses concerning the values of the individual parameters may be tested by the t test, and the significance of the model may be tested by the F test.

To simplify the development of the general multiple linear regression model, we adopt matrix notation and express the n equations in (3.70) as

$$\mathbf{y} = \mathbf{X}\boldsymbol{\beta} + \boldsymbol{\varepsilon} \tag{3.71}$$

where

$$\mathbf{y} = \begin{bmatrix} Y_1 \\ Y_2 \\ \vdots \\ Y_n \end{bmatrix} \qquad \boldsymbol{\beta} = \begin{bmatrix} \beta_0 \\ \beta_1 \\ \vdots \\ \beta_k \end{bmatrix} \qquad \boldsymbol{\varepsilon} = \begin{bmatrix} \varepsilon_1 \\ \varepsilon_2 \\ \vdots \\ \varepsilon_n \end{bmatrix}$$

$$\mathbf{X} = \begin{bmatrix} 1 & X_{11} & X_{21} & \cdots & X_{k1} \\ 1 & X_{12} & X_{22} & \cdots & X_{k2} \\ \vdots & \vdots & \vdots & & \vdots \\ 1 & X_{1n} & X_{2n} & \cdots & X_{kn} \end{bmatrix}$$

Notice that the subscripts in the **X** matrix follow the reverse of the normal pattern where the first subscript usually refers to the row, and the second to the column, of the matrix.

3.3.1 ASSUMPTIONS

Before proceeding with the development of least squares parameter estimation, we state in matrix form the assumptions previously outlined in (3.3), (3.4), and (3.5):

$$E(\boldsymbol{\varepsilon}) = \mathbf{0} \tag{3.72}$$

$$E(\boldsymbol{\varepsilon}\boldsymbol{\varepsilon}') = \sigma^2\mathbf{I} \tag{3.73}$$

$$\mathbf{X} \text{ is an array of fixed numbers} \tag{3.74}$$

In addition, we need the assumption that **X** has *rank* $k + 1 < n$, that is,[4]

$$\operatorname{rank}(\mathbf{X}) = k + 1 < n \tag{3.75}$$

Assumption (3.75) merits further discussion. The assumption that the rank is less than n simply ensures that we have more observations than parameters. The restriction that the rank should equal $k + 1$ implies that the $k + 1$ columns of the matrix **X** are linearly independent of one another. This is a necessary condition for inverting the matrix $\mathbf{X}'\mathbf{X}$ in the least squares estimation procedure described below.

3.3.2 DERIVATION OF THE LEAST SQUARES ESTIMATOR

To derive the least squares estimator, **b**, say, of the vector of regression coefficients, $\boldsymbol{\beta}$, we introduce the vector of residuals, **e**, and express the fitted regression model as

$$\mathbf{y} = \mathbf{X}\mathbf{b} + \mathbf{e} \tag{3.76}$$

where

$$\mathbf{b} = \begin{bmatrix} b_0 \\ b_1 \\ \vdots \\ b_k \end{bmatrix} \qquad \mathbf{e} = \begin{bmatrix} e_1 \\ e_2 \\ \vdots \\ e_n \end{bmatrix}$$

The sum of the squared residuals is

$$\begin{aligned} \sum e_i^2 &= \mathbf{e}'\mathbf{e} \\ &= (\mathbf{y} - \mathbf{X}\mathbf{b})'(\mathbf{y} - \mathbf{X}\mathbf{b}) \\ &= \mathbf{y}'\mathbf{y} - 2\mathbf{b}'\mathbf{X}'\mathbf{y} + \mathbf{b}'\mathbf{X}'\mathbf{X}\mathbf{b} \end{aligned} \tag{3.77}$$

since $\mathbf{b}'\mathbf{X}'\mathbf{y}$ is a scalar and therefore equal to its transpose, $\mathbf{y}'\mathbf{X}\mathbf{b}$. To find the particular vector **b** that minimizes $\mathbf{e}'\mathbf{e}$, we differentiate (3.77) with respect to **b** and set the result equal to **0**:

[4] The rank of a matrix is equal to the number of linearly independent column vectors that it contains. These concepts and their uses are discussed in Chapter 4.

$$\frac{\partial}{\partial \mathbf{b}} \mathbf{e}'\mathbf{e} = -2\mathbf{X}'\mathbf{y} + 2\mathbf{X}'\mathbf{X}\mathbf{b} = \mathbf{0}$$

which reduces to the *normal equations*

$$\mathbf{X}'\mathbf{X}\mathbf{b} = \mathbf{X}'\mathbf{y} \tag{3.78}$$

and, using assumption (3.75),

$$\mathbf{b} = (\mathbf{X}'\mathbf{X})^{-1}\mathbf{X}'\mathbf{y} \tag{3.79}$$

Example. We may illustrate the application of this fundamental result by considering, once again, the simple linear regression model of (3.2):

$$Y_1 = \beta_0 + \beta_1 X_i + \varepsilon_i \qquad (i = 1, 2, \ldots, n)$$

or, in matrix notation,

$$\mathbf{y} = \mathbf{X}\boldsymbol{\beta} + \boldsymbol{\varepsilon}$$

where

$$\mathbf{y} = \begin{bmatrix} Y_1 \\ Y_2 \\ \vdots \\ Y_n \end{bmatrix} \qquad \mathbf{X} = \begin{bmatrix} 1 & X_1 \\ 1 & X_2 \\ \vdots & \vdots \\ 1 & X_n \end{bmatrix} \qquad \boldsymbol{\beta} = \begin{bmatrix} \beta_0 \\ \beta_1 \end{bmatrix} \qquad \boldsymbol{\varepsilon} = \begin{bmatrix} \varepsilon_1 \\ \varepsilon_2 \\ \vdots \\ \varepsilon_n \end{bmatrix}$$

Using (3.78), we have

$$\begin{bmatrix} 1 & 1 & \cdots & 1 \\ X_1 & X_2 & \cdots & X_n \end{bmatrix} \begin{bmatrix} 1 & X_1 \\ 1 & X_2 \\ \vdots & \vdots \\ 1 & X_n \end{bmatrix} \begin{bmatrix} b_0 \\ b_1 \end{bmatrix} = \begin{bmatrix} 1 & 1 & \cdots & 1 \\ X_1 & X_2 & \cdots & X_n \end{bmatrix} \begin{bmatrix} Y_1 \\ Y_2 \\ \vdots \\ Y_n \end{bmatrix}$$

and, therefore,

$$\begin{bmatrix} b_0 \\ b_1 \end{bmatrix} = \begin{bmatrix} n & \sum X_i \\ \sum X_i & \sum X_i^2 \end{bmatrix}^{-1} \begin{bmatrix} \sum Y_i \\ \sum X_i Y_i \end{bmatrix}$$

$$= \frac{1}{n \sum X_i^2 - (\sum X_i)^2} \begin{bmatrix} \sum X_i^2 & -\sum X_i \\ -\sum X_i & n \end{bmatrix} \begin{bmatrix} \sum Y_i \\ \sum X_i Y_i \end{bmatrix}$$

$$= \begin{bmatrix} \dfrac{\sum X_i^2 \sum Y_i - \sum X_i \sum X_i Y_i}{n \sum X_i^2 - (\sum X_i)^2} \\ \\ \dfrac{n \sum X_i Y_i - \sum X_i \sum Y_i}{n \sum X_i^2 - (\sum X_i)^2} \end{bmatrix}$$

a result we first set out in (3.13) and (3.14).

3.3.3 PROPERTIES OF THE LEAST SQUARES ESTIMATOR

To establish the mean and variance of **b**, we substitute (3.71) into (3.79) to find

$$\mathbf{b} = (\mathbf{X}'\mathbf{X})^{-1}\mathbf{X}'(\mathbf{X}\boldsymbol{\beta} + \boldsymbol{\varepsilon})$$
$$= \boldsymbol{\beta} + (\mathbf{X}'\mathbf{X})^{-1}\mathbf{X}'\boldsymbol{\varepsilon} \tag{3.80}$$

since $(\mathbf{X}'\mathbf{X})^{-1}(\mathbf{X}'\mathbf{X}) = \mathbf{I}$. Taking expected values of both sides, we have

$$E(\mathbf{b}) = E(\boldsymbol{\beta}) + E[(\mathbf{X}'\mathbf{X})^{-1}\mathbf{X}'\boldsymbol{\varepsilon}]$$
$$= \boldsymbol{\beta} + (\mathbf{X}'\mathbf{X})^{-1}\mathbf{X}'E(\boldsymbol{\varepsilon})$$

and, using assumptions (3.72) and (3.74), we find

$$E(\mathbf{b}) = \boldsymbol{\beta} \tag{3.81}$$

The variance-covariance matrix of **b**, denoted by Var(**b**), may be found by considering $E[(\mathbf{b} - \boldsymbol{\beta})(\mathbf{b} - \boldsymbol{\beta})']$. From (3.80), we have

$$(\mathbf{b} - \boldsymbol{\beta}) = (\mathbf{X}'\mathbf{X})^{-1}\mathbf{X}'\boldsymbol{\varepsilon}$$

hence

$$\text{Var}(\mathbf{b}) = E[(\mathbf{b} - \boldsymbol{\beta})(\mathbf{b} - \boldsymbol{\beta})']$$
$$= E[(\mathbf{X}'\mathbf{X})^{-1}\mathbf{X}'\boldsymbol{\varepsilon}\boldsymbol{\varepsilon}'\mathbf{X}(\mathbf{X}'\mathbf{X})^{-1}]$$

using the result that $(\mathbf{ABC})' = \mathbf{C}'\mathbf{B}'\mathbf{A}'$ and noting that $(\mathbf{X}'\mathbf{X})^{-1}$ is a symmetric matrix and therefore equal to its transpose. Thus,

$$\text{Var}(\mathbf{b}) = (\mathbf{X}'\mathbf{X})^{-1}\mathbf{X}'E(\boldsymbol{\varepsilon}\boldsymbol{\varepsilon}')\mathbf{X}(\mathbf{X}'\mathbf{X})^{-1}$$
$$= (\mathbf{X}'\mathbf{X})^{-1}\mathbf{X}'\sigma^2\mathbf{I}\mathbf{X}(\mathbf{X}'\mathbf{X})^{-1} \quad \text{by assumption (3.73)}$$
$$= \sigma^2(\mathbf{X}'\mathbf{X})^{-1} \tag{3.82}$$

since σ^2 is a scalar and may be moved to any position on the right-hand side of the equation, and because $(\mathbf{X}'\mathbf{X})^{-1}\mathbf{X}'\mathbf{X} = \mathbf{I}$.

As in simple linear regression, it can be shown that the least squares estimator, **b**, is *linear, unbiased*, has *minimum variance*, and, under the assumption that $\boldsymbol{\varepsilon}$ has a joint normal distribution, is the maximum likelihood estimator of $\boldsymbol{\beta}$.

3.3.4 THE STANDARD ERROR OF THE REGRESSION

The variance-covariance matrix, Var(**b**), depends on σ^2, which is generally unknown and has to be estimated. In the exposition of simple linear regression, it was shown that the best estimate of σ^2 was obtained by dividing $\sum e_i^2$ by $n - 2$. In the same way, it can be shown[5] that for the general model, the best estimate of σ^2 is

$$s^2 = \frac{\mathbf{e}'\mathbf{e}}{n - k - 1} \tag{3.83}$$

A convenient formula for computing $\mathbf{e}'\mathbf{e}$ is offered by (3.77):

$$\begin{aligned} \mathbf{e}'\mathbf{e} &= \mathbf{y}'\mathbf{y} - 2\mathbf{b}'\mathbf{X}'\mathbf{y} + \mathbf{b}'\mathbf{X}'\mathbf{X}\mathbf{b} \\ &= \mathbf{y}'\mathbf{y} - \mathbf{b}'\mathbf{X}'\mathbf{y} \end{aligned} \tag{3.84}$$

since $\mathbf{X}'\mathbf{X}\ \mathbf{b} = \mathbf{X}'\mathbf{y}$.

Rearranging equation (3.84), we have a partitioning of the total sum of squared observations into two parts: the part attributable to the variance about the regression—the "unexplained" part—and that due to the model—the "explained" part:

$$\mathbf{y}'\mathbf{y} = \mathbf{e}'\mathbf{e} + \mathbf{b}'\mathbf{X}'\mathbf{y} \tag{3.85}$$

Since

$$\sum (Y_i - \bar{Y})^2 = \sum Y_i^2 - n\bar{Y}^2 = \mathbf{y}'\mathbf{y} - n\bar{Y}^2$$

we may subtract $n\bar{Y}^2$, the "correction for the mean," from both sides of (3.85) to find the matrix formulation of (3.56):

$$\mathbf{y}'\mathbf{y} - n\bar{Y}^2 = \mathbf{e}'\mathbf{e} + \mathbf{b}'\mathbf{X}'\mathbf{y} - n\bar{Y}^2 \tag{3.86}$$

or

$$\begin{pmatrix} \text{total} \\ \text{sum of squares} \\ \text{about the mean:} \\ SS_T \end{pmatrix} = \begin{pmatrix} \text{error} \\ \text{sum of squares} \\ \text{about regression:} \\ SS_E \end{pmatrix} + \begin{pmatrix} \text{model} \\ \text{sum of squares} \\ \text{due to regression:} \\ SS_M \end{pmatrix}$$

3.3.5 THE *F* STATISTIC

As in simple linear regression, we may define an F statistic by the ratio of the "explained" and "unexplained" sum of squares, each divided the appropriate degress of freedom, to test the hypothesis of no relation between Y and the X's (that is, $H_0: \beta_1 = \beta_2 = \ldots = \beta_k = 0$):

$$F = \frac{(\mathbf{b}'\mathbf{X}'\mathbf{y} - n\bar{Y}^2)/k}{\mathbf{e}'\mathbf{e}/(n - k - 1)} = \frac{SS_M/k}{SS_E/(n - k - 1)} \tag{3.87}$$

[5] For a lucid exposition of the derivation see Johnston (1963), p. 112.

Thus we have the following general analysis of variance table:

Source of Variation	Degrees of Freedom	Sum of Squares	Mean Square	F Ratio
Total (uncorrected for mean)	n	$\mathbf{y}'\mathbf{y}$		
Correction for the Mean (b_0)	1	$n\bar{Y}^2$		
Total (corrected for mean)	$n-1$	$SS_T=\mathbf{y}'\mathbf{y} - n\bar{Y}^2$		
Model ($b_1, b_2, \ldots, b_k \mid b_0$)	k	$SS_M=\mathbf{b}'\mathbf{X}'\mathbf{y}-n\bar{Y}^2$	SS_M/k	$\dfrac{SS_M/k}{SS_E/(n-k-1)}$
Error	$n-k-1$	$SS_E=\mathbf{e}'\mathbf{e}$	$SS_E/(n-k-1)$	

Recalling the definition of the coefficient of determination in (3.58), we have

$$r^2 = \frac{\mathbf{b}'\mathbf{X}'\mathbf{y} - n\bar{Y}^2}{\mathbf{y}'\mathbf{y} - n\bar{Y}^2} = \frac{SS_M}{SS_T} \tag{3.88}$$

and, since

$$1 - r^2 = \frac{\mathbf{y}'\mathbf{y} - n\bar{Y}^2 - \mathbf{b}'\mathbf{X}'\mathbf{y} + n\bar{Y}^2}{\mathbf{y}'\mathbf{y} - n\bar{Y}^2} = \frac{\mathbf{e}'\mathbf{e}}{\mathbf{y}'\mathbf{y} - n\bar{Y}^2}$$

we may express (3.87) as

$$F = \frac{r^2/k}{(1 - r^2)/(n - k - 1)} \tag{3.89}$$

3.3.6 DISTRIBUTIONAL ASSUMPTIONS AND THE t STATISTIC

So far no assumption has been made concerning the distribution of the random error terms, ε_i. If we assume these to be normally distributed, we may, as in simple linear regression, derive significance tests and confidence intervals for the b_i and test the significance of the F statistic defined in (3.87). Hence we add to assumptions (3.72) to (3.75), the assumption

$$\varepsilon_i \quad \text{has a normal distribution} \quad (i = 1, 2, \ldots, n) \tag{3.90}$$

Assumptions (3.72), (3.73), and (3.90) may be rewritten as

$$\boldsymbol{\varepsilon} \text{ is } \text{NORMAL}(\mathbf{0}, \sigma^2\mathbf{I}) \tag{3.91}$$

It follows, then, that **b** has a multivariate normal distribution:

$$\mathbf{b} \text{ is } \text{NORMAL}[\boldsymbol{\beta}, \sigma^2(\mathbf{X'X})^{-1}] \tag{3.92}$$

and it can be shown that **e** and **b** are independently distributed.[6] Hence we may once again use the t distribution to derive tests for individual regression coefficients. The appropriate statistic is

$$t_{b_i} = \frac{b_i - \beta_i}{\sqrt{\mathbf{e'e}/(n-k-1)}\sqrt{c_{ii}}} \tag{3.93}$$

where c_{ii} is the diagonal element in the $(i+1\text{st})$ row and $(i+1\text{st})$ column $(i = 0, 1, \ldots)$ of $(\mathbf{X'X})^{-1}$, and t_{b_i} is distributed with $(n-k-1)$ degrees of freedom. It also follows that a 100 $(1-\alpha)$ percent confidence interval for β_i is given by

$$b_i \pm t_{\alpha/2}\sqrt{\frac{\mathbf{e'e}}{n-k-1}}\sqrt{c_{ii}} \tag{3.94}$$

Finally, by an argument analogous to the one used in the section on the analysis of variance, we may establish that the F statistic defined in (3.87) is distributed according to an F distribution with $(k, n-k-1)$ degrees of freedom. This provides us with a test for the significance of the fit of the multiple linear regression model.

Example. As an illustration of the computations and procedures involved in a multiple linear regression analysis, consider the data in Table 3.9. It will be seen that this is the employment-population data of Table 3.1, to which has been added another variable: distance from center-city.

Table 3.9. Employment-Population-Distance Data

Y (food empl.)	60	75	96	40	54	68	87	64	48	80
X_1 (pop. in thousands)	4	6	8	2	4	6	8	4	2	6
X_2 (distance in quarter-mile units)	3	2	1	4	3	3	1	3	4	2

We begin by expressing the data in matrix form and computing the least squares estimates:

[6] Johnston (1963), p. 118.

$$\mathbf{y} = \begin{bmatrix} 60 \\ 75 \\ 96 \\ 40 \\ 54 \\ 68 \\ 87 \\ 64 \\ 48 \\ 80 \end{bmatrix} \qquad \mathbf{X} = \begin{bmatrix} 1 & 4 & 3 \\ 1 & 6 & 2 \\ 1 & 8 & 1 \\ 1 & 2 & 4 \\ 1 & 4 & 3 \\ 1 & 6 & 3 \\ 1 & 8 & 1 \\ 1 & 4 & 3 \\ 1 & 2 & 4 \\ 1 & 6 & 2 \end{bmatrix} \qquad \mathbf{b} = \begin{bmatrix} b_0 \\ b_1 \\ b_2 \end{bmatrix}$$

$$\mathbf{X}'\mathbf{X} = \begin{bmatrix} 10 & 50 & 26 \\ 50 & 292 & 110 \\ 26 & 110 & 78 \end{bmatrix}$$

$$\mathbf{X}'\mathbf{y} = \begin{bmatrix} 672 \\ 3690 \\ 1583 \end{bmatrix}$$

$$(\mathbf{X}'\mathbf{X})^{-1} = \begin{bmatrix} \frac{2669}{92} & -\frac{65}{23} & -\frac{523}{92} \\ -\frac{65}{23} & \frac{13}{46} & \frac{25}{46} \\ -\frac{523}{92} & \frac{25}{46} & \frac{105}{92} \end{bmatrix}$$

$$\mathbf{b} = (\mathbf{X}'\mathbf{X})^{-1}\mathbf{X}'\mathbf{y} = \begin{bmatrix} \frac{6259}{92} \\ \frac{185}{46} \\ -\frac{741}{92} \end{bmatrix} = \begin{bmatrix} 68.0326 \\ 4.0217 \\ -8.0543 \end{bmatrix}$$

and

$$\hat{Y}_i = 68.0326 + 4.0217X_{1i} - 8.0543X_{2i}$$

The sum of squares due to the model is

$$SS_M = \mathbf{b}'\mathbf{X}'\mathbf{y} - n\overline{Y}^2 = 47{,}808\tfrac{9}{92} - 45{,}158\tfrac{2}{5} = 2{,}649\tfrac{321}{460} = 2{,}649.6978$$

$$\mathbf{y}'\mathbf{y} = 47{,}950$$

and, by (3.85),

$$\mathbf{e}'\mathbf{e} = \mathbf{y}'\mathbf{y} - \mathbf{b}'\mathbf{X}'\mathbf{y} = 47{,}950 - 47{,}808\tfrac{9}{92} = 141\tfrac{83}{92} = 141.9022$$

Hence we may construct the following analysis of variance table:

Source of Variation	Degrees of Freedom	Sum of Squares	Mean Square	F Ratio
Total (uncorrected for mean)	10	47,950.00		
Correction for the Mean (b_0)	1	45,158.40		
Total (corrected for mean)	9	2,791.60		
Model ($b_1, b_2 \mid b_0$)	2	2,649.70	1,324.85	65.35
Error	7	141.90	20.27	

The computed F value exceeds $F_{.05}(2,7) = 4.74$; hence the regression is significant. That is, the hypothesis $\beta_1 = \beta_2 = 0$ is rejected at the five percent level, and a highly significant relationship appears to exist between food store employment, total population, and distance from center-city.

To test the significance of the regression coefficients, we compute the t statistics t_{b_1} and t_{b_2}, under the hypothesis that $\beta_1 = 0$ and $\beta_2 = 0$, respectively:

$$t_{b_1} = \frac{4.0217}{\sqrt{20.2717}\sqrt{0.2826}} = \frac{4.0217}{2.3935} = 1.68$$

and

$$t_{b_2} = \frac{-8.0543}{\sqrt{20.2717}\sqrt{1.1413}} = \frac{-8.0543}{4.8100} = -1.67$$

Both statistics lie outside of the critical region at the five percent level of significance. Hence we cannot reject either hypothesis, and we cannot conclude that total population contributes a significant additional amount of "explanation," after the effects of distance from center-city have been accounted for, and vice versa.

Finally, we compute

$$r^2 = \frac{\mathbf{b}'\mathbf{X}'\mathbf{y} - n\overline{Y}^2}{\mathbf{y}'\mathbf{y} - n\overline{Y}^2} = \frac{2{,}649.6978}{2{,}791.6000} = = 0.9492$$

Recall that in the case of the simple linear regression model, involving only food store employment and total population, r^2 was equal to 0.9288. Thus the introduction of an additional explanatory variable, distance from center-city, has increased our ability to account for variation in food store employment by 2.04 percent. However, the test of b_2 established that this increase is not a statistically significant one, at the five percent level.

3.3.7 APPLICATION: ESTIMATING A POPULATION GROWTH MATRIX FROM A TIME SERIES OF INTERREGIONAL POPULATION DISTRIBUTIONS

Efforts to analyze and forecast interregional population growth frequently are severely constrained by the general paucity of reliable data describing the behavior of the fundamental components of population change. Migration data, for example, are simply not available for most regional subdivisions of the nation. As a result, demographers have had to rely on rather crude methods of estimating migration. Efforts to express the population growth process in matrix form (Section 1.5), however, suggest a means whereby the growth regime of an interregional system may be estimated solely on the basis of a time series of interregional population distributions.

Recall the matrix population model that was defined in (1.19), and consider the population growth process, in this two-region system, that occurs over two sequential periods. Assume that an unknown schedule of growth, defined by the matrix **G**, remains unchanged during this period of time. We have then

$$\begin{bmatrix} w_1(t+1) \\ w_2(t+1) \end{bmatrix} = \begin{bmatrix} g_{11} & g_{21} \\ g_{12} & g_{22} \end{bmatrix} \begin{bmatrix} w_1(t) \\ w_2(t) \end{bmatrix}$$

and

$$\begin{bmatrix} w_1(t+2) \\ w_2(t+2) \end{bmatrix} = \begin{bmatrix} g_{11} & g_{21} \\ g_{12} & g_{22} \end{bmatrix} \begin{bmatrix} w_1(t+1) \\ w_2(t+1) \end{bmatrix}$$

If the w_i's have been observed, and therefore are known, the population growth matrix, **G**, may be derived by solving the following system of four equations in four unknowns[7]:

$$\begin{aligned} w_1(t+1) &= g_{11}w_1(t) + g_{21}w_2(t) \\ w_2(t+1) &= g_{12}w_1(t) + g_{22}w_2(t) \\ w_1(t+2) &= g_{11}w_1(t+1) + g_{21}w_2(t+1) \\ w_2(t+2) &= g_{12}w_1(t+1) + g_{22}w_2(t+1) \end{aligned}$$

[7] Assuming, of course, that the following matrix is nonsingular:

$$\begin{bmatrix} w_1(t) & w_2(t) \\ w_1(t+1) & w_2(t+1) \end{bmatrix}$$

For example, given the 1950-1952 population data in Table 3.10, for the two-region system of California and the rest of the United States, we have

$$11{,}130 = 10{,}643g_{11} + 141{,}225g_{21}$$
$$142{,}852 = 10{,}643g_{12} + 141{,}225g_{22}$$
$$11{,}638 = 11{,}130g_{11} + 142{,}852g_{21}$$
$$144{,}755 = 11{,}130g_{12} + 142{,}852g_{22}$$

Table 3.10. Estimated Total Population of California and the Rest of the United States, 1950–1960 (Population in Thousands)

Year (July 1)	California	Rest of the United States	National Total
1950	10,643	141,225	151,868
1951	11,130	142,852	153,982
1952	11,638	144,755	156,393
1953	12,101	146,855	158,956
1954	12,517	149,367	161,884
1955	13,004	152,065	165,069
1956	13,581	154,507	168,088
1957	14,177	157,010	171,187
1958	14,741	159,408	174,149
1959	15,288	161,637*	176,925*
1960	15,863	163,284*	179,147*

* Continental U.S. only (that is, excluding Alaska and Hawaii).
Source: Economic Development Agency, *California Statistical Abstract*. Sacramento, Calif.: State of California, Documents Section, 1963, p. 44.

The more general problem of estimating such a **G** on the basis of a time series of distributions, however, requires a criterion of fit, since more equations than unknowns are available. One such estimator is the unrestricted least squares (ULS) estimator.

Assume that the observed vectors, **w**, denoting the population in each of m regions over n years, are generated by the linear statistical model

$$\mathbf{w}(t + 1) = \mathbf{G}\mathbf{w}(t) + \boldsymbol{\varepsilon} \tag{3.95}$$

where $\boldsymbol{\varepsilon}$ is an $(mn \times 1)$ vector of error terms. Expressing (3.95) in the more familiar linear regression form, we have

$$\mathbf{y} = \mathbf{X}\mathbf{g} + \boldsymbol{\varepsilon} \tag{3.96}$$

where, for our two-region example,

$$\mathbf{y} = \begin{bmatrix} \mathbf{y}_1 \\ \mathbf{y}_2 \end{bmatrix} \quad \mathbf{g} = \begin{bmatrix} \mathbf{g}_1 \\ \mathbf{g}_2 \end{bmatrix} \quad \boldsymbol{\varepsilon} = \begin{bmatrix} \boldsymbol{\varepsilon}_1 \\ \boldsymbol{\varepsilon}_2 \end{bmatrix} \quad \mathbf{X} = \begin{bmatrix} \mathbf{X}_1 & 0 \\ 0 & \mathbf{X}_2 \end{bmatrix} \quad \mathbf{X}_1 = \mathbf{X}_2$$

Estimator:

$$\mathbf{g} = (\mathbf{X}'\mathbf{X})^{-1}\mathbf{X}'\mathbf{y}$$

Data:

$$\mathbf{X} = \left[\begin{array}{cc:cc} 10643 & 141225 & 0 & 0 \\ 11130 & 142852 & 0 & 0 \\ 11638 & 144755 & 0 & 0 \\ 12101 & 146855 & 0 & 0 \\ 12517 & 149367 & 0 & 0 \\ 13004 & 152065 & 0 & 0 \\ 13581 & 154507 & 0 & 0 \\ 14177 & 157010 & 0 & 0 \\ 14741 & 159408 & 0 & 0 \\ 15288 & 161637 & 0 & 0 \\ \hdashline 0 & 0 & 10643 & 141225 \\ 0 & 0 & 11130 & 142852 \\ 0 & 0 & 11638 & 144755 \\ 0 & 0 & 12101 & 146855 \\ 0 & 0 & 12517 & 149367 \\ 0 & 0 & 13004 & 152065 \\ 0 & 0 & 13581 & 154507 \\ 0 & 0 & 14177 & 157010 \\ 0 & 0 & 14741 & 159408 \\ 0 & 0 & 15288 & 161637 \end{array}\right] \qquad \mathbf{y} = \left[\begin{array}{c} 11130 \\ 11638 \\ 12101 \\ 12517 \\ 13004 \\ 13581 \\ 14177 \\ 14741 \\ 15288 \\ 15863 \\ \hdashline 142852 \\ 144755 \\ 146855 \\ 149367 \\ 152065 \\ 154507 \\ 157010 \\ 159408 \\ 161637 \\ 163284 \end{array}\right]$$

Estimate:

$$\hat{\mathbf{g}} = \left[\begin{array}{c} 1.0149 \\ 0.0022 \\ \hdashline -0.0557 \\ 1.0194 \end{array}\right]$$

Source: Table 3.10.

Figure 3.6. Unrestricted Least Squares Estimate of the Annual Population Growth Matrix for California and the Rest of the United States: 1950–1960 Total Population Time Series

Since the least squares estimator of **g** is one which minimizes the sum of squared deviations of observed from predicted values, we minimize

$$S = \sum (Y_i - \hat{Y}_i) = [\mathbf{y} - \mathbf{X}\mathbf{g}]'[\mathbf{y} - \mathbf{X}\mathbf{g}] \tag{3.97}$$

with respect to **g** and find

$$\hat{\mathbf{g}} = (\mathbf{X}'\mathbf{X})^{-1}\mathbf{X}'\mathbf{y} \tag{3.98}$$

Applying (3.98) to our two-region example in Table 3.10, we have the estimation process illustrated in Figure 3.6 and the estimate

$$\hat{\mathbf{G}} = \begin{bmatrix} 1.0149 & 0.0022 \\ -0.0557 & 1.0194 \end{bmatrix} \tag{3.99}$$

The growth matrix in (3.99) is an unacceptable estimate since it implies a negative migration flow, which is an impossible event. Hence, we need to adopt an estimation procedure that forces the estimates to be nonnegative. Such a procedure is presented in Subsection 5.3.3.

3.4 EXTENSIONS OF THE GENERAL LINEAR MODEL

The above discussion has outlined the basic components of simple and multiple linear regression analysis. In this section we shall sketch out a few extensions of the general linear model that are particularly useful for urban and regional analysis. We begin with an exposition of stepwise regression, then discuss certain nonlinear relationships and transformations that may be analyzed by the general linear model, and consider the use of dummy variables. We then include a very brief consideration of the nature of econometrics and conclude with an application of regression analysis to the study of interregional migration.

3.4.1 STEPWISE REGRESSION

Frequently, we wish to establish a relationship between a particular dependent variable, Y, and some subset of independent variables, $X_1, X_2, \ldots, X_k$, drawn from a larger collection of X's. The problem, then, is one of selecting the best independent variable mix out of the many permutations that are available. Outside of computing all possible combinations, a very cumbersome and time-consuming procedure, no unique method presents itself as being superior to all others. One that has received a great deal of attention and gained considerable popularity is the *stepwise regression procedure*. This procedure begins by selecting the X most highly correlated with Y—X_1, say—and finds the linear regression equation $\hat{Y} = b_0 + b_1X_1$. Next, it selects, for inclusion into the model, the X with the highest *partial correlation coefficient* with Y—X_3, say—and computes a second regression equation, $\hat{Y} = b_0 + b_1X_1 + b_3X_3$. It then examines the significance of X_3 and reexamines the significance of the explanatory contribution made by X_1 after X_3 has been introduced into the model. If this contribution is significant, the procedure continues the search for a third variable; otherwise, the variable X_1 is dropped out of the model prior to the search for another variable. The stepwise procedure terminates when all variables in the independent variable set have been considered.

Example. We may illustrate the stepwise procedure with the numerical

Table 3.11. Employment-Population-Distance Data

Y (food empl.)	60	75	96	40	54	68	87	64	48	80
X_1 (pop. in thousands)	4	6	8	2	4	6	8	4	2	6
X_2 (distance in quarter-mile units)	3	2	1	4	3	3	1	3	4	2
X_3 (total empl.)	240	240	260	200	200	220	260	260	220	240

example in Table 3.11, which adds another variable, total employment, to the example in Table 3.9.

We begin by computing the simple correlation matrix **R**, in which Y is denoted as X_0:

$$\mathbf{R} = \begin{array}{c} \\ X_0 \\ X_1 \\ X_2 \\ X_3 \end{array} \begin{array}{c} \begin{array}{cccc} X_0 & X_1 & X_2 & X_3 \end{array} \\ \begin{bmatrix} 1 & r_{01} & r_{02} & r_{03} \\ r_{10} & 1 & r_{12} & r_{13} \\ r_{20} & r_{21} & 1 & r_{23} \\ r_{30} & r_{31} & r_{32} & 1 \end{bmatrix} \end{array}$$

$$= \begin{bmatrix} 1 & 0.9637 & -0.9637 & 0.7868 \\ 0.9637 & 1 & -0.9569 & 0.6654 \\ -0.9637 & -0.9569 & 1 & -0.7310 \\ 0.7868 & 0.6654 & -0.7310 & 1 \end{bmatrix}$$

where

$$r_{jk} = \frac{\sum (X_{ji} - \bar{X}_j)(X_{ki} - \bar{X}_k)}{\sqrt{[\sum (X_{ji} - \bar{X}_j)^2][\sum (X_{ki} - \bar{X}_k)^2]}} \tag{3.100}$$

Thus the variable X_1 is selected as the first independent variable to enter the regression model, and the fitted equation is

$$\hat{Y}_i = 27.9143 + 7.8571 X_{1i}$$

We have seen earlier that this regression is significant.

Next, computing the partial correlation coefficient between Y and the only two remaining candidates, X_2 and X_3, we have[8]

$$r_{02\cdot1} = \frac{r_{02} - r_{01} r_{21}}{\sqrt{1 - r_{01}^2}\sqrt{1 - r_{21}^2}} = -0.1694$$

$$r_{03\cdot1} = \frac{r_{03} - r_{01} r_{31}}{\sqrt{1 - r_{01}^2}\sqrt{1 - r_{31}^2}} = 0.7245$$

[8] For correlation matrices of higher order, it becomes economical to use the following useful relationship: Let $\mathbf{C} = \mathbf{R}^{-1}$, then

$$r_{jk\cdot1,2,\ldots,j-1,j+1,\ldots,k-1,k+1,\ldots,p} = \frac{-c_{jk}}{c_{jj}c_{kk}}$$

Introducing X_3 into the equation yields

$$\hat{Y}_i = -11.4068 + 6.4407X_{1i} + 0.1983X_{3i}$$

In order to examine the additional contribution of X_3 to the total explanation, we set out the following analysis of variance table, drawing on values derived in earlier computations:

Source of Variation	Degrees of Freedom	Sum of Squares	Mean Square	F Ratio
Total (uncorrected for mean)	10	47,950.00		
Correction for the Mean (b_0)	1	45,158.40		
Total (corrected for mean)	9	2,791.60		
Model ($b_1, b_3 \| b_0$)	2	2,698.92		
($b_1 \| b_0$)	1	2,592.86		
($b_3 \| b_0, b_1$)	1	106.06	106.06	8.01
Error	7	92.68	13.24	

The sum of squares due to X_3 is found by subtraction. The partial F ratio for b_3 exceeds the critical value $F_{.05}$ (1,7) = 5.59. Hence, we enter X_3 into the regression model and reexamine the explanatory contribution of X_1. Specifically, we examine the contribution X_1 would have made if X_3 had been entered first. This may be done by subtracting from the total sum of squares due to the model, with both X_1 and X_3 in the equation, the sum of squares that would have been contributed by X_3 acting alone. The difference is the sum of squares due to the additional contribution of X_1. We may test the significance of this latter sum of squares by means of the following analysis of variance table:

Source of Variation	Degrees of Freedom	Sum of Squares	Mean Square	F Ratio
Total (uncorrected for mean)	10	47,950.00		
Correction for the Mean (b_0)	1	45,158.40		
Total (corrected for mean)	9	2,791.60		
Model ($b_1, b_3 \| b_0$)	2	2,698.92		
($b_3 \| b_0$)	1	1,728.03		
($b_1 \| b_0, b_3$)	1	970.89	970.89	73.33
Error	7	92.68	13.24	

Once again the relevant partial F ratio exceeds the critical value $F_{.05}(1,7) = 5.59$, and we therefore retain X_1 in the regression model. The reader should confirm that the additional explanatory contribution of X_2 is not a statistically significant one and that, therefore, X_2 should not be included in the final regression model [Exercise 1(a)].

3.4.2 NONLINEAR RELATIONSHIPS AND TRANSFORMATIONS

The models discussed thus far have been first-order, linear models involving one or more independent variables. The general methods developed in this chapter, however, may be applied to any model that can be rearranged or transformed into the first-order, linear regression form. Such a case exists when Y is approximated by a polynomial in X. Consider, for example, the simple quadratic relationship,

$$Y = \beta_0 + \beta_1 X + \beta_2 X^2 + \varepsilon \qquad (3.101)$$

This equation may be fitted, using the methods developed for the general linear model, by solving for $\mathbf{b}$ in

$$\mathbf{b} = (\mathbf{XX})^{-1}\mathbf{X}'\mathbf{y}$$

where

$$\mathbf{y} = \begin{bmatrix} Y_1 \\ Y_2 \\ \vdots \\ Y_n \end{bmatrix} \qquad \mathbf{b} = \begin{bmatrix} b_0 \\ b_1 \\ b_2 \end{bmatrix} \qquad \mathbf{X} = \begin{bmatrix} 1 & X_1 & X_1^2 \\ 1 & X_2 & X_2^2 \\ \vdots & \vdots & \vdots \\ 1 & X_n & X_n^2 \end{bmatrix}$$

The significance of b_2 may be tested to determine whether the underlying model is a quadratic one. In general, one begins with a model of degree m and by successive reductions seeks a significant representation of the relationship using a polynomial of the lowest degree possible.

Polynomial models involving powers and cross products of powers of the independent variables $X_1, X_2, \ldots, X_k$, are but one class of nonlinear models that are transformable into the first-order, general linear model. Another class consists of the subset of models, nonlinear in the parameters, that may be defined to be *intrinsically linear*. A model, nonlinear in the parameters, is intrinsically linear if it can be expressed, after suitable transformation of the variables, by the standard linear form. Included in this class are multiplicative models of the general form

$$Y = \delta X_1^{\beta} X_2^{\gamma} \varepsilon \qquad (3.102)$$

where δ, β, and γ are unknown parameters, and ε is a random error term with a unit mean and a finite variance. Taking natural logarithms to the base e of both sides of the equation, we have the linear model

$$\ln Y = \ln \delta + \beta \ln X_1 + \gamma \ln X_2 + \ln \varepsilon \qquad (3.103)$$

The transformed model is linear, and therefore can be dealt with using the methods developed in this chapter. However, by taking logarithms of both sides of the equation, we have introduced a weighting into the least squares fit, such that *relative* rather than *absolute* errors are being given roughly equal weight [Exercise 1(c)]. Moreover, in order to perform tests of significance, we now need to make the assumption that

$$\ln \boldsymbol{\varepsilon} \text{ is NORMAL } (\mathbf{0}, \sigma^2\mathbf{I})$$

The reasonableness of such an assumption should be examined—perhaps by studying the residuals from the fitted equation.

Example. Let us fit the regression model defined in (3.101) to the numerical example described in Table 3.1. We have, then,

$$\mathbf{y} = \begin{bmatrix} 60 \\ 75 \\ 96 \\ 40 \\ 54 \\ 68 \\ 87 \\ 64 \\ 48 \\ 80 \end{bmatrix} \qquad \mathbf{X} = \begin{bmatrix} 1 & 4 & 16 \\ 1 & 6 & 36 \\ 1 & 8 & 64 \\ 1 & 2 & 4 \\ 1 & 4 & 16 \\ 1 & 6 & 36 \\ 1 & 8 & 64 \\ 1 & 4 & 16 \\ 1 & 2 & 4 \\ 1 & 6 & 36 \end{bmatrix} \qquad \mathbf{b} = \begin{bmatrix} b_0 \\ b_1 \\ b_2 \end{bmatrix}$$

$$\mathbf{X'X} = \begin{bmatrix} 10 & 50 & 292 \\ 50 & 292 & 1880 \\ 292 & 1880 & 12880 \end{bmatrix} \qquad \mathbf{X'y} = \begin{bmatrix} 672 \\ 3690 \\ 22940 \end{bmatrix}$$

and

$$(\mathbf{X'X})^{-1} = \begin{bmatrix} \dfrac{295}{84} & -\dfrac{495}{336} & \dfrac{91}{672} \\ -\dfrac{495}{336} & \dfrac{907}{1344} & -\dfrac{175}{2688} \\ \dfrac{91}{672} & -\dfrac{175}{2688} & \dfrac{35}{5376} \end{bmatrix}$$

Thus

$$\mathbf{b} = (\mathbf{X}'\mathbf{X})^{-1}\mathbf{X}'\mathbf{y} = \begin{bmatrix} \frac{2545}{84} \\ \frac{2255}{336} \\ \frac{77}{672} \end{bmatrix} = \begin{bmatrix} 30.2976 \\ 6.7113 \\ 0.1146 \end{bmatrix}$$

and

$$\hat{Y}_i = 30.2976 + 6.7113X_i + 0.1146X_i^2$$

We may compute the following analysis of variance table:

Source of Variation	Degrees of Freedom	Sum of Squares	Mean Square	F Ratio
Total (uncorrected for mean)	10	47,950.00		
Correction for the Mean (b_0)	1	45,158.40		
Total (corrected for mean)	9	2,791.60		
Model ($b_1, b_2 \mid b_0$)	2	2,594.87	1,297.44	46.17
Error	7	196.73	28.10	

The F ratio is significant at the five percent level, and we proceed to test whether the additional explanatory contribution of the nonlinear term also is significant. To do this, we recall the data in an earlier analysis of variance table and proceed as in stepwise regression:

Source of Variation	Degrees of Freedom	Sum of Squares	Mean Square	F Ratio
Total (uncorrected for mean)	10	47,905.00		
Correction for the Mean (b_0)	1	45,158.40		
Total (corrected for mean)	9	2,791.60		
Model ($b_1, b_2 \mid b_0$)	2	2,594.87		
($b_1 \mid b_0$)	1	2,592,86		
($b_2 \mid b_0, b_1$)	1	2.01	2.01	0.07
Error	7	196.73	28.10	

The partial F ratio is not significant; hence we reject the hypothesis that the relationship between food employment and population is quadratic in form.

3.4.3 DUMMY VARIABLES

Occasionally, a few of the variables included in a regression model do not vary over a continuous range, but take on one of several distinct levels or fall into one of several groups. Census tracts in the center of a city, for example, are likely to have more food store employment per capita than suburban census tracts, quite apart from any variations that may be attributed to differences in total population and total retail employment. Economic data collected over the four different quarters of a year may include a seasonal component, the influence of which we may wish to remove. Or economic data collected annually for several years may include a linear trend, the effects of which may be obscuring the underlying relationships. Finally, the dependent variable itself may take on discrete values. A person owns a car or does not, an individual decides to migrate out of the region he is in or does not, and so on. To place such problems into the framework of regression analysis, we assign a combination of zeroes and unities to a set of variables that are included in the regression equation.

For example, suppose we wish to distinguish between observations on food store employment and total population taken in the central city from those taken in the suburban ring. We may achieve this by introducing a dummy variable, as follows:

$$Y = \beta_0 + \beta_1 X_1 + \beta_2 X_2 + \varepsilon \tag{3.104}$$

where

$$Y = \text{food store employment}$$

$$X_1 = \begin{cases} 1 \text{ for observations taken in center-city} \\ 0 \text{ for observations taken in the suburban ring} \end{cases}$$

$$X_2 = \text{total population}$$

The data matrix for a sample of, say, six observations, evenly divided between center-city and the suburban ring, is

$$\mathbf{X} = \begin{bmatrix} 1 & 1 & X_{21} \\ 1 & 1 & X_{22} \\ 1 & 1 & X_{23} \\ \hdashline 1 & 0 & X_{24} \\ 1 & 0 & X_{25} \\ 1 & 0 & X_{26} \end{bmatrix} \quad \begin{matrix} \\ \text{center-city} \\ \\ \\ \text{suburban ring} \\ \\ \end{matrix}$$

The predictive equation for center-city census tracts, then, is

$$\hat{Y} = (b_0 + b_1) + b_2X_2$$

and for suburban census tracts is

$$\hat{Y} = b_0 + b_2X_2$$

The problem of including seasonality effects into a single-equation model may be handled in a similar manner. For quarterly data we would need three dummy variables, as follows:

$$X_1 = \begin{cases} 1 \text{ for observations in the first quarter} \\ 0 \text{ for all others} \end{cases}$$

$$X_2 = \begin{cases} 1 \text{ for observations in the second quarter} \\ 0 \text{ for all others} \end{cases}$$

$$X_3 = \begin{cases} 1 \text{ for observations in the third quarter} \\ 0 \text{ for all others} \end{cases}$$

Thus we would insert the following submatrix into the regular data matrix, **X**:

$$\begin{bmatrix} 1 & 0 & 0 \\ 1 & 0 & 0 \\ \vdots & \vdots & \vdots \\ 1 & 0 & 0 \\ \hdashline 0 & 1 & 0 \\ 0 & 1 & 0 \\ \vdots & \vdots & \vdots \\ 0 & 1 & 0 \\ \hdashline 0 & 0 & 1 \\ 0 & 0 & 1 \\ \vdots & \vdots & \vdots \\ 0 & 0 & 1 \\ \hdashline 0 & 0 & 0 \\ 0 & 0 & 0 \\ \vdots & \vdots & \vdots \\ 0 & 0 & 0 \end{bmatrix}$$

Notice that observations taken during the fourth quarter receive a zero value on all three dummy variables.

Finally, consider the use of a dummy variable for the dependent variable, Y. Assume the following model:

$$Y = \beta_0 + \beta_1 X_1 + \beta_2 X_2 + \varepsilon$$

where

$$Y = \begin{cases} 1 \text{ for households with at least one car} \\ 0 \text{ for households with no car} \end{cases}$$

X_1 = annual household income in dollars

X_2 = distance, in miles, from household to the Central Business District

We may interpret the calculated value of $\hat{Y}$, for any given X_1 and X_2 pair, as an estimate of the *conditional* probability of Y, given X_1 and X_2.

The number of potential applications of dummy variables in regression analysis is large. We have sketched out only a few. For a more definitive discussion, the reader should consult the econometrics literature.[9]

Example. Let us apply the regression model defined in (3.104) to the numerical example described in Table 3.11. We defined *center-city* observations to be those observations that were taken within one-half mile of the city center. We shall call the other observations *suburban-ring* observations. Then

$$\mathbf{y} = \begin{bmatrix} 60 \\ 75 \\ 96 \\ 40 \\ 54 \\ 68 \\ 87 \\ 64 \\ 48 \\ 80 \end{bmatrix} \qquad \mathbf{X} = \begin{bmatrix} 1 & 0 & 4 \\ 1 & 1 & 6 \\ 1 & 1 & 8 \\ 1 & 0 & 2 \\ 1 & 0 & 4 \\ 1 & 0 & 6 \\ 1 & 1 & 8 \\ 1 & 0 & 4 \\ 1 & 0 & 2 \\ 1 & 1 & 6 \end{bmatrix} \qquad \mathbf{b} = \begin{bmatrix} b_0 \\ b_1 \\ b_2 \end{bmatrix}$$

$$\mathbf{X'X} = \begin{bmatrix} 10 & 4 & 50 \\ 4 & 4 & 28 \\ 50 & 28 & 292 \end{bmatrix} \qquad \mathbf{X'y} = \begin{bmatrix} 672 \\ 338 \\ 3690 \end{bmatrix}$$

[9] In particular, see Suits (1957).

and

$$(\mathbf{X}'\mathbf{X})^{-1} = \begin{bmatrix} \frac{24}{23} & \frac{29}{46} & -\frac{11}{46} \\ \frac{29}{46} & \frac{105}{92} & -\frac{5}{23} \\ -\frac{11}{46} & -\frac{5}{23} & \frac{3}{46} \end{bmatrix}$$

Thus

$$\mathbf{b} = (\mathbf{X}'\mathbf{X})^{-1}\mathbf{X}'\mathbf{y} = \begin{bmatrix} \frac{734}{23} \\ \frac{333}{46} \\ \frac{149}{23} \end{bmatrix} = \begin{bmatrix} 31.9130 \\ 7.2391 \\ 6.4783 \end{bmatrix}$$

and

$$\hat{Y}_i = 31.9130 + 7.2391X_{1i} + 6.4783X_{2i}$$

This model yields the following analysis of variance table:

Source of Variation	Degrees of Freedom	Sum of Squares	Mean Square	F Ratio
Total (uncorrected for mean)	10	47,950.00		
Correction for the Mean (b_0)	1	45,158.40		
Total (corrected for mean)	9	2,791.60		
Model ($b_1, b_2 \mid b_0$)	2	2,638.77	1,319.39	60.43
Error	7	152.83	21.83	

The model provides a significant fit, and we now may turn to the examination of the additional explanatory contribution that is provided by the classification scheme. Recalling the analysis of variance table for the simple regression of food store employment on population, we may construct the following analysis of variance table:

Source of Variation	Degrees of Freedom	Sum of Squares	Mean Square	F Ratio
Total (uncorrected for mean)	10	47,950.00		
Correction for the Mean (b_0)	1	45,158.40		
Total (corrected for mean)	9	2,791.60		
Model ($b_1, b_2 \mid b_0$)	2	2,638.77		
($b_2 \mid b_0$)	1	2,592.86		
($b_1 \mid b_0, b_2$)	1	45.92	45.92	2.10
Error	7	152.83	21.83	

Once again the relevant partial F ratio is not significant at the five percent level, and we therefore fail to reject the null hypothesis that the classification system is not a statistically significant one.

3.4.4 ECONOMETRICS

The general multiple linear regression model has been used widely in econometrics, a branch of economics concerned with the empirical validation of mathematically stated economic propositions. Early applications of the single-equation model often were made without a rigorous examination of the validity of the technique for the particular use in question. Over the past years, however, a body of theoretical literature has emerged which is distinctly concerned with the assumptions of the general linear model, with the applicability of these assumptions to the analysis of economic data, and with the things that can be done when some of the assumptions are violated. This body of knowledge may be called the *theory of econometrics.*

Some of the questions that have been raised by econometricians are:

1. *Errors in variables.* Errors of observation and measurement in the Y variable may be merged with the error term, ε, but what happens if these errors are present in the X variables? Such errors produce a dependence between the error term and the observed values of the explanatory variables, thereby invalidating one of the basic assumptions of the linear regression model.

2. *Autocorrelation.* The serial independence of the error term is another critical assumption of the linear model. It implies that successive error terms are drawn independently of one another, an assumption that does not hold in many economic applications. What are the consequences of applying the classical regression formulas in such instances? What if this assumption is violated by the presence of *spatial* autocorrelation, that is, when the data relate to contiguous areal units [King(1969), pp. 157–162]?

3. *Multicollinearity*. The explanatory variables, X_i, may be highly interrelated. Indeed, in some economic models, an explanatory variable X_i may be a previous value of Y. What can be done, in such situations, to disentangle the separate influences of the explanatory variables?

4. *Simultaneous-equation systems*. The essence of most economic phenomena is the interdependence of many simultaneously interacting economic variables and relationships. This presents serious difficulties when one is applying the single-equation model. What can be done to extend regression analysis to take explicit account of a system of relationships?

These and other related questions have stimulated the interest of a generation of econometricians. The econometrics literature is vast, and further discussion of this field is beyond the scope of this text. Entry into the field can be made by consulting any recent text on econometrics.[10]

3.4.5 APPLICATION: ANALYSIS OF INTERREGIONAL MIGRATION FLOWS IN CALIFORNIA

Economists frequently have asserted that the labor market allocates workers more-or-less where they belong in terms of their productive ability. Comparative economic opportunity, they argue, is the driving motivating force that is manifested in interregional migration patterns. According to this thesis, factors such as employment opportunities and salary are major considerations in any decision to move. Thus, internal migration is held to be an important way by which workers respond to changing economic opportunities and thereby redirect the spatial allocation of labor toward a more optimal pattern.

Several models have been suggested for testing the "economic opportunities" hypothesis. One of the more successful of these is

$$M_{ij} = k\left[\frac{WS_j}{WS_i} \cdot \frac{LF_i \cdot LF_j}{D_{ij}}\right]\xi_{ij} \tag{3.105}$$

which, in its generalized log-transformed form, is

$$\begin{aligned} \ln M_{ij} = \beta_0 &+ \beta_1 \ln WS_i + \beta_2 \ln WS_j \\ &+ \beta_3 \ln LF_i + \beta_4 \ln LF_j + \beta_5 \ln D_{ij} + \varepsilon_{ij} \end{aligned} \tag{3.106}$$

where

M_{ij} = number of migrants from i to j;

LF_i, LF_j = labor force eligibles at i and j, respectively;[11]

WS_i, WS_j = average annual per capita wages and salaries at i and j, respectively;

[10] See, for example, Johnston (1963), Goldberger (1964), and Malinvaud (1966).
[11] The number of people in the 15–64 age group.

D_{ij} = shortest highway mileage between the major county seats at i and j, respectively; and

ε_{ij} = error term.

Thus, in matrix form, we have

$$\mathbf{y} = \mathbf{X}\boldsymbol{\beta} + \boldsymbol{\varepsilon} \tag{3.107}$$

where

$$\underset{m(m-1)\times 1}{\mathbf{y}} = \begin{bmatrix} \ln M_{12} \\ \ln M_{13} \\ \vdots \\ \ln M_{1m} \\ \hdashline \ln M_{21} \\ \vdots \\ \hdashline \vdots \\ \hdashline \ln M_{m1} \\ \vdots \\ \ln M_{m,m-1} \end{bmatrix} \qquad \underset{m(m-1)\times 1}{\boldsymbol{\varepsilon}} = \begin{bmatrix} \varepsilon_{12} \\ \varepsilon_{13} \\ \vdots \\ \varepsilon_{1m} \\ \hdashline \varepsilon_{21} \\ \vdots \\ \hdashline \vdots \\ \hdashline \varepsilon_{m1} \\ \vdots \\ \varepsilon_{m,m-1} \end{bmatrix} \qquad \underset{6\times 1}{\boldsymbol{\beta}} = \begin{bmatrix} \beta_0 \\ \beta_1 \\ \beta_2 \\ \beta_3 \\ \beta_4 \\ \beta_5 \end{bmatrix}$$

and

$$\underset{m(m-1)\times 6}{\mathbf{X}} = \begin{bmatrix} 1 & \ln WS_1 & \ln WS_2 & \ln LF_1 & \ln LF_2 & \ln D_{12} \\ 1 & \ln WS_1 & \ln WS_3 & \ln LF_1 & \ln LF_3 & \ln D_{13} \\ \vdots & \vdots & \vdots & \vdots & \vdots & \vdots \\ 1 & \ln WS_1 & \ln WS_m & \ln LF_1 & \ln LF_m & \ln D_{1m} \\ \hdashline 1 & \ln WS_2 & \ln WS_1 & \ln LF_2 & \ln LF_1 & \ln D_{21} \\ \vdots & \vdots & \vdots & \vdots & \vdots & \vdots \\ \hdashline \vdots & \vdots & \vdots & \vdots & \vdots & \vdots \\ \hdashline 1 & \ln WS_m & \ln WS_1 & \ln LF_m & \ln LF_1 & \ln D_{m1} \\ \vdots & \vdots & \vdots & \vdots & \vdots & \vdots \\ 1 & \ln WS_m & \ln WS_{m-1} & \ln LF_m & \ln LF_{m-1} & \ln D_{m,m-1} \end{bmatrix}$$

Let us fit the above model to inter-SMSA[12] flows (10 SMSA's, 90 observations) and then to the full matrix of inter-SEA flows (19 SEA's, 342 observations) shown in Figure 3.7. Using the data in Figure 3.8 and Table 3.12, we first obtain the regression statistics presented in Table 3.13(A) and Table 3.14(A). The fit of the model is impressive. Almost 87 per-

[12] SMSA is the Census Bureau's acronym for Standard Metropolitan Area. SEA is its acronym for Standard Economic Area, a category that includes both SMSA's and non-SMSA's.

cent of the variation is accounted for by five variables, of which three are significantly different from zero at the 0.1 percent confidence level. All five variables have the signs which one would expect on a priori grounds. Migration from i to j is directly related to high per capita wages and salaries at j and to a large labor force at either the origin or the destination. It is inversely related to high per capita wages and salaries at i and increasing distance between i and j.

It is of interest to note, in Table 3.13(B), that when we extend the model to include non-SMSA flows, the r^2 declines from 0.8665 to 0.8045. This is a direct result of an increased number of observations and the mixing of metropolitan and nonmetropolitan flows. To see this more clearly, let us now turn to an analysis of migration streams differentiated by class of subregion at origin and destination.

Demographers have found considerable empirical support for the thesis that factors determining out-migration tend to vary with the type of destination as well as with the type of origin. As a limited test of this hypothesis, we report in Tables 3.15 and 3.16 the four separate fits of the model to the 1955-1960 flow matrix, partitioned by metropolitan and nonmetropolitan origins and destinations.[13]

Table 3.12. Average Annual Per Capita Wages and Salaries and Labor Force Eligibles in 19 California Standard Economic Areas in 1955

Name of SEA	Average Annual Per Capita Wages and Salaries	Labor Force Eligibles
A. San Francisco-Oakland	1,747	1,629,132
B. San Jose	1,225	267,713
C. Sacramento	1,569	236,863
D. Stockton	1,140	142,282
E. Fresno	1,040	190,353
F. Los Angeles-Long Beach	1,671	3,585,361
G. San Diego	1,530	530,544
H. San Bernardino	1,187	381,053
J. Bakersfield	1,233	159,115
K. Santa Barbara	999	69,829
1. Northern Coast	1,385	102,339
2. North Central Coast	935	110,616
3. South Central Coast	1,106	197,817
4. Sacramento Valley	1,044	142,030
5. North San Joaquin Valley	928	133,559
6. South San Joaquin Valley	766	142,280
7. Ventura	1,192	94,085
8. Imperial Valley	973	42,818
9. Sierra	1,138	162,479

Source: Rogers (1965).

[13] An alternative way of introducting such a partitioning is to incorporate dummy variables into the regression model [Exercise 5(a)].

From SEA* \ To SEA*	A	B	C	D	E	F	G	H	J	K
A	2,114,554	50,193	17,333	6,742	4,868	42,524	13,150	6,074	2,818	2,241
B	19,698	354,020	2,279	1,072	1,358	6,648	1,853	1,225	752	591
C	9,236	2,286	305,634	2,353	1,010	5,320	1,267	1,489	518	404
D	6,964	2,546	4,402	185,040	1,017	3,908	866	730	531	103
E	5,890	3,685	2,202	1,259	257,681	8,703	1,181	1,490	2,440	640
F	42,025	24,104	16,885	3,370	7,532	4,939,191	43,158	71,703	11,254	15,316
G	9,776	3,781	1,528	747	776	30,246	646,168	7,340	1,251	1,559
H	4,388	2,066	2,468	425	1,386	35,596	8,748	503,849	2,422	1,724
J	3,173	2,024	1,167	662	2,451	13,358	1,905	2,868	200,990	1,947
K	1,960	936	312	123	440	5,197	696	777	673	87,800
1	5,400	1,329	1,793	713	653	2,349	660	542	288	319
2	9,094	2,054	1,649	522	505	2,672	832	673	288	189
3	9,126	8,225	1,770	974	1,995	7,784	2,229	1,561	1,219	2,202
4	6,026	1,708	8,573	977	894	3,074	898	1,003	654	197
5	5,922	2,809	2,128	3,171	3,105	4,340	958	1,281	699	310
6	3,866	2,641	1,185	814	8,382	7,042	1,240	1,674	3,612	550
7	1,392	1,108	390	88	451	8,004	1,488	1,267	743	1,724
8	484	502	256	246	423	3,283	3,561	1,794	375	148
9	6,683	1,893	8,378	1,787	886	4,817	1,148	1,546	745	277

Figure 3.7. 1955–1960 Migration Flows Between 19 California Standard Economic Areas

From SEA* \ To SEA*	1	2	3	4	5	6	7	8	9
A	5,610	20,271	12,535	8,894	4,928	2,355	1,362	406	10,785
B	807	1,523	6,359	1,327	1,171	815	531	153	2,134
C	609	974	1,561	6,917	1,001	504	161	79	7,380
D	507	697	1,486	1,677	2,831	740	255	204	2,333
E	599	486	2,748	850	2,306	6,960	647	215	1,048
F	2,713	3,712	15,746	6,683	3,829	6,438	17,629	1,575	11,873
G	474	760	1,968	877	510	511	2,100	984	1,009
H	596	664	2,336	1,178	1,284	1,194	1,179	793	2,098
J	459	382	3,024	873	855	3,110	1,470	265	1,028
K	170	132	2,267	258	137	295	1,767	116	335
1	124,730	4,095	1,055	2,285	575	501	136	36	3,251
2	2,279	146,057	953	1,438	466	396	139	12	1,615
3	555	900	240,538	1,081	1,283	1,284	846	399	1,242
4	1,548	1,213	1,332	184,959	814	566	291	121	5,954
5	623	733	1,584	1,165	172,834	1,990	273	149	2,083
6	792	716	2,385	971	2,186	190,393	568	151	1,122
7	173	163	740	417	378	554	118,862	63	622
8	79	40	441	170	284	333	301	51,687	76
9	2,029	1,199	1,529	6,345	1,821	813	325	142	201,170

*A = San Francisco-Oakland SMSA
B = San Jose SMSA
C = Sacramento SMSA
D = Stockton SMSA
E = Fresno SMSA
F = Los Angeles-Long Beach SMSA
G = San Diego SMSA
H = San Bernardino SMSA
J = Bakersfield SMSA
K = Santa Barbara SMSA
1 = Northern Coast SEA
2 = North Central Coast SEA
3 = South Central Coast SEA
4 = Sacramento Valley SEA
5 = North San Joaquin Valley SEA
6 = South San Joaquin Valley SEA
7 = Ventura SEA
8 = Imperial Valley SEA
9 = Sierra SEA

Source: U.S. Bureau of the Census (PC(2)–2B), *U.S. Census of Population, 1960*, *Mobility for State and State Economic Areas*, U.S. Bureau of the Census, Department of Commerce, 1963.

Figure 3.7. 1955–1960 Migration Flows Between 19 California Standard Economic Areas (*Continued*)

	A	B	C	D	E	F	G	H	J	K	1	2	3	4	5	6	7	8	9
A		48	89	83	184	403	522	464	291	337	225	56	171	150	113	221	346	618	245
B	48		125	363	149	366	485	427	254	285	271	102	123	180	99	175	316	581	263
C	89	125		46	166	383	502	444	271	425	252	99	249	77	93	207	398	598	169
D	83	363	46		122	339	458	400	227	74	290	118	197	123	49	161	68	554	185
E	184	149	166	122		217	332	274	105	255	488	240	186	222	119	35	238	428	263
F	403	366	383	339	217		120	62	113	92	622	453	258	430	291	194	65	216	379
G	522	485	502	458	332	120		105	232	221	741	562	377	574	410	313	184	117	485
H	464	427	444	400	274	62	105		174	146	682	514	312	516	352	255	119	159	413
J	291	254	271	227	105	113	232	174		155	442	314	174	343	179	81	128	328	283
K	337	285	425	74	255	92	221	146	155		560	391	166	475	333	236	27	315	446
1	225	271	252	290	488	622	741	682	442	560		170	393	217	330	442	524	826	313
2	56	102	99	118	240	453	562	514	314	391	170		225	154	163	271	418	668	320
3	171	123	249	197	186	258	377	312	174	166	393	225		302	163	164	193	473	349
4	150	180	77	123	222	430	574	516	343	475	217	154	302		172	292	494	670	185
5	113	99	93	49	119	291	410	352	179	333	330	163	163	172		113	306	506	198
6	221	175	207	161	35	194	313	255	81	236	442	271	164	292	113		209	343	290
7	346	316	398	68	238	65	184	119	128	27	524	418	193	494	306	209		280	409
8	618	581	598	554	428	216	117	159	328	315	826	668	473	670	506	343	280		633
9	245	263	169	185	263	379	485	413	283	446	313	320	349	185	198	290	409	633	

Source: Rogers (1965).

Figure 3.8. Inter-SEA Distances [In miles (circa 1955) between major county seats.]

Table 3.13. Regression Statistics for the Migration Model

A. Fitted to 10 × 10 SMSA Flow Matrix			B. Fitted to 19 × 19 SEA Flow Matrix		
Variable	Coefficient	Partial Correlation Coefficient	Variable	Coefficient	Partial Correlation Coefficient
Constant	−9.9527		Constant	−6.2295	
ln LF_i	0.9295*	0.7632	ln LF_i	0.7724*	0.6744
ln LF_j	0.6611*	0.6432	ln LF_j	0.6843*	0.6291
ln D_{ij}	−0.6360*	−0.6484	ln D_{ij}	−0.8058*	−0.6616
ln WS_j	0.5787	0.1237	ln WS_j	0.2716	0.0669
ln WS_i	−0.4409	−0.0945	ln WS_i	−0.2713	−0.0669
r^2	0.8665		r^2	0.8045	

* Significant at the 0.1 percent level.
Source: Calculated using the data in Figures 3.7 and 3.8, and Table 3.12. Computed by Gary Kane.

Table 3.14. Analysis of Variance Statistics for the Migration Model

A. Model Fitted to 10 × 10 SMSA Flow Matrix

Source of Variation	Degrees of Freedom	Sum of Squares	Mean Square	*F* Ratio
Total (uncorrected for mean)	90	5,804.38		
Correction for the Mean (b_0)	1	5,639.20		
Total (corrected for mean)	89	165.18		
Model ($b_1, b_2, b_3, b_4, b_5 \mid b_0$)	5	143.13	28.63	109.05
Error	84	22.05	0.26	

B. Model Fitted to 19 × 19 SEA Flow Matrix

Source of Variation	Degrees of Freedom	Sum of Squares	Mean Square	*F* Ratio
Total (uncorrected for mean)	342	18,266.61		
Correction for the Mean (b_0)	1	17,656.23		
Total (corrected for mean)	341	610.38		
Model ($b_1, b_2, b_3, b_4, b_5 \mid b_0$)	5	491.06	98.21	276.56
Error	336	119.32	0.36	

Source: Same as Table 3.13.

Table 3.15. Regression Statistics for Flows from Metropolitan Subregions

A. Flows from SMSA to SMSA Subregions (10 × 10)			B. Flows from SMSA to Non-SMSA Subregions (10 × 9)		
Variable	Coefficient	Partial Correlation Coefficient	Variable	Coefficient	Partial Correlation Coefficient
Constant	−9.9528		Constant	−15.6364	
ln LF_i	0.9295*	0.7632	ln LF_i	0.8477*	0.7522
ln LF_j	0.6611*	0.6432	ln D_{ij}	−0.9022*	−0.7856
ln D_{ij}	−0.6360*	−0.6484	ln LF_i	1.2506*	0.7388
ln WS_j	0.5787	0.1237	ln WS_j	1.1668*	0.3638
ln WS_i	−0.4409	−0.0945	ln WS_i	−0.8151	−0.1840
r^2	0.8665		r^2	0.8576	

* Significant at the 0.1 percent level.
Source: Same as Table 3.13.

Table 3.16. Regression Statistics for Flows from Nonmetropolitan Subregions

A. Flows from Non-SMSA to Non-SMSA Subregions (9 × 9)			B. Flows from Non-SMSA to SMSA Subregions (9 × 10)		
Variable	Coefficient	Partial Correlation Coefficient	Variable	Coefficient	Partial Correlation Coefficient
Constant	−26.5621		Constant	−8.7055	
ln D_{ij}	−1.2572*	−0.6210	ln LF_j	0.5664*	0.5619
ln LF_j	1.2929*	0.6255	ln D_{ij}	−0.7761*	−0.6978
ln LF_i	0.8561*	0.4689	ln LF_i	0.7719*	0.5161
ln WS_j	1.2566**	0.3254	ln WS_j	0.4954	0.1008
ln WS_i	0.9081***	0.2414	ln WS_i	0.0500	0.0149
r^2	0.7859		r^2	0.7622	

* Significant at the 0.1 percent level.
** Significant at the 1 percent level.
*** Significant at the 5 percent level.
Source: Same as Table 3.13.

Several interesting findings are indicated by the regression statistics. First, it is clear that the model provides a better accounting of flows originating from metropolitan subregions. This may be a reflection of the higher quality of information concerning economic opportunities that exists in metropolitan areas. Second, per capita wages and salaries are significant only in flows to nonmetropolitan subregions. This suggests that people will not move to nonmetropolitan areas unless a definite improvement in per capita earnings is anticipated. Finally, it is encouraging to note that, once again, all five variables have signs which one would expect from a priori considerations. Migration from i to j is directly proportional to per capita wages at j and the product of the "masses" at i and j (as measured by labor force eligibles). It is inversely proportional to per capita wages and salaries at i and to the distance separating i and j.

In sum, the statistics presented in Tables 3.13, 3.14, 3.15, and 3.16 represent a modest attempt to assess the significance and relative weight of a set of economic variables and their differential impact on migrant streams. The results are promising. In every instance, a large proportion of the variation in total flows has been accounted for by a small subset of variables. Thus, on the basis of these regression results, we may reasonably conclude that comparative economic opportunity is a factor that significantly influences interregional movements, at least in California.

EXERCISES

1. (a) Complete the stepwise regression example in the text by introducing distance from center-city into the model. Show that the additional explanatory contribution of that variable is not statistically significant at the five percent level.

(b) Computer programs for carrying out regression analyses generally do not read in the entire data matrix, **X**, before proceeding to form **X′X**. For large data sets, such a procedure would unnecessarily waste (or perhaps exceed) the machine's scarce storage capacity. Most programs, therefore, construct **X′X** by the *slice method*, wherein **X′X** is gradually built up by slices, one slice per observation:

$$\mathbf{X}'\mathbf{X} = \mathbf{x}_1\mathbf{x}_1' + \mathbf{x}_2\mathbf{x}_2' + \cdots + \mathbf{x}_n\mathbf{x}_n'$$

where $\mathbf{x}_i$ denotes the data vector associated with the ith observation. Thus, if n observations are involved in the analysis, only $n^2 + n$ storage locations need to be utilized.

Write a FORTRAN regression program that uses this method to form **X′X**, and demonstrate its use with the numerical example in Table 3.1.

(c) Linearize the following nonlinear model by a logarithmic transformation, and then fit it to the data in Table 3.1:

$$Y_i = bX^c\varepsilon_i$$

Show that a least squares fit made directly to this model in log-linear form is equivalent to a weighted least squares fit made to the model in nonlinear form.

2. (a) Express the consumption function of (3.50) in multiplicative form and then in log-linear form. Fit such a model to the data on housing expenditures and disposable income that appear in Tables 3.3 and 3.4. What is the income elasticity of demand? Repeat the above exercise using permanent income as the income measure.

(b) Analyze the separate and joint explanatory contributions of variables other than income.

(c) Is a classification of households by type of residence (single family houses versus apartments) statistically significant at the five percent level?

3. (a) Repeat the analysis of model life tables that appear in Subsection 3.2.4 using the following expectations of life at 10 years of age, e_{10}, as the independent variable instead of e_0:

	Male	Female
1. Indonesia	46.859	47.561
2. China	48.064	48.830
3. Pakistan	48.302	47.760
4. India	49.183	48.667
5. Korea	53.798	55.053
6. Philippines	56.619	58.429
7. Thailand	57.525	61.790
8. Ceylon	59.871	58.755
9. Japan	55.427	58.524
10. China	54.950	59.843
11. Ceylon	59.834	60.130
12. Japan	59.783	64.539

(b) Demonstrate that improved fits may be obtained for younger and older age groups by using logarithmic transformations.

(c) Construct a life table for Yugoslavian females, using the data in Table 3.7 and an expectation of life at birth of 66.53 years. Compare your results with the empirical life table that appears in Chapter 1.

(d) An early attempt to use regression techniques to construct model life tables [United Nations (1955)] focused on the relationships between successive probabilities of dying and estimated linear regression equations of the form

$$ {}_nq_k = b_0 + b_1\,{}_nq_{k-x} + b_2\,{}_nq_{k-x}^2 $$

That is, ${}_4q_1$ was regressed on ${}_1q_0$, then ${}_5q_5$ on ${}_4q_1$, and so on. In this way, a different life table could be constructed for an arbitrary value of ${}_1q_0$, and using such a process a one-parameter set of model life tables was developed.

Apply this method to the data on Asian mortality that appear in Tables 3.5 and 3.6, and compare the results with those presented in the text. Which method is likely to be more accurate and why?

4. (a) Find the unrestricted least squares (ULS) estimate of the population growth matrix in (3.95), using only the 1950 to 1955 observations in Table 3.10. Repeat, using only the 1955 to 1960 observations. Compare and analyze your results.

(b) Consider the regression equation

$$Y = b_0 + b_1X_1 + b_2X_2$$

Regress Y on X_1 to find $\hat{Y} = a_0 + a_1X_1$, and regress X_2 on X_1 to find $\hat{X}_2 = c_0 + c_1X_1$. Next, regress $(Y - \hat{Y})$ on $(X_2 - \hat{X}_2)$ to find $(Y - \hat{Y}) = d(X_2 - \hat{X}_2)$. (No intercept term is required, since we are dealing with two sets of residuals that sum to zero.) By substitution,

$$Y - (a_0 + a_1X_1) = d[X_2 - (c_0 + c_1X_1)]$$

or, collecting terms,

$$Y = (a_0 - dc_0) + (a_1 - dc_1)X_1 + dX_2 = b_0 + b_1X_1 + b_2X_2$$

Apply the above decomposition procedure to the model in (3.96) to explain why g_{12} is negative, and illustrate graphically the conditions that lead to a negative least squares estimate of g_{12}.

5. (a) Introduce three dummy variables into the migration model defined by (3.104) in order to distinguish between migration flows that have metropolitan and nonmetropolitan origins and destinations. Compare your results with those presented in Tables 3.15 and 3.16.

(b) Compare the fit of the migration model defined by (3.107) with the one that is obtained by removing all of the logarithmic transformations from that model.

(c) Develop and fit a *net* migration model using the data in Subsection 3.4.5.

6. The California Statistical Abstract reports a 1957 unemployment rate of 4.2 percent for the state and the following unemployment rates for eight of the state's SMSA's:

SMSA	1957 Unemployment Rate
1. San Francisco—Oakland	4.2
2. San Jose	5.9
3. Sacramento	4.6
4. Stockton	7.2
5. Fresno	6.8
6. Los Angeles—Long Beach	3.6
7. San Diego	3.1
8. San Bernardino-Riverside-Ontario	5.9

Given this information and the data in Subsection 3.4.5, assume that labor force eligibles (LF) adequately approximate the total number of people that are in the labor force, and fit the following labor force participation model to the eight SMSA's for which data are available:

$$\frac{LF_i}{P_i} = \beta_0 + \beta_1(U_i - U_c) + \beta_2N_i + \varepsilon_i \qquad (i = 1, 2, \ldots, 8)$$

where

U_i = unemployment rate in the ith SMSA;

U_c = unemployment rate for California;

N_i = net migration into the ith SMSA during 1955–1960; and

LF_i/P_i = labor force participation rate in the ith SMSA.

Note that P_i may be found by summing the ith row in Figure 3.7.

7. Transportation planners define a *trip* to be a single, purposeful journey, between two points, that is made by a specified means of transport. Analyses of trip behavior commonly are carried out using regression models that express some measure of trip frequency as a function of such variables as car ownership and distance from center-city.

The following data were adapted from data published by the Penn-Jersey Transportation Study:

Superdistrict of Trip Origin	Total Person Trips (in Thousands) Y	Air Distance to Center-City (in Miles) X_1	Automobiles Owned (in Thousands) X_2	Total Population (in Thousands) X_3
1	592	1.6	69	485
2	307	2.0	41	248
3	132	3.9	20	91
4	478	3.0	60	303
5	262	4.3	36	148
6	82	6.1	15	42
7	392	5.9	64	241
8	439	6.0	67	229
9	88	9.8	13	37
10	136	6.1	22	82
11	36	9.1	7	27

Use these data to estimate the following models:

(a) $Y = \beta_0 + \beta_1 X_1 + \beta_2 X_2 + \beta_3 X_3 + \varepsilon$;

(b) $Y = \beta_0 + \beta_2 X_2 + \beta_3 X_3 + \varepsilon$;

(c) $Y = \beta_0 + \beta_1 X_1 + \varepsilon$;

(d) $Y = \beta_0 + \beta_2 X_2 + \varepsilon$.

Interpret and discuss your results.

8. A *production function* is an economic relationship that expresses output, X, say, as a function of the fundamental factors of production: labor and capital. One of the simplest such functions is called the *Cobb-Douglas* production function, which has the following form:

$$X = aL^b K^c$$

where X, L, and K denote quantities of output and labor and capital inputs, respectively, and b and c are parameters that are to be estimated from cross-sectional data.

The following data describe output levels of gross product, utilized capital stock, and man-hours of employed labor for the private domestic nonfarm sector of the United States (all measured in billions of 1929 dollars):

Year t	Gross Product X_t	Man-Hours Employed L_t	Utilized Capital Stock K_t
1950	163.6	100.4	307.9
1951	173.4	104.8	322.4
1952	178.9	106.2	334.9
1953	186.3	109.2	350.1
1954	183.5	104.5	346.1
1955	198.8	109.9	374.9
1956	205.3	113.1	378.5
1957	206.8	112.4	397.8
1958	198.4	109.1	378.4
1959	216.5	114.4	393.4
1960	221.5	115.2	403.8

Fit the Cobb-Douglas production function to the data, and interpret its parameters.

9. The following data were adapted from those published by the U.S. Department of Commerce that describe, in macro-terms, the state of the U.S. economy during the 1950 to 1960 decade. All variables except the interest rate are measured in billions of 1958 dollars.

Year t	Total Gross Product Y_t	Personal Consumption C_t	Gross Investment I_t	Net Exports E_t	Government Purchases G_t	Interest Rate R_t
1950	355.3	230.5	69.3	2.7	52.8	2.32
1951	383.4	232.8	70.0	5.3	75.4	2.57
1952	395.1	239.4	60.5	3.0	92.1	2.68
1953	412.8	250.8	61.2	1.1	99.8	2.94
1954	407.0	255.7	59.4	3.0	88.9	2.55
1955	438.0	274.2	75.4	3.2	85.2	2.84
1956	446.1	281.4	74.3	5.0	85.3	3.08
1957	452.5	288.2	68.8	6.2	89.3	3.47
1958	447.3	290.1	60.9	2.2	94.2	3.43
1959	475.9	307.3	73.6	0.3	94.7	4.08
1960	487.7	316.1	72.4	4.3	94.9	4.02

Fit the model described in Exercise 10 of Chapter 2 to these data, and estimate the probable impact on output and consumption of:

(a) a drop in the interest rate to two percent;
(b) an increase in the interest rate to eight percent;
(c) a drop in the level of investment to 50 billion dollars; and
(d) an increase in the level of investment to 100 billion dollars.

10. (a) In Table 6.4, we present the minimum car travel times, in minutes, between the 15 commune centers in the Ljubljana Metropolitan Region. Use these data and the data in Section 1.6 to estimate the following model of journey-to-work travel:

$$E_{ij} = k \frac{e_i^a e_j^b}{t_{ij}^c}$$

where

E_{ij} = the number of employees who live in commune i and work in commune j;
e_i, e_j = total employment in communes i and j, respectively;
t_{ij} = minimum car travel time between commune centers i and j; and
a, b, c, k = parameters.

Interpret and analyze your results.

(b) Repeat the above exercise using the slightly modified model [Lakshmanan-Hansen (1965)]:

$$E_{ij} = k e_i^a \left[\frac{e_j^b}{t_{ij}^c \sum_{k=1}^{n} \frac{e_k^b}{t_{ik}^c}} \right]$$

How does this model differ from the previous one, and why is it much more difficult to solve? Can you suggest an estimation method?

REFERENCES AND SELECTED READINGS

THEORY

Draper, N. R. and H. Smith. *Applied Regression Analysis.* New York: John Wiley & Sons, 1966.

Goldberger, A. S. *Econometric Theory.* New York: John Wiley & Sons, 1964.

Hoel, P. G. *Introduction to Mathematical Statistics*, 3rd edition. New York: John Wiley & Sons, 1963.

Johnston, J. *Econometric Methods.* New York: McGraw-Hill, 1963.

King, L.J. *Statistical Analysis in Geography.* Englewood Cliffs, N.J.: Prentice-Hall, 1969.

Malinvaud, E. *Statistical Methods of Econometrics.* Chicago: Rand McNally, 1966.

Mood A. M. *Introduction to the Theory of Statistics.* New York: McGraw-Hill, 1950.

Smiley, K. W. *An Introduction to Regression and Correlation.* New York: Academic Press, 1966.

Suits, D. S. "Use of Dummy Variables in Regression Equations," *Journal of the American Statistical Association*, **LII** : 2, 1957, 548–551.

APPLICATION: THE DEMAND FOR HOUSING

Falcke, C. "The Demand for Housing in Finland," unpublished master's thesis, Department of City and Regional Planning, University of California, Berkeley, 1969.

Friedman, M. *A Theory of the Consumption Function.* Princeton, N. J.: Princeton University Press, 1957.

Lee, T. H. "Housing and Permanent Income: Tests Based on a Three-Year Reinterview Survey," *Review of Economics and Statistics*, **L** : 4, 1968, 480–490.

Maisel, S. and L. Winnick. "Family Housing Expenditures: Elusive Laws and Intrusive Variables," *Consumption and Savings*, **1**, I. Friend and R. Jones, ed. Philadelphia: Wharton School of Finance and Commerce, University of Pennsylvania, 1960, pp. 359–435.

Muth, R. F. *Cities and Housing.* Chicago: The University of Chicago Press, 1969.

APPLICATION: MODEL LIFE TABLES

Coale, A. J. and P. Demeny. *Regional Model Life Tables and Stable Populations.* Princeton, N. J.: Princeton University Press, 1966.

Keyfitz, N. and W. Flieger. *World Population.* Chicago: The University of Chicago Press, 1968.

United Nations, Department of Social Affairs. *Age and Sex Patterns of Mortality.* New York, ST/SOA/Ser.A/22, 1955.

United Nations, Department of Social Affairs. *Methods of Estimating Basic Demographic Measures from Incomplete Data.* New York, ST/SOA/Ser.A/42, 1967.

APPLICATION: ESTIMATING A POPULATION GROWTH MATRIX FROM A TIME SERIES OF INTERREGIONAL POPULATION DISTRIBUTIONS

Miller, G. A. "Finite Markov Processes in Psychology," *Psychometrika*, **XVII** : 2, 1952, 149–167.

Madansky, A. "Least Squares Estimation in Finite Markov Processes," *Psychometrika*, **XXIV** : 2, 1959, 137–144.

Rogers, A. "Estimating Interregional Population and Migration Operators from Interregional Population Distributions," *Demography*, **IV** : 2, 1967, 515–531.

APPLICATION: ANALYSIS OF INTERREGIONAL MIGRATION FLOWS

Greenwood, M. J. "An Analysis of the Determinants of Geographic Labor Mobility in the United States," *Review of Economics and Statistics*, **LI** : 2, 1969, 189–194.

Lowry, I. S. *Migration and Metropolitan Growth: Two Analytical Models*. San Francisco: Chandler, 1966.

Rogers, A. *Projected Population Growth in California Regions: 1960–1980*. Berkeley, Cal.: Center for Planning and Development Research, University of California, 1965.

——— "A Regression Analysis of Interregional Migration in California," *Review of Economics and Statistics*, **XLIX** : 2, 1967, 262–267.

OTHER SELECTED APPLICATIONS

Bell, F. W. "An Econometric Forecasting Model for a Region," *Journal of Regional Science*, **VII** : 2, 1967 109–128.

Berry, B. J. L. *Commercial Structure and Commercial Blight*. Chicago: Department of Geography, University of Chicago, 1963.

Bowen, W. G. and T. A. Finegan. *The Economics of Labor Force Participation*. Princeton, N. J.: Princeton University Press, 1969.

Chapin, F. S., Jr., and S. F. Weiss. *Factors Influencing Land Development*. Chapel Hill, N. C.: Center for Urban and Regional Studies, University of North Carolina, 1962.

——— "Land Development Patterns and Growth Alternatives," *Urban Growth Dynamics*, ed. by F. S. Chapin, Jr., and S. F. Weiss. New York: John Wiley & Sons, 1962, pp. 425–458.

Hill, D. M. "A Growth Allocation Model for the Boston Region," *Journal of the American Institute of Planners*, **XXXI** : 2, 1965, 111–120.

Kosobud, R. "Forecasting Public Education Expenditures," *Papers of the Regional Science Association*, **XI**, 1963, 253–284.

Lakshmanan, T. R. and W. G. Hansen. "A Retail Market Potential Model," *Journal of the American Institute of Planners*, **XXXI** : 2, 1965, 134–143.

Mattila, J. M. and W. R. Thompson. "Toward an Econometric Model of Urban Economic Development," *Issues in Urban Economics*, ed. by H. S. Perloff and L. Wingo, Jr. Baltimore: Johns Hopkins University Press, 1968, pp. 63–78.

Oi, W. Y. and P. W. Shuldiner. *An Analysis of Urban Travel Demand*. Evanston, Ill.: Northwestern University Press, 1962.

four vectors, vector spaces, and simultaneous linear equation systems

In Chapter 1 we frequently encountered matrices with only a single row or a single column. We defined such matrices as row vectors and column vectors, respectively, and found that all of the algebraic operations of matrix addition, matrix subtraction, and matrix multiplication could be carried out with these special matrices. Matrix inversion, however, was defined only for square matrices and, therefore, is not applicable to vectors. Before continuing our discussion of matrix analysis, we will find it useful to review and extend our previous discussion of vectors and vector algebra.

4.1 DEFINITIONS, NOTATION, AND ALGEBRA

Following the notation adopted in Chapter 1, we shall continue to denote column vectors as

$$\underset{m\times 1}{\mathbf{a}} = \begin{bmatrix} a_1 \\ a_2 \\ \vdots \\ a_m \end{bmatrix}$$

and row vectors as

$$\underset{1\times n}{\mathbf{a}'} = [a_1 \quad a_2 \cdots a_n]$$

A vector with all of its elements equal to zero is called a *null vector.* Conversely, a vector with at least a single nonzero element is said to be a *nonnull* vector.

Two vectors of the same order, **a** and **b**, say, can be added to define the vector sum

$$\mathbf{c} = \mathbf{a} + \mathbf{b} = \begin{bmatrix} a_1 + b_1 \\ a_2 + b_2 \\ \vdots \quad \vdots \\ a_m + b_m \end{bmatrix}$$

or

$$\mathbf{c}' = \mathbf{a}' + \mathbf{b}' = [a_1 + b_1 \quad a_2 + b_2 \cdots a_n + b_n]$$

Subtraction may be defined as negative addition.

Successive additions of a vector to itself, λ times, say, results in a vector that is λ times the original vector. For example,

$$\mathbf{a} + \mathbf{a} = \begin{bmatrix} a_1 + a_1 \\ a_2 + a_2 \\ \vdots \quad \vdots \\ a_m + a_m \end{bmatrix} = 2\mathbf{a}$$

or

$$\mathbf{a}' + \mathbf{a}' = [a_1 + a_1 \quad a_2 + a_2 \cdots a_n + a_n] = 2\mathbf{a}'$$

Thus we may view successive additions as the multiplication of a vector by a scalar. That is, if λ is an arbitrary scalar and **a** is any m-dimensional vector, then

$$\lambda\mathbf{a} = \begin{bmatrix} \lambda a_1 \\ \lambda a_2 \\ \vdots \\ \lambda a_m \end{bmatrix}$$

or

$$\lambda\mathbf{a}' = [\lambda a_1 \quad \lambda a_2 \cdots \lambda a_n]$$

A column vector, **b**, say, if premultiplied by a row vector of the same order, **a**′, say, defines the *scalar product*

$$c = \underset{1\times m}{\mathbf{a}'} \underset{m\times 1}{\mathbf{b}} = [a_1 \quad a_2 \cdots a_m] \begin{bmatrix} b_1 \\ b_2 \\ \vdots \\ b_m \end{bmatrix} = \sum_{i=1}^{m} a_i b_i$$

and the same column vector, **b**, if postmultiplied by **a**′, yields the *matrix product*

$$\underset{m\times m}{\mathbf{C}} = \underset{m\times 1}{\mathbf{b}}\ \underset{1\times m}{\mathbf{a}'} = \begin{bmatrix} b_1 \\ b_2 \\ \vdots \\ b_m \end{bmatrix} [a_1 \quad a_2 \cdots a_m] = \begin{bmatrix} a_1b_1 & a_2b_1 & \cdots & a_mb_1 \\ a_1b_2 & a_2b_2 & \cdots & a_mb_2 \\ \vdots & & & \vdots \\ a_1b_m & & \cdots & a_mb_m \end{bmatrix}$$

It is apparent that the operations of addition, subtraction, and multiplication can be carried out only on vectors that have the same order, that is, have the same number of elements.

Let us define the set of all vectors with m elements as the *m-dimensional vector space*, V^m. For example, the collection of all vectors that can be defined in the two-dimensional Euclidean plane will be denoted by V^2. Thus, the vector

$$\mathbf{a} = \begin{bmatrix} a_1 \\ a_2 \end{bmatrix} = \begin{bmatrix} 4 \\ 3 \end{bmatrix}$$

is a member of V^2 and can be plotted as a point in two-dimensional space, as in Figure 4.1.

The straight line connecting the point (4, 3) with the origin is said to be the *length*, denoted by $\|\mathbf{a}\|$, of the vector in V^2. From the Pythagorean theorem of elementary plane geometry, we know that the length of the

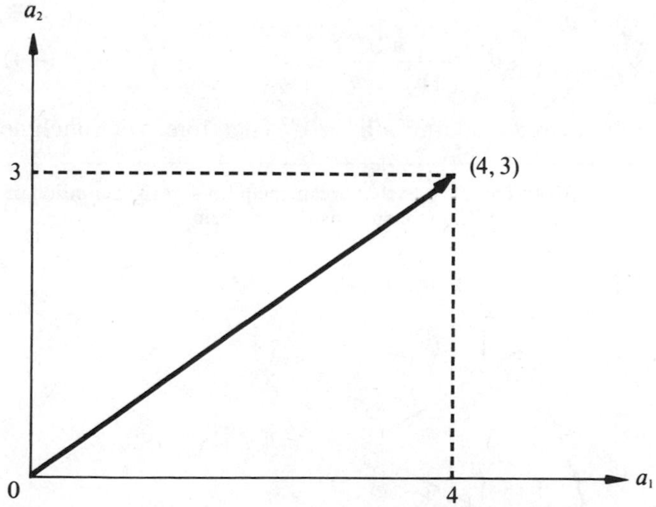

Figure 4.1. A Vector in Two-Dimensional Space

hypotenuse of a right triangle is equal to the square root of the sum of the squares of its two sides. Hence the length of the vector **a** in Figure 4.1 is

$$\begin{aligned}\|\mathbf{a}\| &= \sqrt{a_1^2 + a_2^2} = \sqrt{\mathbf{a}'\mathbf{a}} \\ &= \sqrt{4^2 + 3^2} = \sqrt{25} \\ &= 5\end{aligned}$$

and generalizing this definition to an m-dimensional vector space, we have that

$$\|\mathbf{a}\| = \sqrt{\mathbf{a}'\mathbf{a}} \tag{4.1}$$

Vectors that are perpendicular to each other are said to be *orthogonal.* We can express this condition algebraically by using the *law of cosines*[1] to express the length of the difference of two vectors, **a** and **b**, say, as a function of the lengths of **a** and **b**, respectively, and the cosine of the angle that they define with respect to each other. More specifically, we have that

$$\|\mathbf{a} - \mathbf{b}\|^2 = \|\mathbf{a}\|^2 + \|\mathbf{b}\|^2 - 2\,\|\mathbf{a}\| \cdot \|\mathbf{b}\| \cos\theta \tag{4.2}$$

where θ is the angle between **a** and **b**. But

$$\begin{aligned}\|\mathbf{a} - \mathbf{b}\|^2 &= (\mathbf{a} - \mathbf{b})'(\mathbf{a} - \mathbf{b}) = \mathbf{a}'\mathbf{a} - 2\mathbf{a}'\mathbf{b} + \mathbf{b}'\mathbf{b} \\ &= \|\mathbf{a}\|^2 + \|\mathbf{b}\|^2 - 2\mathbf{a}'\mathbf{b}\end{aligned} \tag{4.3}$$

Thus, equating the right-hand sides of (4.2) and (4.3), we obtain

$$2\mathbf{a}'\mathbf{b} = 2\,\|\mathbf{a}\| \cdot \|\mathbf{b}\| \cos\theta$$

or

$$\cos\theta = \frac{\mathbf{a}'\mathbf{b}}{\|\mathbf{a}\| \cdot \|\mathbf{b}\|} \tag{4.4}$$

Hence, when $\theta = \pm 90°$, $\cos\theta = 0$ and $\mathbf{a}'\mathbf{b} = 0$. Therefore, we conclude

---

[1] The law of cosines can be derived from the Pythagorean theorem and the definition of the sine and cosine functions. For any triangle such as the one below,

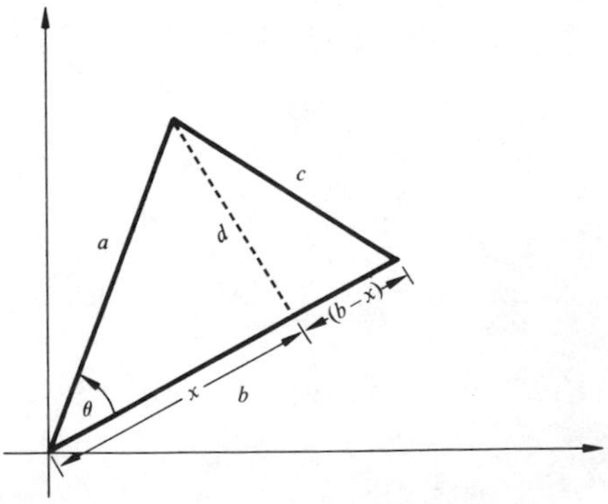

that two vectors, **a** and **b**, say, are *orthogonal* if their scalar product $\mathbf{a}'\mathbf{b}$ is zero.

A vector of unit length is said to be a *normalized vector.* We can normalize any nonnull vector to unit length by dividing each of its elements by its *length.* Normalized vectors that are orthogonal to each other are said to be *orthonormal.*

We can extend the concept of orthogonality to matrices by defining an *orthogonal matrix* as a square matrix consisting of mutually orthonormal column and row vectors. This implies that an orthogonal matrix, **U**, say, is a matrix such that

$$\mathbf{U}'\mathbf{U} = \mathbf{I} \tag{4.5}$$

and since, by definition,

$$\mathbf{U}^{-1}\mathbf{U} = \mathbf{I}$$

we conclude that the transpose of an orthogonal matrix **U** is equal to its inverse, that is,

$$\mathbf{U}'\mathbf{U} = \mathbf{U}^{-1}\mathbf{U} = \mathbf{I}$$

therefore,

$$\mathbf{U}^{-1} = \mathbf{U}' \tag{4.6}$$

Example. To illustrate the above discussion, consider the vectors

$$\mathbf{a} = \begin{bmatrix} 4 \\ 3 \end{bmatrix} \qquad \mathbf{b} = \begin{bmatrix} 3 \\ -4 \end{bmatrix}$$

First, **a** and **b** are orthogonal:

$$\mathbf{a}'\mathbf{b} = [4 \quad 3]\begin{bmatrix} 3 \\ -4 \end{bmatrix} = 0$$

---

we can establish the following relationships:

$$d = a \sin \theta$$
$$x = a \cos \theta$$
$$\begin{aligned} c^2 &= d^2 + (b - x)^2 = d^2 + b^2 - 2bx + x^2 \\ &= a^2 \sin^2 \theta + b^2 - 2ab \cos \theta + a^2 \cos^2 \theta \\ &= a^2 (\sin^2 \theta + \cos^2 \theta) + b^2 - 2ab \cos \theta \end{aligned}$$

and, since $\sin^2 \theta + \cos^2 \theta = 1$, we have that

$$c^2 = a^2 + b^2 - 2ab \cos \theta$$

Carrying out the following substitutions,

$$c = \|\mathbf{a} - \mathbf{b}\|$$
$$a = \|\mathbf{a}\|$$
$$b = \|\mathbf{b}\|$$

we obtain (4.2).

Second, both **a** and **b** have lengths of five units:

$$\|\mathbf{a}\| = \sqrt{\mathbf{a}'\mathbf{a}} = 5 = \sqrt{\mathbf{b}'\mathbf{b}} = \|\mathbf{b}\|$$

Finally, we can normalize **a** and **b** by dividing each of their elements by five:

$$\mathbf{c} = \frac{1}{5}\,\mathbf{a} = \begin{bmatrix} \frac{4}{5} \\ \frac{3}{5} \end{bmatrix} \qquad \mathbf{d} = \frac{1}{5}\,\mathbf{b} = \begin{bmatrix} \frac{3}{5} \\ -\frac{4}{5} \end{bmatrix}$$

and

$$\|\mathbf{c}\| = \sqrt{\mathbf{c}'\mathbf{c}} = 1 = \sqrt{\mathbf{d}'\mathbf{d}} = \|\mathbf{d}\|$$

Since

$$\mathbf{c}'\mathbf{d} = \mathbf{d}'\mathbf{c} = 0$$

the vectors **c** and **d** are also orthogonal to each other; hence they are orthonormal vectors.

We may combine the orthonormal vectors **c** and **d** to define the orthogonal matrix

$$\mathbf{A} = [\mathbf{c} \quad \mathbf{d}] = \begin{bmatrix} \frac{4}{5} & \frac{3}{5} \\ \frac{3}{5} & -\frac{4}{5} \end{bmatrix}$$

Note that $\mathbf{A}'\mathbf{A} = \mathbf{A}^{-1}\mathbf{A} = \mathbf{I}$.

4.2 LINEAR DEPENDENCE

An m-dimensional column vector, $\mathbf{l}$, say, is *linearly dependent* on the m-dimensional column vectors $\mathbf{a}_1, \mathbf{a}_2, \ldots, \mathbf{a}_n$, if there exist scalars $b_1, b_2, \ldots, b_n$ such that

$$b_1\mathbf{a}_1 + b_2\mathbf{a}_2 + \cdots + b_n\mathbf{a}_n = \mathbf{l} \tag{4.7}$$

If such a set of scalars exists, the vector $\mathbf{l}$ is said to be a *linear combination* of the vectors $\mathbf{a}_1, \mathbf{a}_2, \ldots, \mathbf{a}_n$. Otherwise, $\mathbf{l}$ is *linearly independent* of $\mathbf{a}_1, \mathbf{a}_2, \ldots, \mathbf{a}_n$ and cannot be expressed as a linear combination of them. Since (4.7) can be written as

$$\mathbf{Ab} = \mathbf{l} \tag{4.8}$$

we conclude that $\mathbf{l}$ is linearly dependent on the column vectors of **A** if there exists a column vector **b** that satisfies (4.8). If no such vector exists, $\mathbf{l}$ is linearly independent of the column vectors of **A**.

An analogous argument leads to the conclusion that an n-dimensional row vector $\mathbf{p}'$ is linearly dependent on the row vectors of $\mathbf{A}$ if there exists a row vector $\mathbf{c}'$ such that

$$\mathbf{c}'\mathbf{A} = \mathbf{p}' \tag{4.9}$$

If such a vector does not exist, $\mathbf{p}'$ is linearly independent of the row vectors of $\mathbf{A}$.

We can easily establish that the *necessary* and *sufficient* condition for the set of column vectors $\mathbf{a}_1, \mathbf{a}_2, \ldots, \mathbf{a}_n$ to be linearly independent is the nonexistence of scalars $b_1, b_2, \ldots, b_n$, not all of which are zero, such that

$$b_1\mathbf{a}_1 + b_2\mathbf{a}_2 + \cdots + b_n\mathbf{a}_n = \mathbf{0} \tag{4.10}$$

where $\mathbf{0}$ is a column vector of zeroes, that is, a null vector. To prove necessity and sufficiency, we merely assume the converse in each case and show that this leads to contradiction. First, we assume that the column vectors $\mathbf{a}_1, \mathbf{a}_2, \ldots, \mathbf{a}_n$ are linearly independent and observe that (4.10) cannot hold unless all the b's are zero. For if a single b_i is nonzero, we can express $\mathbf{a}_i$ as a linear combination of the other vectors, namely,

$$\mathbf{a}_i = -\frac{b_1}{b_i}\mathbf{a}_1 - \cdots - \frac{b_{i-1}}{b_i}\mathbf{a}_{i-1} - \frac{b_{i+1}}{b_i}\mathbf{a}_{i+1} - \cdots - \frac{b_n}{b_i}\mathbf{a}_n \tag{4.11}$$

Equation (4.11) defines $\mathbf{a}_i$ as being linearly dependent on the vectors $\mathbf{a}_1, \ldots, \mathbf{a}_{i-1}, \mathbf{a}_{i+1}, \ldots, \mathbf{a}_n$. This contradicts our original assumption of linear independence. Hence, if $\mathbf{a}_1, \mathbf{a}_2, \ldots, \mathbf{a}_n$ are linearly independent, then (4.10) can be satisfied only with $b_1 = b_2 = \cdots = b_n = 0$.

Having established the "necessary" condition, we can proceed to establish that this condition is also "sufficient"; that is, if (4.10) can only be satisfied with $b_1 = b_2 = \cdots = b_n = 0$, then $\mathbf{a}_1, \mathbf{a}_2, \ldots, \mathbf{a}_n$ are linearly independent. Again the proof is by contradiction. We assume that all b's are zero and that $\mathbf{a}_1, \mathbf{a}_2, \ldots, \mathbf{a}_n$ are not linearly independent. Then at least one of the vectors, $\mathbf{a}_i$, say, is linearly dependent on the rest, and

$$\mathbf{a}_i = b_1\mathbf{a}_1 + \cdots + b_{i-1}\mathbf{a}_{i-1} + b_{i+1}\mathbf{a}_{i+1} + \cdots + b_n\mathbf{a}_n$$

Therefore,

$$b_1\mathbf{a}_1 + \cdots + b_{i-1}\mathbf{a}_{i-1} - \mathbf{a}_i + b_{i+1}\mathbf{a}_{i+1} + \cdots + b_n\mathbf{a}_n = \mathbf{0} \tag{4.12}$$

and (4.12) satisfies (4.10) with $b_i = -1$. This contradicts our initial assumptions. Hence we have established sufficiency, and from our above discussion it follows that if a vector of a set of vectors can be expressed as a linear combination of the others, then the vectors form a linearly dependent set; conversely, if several vectors form a linearly dependent set, then every vector in that set can be expressed as a linear combination of the others. Furthermore, any subset of a set of linearly independent vectors also forms a linearly independent set, and any set of vectors containing a subset of linearly dependent vectors is also linearly dependent.

As with the definition of linear dependence, we can state the necessary and sufficient conditions for the linear independence of the column vectors of **A** in matrix form. Thus the column vectors of **A** are linearly independent if the only vector **b** for which

$$\mathbf{A}\mathbf{b} = \mathbf{0} \tag{4.13}$$

is the null vector. An analogous statement may be formulated concerning the linear independence of the row vectors of **A**.

A single vector is linearly dependent only if it is the null vector, because for linear dependence it is necessary that

$$b_1 \mathbf{a}_1 = \mathbf{0}$$

where b_1 is nonzero. This can only occur if $\mathbf{a}_1 = \mathbf{0}$. It follows that if a set of vectors contains the null vector, the vectors are linearly dependent.

Example. To illustrate linear dependence and linear independence, let us consider the following set of three-dimensional column vectors:

$$\mathbf{a}_1 = \begin{bmatrix} 3 \\ 2 \\ 1 \end{bmatrix} \qquad \mathbf{a}_2 = \begin{bmatrix} 5 \\ 4 \\ 2 \end{bmatrix} \qquad \mathbf{a}_3 = \begin{bmatrix} 15 \\ 8 \\ 4 \end{bmatrix} \tag{4.14}$$

Substitution of these three vectors into (4.10) yields

$$b_1 \begin{bmatrix} 3 \\ 2 \\ 1 \end{bmatrix} + b_2 \begin{bmatrix} 5 \\ 4 \\ 2 \end{bmatrix} + b_3 \begin{bmatrix} 15 \\ 8 \\ 4 \end{bmatrix} = \begin{bmatrix} 0 \\ 0 \\ 0 \end{bmatrix}$$

or

$$\begin{aligned} 3b_1 + 5b_2 + 15b_3 &= 0 \\ 2b_1 + 4b_2 + 8b_3 &= 0 \\ b_1 + 2b_2 + 4b_3 &= 0 \end{aligned}$$

The above equations have the general solution

$$\mathbf{b} = \begin{bmatrix} b_1 \\ b_2 \\ b_3 \end{bmatrix} = k \begin{bmatrix} 10 \\ -3 \\ -1 \end{bmatrix}$$

where k is an arbitrary constant. We conclude, therefore, that the vectors $\mathbf{a}_1$, $\mathbf{a}_2$, and $\mathbf{a}_3$ satisfy

$$10\mathbf{a}_1 - 3\mathbf{a}_2 - \mathbf{a}_3 = \mathbf{0}$$

or any multiple thereof. Hence the vectors constitute a linearly dependent set.

The two vectors $\mathbf{a}_1$ and $\mathbf{a}_2$, however, form a linearly independent set, since

$$b_1 \mathbf{a}_1 + b_2 \mathbf{a}_2 = \mathbf{0}$$

only if $b_1 = b_2 = 0$. This can be confirmed by solving the equations

$$3b_1 + 5b_2 = 0$$
$$2b_1 + 4b_2 = 0$$
$$b_1 + 2b_2 = 0$$

We now can establish the correspondence between orthogonality and independence by observing that mutually orthogonal vectors are also linearly independent. If $\mathbf{a}_1, \mathbf{a}_2, \ldots, \mathbf{a}_n$ are mutually orthogonal nonnull vectors, then

$$\mathbf{a}_i' \mathbf{a}_j = 0 \qquad \text{for all } i \neq j \qquad (i, j = 1, 2, \ldots, n)$$

If possible, let

$$c_1 \mathbf{a}_1 + c_2 \mathbf{a}_2 + \cdots + c_n \mathbf{a}_n = \mathbf{0}$$

Then

$$\mathbf{a}_i'(c_1 \mathbf{a}_1 + c_2 \mathbf{a}_2 + \cdots + c_n \mathbf{a}_n) = 0 \qquad (i = 1, 2, \ldots, n)$$

and

$$c_i \mathbf{a}_i' \mathbf{a}_i = 0 \qquad (i = 1, 2, \ldots, n)$$

Since $\mathbf{a}_i \neq 0$, $\mathbf{a}_i' \mathbf{a}_i \neq 0$. Hence,

$$c_1 = c_2 = \cdots = c_n = 0$$

and, therefore, the vectors $\mathbf{a}_1, \mathbf{a}_2, \ldots, \mathbf{a}_n$ are linearly independent.

It should be noted that linearly independent vectors are not necessarily mutually orthogonal.

4.3 VECTOR SPACES

The set of column vectors that are linearly dependent on the column vectors $\mathbf{a}_1, \mathbf{a}_2, \ldots, \mathbf{a}_n$ define the *vector space*, $V^m(\mathbf{A})$, say, which is generated by the *space generating vector set* $\mathbf{a}_1, \mathbf{a}_2, \ldots, \mathbf{a}_n$. If the vectors in the space generating set are linearly independent, they are said to form a *basis* of $V^n(\mathbf{A})$. Every vector space containing a nonnull vector has a basis, and any vector in a given vector space can be uniquely expressed as a linear combination of the basis of that vector space. For example, the three vectors $\mathbf{a}_1$, $\mathbf{a}_2$, and $\mathbf{a}_3$ in (4.14) generate the vector space $V^2(\mathbf{A})$ consisting of all vectors **c**, say, of the form

$$\underset{3\times 1}{\mathbf{c}} = \begin{bmatrix} 3c_1 + 5c_2 + 15c_3 \\ 2c_1 + 4c_2 + 8c_3 \\ 1c_1 + 2c_2 + 4c_3 \end{bmatrix} \tag{4.15}$$

and the vector

$$\mathbf{g} = \begin{bmatrix} 11 \\ 8 \\ 4 \end{bmatrix} \tag{4.16}$$

is a member of $V^2(\mathbf{A})$. This can be seen by setting $c_1 = 2$, $c_2 = 1$, and $c_3 = 0$ in (4.15).

A particular vector space can be generated by many different space generating vector sets. For example, the vector space $V^2(\mathbf{A})$ defined by (4.15) could also be generated by the vectors

$$\mathbf{l}_1 = \begin{bmatrix} 30 \\ 20 \\ 10 \end{bmatrix} \qquad \mathbf{l}_2 = \begin{bmatrix} -15 \\ -12 \\ -6 \end{bmatrix} \tag{4.17}$$

which define the vector space containing all vectors, **d**, say, of the form

$$\underset{3\times 1}{\mathbf{d}} = \begin{bmatrix} 30d_1 - 15d_2 \\ 20d_1 - 12d_2 \\ 10d_1 - 6d_2 \end{bmatrix} \tag{4.18}$$

Note that $\mathbf{l}_1$ and $\mathbf{l}_2$ form a basis of $V^2(\mathbf{A})$; hence any member of $V^2(\mathbf{A})$ can be expressed either by (4.18) or by (4.15). The vector **g** in (4.16) was obtained by setting $c_1 = 2$, $c_2 = 1$, and $c_3 = 0$ in (4.15). The same vector is obtained by setting $d_1 = \frac{1}{5}$ and $d_2 = -\frac{1}{3}$ in (4.18).

It can be shown that the dimensions of a vector space remain unchanged by the elementary transformations defined in Section 1.4. Moreover, if the space generating vector set is a basis, elementary transformations will always transform this basis into another basis. Finally, a vector space is unaffected by the inclusion or deletion of a null vector in the space generating vector set.

Example. To illustrate the above properties, let us consider, once again, the vector space generated by the vectors $\mathbf{a}_1$, $\mathbf{a}_2$, and $\mathbf{a}_3$ in (4.14), and show that elementary transformations will transform that space generating vector set into the one which appears in (4.17). We proceed as follows:

1. Multiply $\mathbf{a}_1$ by 10, and denote the resulting vector by $\mathbf{l}_1$. We have then the new space generating vector set $\mathbf{l}_1$, $\mathbf{a}_2$, and $\mathbf{a}_3$.

2. Multiply $\mathbf{a}_2$ by minus three, and denote the resulting vector by $\mathbf{l}_2$. The transformed space generating vector set now is $\mathbf{l}_1$, $\mathbf{l}_2$, and $\mathbf{a}_3$.
3. Subtract $\mathbf{l}_1$ and $\mathbf{l}_2$ from $\mathbf{a}_3$, thereby replacing $\mathbf{a}_3$ with the null vector, which can be deleted from the space generating vector set.

We are left with the space generating vector set $\mathbf{l}_1$ and $\mathbf{l}_2$, as defined by (4.17).

Associated with every vector space, $V^r(\mathbf{A})$, containing nonnull vectors, is a positive integer r, such that there exist r linearly independent vectors in $V^r(\mathbf{A})$, but not more. The integer r is called the *rank* of $V^r(\mathbf{A})$, and *any* r linearly independent vectors in $V^r(\mathbf{A})$ define a basis for $V^r(\mathbf{A})$. This property of vector spaces can be established by noting that $V^r(\mathbf{A})$ has a basis, say $\mathbf{a}_1, \mathbf{a}_2, \ldots, \mathbf{a}_r$, and if $\mathbf{l}_1, \mathbf{l}_2, \ldots, \mathbf{l}_r$ are any r linearly independent vectors in $V^r(\mathbf{A})$, then they also define a basis for $V^r(\mathbf{A})$. For if $\mathbf{l}_1$ is in $V^r(\mathbf{A})$, then it can be expressed as a linear combination of the basis of $V^r(\mathbf{A})$:

$$\mathbf{l}_1 = b_1\mathbf{a}_1 + b_2\mathbf{a}_2 + \cdots + b_r\mathbf{a}_r$$

where at least one of the b's, b_i, say, is nonzero. Because the replacement of a vector in a vector space by its sum with another vector in that space is an elementary transformation, the vector space remains unaffected if we replace $\mathbf{a}_1$ by $\mathbf{l}_1$. Now $\mathbf{l}_2$ is a linear combination of the vectors in the new basis. One of the coefficients of the $\mathbf{a}$'s in this linear combination is nonzero, since otherwise $\mathbf{l}_2$ would be linearly dependent on $\mathbf{l}_1$ and would thereby contradict our initial assumption that $\mathbf{l}_1, \mathbf{l}_2, \ldots, \mathbf{l}_r$ are linearly independent. Hence we can replace one of the $\mathbf{a}$'s, $\mathbf{a}_j$, say, by $\mathbf{l}_2$ and obtain a new basis. Continuing in this manner, we can successively replace the $\mathbf{a}$'s by the $\mathbf{l}$'s and move from one basis to another.

Note that we cannot select more than r linearly independent vectors in $V^r(\mathbf{A})$. If we could, then any r of these vectors would constitute a basis, and the remaining vectors would be linearly dependent on them, thereby contradicting the assumption that there exist more than r linearly independent vectors in $V^r(\mathbf{A})$.

The vector equivalent of the matrix identity

$$\mathbf{AI} = \mathbf{A}$$

is

$$\mathbf{a}'\mathbf{I} = \mathbf{a}' = a_1\mathbf{e}_1 + a_2\mathbf{e}_2 + \cdots + a_m\mathbf{e}_m \tag{4.19}$$

where

$$\mathbf{e}_1 = \begin{bmatrix} 1 \\ 0 \\ 0 \\ \vdots \\ 0 \end{bmatrix} \quad \mathbf{e}_2 = \begin{bmatrix} 0 \\ 1 \\ 0 \\ \vdots \\ 0 \end{bmatrix} \quad \cdots \quad \mathbf{e}_m = \begin{bmatrix} 0 \\ 0 \\ 0 \\ \vdots \\ 1 \end{bmatrix} \tag{4.20}$$

Equation (4.19) states that any m-dimensional row vector, $\mathbf{a}'$, say, can be expressed as a linear combination of the m linearly independent vectors $\mathbf{e}_1, \mathbf{e}_2, \ldots, \mathbf{e}_m$. Thus the m vectors in (4.20) form a basis of $V^m(\mathbf{A})$. It follows that the rank of the vector space containing all vectors with m elements is m, and there cannot exist more than m linearly independent vectors with m elements. Moreover, if r is the rank of the vector space generated by a set of vectors with m elements, then $r \leqq m$. We conclude, therefore, that from any space generating vector set of a vector space with rank r, we can always choose r linearly independent vectors to form a basis of that vector space. And given any two different bases of a vector space, we can always pass from one to the other by means of elementary transformations. These features will prove to be of great importance in our discussion of linear programming in the next chapter.

4.4 THE RANK OF A MATRIX

Having established many of the fundamental concepts involving linear dependence, we now pursue some of their implications, the most important of which revolve around the concept of the *rank* of a matrix.

4.4.1 THE RANK OF A MATRIX: DEFINITION #1

Elementary transformations, carried out in an organized manner—for example, the method of pivotal condensation described in Section 2.4—can always be used to reduce any rectangular matrix, $\mathbf{A}$, say, to its *canonical* form:

$$\left[\begin{array}{c|c} \mathbf{I}_r & \mathbf{0}_3 \\ \hline \mathbf{0}_1 & \mathbf{0}_2 \end{array}\right] = \mathbf{C} \tag{4.21}$$

say, where $\mathbf{I}_r$ is an identity matrix of order r, and $\mathbf{0}_1$, $\mathbf{0}_2$, and $\mathbf{0}_3$ are null matrices. That is, by premultiplying and postmultiplying $\mathbf{A}$ by the appropriate elementary matrices, we can obtain the canonical matrix in (4.21), namely,

$$\mathbf{E}_m \cdots \mathbf{E}_2\mathbf{E}_1\mathbf{A}\mathbf{F}_1\mathbf{F}_2 \cdots \mathbf{F}_n = \mathbf{T}_1\mathbf{A}\mathbf{T}_2 = \mathbf{C} \tag{4.22}$$

where $\mathbf{E}_i$ and $\mathbf{F}_j$ are elementary matrices. *We define the rank of the rectangular matrix* $\mathbf{A}$ *to be the order of the identity matrix in its canonical matrix,* $\mathbf{C}$.

Example. Consider the matrix $\mathbf{A}$ that is defined by the column vectors $\mathbf{a}_1$, $\mathbf{a}_2$, and $\mathbf{a}_3$ of (4.14) and $\mathbf{g}$ of (4.16):

$$\mathbf{A} = \begin{bmatrix} 3 & 5 & 15 & 11 \\ 2 & 4 & 8 & 8 \\ 1 & 2 & 4 & 4 \end{bmatrix} \tag{4.23}$$

Applying the method of pivotal condensation, we obtain the following sequence of transformations:

$\mathbf{E}_1\mathbf{A}$

$$= \begin{bmatrix} \frac{1}{3} & 0 & 0 \\ 0 & 1 & 0 \\ 0 & 0 & 1 \end{bmatrix} \begin{bmatrix} 3 & 5 & 15 & 11 \\ 2 & 4 & 8 & 8 \\ 1 & 2 & 4 & 4 \end{bmatrix} = \begin{bmatrix} 1 & \frac{5}{3} & 5 & \frac{11}{3} \\ 2 & 4 & 8 & 8 \\ 1 & 2 & 4 & 4 \end{bmatrix}$$

$\mathbf{E}_2(\mathbf{E}_1\mathbf{A})$

$$= \begin{bmatrix} 1 & 0 & 0 \\ -2 & 1 & 0 \\ 0 & 0 & 1 \end{bmatrix} \begin{bmatrix} 1 & \frac{5}{3} & 5 & \frac{11}{3} \\ 2 & 4 & 8 & 8 \\ 1 & 2 & 4 & 4 \end{bmatrix} = \begin{bmatrix} 1 & \frac{5}{3} & 5 & \frac{11}{3} \\ 0 & \frac{2}{3} & -2 & \frac{2}{3} \\ 1 & 2 & 4 & 4 \end{bmatrix}$$

$\mathbf{E}_3(\mathbf{E}_2\mathbf{E}_1\mathbf{A})$

$$= \begin{bmatrix} 1 & 0 & 0 \\ 0 & 1 & 0 \\ -1 & 0 & 1 \end{bmatrix} \begin{bmatrix} 1 & \frac{5}{3} & 5 & \frac{11}{3} \\ 0 & \frac{2}{3} & -2 & \frac{2}{3} \\ 1 & 2 & 4 & 4 \end{bmatrix} = \begin{bmatrix} 1 & \frac{5}{3} & 5 & \frac{11}{3} \\ 0 & \frac{2}{3} & -2 & \frac{2}{3} \\ 0 & \frac{1}{3} & -1 & \frac{1}{3} \end{bmatrix}$$

$\mathbf{E}_4(\mathbf{E}_3\mathbf{E}_2\mathbf{E}_1\mathbf{A})$

$$= \begin{bmatrix} 1 & 0 & 0 \\ 0 & \frac{3}{2} & 0 \\ 0 & 0 & 1 \end{bmatrix} \begin{bmatrix} 1 & \frac{5}{3} & 5 & \frac{11}{3} \\ 0 & \frac{2}{3} & -2 & \frac{2}{3} \\ 0 & \frac{1}{3} & -1 & \frac{1}{3} \end{bmatrix} = \begin{bmatrix} 1 & \frac{5}{3} & 5 & \frac{11}{3} \\ 0 & 1 & -3 & 1 \\ 0 & \frac{1}{3} & -1 & \frac{1}{3} \end{bmatrix}$$

$\mathbf{E}_5(\mathbf{E}_4\mathbf{E}_3\mathbf{E}_2\mathbf{E}_1\mathbf{A})$

$$= \begin{bmatrix} 1 & 0 & 0 \\ 0 & 1 & 0 \\ 0 & -\frac{1}{3} & 1 \end{bmatrix} \begin{bmatrix} 1 & \frac{5}{3} & 5 & \frac{11}{3} \\ 0 & 1 & -3 & 1 \\ 0 & \frac{1}{3} & -1 & \frac{1}{3} \end{bmatrix} = \begin{bmatrix} 1 & \frac{5}{3} & 5 & \frac{11}{3} \\ 0 & 1 & -3 & 1 \\ 0 & 0 & 0 & 0 \end{bmatrix}$$

$\mathbf{E}_6\,(\mathbf{E}_5\mathbf{E}_4\mathbf{E}_3\mathbf{E}_2\mathbf{E}_1)\mathbf{A}$

$$= \begin{bmatrix} 1 & -\frac{5}{3} & 0 \\ 0 & 1 & 0 \\ 0 & 0 & 1 \end{bmatrix} \begin{bmatrix} 1 & \frac{5}{3} & 5 & \frac{11}{3} \\ 0 & 1 & -3 & 1 \\ 0 & 0 & 0 & 0 \end{bmatrix} = \begin{bmatrix} 1 & 0 & 10 & 2 \\ 0 & 1 & -3 & 1 \\ 0 & 0 & 0 & 0 \end{bmatrix} \tag{4.24}$$

Let $\mathbf{T}_1 = \mathbf{E}_6\mathbf{E}_5\mathbf{E}_4\mathbf{E}_3\mathbf{E}_2\mathbf{E}_1$; then

$$\mathbf{T}_1\mathbf{A} = \begin{bmatrix} 2 & -\frac{5}{2} & 0 \\ -1 & \frac{3}{2} & 0 \\ 0 & -\frac{1}{2} & 2 \end{bmatrix} \begin{bmatrix} 3 & 5 & 15 & 11 \\ 2 & 4 & 8 & 8 \\ 1 & 2 & 4 & 4 \end{bmatrix} = \begin{bmatrix} 1 & 0 & 10 & 2 \\ 0 & 1 & -3 & 1 \\ 0 & 0 & 0 & 0 \end{bmatrix} \tag{4.25}$$

Now, applying column transformations on $\mathbf{T}_1\mathbf{A}$, we obtain the sequence:

$$(\mathbf{T}_1\mathbf{A})\mathbf{F}_1 = \begin{bmatrix} 1 & 0 & 10 & 2 \\ 0 & 1 & -3 & 1 \\ 0 & 0 & 0 & 0 \end{bmatrix} \begin{bmatrix} 1 & 0 & -10 & 0 \\ 0 & 1 & 0 & 0 \\ 0 & 0 & 1 & 0 \\ 0 & 0 & 0 & 1 \end{bmatrix} = \begin{bmatrix} 1 & 0 & 0 & 2 \\ 0 & 1 & -3 & 1 \\ 0 & 0 & 0 & 0 \end{bmatrix}$$

$$(\mathbf{T}_1\mathbf{A}\mathbf{F}_1)\mathbf{F}_2 = \begin{bmatrix} 1 & 0 & 0 & 2 \\ 0 & 1 & -3 & 1 \\ 0 & 0 & 0 & 0 \end{bmatrix} \begin{bmatrix} 1 & 0 & 0 & -2 \\ 0 & 1 & 0 & 0 \\ 0 & 0 & 1 & 0 \\ 0 & 0 & 0 & 1 \end{bmatrix} = \begin{bmatrix} 1 & 0 & 0 & 0 \\ 0 & 1 & -3 & 1 \\ 0 & 0 & 0 & 0 \end{bmatrix}$$

$$(\mathbf{T}_1\mathbf{A}\mathbf{F}_1\mathbf{F}_2)\mathbf{F}_3 = \begin{bmatrix} 1 & 0 & 0 & 0 \\ 0 & 1 & -3 & 1 \\ 0 & 0 & 0 & 0 \end{bmatrix} \begin{bmatrix} 1 & 0 & 0 & 0 \\ 0 & 1 & 3 & 0 \\ 0 & 0 & 1 & 0 \\ 0 & 0 & 0 & 1 \end{bmatrix} = \begin{bmatrix} 1 & 0 & 0 & 0 \\ 0 & 1 & 0 & 1 \\ 0 & 0 & 0 & 0 \end{bmatrix}$$

$$(\mathbf{T}_1\mathbf{A}\mathbf{F}_1\mathbf{F}_2\mathbf{F}_3)\mathbf{F}_4 = \begin{bmatrix} 1 & 0 & 0 & 0 \\ 0 & 1 & 0 & 1 \\ 0 & 0 & 0 & 0 \end{bmatrix} \begin{bmatrix} 1 & 0 & 0 & 0 \\ 0 & 1 & 0 & -1 \\ 0 & 0 & 1 & 0 \\ 0 & 0 & 0 & 1 \end{bmatrix} = \begin{bmatrix} 1 & 0 & 0 & 0 \\ 0 & 1 & 0 & 0 \\ 0 & 0 & 0 & 0 \end{bmatrix}$$

And letting

$$\mathbf{T}_2 = \mathbf{F}_1\mathbf{F}_2\mathbf{F}_3\mathbf{F}_4 \tag{4.26}$$

we find that

$$\mathbf{T}_1\mathbf{A}\mathbf{T}_2 = \begin{bmatrix} 2 & -\frac{5}{2} & 0 \\ -1 & \frac{3}{2} & 0 \\ 0 & -\frac{1}{2} & 1 \end{bmatrix} \begin{bmatrix} 3 & 5 & 15 & 11 \\ 2 & 4 & 8 & 8 \\ 1 & 2 & 4 & 4 \end{bmatrix} \begin{bmatrix} 1 & 0 & -10 & -2 \\ 0 & 1 & 3 & -1 \\ 0 & 0 & 1 & 0 \\ 0 & 0 & 0 & 1 \end{bmatrix}$$

$$= \left[\begin{array}{cc:cc} 1 & 0 & 0 & 0 \\ 0 & 1 & 0 & 0 \\ \hdashline 0 & 0 & 0 & 0 \end{array}\right] \tag{4.27}$$

Since the identity matrix in the upper left-hand corner of $\mathbf{T}_1\mathbf{A}\mathbf{T}_2$ is of order two, we conclude that the rank of $\mathbf{A}$ is two.

Observe that

$$(\mathbf{T}_1\mathbf{A}\mathbf{T}_2)' = \mathbf{T}_2'\mathbf{A}'\mathbf{T}_1' = \left[\begin{array}{c:c} \mathbf{I}_r & \mathbf{0}_1' \\ \hdashline \mathbf{0}_3' & \mathbf{0}_2' \end{array}\right] = \mathbf{C}' \tag{4.28}$$

We conclude, therefore, that the rank of a rectangular matrix and its transpose are equal:

$$\text{rank } (\mathbf{A}) = \text{rank } (\mathbf{A}') \qquad (4.29)$$

4.4.2 THE RANK OF A MATRIX: DEFINITION #2

Consider the vector space $V(\mathbf{A})$ that is generated by the column vectors of a rectangular matrix **A**, that is, the column vectors $\mathbf{a}_1, \mathbf{a}_2, \ldots, \mathbf{a}_n$. In Section 4.3, we noted that a vector space is unaffected by elementary transformations and the deletion of null vectors from its space generating vector set. Thus the rank of $V(\mathbf{A})$ is also the rank of the vector space $V(\mathbf{T}_1\mathbf{A}\mathbf{T}_2)$, where $\mathbf{T}_1\mathbf{A}\mathbf{T}_2$ is the transformed matrix in (4.22). But the rank of the vector space generated by the column vectors of $\mathbf{T}_1\mathbf{A}\mathbf{T}_2$ is simply r, since the null column vectors can be deleted to leave only the r linearly independent vectors $\mathbf{e}_1, \mathbf{e}_2, \ldots, \mathbf{e}_r$ as the basis of $V(\mathbf{T}_1\mathbf{A}\mathbf{T}_2)$. *Hence we may define the rank of a rectangular matrix to be the rank of the vector space that is generated by its column vectors.* Also, since

$$\text{rank } (\mathbf{A}) = \text{rank } (\mathbf{A}')$$

we have that

$$\text{rank } V(\mathbf{A}) = \text{rank } (\mathbf{A}) = \text{rank } V(\mathbf{A}') \qquad (4.30)$$

and the conclusion that the rank of a matrix is equal to the maximum number of linearly independent column or row vectors in the matrix.

Example. To demonstrate that this alternative definition is consistent with the original one, let us consider once again the matrix **A** in (4.23). We have seen that the first three column vectors of this matrix define a vector space of rank two, and that the fourth column vector is a member of this vector space. Hence the rank of the vector space generated by the column vectors of **A** is two, and both of our definitions yield identical results.

4.4.3 THE RANK OF A MATRIX: DEFINITION #3

The determinant of a square submatrix formed by deleting a number of rows and columns from a rectangular matrix, **A**, say, is called a *partial determinant* of **A**. We may establish a third definition of the rank of a rectangular matrix by noting that the largest order of a nonzero partial determinant of the transformed matrix $\mathbf{T}_1\mathbf{A}\mathbf{T}_2$ in (4.22) is r. Moreover, since elementary transformations affect only the sign and magnitude of a determinant and not its zero or nonzero character (Properties 3, 4, and 6 in Subsection 2.1.2), the largest order of a nonzero partial determinant of **A** is also r. *We conclude, therefore, that the rank of a rectangular matrix* *may be defined to be equal to the order of its largest nonzero partial determinant.* It follows that the rank of an $m \times n$ matrix $(m < n)$ can never be greater than m, and the rank of a nonsingular square matrix of order m is m.

Example. To illustrate the above definition of rank, let us turn once more to the matrix **A** in (4.23). This matrix has four partial determinants of order three:

$$\begin{vmatrix} 3 & 5 & 15 \\ 2 & 4 & 8 \\ 1 & 2 & 4 \end{vmatrix} = 0 \quad \begin{vmatrix} 3 & 5 & 11 \\ 2 & 4 & 8 \\ 1 & 2 & 4 \end{vmatrix} = 0 \quad \begin{vmatrix} 3 & 15 & 11 \\ 2 & 8 & 8 \\ 1 & 4 & 4 \end{vmatrix} = 0 \quad \begin{vmatrix} 5 & 15 & 11 \\ 4 & 8 & 8 \\ 2 & 4 & 4 \end{vmatrix} = 0$$

18 partial determinants of order two, such as

$$\begin{vmatrix} 3 & 5 \\ 2 & 4 \end{vmatrix} = 2 \quad \begin{vmatrix} 3 & 15 \\ 2 & 8 \end{vmatrix} = -6 \quad \begin{vmatrix} 5 & 15 \\ 4 & 8 \end{vmatrix} = -20 \quad \begin{vmatrix} 2 & 4 \\ 1 & 2 \end{vmatrix} = 0$$

and, of course, as many first-order partial determinants as it has elements, that is, 12. All of the third-order partial determinants are zero. Hence the rank of **A** must be less than three. Several nonzero second-order partial determinants can be formed. Hence the largest order of a nonzero partial determinant is two, and we once again have confirmed the result that the rank of the matrix **A** in (4.23) is two.

4.5 SOLUTION OF SQUARE LINEAR EQUATION SYSTEMS

Equations in which unknown quantities appear only to the first power are called *linear equations*. When several such equations, containing common unknowns, are to be solved simultaneously, we have a problem in the solution of a set of simultaneous linear equations, that is, a *linear equation system*. Linear equation systems with an equal number of equations and unknowns are called *square linear equation systems*. A square linear equation system with m equations in m unknowns may be expressed as

$$\begin{aligned} a_{11}x_1 + a_{12}x_2 + \cdots + a_{1m}x_m &= b_1 \\ a_{21}x_1 + a_{22}x_2 + \cdots + a_{2m}x_m &= b_2 \\ &\vdots \\ a_{m1}x_1 + a_{m2}x_2 + \cdots + a_{mm}x_m &= b_m \end{aligned}$$

or, more compactly,

$$\mathbf{Ax} = \mathbf{b}, \tag{4.31}$$

where each x_i is an unknown quantity, the a's are known constant coefficients, and the b's are known quantities. If **b** is a null vector, the equations in (4.31) are called *homogeneous* equations. Otherwise, they are referred to as *nonhomogeneous* equations.

4.5.1 CRAMER'S RULE

Let us defer until later a discussion of the conditions that must be met for solutions to (4.31) to exist, and assume that the simultaneous linear equations in (4.31) are solvable for the m unknowns. Also, let us assume that the square matrix $\mathbf{A}$ is nonsingular, and that the vector $\mathbf{b}$ is not a null vector. We have then that

$$\mathbf{x} = \mathbf{A}^{-1}\mathbf{b} \tag{4.32}$$

and, recalling the definition of the inverse matrix given in (2.9), obtain the following result:

$$\mathbf{x} = \frac{1}{|\mathbf{A}|}\mathbf{A}^a\mathbf{b} = \frac{1}{|\mathbf{A}|}\begin{bmatrix} A_{11}^c & A_{21}^c & \cdots & A_{m1}^c \\ A_{12}^c & A_{22}^c & \cdots & A_{m2}^c \\ \vdots & \vdots & & \vdots \\ A_{1m}^c & A_{2m}^c & \cdots & A_{mm}^c \end{bmatrix}\begin{bmatrix} b_1 \\ b_2 \\ \vdots \\ b_m \end{bmatrix}$$

$$= \frac{1}{|\mathbf{A}|}\begin{bmatrix} b_1A_{11}^c + b_2A_{21}^c + \cdots + b_mA_{m1}^c \\ b_1A_{12}^c + b_2A_{22}^c + \cdots + b_mA_{m2}^c \\ \vdots \qquad \vdots \qquad \qquad \vdots \\ b_1A_{1m}^c + b_2A_{2m}^c + \cdots + b_mA_{mm}^c \end{bmatrix} \tag{4.33}$$

or

$$x_1 = \frac{b_1A_{11}^c + b_2A_{21}^c + \cdots + b_mA_{m1}^c}{|\mathbf{A}|} = \frac{\begin{vmatrix} b_1 & a_{12} & a_{13} & \cdots & a_{1m} \\ b_2 & a_{22} & a_{23} & \cdots & a_{2m} \\ \vdots & \vdots & \vdots & & \vdots \\ b_m & a_{m2} & a_{m3} & \cdots & a_{mm} \end{vmatrix}}{|\mathbf{A}|}$$

$$x_2 = \frac{b_1A_{12}^c + b_2A_{22}^c + \cdots + b_mA_{m2}^c}{|\mathbf{A}|} = \frac{\begin{vmatrix} a_{11} & b_1 & a_{13} & \cdots & a_{1m} \\ a_{21} & b_2 & a_{23} & \cdots & a_{2m} \\ \vdots & \vdots & \vdots & & \vdots \\ a_{m1} & b_m & a_{m3} & \cdots & a_{mm} \end{vmatrix}}{|\mathbf{A}|}$$

$$\vdots$$

$$x_m = \frac{b_1A_{1m}^c + b_2A_{2m}^c + \cdots + b_mA_{mm}^c}{|\mathbf{A}|} = \frac{\begin{vmatrix} a_{11} & a_{12} & \cdots & a_{1,m-1} & b_1 \\ a_{21} & a_{22} & \cdots & a_{2,m-1} & b_2 \\ \vdots & \vdots & & & \vdots \\ a_{m1} & a_{m2} & \cdots & a_{m,m-1} & b_m \end{vmatrix}}{|\mathbf{A}|}$$

Observe that the numerator in each of the above expressions for x_i may be expressed as the determinant of the matrix **A** with its ith column replaced by the vector **b**. The denominator in each case is the determinant of the matrix **A**. Thus we conclude that if a solution to a set of m simultaneous linear equations in m unknowns exists, it can be found by setting the ith unknown equal to the quotient of two determinants: The determinant in the denominator is the determinant of the matrix of coefficients, while the determinant in the numerator is the same determinant, but with the ith column replaced by the column vector on the right-hand side of the equation system. This result is known as *Cramer's Rule* and is a convenient solution method when the number of equations and unknowns is small. When large equation systems are to be solved, other solution methods are more efficient. The latter typically use variants of the *elimination method* of scalar algebra, or the *inverse matrix method.*

Examples. To illustrate the above alternative solution methods, let us consider, once again, the two linear equations in (1.12):

$$3x_1 + 5x_2 = 15$$
$$2x_1 + 4x_2 = 8$$

(i) First, using Cramer's Rule, we have

$$x_1 = \frac{\begin{vmatrix} 15 & 5 \\ 8 & 4 \end{vmatrix}}{\begin{vmatrix} 3 & 5 \\ 2 & 4 \end{vmatrix}} = \frac{20}{2} = 10$$

and

$$x_2 = \frac{\begin{vmatrix} 3 & 15 \\ 2 & 8 \end{vmatrix}}{\begin{vmatrix} 3 & 5 \\ 2 & 4 \end{vmatrix}} = \frac{-6}{2} = -3$$

(ii) Next, using the *elimination method* of scalar algebra, we have, using the first equation, that

$$x_1 = \frac{15 - 5x_2}{3}$$

and, using the second equation, obtain

$$2\left[\frac{15 - 5x_2}{3}\right] + 4x_2 = 8$$

or

$$\frac{2}{3}x_2 = -2$$

Hence

$$x_2 = -3$$

and

$$x_1 = \frac{15 - 5x_2}{3} = \frac{30}{3} = 10$$

(iii) Finally, using the *inverse matrix method,* we have that

$$\mathbf{x} = \mathbf{A}^{-1}\mathbf{b} = \begin{bmatrix} 2 & -\frac{5}{2} \\ -1 & \frac{3}{2} \end{bmatrix} \begin{bmatrix} 15 \\ 8 \end{bmatrix} = \begin{bmatrix} 10 \\ -3 \end{bmatrix}$$

We have assumed, in the above paragraphs, that the simultaneous linear equations in (4.31) were solvable, that is, nad a solution. Now let us consider the conditions that must be met for this to be true. First, let us define simultaneous linear equations to be *consistent* if they are solvable and *inconsistent* if they are not.

4.5.2 HOMOGENEOUS LINEAR EQUATION SYSTEMS

A solution of the linear homogeneous equation system

$$\mathbf{Ax} = \mathbf{0} \tag{4.34}$$

that always exists is the null vector

$$\mathbf{x} = \mathbf{0} \tag{4.35}$$

This solution is called the *trivial solution,* and it rarely is of interest in urban and regional analysis. Rather, we are almost always seeking nontrivial solutions, and these occur only when the matrix **A** is singular. This can be seen by premultiplying both sides of (4.34) by $\mathbf{A}^{-1}$ and using Cramer's Rule to express the solution of each unknown as the ratio of two determinants. For homogeneous equations, the determinant in the numerator always will be zero because of the presence of the null column vector. Hence,

$$x_1 = \frac{0}{|\mathbf{A}|} \qquad x_2 = \frac{0}{|\mathbf{A}|} \qquad \cdots \qquad x_m = \frac{0}{|\mathbf{A}|}$$

or

$$\mathbf{x} = \frac{1}{|\mathbf{A}|}\mathbf{0} \tag{4.36}$$

We can rewrite (4.36) as:

$$|\mathbf{A}|\,\mathbf{x} = \mathbf{0}$$

from which it follows that if $|\mathbf{A}| \neq 0$, then $\mathbf{x} = \mathbf{0}$, and vice versa. Hence a nontrivial solution of (4.34) can only occur when the determinant of **A** is zero, that is, when **A** is a singular matrix. Moreover, we note that if a nonnull vector **x** is a solution of (4.34), then $k\mathbf{x}$ is also a solution, where k is any arbitrary constant. Finally, it can be established that if the rank of **A** is $m - 1$, we can obtain a whole family of solutions of (4.34), namely, $k\mathbf{x}$. If the rank of **A** is $r\,(r < m)$, we can find $m - r$ linearly independent families of solutions of (4.34).

4.5.3 NONHOMOGENEOUS LINEAR EQUATION SYSTEMS

A solution of the nonhomogeneous linear equation system

$$\mathbf{Ax} = \mathbf{b} \tag{4.37}$$

will exist if the ranks of the coefficient matrix **A** and the augmented coefficient matrix

$$\bar{\mathbf{A}} = [\mathbf{A} \quad \mathbf{b}] = \begin{bmatrix} a_{11} & a_{12} & \cdots & a_{1m} & b_1 \\ a_{21} & a_{22} & \cdots & a_{2m} & b_2 \\ \vdots & \vdots & & \vdots & \vdots \\ a_{m1} & a_{m2} & \cdots & a_{mm} & b_m \end{bmatrix} \tag{4.38}$$

are equal. That is, the equations in (4.37) are *consistent* if

$$\text{rank}\,(\mathbf{A}) = \text{rank}\,(\bar{\mathbf{A}})$$

If not, the equations are *inconsistent.* This follows from the fact that the vector **b** must be linearly dependent on the column vectors of **A**, that is, be a member of the same vector space, if it is to be expressed as a linear combination of these vectors. For if (4.37) is consistent, then there exist x_i such that

$$\mathbf{b} = \mathbf{Ax} = x_1\mathbf{a}_1 + x_2\mathbf{a}_2 + \cdots + x_m\mathbf{a}_m \tag{4.39}$$

and by (4.8), **b** is linearly dependent on $\mathbf{a}_1, \mathbf{a}_2, \ldots, \mathbf{a}_m$. Conversely, if **b** is linearly dependent on $\mathbf{a}_1, \mathbf{a}_2, \ldots, \mathbf{a}_m$, then (4.39) can be satisfied and, therefore, (4.37) has a solution.

Note that the above existence condition also holds for homogeneous equations since the rank of a coefficient matrix augmented by the null vector is always equal to the rank of the unaugmented coefficient matrix. Thus homogeneous equations always have a solution, namely the trivial solution.

If the m equations in (4.37) are consistent, and if the matrices $\mathbf{A}$ and $\bar{\mathbf{A}}$ each have a rank of m, then there exists the unique solution

$$\mathbf{x} = \mathbf{A}^{-1}\mathbf{b}$$

If the rank of each matrix is r, say $(r < m)$, then the matrix $\mathbf{A}$ is singular, and the equation system in (4.37) has an infinite number of solutions. In particular, $m - r$ unknowns may be assigned an arbitrary set of values, and the remaining r unknowns will be uniquely related to this set of arbitrarily selected values. This holds true for both homogeneous and nonhomogeneous equation systems. Thus we may summarize the existence conditions for nonhomogeneous equations, as follows:

1. If, in (4.37), $\text{rank}(\mathbf{A}) = \text{rank}(\bar{\mathbf{A}}) = m$, then there exists only the unique solution $\mathbf{x} = \mathbf{A}^{-1}\mathbf{b}$.
2. If, in (4.37), $\text{rank}(\mathbf{A}) = \text{rank}(\bar{\mathbf{A}}) = r < m$, then an infinite number of solutions exist for $\mathbf{x}$, each a function of the values assigned to $m - r$ of the m unknowns.
3. If, in (4.37), $\text{rank}(\mathbf{A}) < \text{rank}(\bar{\mathbf{A}})$, then the equations are inconsistent, and no solution exists.

The first two existence conditions also apply to homogeneous equation systems. In the first instance, we have the unique trivial solution $\mathbf{x} = \mathbf{0}$ and, in the second, an infinite number of solutions.

Example. To illustrate the different classes of solutions described above, consider, once again, the numerical example

$$\begin{aligned} 3x_1 + 5x_2 &= 15 \\ 2x_1 + 4x_2 &= 8 \end{aligned}$$

We have seen that this equation system is consistent and has the solution

$$\mathbf{x} = \begin{bmatrix} 10 \\ -3 \end{bmatrix}$$

This is in accord with the existence conditions listed above, since

$$\text{rank}\left(\begin{bmatrix} 3 & 5 \\ 2 & 4 \end{bmatrix}\right) = 2 = \text{rank}\left(\begin{bmatrix} 3 & 5 & 15 \\ 2 & 4 & 8 \end{bmatrix}\right)$$

The solution to the two equations can be interpreted geometrically as the intersection of two straight lines (Figure 4.2).

Next, consider the two equations

$$\begin{aligned} 3x_1 + 5x_2 &= 15 \\ 6x_1 + 10x_2 &= 30 \end{aligned} \tag{4.40}$$

Since both the coefficient matrix and the augmented coefficient matrix have a rank of one, which is less than the number of equations, the equations have an infinite number of solutions. The solution can be found by solving for x_1 in terms of x_2 from either of the two equations. Thus

$$x_1 = -\frac{5}{3}x_2 + 5 \tag{4.41}$$

and for every value of x_2 we can determine the corresponding value for x_1. Graphically, the two equations represent the same straight line (Figure 4.3).

Finally, consider the two equations

$$3x_1 + 5x_2 = 15$$

$$3x_1 + 5x_2 = 30$$

The rank of the augmented coefficient matrix is two, but the rank of the unaugmented coefficient matrix is unity. Hence the equations are inconsistent and have no solution. Geometrically, the two equations define two parallel lines that do not intersect (Figure 4.4).

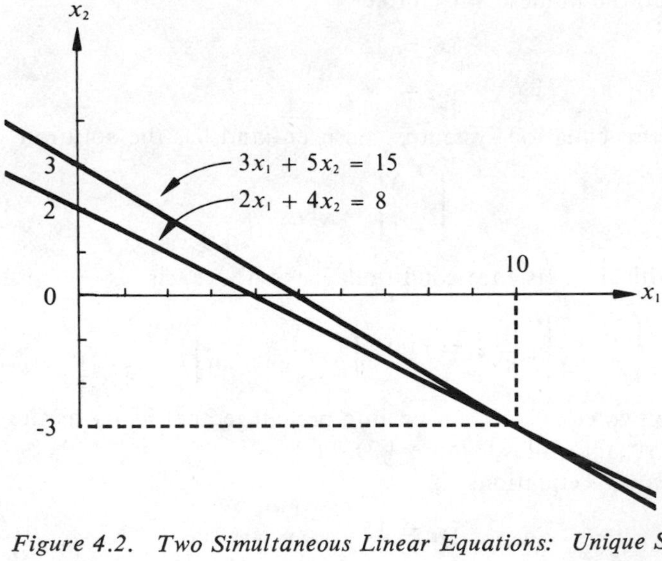

Figure 4.2. Two Simultaneous Linear Equations: Unique Solution

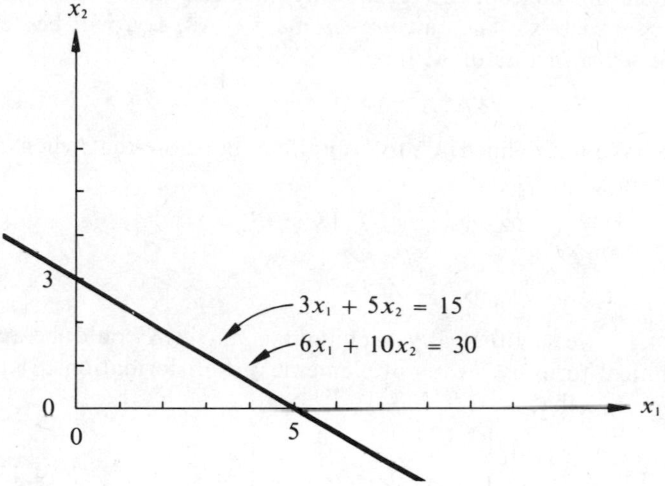

Figure 4.3. Two Simultaneous Linear Equations: Infinite Number of Solutions

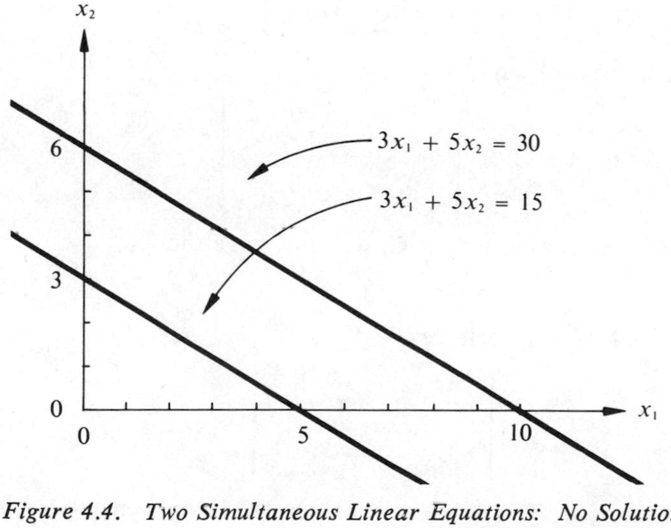

Figure 4.4. Two Simultaneous Linear Equations: No Solution

4.6 GENERALIZED INVERSE MATRICES

The inverse of a nonsingular square matrix was defined in Chapter 2. We shall now generalize this concept to include singular rectangular matrices. Let **A** be any $m \times n$ matrix. Then an $n \times m$ matrix, $\mathbf{A}^*$, say, will be defined to be a *generalized inverse* of **A**, if

$$\mathbf{AA}^*\mathbf{A} = \mathbf{A} \tag{4.42}$$

Observe that we have not defined $\mathbf{A}^*$ to be unique, but note that when **A** is square and nonsingular,

$$\mathbf{A}^{-1}\mathbf{AA}^*\mathbf{AA}^{-1} = \mathbf{A}^{-1}\mathbf{AA}^{-1}$$

whence

$$\mathbf{A}^* = \mathbf{A}^{-1}$$

In Subsection 4.4.1 we saw that any rectangular matrix **A** could be reduced to its canonical form by means of elementary transformations. Recalling (4.22), we have that

$$\underset{m\times m}{\mathbf{T}_1}\ \underset{m\times n}{\mathbf{A}}\ \underset{n\times n}{\mathbf{T}_2} = \left[\begin{array}{c|c} \underset{r\times r}{\mathbf{I}_r} & \underset{r\times(n-r)}{\mathbf{0}_3} \\ \hline \underset{(m-r)\times r}{\mathbf{0}_1} & \underset{(m-r)\times(n-r)}{\mathbf{0}_2} \end{array}\right] = \underset{m\times n}{\mathbf{C}} \tag{4.43}$$

Let

$$\underset{n\times m}{\mathbf{C}^*} = \left[\begin{array}{c|c} \underset{r\times r}{\mathbf{S}} & \underset{r\times(m-r)}{\mathbf{V}} \\ \hline \underset{(n-r)\times r}{\mathbf{U}} & \underset{(n-r)\times(m-r)}{\mathbf{W}} \end{array}\right] \tag{4.44}$$

be any arbitrary matrix. Then

$$\underset{m\times n}{\mathbf{C}}\ \underset{n\times m}{\mathbf{C}^*}\ \underset{m\times n}{\mathbf{C}} = \left[\begin{array}{c|c} \underset{r\times r}{\mathbf{S}} & \underset{r\times(n-r)}{\mathbf{0}_3} \\ \hline \underset{(m-r)\times r}{\mathbf{0}_1} & \underset{(m-r)\times(n-r)}{\mathbf{0}_2} \end{array}\right] \tag{4.45}$$

For $\mathbf{C}^*$ to be a generalized inverse of **C**, we must have that

$$\mathbf{CC}^*\mathbf{C} = \mathbf{C} \tag{4.46}$$

and this will occur if $\mathbf{S} = \mathbf{I}_r$. Hence

$$\underset{n\times m}{\mathbf{C}^*} = \left[\begin{array}{c|c} \underset{r\times r}{\mathbf{I}_r} & \underset{r\times(m-r)}{\mathbf{V}} \\ \hline \underset{(n-r)\times r}{\mathbf{U}} & \underset{(n-r)\times(m-r)}{\mathbf{W}} \end{array}\right] \tag{4.47}$$

where the elements of **U**, **V**, and **W** are arbitrary. Every generalized inverse of **C** is of the form (4.47).

From (4.43) and (4.46), we have that

$$\mathbf{T}_1\mathbf{AT}_2\mathbf{C}^*\mathbf{T}_1\mathbf{AT}_2 = \mathbf{T}_1\mathbf{AT}_2 \tag{4.48}$$

Since $\mathbf{T}_1$ and $\mathbf{T}_2$ are nonsingular, we can premultiply and postmultiply both sides of the equation in (4.48) by their respective inverses to obtain

$$\mathbf{A}\mathbf{T}_2\mathbf{C}^*\mathbf{T}_1\mathbf{A} = \mathbf{A}$$

Hence a generalized inverse of **A** is

$$\underset{n\times n}{\mathbf{T}_2}\ \underset{n\times m}{\mathbf{C}^*}\ \underset{m\times m}{\mathbf{T}_1} \tag{4.49}$$

where $\mathbf{C}^*$ is given by (4.47).

Since the elements of the submatrices **U**, **V**, and **W** in (4.47) have arbitrary values, we may simplify (4.49) by defining **U**, **V**, and **W** to be null matrices. Then $\mathbf{C}^*$ will be equal to the transpose of **C**, and we conclude that another generalized inverse of **A** is

$$\underset{n\times n}{\mathbf{T}_2}\ \underset{n\times m}{\mathbf{C}'}\ \underset{m\times m}{\mathbf{T}_1} \tag{4.50}$$

where

$$\underset{n\times m}{\mathbf{C}'} = \left[\begin{array}{c|c} \underset{r\times r}{\mathbf{I}_r} & \underset{r\times(m-r)}{\mathbf{0}_1'} \\ \hline \underset{(n-r)\times r}{\mathbf{0}_3'} & \underset{(n-r)\times(m-r)}{\mathbf{0}_2'} \end{array}\right] \tag{4.51}$$

Example. To illustrate the computation of a generalized inverse, recall the matrix **A** in (4.23) and the pre- and postmultipliers that reduced it to its canonical form. From (4.27), we have that

$$\underset{3\times 3}{\mathbf{T}_1}\ \underset{3\times 4}{\mathbf{A}}\ \underset{4\times 4}{\mathbf{T}_2} = \begin{bmatrix} 2 & -\frac{5}{2} & 0 \\ -1 & \frac{3}{2} & 0 \\ 0 & -\frac{1}{2} & 1 \end{bmatrix} \begin{bmatrix} 3 & 5 & 15 & 11 \\ 2 & 4 & 8 & 8 \\ 1 & 2 & 4 & 4 \end{bmatrix} \begin{bmatrix} 1 & 0 & -10 & -2 \\ 0 & 1 & 3 & -1 \\ 0 & 0 & 1 & 0 \\ 0 & 0 & 0 & 1 \end{bmatrix}$$

$$= \left[\begin{array}{cc|cc} 1 & 0 & 0 & 0 \\ 0 & 1 & 0 & 0 \\ \hline 0 & 0 & 0 & 0 \end{array}\right] = \underset{3\times 4}{\mathbf{C}}$$

A generalized inverse for the matrix **A**, therefore, is

$$\underset{4\times 3}{\mathbf{A}^*} = \underset{4\times 4}{\mathbf{T}_2}\ \underset{4\times 3}{\mathbf{C}'}\ \underset{3\times 3}{\mathbf{T}_1} = \begin{bmatrix} 1 & 0 & -10 & -2 \\ 0 & 1 & 3 & -1 \\ 0 & 0 & 1 & 0 \\ 0 & 0 & 0 & 1 \end{bmatrix} \begin{bmatrix} 1 & 0 & 0 \\ 0 & 1 & 0 \\ 0 & 0 & 0 \\ 0 & 0 & 0 \end{bmatrix} \begin{bmatrix} 2 & -\frac{5}{2} & 0 \\ -1 & \frac{3}{2} & 0 \\ 0 & -\frac{1}{2} & 1 \end{bmatrix}$$

$$= \begin{bmatrix} 2 & -\frac{5}{2} & 0 \\ -1 & \frac{3}{2} & 0 \\ 0 & 0 & 0 \\ 0 & 0 & 0 \end{bmatrix} \tag{4.52}$$

As a check, we note that

$$\mathbf{AA^*A} = \begin{bmatrix} 3 & 5 & 15 & 11 \\ 2 & 4 & 8 & 8 \\ 1 & 2 & 4 & 4 \end{bmatrix} \begin{bmatrix} 2 & -\frac{5}{2} & 0 \\ -1 & \frac{3}{2} & 0 \\ 0 & 0 & 0 \\ 0 & 0 & 0 \end{bmatrix} \begin{bmatrix} 3 & 5 & 15 & 11 \\ 2 & 4 & 8 & 8 \\ 1 & 2 & 4 & 4 \end{bmatrix}$$

$$= \begin{bmatrix} 3 & 5 & 15 & 11 \\ 2 & 4 & 8 & 8 \\ 1 & 2 & 4 & 4 \end{bmatrix} = \mathbf{A}$$

4.7 SOLUTION OF RECTANGULAR LINEAR EQUATION SYSTEMS[1]

A linear equation system $\mathbf{Ax} = \mathbf{b}$ with a different number of equations from unknowns is called a *rectangular linear equation system.* Such a system is said to be *consistent* if the equations in it have a solution and *inconsistent* if they do not. As with square linear equation systems, if $\mathbf{b}$ is a null vector, the equations are referred to as *homogeneous* equations. Otherwise they are called *nonhomogeneous* equations.

4.7.1 OBTAINING A SOLUTION

A solution of the consistent rectangular linear equation system

$$\mathbf{Ax} = \mathbf{b} \tag{4.53}$$

is

$$\mathbf{x}_0 = \mathbf{A^*b} \tag{4.54}$$

where $\mathbf{A^*}$ is a generalized inverse of $\mathbf{A}$. For if (4.53) is consistent and $\mathbf{A^*}$ is a generalized inverse of $\mathbf{A}$, then there exists a solution $\mathbf{y}$ and

$$\mathbf{b} = \mathbf{Ay} \tag{4.55}$$

But

$$\begin{aligned} \mathbf{Ax}_0 &= \mathbf{AA^*b} \\ &= \mathbf{AA^*Ay} \\ &= \mathbf{Ay} \\ &= \mathbf{b} \end{aligned}$$

which shows that $\mathbf{x}_0$ is a solution of (4.53).

[1] The rest of this chapter draws extensively from the exposition provided by Searle (1966) in Chapter 6 of his book. For a more detailed and definitive exposition, the reader should consult that very readable text.

Examples.

(i) Consider the rectangular linear equation system

$$\underset{3\times 4}{\mathbf{A}}\ \underset{4\times 1}{\mathbf{x}} = \underset{3\times 1}{\mathbf{b}} \tag{4.56}$$

where

$$\mathbf{A} = \begin{bmatrix} 3 & 5 & 15 & 11 \\ 2 & 4 & 8 & 8 \\ 1 & 2 & 4 & 4 \end{bmatrix} \quad \text{and} \quad \mathbf{b} = \begin{bmatrix} 30 \\ 20 \\ 10 \end{bmatrix}$$

In Section 4.3, we saw that **b** lies in the same vector space as do the columns of **A**. Hence the equation system in (4.56) is consistent. Next, recalling (4.52), we note that a generalized inverse for the **A** in (4.56) is

$$\underset{4\times 3}{\mathbf{A}^*} = \begin{bmatrix} 2 & -\frac{5}{2} & 0 \\ -1 & \frac{3}{2} & 0 \\ 0 & 0 & 0 \\ 0 & 0 & 0 \end{bmatrix}$$

Therefore, by (4.54),

$$\mathbf{x}_0 = \mathbf{A}^*\mathbf{b} = \begin{bmatrix} 2 & -\frac{5}{2} & 0 \\ -1 & \frac{3}{2} & 0 \\ 0 & 0 & 0 \\ 0 & 0 & 0 \end{bmatrix} \begin{bmatrix} 30 \\ 20 \\ 10 \end{bmatrix}$$

$$= \begin{bmatrix} 10 \\ 0 \\ 0 \\ 0 \end{bmatrix}$$

is a solution of (4.56).

(ii) Next, consider the rectangular linear equation system

$$\underset{3\times 2}{\mathbf{A}}\ \underset{2\times 1}{\mathbf{x}} = \underset{3\times 1}{\mathbf{b}} \tag{4.57}$$

where

$$\mathbf{A} = \begin{bmatrix} 3 & 5 \\ 2 & 4 \\ 1 & 2 \end{bmatrix} \quad \text{and} \quad \mathbf{b} = \begin{bmatrix} 15 \\ 8 \\ 4 \end{bmatrix}$$

Since the columns of **A** and the vector **b** lie in the same vector space, the equation system in (4.57) is consistent. Thus we may find

$$\underset{2\times 3}{\mathbf{A}^*} = \begin{bmatrix} 2 & -\frac{5}{2} & 0 \\ -1 & \frac{3}{2} & 0 \end{bmatrix}$$

and obtain a solution:

$$\mathbf{x}_0 = \mathbf{A}^*\mathbf{b} = \begin{bmatrix} 2 & -\frac{5}{2} & 0 \\ -1 & \frac{3}{2} & 0 \end{bmatrix} \begin{bmatrix} 15 \\ 8 \\ 4 \end{bmatrix}$$

$$= \begin{bmatrix} 10 \\ -3 \end{bmatrix}$$

4.7.2 NONHOMOGENEOUS RECTANGULAR LINEAR EQUATION SYSTEMS

In the preceding paragraphs we have shown how a solution to the consistent rectangular linear equation system $\mathbf{Ax} = \mathbf{b}$ may be obtained using the generalized inverse $\mathbf{A}^*$. But, as we saw earlier, when the rank of $\mathbf{A}$ is less than the number of unknowns, an infinite number of solutions exist for $\mathbf{x}$. To obtain this multitude of solutions, we first select an arbitrary vector $\mathbf{z}$ of order n, where n is the number of columns in $\mathbf{A}$. Next, we define $\mathbf{D} = \mathbf{A}^*\mathbf{A}$ and solve for the solution vector $\mathbf{x}_0$ in

$$\mathbf{x}_0 = \mathbf{A}^*\mathbf{b} + (\mathbf{D} - \mathbf{I})\mathbf{z} \tag{4.58}$$

To prove that (4.58) is a general solution of the consistent equations $\mathbf{Ax} = \mathbf{b}$, we adopt the following argument presented in Searle (1966). If

$$\mathbf{x}_0 = \mathbf{A}^*\mathbf{b} + (\mathbf{D} - \mathbf{I})\mathbf{z}$$

then

$$\begin{aligned} \mathbf{Ax}_0 &= \mathbf{AA}^*\mathbf{b} + \mathbf{A}(\mathbf{D} - \mathbf{I})\mathbf{z} \\ &= \mathbf{AA}^*\mathbf{b} + (\mathbf{AA}^*\mathbf{A} - \mathbf{A})\mathbf{z} \\ &= \mathbf{AA}^*\mathbf{b} \qquad \text{since} \quad \mathbf{AA}^*\mathbf{A} = \mathbf{A} \\ &= \mathbf{AA}^*\mathbf{Ax} \qquad \text{because} \quad \mathbf{Ax} = \mathbf{b} \\ &= \mathbf{Ax} \\ &= \mathbf{b} \end{aligned}$$

Hence $\mathbf{x}_0$ is a solution of $\mathbf{Ax} = \mathbf{b}$, for any vector $\mathbf{z}$ of order n.

Examples.

(i) To illustrate the application of (4.58), let us obtain the general solution of the rectangular linear equation system in (4.56). We first compute

$$\mathbf{D} = \mathbf{A}^*\mathbf{A} = \begin{bmatrix} 2 & -\frac{5}{2} & 0 \\ -1 & \frac{3}{2} & 0 \\ 0 & 0 & 0 \\ 0 & 0 & 0 \end{bmatrix} \begin{bmatrix} 3 & 5 & 15 & 11 \\ 2 & 4 & 8 & 8 \\ 1 & 2 & 4 & 4 \end{bmatrix}$$

$$= \begin{bmatrix} 1 & 0 & 10 & 2 \\ 0 & 1 & -3 & 1 \\ 0 & 0 & 0 & 0 \\ 0 & 0 & 0 & 0 \end{bmatrix} \tag{4.59}$$

Then we solve for $\mathbf{x}_0$ in

$$\mathbf{x}_0 = \mathbf{A}^*\mathbf{b} + (\mathbf{D} - \mathbf{I})\mathbf{z}$$

$$= \begin{bmatrix} 10 \\ 0 \\ 0 \\ 0 \end{bmatrix} + \begin{bmatrix} 0 & 0 & 10 & 2 \\ 0 & 0 & -3 & 1 \\ 0 & 0 & -1 & 0 \\ 0 & 0 & 0 & -1 \end{bmatrix} \begin{bmatrix} z_1 \\ z_2 \\ z_3 \\ z_4 \end{bmatrix}$$

$$= \begin{bmatrix} 10 + 10z_3 + 2z_4 \\ -3z_3 + z_4 \\ -z_3 \\ -z_4 \end{bmatrix}$$

(ii) Another illustration is offered by the rectangular linear equation system in (4.57). Here

$$\mathbf{D} = \mathbf{A}^*\mathbf{A} = \begin{bmatrix} 2 & -\frac{5}{2} & 0 \\ -1 & \frac{3}{2} & 0 \end{bmatrix} \begin{bmatrix} 3 & 5 \\ 2 & 4 \\ 1 & 2 \end{bmatrix}$$

$$= \begin{bmatrix} 1 & 0 \\ 0 & 1 \end{bmatrix} \tag{4.60}$$

$$\mathbf{x}_0 = \mathbf{A}^*\mathbf{b} + (\mathbf{D} - \mathbf{I})\mathbf{z}$$

$$= \begin{bmatrix} 10 \\ -3 \end{bmatrix}$$

and we conclude that the equation system in (4.57) has only the above unique solution.

4.7.3 HOMOGENEOUS RECTANGULAR LINEAR EQUATION SYSTEMS

The solution for $\mathbf{x}_0$ in (4.58) also applies to cases where $\mathbf{b}$ is a null vector. And by the definition of consistency, it is clear that the homogeneous rectangular linear equation system

$$\mathbf{Ax} = \mathbf{0} \tag{4.61}$$

is always consistent. Hence, setting $\mathbf{b} = \mathbf{0}$ in (4.58), we obtain the following general solution for (4.60):

$$\mathbf{x}_0 = (\mathbf{D} - \mathbf{I})\mathbf{z} \tag{4.62}$$

for arbitrary $\mathbf{z}$ of order n.

Examples.

(i) Let us set $\mathbf{b} = \mathbf{0}$ in (4.56). We then have the solution

$$\begin{aligned} \mathbf{x}_0 &= (\mathbf{D} - \mathbf{I})\mathbf{z} \\ &\doteq \begin{bmatrix} 0 & 0 & 10 & 2 \\ 0 & 0 & -3 & 1 \\ 0 & 0 & -1 & 0 \\ 0 & 0 & 0 & -1 \end{bmatrix} \begin{bmatrix} z_1 \\ z_2 \\ z_3 \\ z_4 \end{bmatrix} \\ &= \begin{bmatrix} 10z_3 + 2z_4 \\ -3z_3 + z_4 \\ -z_3 \\ -z_4 \end{bmatrix} \end{aligned}$$

(ii) Setting $\mathbf{b} = \mathbf{0}$ in (4.57), we obtain

$$\begin{aligned} \mathbf{x}_0 &= (\mathbf{D} - \mathbf{I})\mathbf{z} \\ &= \begin{bmatrix} 0 \\ 0 \end{bmatrix} \end{aligned}$$

and conclude that the null vector is the only solution.

The condition under which $\mathbf{Ax} = \mathbf{0}$ has nonnull solutions is worth exploring further. We begin by deriving three important properties of the matrix $\mathbf{D} = \mathbf{A}^*\mathbf{A}$:

1. The matrices $\mathbf{D}$ and $\mathbf{A}$ have the same rank, that is, rank $(\mathbf{D})$ = rank $(\mathbf{A})$.
2. $\mathbf{D}^2 = \mathbf{D}$. Matrices having this property are said to be *idempotent.*
3. If $\mathbf{A}$ is an $m \times n$ matrix with rank r, then $(\mathbf{D} - \mathbf{I})$ is of rank $n - r$.

The first of the above three properties follows from the fact that the rank of a product matrix $\mathbf{AB}$ cannot exceed the rank of either $\mathbf{A}$ or $\mathbf{B}$ [Exercise 3(b)]. Hence, since $\mathbf{D} = \mathbf{A}^*\mathbf{A}$, rank $(\mathbf{D}) \leqq$ rank $(\mathbf{A})$. But because $\mathbf{A} = \mathbf{AA}^*\mathbf{A} = \mathbf{AD}$, rank $(\mathbf{A}) \leqq$ rank $(\mathbf{D})$. Therefore, rank $(\mathbf{D})$ = rank $(\mathbf{A})$.

The second property of the matrix $\mathbf{D}$ easily can be established by noting that $\mathbf{D}^2 = (\mathbf{A}^*\mathbf{A})^2 = \mathbf{A}^*(\mathbf{AA}^*\mathbf{A}) = \mathbf{A}^*\mathbf{A} = \mathbf{D}$.

Finally, the third property follows from the relationships between $\mathbf{A}^*$ and $\mathbf{A}$. We recall from (4.22) and (4.50) that $\mathbf{T}_1\mathbf{A}\mathbf{T}_2 = \mathbf{C}$ and $\mathbf{A}^* = \mathbf{T}_2\mathbf{C}'\mathbf{T}_1$, respectively. Since $\mathbf{T}_1$ and $\mathbf{T}_2$ are nonsingular matrices, $\mathbf{A} = \mathbf{T}_1^{-1}\mathbf{C}\mathbf{T}_2^{-1}$ and we have that

$$\mathbf{D} = \mathbf{A}^*\mathbf{A} = \mathbf{T}_2\mathbf{C}'\mathbf{T}_1\mathbf{T}_1^{-1}\mathbf{C}\mathbf{T}_2^{-1} = \mathbf{T}_2\left[\begin{array}{c|c} \mathbf{I}_r & \mathbf{0}_6 \\ \hline \mathbf{0}_4 & \mathbf{0}_5 \end{array}\right]\mathbf{T}_2^{-1}$$

Hence

$$\mathbf{D} - \mathbf{I}_n = \mathbf{T}_2\left\{\left[\begin{array}{c|c} \mathbf{I}_r & \mathbf{0}_6 \\ \hline \mathbf{0}_4 & \mathbf{0}_5 \end{array}\right] - \mathbf{I}_n\right\}\mathbf{T}_2^{-1}$$

and, because the multiplication of any matrix by an elementary matrix does not alter rank [Exercise 3(a)],

$$\text{rank}\,(\mathbf{D} - \mathbf{I}_n) = \text{rank}\left\{\left[\begin{array}{c|c} \mathbf{I}_r & \mathbf{0}_6 \\ \hline \mathbf{0}_4 & \mathbf{0}_5 \end{array}\right] - \mathbf{I}_n\right\} = n - r$$

Since the rank of $(\mathbf{D} - \mathbf{I})$ is $n - r$, clearly when $r = n$, $\mathbf{D} - \mathbf{I}$ is null and, therefore, so is the solution vector $\mathbf{x}_0$ in (4.62). This explains the result found in the second example above. When $r < n$, however, the solution vector can be nonnull. We conclude, therefore, that a homogeneous rectangular linear equation system $\mathbf{Ax} = \mathbf{0}$ has nonnull solutions if, and only if, the rank of $\mathbf{A}$ is less than n.

4.7.4 INDEPENDENT SOLUTIONS AND LINEAR COMBINATIONS OF SOLUTIONS

Since the solution vector, $\mathbf{x}_0$, in (4.58) is of order n, there cannot exist more than n linearly independent nonnull solution vectors to the consistent rectangular linear equation system $\mathbf{Ax} = \mathbf{b}$. In fact, there are fewer, and all other solutions are particular linear combinations of this set of independent solution vectors. Furthermore, linear combinations of the elements of any solution vector are unique for a restricted class of linear functions. These results, set out in the form of theorems by Searle (1966), are presented here without proof. They will have important applications in our subsequent expositions of linear statistical models in Section 4.8 and of linear programming in the next chapter.

Theorem 1. *If* $\mathbf{A}$ *is an* $m \times n$ *matrix with rank* r, *then the number of linearly independent nonnull solutions to the consistent rectangular nonhomogeneous linear equation system* $\mathbf{Ax} = \mathbf{b}$ *is* $n - r + 1$.

This theorem asserts that $\mathbf{x}_0 = \mathbf{A}^*\mathbf{b}$ and $\mathbf{x}_0 = \mathbf{A}^*\mathbf{b} + (\mathbf{D} - \mathbf{I})\mathbf{z}$, for $n - r$ linearly independent nonnull vectors $\mathbf{z}$, are linearly independent nonnull solution vectors of $\mathbf{Ax} = \mathbf{b}$. Hence all other solutions will be particular linear combinations of these $n - r + 1$ linearly independent nonnull solution vectors. It follows that for the homogeneous case, $\mathbf{A}^*\mathbf{b}$ is a null vector, and so there are then only $n - r$ linearly independent nonnull solutions.

Theorem 2. *If* $\mathbf{x}_1, \mathbf{x}_2, \ldots, \mathbf{x}_k$ *are any* k *solutions of the consistent rectangular nonhomogeneous linear equation system* $\mathbf{Ax} = \mathbf{b}$, *then any linear combination of these solutions*

$$\tilde{\mathbf{x}} = \sum_{i=1}^{k} \lambda_i \mathbf{x}_i$$

is also a solution if, and only if,

$$\sum_{i=1}^{k} \lambda_i = 1$$

Theorem 2 states that a linear combination of any k solutions of $\mathbf{Ax} = \mathbf{b}$, be they linearly independent or not, is itself a solution if the coefficients of that combination sum to unity. Such linear combinations are frequently referred to as *convex combinations.*

Theorem 3. *If* $\mathbf{x}_0$ *is any solution of the consistent rectangular linear equation system* $\mathbf{Ax} = \mathbf{b}$, *for which* $\mathbf{AA}^*\mathbf{A} = \mathbf{A}$ *and* $\mathbf{D} = \mathbf{A}^*\mathbf{A}$, *then the linear combination* $\mathbf{c}'\mathbf{x}_0$ *is unique if, and only if,* $\mathbf{c}'\mathbf{D} = \mathbf{c}'$.

As a consequence of Theorem 3 and the idempotency property of $\mathbf{D}$, we have that $\mathbf{c}' = \mathbf{v}'\mathbf{D}$ is a solution of $\mathbf{c}'\mathbf{D} = \mathbf{c}'$ for any arbitrary vector $\mathbf{v}$. Hence, for any vector $\mathbf{v}'$, $\mathbf{c}' = \mathbf{v}'\mathbf{D}$, and

$$\begin{aligned} \mathbf{c}'\mathbf{x}_0 &= \mathbf{v}'\mathbf{D}\mathbf{x}_0 = \mathbf{v}'\mathbf{D}\mathbf{A}^*\mathbf{b} + \mathbf{v}'\mathbf{D}(\mathbf{D} - \mathbf{I})\mathbf{z} \\ &= \mathbf{v}'\mathbf{D}\mathbf{A}^*\mathbf{b} \\ &= \mathbf{v}'\mathbf{A}^*\mathbf{A}\mathbf{A}^*\mathbf{b} \end{aligned}$$

and if the generalized inverse of $\mathbf{A}$ is such that $\mathbf{A}^*\mathbf{A}\mathbf{A}^* = \mathbf{A}^*$, then

$$\mathbf{c}'\mathbf{x}_0 = \mathbf{v}'\mathbf{A}^*\mathbf{b} \tag{4.63}$$

Thus, for any $\mathbf{v}'$ and $\mathbf{c}' = \mathbf{v}'\mathbf{D}$, $\mathbf{c}'\mathbf{x}_0 = \mathbf{v}'\mathbf{A}^*\mathbf{b}$ is unique for all solutions $\mathbf{x}_0$. And since the rank of $\mathbf{D}$ is r, $\mathbf{c}' = \mathbf{v}'\mathbf{D}$ produces a set of r linearly independent nonnull vectors $\mathbf{c}'$ that have this property.

Example. We can illustrate the salient points of Theorems 1, 2, and 3 with the numerical example in (4.56). Earlier, we established that for this particular rectangular linear equation system,

$$\mathbf{A}^* = \begin{bmatrix} 2 & -\frac{5}{2} & 0 \\ -1 & \frac{3}{2} & 0 \\ 0 & 0 & 0 \\ 0 & 0 & 0 \end{bmatrix} \qquad \mathbf{D} = \mathbf{A}^*\mathbf{A} = \begin{bmatrix} 1 & 0 & 10 & 2 \\ 0 & 1 & -3 & 1 \\ 0 & 0 & 0 & 0 \\ 0 & 0 & 0 & 0 \end{bmatrix}$$

and

$$\mathbf{x}_0 = \begin{bmatrix} 10 + 10z_3 + 2z_4 \\ -3z_3 + z_4 \\ -z_3 \\ -z_4 \end{bmatrix} \tag{4.64}$$

Adopting the arbitrary vector $\mathbf{v}' = [v_1 \;\; v_2 \;\; v_3 \;\; v_4]$, we can obtain unique values $\mathbf{c}'\mathbf{x}_0$ for any $\mathbf{c}'$ of the form

$$\mathbf{c}' = \mathbf{v}'\mathbf{D} = [v_1 \quad v_2 \quad (10v_1 - 3v_2) \quad (2v_1 + v_2)] \tag{4.65}$$

The corresponding value of $\mathbf{c}'\mathbf{x}_0$ is

$$\mathbf{c}'\mathbf{x}_0 = \mathbf{v}'\mathbf{A}^*\mathbf{b} = 10 \tag{4.66}$$

where $\mathbf{x}_0$ is the solution in (4.64).

Since $n = 4$ and rank $(\mathbf{A}) =$ rank $(\mathbf{D}) = 2$, then $4 - 2 + 1 = 3$ linearly independent nonnull solutions can be found. For example, on setting $z_3 = z_4 = 1$, we obtain

$$\mathbf{x}_1 = \begin{bmatrix} 22 \\ -2 \\ -1 \\ -1 \end{bmatrix}$$

For $z_3 = 1$ and $z_4 = 2$, we have

$$\mathbf{x}_2 = \begin{bmatrix} 24 \\ -1 \\ -1 \\ -2 \end{bmatrix}$$

And, finally, for $z_3 = 3$ and $z_4 = 1$, we find

$$\mathbf{x}_3 = \begin{bmatrix} 42 \\ -8 \\ -3 \\ -1 \end{bmatrix}$$

Any other solution vector will be a linear convex combination of $\mathbf{x}_1$, $\mathbf{x}_2$, and $\mathbf{x}_3$. For example,

$$\mathbf{x}_4 = \begin{bmatrix} 80 \\ -21 \\ -7 \\ 0 \end{bmatrix}$$

is a solution, and $\mathbf{x}_4 = 3\mathbf{x}_3 - \mathbf{x}_2 - \mathbf{x}_1$.

Since rank $(\mathbf{D}) = 2$, there will be two linearly independent nonnull vectors $\mathbf{c}'$ which satisfy (4.65). For example,

$$\mathbf{c}_1' = [1 \quad 0 \quad 10 \quad 2] \quad \text{and} \quad \mathbf{c}_2' = [0 \quad 1 \quad -3 \quad 1]$$

are linearly independent nonnull vectors which satisfy (4.65). They yield the following values for $\mathbf{c}'\mathbf{x}_0$:

$$\mathbf{c}_1'\mathbf{x}_0 = 10 \qquad \mathbf{c}_2'\mathbf{x}_0 = 0$$

respectively. Any other $\mathbf{c}'$ satisfying (4.65) will be a linear combination of $\mathbf{c}_1'$ and $\mathbf{c}_2'$, and the corresponding value of $\mathbf{c}'\mathbf{x}_0$ will be the same linear combination of $\mathbf{c}_1'\mathbf{x}_0$ and $\mathbf{c}_2'\mathbf{x}_0$. Finally, note that although $\mathbf{c}_1'\mathbf{x}_0$ and $\mathbf{c}_2'\mathbf{x}_0$ are different, each yields a value that is unique for all solution vectors $\mathbf{x}_0$.

4.8 APPLICATION: LINEAR STATISTICAL MODELS

In Chapter 3, we developed the regression model in matrix form and found that the least squares estimator of $\boldsymbol{\beta}$ in the model

$$\mathbf{y} = \mathbf{X}\boldsymbol{\beta} + \boldsymbol{\varepsilon} \tag{4.67}$$

was

$$\mathbf{b} = (\mathbf{X}'\mathbf{X})^{-1}\mathbf{X}'\mathbf{y} \tag{4.68}$$

The matrix $(\mathbf{X}'\mathbf{X})$ was always assumed to be nonsingular; consequently, a unique solution always existed.

The introduction, in this chapter, of the concept of the generalized inverse suggests the following two related questions: are there linear models of the form (4.67) for which the product matrix $(\mathbf{X}'\mathbf{X})$ is singular, and can the generalized inverse $(\mathbf{X}'\mathbf{X})^*$ be used to obtain a meaningful solution in such cases? The answer to both questions is yes. Such models fall under the general heading of linear statistical models, and their exposition is the subject of numerous texts, such as, Graybill (1961), Morrison (1967), Searle (1966), and Scheffé (1959).

In this section, we shall touch on the topic of linear statistical models. Because of the subject's vastness, only the very basic concepts will be discussed, and particular attention will be given to the use of the generalized inverse in solving such models. For a more definitive discussion, the reader should consult the texts mentioned above.

4.8.1 THE SIMPLE LINEAR STATISTICAL MODEL WITH ONE-WAY CLASSIFICATION

The simplest linear statistical model is one which seeks to account for variation in a dependent variable by introducing a one-way classification system. Such models assume that variation in the dependent variable Y_{ij} (ith class, jth observation) is the sum of three parts, that is,

$$Y_{ij} = \mu + \alpha_i + \varepsilon_{ij} \tag{4.69}$$

where μ denotes the grand mean, α_i is the effect of membership in the ith class, and ε_{ij} is a random error term associated with Y_{ij}. As in regression analysis, it is assumed that the ε_{ij}'s are independently normally distributed with

$$\begin{aligned} E(\boldsymbol{\varepsilon}) &= \mathbf{0} \\ E(\boldsymbol{\varepsilon}\boldsymbol{\varepsilon}') &= \sigma^2 \mathbf{I} \\ E(Y_{ij}) &= \mu + \alpha_i \end{aligned} \tag{4.70}$$

The problem, then, is to estimate the parameters μ and α_i, and also σ^2. As we shall see below, the singularity of the product matrix $(\mathbf{X}'\mathbf{X})$ will impose restrictions on what can be estimated. In particular, it will be shown that only certain linear functions of the parameters μ and α_i can be estimated.

Example.

Table 4.1. Employment-Distance Data Classified by Location Category

	j	Food Store Employment
Center-City $i = 1$	1	75
	2	96
	3	87
	4	80
Suburban Ring $i = 2$	1	60
	2	40
	3	54
	4	68
	5	64
	6	48

Recall the numerical example that was introduced in Chapter 3. There we attempted to "explain" variation in the dependent variable, food store employment, by associating this variation with differences in total census tract population, distance to the center-city, and total retail employment. Let us now attempt to account for the variation in food store employment in another way. We define two classes of observations: *center-city* observations and *suburban-ring* observations, and classify the 10 observations into these two categories according to whether they lie within one-half mile of the city center or not. This classification procedure produces the four center-city and six suburban-ring observations that are presented in Table 4.1 and illustrated in Figure 4.5.

Expressing the 10 observations in terms of the model defined in (4.69), we have

$$\begin{aligned}
Y_{11} &= 75 = \mu + \alpha_1 \qquad\quad + \varepsilon_{11} \\
Y_{12} &= 96 = \mu + \alpha_1 \qquad\quad + \varepsilon_{12} \\
Y_{13} &= 87 = \mu + \alpha_1 \qquad\quad + \varepsilon_{13} \\
Y_{14} &= 80 = \mu + \alpha_1 \qquad\quad + \varepsilon_{14} \\
Y_{21} &= 60 = \mu \qquad\quad + \alpha_2 + \varepsilon_{21} \\
Y_{22} &= 40 = \mu \qquad\quad + \alpha_2 + \varepsilon_{22} \\
Y_{23} &= 54 = \mu \qquad\quad + \alpha_2 + \varepsilon_{23} \\
Y_{24} &= 68 = \mu \qquad\quad + \alpha_2 + \varepsilon_{24} \\
Y_{25} &= 64 = \mu \qquad\quad + \alpha_2 + \varepsilon_{25} \\
Y_{26} &= 48 = \mu \qquad\quad + \alpha_2 + \varepsilon_{26}
\end{aligned}$$

or, in matrix form,

$$\mathbf{y} = \mathbf{X}\boldsymbol{\beta} + \boldsymbol{\varepsilon} \tag{4.71}$$

where

$$\mathbf{y} = \begin{bmatrix} 75 \\ 96 \\ 87 \\ 80 \\ 60 \\ 40 \\ 54 \\ 68 \\ 64 \\ 48 \end{bmatrix} \qquad \mathbf{X} = \begin{bmatrix} 1 & 1 & 0 \\ 1 & 1 & 0 \\ 1 & 1 & 0 \\ 1 & 1 & 0 \\ 1 & 0 & 1 \\ 1 & 0 & 1 \\ 1 & 0 & 1 \\ 1 & 0 & 1 \\ 1 & 0 & 1 \\ 1 & 0 & 1 \end{bmatrix} \qquad \boldsymbol{\beta} = \begin{bmatrix} \mu \\ \alpha_1 \\ \alpha_2 \end{bmatrix} \qquad \boldsymbol{\varepsilon} = \begin{bmatrix} \varepsilon_{11} \\ \varepsilon_{12} \\ \varepsilon_{13} \\ \varepsilon_{14} \\ \varepsilon_{21} \\ \varepsilon_{22} \\ \varepsilon_{23} \\ \varepsilon_{24} \\ \varepsilon_{25} \\ \varepsilon_{26} \end{bmatrix}$$

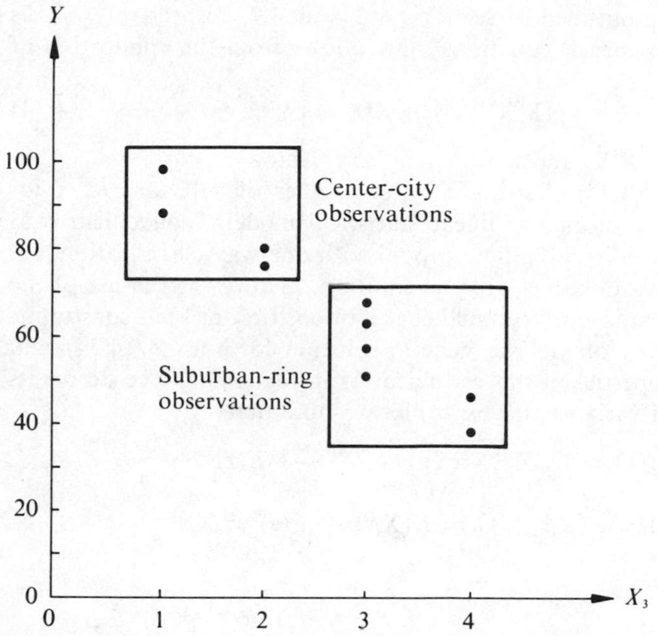

Figure 4.5. Scatter Diagram of Food Store Employment on Distance

Notice that the linear statistical model in (4.71) and the regression model in (4.67) have exactly the same matrix expression. In both models, **y** is a vector of dependent variables, the variation of which we seek to explain. The only difference appears in the elements of **X**. In regression, its elements are observations on the independent variables, whereas in (4.71) they all take on values of unity or zero in order to express the presence or absence of particular parameters in the model. Thus the problem of parameter estimation in (4.71) differs from that in (4.67) only in that $(\mathbf{X}'\mathbf{X})^{-1}$ does not exist in the former model and is therefore replaced, in (4.68), by $(\mathbf{X}'\mathbf{X})^*$, to form

$$\mathbf{b} = (\mathbf{X}'\mathbf{X})^*\mathbf{X}'\mathbf{y} \tag{4.72}$$

4.8.2 PARAMETER ESTIMATION

As in the regression model, the equations

$$\mathbf{X}'\mathbf{X}\mathbf{b} = \mathbf{X}'\mathbf{y} \tag{4.73}$$

are called the *normal equations* of the linear statistical model defined by (4.71). We seek an estimator for $\boldsymbol{\beta}$, and a solution is provided by (4.72). The generalized inverse $(\mathbf{X}'\mathbf{X})^*$ may be obtained, and (4.72) solved, by methods such as are outlined in Sections 4.6 and 4.7, respectively. Thus the solution to the normal equations that follows from the application of (4.58) is

$$\mathbf{b} = (\mathbf{X}'\mathbf{X})^*\mathbf{X}'\mathbf{y} + (\mathbf{D} - \mathbf{I})\mathbf{z} \tag{4.74}$$

where $\mathbf{D} = (\mathbf{X}'\mathbf{X})^*(\mathbf{X}'\mathbf{X})$ and $\mathbf{z}$ is an arbitrary vector.

It is clear from (4.74) that an infinite number of solutions exist for $\mathbf{b}$, and in many expositions of linear statistical models "convenient constraints," such as $\alpha_1 + \alpha_2 = 0$ in our model with one-way classification, are adopted in order to obtain a unique solution. However, the use of the concept of the generalized inverse makes the imposition of such constraints unnecessary. We can obtain the general solution for $\mathbf{b}$ using (4.74) and then derive the properties of this estimator as in regression. To derive its expected value and variance, for example, we note that

$$E(\mathbf{b}) = (\mathbf{X}'\mathbf{X})^*\mathbf{X}'E(\mathbf{y}) + (\mathbf{D} - \mathbf{I})E(\mathbf{z})$$

But

$$E(\mathbf{y}) = E(\mathbf{X}\boldsymbol{\beta} + \boldsymbol{\varepsilon}) = E(\mathbf{X}\boldsymbol{\beta}) + E(\boldsymbol{\varepsilon}) = \mathbf{X}\boldsymbol{\beta}$$

and

$$E(\mathbf{z}) = \mathbf{z}$$

Hence

$$E(\mathbf{b}) = (\mathbf{X}'\mathbf{X})^*\mathbf{X}'\mathbf{X}\boldsymbol{\beta} + (\mathbf{D} - \mathbf{I})\mathbf{z} = \mathbf{D}\boldsymbol{\beta} + (\mathbf{D} - \mathbf{I})\mathbf{z} \tag{4.75}$$

and $\mathbf{b}$ is a *biased* estimator of $\boldsymbol{\beta}$.

Since $\mathbf{z}$ is an arbitrary vector of constants, it does not affect the variance of $\mathbf{b}$. Thus the variance-covariance matrix,

$$\begin{aligned}
\text{Var}(\mathbf{b}) &= E[\mathbf{b} - E(\mathbf{b})][\mathbf{b} - E(\mathbf{b})]' \\
&= E[(\mathbf{X}'\mathbf{X})^*\mathbf{X}'\mathbf{y} - \mathbf{D}\boldsymbol{\beta}][\mathbf{y}'\mathbf{X}(\mathbf{X}'\mathbf{X})^* - \boldsymbol{\beta}'\mathbf{D}'] \\
&= (\mathbf{X}'\mathbf{X})^*\mathbf{X}'E[(\mathbf{y} - \mathbf{X}\boldsymbol{\beta})(\mathbf{y}' - \boldsymbol{\beta}'\mathbf{X}')]\mathbf{X}(\mathbf{X}'\mathbf{X})^* \\
&= (\mathbf{X}'\mathbf{X})^*\mathbf{X}'E(\boldsymbol{\varepsilon}\boldsymbol{\varepsilon}')\mathbf{X}(\mathbf{X}'\mathbf{X})^* \\
&= (\mathbf{X}'\mathbf{X})^*\mathbf{X}'\sigma^2\mathbf{I}\mathbf{X}(\mathbf{X}'\mathbf{X})^* \\
&= \sigma^2(\mathbf{X}'\mathbf{X})^*
\end{aligned} \tag{4.76}$$

This result is directly analogous to the one derived for the regression model in (3.82). And, as in regression, it can be shown that an unbiased estimator of σ^2 is

$$s^2 = \frac{\mathbf{e}'\mathbf{e}}{n - r} \tag{4.77}$$

where r is the rank of $\mathbf{X}$, n is the number of observations, and

$$\mathbf{e}'\mathbf{e} = \mathbf{y}'\mathbf{y} - \mathbf{b}'\mathbf{X}'\mathbf{y} \tag{4.78}$$

as in (3.84). What is interesting in this result is that (4.78) remains constant for any of the infinite number of solutions for $\mathbf{b}$ in (4.74). Thus we can set $\mathbf{z} = \mathbf{0}$ in (4.74) and obtain a solution for $\mathbf{b}$, substitute that expression into (4.78), and use the symmetric property of $(\mathbf{X}'\mathbf{X})^*$ to obtain the result

$$\mathbf{e}'\mathbf{e} = \mathbf{y}'\mathbf{y} - \mathbf{y}'\mathbf{X}(\mathbf{X}'\mathbf{X})^*\mathbf{X}'\mathbf{y} \tag{4.79}$$

The similarities between the regression model of Chapter 3 and the linear statistical models discussed in this section are many, and, indeed, the former can be viewed as a special case of the latter. Table 4.2 lists a few of the points of correspondence between the two classes of models.

The "forcing" of simple linear statistical models into the form of the regression model, and the consequent reliance on the concept of the generalized inverse, may seem, at first, to be unnecessarily cumbersome. However, it is the universality of the matrix approach that merits our attention. Unlike the common analysis of variance formulas found in most elementary statistics texts, the formulation developed here is applicable to all possible situations. Thus, for example, the method can be used in instances where the data are unbalanced between classes, that is, when an unequal number of observations are found in the smallest subclassifications of the data, or when some subclassifications are empty.

Table 4.2. Corresponding Formulas in the Regression and the Linear Statistical Models

	Regression Model	Equation Number in Text	Linear Statistical Model	Equation Number in Text
Model	$\mathbf{y} = \mathbf{X}\boldsymbol{\beta} + \boldsymbol{\varepsilon}$, rank$(\mathbf{X}) = k + 1$	(3.71)	$\mathbf{y} = \mathbf{X}\boldsymbol{\beta} + \boldsymbol{\varepsilon}$ rank$(\mathbf{X}) = r$	(4.71)
Normal Equations	$\mathbf{X}'\mathbf{X}\mathbf{b} = \mathbf{X}'\mathbf{y}$	(3.78)	$\mathbf{X}'\mathbf{X}\mathbf{b} = \mathbf{X}'\mathbf{y}$	(4.73)
Parameter Estimator	$\mathbf{b} = (\mathbf{X}'\mathbf{X})^{-1}\mathbf{X}'\mathbf{y}$	(3.79)	$\mathbf{b} = (\mathbf{X}'\mathbf{X})^*\mathbf{X}'\mathbf{y} + (\mathbf{D} - \mathbf{I})\mathbf{z}$	(4.74)
$E(\mathbf{b})$	$E(\mathbf{b}) = \boldsymbol{\beta}$	(3.81)	$E(\mathbf{b}) = \mathbf{D}\boldsymbol{\beta} + (\mathbf{D} - \mathbf{I})\mathbf{z}$	(4.75)
Var$(\mathbf{b})$	Var$(\mathbf{b}) = \sigma^2(\mathbf{X}'\mathbf{X})^{-1}$	(3.82)	Var$(\mathbf{b}) = \sigma^2(\mathbf{X}'\mathbf{X})^*$	(4.76)
$\mathbf{e}'\mathbf{e}$	$\mathbf{e}'\mathbf{e} = \mathbf{y}'\mathbf{y} - \mathbf{b}'\mathbf{X}'\mathbf{y}$	(3.84)	$\mathbf{e}'\mathbf{e} = \mathbf{y}'\mathbf{y} - \mathbf{b}'\mathbf{X}'\mathbf{y}$	(4.78)
s^2	$s^2 = \mathbf{e}'\mathbf{e}/(n - k - 1)$	(3.83)	$s^2 = \mathbf{e}'\mathbf{e}/(n - r)$	(4.77)

Examples.

(i) Returning to our numerical example, we now can derive a *biased* estimate of $\boldsymbol{\beta}$ and the unbiased estimate of σ^2. First, we form $(\mathbf{X}'\mathbf{X})$ and obtain its generalized inverse. Thus

$$(\mathbf{X}'\mathbf{X}) = \begin{bmatrix} 10 & 4 & 6 \\ 4 & 4 & 0 \\ 6 & 0 & 6 \end{bmatrix} \qquad (\mathbf{X}'\mathbf{X})^* = \begin{bmatrix} \frac{1}{6} & -\frac{1}{6} & 0 \\ -\frac{1}{6} & \frac{5}{12} & 0 \\ 0 & 0 & 0 \end{bmatrix}$$

Next, we find

$$\mathbf{X}'\mathbf{y} = \begin{bmatrix} 672 \\ 338 \\ 334 \end{bmatrix} \qquad \mathbf{D} = (\mathbf{X}'\mathbf{X})^*(\mathbf{X}'\mathbf{X}) = \begin{bmatrix} 1 & 0 & 1 \\ 0 & 1 & -1 \\ 0 & 0 & 0 \end{bmatrix}$$

and

$$\mathbf{b} = (\mathbf{X}'\mathbf{X})^*\mathbf{X}'\mathbf{y} + (\mathbf{D} - \mathbf{I})\mathbf{z} = \begin{bmatrix} \frac{167}{3} - z_3 \\ \frac{173}{6} - z_3 \\ -z_3 \end{bmatrix}$$

Then

$$\begin{aligned} \mathbf{e}'\mathbf{e} &= \mathbf{y}'\mathbf{y} - \mathbf{b}'\mathbf{X}'\mathbf{y} \\ &= \mathbf{y}'\mathbf{y} - \mathbf{y}'\mathbf{X}(\mathbf{X}'\mathbf{X})^*\mathbf{X}'\mathbf{y} \\ &= 47{,}950 - 47{,}153\tfrac{2}{3} = 796\tfrac{1}{3} \end{aligned}$$

and

$$s^2 = \frac{\mathbf{e}'\mathbf{e}}{n - r} = \frac{796\frac{1}{3}}{8} = 99\tfrac{13}{24}$$

Recalling that the total "corrected" sum of squares, SS_T, say, is

$$SS_T = \mathbf{y}'\mathbf{y} - n\bar{Y}^2 = 47{,}950 - 45{,}158\tfrac{2}{5} = 2{,}791\tfrac{3}{5}$$

we can obtain the sum of squares due to the fit of the linear model, SS_M, by subtraction:

$$SS_M = SS_T - \mathbf{e}'\mathbf{e} = 2{,}791\tfrac{3}{5} - 796\tfrac{1}{3} = 1{,}995\tfrac{4}{15}$$

and develop the following analysis of variance table:

Source	D.F.	Sum of Squares	Mean Square	*F* Ratio
Total (uncorr.)	10	47,950.00		
Correction for the Mean (u)	1	45,158.40		
Total (corr.)	9	2,791.60		
Model ($a_1, a_2 \mid u$)	1	1,995.27	1,995.27	20.04
Error	8	796.33	99.54	

(ii) The above numerical example illustrates the linear statistical model with one-way classification. Exactly the same procedure, however, applies for many other classes of linear models. For example, we may wish to introduce a second classification and adopt the model

$$Y_{ijk} = \mu + \alpha_i + \beta_j + \varepsilon_{ijk} \tag{4.80}$$

Equation (4.80) is called *the linear statistical model with two-way classification and no interactions.*

To illustrate the linear statistical model with two-way classification and no interaction, let us turn, once again, to our numerical example, and classify the 10 census tracts into two groups: *light* and *heavy* concentrations of *total* employment. If total employment in a census tract is less than or equal to 220 people, we shall place the tract into the *light* concentration category; otherwise, we shall classify the tract as having a *heavy* concentration of employment. This classification leads to the cross-classification presented in Table 4.3 below. The data are said to be "unbalanced," because the cross-classification leads to an uneven number of observations in some cells. Note that no census tract falls into both location class 1 and total employment class 1 (that is, center-city and light employment).

To test the significance of "employment concentration" effects and "location" effects we adopt the model

$$\mathbf{y} = \mathbf{X}\boldsymbol{\beta} + \boldsymbol{\varepsilon} \tag{4.81}$$

Table 4.3. Food Store Employment by Location and Total Employment Category

	Total Employment Category				Total
Location Category	$j = 1$		$j = 2$		
$i = 1$			$k = 1$	75	338
			2	96	
			3	87	
			4	80	
$i = 2$	$k = 1$	40	$k = 1$	60	334
	2	54	2	64	
	3	68			
	4	48			
Total		210		462	672

where

$$\mathbf{y} = \begin{bmatrix} Y_{211} \\ Y_{212} \\ Y_{213} \\ Y_{214} \\ \hline Y_{121} \\ Y_{122} \\ Y_{123} \\ Y_{124} \\ \hline Y_{221} \\ Y_{222} \end{bmatrix} = \begin{bmatrix} 40 \\ 54 \\ 68 \\ 48 \\ \hline 75 \\ 96 \\ 87 \\ 80 \\ \hline 60 \\ 64 \end{bmatrix} \qquad \mathbf{X} = \begin{bmatrix} 1 & 0 & 1 & 1 & 0 \\ 1 & 0 & 1 & 1 & 0 \\ 1 & 0 & 1 & 1 & 0 \\ 1 & 0 & 1 & 1 & 0 \\ \hline 1 & 1 & 0 & 0 & 1 \\ 1 & 1 & 0 & 0 & 1 \\ 1 & 1 & 0 & 0 & 1 \\ 1 & 1 & 0 & 0 & 1 \\ \hline 1 & 0 & 1 & 0 & 1 \\ 1 & 0 & 1 & 0 & 1 \end{bmatrix}$$

$$\boldsymbol{\beta} = \begin{bmatrix} \mu \\ \alpha_1 \\ \alpha_2 \\ \beta_1 \\ \beta_2 \end{bmatrix} \qquad \boldsymbol{\varepsilon} = \begin{bmatrix} \varepsilon_{211} \\ \varepsilon_{212} \\ \varepsilon_{213} \\ \varepsilon_{214} \\ \hline \varepsilon_{121} \\ \varepsilon_{122} \\ \varepsilon_{123} \\ \varepsilon_{124} \\ \hline \varepsilon_{221} \\ \varepsilon_{222} \end{bmatrix}$$

We proceed, as before, to find

$$(\mathbf{X}'\mathbf{X}) = \begin{bmatrix} 10 & 4 & 6 & 4 & 6 \\ 4 & 4 & 0 & 0 & 4 \\ 6 & 0 & 6 & 4 & 2 \\ 4 & 0 & 4 & 4 & 0 \\ 6 & 4 & 2 & 0 & 6 \end{bmatrix} \qquad (\mathbf{X}'\mathbf{X})^* = \begin{bmatrix} \frac{1}{2} & -\frac{1}{2} & 0 & -\frac{1}{2} & 0 \\ -\frac{1}{2} & \frac{3}{4} & 0 & \frac{1}{2} & 0 \\ 0 & 0 & 0 & 0 & 0 \\ -\frac{1}{2} & \frac{1}{2} & 0 & \frac{3}{4} & 0 \\ 0 & 0 & 0 & 0 & 0 \end{bmatrix}$$

$$\mathbf{X}'\mathbf{y} = \begin{bmatrix} 672 \\ 338 \\ 334 \\ 210 \\ 462 \end{bmatrix} \qquad \mathbf{D} = (\mathbf{X}'\mathbf{X})^*(\mathbf{X}'\mathbf{X}) = \begin{bmatrix} 1 & 0 & 1 & 0 & 1 \\ 0 & 1 & -1 & 0 & 0 \\ 0 & 0 & 0 & 0 & 0 \\ 0 & 0 & 0 & 1 & -1 \\ 0 & 0 & 0 & 0 & 0 \end{bmatrix}$$

Substituting into (4.74), we obtain

$$\mathbf{b} = \begin{bmatrix} 62 + z_3 + z_5 \\ \frac{45}{2} - z_3 \\ -z_3 \\ -\frac{19}{2} - z_5 \\ -z_5 \end{bmatrix}$$

and find

$$\mathbf{e}'\mathbf{e} = \mathbf{y}'\mathbf{y} - \mathbf{y}'\mathbf{X}(\mathbf{X}'\mathbf{X})^*\mathbf{X}'\mathbf{y} = 47{,}950 - 47{,}274 = 676$$

Consequently,

$$s^2 = \frac{\mathbf{e}'\mathbf{e}}{n - r} = \frac{676}{7}$$

Thus we have the following analysis of variance table:

Source	D.F.	Sum of Squares	Mean Square	*F* Ratio
Total (uncorr.)	10	47,950.00		
Correction for the Mean (u)	1	45,158.40		
Total (corr.)	9	2,791.60		
Model ($a_1, a_2, b_1, b_2 \mid u$)	2	2,115.60	1,057.80	10.95
Error	7	676.00	96.57	

4.8.3 ESTIMABLE FUNCTIONS

In (4.75) we saw that $\mathbf{b}$ is a *nonunique, biased* estimator of $\boldsymbol{\beta}$. We now wish to consider a class of *unique, unbiased* estimators of certain linear combinations of the elements of $\boldsymbol{\beta}$. To do this, we shall draw on some of the results presented in Section 4.7. In particular, we recall Theorem 3, in Subsection 4.7.4, which states that certain linear combinations of the elements of a solution $\mathbf{b}$ have a unique value no matter which particular solution for $\mathbf{b}$ is obtained from (4.74). These linear combinations are given by $\mathbf{w}'\mathbf{b}$, for those $\mathbf{w}'$ for which $\mathbf{w}'\mathbf{D} = \mathbf{w}'$. Recall that any $\mathbf{w}'$ that has the form $\mathbf{w}' = \mathbf{v}'\mathbf{D}$ satisfies this condition, because then $\mathbf{w}'\mathbf{D} = \mathbf{v}'\mathbf{D}^2 = \mathbf{v}'\mathbf{D} = \mathbf{w}'$, since $\mathbf{D}$ is an idempotent matrix. Hence, for any arbitrary $\mathbf{v}'$, $\mathbf{v}'\mathbf{D}\mathbf{b}$ is unique.

Recall (4.74), and let

$$\mathbf{w}' = \mathbf{v}'\mathbf{D} \tag{4.82}$$

Then

$$\begin{aligned}\mathbf{w}'\mathbf{b} &= \mathbf{v}'\mathbf{D}\mathbf{b}\\ &= \mathbf{v}'\mathbf{D}[(\mathbf{X}'\mathbf{X})^*\mathbf{X}'\mathbf{y} + (\mathbf{D} - \mathbf{I})\mathbf{z}]\\ &= \mathbf{v}'\mathbf{D}(\mathbf{X}'\mathbf{X})^*\mathbf{X}'\mathbf{y}, \qquad \text{since } \mathbf{D}^2 = \mathbf{D} \qquad (4.83)\\ &= \mathbf{v}'(\mathbf{X}'\mathbf{X})^*\mathbf{X}'\mathbf{y}, \qquad \text{since } \mathbf{D}(\mathbf{X}'\mathbf{X})^* = (\mathbf{X}'\mathbf{X})^* \qquad (4.84)\\ &= \mathbf{v}'\mathbf{b} \qquad \text{when } \mathbf{b} = (\mathbf{X}'\mathbf{X})^*\mathbf{X}'\mathbf{y}\end{aligned}$$

and

$$\begin{aligned}E(\mathbf{w}'\mathbf{b}) &= \mathbf{v}'(\mathbf{X}'\mathbf{X})^*\mathbf{X}'E(\mathbf{y}) \qquad \text{by (4.84)}\\ &= \mathbf{v}'(\mathbf{X}'\mathbf{X})^*\mathbf{X}'\mathbf{X}\boldsymbol{\beta}\\ &= \mathbf{v}'\mathbf{D}\boldsymbol{\beta}\\ &= \mathbf{w}'\boldsymbol{\beta}\end{aligned}$$

Consequently, any linear function of the parameter estimator **b** that is unique is unbiased. And linear functions of **b** that are unique are the unique, unbiased estimators of the same linear functions of $\boldsymbol{\beta}$.[2] Such functions are called *linearly estimable functions*, and they are the only linear functions of the parameters that can be so estimated. Thus, if $\mathbf{w}'$ is such that $\mathbf{w}'\mathbf{b}$ is unique, then $\mathbf{w}'\mathbf{b}$ is the unique, unbiased estimator of the *linearly estimable function* $\mathbf{w}'\boldsymbol{\beta}$.

To find the variance of the estimator of a linearly estimable function, recall that in (4.83) we had that

$$\mathbf{w}'\mathbf{b} = \mathbf{v}'\mathbf{D}(\mathbf{X}'\mathbf{X})^*\mathbf{X}'\mathbf{y}$$

where, by (4.82), $\mathbf{w}' = \mathbf{v}'\mathbf{D}$. Hence,

$$\begin{aligned}\mathbf{w}'\mathbf{b} &= \mathbf{w}'(\mathbf{X}'\mathbf{X})^*\mathbf{X}'\mathbf{y}\\ &= \mathbf{w}'(\mathbf{X}'\mathbf{X})^*\mathbf{X}'[\mathbf{X}\boldsymbol{\beta} + \boldsymbol{\varepsilon}]\\ &= \mathbf{w}'\boldsymbol{\beta} + \mathbf{w}'(\mathbf{X}'\mathbf{X})^*\mathbf{X}'\boldsymbol{\varepsilon}\end{aligned}$$

or

$$\mathbf{w}'\mathbf{b} - \mathbf{w}'\boldsymbol{\beta} = \mathbf{w}'(\mathbf{X}'\mathbf{X})^*\mathbf{X}'\boldsymbol{\varepsilon}$$

Therefore,

$$\begin{aligned}\operatorname{Var}(\mathbf{w}'\mathbf{b}) &= E[(\mathbf{w}'\mathbf{b} - \mathbf{w}'\boldsymbol{\beta})(\mathbf{w}'\mathbf{b} - \mathbf{w}'\boldsymbol{\beta})']\\ &= E[\mathbf{w}'(\mathbf{X}'\mathbf{X})^*\mathbf{X}'\boldsymbol{\varepsilon}\boldsymbol{\varepsilon}'\mathbf{X}(\mathbf{X}'\mathbf{X})^*\mathbf{w}]\end{aligned}$$

since $(\mathbf{X}'\mathbf{X})^*$ is symmetric and therefore equal to its transpose. Thus

$$\begin{aligned}\operatorname{Var}(\mathbf{w}'\mathbf{b}) &= \mathbf{w}'(\mathbf{X}'\mathbf{X})^*\mathbf{X}'E(\boldsymbol{\varepsilon}\boldsymbol{\varepsilon}')\mathbf{X}(\mathbf{X}'\mathbf{X})^*\mathbf{w}\\ &= \mathbf{w}'(\mathbf{X}'\mathbf{X})^*\mathbf{w}\sigma^2 \qquad \text{by (4.70)}\\ &= \mathbf{v}'\mathbf{D}(\mathbf{X}'\mathbf{X})^*\mathbf{D}'\mathbf{v}\sigma^2 \qquad \text{by (4.82)}\\ &= \mathbf{v}'(\mathbf{X}'\mathbf{X})^*\mathbf{v}\sigma^2 \qquad (4.85)\end{aligned}$$

[2] Since rank $(\mathbf{D})$ = rank $(\mathbf{X}) = r$, there are only r linearly independent vectors $\mathbf{w}' = \mathbf{v}'\mathbf{D}$ and, therefore, only r linearly independent linearly estimable functions.

because $\mathbf{D} = (\mathbf{X}'\mathbf{X})^*(\mathbf{X}'\mathbf{X})$. Note that (4.85) is exactly analogous to the corresponding result in regression analysis. And, as in regression, it can be shown that $\mathbf{w}'\mathbf{b}$, where $\mathbf{b}$ is obtained from (4.74), is the minimum variance estimator; that is, no linear unbiased estimator of $\mathbf{w}'\boldsymbol{\beta}$ has a variance smaller than $\mathbf{v}'(\mathbf{X}'\mathbf{X})^*\mathbf{v}\sigma^2$ [Rao (1962)].

Examples.

(i) Returning to our numerical example of the simple linear statistical model with one-way classification, we have, for the arbitrary vector $\mathbf{v}' = [v_1\ v_2\ v_3]$ and the vector of parameters $\boldsymbol{\beta}' = [\mu\ \alpha_1\ \alpha_2]$, the linearly estimable functions

$$\mathbf{w}'\boldsymbol{\beta} = \mathbf{v}'\mathbf{D}\boldsymbol{\beta} = v_1(\mu + \alpha_2) + v_2(\alpha_1 - \alpha_2) \tag{4.86}$$

for which estimators are, by (4.84),

$$\mathbf{w}'\mathbf{b} = \mathbf{v}'(\mathbf{X}'\mathbf{X})^*\mathbf{X}'\mathbf{y} = \frac{167}{3}v_1 + \frac{173}{6}v_2 \tag{4.87}$$

Note that (4.86) and (4.87) hold true for any values of v_1 and v_2. Thus we can obtain particular linearly estimable functions from (4.86) by giving specific values to v_1 and v_2. And we can obtain the estimator of this particular function by giving the same specific values to v_1 and v_2 in (4.87). Conversely, we can ascertain whether a particular linear function of the parameters is linearly estimable by seeing if (4.86) reduces to it for some specific set of values for the v's. Thus, in the above example, $\alpha_1 - \alpha_2$ is linearly estimable, since $\mathbf{w}'\boldsymbol{\beta} = \alpha_1 - \alpha_2$ in (4.86), if $v_1 = 0$ and $v_2 = 1$. This, of course, is equivalent to testing whether for a particular $\mathbf{w}'\boldsymbol{\beta}$, $\mathbf{w}'$ satisfies $\mathbf{w}'\mathbf{D} = \mathbf{w}'$. In our example, for $\mathbf{w}'\boldsymbol{\beta} = \alpha_1 - \alpha_2$, $\mathbf{w}' = [0\ 1\ -1]$ and

$$\mathbf{w}'\mathbf{D} = [0 \quad 1 \quad -1]\begin{bmatrix} 1 & 0 & 1 \\ 0 & 1 & -1 \\ 0 & 0 & 0 \end{bmatrix} = [0 \quad 1 \quad -1] = \mathbf{w}'$$

and $\alpha_1 - \alpha_2$, therefore, is linearly estimable. Its minimum variance, linear, unbiased estimate is, by (4.87),

$$\mathbf{w}'\mathbf{b} = \frac{173}{6}$$

(ii) In our numerical example of a linear statistical model with two-way classification, we have, for the arbitrary vector $\mathbf{v}' = [v_1\ v_2\ v_3\ v_4\ v_5]$ and the vector of parameters $\boldsymbol{\beta}' = [\mu\ \alpha_1\ \alpha_2\ \beta_1\ \beta_2]$, the linearly estimable functions

$$\mathbf{w}'\boldsymbol{\beta} = \mathbf{v}'\mathbf{D}\boldsymbol{\beta} = v_1(\mu + \alpha_2 + \beta_2) + v_2(\alpha_1 - \alpha_2) + v_4(\beta_1 - \beta_2) \tag{4.88}$$

for which estimators are

$$\mathbf{w}'\mathbf{b} = \mathbf{v}'(\mathbf{X}'\mathbf{X})^*\mathbf{X}'\mathbf{y} = 62\,v_1 + \frac{45}{2}v_2 + \frac{19}{2}v_4 \tag{4.89}$$

Thus, for example, $\alpha_1 - \alpha_2$ is linearly estimable, and its minimum variance, linear, unbiased estimate is

$$\mathbf{w}'\mathbf{b} = \frac{45}{2}$$

4.8.4 HYPOTHESIS TESTING

Let us now consider the problem of testing *linear hypotheses*, that is, hypotheses stating that some linear function of the parameters has the value of a given constant, q_0 say. Only linearly estimable functions of the parameters are of interest, since they are the only ones that can be tested. For example, if the function $\alpha_1 - \alpha_2$ is linearly estimable, then one can test the hypothesis that $\alpha_1 - \alpha_2 = q_0$, where q_0 is an arbitrary constant.

The general procedure that is followed in testing a linear hypothesis that $\mathbf{w}'\boldsymbol{\beta} = q_0$, where q_0 is a constant and $\mathbf{w}'\boldsymbol{\beta}$ is linearly estimable, is analogous to the procedure used in stepwise regression, described in Subsection 3.4.1. First, we amend the model to take into account the hypothesis. Next, we obtain the sum of squares due to the original model, called the *full model*, and the sum of squares due to the amended model, called the *reduced model*. The difference between these two sums of squares, $SS_M\,(\text{full}) - SS_M\,(\text{reduced})$, say, forms the numerator of the F ratio, which is the test statistic that determines whether the explanatory contribution of the extra components in the full model is statistically significant. The denominator, as before, is the mean square due to error, s^2. Thus, if $\mathbf{y} = \mathbf{X}\boldsymbol{\beta} + \boldsymbol{\varepsilon}$ is the *full model*, and the hypothesis that $\mathbf{w}'\boldsymbol{\beta} = q_0$ leads to $\boldsymbol{\beta}$ being changed into $\boldsymbol{\beta}_r$, say, then the *reduced model* is $\mathbf{y} = \mathbf{X}_r\boldsymbol{\beta}_r + \boldsymbol{\varepsilon}$, where $\mathbf{X}_r$ is the matrix $\mathbf{X}$ that corresponds to $\boldsymbol{\beta}_r$, and

$$SS_M\,(\text{full}) = \mathbf{y}'\mathbf{X}(\mathbf{X}'\mathbf{X})^*\mathbf{X}'\mathbf{y} - n\bar{Y}^2 \tag{4.90}$$

$$SS_M\,(\text{reduced}) = \mathbf{y}'\mathbf{X}_r(\mathbf{X}_r'\mathbf{X}_r)^*\mathbf{X}_r'\mathbf{y} - n\bar{Y}^2 \tag{4.91}$$

Hence,

$$F = \frac{SS_M\,(\text{full}) - SS_M\,(\text{reduced})}{s^2} \tag{4.92}$$

where

$$s^2 = \frac{\mathbf{e}'\mathbf{e}}{n - r} \tag{4.93}$$

and by comparing F with tabulated values of the F distribution with r and $n - r$ degrees of freedom, we test the linear null hypothesis that $\mathbf{w}'\boldsymbol{\beta} = q_0$.

Frequently, linear hypotheses cannot be represented by the single equation $\mathbf{w}'\boldsymbol{\beta} = q_0$, but require several such equations. These may be expressed as $\mathbf{W}'\boldsymbol{\beta} = \mathbf{q}$, where the rows of $\mathbf{W}'\boldsymbol{\beta}$ are linearly independent, linearly estimable functions. Thus the rank of a matrix $\mathbf{W}$ with m rows is m, and $\mathbf{W}'\mathbf{D} = \mathbf{W}'$.

The null hypothesis $\mathbf{W}'\boldsymbol{\beta} = \mathbf{q}$ is commonly referred to as the *general linear hypothesis*, and a test of this hypothesis may be carried out by computing [Searle (1966)] the F statistic

$$F = \frac{(\mathbf{W}'\mathbf{b} - \mathbf{q})'[\mathbf{W}'(\mathbf{X}'\mathbf{X})^*\mathbf{W}]^{-1}(\mathbf{W}'\mathbf{b} - \mathbf{q})}{ms^2} \tag{4.94}$$

and entering a table of the F distribution with m and $n - r$ degrees of freedom.[3]

Examples.

(i) In the first numerical example of this section, we adopted the *full model*,

$$Y_{ij} = \mu + \alpha_i + \varepsilon_{ij}$$

The sum of squares due to the fitting of this model was found to be $SS_M\,(\text{full}) = 1{,}995\tfrac{4}{15}$ and the estimate of σ^2 was $s^2 = 99\tfrac{13}{24}$. We also have seen that $\alpha_1 - \alpha_2$ is linearly estimable; consequently, a testable null hypothesis is that $\alpha_1 - \alpha_2 = 0$, or $\alpha_1 = \alpha_2$. The *reduced* model under this hypothesis is

$$Y_j = \mu + \alpha + \varepsilon_j$$

where $\alpha = \alpha_1 = \alpha_2$, and the corresponding normal equations are

$$\begin{bmatrix} 10 & 10 \\ 10 & 10 \end{bmatrix} \begin{bmatrix} \mu \\ \alpha \end{bmatrix} = \begin{bmatrix} 672 \\ 672 \end{bmatrix}$$

The generalized inverse of $(\mathbf{X}_r'\mathbf{X}_r)$ is

$$(\mathbf{X}_r'\mathbf{X}_r)^* = \begin{bmatrix} \frac{1}{10} & 0 \\ 0 & 0 \end{bmatrix}$$

and the sum of squares due to the reduced model is

$$\begin{aligned} SS_M\,(\text{reduced}) &= \mathbf{y}'\mathbf{X}_r(\mathbf{X}_r'\mathbf{X}_r)^*\mathbf{X}_r'\mathbf{y} - n\bar{Y}^2 \\ &= 45{,}158\tfrac{2}{5} - 45{,}158\tfrac{2}{5} \\ &= 0 \end{aligned}$$

[3]Since $\mathbf{W}'\mathbf{b}$ is the estimator of the linearly estimable functions $\mathbf{W}'\boldsymbol{\beta}$ in the full model, F is readily obtainable once $\mathbf{b} = (\mathbf{X}'\mathbf{X})^*\mathbf{X}'\mathbf{y}$ has been calculated. Note that when $\mathbf{q} = \mathbf{0}$, (4.94) reduces to

Hence the F statistic for testing the null hypothesis that $\alpha_1 = \alpha_2$ is

$$F = \frac{1{,}995.27 - 0}{99.54} = 20.04$$

with (1, 8) degrees of freedom. Consequently, we reject the null hypothesis at the five percent level and conclude that one cannot account for the variation in the dependent variable solely by the variation in the error term.

(ii) For our second numerical example, we adopted the *full model,*

$$Y_{ijk} = \mu + \alpha_i + \beta_j + \varepsilon_{ijk} \tag{4.96}$$

The sum of squares due to this model was SS_M (full) $= 2{,}115\frac{3}{5}$, and the estimate of σ^2 was

$$s^2 = \frac{\mathbf{e}'\mathbf{e}}{n - r} = \frac{676}{7}$$

The linear function $\beta_1 - \beta_2$ was found to be linearly estimable. Consequently, a testable null hypothesis is that $\beta_1 - \beta_2 = 0$, or $\beta_1 = \beta_2$. The *reduced* model under this null hypothesis is

$$Y_{ik} = \mu + \alpha_i + \beta + \varepsilon_{ik} \tag{4.97}$$

where $\beta = \beta_1 = \beta_2$. The corresponding normal equations are

$$\begin{bmatrix} 10 & 4 & 6 & 10 \\ 4 & 4 & 0 & 4 \\ 6 & 0 & 6 & 6 \\ 10 & 4 & 6 & 10 \end{bmatrix} \begin{bmatrix} \mu \\ \alpha_1 \\ \alpha_2 \\ \beta \end{bmatrix} = \begin{bmatrix} 672 \\ 338 \\ 334 \\ 672 \end{bmatrix}$$

and the generalized inverse, in this case, is

$$(\mathbf{X}_r'\mathbf{X}_r)^* = \begin{bmatrix} \frac{1}{6} & -\frac{1}{6} & 0 & 0 \\ -\frac{1}{6} & \frac{5}{12} & 0 & 0 \\ 0 & 0 & 0 & 0 \\ 0 & 0 & 0 & 0 \end{bmatrix}$$

The sum of squares due to the reduced model is

$$\begin{aligned} SS_M \text{ (reduced)} &= \mathbf{y}'\mathbf{X}_r(\mathbf{X}_r'\mathbf{X}_r)^*\mathbf{X}_r'\mathbf{y} - n\bar{Y}^2 \\ &= 47{,}153\tfrac{2}{3} - 45{,}158\tfrac{2}{5} \\ &= 1{,}995\tfrac{4}{5} \end{aligned}$$

Hence

$$F = \frac{2{,}115.60 - 1{,}995.27}{96.57} = \frac{120.33}{96.57} = 1.25 \tag{4.98}$$

with (1, 7) degrees of freedom, and we fail to reject the null hypothesis that $\beta_1 = \beta_2$. Note that the same result may be obtained by using (4.95). Thus,

$$F = \frac{\mathbf{b}'\mathbf{w}[\mathbf{w}'(\mathbf{X}'\mathbf{X})^*\mathbf{w}]^{-1}\mathbf{w}'\mathbf{b}}{s^2} = \frac{(-19/2)(4/3)(-19/2)}{96.57} = \frac{120.33}{96.57} = 1.25$$

Alternatively, we may wish to test the significance of the explanatory contribution of the total employment classification, after the explanatory contribution of location has been taken into account. First, we fit the full model and obtain the sum of squares due to that fit, SS_M (full), say. We have seen that SS_M (full) $= 2{,}115\,\frac{3}{5}$. Next, we fit the reduced model

$$Y_{ik} = \mu + \alpha_i + \varepsilon_{ik} \tag{4.99}$$

and obtain the corresponding sum of squares, SS_M (reduced), say. This too was done earlier, and we recall that SS_M (reduced) $= 1{,}995\,\frac{4}{15}$. Hence

$$F = \frac{2{,}115.60 - 1{,}995.27}{96.57} = \frac{120.33}{96.57} = 1.25$$

But this is precisely the F statistic obtained in (4.98) to test the null hypothesis $\beta_1 = \beta_2$! Yet our linear hypothesis in this latter case was $\beta_1 = \beta_2 = 0$. The reason for this apparent paradox is clear if we rewrite the reduced model in (4.97) as follows:

$$Y_{ik} = (\mu + \beta) + \alpha_i + \varepsilon_{ik} = \bar{\mu} + \alpha_i + \varepsilon_{ik} \tag{4.100}$$

which is equivalent to the reduced model in (4.99).

The results of the above calculations may be set out in an analysis of variance table, as follows:

Source	D.F.	Sum of Squares	Mean Square	F Ratio
Total (uncorr.)	10	47,950.00		
Correction for the Mean (u)	1	45,158.40		
Total (corr.)	9	2,791.60		
Model ($a_1, a_2, b_1, b_2 \mid u$)	2	2,115.60		
Location ($a_1, a_2 \mid u$)	1	1,995.27		
Employment| Location ($b_1, b_2 \mid u, a_1, a_2$)	1	120.33	120.33	1.25
Error	7	676.00	96.57	

Similar procedures may be used to test the significance of the contribution of the location effects, after the total employment effect has been taken into account.

4.8.5 ANALYSIS OF COVARIANCE

In Chapter 3 we dealt with regression models, and in the preceding sections we introduced linear statistical models with one-way and two-way classifications. Occasionally, however, we may wish to use a combination of both models. For example, we may wish to adopt the model

$$Y_{ij} = \mu + \alpha_i + \beta X_{ij} + \varepsilon_{ij} \tag{4.101}$$

where μ is the grand mean, α_i denotes the location effect, βX_{ij} represents the population effect, and ε_{ij} is a random error term. The application of this more general linear statistical model proceeds exactly as before, only **X** now is a matrix which also includes observations on the independent variable X_{ij}.[4]

Example. To illustrate the covariance model defined in (4.101), we shall fit it to the numerical example that we have been using throughout our discussion of regression and linear statistical models. Recalling the data presented in Table 3.11, we can express the 10 observations in terms of the covariance model defined in (4.101), as follows:

$$\begin{aligned}
Y_{11} &= 75 = \mu + \alpha_1 && + 6\beta + \varepsilon_{11}\\
Y_{12} &= 96 = \mu + \alpha_1 && + 8\beta + \varepsilon_{12}\\
Y_{13} &= 87 = \mu + \alpha_1 && + 8\beta + \varepsilon_{13}\\
Y_{14} &= 80 = \mu + \alpha_1 && + 6\beta + \varepsilon_{14}\\
Y_{21} &= 60 = \mu && + \alpha_2 + 4\beta + \varepsilon_{21}\\
Y_{22} &= 40 = \mu && + \alpha_2 + 2\beta + \varepsilon_{22}\\
Y_{23} &= 54 = \mu && + \alpha_2 + 4\beta + \varepsilon_{23}\\
Y_{24} &= 68 = \mu && + \alpha_2 + 6\beta + \varepsilon_{24}\\
Y_{25} &= 64 = \mu && + \alpha_2 + 4\beta + \varepsilon_{25}\\
Y_{26} &= 48 = \mu && + \alpha_2 + 2\beta + \varepsilon_{26}
\end{aligned}$$

or, in matrix form,

$$\mathbf{y} = \mathbf{X}\boldsymbol{\beta} + \boldsymbol{\varepsilon} \tag{4.102}$$

[4] Note that the adoption of the model in (4.101) implies the following strict assumptions:
(a) the dependent variable Y is *homoscedastic*, that is, $\text{Var}(Y_{ij}) = \sigma^2$;
(b) the regressions are *linear*; and
(c) the class-specific regression lines are *parallel* to each other.
Hence, what covariance analysis is testing, in this case, is whether the intercepts of the two regression lines are significantly different. And for a truly rigorous test of such an hypothesis, one should first test whether the above three assumptions are justified.

where

$$\mathbf{y} = \begin{bmatrix} 75 \\ 96 \\ 87 \\ 80 \\ 60 \\ 40 \\ 54 \\ 68 \\ 64 \\ 48 \end{bmatrix} \qquad \mathbf{X} = \begin{bmatrix} 1 & 1 & 0 & 6 \\ 1 & 1 & 0 & 8 \\ 1 & 1 & 0 & 8 \\ 1 & 1 & 0 & 6 \\ 1 & 0 & 1 & 4 \\ 1 & 0 & 1 & 2 \\ 1 & 0 & 1 & 4 \\ 1 & 0 & 1 & 6 \\ 1 & 0 & 1 & 4 \\ 1 & 0 & 1 & 2 \end{bmatrix} \qquad \boldsymbol{\beta} = \begin{bmatrix} \mu \\ \alpha_1 \\ \alpha_2 \\ \beta \end{bmatrix} \qquad \boldsymbol{\varepsilon} = \begin{bmatrix} \varepsilon_{11} \\ \varepsilon_{12} \\ \varepsilon_{13} \\ \varepsilon_{14} \\ \varepsilon_{21} \\ \varepsilon_{22} \\ \varepsilon_{23} \\ \varepsilon_{24} \\ \varepsilon_{25} \\ \varepsilon_{26} \end{bmatrix}$$

Thus

$$\mathbf{X'X} = \begin{bmatrix} 10 & 4 & 6 & 50 \\ 4 & 4 & 0 & 28 \\ 6 & 0 & 6 & 22 \\ 50 & 28 & 22 & 292 \end{bmatrix} \qquad (\mathbf{X'X})^* = \begin{bmatrix} \frac{24}{23} & \frac{29}{46} & 0 & -\frac{11}{46} \\ \frac{29}{46} & \frac{105}{92} & 0 & -\frac{5}{23} \\ 0 & 0 & 0 & 0 \\ -\frac{11}{46} & -\frac{5}{23} & 0 & \frac{3}{46} \end{bmatrix}$$

$$\mathbf{X'y} = \begin{bmatrix} 672 \\ 338 \\ 334 \\ 3690 \end{bmatrix} \qquad \mathbf{D} = (\mathbf{X'X})^*(\mathbf{X'X}) = \begin{bmatrix} 1 & 0 & 1 & 1 \\ 0 & 1 & -1 & 0 \\ 0 & 0 & 0 & 0 \\ 0 & 0 & 0 & 1 \end{bmatrix}$$

Letting $\mathbf{v}' = [v_1 \;\; v_2 \;\; v_3 \;\; v_4]$ be the arbitrary vector in (4.82) and (4.84), we obtain the linearly estimable functions,

$$\mathbf{w}'\boldsymbol{\beta} = \mathbf{v}'\mathbf{D}\boldsymbol{\beta} = v_1(\mu + \alpha_2) + v_2(\alpha_1 - \alpha_2) + v_4\beta$$

and their estimators

$$\mathbf{w}'\mathbf{b} = \mathbf{v}'(\mathbf{X'X})^*\mathbf{X'y} = \mathbf{v}'\mathbf{b} = \frac{734}{23}v_1 + \frac{333}{46}v_2 + \frac{149}{23}v_4$$

We note that β and $\alpha_1 - \alpha_2$ are both linearly estimable functions with estimators

$$b = \frac{149}{23}$$

for $v_1 = v_2 = 0$ and $v_4 = 1$, and

$$a_1 - a_2 = \frac{333}{46}$$

for $v_1 = v_4 = 0$ and $v_2 = 1$.

Recalling (4.85), we obtain the variance of the estimator of a linearly estimable function. Thus

$$v'(\mathbf{X}'\mathbf{X})^* v\sigma^2 = \left[\frac{v_1}{92}(96v_1 + 58v_2 - 22v_4) + \frac{v_2}{92}(58v_1 + 105v_2 - 20v_4) - \frac{v_4}{92}(22v_1 + 20v_2 - 6v_4)\right]\sigma^2$$

which for b is

$$\text{Var}(b) = \frac{3}{46}\sigma^2$$

and for $a_1 - a_2$ is

$$\text{Var}(a_1 - a_2) = \frac{105}{92}\sigma^2$$

The estimator of σ^2 can be found using (4.77). Thus

$$s^2 = \frac{\mathbf{e}'\mathbf{e}}{n-r} = \frac{\mathbf{y}'\mathbf{y} - \mathbf{b}'\mathbf{X}'\mathbf{y}}{n-r} = \frac{47{,}950 - 47{,}797\frac{4}{23}}{10-3} = \frac{152\frac{19}{23}}{7} = \frac{3{,}515}{161}$$

Finally, computing the total corrected sum of squares, SS_T, we find

$$SS_T = \mathbf{y}'\mathbf{y} - n\bar{Y}^2 = 47{,}950 - 45{,}158\tfrac{2}{5} = 2{,}791\tfrac{3}{5}$$

and, by subtraction, obtain the sum of squares due to the fit of the model, SS_M, say,

$$SS_M = SS_T - \mathbf{e}'\mathbf{e} = 2{,}791\tfrac{3}{5} - 152\tfrac{19}{23} = 2{,}638\tfrac{89}{115}$$

These results may be presented in an analysis of variance table, as follows:

Source	D.F.	Sum of Squares	Mean Square	F Ratio
Total (corr.)	9	2,791.60		
Model ($a_1, a_2, b \mid u$)	2	2,638.77	1,319.39	60.43
Error	7	152.83	21.83	

Let us now test whether the location effects are a significant influence on food store employment, after the effects of total population have been accounted for. To carry out this test, we need the sum of squares due to the reduced model

$$Y_{ij} = \mu + \beta X_{ij} + \varepsilon_{ij} \tag{4.103}$$

This quantity, SS_M (reduced), say, was computed in Chapter 3 and was found to be equal to 2,592.86. However, since $\alpha_1 - \alpha_2$ is linearly estimable, we can obtain SS_M (reduced) by considering the linear hypothesis $\alpha_1 - \alpha_2 = 0$, for which $\mathbf{w}' = [0\ 1\ -1\ 0]$. A solution of the normal equations is

$$\mathbf{b} = (\mathbf{X}'\mathbf{X})^*\mathbf{X}'\mathbf{y} = \begin{bmatrix} \frac{734}{23} \\ \frac{333}{46} \\ 0 \\ \frac{149}{23} \end{bmatrix}$$

Hence $\mathbf{w}'\mathbf{b} = 333/46$, and $\mathbf{w}'(\mathbf{X}'\mathbf{X})^*\mathbf{w} = 105/92$. Thus, using the formula for the numerator of the F statistic in (4.95), we have that

$$\begin{aligned} SS_M \text{ (full)} - SS_M \text{ (reduced)} &= 2{,}638\tfrac{89}{115} - SS_M \text{ (reduced)} \\ &= \frac{333}{46}\left(\frac{92}{105}\right)\frac{333}{46} = 45.92 \end{aligned}$$

which yields

$$SS_M \text{ (reduced)} = 2{,}592.86$$

as in Chapter 3. The associated analysis of variance table, therefore, is as follows:

Source	D.F.	Sum of Squares	Mean Square	F Ratio
Total (corr.)	9	2,791.60		
Model $(a_1, a_2, b \mid u)$	2	2,638.77		
Population $(b \mid u)$	1	2,592.86		
Location | Population $(a_1, a_2 \mid u, b)$	1	45.92	45.92	2.10
Error	7	152.83	21.83	

The F statistic for testing the significance of the location effect is not significant at the five percent level.

Several related hypotheses could be tested at this point. For example, we could test whether $\beta = 0$. Or we could fit a separate regression equation for each of the two location classes and test whether $\beta_1 = \beta_2$. Alternatively, we could adopt a more complex model by including additional regression variables—total employment, for example (Exercise 1).

4.8.6 LINEAR STATISTICAL MODELS: A RECAPITULATION

In our discussion of regression models and linear statistical models, we began with a model that purported to "explain" the relationship between a particular variable, called a *dependent* variable, and a set of other factors, called *independent* variables. No cause and effect relationships were postulated, and all inferences were derived from a theoretical interpretation of the purely statistical results. We assumed that the mean values of the dependent variable and the independent variables were given and were not subjects for explanation. Only the variation in the dependent variable from its mean value was to be explained, and this explanation proceeded in terms of the concomitant variation of the independent variables from their mean values.

The variation of a dependent variable from its mean value typically is summarized by an index called *variance*, which is the sum of squares of the deviations of the observations from their mean divided by the total number of observations.[5] Thus variance is a measure of average variation per observation. When such deviations for a dependent variable are measured from the grand mean for the sample, the resulting index of variation is referred to as *total variance*. The numerator of this index is called *total variation* or *total sum of squares*, and the denominator is defined as the *degrees of freedom* carried by this sum of squares. Their quotient is total variance. A graphical illustration of the total variation in the numerical example that has been used throughout our discussion of regression and linear statistical models appears in Figure 4.6(a), and numerical values for this quantity and for total variance are set out in Table 4.4(A).

A statistical explanation of the behavior of a dependent variable may be interpreted as an attempt to reduce the total variance of the dependent variable by measuring deviations from some point other than the grand mean. This form of statistical accounting may be accomplished in one of two ways: by classifying the sample observations into groups and introducing subgroup means, or by regressing the dependent variable on one or

[5] When used as an estimator of the population variance, the denominator is $n - 1$ instead of n, in order to give the estimator the property of unbiasedness.

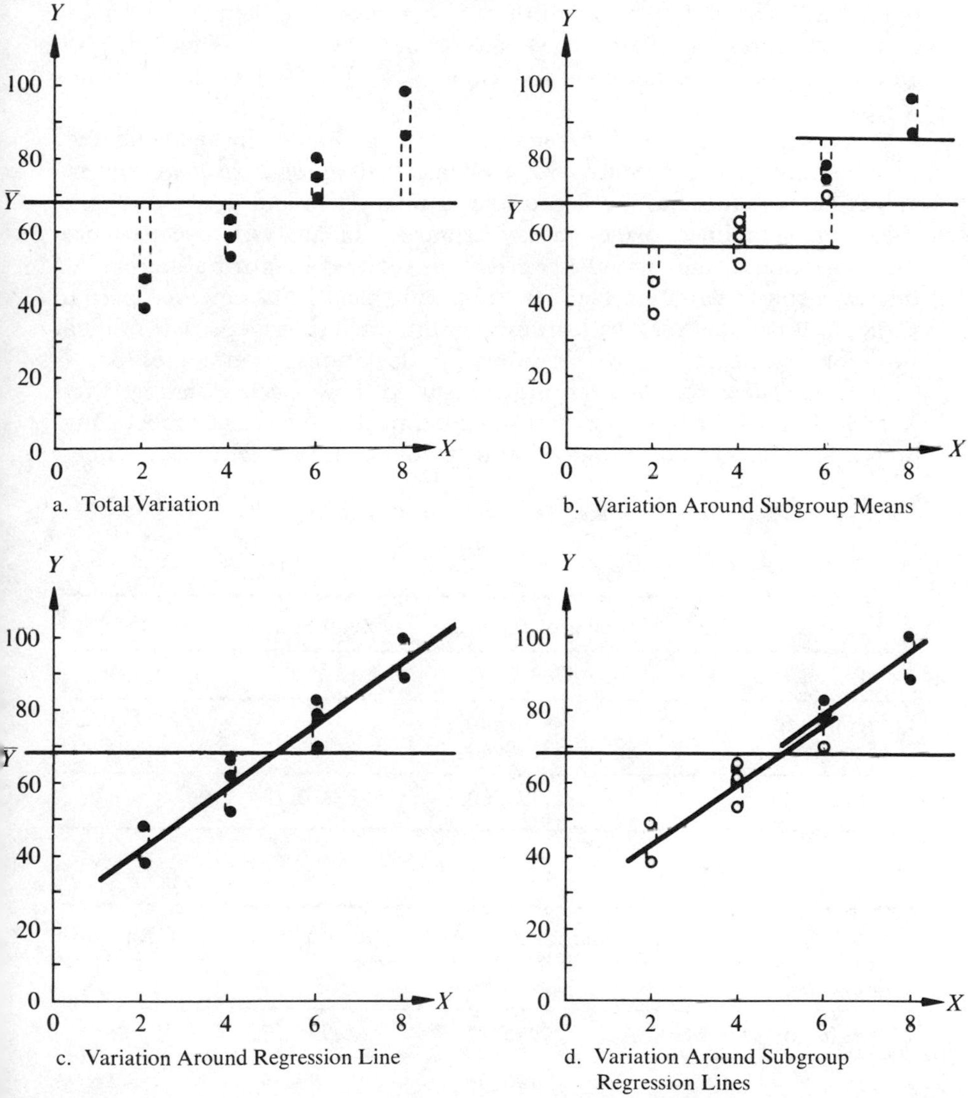

Figure 4.6. Graphic Illustrations of Classification, Regression, and Covariance Models

more independent variables. In the former method, the deviations of the dependent variable are measured from the subgroup means instead of from the single grand mean for the entire sample; in the latter method, the deviations are measured from the fitted regression line, regression plane, or regression hyperplane. If the total variance of the dependent variable is significantly reduced by either of these two procedures, then the classification or the regression is said to have an explanatory value.[6] Figures 4.6(b)–4.6(c) illustrate these concepts, and Tables 4.4(B)–4.4(C) set out their numerical values.

Occasionally, it is useful to combine the two methods for reducing total variation. Such a procedure is known as *analysis of covariance* and involves the simultaneous use of a classification system and a series of parallel regression lines, planes, or hyperplanes. In analysis of covariance, total variation in the dependent variable is reduced by attributing part of this variation to variation between subgroup means and another part to variation accounted for by a regression within each subgroup. The residual variation, consisting of within-subgroup deviations from regression, is called *unexplained variation* and is a measure of how much variation is left to be accounted for by factors not included in the covariance model. Figure 4.6(d) illustrates the application of a covariance model to our numer-

Table 4.4. Analysis of Variance and Covariance Tables

A. Total Variance

Source	D.F.	Sum of Squares	Mean Square	*F* Ratio
Total	10	47,950.00		
Correction for the Mean	1	45,158.40		
Total (corr.)	9	2,791.60	310.18	

B. Analysis of Variance of Classification Model

Source	D.F.	Sum of Squares	Mean Square	*F* Ratio
Total (corr.)	9	2,791.60		
Model $(a_1, a_2 \mid u)$	1	1,995.27	1,995.27	20.04
Error	8	796.33	99.54	

[6] By "significantly reduced" we mean a reduction in excess of the reduction that would result from a random assignment of means or regression lines.

Table 4.4. Analysis of Variance and Covariance Tables (Continued)

C. Analysis of Variance of Regression Model

Source	D.F.	Sum of Squares	Mean Square	F Ratio
Total (corr.)	9	2,791.60		
Model $(b\|u)$	1	2,592.86	2,592.86	104.37
Error	8	198.74	24.84	

D. Analysis of Covariance

Source	D.F.	Sum of Squares	Mean Square	F Ratio
Total (corr.)	9	2,791.60		
Model $(a_1, a_2, b\|u)$	2	2,638.77	1,319.39	60.43
Error	7	152.83	21.83	

E. Significance of Classification after Regression: Location Effects

Source	D.F.	Sum of Squares	Mean Square	F Ratio
Total (corr.)	9	2,791.60		
Model				
$(a_1, a_2, b\|u)$	2	2,638.77		
$(b\|u)$	1	2,592.86		
$(a_1, a_2\|u, b)$	1	45.92	45.92	2.10
Error	7	152.83	21.83	

F. Significance of Regression after Classification: Population Effects

Source	D.F.	Sum of Squares	Mean Square	F Ratio
Total (corr.)	9	2,791.60		
Model				
$(a_1, a_2, b\|u)$	2	2,638.77		
$(a_1, a_2\|u)$	1	1,995.27		
$(b\|u, a_1, a_2)$	1	643.51	643.51	29.47
Error	7	152.83	21.83	

ical example, and Table 4.4(D) sets out the reduction in total variance that is achieved by this model.

In conclusion, a statistical explanation of a phenomenon that may be represented by a dependent variable is carried out by measuring the deviation of this variable from (a) subgroup means of categories introduced by the adoption of a classification system, or (b) the regression line, plane, or hyperplane of the dependent variable on an independent variable or set of independent variables, or (c) a combination of subgroup means and regressions. If such procedures lead to a significant reduction of the variance, the independent categories or variables that are used may be said to have partially explained the variation of the dependent variable about its mean. Such explanations, however, are purely associational in character, and causal relationships can be inferred only if appropriate theoretical considerations support such an interpretation.

4.8.7 APPLICATION: ANALYSIS OF INTERREGIONAL MIGRATION FLOWS IN CALIFORNIA (CONTINUED)

To illustrate the application of a covariance model to real data, let us return to the analysis of migration flows between California regions that was described in Subsection 3.4.5. There we found that the "economic opportunities" hypothesis, as reflected in the model in (3.102) and (3.103), provided a satisfactory explanation for differences in the volumes of interregional migration flows. It was further noted in Subsection 3.4.5 that factors determining out-migration tend to vary with the type of destination as well as with the type of origin. This led to a classification of flows by category of origin and category of destination, which produced the following four migrant flow classes:

1. flows from metropolitan to metropolitan subregions [Table 3.15(A)];
2. flows from metropolitan to nonmetropolitan subregions [Table 3.15 (B)];
3. flows from nonmetropolitan to metropolitan subregions [Table 3.16 (A)];
4. flows from nonmetropolitan to nonmetropolitan subregions [Table 3.16(B)].

Two important findings that emerged from this classification were that the model provides a better accounting of flows originating from metropolitan subregions and that per capita wages and salaries are significant only in explaining flows to nonmetropolitan subregions.

Consider the following restatement of the model defined in (3.103):

$$\ln M_{ijk} = \mu + \alpha_k + \beta_1 \ln WS_i + \beta_2 \ln WS_j + \beta_3 \ln LF_i + \beta_4 \ln LF_j + \beta_5 \ln D_{ij} + \varepsilon_{ij} \qquad (4.104)$$

where the independent variables have the same definition as before, μ is the grand mean, and the α_k ($k = 1, 2, 3, 4$) denote the effects of the four flow classes defined above. Table 4.5 presents the results of the covariance analysis and also includes the corresponding analysis of variance tables for the classification and the regression models. The findings in all cases confirm those of Subsection 3.4.5, as indeed they must. The classification system contributes a significant statistical explanation when applied alone or when applied in conjunction with the regression model. Similarly, the "economic opportunities" regression model also is significant when applied alone or when applied after the explanatory contribution of the classification system has been accounted for.

Table 4.5. Analysis of Variance and Covariance Tables for the Analysis of Interregional Migration

A. Total Variance

Source	D.F.	Sum of Squares	Mean Square	F Ratio
Total	342	18,266.61		
Correction for the Mean	1	17,656.23		
Total (corr.)	341	610.38	1.79	

B. Analysis of Variance of Classification Model

Source	D.F.	Sum of Squares	Mean Square	F Ratio
Total (corr.)	341	610.38		
Model ($a_1, a_2, a_3, a_4 \mid u$)	3	96.63	32.21	21.19
Error	338	513.75	1.52	

C. Analysis of Variance of Regression Model

Source	D.F.	Sum of Squares	Mean Square	F Ratio
Total (corr.)	341	610.38		
Model ($b_1, b_2, b_3, b_4, b_5 \mid u$)	5	491.06	98.21	276.56
Error	336	119.32	0.36	

Table 4.5. Analysis of Variance and Covariance Tables for the Analysis of Interregional Migration (Continued)

D. Analysis of Covariance

Source	D.F.	Sum of Squares	Mean Square	F Ratio
Total (corr.)	341	610.38		
Model ($a_1, a_2, a_3, a_4, b_1, b_2, b_3, b_4, b_5 \| u$)	8	498.15	62.27	184.76
Error	333	112.23	0.34	

E. Significance of Classification after Regression: Flow Category Effects

Source	D.F.	Sum of Squares	Mean Square	F Ratio
Total (corr.)	341	610.38		
Model (a_1, a_2, a_3, a_4 $b_1, b_2, b_3, b_4, b_5 \| u$)	8	498.15		
($b_1, b_2, b_3, b_4, b_5 \| u$)	5	491.06		
($a_1, a_2, a_3, a_4 \| u, b_1, b_2, b_3, b_4, b_5$)	3	7.09	2.36	7.01
Error	333	112.23	0.34	

F. Significance of Regression after Classification: Economic Opportunity Effects

Source	D.F.	Sum of Squares	Mean Square	F Ratio
Total (corr.)	341	610.38		
Model (a_1, a_2, a_3, a_4 $b_1, b_2, b_3, b_4, b_5 \| u$)	8	498.15		
($a_1, a_2, a_3, a_4 \| u$)	3	96.63		
($b_1, b_2, b_3, b_4, b_5 \| u, a_1, a_2, a_3, a_4$)	5	401.52	80.30	238.27
Error	333	112.23	0.34	

Source: Calculated using the data in Figures 3.7 and 3.8, and in Table 3.12. Programmed by Caj Falcke.

EXERCISES

1. Introduce total employment as an additional independent variable into the numerical example in (4.102), and test whether the additional explanatory contribution of that variable is statistically significant at the five percent level, after the effects of location and population have been taken into account.

2. Contrast analysis of covariance models with regression models that include dummy variables. Refer to the numerical examples in Subsections 3.4.3 and 4.8.5 to illustrate your points.

3. (a) Prove that the multiplication of a matrix by a nonsingular matrix does not change its rank.

(b) Prove that the rank of **AB** is less than or equal to the rank of either **A** or **B**.

4. Write a FORTRAN subroutine that will calculate a generalized inverse for an arbitrary rectangular matrix and, with this subroutine, develop a general program that will estimate the parameters and compute the analysis of variance table of any linear statistical model.

5. (a) Show that if $\mathbf{AX} = \mathbf{B}$, then

$$\mathbf{X}_0 = \mathbf{A}^*\mathbf{B} + (\mathbf{A}^*\mathbf{A} - \mathbf{I})\,\mathbf{Z}$$

and, if $\mathbf{XA} = \mathbf{B}$, then

$$\mathbf{X}_0 = \mathbf{BA}^* + \mathbf{Z}(\mathbf{AA}^* - \mathbf{I})$$

where **A** and **Y** are known matrices, **X** is unknown, $\mathbf{A}^*$ is a generalized inverse of **A**, and **Z** is an arbitrary matrix.

(b) Use the above results to prove that the *deconsolidation* of the consolidated population growth matrix $\hat{\mathbf{G}}$ in (1.27) may be expressed as follows:

$$\mathbf{G} = \mathbf{C}^*\hat{\mathbf{G}}\mathbf{D}^*(t) + (\mathbf{C}^*\mathbf{C} - \mathbf{I})\,\mathbf{Z}_c\,\mathbf{D}^*(t)\,\mathbf{Z}_d[\mathbf{D}(t)\mathbf{D}^*(t) - \mathbf{I}]$$

(c) Use the deconsolidation formula in (b) to express the deconsolidation of the consolidated population growth matrix $\hat{\mathbf{G}}$ in (2.41) into the unconsolidated population growth matrix **G** in (1.20).

6. Carry out an analysis of covariance of housing demand in Finland (Tables 3.2 and 3.3). Classify households by size, location, socioeconomic class, and dwelling type (that is, single family houses and apartments). Discuss your findings.

7. Carry out an analysis of covariance of mortality in 12 Asian countries (Tables 3.4 and 3.5). Classify the data by sex. Discuss your findings.

8. The analysis of covariance of interregional migration flows in Subsection 4.8.7 implicitly assumed that the regression hyperplanes in the four flow classes were parallel to each other. Is this assumption justified by the data? (Hint: The error sum of squares of the covariance model is 112.23 and carries $n - m - k + 1 = 333$ degrees of freedom. Find the error sum of squares of the four individual regressions, separately fitted to each of the four classes, and add them up. Their total error sum of squares carries $n - mk = 318$ degress of freedom. The difference between the two error sums of squares is the sum of squares attributable to differences in the regression coefficients between subgroup regressions, which, divided by its 15 degrees of freedom, forms the numerator of the F statistic for testing the null hypothesis that the four regression hyperplanes are parallel.)

9. Carry out an analysis of covariance of travel behavior using the data presented in Exercise 7 of Chapter 3. Classify the observations into two groups: (a) those within five miles of center-city Philadelphia, and (b) those beyond.

10. Carry out an analysis of covariance of the time series data on gross national product that appear in Exercises 8 and 9 of Chapter 3. Classify the observations into two groups: (a) those measured in 1929 dollars, and (b) those measured in 1958 dollars, and fit the model

$$Y_t = \mu + \alpha_k + \beta t + \varepsilon$$

$k = 1, 2$. Are the two regression lines parallel?

REFERENCES AND SELECTED READINGS

THEORY

Almon, C., Jr. *Matrix Methods in Economics.* Reading, Mass.: Addison-Wesley, 1967.

Gantmacher, F. R. *The Theory of Matrices,* **I** and **II**. New York: Chelsea, 1959.

Gere, J. M. and W. Weaver, Jr. *Matrix Algebra for Engineers.* Princeton, N. J.: D. van Nostrand, 1965.

Hadley, G. *Linear Algebra.* Reading, Mass.: Addison-Wesley, 1961.

Lancaster, P. *Theory of Matrices.* New York: Academic Press, 1969.

Noble, B. *Applied Linear Algebra.* Englewood Cliffs, N. J.: Prentice-Hall. 1969.

Schneider, H. and G. P. Barker. *Matrices and Linear Algebra.* New York: Holt, Rinehart & Winston, 1968.

Searle, S. R. *Matrix Algebra for the Biological Sciences.* New York: John Wiley & Sons, 1966.

APPLICATION: LINEAR STATISTICAL MODELS

Graybill, F. A. *An Introduction to Linear Statistical Models.* New York: McGraw-Hill, 1961.

Morrison, D. F. *Multivariate Statistical Methods.* New York: McGraw-Hill, 1967.

Rao, C. R. "A Note on a Generalized Inverse of a Matrix with Applications to Problems in Mathematical Statistics," *Journal of the Royal Statistical Society,* Series B, **XXIV**, 1962, 152–158.

Scheffé, H. *The Analysis of Variance.* New York: John Wiley & Sons, 1959.

Searle, S. R. *Matrix Algebra for the Biological Sciences* (Ch. 10, pp. 254–289). New York: John Wiley & Sons, 1966.

five linear programming and the theory of games

Linear programming deals with the problem of allocating scarce resources among competing activities in a way that satisfies a desired objective in an optimal manner. The allocation problem is characterized by the presence of a set of constraints that reflect limited resources, and by the existence of a large number of possible solutions that satisfy these constraints. Procedures for selecting the "best" allocation, without having to consider and evaluate all of the possible solutions, are the principal concern of the theory of *mathematical programming*. And when both the objective and the resource constraints can be expressed in *linear form*, *linear programming* can be used to obtain a solution that does not violate the constraints and which is optimal in the sense that no other such solution better satisfies the objective.

5.1 BASIC CONCEPTS OF LINEAR PROGRAMMING

The general linear programming problem can be defined as follows: Given a set of m resource restrictions expressed as linear inequalities in k variables, find a set of nonnegative values for these variables such that the restrictions are satisfied and some particular linear function of these k variables is maximized (or minimized, as the case may be). The mathematical statement of the maximizing linear programming problem can be expressed as follows: Maximize the linear objective function

$$z = c_1x_1 + c_2x_2 + \cdots + c_kx_k \tag{5.1}$$

subject to the linear restrictions

$$\begin{aligned} a_{11}x_1 + a_{12}x_2 + \cdots + a_{1k}x_k &\leqq b_1 \\ a_{21}x_1 + a_{22}x_2 + \cdots + a_{2k}x_k &\leqq b_2 \\ &\vdots \\ a_{m1}x_1 + a_{m2}x_2 + \cdots + a_{mk}x_k &\leqq b_m \end{aligned} \tag{5.2}$$

and

$$x_1 \geqq 0, x_2 \geqq 0, \cdots, x_k \geqq 0 \tag{5.3}$$

where the a_{ij}, b_i (> 0), and c_j are given constants. The function to be maximized is called the *objective function*, the restrictions are generally referred to as *constraints*, and the variables x_i ($i = 1, 2, \ldots, k$) sometimes are called the *decision variables*.

We may express (5.1), (5.2), and (5.3) in matrix form as

$$\text{maximize:} \quad z = \mathbf{c}'\mathbf{x} \tag{5.4}$$

$$\text{subject to:} \quad \mathbf{Ax} \leqq \mathbf{b} \tag{5.5}$$

$$\mathbf{x} \geqq \mathbf{0} \tag{5.6}$$

A more manageable formulation of the optimization problem can be obtained by introducing *slack* variables, which transform the inequalities of (5.2) and (5.5) into equalities. For example, the ith inequality of (5.2),

$$a_{i1}x_1 + a_{i2}x_2 + \cdots + a_{ik}x_k \leqq b_i \tag{5.7}$$

can be expressed as an equation by introducing an additional variable, x_{k+i}, say, such that

$$a_{i1}x_1 + a_{i2}x_2 + \cdots + a_{ik}x_k + x_{k+i} = b_i \tag{5.8}$$

where $x_{k+i} \geqq 0$. Any set of decision variables $x_1, x_2, \ldots, x_k$ that satisfies (5.7) will satisfy (5.8), and conversely. Hence we may restate our linear programming problem of (5.1), (5.2), and (5.3), as follows: Find $x_1, x_2, \cdots, x_k, x_{k+1}, \cdots, x_n$ such that

$$z = c_1x_1 + c_2x_2 + \cdots + c_kx_k + 0 \cdot x_{k+1} + \cdots + 0 \cdot x_n \tag{5.9}$$

is as great as possible and

$$\begin{aligned} a_{11}x_1 + a_{12}x_2 + \cdots + a_{1k}x_k + x_{k+1} \qquad\qquad &= b_1 \\ a_{21}x_1 + a_{22}x_2 + \cdots + a_{2k}x_k \qquad + x_{k+2} \qquad &= b_2 \\ \vdots \qquad\qquad\qquad\qquad & \\ a_{m1}x_1 + a_{m2}x_2 + \cdots + a_{mk}x_k \qquad\qquad + x_n &= b_m \end{aligned} \tag{5.10}$$

$$x_1 \geqq 0, x_2 \geqq 0, \ldots, x_k \geqq 0, x_{k+1} \geqq 0, \ldots, x_n \geqq 0 \tag{5.11}$$

With the appropriate redefinition of the matrix **A**, we may express (5.9), (5.10), and (5.11) in matrix form as

$$\text{maximize:} \quad z = \underset{1\times n}{\mathbf{c}'}\ \underset{n\times 1}{\mathbf{x}} \tag{5.12}$$

$$\text{subject to:} \quad \underset{m\times n}{\mathbf{A}}\ \underset{n\times 1}{\mathbf{x}} = \underset{m\times 1}{\mathbf{b}} \tag{5.13}$$

$$\underset{n\times 1}{\mathbf{x}} \geqq \underset{n\times 1}{\mathbf{0}} \tag{5.14}$$

In the following sections, we shall discuss the solution of the maximization problem in (5.12). The solution of the minimization problem follows from the fact that minimizing z is equivalent to maximizing $-z$; hence a minimization problem can easily be converted into an equivalent maximization problem.

Any vector $\mathbf{x}$ that satisfies (5.13) will be called a *solution*, and any solution that satisfies (5.14) will be called a *feasible solution*. Any feasible solution that makes (5.12) as large as possible will be called an *optimal solution*. There may be more than one. A *basic solution* is a vector $\mathbf{x}$ which is obtained from (5.13) by solving for m variables in terms of the remaining $n - m$ variables and setting these $n - m$ variables equal to zero.[1] Thus a *basic feasible solution* is a basic solution that also is feasible, and a *nondegenerate basic feasible solution* is a basic feasible solution in which the m nonzero variables are all positive. These m variables are generally referred to as *basic* variables or as the variables in the *basis*. The other $n - m$ variables are called *nonbasic* variables.

The set of all solutions, $\mathbf{x}_0$, say, to the rectangular equation system in (5.13) may be found by using a generalized inverse, as described in Sections 4.6 and 4.7. Thus, recalling (4.58), we have that

$$\underset{n\times 1}{\mathbf{x}_0} = \underset{n\times m}{\mathbf{A}^*}\ \underset{m\times 1}{\mathbf{b}} + (\underset{n\times n}{\mathbf{D}} - \underset{n\times n}{\mathbf{I}})\ \underset{n\times 1}{\mathbf{q}} \tag{5.15}$$

where, as before, $\mathbf{D} = \mathbf{A}^*\mathbf{A}$, and $\mathbf{q}$ is an arbitrary vector. Not all of these solutions, however, will be feasible solutions, since some of them will not satisfy (5.14). To obtain a feasible solution, therefore, the elements of $\mathbf{q}$ must be selected such that $\mathbf{x}_0 \geqq 0$. And to find a nondegenerate basic feasible solution, the values assumed by the elements of $\mathbf{q}$ must produce exactly m positive elements and $n - m$ zero elements in $\mathbf{x}_0$. Finally, no direct method for finding an optimal solution to linear programming problems is known. That is, there is no direct formula into which data

[1] We shall assume that such a solution exists and is unique. This assumption is not a necessary one, but it greatly simplifies the exposition. For a discussion of how to resolve the problems that stem from the violation of this assumption, commonly referred to as *degeneracy* problems, see, for example, Hadley (1962), pp. 174–196.

may be substituted to yield an optimal solution to a linear programming problem. This lack of direct solutions forces us to resort to iterative step-by-step procedures that converge to an optimal solution in a finite number of steps. Such procedures are sometimes called *algorithms.*

Examples.

(i) To illustrate a few of the concepts discussed above, let us consider a hypothetical isolated regional economy, which desires to maximize the new income that is generated by its two economic activities, Agriculture and Manufacturing, and which has available for such purposes only a limited quantity of two resources, Labor and Capital. To generate a dollar of new income, that is, a dollar of "profit" to the economy, each of these two activities requires a set of inputs of these two scarce resources, in the amounts listed in Table 5.1.

Table 5.1. Resource Requirements per Dollar of New Income

Units Required	Activity	
	1. Agriculture	2. Manufacturing
Labor	$\frac{2}{5}$	$\frac{1}{5}$
Capital	1	2

We define the unit level of operation of each activity as that level which generates a dollar of new income. Our production problem, therefore, is to find the optimal mix of activity levels at which to operate the economy. These levels are multiples of the unit-level operations defined in Table 5.1, and will be denoted by x_1 and x_2, respectively. The resource limitations are 30 units of Labor and 150 units of Capital.

Expressing the above production problem in equation form, we have the constraints

$$\begin{aligned} \tfrac{2}{5}x_1 + \tfrac{1}{5}x_2 &\leqq 30 \\ x_1 + 2x_2 &\leqq 150 \\ x_1 \geqq 0 \qquad x_2 &\geqq 0 \end{aligned} \tag{5.16}$$

and the objective function

$$z = x_1 + x_2 \tag{5.17}$$

Thus our linear programming problem is to maximize (5.17), subject to the constraints listed in (5.16).

We begin by introducing the slack variables x_3 and x_4, such that

$$\begin{aligned} \tfrac{2}{5}x_1 + \tfrac{1}{5}x_2 + x_3 \qquad &= 30 \\ x_1 + 2x_2 \qquad + x_4 &= 150 \end{aligned} \tag{5.18}$$

which in matrix form is

$$\mathbf{Ax} = \mathbf{b} \tag{5.19}$$

where

$$\mathbf{A} = \begin{bmatrix} \frac{2}{5} & \frac{1}{5} & 1 & 0 \\ 1 & 2 & 0 & 1 \end{bmatrix} \quad \mathbf{x} = \begin{bmatrix} x_1 \\ x_2 \\ x_3 \\ x_4 \end{bmatrix} \quad \text{and } \mathbf{b} = \begin{bmatrix} 30 \\ 150 \end{bmatrix}$$

Thus the set of all solutions, $\mathbf{x}_0$, say, to (5.19) is given by (5.15), where

$$\mathbf{A}^* = \begin{bmatrix} \frac{10}{3} & -\frac{1}{3} \\ -\frac{5}{3} & \frac{2}{3} \\ 0 & 0 \\ 0 & 0 \end{bmatrix} \quad \mathbf{D} = \mathbf{A}^*\mathbf{A} = \begin{bmatrix} 1 & 0 & \frac{10}{3} & -\frac{1}{3} \\ 0 & 1 & -\frac{5}{3} & \frac{2}{3} \\ 0 & 0 & 0 & 0 \\ 0 & 0 & 0 & 0 \end{bmatrix}$$

Hence

$$\mathbf{x}_0 = \begin{bmatrix} x_1 \\ x_2 \\ x_3 \\ x_4 \end{bmatrix} = \begin{bmatrix} \frac{10}{3} & -\frac{1}{3} \\ -\frac{5}{3} & \frac{2}{3} \\ 0 & 0 \\ 0 & 0 \end{bmatrix} \begin{bmatrix} 30 \\ 150 \end{bmatrix} + \begin{bmatrix} 0 & 0 & \frac{10}{3} & -\frac{1}{3} \\ 0 & 0 & -\frac{5}{3} & \frac{2}{3} \\ 0 & 0 & -1 & 0 \\ 0 & 0 & 0 & -1 \end{bmatrix} \begin{bmatrix} q_1 \\ q_2 \\ q_3 \\ q_4 \end{bmatrix}$$

$$= \begin{bmatrix} 50 + \frac{10}{3}q_3 - \frac{1}{3}q_4 \\ 50 - \frac{5}{3}q_3 + \frac{2}{3}q_4 \\ -q_3 \\ -q_4 \end{bmatrix} \tag{5.20}$$

To obtain a feasible solution, we must select $q_3 \leqq 0$ and $q_4 \leqq 0$. And to obtain a basic feasible solution, two of the elements of $\mathbf{x}_0$ in (5.20) must become zero when q_3 and q_4 are set equal to their respective nonpositive values. For example, setting $q_3 = -3$ and $q_4 = 0$ yields the feasible solution vector

$$\mathbf{x}_f = \begin{bmatrix} 40 \\ 55 \\ 3 \\ 0 \end{bmatrix} \tag{5.21}$$

and the objective function

$$z = 40 + 55 = \$95$$

Setting $q_3 = q_4 = 0$, produces the basic feasible solution vector

$$\mathbf{x}_b = \begin{bmatrix} 50 \\ 50 \\ 0 \\ 0 \end{bmatrix} \tag{5.22}$$

and the objective function

$$z = 50 + 50 = \$100$$

A few more trial values for q_3 and q_4 may be substituted into (5.20). The results will indicate that (5.22) is the optimal solution of the linear programming problem defined in (5.16) and (5.17).

We may complicate matters somewhat by introducing additional activity vectors or by adding more resource constraints. However, the procedure of using the generalized inverse to obtain the set of all solutions remains unchanged. To illustrate this, let us introduce another resource, Land, and assume that to produce a dollar of new income Agriculture and Manufacturing require $1\frac{1}{2}$ units and 1 unit, respectively, of this scarce resource. Moreover, assume that only 120 units of Land are available to the economy. Then, in addition to the constraints in (5.16), we have the restriction that

$$\frac{3}{2}x_1 + x_2 \leqq 120 \tag{5.23}$$

The objective function remains unchanged. Our new linear programming problem, including slack variables, is

$$\text{maximize:} \quad z = \mathbf{c}'\mathbf{x} \tag{5.24}$$

$$\text{subject to:} \quad \mathbf{Ax} = \mathbf{b} \tag{5.25}$$

$$\mathbf{x} \geqq \mathbf{0} \tag{5.26}$$

where

$$\mathbf{A} = \begin{bmatrix} \frac{2}{5} & \frac{1}{5} & 1 & 0 & 0 \\ 1 & 2 & 0 & 1 & 0 \\ \frac{3}{2} & 1 & 0 & 0 & 1 \end{bmatrix} \quad \mathbf{x} = \begin{bmatrix} x_1 \\ x_2 \\ x_3 \\ x_4 \\ x_5 \end{bmatrix} \quad \mathbf{c} = \begin{bmatrix} 1 \\ 1 \\ 0 \\ 0 \\ 0 \end{bmatrix} \quad \text{and } \mathbf{b} = \begin{bmatrix} 30 \\ 150 \\ 120 \end{bmatrix}$$

The set of all solutions is

$$\mathbf{x}_0 = \begin{bmatrix} x_1 \\ x_2 \\ x_3 \\ x_4 \\ x_5 \end{bmatrix} = \begin{bmatrix} 0 & -\frac{1}{2} & 1 \\ 0 & \frac{3}{4} & -\frac{1}{2} \\ 1 & \frac{1}{20} & -\frac{3}{10} \\ 0 & 0 & 0 \\ 0 & 0 & 0 \end{bmatrix} \begin{bmatrix} 30 \\ 150 \\ 120 \end{bmatrix}$$

$$+ \begin{bmatrix} 0 & 0 & 0 & -\frac{1}{2} & 1 \\ 0 & 0 & 0 & \frac{3}{4} & -\frac{1}{2} \\ 0 & 0 & 0 & \frac{1}{20} & -\frac{3}{10} \\ 0 & 0 & 0 & -1 & 0 \\ 0 & 0 & 0 & 0 & -1 \end{bmatrix} \begin{bmatrix} q_1 \\ q_2 \\ q_3 \\ q_4 \\ q_5 \end{bmatrix} = \begin{bmatrix} 45 - \frac{1}{2}q_4 + q_5 \\ 52\frac{1}{2} + \frac{3}{4}q_4 - \frac{1}{2}q_5 \\ 1\frac{1}{2} + \frac{1}{20}q_4 - \frac{3}{10}q_5 \\ -q_4 \\ -q_5 \end{bmatrix} \tag{5.27}$$

Setting $q_4 = -10$ and $q_5 = 0$, we find the feasible solution

$$\mathbf{x}_f = \begin{bmatrix} 50 \\ 45 \\ 1 \\ 10 \\ 0 \end{bmatrix} \tag{5.28}$$

and the objective function

$$z = 50 + 45 = \$95$$

Setting $q_4 = q_5 = 0$, we obtain the basic optimal solution,

$$\mathbf{x}_{\text{opt}} = \begin{bmatrix} 45 \\ 52\frac{1}{2} \\ 1\frac{1}{2} \\ 0 \\ 0 \end{bmatrix} \tag{5.29}$$

and the objective function,

$$z = 45 + 52\tfrac{1}{2} = \$97\tfrac{1}{2}$$

(ii) The input-output model defined in Sections 1.7 and 2.9 may be interpreted as a special case of the linear programming production model described above. Recall the numerical example of the static open model in Table 1.14, for which

$$(\mathbf{I} - \mathbf{A})\mathbf{x} = \mathbf{y} \tag{5.30}$$

where

$$(\mathbf{I} - \mathbf{A}) = \begin{bmatrix} \frac{4}{5} & -\frac{1}{5} \\ -\frac{2}{5} & \frac{2}{5} \end{bmatrix} \quad \mathbf{x} = \begin{bmatrix} X_1 \\ X_2 \end{bmatrix} \quad \text{and } \mathbf{y} = \begin{bmatrix} 100 \\ 40 \end{bmatrix}$$

The input-output problem was to find a vector **x** that satisfied (5.30). Since (**I** − **A**) was found to be nonsingular, the solution was

$$\mathbf{x} = (\mathbf{I} - \mathbf{A})^{-1}\mathbf{y} = \begin{bmatrix} \frac{5}{3} & \frac{5}{6} \\ \frac{5}{3} & \frac{10}{3} \end{bmatrix} \begin{bmatrix} 100 \\ 40 \end{bmatrix} = \begin{bmatrix} 200 \\ 300 \end{bmatrix}$$

This same input-output problem can be viewed as a linear programming problem by expressing the equations in (5.30) as inequalities and by adopting an objective function. First, we specify that it is only necessary for the output of each industry to be no less than the total final demand for it. Thus (5.30) becomes

$$(\mathbf{I} - \mathbf{A})\mathbf{x} \geqq \mathbf{y} \tag{5.31}$$

Next, we assume that it is desired to achieve this level of total final demand with minimum use of labor. That is, we seek to minimize

$$z = \mathbf{c}'\mathbf{x} = a_{31}X_1 + a_{32}X_2 = \tfrac{2}{5}X_1 + \tfrac{1}{5}X_2 \tag{5.32}$$

where z denotes total labor required, and $\mathbf{c}'$ denotes the row vector of labor input coefficients derived from Table 1.16. In addition, since the output levels X_j can never be negative, we impose the restriction $\mathbf{x} \geqq \mathbf{0}$. Thus we have the following linear programming problem:

$$\text{minimize:} \qquad z = \mathbf{c}'\mathbf{x} \tag{5.33}$$

$$\text{subject to:} \quad (\mathbf{I} - \mathbf{A})\mathbf{x} \geqq \mathbf{y} \tag{5.34}$$

$$\mathbf{x} \geqq \mathbf{0} \tag{5.35}$$

where

$$(\mathbf{I} - \mathbf{A}) = \begin{bmatrix} \frac{4}{5} & -\frac{1}{5} \\ -\frac{2}{5} & \frac{2}{5} \end{bmatrix} \quad \mathbf{x} = \begin{bmatrix} X_1 \\ X_2 \end{bmatrix} \quad \mathbf{y} = \begin{bmatrix} 100 \\ 40 \end{bmatrix} \quad \text{and } \mathbf{c} = \begin{bmatrix} \frac{2}{5} \\ \frac{1}{5} \end{bmatrix}$$

Introducing slack variables, we have

$$\begin{aligned} \tfrac{4}{5}X_1 - \tfrac{1}{5}X_2 - X_3 \qquad &= 100 \\ -\tfrac{2}{5}X_1 + \tfrac{2}{5}X_2 \qquad - X_4 &= \ \ 40 \end{aligned}$$

and, by (5.15), we have the set of solutions

$$\mathbf{x}_0 = \begin{bmatrix} X_1 \\ X_2 \\ X_3 \\ X_4 \end{bmatrix} = \begin{bmatrix} \frac{5}{3} & \frac{5}{6} \\ \frac{5}{3} & \frac{10}{3} \\ 0 & 0 \\ 0 & 0 \end{bmatrix} \begin{bmatrix} 100 \\ 40 \end{bmatrix} + \begin{bmatrix} 0 & 0 & -\frac{5}{3} & -\frac{5}{6} \\ 0 & 0 & -\frac{5}{3} & -\frac{10}{3} \\ 0 & 0 & -1 & 0 \\ 0 & 0 & 0 & -1 \end{bmatrix} \begin{bmatrix} q_1 \\ q_2 \\ q_3 \\ q_4 \end{bmatrix}$$

$$= \begin{bmatrix} 200 - \frac{5}{3}q_3 - \frac{5}{6}q_4 \\ 300 - \frac{5}{3}q_3 - \frac{10}{3}q_4 \\ -q_3 \\ -q_4 \end{bmatrix} \tag{5.36}$$

Feasible solutions are those for which q_3 and q_4 are zero or negative, and the input-output solution appears when $q_3 = q_4 = 0$. This nondegenerate basic feasible solution is the optimal solution, since any other feasible values of q_3 and q_4 in (5.36) will increase X_1 and X_2, and therefore will increase the objective function which is to be minimized.

Having illustrated the linear programming problem with two numerical examples, let us now conclude by identifying some of the formal characteristics of such problems.

First, all linear programming problems are concerned with maximizing or minimizing a quantity called the *objective function*. We do not need to distinguish between maximizing and minimizing problems, because there is no real difference between the two operations. Each time a quantity is maximized, some other quantity, such as its negative, is minimized.

Second, present in all linear programming problems are certain restricting conditions called *constraints*, which prevent us from arbitrarily increasing (or decreasing) the objective function. These constraints are of two kinds. There are the nonnegativity constraints which are general to all linear programming problems, and there are constraints that express the particular conditions of a specific problem.

Finally, embedded in every linear programming problem are variables, which are assigned values so as to maximize (or minimize) the objective function. These variables are called *decision variables*, and they appear both in the objective function and in the constraints.

In economic applications of linear programming, the decision variables of the problem frequently represent the extent to which some process is to be carried out. Thus it is convenient to consider each decision variable as an indicator of the level of some operation, called an *activity*. An activity may be interpreted as almost any physical operation that is carried out on a set of resource or commodity inputs. For example, production, consumption, storage, sales, and disposal all can be thought of as activities.

The fundamental characteristics of activities in linear programming problems stem from the way these activities are introduced into the objective function and the constraints. In particular, these characteristics are reflected in the coefficients by which each activity variable is multiplied in the objective function and in the constraints. The coefficient by which the activity variable is multiplied in the objective function is generally referred to as the *value* of the activity. The vector of coefficients by which that same activity variable is multiplied in the constraints is known as the *activity vector.*

A list specifying the levels at which all of the activities in a linear programming problem are to be carried out is called a *program.* All such lists that simultaneously satisfy all of the constraints are called *feasible programs,* and those that maximize (or minimize) the objective function are called *optimal programs.* Linear programming, therefore, is concerned with the identification of optimal programs and their characteristics.

5.2 THE GEOMETRY OF LINEAR PROGRAMMING: THE GRAPHICAL SOLUTION

Linear programming problems that involve only two decision variables can be expressed and solved graphically. Such geometrical interpretations are useful because the insights they provide, in problems involving only two variables, usually may be carried over to the more general case with any number of variables.

The first step in the graphical solution method is the graphical identification of all values of the two variables, x_1 and x_2, say, that are permitted by the constraints. Such values are feasible solutions and may be located in an x_1-x_2 coordinate system such as the one in Figure 5.1. We note that because of the nonnegativity restrictions, all feasible solutions must lie in the nonnegative quadrant of the coordinate system. That is, any point lying in the nonnegative quadrant has $x_1 \geqq 0$, $x_2 \geqq 0$ and therefore satisfies the nonnegativity constraints. Next, we observe that a constraint such as $x_1 \leqq 2$ means that the point (x_1, x_2) cannot lie to the right of the line $x_1 = 2$, and a constraint such as $x_2 \leqq 2$ restricts all feasible solutions to points lying below or on the line $x_2 = 2$. Finally, a constraint such as $x_1 + x_2 \leqq 3$ excludes all points lying above the line $x_1 + x_2 = 3$. This can easily be established by noting that the origin (0, 0) satisfies the inequality and therefore must lie below the line.

The only points (x_1, x_2) that simultaneously satisfy all of the above constraints lie in the shaded region in Figure 5.1. This region is called the

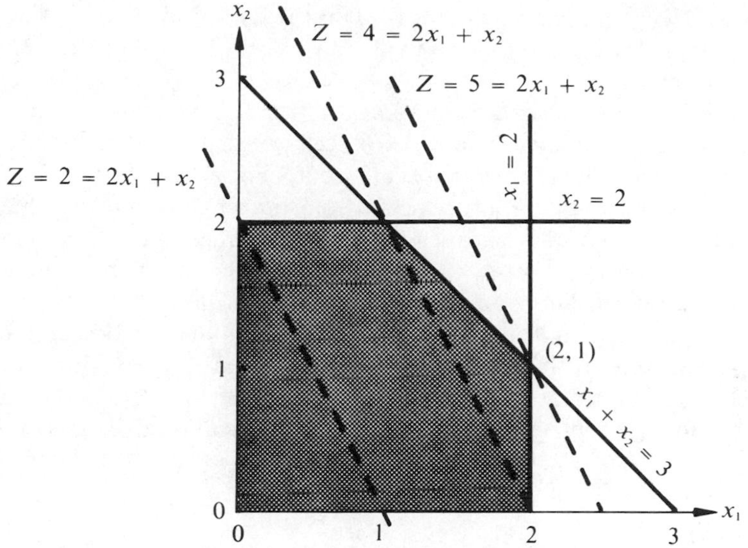

Figure 5.1. Graphical Solution of a Simple Linear Programming Problem

feasible region, and only the points lying in this region are feasible solutions. Points lying on the lines that define the feasible region are said to be located on the *boundary* of this region. And points lying on the corner points (that is, at the intersection of two constraint lines) of the boundary are called *extreme points*. Five extreme points appear in Figure 5.1. They are (0, 0), (0, 2), (1, 2), (2, 1), and (2, 0). It can be shown that basic feasible solutions are extreme points and vice versa [Hadley (1962), pp. 100–102].

The second and final step in the graphical solution method is the identification of the point or points, in the feasible region, that maximize the value of the objective function. For any particular function, $z = 2x_1 + x_2$, say, and any fixed value of z, $z = 2$, say, the objective function can be depicted as a straight line. In Figure 5.1 this straight line is denoted by the dotted line that crosses the coordinate axes at $x_1 = 1$ and $x_2 = 2$, respectively. All points on this line, which also lie in the feasible region [for example, (1, 0), ($\frac{1}{2}$, 1), and (0, 2)], represent feasible solutions that give the objective function the same value of two. For each different value of z, we obtain a different, *but parallel*, straight line. This is because any line $z = c_1x_1 + c_2x_2$ may be expressed as $x_2 = z/c_2 - (c_1/c_2)x_1$, from which it follows that the slope of the objective function is $-c_1/c_2$ no matter what value is assumed by z. Thus it becomes clear that the maximization problem involves nothing more than drawing a family of parallel lines that have at least one point in the feasible region and then selecting the line that is furthest away from the origin. In Figure 5.1 this line is $z = 2x_1 + x_2 = 5$. Hence the extreme point (2, 1) is the optimal solution. Any other point either gives a lower value to the objective function or lies outside of the feasible region.

The above example illustrated the graphical solution of a "well-behaved" linear programming problem. The same procedure easily can be used to illustrate certain exceptional cases that can occur. For example, if the inequalities $x_1 \leqq 2$ and $x_2 \leqq 2$ are reversed, we no longer have any feasible solutions, since any point that satisfies these reversed inequalities will no longer satisfy the constraint $x_1 + x_2 = 3$. Alternatively, if we retain the original feasible region, but change the objective function to $z = x_1 + x_2$, we obtain an infinity of optimal solutions, for any point that lies in the feasible region and on the line $x_1 + x_2 = 3$ is an optimal solution. Finally, if we delete the constraints $x_1 \leqq 2$ and $x_1 + x_2 \leqq 3$, we are left with a linear programming problem that has an unbounded solution. This gene-

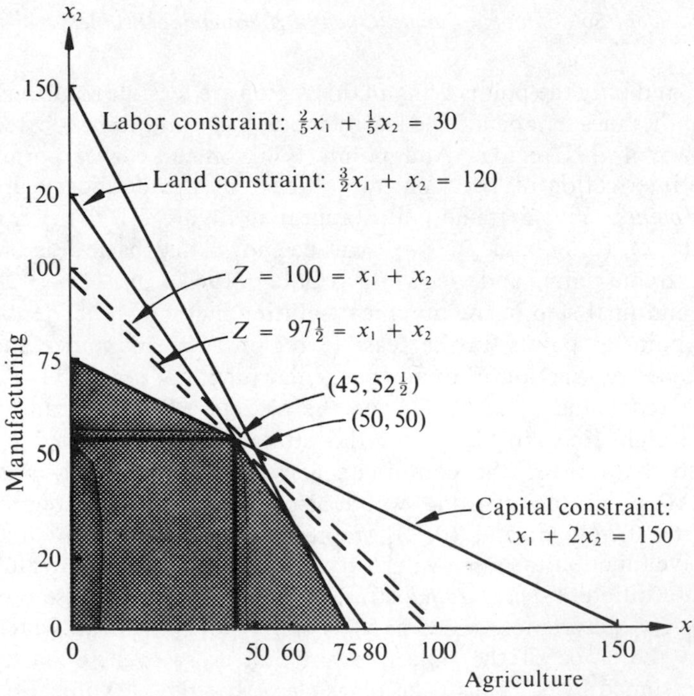

Figure 5.2. Graphical Solution of the Production Problem

rally is an indication that a mistake has been made in the formulation of an actual problem.

Examples.

(i) Our earlier numerical example of the production problem, with the three resource constraints of Labor, Capital, and Land, can be solved graphically, because it only involves two activities: Agriculture and Manufacturing. We begin by associating these two variables with the two axes of an x_1-x_2 coordinate system and then delineate the feasible region that is defined by the various constraints. This results in the shaded feasible region in Figure 5.2. Next we find that the optimal solution is, as before, $x_1 = 45$ and $x_2 = 52\frac{1}{2}$. Finally, we note that without the constraint on Land, the feasible region expands to include the point (50, 50), and that this then is the optimal solution for that particular subproblem.

(ii) The graphical solution of the input-output problem is straightforward. Again we associate the two axes of an x_1-x_2 coordinate system with the two activities, Agriculture and Manufacturing, and again we delineate the feasible region with the set of constraints. This produces the shaded region in Figure 5.3. In this problem, however, our concern is to

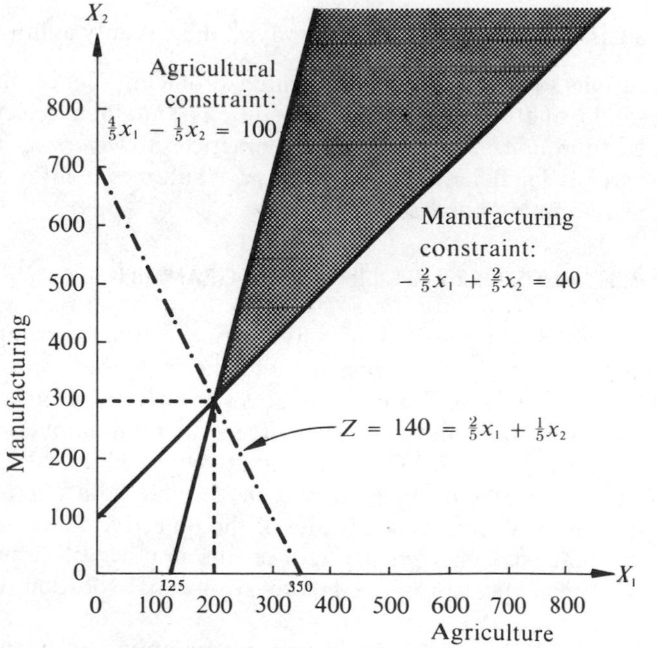

Figure 5.3. Graphical Solution of the Input-Output Problem

minimize the objective function. Hence, from among the family of parallel lines representing various values of the objective function, we now seek that line which has at least one point in the feasible region and which is *closest* to the origin. In Figure 5.3, this line is seen to be the one that yields an objective function with a value of 140 units of labor. Thus the optimal solution is represented by the point (200, 300). Note that if less than 140 units of labor were available to the economy for productive activities, no feasible solution would exist, and we would conclude that the economy did not have at its disposal enough labor to produce the specified final demands.

5.3 THE ALGEBRA OF LINEAR PROGRAMMING

In this section we shall show that an optimal solution to a linear programming problem is contained in the set of basic feasible solutions to that problem. Recall that a basic solution to the consistent rectangular equation in (5.13) is a solution that uses only linearly independent activities (that is, column vectors of **A**). Thus, if we set $n - m$ of the elements of $\mathbf{x}$ equal to zero, there will remain an ordinary set of m equations in m unknowns which will yield a basic solution involving no more than m of the variables. And since we can select m unknowns from a set of n in only a finite number of ways $\left[\text{that is, } \binom{n}{m} = \frac{n!}{m!\,(n-m)!} \text{ ways}\right]$, there is only a finite number of basic solutions to any linear programming problem. Hence, in theory at least, we could find all basic feasible solutions and then select the one that optimizes the objective function. In practice, however, such a method would be grossly inefficient and, in addition, would never inform us that a problem had an unbounded solution.

5.3.1 THE FUNDAMENTAL THEOREM OF LINEAR PROGRAMMING

We have noted that no direct method of solving linear programming problems exists. That is, there is no expression which, with the appropriate substitution of data, will yield the optimal solution immediately. However, we do have available a compromise between the total enumeration method and the direct method. This is an iterative procedure called the *simplex method,* which carries us from one basic feasible solution to another in a way that never decreases the value of the objective function from one iteration to the next. This greatly reduces the number of basic feasible solutions that must be examined before an optimal solution is found.

Recall the general formulation of the linear programming problem presented in (5.12), (5.13), and (5.14). If the equations in (5.13) are consistent, and if a nondegenerate basic feasible solution exists, then the column vector **b**, on the right-hand side of the equation system, cannot be expressed as a linear combination of less than m columns of coefficients on the left-hand side of those equations. Hence any solution vector of (5.13) must have at least m nonzero elements in it, and there must exist at least one set of m linearly independent columns in the **A** matrix.

If the linear programming problem in (5.12), (5.13), and (5.14) has a feasible solution, $\mathbf{x}_f$, *say, then it has a basic feasible solution,* $\mathbf{x}_b$, *say.* This can be shown by observing that if $\mathbf{x}_f$ is a nonbasic feasible solution, with, say, $p \leqq n$ positive variables $(m < n)$, then if we renumber the variables so that the first p are positive, the feasible solution can be expressed as

$$x_1\mathbf{a}_1 + x_2\mathbf{a}_2 + \cdots + x_p\mathbf{a}_p = \sum_{i=1}^{n} x_i\mathbf{a}_i = \mathbf{A}\mathbf{x}_f = \mathbf{b} \tag{5.37}$$

where

$$x_i = \begin{cases} > 0 & i = 1, 2, \ldots, p \\ = 0 & i = p + 1, \ldots, n \end{cases}$$

Now the vectors $\mathbf{a}_1, \mathbf{a}_2, \ldots, \mathbf{a}_p$ are either linearly independent or linearly dependent. If they are linearly independent, then $p=m$ and the feasible solution is a basic feasible solution. If these vectors are linearly dependent, then there must exist y_i, not all zero, such that

$$y_1\mathbf{a}_1 + y_2\mathbf{a}_2 + \cdots + y_p\mathbf{a}_p = \sum_{i=1}^{n} y_i\mathbf{a}_i = \mathbf{A}\mathbf{y} = \mathbf{0} \tag{5.38}$$

where

$$y_i = \begin{cases} \neq 0 & \text{for at least one } i = 1, 2, \ldots, p \\ = 0 & i = p + 1, \ldots, n \end{cases}$$

We may express any vector $\mathbf{a}_j$ in (5.38), for which $y_j \neq 0$, in terms of the remaining $p - 1$ vectors. Thus,

$$\mathbf{a}_j = -\frac{y_1}{y_j}\mathbf{a}_1 - \cdots - \frac{y_p}{y_j}\mathbf{a}_p = -\sum_{\substack{i=1 \\ i \neq j}}^{p} \frac{y_i}{y_j}\mathbf{a}_i \tag{5.39}$$

Substituting (5.39) into (5.38), we obtain

$$x_1\mathbf{a}_1 + \cdots + x_j\left[-\frac{y_1}{y_j}\mathbf{a}_1 - \cdots - \frac{y_p}{y_j}\mathbf{a}_p\right] + \cdots + x_p\mathbf{a}_p = \mathbf{b}$$

or, more compactly,

$$\sum_{\substack{i=1 \\ i \neq j}}^{p} \left(x_i - x_j\frac{y_i}{y_j}\right)\mathbf{a}_i = \sum_{i=1}^{n} (x_i - \theta y_i)\mathbf{a}_i = \mathbf{A}(\mathbf{x}_f - \theta\mathbf{y}) = \mathbf{b} \tag{5.40}$$

where

$$\theta = \frac{x_j}{y_j} \text{ and } x_i = \begin{cases} > 0 & i = 1, 2, \ldots, p \\ = 0 & i = p+1, \ldots, n \end{cases}$$

Since $[x_j - x_j(y_j/y_j)] = 0$, we may extend the summation to include it without affecting the equality.[2]

Equation (5.40) provides a solution to (5.13) with only $p - 1$ nonzero variables. If these variables are all nonnegative, then they represent a feasible solution that has one fewer nonzero variable than our initial feasible solution $\mathbf{x}_f$. To ensure that they satisfy this condition, we must restrict the range of values that θ can take on.

Consider what happens in (5.40) if θ is set equal to zero and then is gradually increased. As θ increases, the values of the variables $x_1 - \theta y_1, \ldots, x_p - \theta y_p$, may increase or decrease, depending on the signs of the y_i. If at least one y is positive, then we can increase θ until one of the variables, $x_r - \theta y_r$, say, becomes zero.[3] Any further increase in θ would result in this number becoming negative and a solution that was no longer feasible. Therefore, θ must not exceed x_r/y_r. Hence, if we choose

$$\theta = \min_{i} \left\{\frac{x_i}{y_i},\ y_i > 0\right\} = \frac{x_r}{y_r}, \text{ say,} \tag{5.41}$$

then each of the p variables $x_1 - \theta y_1, \ldots, x_p - \theta y_p$, will be nonnegative and one of them, $x_r - \theta y_r$, will be zero.[4]

The above process can now be repeated until there are only m positive variables in the solution. At this point, we shall have a basic feasible solution, $\mathbf{x}_b$, say. Thus we have shown that if a feasible solution to a nondegenerate linear programming problem exists, then so does a basic feasible solution.

Consider now what happens to the objective function as we use the above procedure to move from a feasible solution to a basic feasible solution.

[2] Equation (5.40) may be derived in a shorter way: Since $\mathbf{Ax}_f = \mathbf{b}$ and $\mathbf{Ay} = \mathbf{0}$, then $\theta\mathbf{Ay} = \mathbf{0}$ for any θ; therefore, $\mathbf{A}(\mathbf{x}_f - \theta\mathbf{y}) = \mathbf{b}$ for any θ. The longer derivation, however, is useful because it suggests what value θ should take on.

[3] There must always be at least one y_i that is positive, since if all $y_i \leqq 0$, we can simply multiply (5.38) by minus one to obtain y_i that are all nonnegative, with at least one y_i that is positive.

[4] Instead of setting θ equal to zero and then gradually increasing it, we could operate in the opposite direction; that is, we could set θ equal to zero and then gradually increase it in the negative direction. Then (5.41) would become $\theta = \max_i \{x_i/y_i,\ y_i < 0\} = x_s/y_s$, say, and this choice also would lead to a feasible solution with $p - 1$ nonzero variables. However, the vector chosen in this way will not be the same as the one obtained from (5.41).

Let z_f be the value of the objective function that corresponds to the original feasible solution $\mathbf{x}_f$, and let $z(\theta)$ denote the value of the objective function that is associated with the solution $(\mathbf{x}_f - \theta\mathbf{y})$. Then, by direct substitution,

$$z(\theta) = \mathbf{c}'(\mathbf{x}_f - \theta\mathbf{y}) = \mathbf{c}'\mathbf{x}_f - \theta\mathbf{c}'\mathbf{y} = z_f - \theta\mathbf{c}'\mathbf{y} \tag{5.42}$$

If $\mathbf{y}$ satisfies (5.38), then so does $-\mathbf{y}$; therefore, we can always choose a $\mathbf{y}$ such that $\mathbf{c}'\mathbf{y} \leqq 0$. Hence, since $\theta > 0$, we can increase the objective function if $\mathbf{c}'\mathbf{y} < 0$. If $\mathbf{c}'\mathbf{y} = 0$, we can vary θ without changing the objective function. *In either case, we end up with a feasible solution that has one fewer positive variable and an objective function that is not less than* z_f. Note, however, that if $\mathbf{c}'\mathbf{y} < \mathbf{0}$ and none of the y_i is positive, then (5.40) shows that θ can be increased indefinitely without creating a nonfeasible solution. In that case, the objective function $z(\theta)$ is unbounded.

In the above paragraphs, we have presented the fundamental rationale for the simplex method that will be described in the next section. We have shown how one can obtain a basic feasible solution from any feasible solution in a finite number of steps, without ever decreasing the objective function along the way. The same procedure can be applied to move from one basic feasible solution to another, again without decreasing the objective function. Since there is only a finite number of basic feasible solutions to (5.13), ultimately this procedure will bring us to a basic feasible solution that is optimal. This is the crux of the simplex method. All that remains is the development of the computational details.

We many summarize the results of this section with the following fundamental theorem of linear programming.

Fundamental Theorem. *If a nondegenerate linear programming problem has a feasible solution* $\mathbf{x}_f$, *say, then it has a basic feasible solution,* $\mathbf{x}_b$, *say, that gives at least as high a value to the objective function z as does* $\mathbf{x}_f$, *or z can be increased indefinitely. Consequently, if a nondegenerate linear programming problem has an optimal solution, then it has an optimal solution that is also a basic solution.*

The Fundamental Theorem allows us to restrict our attention solely to basic solutions of a linear programming problem. For if such a problem has an optimal solution, one of its basic solutions will be an optimal solution.

Example. Recall the numerical example described in (5.16) and (5.17). A feasible solution for this linear programming problem appears in (5.21). Expressing this solution in the form of (5.37), we find that

$$40\mathbf{a}_1 + 55\mathbf{a}_2 + 3\mathbf{a}_3 = \mathbf{b} \tag{5.43}$$

or

$$40\begin{bmatrix} \frac{2}{5} \\ 1 \end{bmatrix} + 55\begin{bmatrix} \frac{1}{5} \\ 2 \end{bmatrix} + 3\begin{bmatrix} 1 \\ 0 \end{bmatrix} = \begin{bmatrix} 30 \\ 150 \end{bmatrix}$$

The three vectors $\mathbf{a}_1$, $\mathbf{a}_2$, and $\mathbf{a}_3$ are of order two; therefore, they are linearly dependent. Hence,

$$y_1\begin{bmatrix} \frac{2}{5} \\ 1 \end{bmatrix} + y_2\begin{bmatrix} \frac{1}{5} \\ 2 \end{bmatrix} + y_3\begin{bmatrix} 1 \\ 0 \end{bmatrix} = \begin{bmatrix} 0 \\ 0 \end{bmatrix} \tag{5.44}$$

and a solution to (5.44) is $y_1 = -\frac{20}{3}$, $y_2 = \frac{10}{3}$, and $y_3 = 2$. Thus we may express one of the $\mathbf{a}$ vectors, $\mathbf{a}_3$, say, as the following linear combination of the other two:

$$\mathbf{a}_3 = -\frac{(-20/3)}{2}\mathbf{a}_1 - \frac{(10/3)}{2}\mathbf{a}_2 \tag{5.45}$$

$$= \frac{10}{3}\begin{bmatrix} \frac{2}{5} \\ 1 \end{bmatrix} - \frac{5}{3}\begin{bmatrix} \frac{1}{5} \\ 2 \end{bmatrix} = \begin{bmatrix} 1 \\ 0 \end{bmatrix}$$

Substituting (5.45) into (5.43), we have

$$40\mathbf{a}_1 + 55\mathbf{a}_2 + 3\left[-\frac{(-20/3)}{2}\mathbf{a}_1 - \frac{(10/3)}{2}\mathbf{a}_2\right] = \mathbf{b}$$

or

$$\begin{aligned} \mathbf{b} &= (x_1 - \theta_3 y_1)\mathbf{a}_1 + (x_2 - \theta_3 y_2)\mathbf{a}_2 \\ &= [40 - \tfrac{3}{2}(-\tfrac{20}{3})]\,\mathbf{a}_1 + [55 - \tfrac{3}{2}(\tfrac{10}{3})]\,\mathbf{a}_2 \\ &= (40 + 10)\mathbf{a}_1 + (55 - 5)\mathbf{a}_2 \\ &= 50\mathbf{a}_1 + 50\mathbf{a}_2 \\ &= 50\begin{bmatrix} \frac{2}{5} \\ 1 \end{bmatrix} + 50\begin{bmatrix} \frac{1}{5} \\ 2 \end{bmatrix} = \begin{bmatrix} 30 \\ 150 \end{bmatrix} \end{aligned} \tag{5.46}$$

Equation (5.46) is a basic feasible solution of (5.16). Indeed, it is the optimal basic feasible solution that appears in (5.22).

The above argument also may be expressed in matrix form, as follows:

$$\mathbf{A}\mathbf{x}_f = \begin{bmatrix} \frac{2}{5} & \frac{1}{5} & 1 & 0 \\ 1 & 2 & 0 & 1 \end{bmatrix}\begin{bmatrix} 40 \\ 55 \\ 3 \\ 0 \end{bmatrix} = \begin{bmatrix} 30 \\ 150 \end{bmatrix} = \mathbf{b}$$

$$\mathbf{Ay} = \begin{bmatrix} \frac{2}{5} & \frac{1}{5} & 1 & 0 \\ 1 & 2 & 0 & 1 \end{bmatrix} \begin{bmatrix} -\frac{20}{3} \\ \frac{10}{3} \\ 2 \\ 0 \end{bmatrix} = \begin{bmatrix} 0 \\ 0 \end{bmatrix} = \mathbf{0}$$

and, because $\mathbf{A}\theta\mathbf{y} = \mathbf{0}$,

$$\mathbf{A}(\mathbf{x}_f - \theta\mathbf{y}) = \begin{bmatrix} \frac{2}{5} & \frac{1}{5} & 1 & 0 \\ 1 & 2 & 0 & 1 \end{bmatrix} \begin{bmatrix} 40 + \frac{20}{3}\theta \\ 55 - \frac{10}{3}\theta \\ 3 - 2\theta \\ 0 \end{bmatrix} = \begin{bmatrix} 30 \\ 150 \end{bmatrix} = \mathbf{b}$$

If θ is assigned any value greater than $\frac{3}{2}$, then the third element of $(\mathbf{x}_f - \theta\mathbf{y})$ becomes negative. Therefore, to obtain a basic solution that is also feasible, we set $\theta = \frac{3}{2}$ and obtain

$$\mathbf{Ax}_b = \begin{bmatrix} \frac{2}{5} & \frac{1}{5} & 1 & 0 \\ 1 & 2 & 0 & 1 \end{bmatrix} \begin{bmatrix} 50 \\ 50 \\ 0 \\ 0 \end{bmatrix} = \begin{bmatrix} 30 \\ 150 \end{bmatrix} = \mathbf{b}$$

5.3.2 THE SIMPLEX METHOD

The simplex method or algorithm is a procedure for transforming an initial basic feasible solution into another one by substituting a vector not in the basis for one formerly in it or, equivalently, by substituting a variable not in the basic feasible solution for one formerly in it. *The entering vector is chosen so that the substitution will increase the objective function, and the vector leaving the basis is selected so that the new basic feasible solution remains feasible.* These two rules for determining which vectors should enter and leave the basis form the core of the simplex method. For once the appropriate basic variables have been identified, their levels can be found by a straightforward solution of a square linear equation system.

To develop the computational steps in greater detail, let us apply the simplex algorithm to the linear programming problem defined in (5.9), (5.10), and (5.11). Assume that an initial basic feasible solution is available. Often one is obvious.[5] For example, the slack variables provide

[5] If no such solution is obvious, we may augment the problem by introducing "artificial variables" and take as an objective the minimization of the use of these artificial activities. Upon solving this augmented linear programming problem, we find an initial feasible solution to the original problem. For a detailed exposition of this procedure, see Hadley (1962), pp. 116–124.

such a solution in (5.10) when the $n - m$ variables $x_1, x_2, \ldots, x_k$, are set equal to zero. Then

$$\begin{aligned} x_{k+1} &= b_1 \\ x_{k+2} &= b_2 \\ &\vdots \\ x_n &= b_m \end{aligned} \tag{5.47}$$

We must now select one of the $n - m$ nonbasic variables, $x_1, x_2, \cdots, x_k$, to enter the solution vector. (Or, equivalently, we must choose one of the $n - m$ nonbasic vectors, $\mathbf{a}_1, \mathbf{a}_2, \cdots, \mathbf{a}_k$, to enter the basis.)

Now, recall from (5.42) that

$$z(\theta) = \mathbf{c}'\mathbf{x} - \theta\mathbf{c}'\mathbf{y} = z - \theta\mathbf{c}'\mathbf{y}$$

Consequently, $z(\theta) > z$ if $\mathbf{c}'\mathbf{y} < 0$. But we no longer are interested in moving from a nonbasic to a basic feasible solution. Rather, we wish to shift from one basic feasible solution to another. Hence we must modify (5.42) to take into account the contribution to $z(\theta)$ that is made by the newly entering variable, x_k, say. To maintain feasibility, the maximum value that this variable may take on is θ, as defined by (5.41); we therefore have that

$$z(\theta) = \mathbf{c}'\mathbf{x}_b - \theta\mathbf{c}'\mathbf{y} + c_k\theta = z + \theta(c_k - \mathbf{c}'\mathbf{y})$$

whence $z(\theta) > z$ if $c_k - \mathbf{c}'\mathbf{y} > 0$. Thus, given a basic feasible solution, $\mathbf{x}_b$, if $c_k - \mathbf{c}'\mathbf{y} > 0$ holds for any vector $\mathbf{y}$ not currently in the basis, and if at least one $y_i > 0$, then it is possible to obtain a new basic feasible solution that will increase the value of the objective function.

Most versions of the simplex algorithm rely on the inequality check $c_k - \mathbf{c}'\mathbf{y} > 0$, sometimes called the *simplex criterion*, to establish whether the value of the objective function can be increased. Others, however, take advantage of the fact that if the current objective function is always expressed in terms of only the currently nonbasic variables, then the current vector of constants that defines this relationship is such that $\mathbf{c}'\mathbf{y}$ is always equal to the null vector for any variable not currently in the basis. More specifically, by treating z as just another basic variable and the objective function as an additional constraint, which is transformed along with the rest of the constraints, we maintain $\mathbf{c}'\mathbf{y} = 0$ throughout the iterative procedure. Therefore,

$$z(\theta) = z + \theta(c_k - \mathbf{c}'\mathbf{y}) = z + \theta c_k$$

Consequently, since $\theta > 0$, any $c_k > 0$ is an indication that it is possible to obtain a new basic feasible solution that will yield a higher valued objective function. Thus our selection principle is simply:

Introduction Rule. Scan the magnitudes of the coefficients in the current objective function and enter into the basic feasible solution the nonbasic variable that has associated with it the largest positive coefficient. In case of a tie, the selection between the tied contenders may be made arbitrarily. If no positive coefficients exist, then the current solution is optimal. A nonbasic variable with a zero coefficient is an indication that multiple solutions exist.

Having selected a new entering basic variable, x_k, say, we must next determine which of the former basic variables must leave the basis. We need a rule to identify the basic variable that is forced to zero first as the entering basic variable is increased. Such a rule, already derived in (5.41), is:

Elimination Rule. Remove the basic variable that reaches zero first as the entering basic variable is increased. That is, choose the variable x_r for which

$$\theta_r = \min_i \left\{\frac{x_i}{y_{ik}},\ y_{ik} > 0\right\}$$

If the entering variable can be increased indefinitely without driving any of the former basic variables to assume a negative value, that is, if all $y_{ik} \leq 0$, then the linear programming problem has an unbounded solution.

After determining which variable is to enter the basic feasible solution and which of the former basic variables it is to replace, we must solve for the new values of the remaining basic variables. This operation can be conveniently carried out by performing appropriate elementary operations on the equations, such that the basic variables and the objective function are expressed in terms of only the nonbasic variables. This implies that each basic variable must appear in exactly one equation, and that no other basic variable be contained in this same equation. Recall that the objective function is treated as one of the constraint equations, with z playing the role of the basic variable. Thus, for the linear programming problem defined in (5.9), (5.10), and (5.11), we have

$$\begin{aligned}
z - c_1x_1 - c_2x_2 - \cdots - c_kx_k - 0\cdot x_{k+1} - 0\cdot x_{k+2} - \cdots - 0\cdot x_n &= 0\\
a_{11}x_1 + a_{12}x_2 + \cdots + a_{1k}x_k + x_{k+1} \qquad\qquad &= b_1\\
a_{21}x_1 + a_{22}x_2 + \cdots + a_{2k}x_k \qquad + \quad x_{k+2} \qquad &= b_2\\
\vdots \qquad\qquad\qquad\qquad &\\
a_{m1}x_1 + a_{m2}x_2 + \cdots + a_{mk}x_k \qquad\qquad + x_n &= b_m
\end{aligned} \tag{5.48}$$

which, with the initial basic feasible solution described in (5.47), reduces to

$$\begin{aligned} z &= 0 \\ x_{k+1} &= b_1 \\ x_{k+2} &= b_2 \\ &\vdots \\ x_n &= b_m \end{aligned} \tag{5.49}$$

A notational shorthand for the simplex method is afforded by the use of *simplex tableaus,* which record only the essential information of a linear programming problem. For example, we may express the equations in (5.48) in the following tableau form:

Basic Variables	Coefficients									Right-Hand Side of the Equations
	z	x_1	x_2	$\cdots$	x_k	x_{k+1}	x_{k+2}	$\cdots$	x_n	
z	1	$-c_1$	$-c_2$	$\cdots$	$-c_k$	0	0	$\cdots$	0	0
x_{k+1}	0	a_{11}	a_{12}	$\cdots$	a_{1k}	1	0	$\cdots$	0	b_1
x_{k+2}	0	a_{21}	a_{22}	$\cdots$	a_{2k}	0	1	$\cdots$	0	b_2
$\vdots$	$\vdots$	$\vdots$	$\vdots$	$\vdots$	$\vdots$	$\vdots$	$\vdots$	$\vdots$	$\vdots$	$\vdots$
x_n	0	a_{m1}	a_{m2}	$\cdots$	a_{mk}	0	0	$\cdots$	1	b_m

The simplex method may then be applied as follows:

1. Scan the coefficients in the first row and identify the largest negative coefficient, c_k, say. (In transferring the right-hand side of the objective function to the left-hand side, we have, of course, reversed the signs of the coefficients. Hence, our introduction rule must be modified accordingly.) Enter the variable x_k into the basic feasible solution. If no negative coefficient exists, we have an optimal solution. STOP. Otherwise go on to Step 2.

2. Next, consider the positive elements in the column labeled x_k (excluding the first row), and identify the smallest value of $\theta_i = x_i/y_{ik}$, where x_i is the value of any current basic variable.

For example, in the first tableau, $a_{ij} = y_{ij}$ and the m basic variables x_{k+1}, $x_{k+2}, \ldots, x_n$ are equal to $b_1, b_2, \ldots, b_m$, respectively. Hence

$$\theta = \min_i \left\{ \frac{b_i}{a_{ik}},\ a_{ik} > 0 \right\} = \frac{b_r}{a_{rk}}, \text{ say.}$$

If all $a_{ik} \leqq 0$, the linear programming problem has an unbounded solution. STOP. Otherwise go on to Step 3.

3. Replace x_r by x_k in the basic variable column, divide that entire row by the current coefficient of x_k in Row k, and add or subtract appropriate multiples of Row k from all other rows so as to reduce all other elements in Column x_k to zero.
4. Return to Step 1.

Example. Consider, once again, the numerical example in (5.16) and (5.17). Introducing slack variables, we have the following linear programming problem:

$$\text{maximize:} \quad z = x_1 + x_2 \tag{5.50}$$

$$\begin{aligned} \text{subject to:} \quad \tfrac{2}{5}x_1 + \tfrac{1}{5}x_2 + x_3 \quad &= 30 \\ x_1 + 2x_2 \quad + x_4 &= 150 \end{aligned} \tag{5.51}$$

Setting $x_1 = x_2 = 0$, we obtain the initial basic feasible solution $x_3 = 30$, $x_4 = 150$, and an objective function that is equal to zero. The associated initial simplex tableau is

Basic Variables	Coefficients					Right-Hand Side of the Equations
	z	x_1	x_2	x_3	x_4	
z	1	-1	-1	0	0	0
x_3	0	$\frac{2}{5}$	$\frac{1}{5}$	1	0	30
x_4	0	1	2	0	1	150

Applying the introduction rule, we observe that either x_1 or x_2 may be introduced into the basis, since both have the same coefficient in the objective function. Arbitrarily, we enter x_1 into the basis and now wish to assign to it some positive value. The value of x_2 remains zero. Therefore, according to the constraints in (5.51), x_1 must not exceed $30/\frac{2}{5} = 75$, otherwise x_3 will become negative and our solution will no longer be feasible. Next, by virtue of the second equation in (5.51), x_1 cannot exceed $150/1 = 150$, lest x_4 become negative. The smallest of these two ratios is

$$\theta = \min\left\{\frac{30}{2/5}, \quad \frac{150}{1}\right\} = 75$$

and by setting $x_1 = 75$, we get $x_3 = 0$. Thus x_1 becomes the new basic variable in place of x_3.

We now perform the necessary algebraic manipulation in order to ensure that each basic variable appears only in one equation. This is achieved by dividing the first equation in (5.51) by the coefficient of x_1, as follows:

$$x_1 + \tfrac{1}{2}x_2 + \tfrac{5}{2}x_3 = 75$$

and then using this new equation to eliminate x_1 from the other equation and the objective function. We have, then, the constraint

$$(75 - \tfrac{1}{2}x_2 - \tfrac{5}{2}x_3) + 2x_2 + x_4 = 75 + \tfrac{3}{2}x_2 - \tfrac{5}{2}x_3 + x_4 = 150$$

the objective function

$$z = 75 - \tfrac{1}{2}x_2 - \tfrac{5}{2}x_3 + x_2 = 75 + \tfrac{1}{2}x_2 - \tfrac{5}{2}x_3$$

and the basic feasible solution $x_1 = 75$, $x_4 = 75$, $x_2 = x_3 = 0$ which yields an objective function with a value of 75.

At the end of the first simplex iteration, therefore, we have transformed the equations in (5.50) and (5.51) into

$$\begin{aligned} z \qquad - \tfrac{1}{2}x_2 + \tfrac{5}{2}x_3 \qquad &= 75 \\ x_1 + \tfrac{1}{2}x_2 + \tfrac{5}{2}x_3 \qquad &= 75 \\ \tfrac{3}{2}x_2 - \tfrac{5}{2}x_3 + x_4 &= 75 \end{aligned} \tag{5.52}$$

The associated simplex tableau is

Basic Variables	Coefficients					Right-Hand Side of the Equations
	z	x_1	x_2	x_3	x_4	
z	1	0	$-\frac{1}{2}$	$\frac{5}{2}$	0	75
x_1	0	1	$\frac{1}{2}$	$\frac{5}{2}$	0	75
x_4	0	0	$\frac{3}{2}$	$-\frac{5}{2}$	1	75

Note that the simplex method could have been applied directly to the first tableau to obtain the second one. To illustrate the tableau operations, let us now transform the above tableau into a third one. First, scan the first row and note that a single negative coefficient is still available. This is a signal that the objective function can be increased by introducing x_2 into the basic solution. Second, consider the ratios $\theta_1 = 75/\frac{1}{2}$ and $\theta_4 = 75/\frac{3}{2}$. The smallest θ is $\theta_4 = 50$; hence, we replace the basic variable x_4 with x_2. Third, divide through the third row of the tableau by the coefficient of x_2, that is, $\frac{3}{2}$, and reduce the other elements of Column x_2 to zero by adding one-half of the third row to the first row and subtracting one-half of the third row from the second row. These steps produce the third tableau

Basic Variables	Coefficients					Right-Hand Side of the Equations
	z	x_1	x_2	x_3	x_4	
z	1	0	0	$\frac{5}{3}$	$\frac{1}{3}$	100
x_1	0	1	0	$\frac{10}{3}$	$-\frac{1}{3}$	50
x_2	0	0	1	$-\frac{5}{3}$	$\frac{2}{3}$	50

We immediately see that we are at an optimal solution, since no negative coefficients appear in the first row of the tableau. Therefore, the optimal solution vector is

$$x_{\text{opt}} = \begin{bmatrix} 50 \\ 50 \\ 0 \\ 0 \end{bmatrix}$$

and $z = 50 + 50 = 100$, which is precisely the result we obtained earlier using the graphical solution method.

5.3.3 APPLICATION: ESTIMATING A POPULATION GROWTH MATRIX FROM A TIME SERIES OF INTERREGIONAL POPULATION DISTRIBUTIONS (CONTINUED)

To illustrate the application of linear programming to empirical data, let us return to the estimation problem discussed in Subsection 3.3.7. There we found that the use of the unrestricted least squares (ULS) estimator produced a negative migration rate in the estimated population growth matrix **G**. It appears, therefore, that for more reasonable results, one must adopt a method that incorporates a nonnegativity constraint in the estimation procedure. Such a restriction may be introduced by a linear programming formulation of the estimation problem and the use of the minimum absolute deviations (MAD) estimator.

The minimum absolute deviations estimator finds the vector of parameter estimates that minimizes the sum of the *absolute values* of the deviations between observed and predicted values. That is, it derives the vector, **g**, say, that minimizes

$$S = \Sigma \mid Y_i - \hat{Y}_i \mid = \mid \mathbf{y} - \mathbf{Xg} \mid '\mathbf{1} \tag{5.53}$$

subject to the constraints

$$\mathbf{y} = \mathbf{Xg} + \boldsymbol{\varepsilon} \tag{5.54}$$

$$\mathbf{g} \geqq \mathbf{0} \tag{5.55}$$

To transform (5.53) into a form that is solvable by linear programming methods, we must express each ε_i as the difference of two nonnegative variables u_i and v_i, say.[6] Thus we now seek the vector **g** that minimizes

$$S = |\mathbf{u} - \mathbf{v}|'\mathbf{1} = [\mathbf{u} + \mathbf{v}]'\mathbf{1} \tag{5.56}$$

[6] Any variable that may assume a negative value can be expressed as the difference of two nonnegative variables. Since negative-valued variables cannot appear in linear programming problems, we have to use this trick in order to formulate the estimation problem as a linear programming problem.

subject to the constraints

$$\mathbf{y} = \mathbf{X}\mathbf{g} + \boldsymbol{\varepsilon} = \mathbf{X}\mathbf{g} + [\mathbf{I} \quad -\mathbf{I}]\begin{bmatrix} \mathbf{u} \\ \mathbf{v} \end{bmatrix} \tag{5.57}$$

$$\mathbf{g}, \mathbf{u}, \mathbf{v} \geqq \mathbf{0} \tag{5.58}$$

The problem can be solved by applying the simplex algorithm to the tableau presented in Table 5.2. Since in (5.57) the vectors **u** and **v** are linearly dependent, elements of one or the other, but not both, will enter the optimal solution.[7]

A simplex tableau made up of the population data in Table 3.10 appears in Table 5.3. The estimate of the population growth matrix that results is

$$\hat{\mathbf{G}} = \begin{bmatrix} 1.0057 & 0.0030 \\ 0.0774 & 1.0083 \end{bmatrix} \tag{5.59}$$

The MAD estimator appears to resolve one of the problems presented by the ULS estimator: namely, that of the possible entry of negative elements into the growth operator. However, the MAD estimator does not seem to provide improved results in two important respects [Rogers (1967)]:

1. Although the MAD estimator is sure to produce a nonnegative population growth matrix, what appears as a negative element in the ULS estimate often merely assumes a zero value in the MAD estimate. Zero migration, though a more reasonable result than negative migration, is still a rather improbable event.

2. The elements of the population growth matrix occasionally take on very unlikely dimensions. In particular, the diagonal elements frequently are less than unity, and the off-diagonal entries become excessively large in order to compensate for this.

Table 5.2. Simplex Tableau for Finding the Minimum Absolute Deviations Estimate

Basic Variables	Coefficients													Right-Hand Side of the Equations
	z	$\mathbf{g}_1'$	$\mathbf{g}_2'$	$\cdots$	$\mathbf{g}_r'$	$\mathbf{u}_1'$	$\mathbf{u}_2'$	$\cdots$	$\mathbf{u}_r'$	$\mathbf{v}_1'$	$\mathbf{v}_2'$	$\cdots$	$\mathbf{v}_r'$	
z	1	$\mathbf{0}'$	$\mathbf{0}'$	$\cdots$	$\mathbf{0}'$	$-\mathbf{1}'$	$-\mathbf{1}'$	$\cdots$	$-\mathbf{1}'$	$-\mathbf{1}'$	$-\mathbf{1}'$	$\cdots$	$-\mathbf{1}'$	0
$\mathbf{u}_1$		$\mathbf{X}_1$				$\mathbf{I}_n$				$-\mathbf{I}_n$				$\mathbf{y}_1$
$\mathbf{u}_2$			$\mathbf{X}_2$				$\mathbf{I}_n$				$-\mathbf{I}_n$			$\mathbf{y}_2$
$\vdots$				$\ddots$				$\ddots$				$\ddots$		$\vdots$
$\mathbf{u}_r$					$\mathbf{X}_r$				$\mathbf{I}_n$				$-\mathbf{I}_n$	$\mathbf{y}_r$

[7] If a particular u_i and v_i were both strictly positive, with $u_i > v_i$, say, the solution could not be optimal, since it would be possible to find a smaller value for S in (5.56) by replacing u_i by $u_i - v_i$ and setting the original v_i equal to zero.

Table 5.3. Simplex Tableau for the Minimum Deviations Estimate of the Annual Population Growth Operator for California and the Rest of the United States: 1950-1960 Total Population Time Series

Basic Variables	Coefficients											Right-Hand Side of the Equations
	z	g_{11}	g_{21}	g_{12}	g_{22}	u_{11}	u_{12}	...	v_{11}	v_{12}	...	
z	1	0	0	0	0	−1	−1	...	−1	−1	...	0
u_{11}		10,643	141,225			1			−1			11,130
u_{12}		11,130	142,852				1			−1		11,638
u_{13}		11,638	144,755									12,101
u_{14}		12,101	146,855									12,517
u_{15}		12,517	149,367									13,004
u_{16}		13,004	152,065				.			.		13,581
u_{17}		13,581	154,507									14,177
u_{18}		14,177	157,010									14,741
u_{19}		14,741	159,408									15,288
u_{20}		15,288	161,637					.			.	15,863
u_{21}				10,643	141,225							142,852
u_{22}				11,130	142,852							144,755
u_{23}				11,638	144,755							146,855
u_{24}				12,101	146,855			.			.	149,367
u_{25}				12,517	149,367							152,065
u_{26}				13,004	152,065							154,507
u_{27}				13,581	154,507							157,010
u_{28}				14,177	157,010							159,408
u_{29}				14,741	159,408							161,637
u_{30}				15,288	161,637			1			−1	163,284

Source: Table 3.10.

5.4 DUALITY

Linear programming problems come in pairs. With every maximization problem of the kind

$$\text{maximize:} \quad z = \mathbf{c}'\mathbf{x} \tag{5.60}$$

$$\text{subject to:} \quad \mathbf{A}\mathbf{x} \leqq \mathbf{b} \tag{5.61}$$

$$\mathbf{x} \geqq \mathbf{0} \tag{5.62}$$

there exists the associated problem

$$\text{minimize:} \quad Z = \mathbf{b}'\mathbf{w} \tag{5.63}$$

$$\text{subject to:} \quad \mathbf{A}'\mathbf{w} \geqq \mathbf{c} \tag{5.64}$$

$$\mathbf{w} \geqq \mathbf{0} \tag{5.65}$$

The latter problem is called the *dual* of the first one, which is called the *primal*. The m coefficients of the jth decision variable in the primal constraints are the coefficients of the m variables in the jth dual constraint, and vice versa. Moreover, the coefficients of the m decision variables in the primal objective function form the right-hand side of the m constraints in the dual. Hence, there is one dual decision variable associated with each primal constraint and one dual constraint associated with each primal decision variable.

Several important relationships exist between a primal linear programming problem and its dual. These are summarized in the following theorem:

The Duality Theorem of Linear Programming. *If a primal linear programming problem and its dual both have feasible solutions, then both problems have optimal solutions, and the maximum value of z corresponding to the primal is equal to the minimum value of Z corresponding to the dual. If the primal has an unbounded solution, the dual has no feasible solution.*

Finally, the following *complementary slackness conditions* hold in an optimal solution for a primal and a dual:

a. If a slack variable in the primal appears in an optimal basic feasible solution, then the value of its associated decision variable in the dual is zero.
b. If a decision variable in the primal appears in an optimal basic feasible solution, then the value of its associated slack variable in the dual is zero, that is, the dual constraint associated with that decision variable holds as a strict equality.

The proofs of the above relationships can be found in Hadley (1962).

The symmetrical relationships between a primal linear programming problem and its dual, which are identified by the duality theorem, have two important implications. They suggest that the dual can serve as a computational stand-in for the primal. And they frequently have a distinct and significant economic interpretation.

If a primal linear programming problem contains many constraints and only a few decision variables, it is generally simpler to solve the dual problem and from that solution obtain the solution to the primal, than to solve the primal problem directly. This is because the large number of constraints in the primal will result in the introduction of a large number of slack variables and, therefore, a large basis. However, the dimension of the basis in the dual is simply equal to the number of decision variables in the primal. Thus, solving the dual generally requires a smaller computational effort.

The optimal solution to a dual linear programming problem provides a very important interpretation of the primal problem. To develop this interpretation, consider the general nature and unit of measure of the dual variables, w_i. In particular, consider the meaning of the jth constraint in (5.64):

$$a_{1j}w_1 + a_{2j}w_2 + \cdots + a_{mj}w_m \geqq c_j \tag{5.66}$$

Recall that in the primal, a_{ij} denotes the units of resource i that are required to produce a unit of output of the jth activity and c_j denotes the value of such a unit of output. Therefore, (5.66) states that a linear combination of the inputs used to produce one unit of output of the jth activity should not be less than the value of such a unit of output. Hence, w_i may be interpreted as the price of a unit of the ith resource, and the left-hand side of (5.66) then expresses the proposition that the value of the inputs used to produce a unit of output must not be less than the value of this unit of output.

However, w_i is not a *market* price but a very special kind of price. Namely, it is the value that is *imputed* to the resource by the consumer of that resource. And since costs never appear anywhere in the problem, these imputed values have nothing to do with the actual market costs of the resource, but merely reflect a kind of "shadow" or "opportunity" cost.

Consider, next, the dual objective function in (5.63), which states that resource prices should be chosen so as to minimize the total value that is imputed to the available resources. The duality theorem informs us that this total resource value will equal the value of the total output of the activities that consume these resources in an optimal manner. And the complementary slackness conditions indicate that the imputed value of resource i is zero whenever the supply of that resource is not totally exhausted by the activities. (Such a resource, in the jargon of economists, becomes a "free good.") Consequently, we also can interpret the objective function as measuring the total cost of resources consumed.

Example. Let us interpret the dual program of the production problem defined in (5.16) and (5.17):

$$\text{maximize: } z = x_1 + x_2$$
$$\text{subject to: } \tfrac{2}{5}x_1 + \tfrac{1}{5}x_2 \leqq 30$$
$$x_1 + 2x_2 \leqq 150$$
$$x_1 \geqq 0 \qquad x_2 \geqq 0$$

The dual of this primal is

$$\text{minimize: } Z = 30w_1 + 150w_2 \tag{5.67}$$
$$\left.\begin{aligned} \text{subject to: } \tfrac{2}{5}w_1 + w_2 &\geqq 1 \\ \tfrac{1}{5}w_1 + 2w_2 &\geqq 1 \end{aligned}\right. \tag{5.68}$$
$$w_1 \geqq 0 \qquad w_2 \geqq 0 \tag{5.69}$$

Recall that the objective in the primal was the maximization of new income generated by the production of Agricultural and Manufacturing output. Thus z is measured in dollars. Consequently, Z should also be valued in dollars. Since the numbers 30 and 150 in (5.67) denote the total quantities of Labor and Capital that are available as resource inputs, the symbols w_1 and w_2 must be expressed in dollar units per unit of Labor and Capital, respectively, for only then will $30w_1$ and $150w_2$ come out in dollar units. Thus w_1 and w_2 denote the *imputed values* of the two resources in question.

Let us now describe the economic meaning of the linear programming problem defined by (5.67), (5.68), and (5.69). First, the nonnegativity restrictions in (5.69) state that the imputed value of Labor and Capital must be nonnegative. This is certainly an economically sensible restriction. Second, the constraints in (5.68) specify that the imputed value of the total amounts of Labor and Capital that are used to produce a unit of Agricultural or Manufacturing output must be no less than the "profit" to the economy that comes from producing a unit of such an output. Since we have defined the unit level of operation of each activity as that level which generates a profit of a dollar of new income, the right-hand side of the constraints consists of unities. Finally, the objective function in (5.67) describes the total value imputed to the economy's resources, and it is the idea of the linear program to minimize this quantity while satisfying the constraints as interpreted above. Thus the correspondence between this dual program and its associated primal is that maximizing the new income that is generated by production is equivalent to minimizing the total imputed value of the economy's resources, with the restriction that the imputed cost of production of each output must not be less than the profit derivable from it.

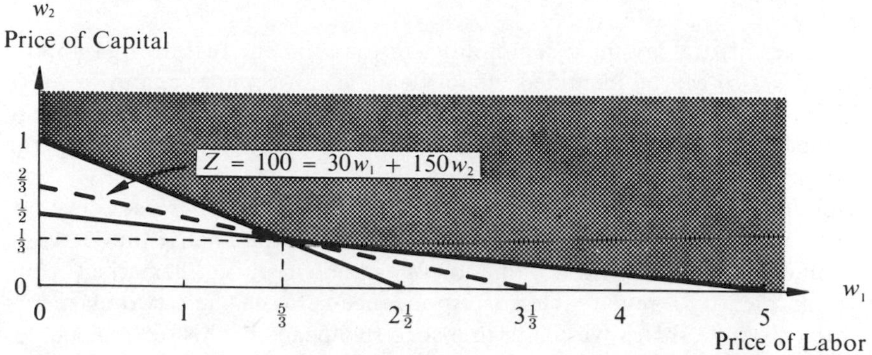

Figure 5.4. Graphical Solution of the Dual to the Production Problem

The dual problem in (5.67), (5.68), and (5.69) has only two variables. Hence we can solve it graphically, as in Figure 5.4, to find that $w_1 = \frac{5}{3}$ and $w_2 = \frac{1}{3}$, and $Z = 30(\frac{5}{3}) + 150(\frac{1}{3}) = \$100$. However, this is unnecessary, because in solving the primal problem with the simplex tableau method, we already have the optimal solution to the dual contained in the *first* row of the final simplex tableau. If we take the *absolute values* of the entries that appear in the slack variable columns, we get the numbers $\frac{5}{3}$ and $\frac{1}{3}$, arranged in the proper order. (Taking absolute values is necessary because the w_i's always must be nonnegative.)

In a previous numerical example, we have shown how an input-output model can be interpreted as an extremely simplified linear programming model. The above discussion of the dual to a production problem suggests that a similar dual may exist for the input-output model. This indeed is the case, and we leave as an exercise to the reader (Exercise 4) the verification of the proposition that in *selecting gross outputs to minimize the total consumption of labor in an input-output model, subject to the production of a specified bill of goods,* we are, simultaneously, *choosing prices to maximize the value of net output, subject to a set of price-cost inequalities.*

5.5 APPLICATION: THE THEORY OF GAMES

A *game* is a situation in which two or more participants pursue mutually conflicting objectives. There are basically two major categories of games: *games of chance,* such as dice and roulette, and *games of strategy,* such as bridge and chess. No skill is involved in playing games of chance, since their outcomes are determined by the laws of probability and not by the particular actions taken by the participants. Skill is involved, however, in playing games of strategy, and the identification of the optimal course of action for each participant in such games is the goal of game theory.

Games of strategy most commonly are found in the realm of gambling; but they also can be identified in political, social, economic, and military affairs. The underlying common dimension in all such games of strategy is the presence of a conflict of interests that ultimately is resolved by the *collective* actions of all of the participants.

Both linear programming and game theory are relatively recent developments in mathematics. But this is not the only property that they have in common. By expressing a game theory problem in mathematical form, we can identify a remarkable correspondence between these two classes of problems. We shall investigate this correspondence in this section, pursuing it only far enough to develop the basic concepts of game theory and to illustrate their potential application to the analysis of urban and regional problems.

5.5.1 BASIC CONCEPTS OF TWO-PERSON CONSTANT-SUM GAMES

Game theory is concerned with the analysis of situations in which two or more participants, with conflicting interests, choose courses of action that individually influence but do not completely determine the outcome of a certain event, called a *game*. The elements of a game are a set of participants, called *players*, a list of alternative courses of action, called *strategies*, that are available to each player, and a specification of the way in which these strategies collectively determine the gains and losses, called *payoffs*, that are realized by each player. At the end of each play of the game some players win and receive a *positive payoff*, whereas others lose and receive a *negative payoff*. If the sum of the payoffs realized by all the players at the end of each play is constant, then the game is called a *constant-sum* game; otherwise, the game is a *nonconstant-sum* game.

Games may be classified according to the number of players who participate in them. The basic categories in game theory are *two-person* games and *more-than-two-person* games. Moreover, games with a finite number of strategies are distinguished from those with an infinite number. Finally, games may be characterized as being cooperative or noncooperative. In the former, the players may form coalitions, while in the latter they may not. Two-person games are noncooperative by definition.

We shall confine our attention to two-person constant-sum games with a finite number of possible outcomes. Such games may be expressed in the form of an m-by-n *payoff matrix*,

$$\mathbf{A} = \begin{bmatrix} a_{11} & a_{12} & \cdots & a_{1n} \\ a_{21} & a_{22} & \cdots & a_{2n} \\ \vdots & \vdots & \ddots & \vdots \\ a_{m1} & a_{m2} & \cdots & a_{mn} \end{bmatrix} \tag{5.70}$$

in which the elements a_{ij}, by convention, denote the payments made to Player 1 by Player 2 if the former selects the strategy associated with the ith row and the latter adopts the strategy associated with the jth column. If chance determines certain strategies or their payoffs, and the game therefore is not completely determined by the actions of the players, we may interpret the a_{ij} as expected payoffs. Notice that in (5.70) we have assumed that Player 1 has m strategies available, while Player 2 has n. The total number of possible outcomes of this game, therefore, is mn.

The matrix $\mathbf{A}$ in (5.70) defines the payoffs to Player 1 by Player 2. We also may describe the payoffs to Player 2 by Player 1 with another m-by-n payoff matrix:

$$\mathbf{B} = \begin{bmatrix} b_{11} & b_{12} & \cdots & b_{2n} \\ b_{21} & b_{22} & \cdots & b_{2n} \\ \vdots & \vdots & \ddots & \vdots \\ b_{m1} & b_{m2} & \cdots & b_{mn} \end{bmatrix} \tag{5.71}$$

where the elements b_{ij} denote the payments made to Player 2 by Player 1 if the latter selects the ith strategy and the former adopts the jth strategy. However, since we are restricting our discussion to constant-sum games, there is no need for this matrix, because Player 2's payoffs are simply the constant-sum of the game less the payoffs to Player 1. Thus, if k denotes the constant-sum, then

$$\mathbf{B} = k - \mathbf{A} \tag{5.72}$$

and, in the particular case of a zero-sum game,

$$\mathbf{B} = -\mathbf{A} \tag{5.73}$$

A nonzero constant-sum game always can be transformed into a zero-sum one, because a game with a payoff matrix consisting of elements $ca_{ij} + d$, where c and d are constants, has the same fundamental structure and solution as a game with the payoff matrix $\mathbf{A}$ [Kemeny, *et al.* (1962), pp. 422–424]. Therefore, we shall henceforth, without loss of generality, consider only zero-sum games in our discussion of methods for solving constant-sum games.

A solution to a game is obtained when an optimal strategy is found for each player. A strategy is optimal only with respect to a particular objective function, however. And the choice of an objective function depends on the kind of information that players have regarding each other's strategies. For example, if Player 1 knows that Player 2 is going to adopt Strategy j, say, then the appropriate objective function for him is to maximize his payoff by choosing the strategy associated with the row containing the largest element in the jth column of the payoff matrix **A**. And if Player 1's information is only probabilistic in character, then an appropriate objective for him is to try to maximize his *expected* payoff. But if Player 1 has no knowledge about the strategy that Player 2 is going to adopt, then it becomes necessary to assume an objective function for each player before proceeding to derive optimal strategies.

In game theory it is generally assumed that players are conservative in their choice of objective functions and that each player will strive to minimize his opponent's winnings while at the same time maximizing his own payoffs. Hence, in the game described by the payoff matrix in (5.70), Player 1 will be striving to realize the largest possible payoff in the **A** matrix, while Player 2 will try to realize the smallest possible payoff. Consequently, we shall call Player 1 the *maximizing player* and Player 2 the *minimizing player*.

By an appropriate choice of strategy, the maximizing player, Player 1, can assure himself of winning an amount at least as large as the largest member of the set consisting of the smallest element of each row in the payoff matrix, that is, the greatest of the row minima, irrespective of Player 2's actions. This lower bound for his winnings is called the *max-min* and represents what the game is *worth* to him, since his opponent cannot prevent him from winning it.

Conversely, Player 2, by an equally appropriate choice of strategy, can ensure that Player 1's payoffs never are greater than the smallest member of the set consisting of the largest element of each column in the same payoff matrix, that is, the smallest of the column maxima, irrespective of Player 1's actions. This upper bound for Player 2's losses is called the *min-max* and represents the worth of the game to him, since Player 1 cannot make him lose more. If the max-min is equal to the min-max, then the game is said to have a *saddle-point* at the common row minimum and column maximum. A saddle-point, therefore, must be simultaneously the maximum of its column and the minimum of its row.

Although a single payoff matrix, **A**, say, completely describes a two-person constant-sum game, it by itself does not enable us to identify the final outcome of the game. To do this, we must specify how each of the two players will play the game, and this cannot be done without prior knowledge of each player's objective function and his behavior pattern.

In the theory of two-person zero-sum games it is assumed that players are conservative in their outlook. Specifically, it is assumed that each player acts so as to avoid the less-favorable outcome, even though by adopting such a course of action he forsakes the possibility of ever realizing the best possible outcome.

If Player 1 chooses Strategy i, he is sure of winning at least the smallest element in the ith row of the payoff matrix $\mathbf{A}$, that is,

$$\min_j a_{ij}$$

irrespective of the strategy adopted by Player 2. Thus it would seem wise for Player 1 to choose the strategy that is associated with the maximum of these respective minima:

$$\max_i \min_j a_{ij}$$

Conversely, since Player 2 is striving to prevent Player 1 from winning any more than necessary, it seems reasonable for him to select a strategy that would minimize his maximum loss.[8] Thus he should choose the strategy associated with

$$\min_j \max_i a_{ij}$$

If the payoff matrix contains an element (or elements) a_{rs}, such that

$$a_{rs} = \max_i \min_j a_{ij} = \min_j \max_i a_{ij} \tag{5.74}$$

then the game has a saddle-point at a_{rs}. In such cases, Player 1 can be sure of receiving at least a payoff of a_{rs}, by adopting Strategy r, and Player 2 can be sure that he will lose no more than a_{rs}, by adopting Strategy s. Hence such a *saddle-point solution* to a game, when it exists, is always the optimal solution, and a_{rs} is called the *value* of the game. Any deviation from it by Player 1 lowers his opportunity for winning at least a_{rs}, and any deviation from it by Player 2 raises Player 1's opportunity for winning more than a_{rs}.

Before discussing the solution of a two-person zero-sum game that has no saddle-point solution, we should note a special phenomenon that occasionally is present in some payoff matrices: the existence of ***dominated strategies***. Strategy k is said to be dominated by Strategy l if an element-by-element comparison of these two strategies reveals an inferior payoff to

[8] Because of the constant-sum nature of the game, choosing the minimum of the column maxima in the payoff matrix $\mathbf{A}$ is equivalent to choosing the maximum of the column minima in the payoff matrix $\mathbf{B}$.

the player whenever the former is used instead of the latter, irrespective of what strategy is adopted by the opponent. In such instances, there is no reason for the player to ever consider selecting Strategy k, and it may therefore be deleted from the payoff matrix without affecting the final solution of the game.

Examples.

(i) We may illustrate the fundamental character of those constant-sum games that have a saddle-point solution with the following location problem, first posed by Hotelling (1929). Two competing gasoline stations, A and B, say, plan to locate at one of five possible locations along a stretch of highway: at the end-points or at one of the quarter-points, that is, 0, $\frac{1}{4}$, $\frac{1}{2}$, $\frac{3}{4}$, or 1. Assume that the total demand for gasoline remains the same wherever the two stations locate and that this demand is uniformly distributed over the length of the highway, such that the distance from the beginning of the highway to any other point on it measures the proportion of total demand to the left of that point. Moreover, assume that customers will patronize the gasoline station that is closest to them or, if both stations are an equal distance away, half will patronize one station and half will patronize the other. Where should the two stations locate and why?

This problem may be described in the format of a two-person constant-sum game. For example, if both stations locate at the beginning of the highway, they will split the market between them, and the payoff to Station A would be $\frac{1}{2}$. The same payoff is realized by Station A if both locate at the mid-point, the quarter-points, or at the end of the highway.

Table 5.4. Payoff Matrix for Station A in the Hotelling Location Problem

Location of Station A	Location of Station B: 0	$\frac{1}{4}$	$\frac{1}{2}$	$\frac{3}{4}$	1	Row Minimum
0	$\frac{1}{2}$	$\frac{1}{8}$	$\frac{1}{4}$	$\frac{3}{8}$	$\frac{1}{2}$	$\frac{1}{8}$
$\frac{1}{4}$	$\frac{7}{8}$	$\frac{1}{2}$	$\frac{3}{8}$	$\frac{1}{2}$	$\frac{5}{8}$	$\frac{3}{8}$
$\frac{1}{2}$	$\frac{3}{4}$	$\frac{5}{8}$	($\frac{1}{2}$)	$\frac{5}{8}$	$\frac{3}{4}$	($\frac{1}{2}$) max-min
$\frac{3}{4}$	$\frac{5}{8}$	$\frac{1}{2}$	$\frac{3}{8}$	$\frac{1}{2}$	$\frac{7}{8}$	$\frac{3}{8}$
1	$\frac{1}{2}$	$\frac{3}{8}$	$\frac{1}{4}$	$\frac{1}{8}$	$\frac{1}{2}$	$\frac{1}{8}$
Column Maximum	$\frac{7}{8}$	$\frac{5}{8}$	($\frac{1}{2}$)	$\frac{5}{8}$	$\frac{7}{8}$	
			↑ min-max			

A little more arithmetic yields the payoff matrix in Table 5.4, where Station *A* is the maximizing player.

Notice that the end-points are never seriously considered, because they are dominated strategies, and observe that the payoff matrix in Table 5.4 has a saddle-point in the center. Thus, each of the two stations will locate at the mid-point of the stretch of highway in order to capture a half of the market, regardless of the location selected by its competitor. This is not the socially optimal solution, however, because by locating at the two quarter-points each station could still capture a half of the market, yet be closer to its customers. But since the game is assumed to be a noncooperative one, one station would move toward the mid-point of the highway to gain an advantage over its competitor, thereby causing the other station also to move to the same location.

Now assume that Stations *A* and *B*, having located at the mid-point of the highway, are faced with the following pricing problem. They can sell their gasoline for 30 cents or 40 cents a gallon, and their total profit will depend on how much the other charges for its gasoline. Specifically, let the payoff matrix for each be the one set out in Table 5.5.

Since the game described in Table 5.5 is a constant-sum game (that is, the total payoff to each player is always 1,000 dollars), we may focus solely on the payoffs to the maximizing player, as set out in Table 5.6.

According to Table 5.5, the optimal strategy for each station is to sell its gasoline for 30 cents a gallon. In this way Station *A* is assured of a daily profit of 600 dollars, and Station *B* is certain of realizing a daily profit of 400 dollars. The worth of this game to the maximizing player, Station *A*, is 600 dollars, and he can obtain this payoff regardless of what Station *B* charges for its gasoline. Conversely, the worth of this game to the minimizing player, Station *B*, is also 600 dollars, because he can

Table 5.5. Payoff Matrices for the Two Gasoline Stations: Constant-Sum Game with a Saddle-Point

Station *A*'s Price	Payoff Matrix for Station *A* (Station *A*'s Daily Profit in Dollars)		Payoff Matrix for Station *B* (Station *B*'s Daily Profit in Dollars)	
	Station *B*'s Price		Station *B*'s Price	
	30 cents	40 cents	30 cents	40 cents
30 cents	600	700	400	300
40 cents	400	500	600	500

Table 5.6. Payoff Matrix for Station A: Constant-Sum Game with a Saddle-Point

Station A's Price	Payoff Matrix for Station A (Station A's Daily Profit in Dollars) Station B's Price: 30 cents	40 cents	Row Minimum
30 cents	(600)	700	600
40 cents	400	500	400
Column Maximum	600	700	

prevent Station *A* from realizing a profit that exceeds this amount. The value of the game to each player is also 600 dollars. However, this equality between the worth and the value of the game to each player occurs only if a saddle-point solution exists.

(ii) Consider the following game-theoretic formulation of a population projection problem posed by Muhsam (1956). Assume that a planner is provided with the following five alternative population projections: $X - 2a$, $X - a$, X, $X + a$, and $X + 2a$, where X and a are particular values. Let x_0 denote his choice of one of these five projections, and let x denote the population that ultimately occurs. Hence $x_0 - x$ is the error that he has made by adopting the projection x_0 instead of working with the actual value x.

Let $L(x_0, x)$ be a *loss function*, which expresses in some suitable quantitative units the loss that is suffered by the people who follow the planner's advice. For a concrete illustration, consider Muhsam's example of the planning of an additional water supply system for a city which currently has a satisfactory supply that cannot be expanded. For simplicity, assume that the new supply system only needs to satisfy the additional demands generated by the population of this city until the year t and may ignore any demands beyond that year. Then suppose that an additional water supply system is built on the expectation that the city's population at time t will be x_0. If the population actually numbers x_0 in the year t, then no loss is suffered because the system exactly serves the needs of the population. However, if $x \neq x_0$, a loss will be incurred, since the system then will be either underdesigned or overdesigned with respect to the demand. Thus, in the former case, another supply system will have to be built or, in the latter case, a smaller supply system would have been sufficient.

Assume that the loss function is symmetric (that is, an underprojection

Table 5.7. Payoff Matrix for the Population Projection Problem: Symmetric Loss Function

Projection of Population x_0	Actual Population at Time t, x: $X-2a$	$X-a$	X	$X+a$	$X+2a$	Row Maximum
$X-2a$	0	ba	$2ba$	$3ba$	$4ba$	$4ba$
$X-a$	ba	0	ba	$2ba$	$3ba$	$3ba$
X	$2ba$	ba	0	ba	$2ba$	$2ba$ min-max loss
$X+a$	$3ba$	$2ba$	ba	0	ba	$3ba$
$X+2a$	$4ba$	$3ba$	$2ba$	ba	0	$4ba$

of the actual total is as costly an error as an overprojection) and that it has the linear form

$$L(x_0, x) = b \mid x_0 - x \mid \tag{5.75}$$

where $\mid x_0 - x \mid$ denotes the absolute value of the difference between x_0 and x, and b is a specified constant. What is the min-max loss projection? (Note that in this case the planner will be a minimizing player.)

Table 5.7 sets out the payoff matrix that is associated with the loss function defined in (5.75). Note that if the planner's policy is to minimize the maximum loss that can be incurred, then his optimal strategy is to use the population projection: $x_0 = X$.

Let us now complicate the problem somewhat by associating the following probabilities with each of the five alternative population totals for x:

$$p(x) = \begin{cases} \frac{3}{13} & \text{for } x = X - 2a \\ \frac{4}{13} & \text{for } x = X - a \\ \frac{3}{13} & \text{for } x = X \\ \frac{2}{13} & \text{for } x = X + a \\ \frac{1}{13} & \text{for } x = X + 2a \end{cases} \tag{5.76}$$

What is the population projection that minimizes the *expected* loss?

We begin by denoting the payoff matrix in Table 5.7 by **L** and the probability distribution in (5.76) by the vector **p**. Then

$$\mathbf{r} = \mathbf{L}\mathbf{p} = \frac{ba}{13}\begin{bmatrix} 0 & 1 & 2 & 3 & 4 \\ 1 & 0 & 1 & 2 & 3 \\ 2 & 1 & 0 & 1 & 2 \\ 3 & 2 & 1 & 0 & 1 \\ 4 & 3 & 2 & 1 & 0 \end{bmatrix}\begin{bmatrix} 3 \\ 4 \\ 3 \\ 2 \\ 1 \end{bmatrix}$$

$$= \frac{ba}{13}\begin{bmatrix} 20 \\ 13 \\ 14 \\ 21 \\ 32 \end{bmatrix} \begin{matrix} \\ \\ \leftarrow \text{min-expected loss} \\ \\ \\ \end{matrix} \tag{5.77}$$

where **r** is the vector of expected losses associated with the five alternative projections. Hence, according to (5.77), *the loss function* in (5.75), *the probability distribution* in (5.76), and *the policy criterion* of minimizing expected loss lead to the selection of the population projection: $x_0 = X - a$.

Assume now that underprojection is more costly than overprojection, and consider the effects of introducing the asymmetric loss function

$$L(x_0, x) = \begin{cases} b \mid x_0 - x \mid & \text{if } x \leqq x_0 \\ c \mid x_0 - x \mid & \text{if } x > x_0 \end{cases} \tag{5.78}$$

where $c = 2b$, say. What are the min-max loss and min-expected loss projections?

The loss function in (5.78) generates the loss matrix

$$\mathbf{L} = ba\begin{bmatrix} 0 & 2 & 4 & 6 & 8 \\ 1 & 0 & 2 & 4 & 6 \\ 2 & 1 & 0 & 2 & 4 \\ 3 & 2 & 1 & 0 & 2 \\ 4 & 3 & 2 & 1 & 0 \end{bmatrix}$$

which identifies $x_0 = X + a$ as the projection that minimizes maximum loss. Next, adopting the probability distribution in (5.76), we find that

$$\mathbf{r} = \mathbf{L}\mathbf{p} = \frac{ba}{13}\begin{bmatrix} 40 \\ 23 \\ 18 \\ 22 \\ 32 \end{bmatrix} \begin{matrix} \\ \\ \leftarrow \text{min-expected loss} \\ \\ \\ \end{matrix} \tag{5.79}$$

and that $x_0 = X$ is the minimum expected loss projection.

We conclude, therefore, that the problem of selecting the optimal population projection depends essentially on three considerations: the loss function, the probability distribution, and the policy criterion. A change in any one of these will, in general, lead to a change in the optimal population projection (Exercise 8).

5.5.2 MIXED STRATEGIES

The presence of a saddle-point in a payoff matrix determines a solution to the game. Difficulties arise, however, when no saddle-point exists—that is, when

$$a_{rs} = \max_i \min_j a_{ij} < \min_j \max_i a_{ij} = a_{uv} \tag{5.80}$$

On such occasions, Player 1 should be able to win more than a_{rs}, and Player 2 should be able to lose less than a_{uv}. The exact amount will depend on the strategy that is adopted by each of the two players. To resolve this problem, we need to introduce the concept of a *mixed strategy*.

A mixed strategy is a particular combination of pure strategies. We say that a player is following a mixed strategy if he selects randomly from among his available pure strategies according to a fixed set of probabilities of selecting each. To solve a two-person constant-sum game that has no saddle-point, therefore, we must determine these probabilities.

The principal characteristic of mixed strategies is that each player should avoid using the same pure strategy in repeated plays of the game, because this will place him at a distinct disadvantage. This does not mean, however, that players should select their strategies completely at random. It merely means that the exact sequence in which different pure strategies are used in different plays of the game must be unpredictable, while the *relative frequency* with which each is adopted is determinate and known. In this way, each player realizes the most desirable expected payoff that he can attain against a rational and intelligent opponent.

Assume that Player 1 uses some chance mechanism, such as flipping a coin or drawing a card out of a deck, to select Strategy i with probability $p_i \geqq 0$, $\sum_{i=1}^{m} p_i = 1$, and that Player 2 uses a similar device to select Strategy j with probability $q_j \geqq 0$, $\sum_{j=1}^{n} q_j = 1$. In this way, both players are ignorant of each other's strategy, and the only thing that is known to each player is the relative frequency with which each available strategy should be adopted.

When players adopt mixed strategies, it is no longer possible to determine what the outcome of a particular game will be. We can only focus on the expected winnings for Player 1 and on the expected losses for Player 2. For example, if in a game described by the payoff matrix

$$\mathbf{A} = \begin{bmatrix} a_{11} & a_{12} \\ a_{21} & a_{22} \end{bmatrix}$$

Player 1 chooses the mixed strategy defined by

$$\mathbf{p} = \begin{bmatrix} p_1 \\ p_2 \end{bmatrix}$$

and Player 2 selects the mixed strategy defined by

$$\mathbf{q} = \begin{bmatrix} q_1 \\ q_2 \end{bmatrix}$$

then Player 1 may expect to realize the payoff a_{11} with probability p_1q_1, the payoff a_{12} with probability p_1q_2, the payoff a_{21} with probability p_2q_1, and the payoff a_{22} with probability p_2q_2. Hence his expected winnings are

$$E(\mathbf{p}, \mathbf{q}) = a_{11}p_1q_1 + a_{12}p_1q_2 + a_{21}p_2q_1 + a_{22}p_2q_2$$

or, in general,

$$E(\mathbf{p}, \mathbf{q}) = \sum_i^m \sum_j^n p_i a_{ij} q_j = \mathbf{p}'\mathbf{A}\mathbf{q} \tag{5.81}$$

Since in a two-person zero-sum game, Player 1's winnings are Player 2's losses, we conclude that Player 2's expected losses are $-\ \mathbf{p}'\mathbf{A}\mathbf{q}$.

Now consider the problem of determining the probability vectors, $\mathbf{p}^0$ and $\mathbf{q}^0$, say, that define the optimal mix of strategies for Players 1 and 2, respectively. Player 1 seeks a $\mathbf{p}$ that will maximize his expected winnings. For any $\mathbf{p}$ he chooses, he is sure that his expected winnings will be not less than

$$\min_{\mathbf{q}} E(\mathbf{p}, \mathbf{q}) = W_1, \text{ say} \tag{5.82}$$

Hence he seeks the mixed strategy $\mathbf{p}^0$ that maximizes this quantity, that is,

$$\max_{\mathbf{p}} \min_{\mathbf{q}} E(\mathbf{p}, \mathbf{q}) = \max W_1 \tag{5.83}$$

Analogously, Player 2 seeks a mixed strategy $\mathbf{q}^0$ that minimizes the largest expected loss that he can incur, that is,

$$\min_{\mathbf{q}} \max_{\mathbf{p}} E(\mathbf{p}, \mathbf{q}) = \min W_2 \tag{5.84}$$

If there exist vectors $\mathbf{p}^0$ and $\mathbf{q}^0$ such that $W_1 = W_2$, then Player 1 should use the mixed strategy defined by $\mathbf{p}^0$, and Player 2 should adopt the mixed strategy defined by $\mathbf{q}^0$.[9] The common value $W = W_1 = W_2$ is called the *value* of the game, and the problem of solving any two-person zero-sum game, therefore, reduces to one of finding the optimal mixed strategy vectors, $\mathbf{p}^0$ and $\mathbf{q}^0$, and the value of the game, W.

[9] Such a $\mathbf{p}^0$ and $\mathbf{q}^0$ always exist. This property, commonly referred to as the *fundamental theorem for two-person zero-sum games*, follows directly from the duality theorem of linear programming, as we shall show in Subsection 5.5.3.

Example. Consider the consequences of the slight modifications of the payoff matrix in Table 5.6 that appear in Table 5.8. Now it seems that the most profitable course of action for Station *A* is to charge 40 cents a gallon in the hope that Station *B* also will charge 40 cents, thereby allowing *A* to realize a profit of 700 dollars. But this is a dangerous choice for *A*, since *B* could anticipate this decision and charge 30 cents a gallon, thereby reaping a profit of 600 dollars and leaving *A* only a 400-dollar profit. So it appears that *A* should charge only 30 cents a gallon in the expectation that *B* also is going to charge 30 cents a gallon. In this way, *A* can expect to realize a profit of 600 dollars. But what if *B* anticipates *A*'s reasoning to this point? Then *B* will expect *A* to charge 30 cents and on this basis will sell his gasoline for 40 cents a gallon, hoping for a profit of 500 dollars. If this happens then perhaps *A* should charge 40 cents after all, for if *B* is going to charge 40 cents a gallon, then the profit of 700 dollars may be attainable after all. However, should *B* anticipate. . . .

Clearly, the above argument has no end and offers no solution. A way of bypassing the dilemma of circularity is to consider a mixed strategy for each station.

It can be shown (Exercise 9) that the optimal mixed strategies in a two-by-two game, with no saddle-point solution, may be found by solving the equations

$$\frac{p_1}{p_2} = \frac{a_{22} - a_{21}}{a_{11} - a_{12}} \tag{5.85}$$

and

$$\frac{q_1}{q_2} = \frac{a_{22} - a_{12}}{a_{11} - a_{21}} \tag{5.86}$$

where the a_{ij} are the elements of the payoff matrix $\mathbf{A}$. Substituting the data in Table 5.8 into (5.85) and (5.86), we conclude that the optimal

Table 5.8. Payoff Matrix for Station A: Constant-Sum Game with No Saddle-Point

Station *A*'s Price	Payoff Matrix for Station *A* (Station *A*'s Daily Profit in Dollars) — Station *B*'s Price: 30 cents	40 cents	Row Minimum
30 cents	600	500	500
40 cents	400	700	400
Column Maximum	600	700	

strategy for Station A is to charge 30 cents a gallon three-fourths of the time and 40 cents a gallon the rest of the time. The optimal strategy for Station B, on the other hand, is to charge 30 cents and 40 cents a gallon an equal proportion of the time. That is,

$$p_1 = \tfrac{3}{4}$$
$$p_2 = \tfrac{1}{4}$$
$$q_1 = \tfrac{1}{2}$$
$$q_2 = \tfrac{1}{2}$$

The worth of the game to Station A is 500 dollars. The worth of the game to Station B is 600 dollars. The dollar value of the game is (Exercise 9)

$$W = \frac{a_{11}a_{22} - a_{12}a_{21}}{a_{11} + a_{22} - (a_{12} + a_{21})} = 550$$

5.5.3 REDUCTION OF A TWO-PERSON CONSTANT-SUM GAME TO A LINEAR PROGRAMMING PROBLEM

In the previous section, we observed that in a two-person constant-(zero)-sum game, the maximizing player, Player 1, seeks a set of probabilities p_1, $p_2, \ldots, p_m$, that will make his minimum expected winnings, W_1, as large as possible. In doing so, however, he is restricted by the constraints implicit in (5.82), which may be expressed in the form of the following set of inequalities:

$$a_{1j}p_1 + a_{2j}p_2 + \cdots + a_{mj}p_m \geqq W_1 \quad (j = 1, 2, \ldots, n) \qquad (5.87)$$

Moreover, since the p_i are probabilities, they must be nonnegative, and their sum must be equal to unity. Finally, because increasing the elements of a payoff matrix by a constant amount does not affect the relative desirability of the various strategies of a game, we can assume, without loss of generality, that the payoff matrix is a positive matrix and, therefore, that W_1 is positive.[10] Player 1's decision problem, therefore, can be expressed as the following linear programming problem: Choose numbers $p_1, p_2, \ldots, p_m$ so as to

$$\text{maximize:} \quad W_1(> 0) \qquad (5.88)$$
$$\text{subject to:} \quad \mathbf{A'p} \geqq W_1\mathbf{1} \qquad (5.89)$$
$$\mathbf{p} \geqq \mathbf{0} \qquad (5.90)$$
$$\mathbf{1'p} = 1 \qquad (5.91)$$

[10] For example, to get a positive payoff matrix from one containing negative entries, we could add one minus its most negative entry to every element and thereby obtain positive values throughout the matrix.

The situation facing the minimizing player, Player 2, is similar. He is seeking a set of probabilities $q_1, q_2, \ldots, q_n$ that will make his maximum expected loss, W_2, as small as possible. Hence his problem can be defined as the following linear programming problem: Choose numbers $q_1, q_2, \ldots, q_n$ so as to

$$\text{minimize:} \quad W_2 \ (> 0) \tag{5.92}$$

$$\text{subject to:} \quad \mathbf{Aq} \leqq W_2\mathbf{1} \tag{5.93}$$

$$\mathbf{q} \geqq 0 \tag{5.94}$$

$$\mathbf{1}'\mathbf{q} = 1 \tag{5.95}$$

Now let

$$x_i = \frac{p_i}{W_1} \ (i = 1, 2, \ldots, m) \text{ and } y_j = \frac{q_j}{W_2} \ (j = 1, 2, \ldots, n)$$

then

$$\sum_{i=1}^{m} x_i = \mathbf{1}'\mathbf{x} = \frac{1}{W_1}$$

$$\sum_{j=1}^{n} y_j = \mathbf{1}'\mathbf{y} = \frac{1}{W_2}$$

and the above two linear programming problems may be expressed as

$$\text{minimize:} \quad z = \mathbf{1}'\mathbf{x} \tag{5.96}$$

$$\text{subject to:} \quad \mathbf{A}'\mathbf{x} \geqq \mathbf{1} \tag{5.97}$$

$$\mathbf{x} \geqq \mathbf{0} \tag{5.98}$$

and

$$\text{maximize:} \quad Z = \mathbf{1}'\mathbf{y} \tag{5.99}$$

$$\text{subject to:} \quad \mathbf{Ay} \leqq \mathbf{1} \tag{5.100}$$

$$\mathbf{y} \geqq \mathbf{0} \tag{5.101}$$

Observe that by minimizing $\mathbf{1}'\mathbf{x}$, Player 1 will in fact be maximizing W_1, and by maximizing $\mathbf{1}'\mathbf{y}$, Player 2 will be minimizing W_2.

Comparing the two linear programming problems defined by (5.96) through (5.101), we see that they are duals of each other. Furthermore, we note that feasible solutions always exist to these two problems, because each player always has the option of using a pure strategy. Since the primal has a feasible solution, it has either an optimal or an unbounded solution. However, if it has an unbounded solution, then the dual will have no solution. But we already have established that the dual has a feasible solution. Therefore, the primal must have an optimal solution. An analogous argument leads to the conclusion that the dual also has an optimal solution. Hence we have proved the fundamental theorem of game theory and have established that

$$\min z = \max Z$$

or, equivalently, that

$$\max W_1 = \min W_2 = W \tag{5.102}$$

say.

Example. Recall the payoff matrix in Table 5.8, and consider the reduction of that game to the following pair of linear programming problems:

Primal

$$\begin{aligned} \text{minimize:} \quad & z = x_1 + x_2 \\ \text{subject to:} \quad & 600\, x_1 + 400\, x_2 \geqq 1 \\ & 500\, x_1 + 700\, x_2 \geqq 1 \\ & x_1, x_2 \geqq 0 \end{aligned}$$

Dual

$$\begin{aligned} \text{maximize:} \quad & Z = y_1 + y_2 \\ \text{subject to:} \quad & 600\, y_1 + 500\, y_2 \leqq 1 \\ & 400\, y_1 + 700\, y_2 \leqq 1 \\ & y_1, y_2 \geqq 0 \end{aligned}$$

The reader should confirm that the optimal solution to the primal problem is $x_1 = 3/2{,}200$, $x_2 = 1/2{,}200$, and to the dual problem is $y_1 = y_2 = 1/1{,}100$. The value of the objective function in both cases is $z = Z = 1/500$. Recalling the definitions of these variables, we note that the results are in agreement with those found earlier using the method described in Exercise 9.

5.5.4 APPLICATION: THE PRISONER'S DILEMMA AND GHETTO EXPANSION

The theory of two-person constant-sum games is the most orderly and best developed branch of game theory. Unfortunately, many of the conflict situations that are subjects for urban and regional analysis cannot be expressed as two-person constant-sum games. One of the more interesting of these is the question of racial discrimination in the housing market and its effect on ghetto expansion. Such problems tend rather naturally to take on the form of the two-person nonconstant-sum game known as the *Prisoner's Dilemma*.

The Prisoner's Dilemma game derives its name from the following story

[Luce and Raiffa (1957)]. A district attorney visits two suspects who have been taken into custody and kept in separate cells. He is certain that they are guilty of a specific crime, but does not have sufficient evidence for a conviction. He therefore offers each one a chance to confess. If neither confesses, then he will book them both on some minor charge, and both suspects will receive a minor sentence. If both confess, then they will be prosecuted, but will receive less than the usual punishment. However, if one confesses and the other does not, then the confessor will receive a lenient sentence, whereas the other will get the most severe punishment that the law allows. The nature of the dilemma is that, in the absence of collusion, the individually rational action for each suspect is to confess.

Several attempts have been made to describe aspects of the housing market with the Prisoner's Dilemma model [Davis and Whinston (1961), and Smolensky, Becker, and Molotch (1968)]. The latter article seeks to determine the reason for the failure of blacks to acquire housing at the boundary of the ghetto, when they are willing and able to pay for it. The model is applied in the following way. A black man wishes to rent one of two adjacent houses that are vacant in a neighborhood of single-family dwelling units that have been rented to white families by profit-maximizing owners. Assume that the owners of the vacant houses do not communicate with each other. Should the owner who is approached first rent, and if so at what price? Is there a rational economic reason for the owner not to rent, when the prospective tenant is willing to pay the prevailing rent?

To simplify the exposition, assume that the two property owners perceive the situation as the nonconstant-sum game described in Table 5.9. If both of them refuse to rent to blacks, they each will continue to receive a rental of 120 dollars a month from whites. If one of the owners rents to blacks while the other does not, then the former will receive 130 dollars a month, whereas the latter will receive only 100 dollars. This reflects the assumption that the black tenant is willing to pay a slight premium only as long as his is the sole black household in the neighborhood. Finally, if both

Table 5.9. Payoff Matrix for Ghetto Expansion Problem: Nonconstant-Sum Game

Owner *A*'s Decision	Payoff to Owner *A*		Payoff to Owner *B*	
	Owner *B*'s Decision		Owner *B*'s Decision	
	Not Rent	Rent	Not Rent	Rent
Not Rent	120	100	120	130
Rent	130	110	100	110

owners rent to blacks, then the two black families will insist on rents below those now paid by whites, and each owner will receive only 110 dollars for monthly rental.

If the payoff matrix in Table 5.9 accurately describes a neighborhood rental situation, then the two owners will be caught in the Prisoner's Dilemma. And if exclusion of blacks does occur, then collusion is probably present, for the bulk of the experimental evidence so far indicates that when the Prisoner's Dilemma game is played experimentally by two people with no specific instructions that suggest collusion, they in fact do not collude, thus failing to maximize their joint profit [Rapaport (1965)]. Thus, if the two owners in Table 5.9 were acting to maximize their own profits rather than their joint profit, then we would expect them to rent to blacks. The fact that in so many neighborhoods they do not, therefore, is an indication that there may be communication and collusion to realize maximum joint profit.

To test whether the Prisoner's Dilemma model successfully accounts for the exclusion of blacks at the boundary of the ghetto, Smolensky, Becker, and Molotch (1968) interviewed a moderately large sample of real estate agents in Chicago. From their responses, payoff matrices were constructed and studied to see if they conformed to the Prisoner's Dilemma model. The conclusion reached by the study team was that the model does not have great explanatory power. For a detailed analysis and discussion of the major findings of this study, the reader should consult the Smolensky, Becker, and Molotch (1968) article that is included in the list of readings at the end of this chapter.

EXERCISES

1. Education and training are the means with which society develops its human resources, and linear programming models have been used in the planning of such programs. Consider, for example, the following numerical illustration adapted from Bowles (1969). An underdeveloped country is faced with the problem of deciding how many students to admit to each of two categories of schools: general secondary schools and vocational secondary schools. Assume that both school systems use the same types of teachers and other professional staff, and that the student input available to both is a fixed number of graduates from primary schools, p. For simplicity, assume that the country has available only a fixed number of two types of teachers: science teachers, T_s, and humanities teachers, T_h. Then if x_g and x_v denote the number of students (in thousands) to be admitted to general and vocational schools, respectively, we have the constraints

$$x_g + x_v \leqq p$$
$$a_{sg}x_g + a_{sv}x_v \leqq T_s$$
$$a_{hg}x_g + a_{hv}x_v \leqq T_h$$

and

$$x_g, x_v \geqq 0$$

The above constraints delimit an infinite number of feasible admissions plans. In order to select one that is in some sense optimal, let us assume that in the view of the educational planners in this country, a year of vocational schooling is twice as socially valuable as a year of general secondary education. Thus (ignoring dropouts) we wish to maximize

$$z = x_g + 2x_v$$

(a) What do the a_{ij} coefficients in the constraints represent?

(b) Let $a_{sg} = 4$, $a_{sv} = 10$, $a_{hg} = 22$, $a_{hv} = 11$, $p = 400$, $T_s = 3{,}400$, and $T_h = 6{,}600$. Find the optimal x_g and x_v.

(c) Interpret the dual.

(d) Change the objective function to $Z = x_g + x_v$, and solve the linear programming problem once again.

(e) What are some of the logical and statistical problems in using such a model in a real educational planning situation?

2. Linear programming models have been used effectively in studies of capital budgeting decisions [Weingartner (1963)]. A popular formulation is the following one. A local government is faced with the decision of how best to allocate its scarce budget, b_j, over the next n years, among several independent projects. It has established the net present value, c_i, of each alternative and has estimated the required outlays in dollars, a_{ij}, for each of the m projects in each of the n years. The government wishes to determine the levels at which it should financially support each of the m projects so as to maximize the total net present value of the accepted projects, while simultaneously satisfying the budgetary constraints on outlays in each of the n years.

Formulate the above capital budgeting problem as a linear programming model. Illustrate its characteristics with a numerical example, and interpret the dual.

3. Repeat the estimation carried out in Subsection 5.3.3, using only the 1950 to 1955 time series of interregional population distributions. Contrast your results with those that arise if only the 1955 to 1960 time series is used. How do these results compare with those found in Chapter 3 using regression methods?

4. Prove that in selecting gross outputs to minimize the total consumption of labor in an input-output model, subject to the production of a specified bill of goods, we are simultaneously choosing prices to maximize the value of net output, subject to a set of price-cost inequalities. Illustrate your arguments with the numerical example in Chapters 1 and 2.

5. Express the numerical dynamic input-output example in Chapters 1 and 2 as a linear programming problem in which the objective function is the maximization of available capital stock at the end of an n-year time period. Assume that consumption over the n years and the initial capital stock are given, and show how one can find a capital program that is efficient in the sense of maximizing an appropriately weighted terminal stock of capital. Interpret the dual.

6. Frequently, it is useful to study the behavior of an optimal solution to a linear programming problem when some of the parameters in the model are allowed to vary over a certain range. For example, recall the linear programming problem described in (5.16) and (5.17), and consider the impact of the following change in the objective function:

$$z = x_1 + kx_2$$

For what values of k will the original optimal solution of $x_1 = x_2 = 50$ still be optimal?

Recall the constraint equations of the dual problem set out in (5.68):

$$\begin{aligned} \tfrac{2}{5} w_1 + w_2 &\geqq 1 \\ \tfrac{1}{5} w_1 + 2w_2 &\geqq 1 \end{aligned}$$

Replace the unity on the right-hand side of the second equation by k, solve, and show that the original optimal solution will remain optimal if $\frac{1}{2} \leqq k \leqq 2$. Next, replace b_1 by $b_1 + K$ in the original formulation of the primal, and find the range of values that K may take on if the original optimal solution is to be maintained.

7. Two department stores, one large and one small, wish to locate in one of four suburban towns that are situated on either side of a large city with a "dying" Central Business District. The percentage distribution of the total metropolitan population and the distances, in miles, between the city and the four towns are as shown in the accompanying figure. Assume that the large department store will capture $\frac{4}{5}$ of the total available business if it is nearer to the market than the other store, $\frac{3}{5}$ if it and its competitor are an equal distance away from the market, and only $\frac{2}{5}$ if the small department store is nearer to the market.

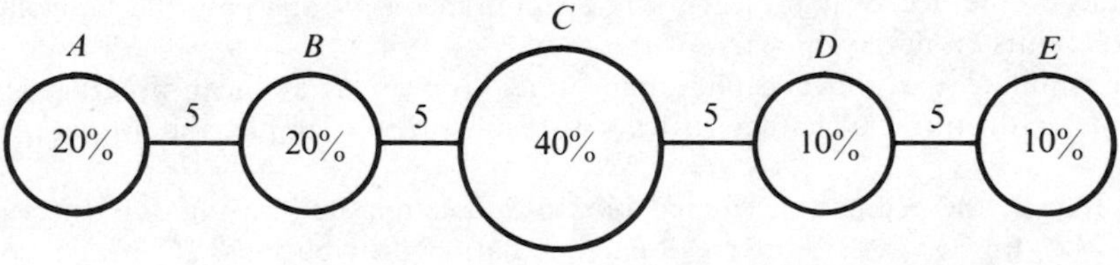

Set up the payoff matrix for this game and determine the optimal strategy for each store.

8. Given the five alternative population projections and associated probabilities in (5.76), find the min-expected loss projection for a loss function with the quadratic form

$$L(x_0, x) = \begin{cases} b(x_0 - x)^2 & \text{for } x \leqq x_0 \\ c(x_0 - x)^2 & \text{for } x > x_0 \end{cases}$$

where $c = 2b$.

Next, generalize your result to include all $c = \theta b$ for $1 \leqq \theta \leqq 16$. Contrast your findings with those that arise if the loss function is the linear one defined in (5.75).

Finally, repeat the above analysis after changing the probability distribution to a rectangular one, that is, one in which all $p_i = \frac{1}{5}$.

9. Show that if a two-by-two constant-sum game has no saddle-point, then the value of the game and the optimal mixed strategies for each of its two players may be found by solving the following equations:

$$\frac{p_1}{p_2} = \frac{a_{22} - a_{21}}{a_{11} - a_{12}} \qquad \frac{q_1}{q_2} = \frac{a_{22} - a_{12}}{a_{11} - a_{21}}$$

and

$$W = \frac{a_{11}a_{22} - a_{12}a_{21}}{a_{11} + a_{22} - (a_{12} + a_{21})}$$

where the respective a_{ij} are the elements of the two-by-two payoff matrix **A**.

10. In examing the question of why urban renewal is necessary, Davis and Whinston (1961) use the Prisoner's Dilemma game to illustrate how interdependence among the conditions of adjacent properties (the "neighborhood effect") can cause urban blight. Consider the following adaptation of their argument. Two owners of adjacent properties are confronted with the following payoff matrix as they try to determine whether or not to make an additional investment for redeveloping their property.

Owner *A*'s Decision	Payoff to Owner *A*		Payoff to Owner *B*	
	Owner *B*'s Decision		Owner *B*'s Decision	
	Invest	Not Invest	Invest	Not Invest
Invest	0.08	0.04	0.08	0.11
Not Invest	0.11	0.05	0.04	0.05

Each owner has made an initial investment in his property and another one in the stock market. Currently, the average return on both these investments is five percent a year. This situation is represented by the entries in the lower right-hand corner of the two payoff matrices, A and B. If both property owners decide to sell their stocks and invest the proceeds in redeveloping their property, they each will realize an annual eight percent return on their investment. Finally, if only one of the two owners decides to invest, then the noninvesting owner will reap some economic benefits without having to pay for them, while the investor will find that his return will be lowered because of the negative neighborhood effects caused by his neighbor's unimproved property. Thus the average return on his total investment will decline to four percent, while that of his neighbor will increase to 11 percent.

(a) Describe the decision making process and its probable results.
(b) Develop the conditions under which urban renewal is warranted.
(c) Extend your argument to the case of more than two owners and more than two properties.

REFERENCES AND SELECTED READINGS

LINEAR PROGRAMMING: THEORY

Dantzig, G. B. *Linear Programming and Extensions.* Princeton, N. J.: Princeton University Press, 1963.

Dorfman, R., P. Samuelson, and R. Solow. *Linear Programming and Economic Analysis.* New York: McGraw-Hill, 1958.

Gass, S. I. *Linear Programming*, 2d ed. New York: McGraw-Hill, 1964.

Hadley, G. *Linear Programming.* Reading, Mass.: Addison-Wesley, 1962.

LINEAR PROGRAMMING: APPLICATIONS

Bowles, S. *Planning Educational Systems for Economic Growth.* Cambridge, Mass.: Harvard University Press, 1969.

Eckaus, R. S. and K. S. Parikh. *Planning for Growth: Multisectoral, Intertemporal Models Applied to India.* Cambridge, Mass.: The M.I.T. Press, 1968.

Fisher, W.D. "A Note on Curve Fitting with Minimum Deviations by Linear Programming," *Journal of the American Statistical Association*, **LVI**, 1961, 359–362.

Herbert, J. D. and B. H. Stevens. "A Model for the Distribution of Residential Activity in Urban Areas," *Journal of Regional Science*, **II**, 1960, 21–36.

Howes, R. "A Test of a Linear Programming Model of Agriculture," *Papers of the Regional Science Association*, **XIX**, 1967, 123–140.

Lee, T. C., G. G. Judge, and T. Takayama. "On Estimating the Transition Probabilities of a Markov Process," *Journal of Farm Economics*, **XLIII**, 1965, 742–762.

Rogers, A. "Estimating Interregional Population and Migration Operators from Interregional Population Distributions," *Demography*, **IV**: 2, 1967, 515–531.

Schlager, K. J. "A Land Use Plan Design Model," *Journal of the American Institute of Planners*, **XXXI**: 2, 1965, 103–111.

Stevens, B. H. "Linear Programming and Location Rent," *Journal of Regional Science*, **III**: 2, 1961, 15–26.

Weingartner, H. M. *Mathematical Programming and the Analysis of Capital Budgeting Problems.* Englewood Cliffs, N.J.: Prentice-Hall, 1963.

THE THEORY OF GAMES: THEORY

Kemeny, J. G., A. Schleifer, J. L. Snell, and G. L. Thompson. *Finite Mathematics with Business Applications.* Englewood Cliffs, N. J.: Prentice-Hall, 1962, pp. 402–464.

Luce, R. D. and H. Raiffa. *Games and Decisions: Introduction and Critical Survey.* New York: John Wiley & Sons, 1957.

McKinsey, J. C. C. *Introduction to the Theory of Games.* New York: McGraw-Hill, 1952.

Rapaport, A. *Prisoner's Dilemma.* Ann Arbor, Mich.: University of Michigan Press, 1965.

von Neumann, J. and O. Morgenstern. *Theory of Games and Economic Behavior.* Princeton, N. J.: Princeton University Press, 1944.

Williams, J. D. *The Compleat Strategyst.* New York: McGraw-Hill, 1954.

THE THEORY OF GAMES: APPLICATIONS

Davis, O. A. and A. B. Whinston. "The Economics of Urban Renewal," *Law and Contemporary Problems,* **XXVI**: 1, 1961, 105–117.

Hotelling, H. "Stability in Competition," *Economic Journal,* **XXXIX**, 1929, 41–57.

Isard, W. and T. A. Reiner. "Aspects of Decision-Making Theory and Regional Science," *Papers of the Regional Science Association,* **IX**, 1962, 25–33.

Muhsam, H. V. "The Utilization of Alternative Population Forecasts in Planning," *Bulletin of the Research Council of Israel,* **V**: 2, 1956, 133–146.

Shubik, M. *Game Theory and Related Approaches to Social Behavior.* New York: John Wiley & Sons, 1964.

Smolensky, E., S. Becker, and H. Molotch. "The Prisoner's Dilemma," *Land Economics,* **XLIV**: 4, 1968, 419–430.

Stevens, B. H. "An Application of Game Theory to a Problem in Location Strategy," *Papers and Proceedings of the Regional Science Association,* **VII**, 1961, 143–157.

six network analysis*

In the last chapter, we considered a class of optimization problems called linear programming problems. These were expressed in matrix form as

$$\text{maximize (or minimize): } z = \mathbf{c}'\mathbf{x} \tag{6.1}$$

$$\text{subject to: } \mathbf{Ax} \leqq \mathbf{b} \text{ (or } \mathbf{Ax} \geqq \mathbf{b}) \tag{6.2}$$

$$\mathbf{x} \geqq \mathbf{0} \tag{6.3}$$

In this chapter, we shall devote our attention to those linear programming problems that can be described as flows through networks. Although such problems can be expressed in the form of (6.1), (6.2), (6.3) and solved with the simplex algorithm, more efficient solution techniques are provided by a methodology that falls under the general heading of network flow theory. This theory and the procedures for solving some of the more interesting problems in urban and regional analysis to which it applies are introduced below.

6.1 GRAPHS AND NETWORKS

In the last few decades, the generic name of *graph* has been given to descriptions of problems in terms of a collection of points, certain pairs of which are joined by one or more lines. The theory of graphs has demonstrated its usefulness in many fields that deal with the spatial arrangement of, and interlinkages between, several discrete objects. Examples may be drawn from such diverse fields as sociology, economics, and transportation planning.

* The focus of this chapter differs somewhat from that of the rest of the text. Consequently, this chapter may be omitted without loss of continuity.

6.1.1 DEFINITIONS AND NOTATION

A *graph* consists of a set of two or more points called *vertices*, each joined to one or more of the others by lines called *edges*.

The vertices of a graph will be denoted by numbers, that is, 1, 2, 3, . . . , *m*. Every edge of a graph may be defined by the pair of vertices that it joins. Thus, in Figure 6.1, edge (3, 5) is the line that connects vertex 3 with vertex 5. More than one edge may connect the same pair of vertices. A *chain* is a sequence of edges connecting vertex *i* to vertex *j*. For example, the sequence of edges (2, 3), (3, 4), (4, 5) forms a chain connecting vertices 2 and 5. A *loop* is a chain connecting a vertex to itself. Thus edges (2, 3), (3, 4), and (4, 2) form a loop. A graph is said to be *connected* if there exists a chain connecting every pair of vertices. A *connected graph* containing no loops is called a *tree*. Removing edges (4, 5), (2, 5), (2, 3), (1, 4), and (3, 4) from the graph in Figure 6.1 produces a tree.

It is often useful to attribute a precedence or orientation between pairs of vertices in a graph by considering one vertex as the point of origin and the other as the point of destination. Such a relationship may be defined by means of a *directed edge*: an edge with an arrowhead at the appropriate vertex. A directed edge originating at vertex *i* and destined for vertex *j* may be represented algebraically by (*i*, *j*). A *directed graph* is a graph composed entirely of directed edges. Figure 6.2 depicts such a graph.

A directed graph can be expressed in matrix form by means of a *node-arc incidence matrix*, **A**, say, in which the row subscripts refer to the graph's nodes and the column subscripts to its arcs. Such a matrix is formed by recording, in the column corresponding to arc (*i*, *j*), a "one" in the row corresponding to node *i*, a "minus one" in the row corresponding to *j*, and

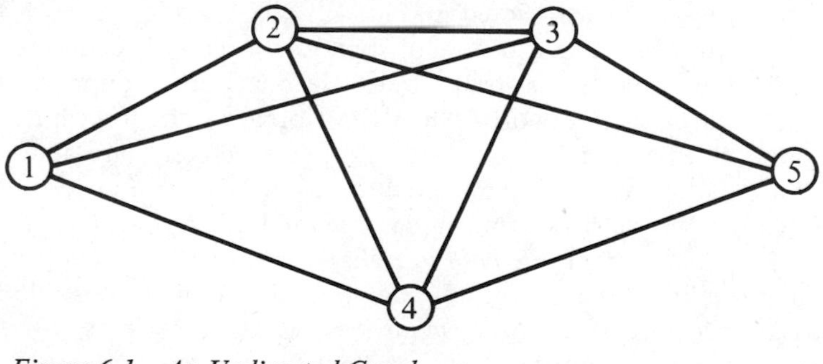

Figure 6.1. An Undirected Graph

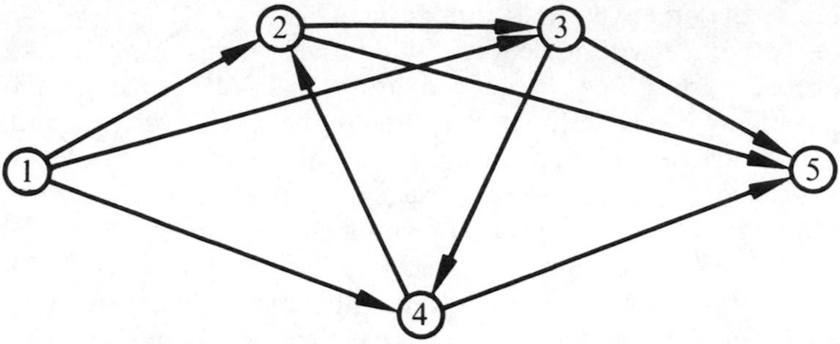

Figure 6.2. A Directed Graph

zeroes elsewhere. For example, the directed graph in Figure 6.2 has the incidence matrix

$$
\mathbf{A} = \begin{array}{c} \\ 1 \\ 2 \\ 3 \\ 4 \\ 5 \end{array}
\begin{array}{c}
\begin{array}{ccccccccc} (1,2) & (1,3) & (1,4) & (2,3) & (2,5) & (3,4) & (3,5) & (4,2) & (4,5) \end{array} \\
\begin{bmatrix}
1 & 1 & 1 & 0 & 0 & 0 & 0 & 0 & 0 \\
-1 & 0 & 0 & 1 & 1 & 0 & 0 & -1 & 0 \\
0 & -1 & 0 & -1 & 0 & 1 & 1 & 0 & 0 \\
0 & 0 & -1 & 0 & 0 & -1 & 0 & 1 & 1 \\
0 & 0 & 0 & 0 & -1 & 0 & -1 & 0 & -1
\end{bmatrix}
\end{array}
$$

Note that implicit in our definition of the node-arc incidence matrix is the convention that arcs directed out of a node are positive and arcs directed into a node are negative.

A *network* is a graph that has quantitative attributes assigned to its purely structural relationships. The *nodes* and *arcs* of a network are the vertices and edges, respectively, of its associated graph.

It is often useful to imagine that a flow of some sort occurs through the arcs of a network. For example, we speak of electrical networks, communications networks, and project networks when describing graphs for which quantitative flows of energy, messages, and effort, respectively, are associated with the arcs. One may describe these flows by nonnegative integers, $f(i, j)$, say, which denote the flow from nodes i to nodes j, via arcs (i, j), where $i, j = 1, 2, \ldots, m$ $(i \neq j)$. A *path* is a chain traversing no arc more than once. The *capacity* of an arc is simply the upper bound of the possible flow across the arc per unit time. A *capacitated network* is a network with capacity constraints imposed on its arcs. If a flow through an arc equals its capacity, we say the arc is *saturated*. The *source* of a network is a node

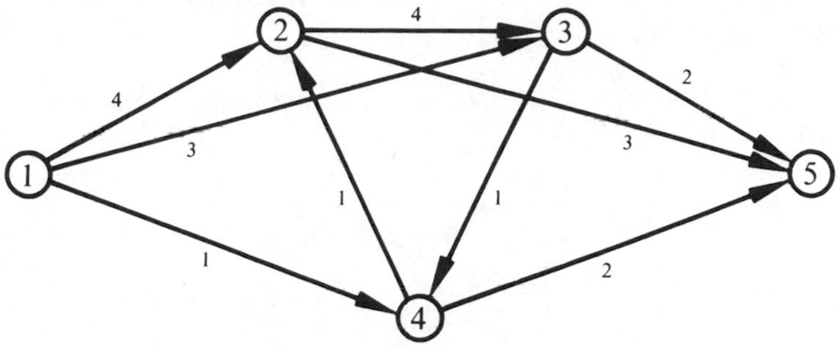

Figure 6.3. A Capacitated Directed Network

with all of its arcs directed *away* from it. The *sink* of a network is a node with all of its arcs directed *toward* it. In network problems, one typically associates the source node with the origin of a flow and the sink node with the destination of the flow. Figure 6.3 is an illustration of a directed capacitated network. The flow capacity of each arc is denoted by the number alongside it. [For example, the flow capacity of arc (2, 5) is equal to three units.]

One final concept is needed for the development of the maximal flow problem in Section 6.2. This is the definition of a *cut*. A cut, with respect to a source node, s, and a sink node, t, is a set of arcs, $(X, \bar{X})$, say, where s is in X and t is in $\bar{X}$. Such a *cut set* contains one arc of every path of positive capacity leading from s to t. The *capacity*, k, say, of the cut is the sum of the capacities of the arcs that cross the cut in the direction of the orientation of the cut. Thus the capacity of the cut $(X, \bar{X})$ is $k(X, \bar{X}) = \sum_{\substack{i \text{ in } X \\ j \text{ in } \bar{X}}} k(i, j)$. A cut with a capacity that is as small as possible is called a *minimal cut*.

In the network in Figure 6.3, the set of arcs $\{(1, 2), (1, 3), (1, 4)\}$ with $X = \{1\}$ is a cut with a capacity of eight units.

6.1.2 APPLICATION: THE STRUCTURE OF THE HIGHWAY NETWORK AROUND SAO PAULO, BRAZIL

Several studies have used concepts drawn from graph theory to examine the spatial structure of transportation networks [for example, Garrison (1960) and Kansky (1963)]. Such studies generally view a transportation network that connects m places with n routes as an undirected graph consisting of m vertices and n edges, and describe the interconnections between these with a *connectivity matrix*, $\mathbf{X}$, say, which has unities associated with pairs of places that have a direct connection and zeroes elsewhere. That is, $x_{ij} = 1$ if, and only if, an edge connects vertex i to vertex j; otherwise, $x_{ij} = 0$. Table 6.1 presents such a connectivity matrix for the highway network around Sao Paulo, Brazil, in 1940 and in 1950.

Table 6.1. Connectivity Matrix for the Highway Network around Sao Paulo, Brazil: 1940 and 1950

A. 1940 Network

Place	Direct Connections														
	1	2	3	4	5	6	7	8	9	10	11	12	13	14	15
1. Sao Paulo	0	1	0	1	0	0	1	0	0	0	0	0	0	0	0
2. Mogi das Cruzes	1	0	1	0	0	0	0	0	0	0	0	0	0	0	0
3. Sao Jose dos Campos	0	1	0	0	0	0	0	0	0	0	0	0	0	0	0
4. Atibaia	1	0	0	0	1	1	0	0	0	0	0	0	0	0	0
5. Piracaia	0	0	0	1	0	0	0	0	0	0	0	0	0	0	0
6. Braganca Paulista	0	0	0	1	0	0	0	0	0	0	0	0	0	0	0
7. Franco da Rocha	1	0	0	0	0	0	0	1	0	0	0	0	0	0	0
8. Jundiai	0	0	0	0	0	0	1	0	1	0	0	0	0	0	0
9. Campinas	0	0	0	0	0	0	0	1	0	1	1	0	0	0	0
10. Jaguariuna	0	0	0	0	0	0	0	0	1	0	0	0	0	0	0
11. Americana	0	0	0	0	0	0	0	0	1	0	0	1	1	0	0
12. Piracicaba	0	0	0	0	0	0	0	0	0	0	1	0	1	0	0
13. Limeira	0	0	0	0	0	0	0	0	0	0	1	1	0	1	1
14. Araras	0	0	0	0	0	0	0	0	0	0	0	0	1	0	1
15. Rio Claro	0	0	0	0	0	0	0	0	0	0	0	0	1	1	0

B. 1950 Network

Place	Direct Connections														
	1	2	3	4	5	6	7	8	9	10	11	12	13	14	15
1. Sao Paulo	0	1	1	1	1	0	1	1	0	0	0	0	0	0	0
2. Mogi das Cruzes	1	0	1	0	0	0	0	0	0	0	0	0	0	0	0
3. Sao Jose dos Campos	1	1	0	0	0	0	0	0	0	0	0	0	0	0	0
4. Atibaia	1	0	0	0	1	1	0	1	0	0	0	0	0	0	0
5. Piracaia	1	0	0	1	0	1	0	0	0	0	0	0	0	0	0
6. Braganca Paulista	0	0	0	1	1	0	0	0	0	0	0	0	0	0	0
7. Franco da Rocha	1	0	0	0	0	0	0	1	0	0	0	0	0	0	0
8. Jundiai	1	0	0	1	0	0	1	0	1	0	0	0	0	0	0
9. Campinas	0	0	0	0	0	0	0	1	0	1	1	0	0	0	0
10. Jaguariuna	0	0	0	0	0	0	0	0	1	0	0	0	0	0	0
11. Americana	0	0	0	0	0	0	0	0	1	0	0	1	1	0	0
12. Piracicaba	0	0	0	0	0	0	0	0	0	0	1	0	1	0	1
13. Limeira	0	0	0	0	0	0	0	0	0	0	1	1	0	1	1
14. Araras	0	0	0	0	0	0	0	0	0	0	0	0	1	0	1
15. Rio Claro	0	0	0	0	0	0	0	0	0	0	0	1	1	1	0

Source: Adapted from Gauthier (1968).

The connectivity matrix of a transportation network suggests a method for examining the connectiveness or cohesiveness of that network. For example, the ith row of the $\mathbf{X}$ matrix describes the number of transportation routes that originate from the ith place, and the kth power of $\mathbf{X}$ contains elements that indicate the number of ways the ith place may be reached from the jth place in exactly k steps. Another notion of connectivity may be obtained from the matrix $\mathbf{T}$, where $\mathbf{T} = \mathbf{X} + \mathbf{X}^2 + \mathbf{X}^3 + \cdots + \mathbf{X}^s$, and s is the lowest power to which $\mathbf{X}$ must be raised for $\mathbf{T}$ to have no zero elements. Elements of $\mathbf{T}$ describe the number of ways that place j may be reached from place i in s steps or less, and a summation across the columns (or down the rows) of this matrix provides an index of the general accessibility of a place. That is,

$$a_i = \sum_{j=1}^{m} t_{ij}$$

may be defined to be the *accessibility index* of place i, where t_{ij} is the element in the ith row and jth column of $\mathbf{T}$. Columns 1 and 4 in Table 6.2 present the accessibility indices associated with each of the 15 places in the highway network around Sao Paulo in 1940 and in 1950, respectively.

Table 6.2. Accessibility Indices, Associate Numbers, and Relative Distances of Places in the Highway Network around Sao Paulo, Brazil: 1940 and 1950

Place	1940 Network			1950 Network		
	Accessibility Index **a** (1)	Associated Number **v** (2)	Relative Distance **d** (3)	Accessibility Index **a** (4)	Associated Number **v** (5)	Relative Distance **d** (6)
1. Sao Paulo	1,455	6	44	(3,901)	5	34
2. Mogi das Cruzes	786	7	55	1,571	6	46
3. Sao Jose dos Campos	371	8	68	1,571	6	46
4. Atibaia	1,067	7	53	3,141	5	36
5. Piracaia	507	8	66	2,476	6	44
6. Braganca Paulista	507	8	66	1,589	6	48
7. Franco da Rocha	1,300	5	41	1,987	5	39
8. Jundiai	1,736	(4)	(40)	3,011	4	(30)
9. Campinas	2,951	5	41	1,412	(3)	31
10. Jaguariuna	1,159	6	54	428	4	44
11. Americana	4,939	6	46	1,348	4	36
12. Piracicaba	4,088	7	56	1,311	5	45
13. Limeira	(6,008)	7	54	1,526	5	44
14. Araras	3,574	8	66	887	6	56
15. Rio Claro	3,574	8	66	1,207	6	55

Source: Calculated using the data in Table 6.1. Programmed by Oscar Yujnovsky.

Notice that, according to this measure, the most "accessible" place in 1940 was Limeira and in 1950 was Sao Paulo.

The accessibility index of a place is but one of several measures that graph theory suggests as descriptors of the relative position of individual places in a transportation network. Two other commonly used measures are the *associated number* of a place and its *relative distance.* The associated number of place i, v_i, say, is the maximum distance between it and the other places in the network, where the *distance,* $d(i, j)$, say, between two places is defined to be the *length* of the shortest path that joins them, and where the length of a path is measured by the number of edges in it. The *relative distance* of place i, d_i, say, is simply the sum of the distances from that place to all other places. Thus,

$$v_i = \max_j d(i, j)$$

and

$$d_i = \sum_{j=1}^{m} d(i, j)$$

Columns 2, 3, 5, and 6 present, respectively, the associated numbers and relative distances of each of the 15 places in the Sao Paulo highway network in 1940 and 1950. Notice that the place with the smallest associated number, sometimes called the *central place,* was Jundiai in 1940, but changed to Campinas in 1950. The relative distance of Jundiai, however, was the shortest in both years. Thus we see that our three graph-theoretic measures are not consistent in their description of the relative position of places in the highway network. Why? Are they in fact measuring different attributes?

Several graph-theoretic measures may be applied to describe the structure of an entire transportation network. One such index is the *degree of connectivity* of the graph that describes the network. A graph with m vertices and n edges can have at most $m(m - 1)/2$ edges. Hence, we may define

$$K = \frac{m(m - 1)/2}{n}$$

to be its degree of connectivity. For example, the degree of connectivity of the Sao Paulo highway network in 1940 was

$$K(1940) = \frac{15(14)/2}{16} = 6.5625$$

and in 1950 was

$$K(1950) = \frac{15(14)/2}{22} = 4.7727$$

Since the maximum degree of connectivity for any graph is unity and the minimum is $m/2$, it is possible to compare the degrees of connectivity of different graphs by transforming the degree of connectivity values into percentages.

Another useful measure of the cohesiveness of a graph is its *index of dispersion.* This index, D, say, is the sum of the distances from all vertices to all other vertices:

$$D = \sum_{i=1}^{m} \sum_{j=1}^{m} d(i, j) = \sum_{i=1}^{m} d_i$$

For the Sao Paulo highway network, we have

$$D(1940) = 816$$

and

$$D(1950) = 634$$

We conclude, therefore, that the network was less dispersed, and therefore more cohesive, in 1950 than it was in 1940.

Finally, a graph's maximum associated number, V, say, is called its *diameter* and is a crude measure of its shape or extent. The diameter of the Sao Paulo highway network in 1940 was eight and in 1950 was six. Thus the routes that were added to the highway network during the decade made it more compact.

The use of descriptive indices, drawn from graph theory, to describe the structure of transportation networks allows us to compare one region's transportation network with another's, or to follow the development of the same transportation network over time. Alternatively, an observed transportation network may be compared to a theoretically constructed one in order, for example, to test hypotheses regarding hierarchical orderings or spatial arrangements, Finally, Kansky (1963) has produced some evidence in support of the thesis that a relationship exists between the geometry of a region's transportation network and its level of economic development.

6.2 THE MAXIMAL FLOW PROBLEM

Imagine a capacitated network through which there is a flow of, say, fluids, people, electricity, or automobiles. Deriving the maximal rate of flow from source to sink in such a network is the *maximal flow problem.*

6.2.1 THE LINEAR PROGRAMMING FORMULATION

Consider a connected network with a single source node, s, a single sink node, t, m other nodes, and n directed arcs, (i, j), with associated flows,

$f(i, j)$, and capacities, $k(i, j)$. Then

$$0 \leq f(i, j) \leq k(i, j) \quad \text{for each arc } (i, j)$$

or, in matrix form,

$$\mathbf{0} \leq \mathbf{x} \leq \mathbf{k} \tag{6.4}$$

where

$$\underset{n\times 1}{\mathbf{x}} = \begin{bmatrix} f(s, 1) \\ f(s, 2) \\ \vdots \\ f(m, t) \end{bmatrix} \quad \text{and} \quad \underset{n\times 1}{\mathbf{k}} = \begin{bmatrix} k(s, 1) \\ k(s, 2) \\ \vdots \\ k(m, t) \end{bmatrix}$$

Assume that flow is conserved at every node other than the source and sink, such that the sum of the flows directed into a node and the sum of the flows directed out of a node are equal. Since we are interested in the static and not the dynamic formulation of the problem, assume also that the flow in each arc does not change with time. Then, recalling our sign convention for arcs directed into and out of nodes, we have that

$$\sum_j f(s, j) = z$$

$$\sum_j f(i, j) - \sum_j f(j, i) = 0$$

for all arcs (i, j) with $i \neq s$ and $j \neq t$, and

$$-\sum_j f(j, t) = -z$$

We may express the above equations in matrix form as

$$\mathbf{Ax} = \mathbf{b} \tag{6.5}$$

where $\mathbf{A}$ is the $(m + 2) \times n$ node-arc incidence matrix of the network, and

$$\underset{(m+2)\times 1}{\mathbf{b}} = \begin{bmatrix} z \\ 0 \\ \vdots \\ 0 \\ -z \end{bmatrix}$$

Since the flow, z, through the network may be represented as the flow out of the source node, s,

$$z = \sum_j f(s, j)$$

or, in matrix form,

$$z = \mathbf{c}'\mathbf{x} \tag{6.6}$$

where $\mathbf{c}'$ is a row vector with unities in the positions corresponding to the arcs leading away from the source and zeroes elsewhere.

It follows that the problem of deriving the maximal flow that can be carried over this network is simply the linear programming problem of maximizing (6.6) subject to the constraints (6.4) and (6.5). Hence we can solve the maximal flow problem using the simplex algorithm. However, a much more efficient computational procedure is derivable from a network theorem called the *maximal flow-minimal cut theorem,* hereafter referred to as the *max flow-min cut theorem.*

6.2.2 THE MAX FLOW-MIN CUT THEOREM

Consider the capacitated directed network in Figure 6.3. Earlier, we noted that the capacity of the cut $\{1|2, 3, 4, 5\}$ is eight units. It is clear that this cut defines an upper bound for the maximal flow. However, its capacity does not necessarily constitute the smallest upper bound, since other cuts may have smaller capacities. By inspection, we can determine that the smallest capacities are those of the cuts $\{1, 2, 3 \mid 4, 5\}$ and $\{1, 2, 3, 4 \mid 5\}$. Each of these cuts is a minimal cut, and the value of the minimal cut is seven units. Hence the maximal flow cannot exceed this number. It also can be shown that the maximal flow cannot be less than seven units, since otherwise one could send more flow through the network. This result is formally known as the max flow-min cut theorem.

The Max Flow-Min Cut Theorem. *For any network, the value of the maximal flow that can be sent from source to sink is equal to the capacity of the minimal cut with respect to that source and sink.*

The max flow-min cut theorem provides us with a means of verifying that a given flow is optimal. One merely looks for a cut with a capacity that is equal to this flow. If such a cut is found, then the flow is optimal. Finding such a cut in large networks, however, can be a very time-consuming and tedious job. Fortunately, a more efficient method is available—the *maximal flow labeling algorithm.*

6.2.3 THE MAXIMAL FLOW LABELING ALGORITHM

The maximal flow labeling algorithm is initiated with a network carrying zero flows through all its arcs. The algorithm first sends a positive flow along any unsaturated path from source to sink. It then systematically searches for other unsaturated paths from the source node to the destination node by using a labeling procedure which moves outward from the source, labeling each node in its way. It considers all possible paths at each step until the sink is labeled. At each iteration, the labeling process determines whether an increase in the flow through the network is possible: (a) directly, or (b) by rearranging the flow pattern. Rearrangement of the flow pattern is effected by using the artifice of assigning fictional flows in the "wrong" direction along an arc. The effect of this is to cancel out part or all of the previously assigned flow in the "right" direction and to reroute it along another arc. At its termination, the labeling process defines both the maximal flow and the minimal cut. The former is the flow in the network at the end of the algorithm; the latter consists of the set of arcs leading from labeled to unlabeled nodes.

Algorithm.

1. Assign a zero flow to all arcs.
2. Label the source node $[-, \infty]$.
3. Select any labeled node i (for example, the node with the lowest index). Suppose it is labeled $[x^{\pm}, \delta(i)]$. Look for all unlabeled nodes j such that $f(i, j) < k(i, j)$ and label them $[i^{+}, \delta(j)]$, where

$$\delta(j) = \min\,[\delta(i), k(i, j) - f(i, j)]$$

   Scan all nodes that are still unlabeled. To those nodes j for which $f(j, i) > 0$, assign the label $[i^{-}, \delta(j)]$, where

$$\delta(j) = \min\,[\delta(i), f(j, i)]$$

4. Continue labeling until: (a) the sink t is labeled $[j^{\pm}, \delta(t)]$, or (b) the sink cannot be reached (that is, until no more nodes can be labeled and the sink is unlabeled). If (b), terminate the algorithm; the existing flow is maximal. Otherwise, go on to Step 5.
5. If t has the label $[j^{+}, \delta(t)]$, increase $f(j, t)$ by $\delta(t)$. If t has the label $[j^{-}, \delta(t)]$, decrease $f(t, j)$ by $\delta(t)$. Repeat this procedure for node j, and continue in this manner until the source is reached.
6. Erase the old labels and begin again at Step 2.

Example. The labeling algorithm will be illustrated for the network shown in Figure 6.4. The pair of numbers, $f(i, j)$ and $k(i, j)$, is written in that order adjacent to each arc, (i, j).

Begin the labeling algorithm by assigning a zero flow to every arc, and label the source node $[-, \infty]$. From the source, label the nodes that are joined to it by arcs of positive capacity, that is, label nodes 2 and 4. Since there are no arcs leading into the source node, select from the set just labeled the node with the lowest index, that is, node 2, and continue on with Step 4 of the algorithm. From node 2 label nodes 3 and 5. Label the sink from node 3 and increase by two units the flow along the path [(1, 2), (2, 3),

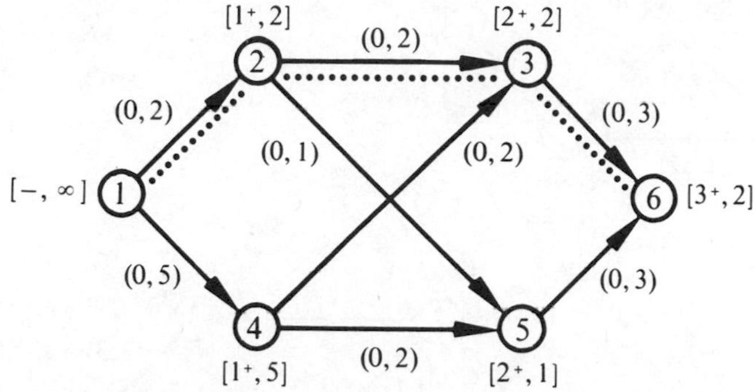

Figure 6.4. A Labeled Capacitated Directed Network

(3, 6)]. Erase the labels and begin again. Continue adding increments of flow in this manner until the sink cannot be labeled. The sequence of labelings and network flow patterns that such a procedure will produce is illustrated in Figure 6.5. The maximal flow is equal to six units, and the minimal cut set consists of the arcs (1, 2), (4, 3), and (4, 5). As a check, note that the capacity of the minimal cut equals the value of the maximal flow. Also note that the artifice of sending a flow in the "wrong" direction is used in Figure 6.5(c).

6.2.4 APPLICATION: A HOUSEHOLD ASSIGNMENT MODEL

Several model formulations in urban analysis at some point require an allocation, or matching, of m objects to n classes or regions. For example, in some simulation models of the housing market one has to assign households to sites or to a housing stock. Such problems often may be formulated as network problems and solved by means of the maximal flow labeling algorithm.

Consider, for example, a residential assignment model that matches m households with n homes according to the following procedure:

1. Each household selects a subset of preferred homes among which it is indifferent.
2. A household is assigned to one of the homes that is contained in its preferred subset.

Given the preference schedule shown in Table 6.3, is it possible to match each of the four households with a home that it prefers? If so, what is the proper allocation? How can we use an appropriate directed network and the maximal flow labeling algorithm to derive this allocation?

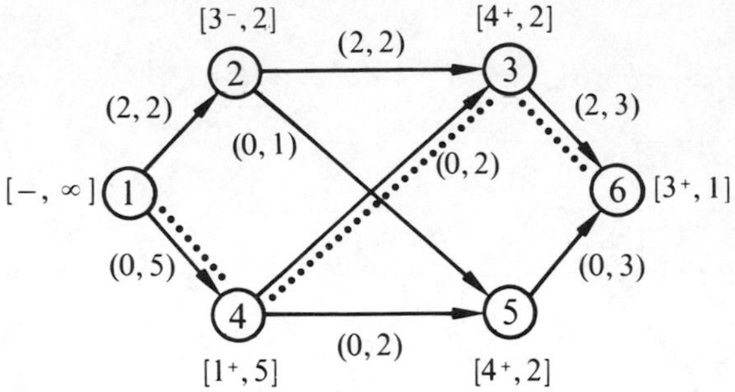

a. Second Iteration: $z = 2 + 1$

b. Third Iteration: $z = 3 + 2$

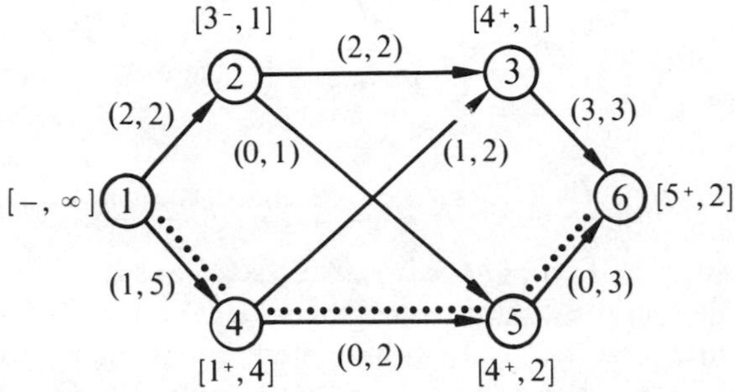

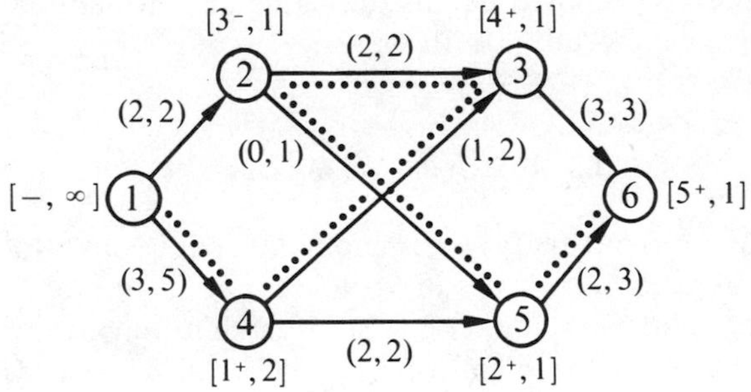

c. Fourth Iteration: $z = 5 + 1$

d. Fifth Iteration: $z = 6 + 0$

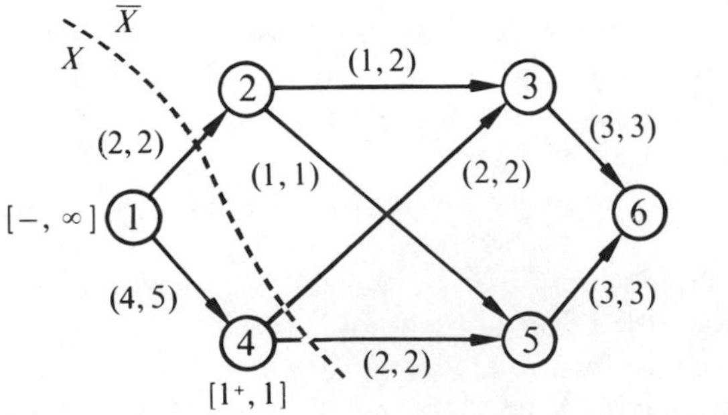

Figure 6.5. Labeling Sequence

Table 6.3. Preference Schedule (0 Denotes Non-Preference; 1 Denotes Preference.)

Households	Homes				
	1	2	3	4	5
A	0	1	0	1	0
B	0	1	0	0	0
C	1	0	1	0	1
D	1	0	1	0	0

We begin by formulating the assignment problem as a network problem. First, we introduce a source node which is connected by directed arcs with unit capacity to the $m(=4)$ "household nodes" and a sink node which is similarly linked to the $n(=5)$ "home nodes." Then we join each household node to every home node that it prefers by a directed arc with infinite capacity. Figure 6.6 illustrates the resulting directed network. Finally, we maximize the flow over this network. This yields a maximal flow of four units and the household-to-home assignment: $A \to 4$, $B \to 2$, $C \to 5$ or 1 or 3, $D \to 1$ or 3, whichever is left unassigned.

Suppose we now introduce an additional household, E, which will only accept home 3 as a residence. Is it still possible to match each household with a home? If so, what is the proper allocation?

The introduction of household E does not alter the allocation very much. Application of the labeling algorithm to the network, suitably revised by

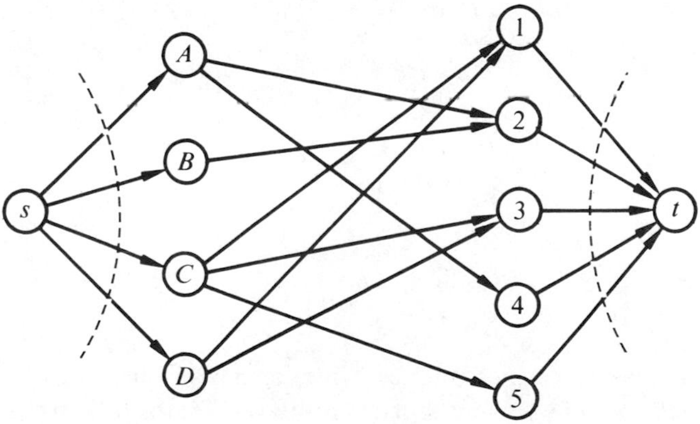

Figure 6.6. Network for an Assignment Problem

the inclusion of an additional "household node," E, yields the following assignment:

$$A \rightarrow 4$$
$$B \rightarrow 2$$
$$C \rightarrow 5$$
$$D \rightarrow 1$$
$$E \rightarrow 3$$

Suppose D now changes its preference schedule and decides that it will only accept home 4. Is it still possible to match each household with a home? The answer to this question is no, since one finds that the algorithm terminates with household A, household D, or household B unassigned to a home.

6.3 THE SHORTEST ROUTE PROBLEM

Imagine a directed network with arcs which have associated with them a measure of the "friction cost" that is incurred in crossing over them. Finding the shortest route through such a network is one of the simplest yet most useful problems in network analysis.

6.3.1 THE LINEAR PROGRAMMING FORMULATION

Once again, we take up a network with a source and a sink. Associated with each arc is a nonnegative number, $c(i, j)$, say, called the *friction cost* of the arc (i, j). Hence

$$c(i, j) \geqq 0 \quad \text{for all arcs } (i, j)$$

or, in matrix form,

$$\mathbf{c} \geqq \mathbf{0} \tag{6.7}$$

where

$$\underset{n\times 1}{\mathbf{c}} = \begin{bmatrix} c(s, 1) \\ c(s, 2) \\ \vdots \\ c(m, t) \end{bmatrix}$$

Typically, $c(i, j)$ is a measure of the distance, time, or money that must be used to get from node i to node j. The shortest route problem is to find the path of minimal friction cost from source to sink. Therefore, the network flow formulation may be visualized as a search for the routing of a unit of flow, from source to sink, that will minimize friction cost. Thus the objective is to minimize

$$z = \sum_i \sum_j c(i, j) f(i, j) \quad \text{for all arcs } (i, j)$$

subject to the conservation-of-flow equations

$$\sum_j f(s, j) = 1$$

$$\sum_j f(i, j) - \sum_j f(j, i) = 0$$

for all arcs (i, j) with $i \neq s$, $j \neq t$, and

$$-\sum_j f(j, t) = -1$$

Hence we may express the shortest route problem in matrix form, as follows:

$$\text{minimize:} \quad z = \mathbf{c}'\mathbf{x} \tag{6.8}$$

$$\text{subject to:} \quad \mathbf{Ax} = \mathbf{b} \tag{6.9}$$

$$\mathbf{x} \geqq \mathbf{0} \tag{6.10}$$

where $\mathbf{A}$ is the $(m + 2) \times n$ node-arc incidence matrix of the network, and

$$\underset{(m+2)\times 1}{\mathbf{b}} = \begin{bmatrix} 1 \\ 0 \\ \vdots \\ 0 \\ -1 \end{bmatrix} \qquad \underset{n\times 1}{\mathbf{x}} = \begin{bmatrix} f(s, 1) \\ f(s, 2) \\ \vdots \\ f(m, t) \end{bmatrix}$$

Since the shortest route problem is reducible to linear programming form, we have a solution method in the simplex algorithm. However, as in the case of the maximal flow problem, much more efficient procedures are provided by network labeling algorithms, such as the one outlined in the next section.

6.3.2 THE SHORTEST ROUTE LABELING ALGORITHM

Several alternative algorithms have been proposed for the solution of the shortest route problem. One of simplest and most elegant is described here. It is a labeling procedure which fans out from the source and successively identifies the shortest path from the source to every node until the sink is reached.

Algorithm.

1. Let M be the set of all labeled nodes at any stage, N the set of all nodes in the network, and $v(k)$ the shortest route between the source node s and node k.
2. Label the source node $[-, 0]$ and set $M = \{s\}$.
3. Find an unlabeled node j such that

$$\begin{aligned} v(j) &= \min_{x \text{ in } M} [v(x) + \min_{y \text{ in } \overline{M}} c(x, y)] \\ &= v(i) + c(i, j) \text{ for some } i \text{ in } M \end{aligned}$$

   Assign to node j the label $[i, v(j)]$. In the event of a tie, label the node with the lowest index.
4. Add node j to the set M and delete it from the set $\overline{M}$. If $\overline{M}$ is empty, terminate the algorithm. Otherwise, go to Step 3.

Example. We shall demonstrate the labeling algorithm on the network in Figure 6.7. The number along each arc (i, j) is its associated friction cost $c(i, j)$.

Begin by assigning the label $[-, 0]$ to the source node and setting $M = \{1\}$. Now scan the unlabeled nodes that are connected to the source node and identify its nearest unlabeled neighbor. This happens to be node 2, which is three units away from the source. Assign to it the label [1, 3], and enter it into the set of labeled nodes M. Next, for each node in M find its nearest unlabeled neighbor in $\overline{M}$, and out of this subset label the node that is closest to the source. Continue labeling until all nodes have been labeled, and then use the information carried along by the labels to identify both the value of the shortest path and the arcs that form it. Figure 6.8 presents the sequence of labelings that lead to the final solution for our

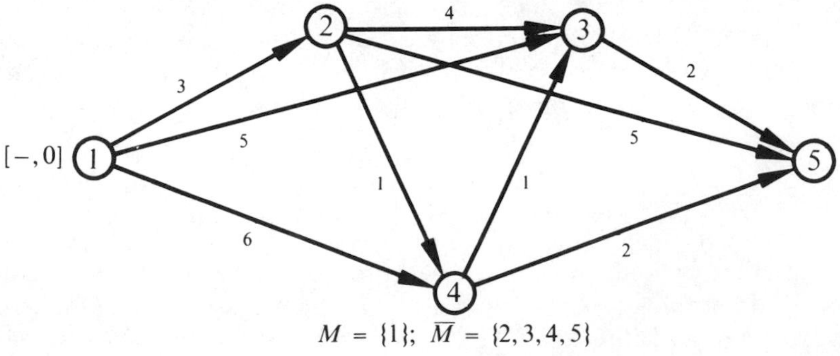

Figure 6.7. A Directed Network with Friction Costs

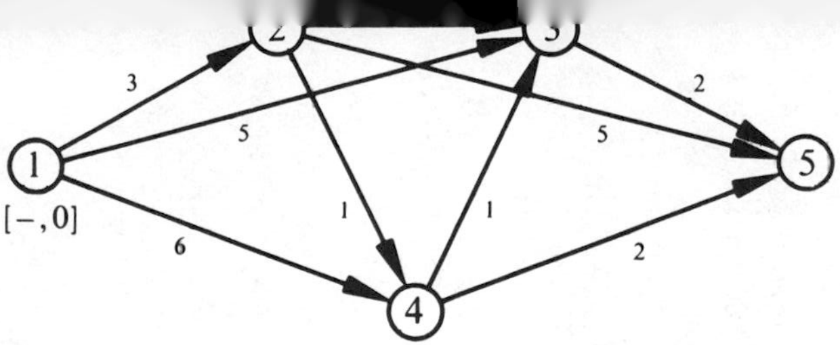

$$v(j) = \min \left\{ 0 + \min \begin{bmatrix} 3 \\ 5 \\ 6 \end{bmatrix} \right\}$$

$v(2) = 0 + 3 = 3$

$M = \{1,2\};\ \overline{M} = \{3,4,5\}$

a. First Iteration

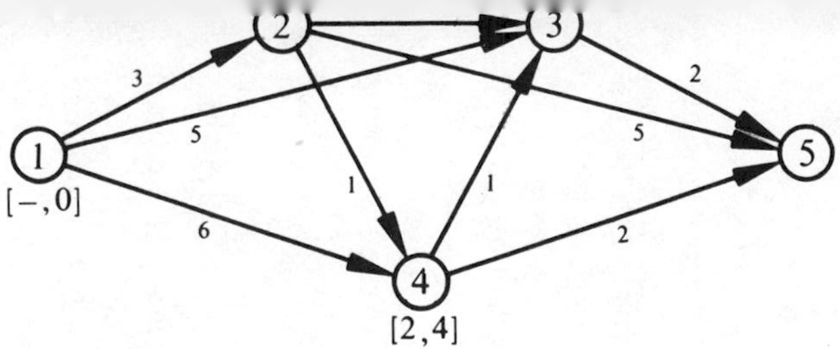

$$v(j) = \min \left\{ 0 + \min \begin{bmatrix} 5 \\ 6 \end{bmatrix};\ 3 + \min \begin{bmatrix} 4 \\ 5 \\ 1 \end{bmatrix} \right\}$$

$v(4) = 3 + 1 = 4$

$M = \{1,2,4\};\ \overline{M} = \{3,5\}$

b. Second Iteration

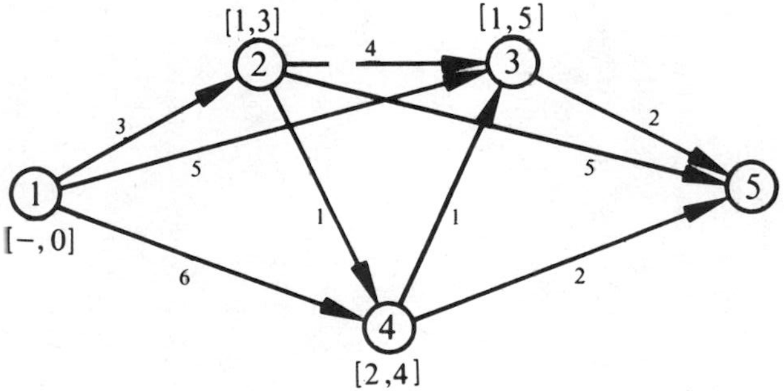

$$v(j) = \min \left\{ 0 + \min [5];\ 3 + \min \begin{bmatrix} 4 \\ 5 \end{bmatrix};\ 4 + \min \begin{bmatrix} 1 \\ 2 \end{bmatrix} \right\}$$

$v(3) = 0 + 5 = 5$

$M = \{1,2,3,4\};\ \overline{M} = \{5\}$

c. Third Iteration

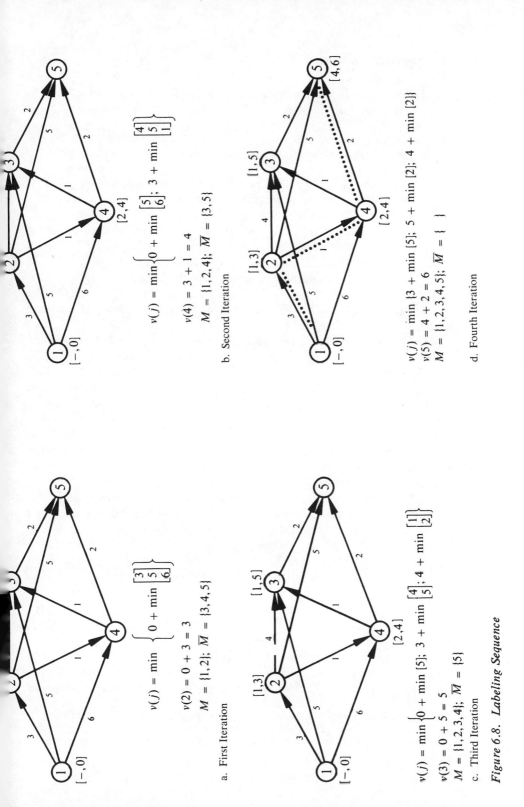

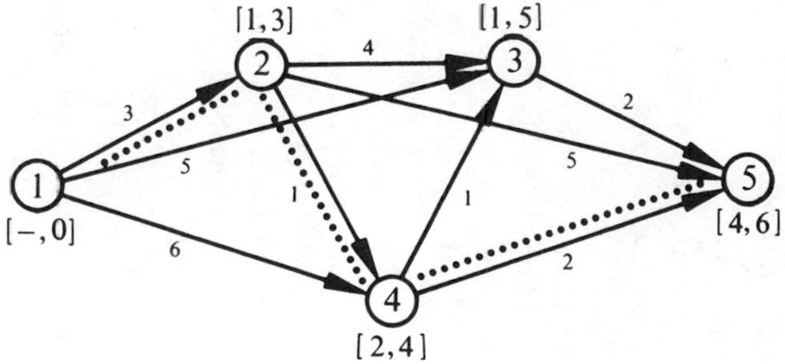

$v(j) = \min \{3 + \min [5];\ 5 + \min [2];\ 4 + \min [2]\}$

$v(5) = 4 + 2 = 6$

$M = \{1,2,3,4,5\};\ \overline{M} = \{\ \ \}$

d. Fourth Iteration

Figure 6.8. Labeling Sequence

example. The arcs in the minimal path are (1, 2), (2, 4), and (4, 5). The shortest route is six units long.

6.3.3 APPLICATION: ASSIGNING TRAFFIC TO THE ROAD NETWORK IN THE LJUBLJANA METROPOLITAN REGION IN NORTHERN YUGOSLAVIA

Traffic assignment using the shortest route algorithm is perhaps the most important analytical technique developed in transportation studies conducted during the past decade. First used in the pioneering Chicago Area Transportation Study, this technique provides the transportation planner with a systematic means for analyzing and forecasting the traffic load on a complex network. Using a network describing a transportation system and a trip volume matrix describing interzonal traffic movements, the assignment process estimates the traffic volume on each link of the system by assuming that people try to minimize travel friction (as measured by time, distance, or cost).

In the simplest formulation of the traffic assignment process, it is assumed that every person will select the shortest path from node i to node j. Relationships between flow volume and travel time are not taken into account, and capacity restrictions and turning penalties are ignored. To illustrate this method, we will use the intercommunal car and bus travel times for the Ljubljana Metropolitan Region that appear in Table 6.4, and assign to that road network the person work trips that were presented earlier in Table 1.11.

First, we use the shortest route algorithm to find the car and bus minimal paths from each node to every other node, that is, the car and bus *minimal path trees*. An example of a car and a bus minimal path tree appears in Figure 6.9. (Note the alternative minimal paths that are identified by the dotted lines.) Using such minimal path trees, we obtain the results listed in Table 6.5. Next, we recall the data on the journey to work in the Ljubljana Metropolitan Region that were set out in Table 1.11. Assuming a balanced daily flow over the network, the actual work trip volume from commune i to commune j should be the work trips made by persons living in i and working in j, plus the returning trips made by persons working in i but living in j. Thus we have the daily intercommunal person work trips in Table 6.6, and, assigning all of these trips to the bus minimal path trees, we obtain the results set out in Table 6.7.[1]

Not all person work trips will be made by bus, however. A way of diverting some of the daily person work trips in Table 6.6 to cars is provided by the notion of a *diversion curve*. A diversion curve is simply a

[1] In instances of more than one minimal path between two nodes, we have arbitrarily assigned all trips to the path with the minimum number of intervening nodes. Another valid procedure would be to distribute the total number of trips equally among the alternative minimal paths.

Table 6.4. Car and Bus Travel Times in Minutes, between Commune Centers in the Ljubljana Metropolitan Region in 1963: Direct Connections Only

Commune of Origin (From) \ Commune of Destination (To)	1. Kranj	2. Skofja Loka	3. Trzic	4. Cerknica	5. Domzale	6. Grosuplje	7. Kamnik	8. Litija	9. Ljubljana-Bezigrad	10. Ljubljana-Center	11. Ljubljana-Moste-Polje	12. Ljubljana-Siska	13. Ljubljana-Vic-Rudnik	14. Logatec	15. Vrhnika
1. Kranj		11(25)	18(26)				23(35)					25(31)			
2. Skofja Loka	11(25)											23(31)			
3. Trzic	18(26)														
4. Cerknica														29(40)	
5. Domzale							10(20)	50(105)	14(16)	22(30)					
6. Grosuplje										26(36)					
7. Kamnik	23(35)				10(20)				20(24)						
8. Litija					50(105)				37(80)	44(80)					
9. Ljubljana-Bezigrad					14(16)		20(24)	37(80)		8(10)	17(25)	15(15)			
10. Ljubljana-Center					22(30)	26(36)		44(80)	8(10)		10(15)	8(20)	5(10)		
11. Ljubljana-Moste-Polje									17(25)	10(15)					
12. Ljubljana-Siska	25(31)	23(31)							15(15)	8(20)					
13. Ljubljana-Vic-Rudnik										5(10)					20(22)
14. Logatec				29(40)											10(12)
15. Vrhnika													20(22)	10(12)	

Source: Town Planning Institute of Slovenia, Ljubljana, Yugoslavia.

Table 6.5. Car and Bus Travel Times, in Minutes, between Commune Centers in the Ljubljana Metropolitan Region in 1963: Minimal Path Travel Times

From \ To	1	2	3	4	5	6	7	8	9	10	11	12	13	14	15
1		11(25)	18(26)	97(135)	33(55)	59(87)	23(35)	77(126)	40(46)	33(51)	43(66)	25(31)	38(61)	68(95)	58(83)
2	11(25)		29(51)	95(135)	44(62)	57(87)	34(60)	75(126)	38(46)	31(51)	41(66)	23(31)	36(61)	66(95)	56(83)
3	18(26)	29(51)		115(161)	51(81)	77(113)	41(61)	95(152)	58(72)	51(77)	61(92)	43(57)	56(87)	86(121)	76(109)
4	97(135)	95(135)	115(161)		86(110)	90(120)	92(118)	108(164)	72(94)	64(84)	74(99)	72(104)	59(74)	29(40)	39(52)
5	33(55)	44(62)	51(81)	86(110)		48(62)	10(20)	50(96)	14(16)	22(26)	31(41)	29(31)	27(36)	57(70)	47(58)
6	59(87)	57(87)	77(113)	90(120)	48(62)		54(70)	70(116)	34(46)	26(36)	36(51)	34(56)	31(46)	61(80)	51(68)
7	23(35)	34(60)	41(61)	92(118)	10(20)	54(70)		57(104)	20(24)	28(34)	37(49)	35(39)	33(44)	63(78)	53(66)
8	77(126)	75(126)	95(152)	108(164)	50(96)	70(116)	57(104)		37(80)	44(80)	54(95)	52(95)	49(90)	79(124)	69(112)
9	40(46)	38(46)	58(72)	72(94)	14(16)	34(46)	20(24)	37(80)		8(10)	17(25)	15(15)	13(20)	43(54)	33(42)
10	33(51)	31(51)	51(77)	64(84)	22(26)	26(36)	28(34)	44(80)	8(10)		10(15)	8(20)	5(10)	35(44)	25(32)
11	43(66)	41(66)	61(92)	74(99)	31(41)	36(51)	37(49)	54(95)	17(25)	10(15)		18(35)	15(25)	45(59)	35(47)
12	25(31)	23(31)	43(57)	72(104)	29(31)	34(56)	35(39)	52(95)	15(15)	8(20)	18(35)		13(30)	43(64)	33(52)
13	38(61)	36(61)	56(87)	59(74)	27(36)	31(46)	33(44)	49(90)	13(20)	5(10)	15(25)	13(30)		30(34)	20(22)
14	68(95)	66(95)	86(121)	29(40)	57(70)	61(80)	63(78)	79(124)	43(54)	35(44)	45(59)	43(64)	30(34)		10(12)
15	58(83)	56(83)	76(109)	39(52)	47(58)	51(68)	53(66)	69(112)	33(42)	25(32)	35(47)	33(52)	20(22)	10(12)	

Source: Calculated using the data in Table 6.4. Programmed by Chui Kang Lu.

Table 6.6. Daily Person Work Trips between Commune Centers in the Ljubljana Metropolitan Region in 1963

From \ To	1	2	3	4	5	6	7	8	9	10	11	12	13	14	15
1		349	310		6		47		12	46	19	542	34		1
2	349		3		1				41	61	9	189	6	20	
3	310	3								1		7	1		
4										5			21	9	7
5	6	1					512	19	432	89	87	149	26	1	
6								4	9	245	12	20	51		1
7	47				512				55	37	3	35	5		1
8					19	4			12	100	171	37	9		1
9	12	41			432	9	55	12		1,069	279	816	175	4	11
10	46	61	1	5	89	245	37	100	1,069		1,398	2,028	1,809	9	116
11	19	9			87	12	3	171	279	1,398		194	232		13
12	542	189	7		149	20	35	37	816	2,028	194		249	5	51
13	34	6	1	21	26	51	5	9	175	1,809	232	249		5	132
14		20		9	1				4	9		5	5		23
15	1			7		1	1	1	11	116	13	51	132	23	

Source: Table 1.11. Travel into and out of the Ljubljana Metropolitan Region is ignored.

Table 6.7. Assignment of Total Daily Person Work Trips to the Bus Minimal Path Trees

From \ To	1	2	3	4	5	6	7	8	9	10	11	12	13	14	15
1		352	322				53					663			
2	352											327			
3	322														
4														42	
5							518		804						
6										342					
7	53				518				136						
8									68	285					
9					804		136	68		1,427	369	1,091			
10						342		285	1,427		2,048	2,745	2,836		
11									369	2,048					
12	663	327							1,091	2,745					
13										2,836					397
14				42											100
15													397	100	

Source: Calculated using the data in Tables 6.5 and 6.6. Programmed by Chui Kang Lu.

Table 6.8. Proportion of Total Daily Person Work Trips that Are Diverted to the Car Minimal Path Trees

From \ To	1	2	3	4	5	6	7	8	9	10	11	12	13	14	15
1		0.9838	0.8628	0.8393	0.9279	0.8746	0.8908	0.9215	0.6679	0.8981	0.8949	0.7457	0.9142	0.8418	0.8572
2	0.9838		0.9439	0.8528	0.8474	0.8923	0.9448	0.9305	0.7222	0.9234	0.9153	0.8164	0.9332	0.8607	0.8773
3	0.8628	0.9439		0.8432	0.9100	0.8719	0.8794	0.9129	0.7467	0.8869	0.8864	0.8036	0.9005	0.8465	0.8585
4	0.8393	0.8528	0.8432		0.7739	0.8082	0.7763	0.8898	0.7914	0.7957	0.8108	0.8628	0.7563	0.8331	0.8082
5	0.9279	0.8474	0.9100	0.7739		0.7824	0.9697	0.9631	0.6610	0.6975	0.8019	0.5826	0.8082	0.7364	0.7411
6	0.8746	0.8923	0.8719	0.8082	0.7824		0.7854	0.9259	0.8193	0.8358	0.8509	0.9238	0.8780	0.7951	0.8082
7	0.8908	0.9448	0.8794	0.7763	0.9697	0.7854		0.9529	0.7133	0.7253	0.8029	0.6321	0.8082	0.7442	0.7497
8	0.9215	0.9305	0.9129	0.8898	0.9631	0.9259	0.9529		0.9793	0.9521	0.9440	0.9532	0.9543	0.9050	0.9185
9	0.6679	0.7222	0.7467	0.7914	0.6610	0.8193	0.7133	0.9793		0.7532	0.8731	0.5000	0.8960	0.7575	0.7696
10	0.8981	0.9234	0.8869	0.7957	0.6975	0.8358	0.7253	0.9521	0.7532		0.8836	0.9899	0.9697	0.7585	0.7746
11	0.8949	0.9153	0.8864	0.8108	0.8019	0.8509	0.8029	0.9440	0.8731	0.8836		0.9653	0.9279	0.7948	0.8137
12	0.7457	0.8164	0.8036	0.8628	0.5826	0.9238	0.6321	0.9532	0.5000	0.9899	0.9653		0.9850	0.8796	0.9067
13	0.9142	0.9332	0.9005	0.7563	0.8082	0.8780	0.8082	0.9543	0.8960	0.9697	0.9279	0.9850		0.6515	0.6169
14	0.8418	0.8607	0.8465	0.8331	0.7364	0.7951	0.7442	0.9050	0.7575	0.7585	0.7948	0.8796	0.6515		0.7133
15	0.8572	0.8773	0.8585	0.8082	0.7411	0.8082	0.7497	0.9185	0.7696	0.7746	0.8137	0.9067	0.6169	0.7133	

Source: Calculated using the data in Table 6.5. Programmed by Chui Kang Lu.

Table 6.9. Daily Person Work Trips between Commune Centers in the Ljubljana

From \ To	1	2	3	4	5	6	7	8
1		343 (6)	267 (43)		6 (0)		42 (5)	
2	343 (6)		3 (0)		1 (0)			
3	267 (43)	3 (0)						
4								
5	6 (0)	1 (0)					496 (16)	18 (1)
6								4 (0)
7	42 (5)				496 (16)			
8					18 (1)	4 (0)		
9	8 (4)	30 (11)			286 (146)	7 (2)	39 (16)	12 (0)
10	41 (5)	56 (5)	1 (0)	4 (1)	62 (27)	205 (40)	27 (10)	95 (5)
11	17 (2)	8 (1)			70 (17)	10 (2)	2 (1)	161 (10)
12	404 (138)	154 (35)	6 (1)		87 (62)	18 (2)	22 (13)	35 (2)
13	31 (3)	6 (0)	1 (0)	16 (5)	21 (5)	45 (6)	4 (1)	9 (0)
14		17 (3)		7 (2)	1 (0)			
15	1 (0)			6 (1)		1 (0)	1 (0)	1 (0)

Source: Calculated using the data in Tables 6.6 and 6.8. Programmed by Chiu Kang Lu.

formula or graph that uses the comparative costs of travel by two or more different modes to establish the proportion of trips that will be made by each mode of travel. We shall assume the following formula:

$$P = \frac{1}{1 + R^5}$$

where R is the ratio of the minimal travel time by car and bus, and P is the proportion of total daily person work trips that will be made using cars. For example, consider the minimal path between commune 5 and commune 7. The travel time by bus is exactly twice as long as by car.

Metropolitan Region in 1963: Car and Bus Person Work Trips

9	10	11	12	13	14	15
8	41	17	404	31		1
(4)	(5)	(2)	(138)	(3)		(0)
30	56	8	154	6	17	
(11)	(5)	(1)	(35)	(0)	(3)	
	1		6	1		
	(0)		(1)	(0)		
	4			16	7	6
	(1)			(5)	(2)	(1)
286	62	70	87	21	1	
(146)	(27)	(17)	(62)	(5)	(0)	
7	205	10	18	45		1
(2)	(40)	(2)	(2)	(6)		(0)
39	27	2	22	4		1
(16)	(10)	(1)	(13)	(1)		(0)
12	95	161	35	9		1
(0)	(5)	(10)	(2)	(0)		(0)
	805	244	408	157	3	8
	(264)	(35)	(408)	(18)	(1)	(3)
805		1,235	2,007	1,754	7	90
(264)		(163)	(21)	(55)	(2)	(26)
244	1,235		187	215		11
(35)	(163)		(7)	(17)		(2)
408	2,007	187		245	4	46
(408)	(21)	(7)		(4)	(1)	(5)
157	1,754	215	245		3	81
(18)	(55)	(17)	(4)		(2)	(51)
3	7		4	3		16
(1)	(2)		(1)	(2)		(7)
8	90	11	46	81	16	
(3)	(26)	(2)	(5)	(51)	(7)	

Hence $R = \frac{1}{2}$, $R^5 = \frac{1}{32}$, and $P = 0.9697$. Thus 96.97 percent of the total daily person work trips made between communes 5 and 7 will be made in cars, that is,

$$512 \times 0.9697 = 495$$

person work trips, and $512 - 495 = 17$ person work trips will be made in buses. Table 6.8 presents proportions of total daily person work trips that are diverted to the car minimal path trees, and Table 6.9 lists the division of total daily person work trips into car person work trips and bus person work trips. Finally, Table 6.10 describes the assignment of these car and bus person work trips to the car and bus minimal path trees.

Table 6.10. Assignment of Total Daily Car and Bus Person Work Trips to the Car

From \ To	1	2	3	4	5	6	7	8
1		347 (6)	278 (44)				48 (6)	
2	347 (6)							
3	278 (44)							
4								
5							503 (16)	18 (0)
6								
7	48 (6)				503 (16)			
8					18 (0)			
9					442 (259)		95 (41)	208 (3)
10					84 (0)	290 (52)		108 (15)
11								
12	510 (153)	271 (55)						
13								
14				33 (9)				
15								

Source: Calculated using the data in Tables 6.8 and 6.9. Programmed by Chiu Kang Lu.

In assigning the daily person work trips to the Ljubljana Metropolitan Region's road network, we have made many simplifying assumptions. First, in calculating the car travel times, we have not given any consideration to terminal times, that is, the time spent in finding a parking space and walking from that space to the ultimate destination. In central areas, terminal times may be an important factor. Second, in calculating bus travel times, we have not taken into account the effects of the frequency of the bus service. Clearly, this is also an important variable, and some measure of waiting time should be included. Third, we have not incorporated the influences

and Bus Minimal Path Trees

9	10	11	12	13	14	15
			510 (153) 271 (55)			
					33 (9)	
442 (259)	84 (0) 290 (52)					
95 (41)						
208 (3)	108 (15)					
	1,012 (331)	477 (53)	590 (500)			
1,012 (331) 477 (53) 590 (500)		1,684 (203)	2,688 (57)	2,682 (154)		
	1,684 (203) 2,688 (57) 2,682 (154)					
						295 (102) 77 (23)
				295 (102)	77 (23)	

of factors other than travel time on the choice of travel mode, factors such as car ownership, trip purpose, and trip length. Fourth, capacity restraints have not been considered, nor have the obvious relationships between traffic volume and travel time been taken into account. Finally, our diversion curve describes a modal choice situation that is likely to be found only in a highly motorized society, such as exists in the United States today; thus it does not adequately represent the conditions that currently prevail in Yugoslavia. Some of these refinements are left as an exercise for the reader (Exercise 5).

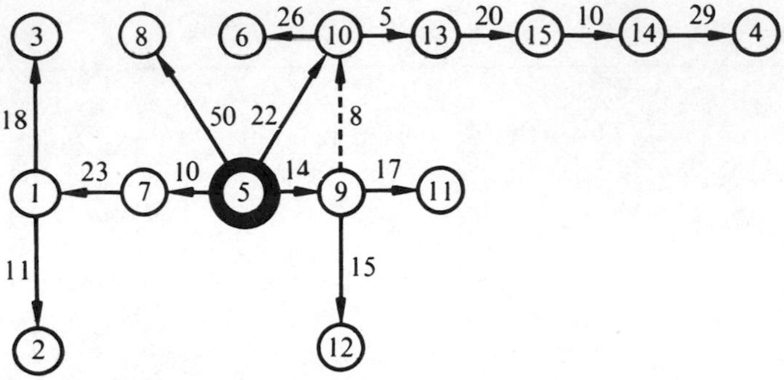

a. Car Minimal Path Tree

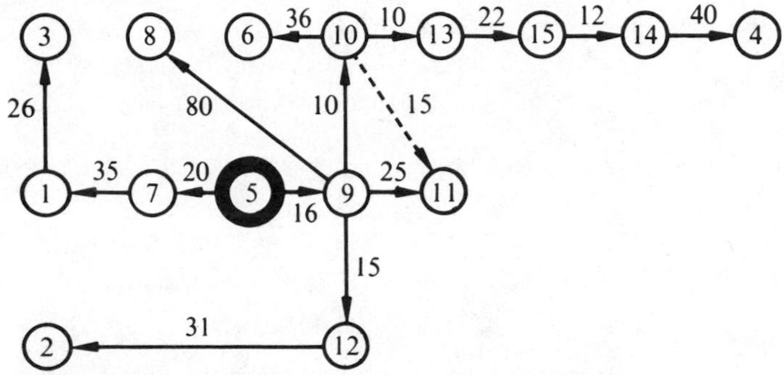

b. Bus Minimal Path Tree

Source: Calculated using the data in Table 6.4. Programmed by Chui Kang Lu.

Figure 6.9. Car and Bus Minimal Path Trees from Domzale

6.4 CRITICAL PATH ANALYSIS: THE LONGEST ROUTE PROBLEM

The need for analyzing and coordinating complex projects composed of a large number of interrelated activities has led to the development of a set of project management techniques known as *critical path methods.* Critical path analysis may be used to determine the earliest possible completion time of a large-scale project. It also can identify the most likely bottlenecks in a sequence of tasks to be performed and evaluate the effect of changes in activity completion times on the overall project duration. This information alerts project managers to the possibility of shifting resources away from less critical activities to those that have been identified as probable bottlenecks, and it allows them to assess the implications of deviations of actual from predicted completion times, for particular activities.

6.4.1 THE PROJECT NETWORK

The first step in critical path analysis is to identify all the activities that have to be performed in the course of completing a complex project. Next, a precedence relationship must be established among the activities, and the time necessary to perform each activity has to be estimated. Finally, all this information is summarized by a network in which each activity is represented as a directed arc with an associated expected activity duration time. An example of such a network appears in Figure 6.10. The time, in days, required to perform each activity is denoted by the number along each arc. The network is *node-ordered* for subsequent computational convenience [that is, for every activity (i, j), $i<j$].

Each node in the network represents an *event,* a point in time at which a particular set of activities is completed. The configuration of the directed arcs indicates the specific activity sequence that must be followed. For example, in Figure 6.10, activity (4, 6) cannot be initiated until activities (1, 4), (2, 4), and (3, 4) have been concluded, an event which is not expected to occur until 10 days after the project is started. The entire project is terminated when both activities (8, 10) and (9, 10) have been completed.

Generally, several paths lead from the starting node to the completion node of a project network. The length of each path is simply the sum of the estimated completion times for every activity on the path. Thus the longest path is the critical one. It defines the minimal length of time required to complete the entire project. In relatively simple networks, one can readily find the critical path by inspection. For complex networks, however, it becomes necessary to adopt a more efficient computational procedure.

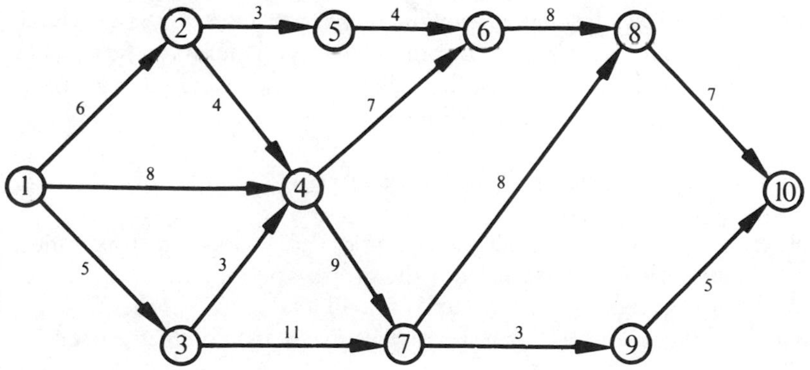

Figure 6.10. A Project Network

6.4.2 THE LINEAR PROGRAMMING FORMULATION

The critical path problem and the shortest route problem, in their linear programming form, differ only in their respective objective functions. Whereas the latter formulation seeks a minimum, the former searches for a maximum. Hence, to express the critical path problem in linear programming form, we need only to replace the "minimize" in (6.8) with a "maximize." The constraints in (6.9) and (6.10) remain unchanged.

As in the case of the shortest route, the critical path, or longest route, problem can be solved with the simplex algorithm. But more efficient procedures rely on network labeling algorithms, such as the one presented in Subsection 6.4.4.

6.4.3 DEFINITIONS

Before proceeding with an exposition of the critical path labeling algorithm, a few definitions are in order.

Recall that a *tree* is a connected graph containing no loops. An *early tree* is a tree that contains all the nodes of a network, such that every node is connected to the source by a path of maximal length. A *late tree* is an early tree with respect to the sink.

The *earliest occurrence time* of an event is the time at which the event will be realized if preceding activities are started as early as possible. The *latest occurrence time* of an event is the latest time at which the event may be realized without delaying the completion of the overall project beyond its earliest occurrence time.

Slack time is the difference between the latest and earliest occurrence times of an event.

The *earliest starting time* of an activity (i, j) is the earliest occurrence time of event i. The *latest completion time* of an activity (i, j) is the latest occurrence time of event j. The *earliest completion time* of an activity is the sum of its earliest starting time and its activity duration time. The *latest starting time* of an activity is the difference between its latest completion time and its activity duration time.

6.4.4 THE CRITICAL PATH LABELING ALGORITHM

The critical path labeling algorithm begins by node ordering the project network. It then moves outward from the origin node to find an early tree and moves backward from the sink node to find a late tree. It identifies the earliest and the latest occurrence times of each event and connects the events for which these two times are equal, that is, events for which the slack time is zero. The resulting path is the *critical path.*

Algorithm.

Early Tree:

1. Let $t(i, j)$ denote the time required to perform activity (i, j); let $L(i)$ denote the earliest occurrence time of event i; let $L^s(i, j)$ denote the earliest starting time of activity (i, j); and let $L^c(i, j)$ denote the earliest completion time of activity (i, j). Set all $L(i) = 0$, and start the algorithm with $i = 1$.
2. Scan activity (i, j), and set

$$L^s(i, j) = L(i) \quad \text{and} \quad L^c(i, j) = L(i) + t(i, j)$$

If $L^c(i, j) > L(j)$, set $L(j) = L^c(i, j)$ and go to Step 3; otherwise, do nothing and go to Step 3.

3. Look for another activity, (i, k), say. If one exists, go to Step 2; otherwise, increase i by one. If the new $i < n$, the number of nodes in the network, go to Step 2; otherwise, go to Step 4.

Late Tree:

4. Let $U(i)$ denote the latest occurrence time of event i; let $U^s(i, j)$ denote the latest starting time of activity (i, j); and let $U^c(i, j)$ denote the latest completion time of activity (i, j). Set all $U(i) = L(n)$, and begin with $j = n$.
5. Scan activity (i, j), and set

$$U^c(i, j) = U(j) \quad \text{and} \quad U^s(i, j) = U(j) - t(i, j)$$

If $U^s(i, j) < U(i)$, set $U(i) = U^s(i, j)$, and go to Step 6; otherwise, do nothing and go to Step 6.

6. Look for another activity, (k, j), say. If one exists, go to Step 5; otherwise, decrease j by one. If the new $j > 1$, go to Step 5; otherwise, go to Step 7.

Critical Path:

7. Identify the path leading from source to sink over nodes for which $L(i) = U(i)$. This is the critical path.

Example. Let us illustrate the critical path labeling algorithm on the project network shown in Figure 6.11.

Set all $L(i) = 0$ and begin with $i = 1$. Scan activity (1, 2) and set $L^s(1, 2) = L(1) = 0$. Set $L^c(1, 2) = L(1) + 6 = 6$. Since $L^c(1, 2) > L(2)$, set $L(2) = L^c(1, 2) = 6$. Repeat this procedure for activities (1, 4) and (1, 3). This results in $L(4) = 8$ and $L(3) = 5$. At this point, increase i by one and scan the activities leading from node 2. Repeated application of

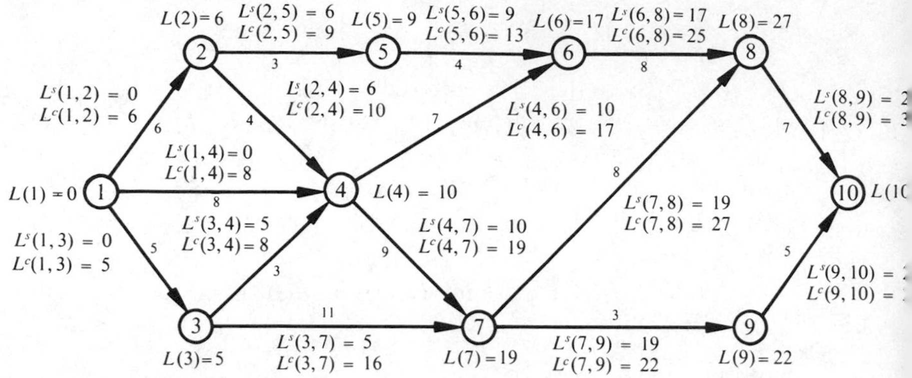

a. Early Tree Labels

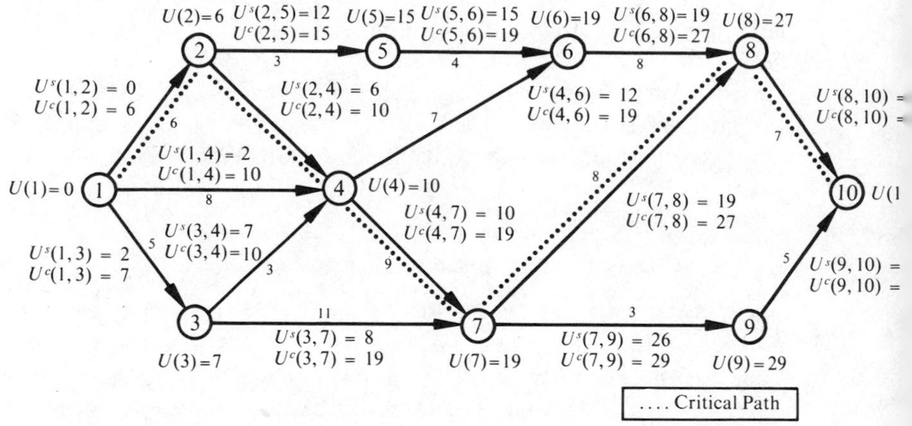

b. Late Tree Labels and the Critical Path

Figure 6.11. The Early Tree, the Late Tree, and the Critical Path

the early tree portion of the algorithm results in the labelings shown in Figure 6.11(a). [Notice that $L(4)$ gets changed to 10.]

The late tree portion of the algorithm is now initiated. Set all $U(i) = 34$ and begin with $j = 10$. Scan activity (9, 10) and set $U^c(9, 10) = U(10) = 34$. Set $U^s(9, 10) = U(10) - 5 = 29$. Since $U^s(9, 10) < U(9)$, set $U(9) = U^s(9, 10) = 29$. Repeat this procedure for activity (8, 10). The result is $U(8) = 27$. At this point, decrease j by one and scan the activities leading into node 9. Repeated application of the late tree portion of the algorithm results in the labelings shown in Figure 6.11(b).

Now find the path connecting nodes with zero slack. The critical path is defined by the arcs (1, 2), (2, 4), (4, 7), (7, 8), and (8, 10). The minimal project duration time is 34 days.

6.4.5 PROGRAM EVALUATION AND REVIEW TECHNIQUE (PERT)

An extension of critical path analysis, the Program Evaluation and Review Technique (PERT), may be used to determine the probabilities associated with various project duration times. In this method, each activity's duration time is viewed as a random variable drawn from a hypothesized probability distribution (generally the beta distribution). Two numbers are now associated with each activity: its mean duration time, $\bar{t}$, and its variance, s^2. Commonly, these are calculated on the basis of the "optimistic," "most likely," and "pessimistic" estimates of the time required to complete a specified activity. In particular, if the duration variable is assumed to approximately follow a beta distribution (a nonsymmetric bell-shaped distribution), then it can be shown that the mean activity duration is approximately

$$\bar{t} = \frac{a + 4m + b}{6}$$

and the variance is approximately

$$s^2 = \left[\frac{b - a}{6}\right]^2$$

where

m = most likely estimate of activity duration time;
a = optimistic estimate of activity duration time; and
b = pessimistic estimate of activity duration time

With estimates of the mean activity duration time and variance for each activity in the project network, a few simplifying assumptions allow the application of the Central Limit Theorem of probability theory. This is to establish that the overall project duration time is a random variable drawn from an approximately normal distribution with a mean and variance equal to, respectively, the sum of the individual activity duration means and the sum of the individual variances along the critical path. With this information, standard tables for normal deviates may be entered to obtain the probabilities associated with various completion times.

Example. Consider the project network in Figure 6.12. This same network appears in Figure 6.10. There, one number is associated with each activity. Here there are three. These numbers denote, respectively, the optimistic, most likely, and pessimistic estimates of each activity's duration time. Find the probabilities of meeting various project deadlines.

Consider activity (1, 2), for example. The optimistic estimate of this

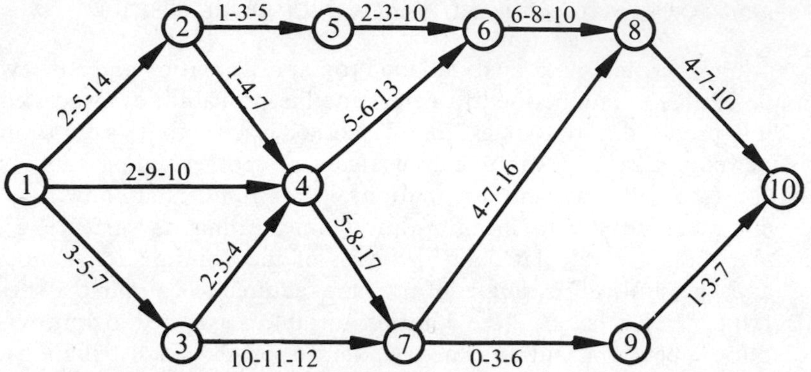

Figure 6.12. PERT Project Network

activity's duration is two days, the most likely estimate is five days, and the pessimistic estimate is 14 days. Hence, for this activity we find the following approximate mean duration time and variance:

$$\bar{t}(1, 2) = \frac{2 + 20 + 14}{6} = 6$$

$$s^2(1, 2) = \left[\frac{14 - 2}{6}\right]^2 = 4$$

In a similar manner, we may find the means and variances for all other activities in the network. Notice that the numbers associated with the arcs of the network in Figure 6.10 are, in fact, mean activity duration times. Thus we do not need to recompute the critical path but may use the solution found earlier. Summing the means and variances of activities lying on this critical path, we have the following mean and variance for the total project duration time:

$$\bar{T} = 34$$

$$S^2 = 14$$

With the mean and variance of a normally distributed project duration time, we may compute the normal deviate Z:

$$Z = \frac{T - \bar{T}}{\sqrt{S^2}}$$

and enter an appropriate statistical table to find the associated probability.

Thus, to find the probability of completing the project in 30 days or less, for example, we compute

$$Z = \frac{30 - 34}{\sqrt{14}} = -1.07$$

and find that the associated probability is 0.15. The probability of completing the project in 31 days or less is 0.21, and so on.

The same computations may be applied to find the probabilities of completing, on schedule, any of the intervening events in a project network. Indeed, one can find the means and variances, and therefore the probabilities, associated with the various earliest and latest occurrence times. For example, for the project network in Figure 6.12, the probability of event 9 occurring on or before its expected latest occurrence time of 29 days is 0.99.

6.4.6 APPLICATION: A PERT ANALYSIS OF AN URBAN DEVELOPMENT PLAN PROJECT IN SAN ANTONIO, CHILE

Table 6.11 presents the data for the PERT network in Figure 6.13, which describes the sequence of activities that are to be carried out by the city of San Antonio, Chile, in the course of preparing an urban development plan. The optimistic, most likely, and pessimistic estimates of activity duration times are taken from a recent study by Lopez and Wellborn (1966), who assumed that an office staff consisting of two principals and two assistants would be assigned to each activity. The reader should confirm that the expected duration time of the overall project is 202 days and that there exist three critical paths (Exercise 7).

Table 6.11. Activity Duration Times for the Planning Studies of San Antonio, Chile

Starting Event	Completion Event	Activity Description	Estimates of Duration Time (in Days)		
			Optimistic	Most Likely	Pessimistic
1	2	Obtain Primary Information	5	8	15
1	3	Obtain Secondary Information	10	15	20
1	4	Obtain Tertiary Information	15	20	25
1	25	Obtain Plans for Specific Projects	5	8	15
1	30	Conduct and Analyze Soil Study	10	15	20
1	55	Obtain Existing Master Plan	1	3	5
2	5	Extract Regional Data from Primary Information	5	10	15
2	10	Extract Communal Census Data	1	2	3
2	26	Extract Urban Data from Primary Information	5	8	12

Table 6.11. Activity Duration Times for the Planning Studies of San Antonio, Chile (Continued)

Starting Event	Completion Event	Activity Description	Estimates of Duration Time (in Days)		
			Optimistic	Most Likely	Pessimistic
2	34	Extract Housing Data from Primary Information	3	6	10
3	5	Extract Regional Data from Secondary Information	1	2	3
3	19	Extract and Display Communal and Urban Industrial Data from Secondary Information	1	2	3
3	26	Extract Urban Data from Secondary Information	1	2	3
4	19	Extract and Display Communal and Urban Industrial Data from Tertiary Information	1	2	3
4	26	Extract and Display Urban Data from Tertiary Information	1	2	3
4	33	Extract and Analyze Community Facilities Data from Tertiary Information	3	6	10
4	35	Extract and Analyze Infrastructure Data from Tertiary Information	3	6	10
4	54	Extract and Apply Standards for Housing, Community Facilities, and Infrastructure	5	8	15
5	6	Analyze Regional Data	5	10	15
6	7	Determine Boundaries of Micro-Region	1	2	3
7	8	Determine Areas of Future Growth	4	6	12
8	9	Prepare Drawings and Text for Regional Analysis	5	10	15
9	23	Administrative Delay	0	0	1
10	11	Display 1960 Census Data	5	8	12
10	12	Display 1940 and 1952 Census Data	5	8	12
11	13	Analyze 1960 Census Data for Survey of Population	1	3	6
11	24	Analyze 1960 Census Data for Projection of Population	1	3	5
12	24	Analyze 1940 and 1952 Census Data for Projection of Population	1	3	5
13	14	Determine Sample for Population Survey	1	2	3
14	15	Design Survey	5	8	12
15	16	Conduct Survey	3	5	15
16	17	Display Survey Data	8	15	20
17	18	Analyze Survey Data and Prepare Preliminary Text of Report	10	15	20

Table 6.11. Activity Duration Times for the Planning Studies of San Antonio, Chile (Continued)

Starting Event	Completion Event	Activity Description	Estimates of Duration Time (in Days)		
			Optimistic	Most Likely	Pessimistic
18	32	Determine Housing Demand	2	5	8
18	44	Determine Labor Supply	1	2	3
18	54	Determine Partial Definition of Neighborhoods	3	5	8
18	60	Estimate Social Benefits	5	8	10
19	20	Design Survey of Industries	3	5	10
19	36	Determine Partial Estimate of the Demand for Community Facilities	1	2	3
19	37	Determine Partial Estimate of the Demand for Infrastructure	1	2	3
20	21	Conduct Survey of Industries	5	10	20
21	22	Determine Job Opportunity Characteristics and Prepare the Text of Report	3	8	12
22	23	Prepare Microregion Summary Report	3	8	12
23	64	Prepare Section for Final Report	0	0	1
24	32	Analyze the Effect of Projected Population on the Demand for Housing	3	5	8
24	44	Analyze Population Projection by Occupational Groups	1	2	3
25	37	Analyze the Effect of Projected Population on the Demand for Infrastructure	5	10	15
26	27	Prepare Field Study	3	5	8
27	28	Conduct Field Study	3	5	10
28	29	Display Field Study Data	5	10	15
29	30	Analyze Field Study Data and Other Urban Data	3	5	10
29	33	Determine Supply of Community Facilities	1	3	5
29	35	Determine Infrastructure Supply	1	3	5
29	36	Determine Partial Demand for Community Facilities	1	3	5
29	37	Administrative Delay	1	3	5
29	42	Determine Supply of Construction Materials	3	5	8
29	46	Determine Supply of Construction Organizations	3	5	8
29	54	Determine Partial Definition of Neighborhoods	3	5	8
30	31	Prepare Urban Data Report	5	8	10
31	64	Prepare Section for Final Report	0	0	1
32	39	Project Housing Demand	1	3	5

Table 6.11. Activity Duration Times for the Planning Studies of San Antonio, Chile (Continued)

Starting Event	Completion Event	Activity Description	Estimates of Duration Time (in Days)		
			Optimistic	Most Likely	Pessimistic
33	40	Project Supply of Community Facilities	1	2	3
34	36	Determine Partial Estimate of the Demand for Community Facilities	1	3	5
34	37	Determine Partial Estimate of the Demand for Infrastructure	1	2	3
34	39	Project Housing Supply	1	3	5
35	38	Project Infrastructure Supply	1	2	3
36	40	Project Demand for Community Facilities	1	2	3
37	38	Project Demand for Infrastructure	1	2	3
38	41	Prepare Infrastructure Summary	3	5	8
39	41	Prepare Housing Summary	3	5	8
40	41	Prepare Community Facilities Summary	3	5	8
41	43	Analyze Development Requirements for Demand on Construction Materials	5	8	10
41	45	Analyze Development Requirements for Demand on Labor Force	5	8	10
41	47	Analyze Development Requirements for Demand on Construction Organizations	5	8	10
41	52	Summarize Urban Development Requirements	5	8	10
42	48	Project Supply of Construction Materials	2	4	6
43	48	Project Demand for Construction Materials	2	4	6
44	49	Project Labor Supply	3	5	8
45	49	Project Labor Demand	3	5	8
46	50	Project Supply of Construction Organizations	2	4	6
47	50	Project Demand for Construction Organizations	2	4	6
48	51	Prepare Construction Materials Summary	3	5	8
49	51	Prepare Labor Summary	2	4	6
50	51	Prepare Construction Organizations Summary	3	5	8
51	52	Summarize Urban Development Capacities	5	8	10
52	53	Prepare Quantitative Program for Urban Development	10	15	20
53	54	Administrative Delay	0	0	1
54	56	Prepare Locational Program for Urban Development	10	15	20
55	57	Analyze Existing Master Plan	3	5	8
56	57	Propose Changes in Master Plan	1	8	10
56	58	Estimate Project Costs	10	15	20

Table 6.11. Activity Duration Times for the Planning Studies of San Antonio, Chile (Continued)

Starting Event	Completion Event	Activity Description	Estimates of Duration Time (in Days)		
			Optimistic	Most Likely	Pessimistic
56	59	Prepare Recommendations for Organization, Administration, and Maintenance	5	8	10
56	60	Determine Benefits of Each Project	5	8	10
57	64	Prepare Section for Final Report	0	0	1
58	60	Estimate Project Administration Costs	5	8	10
59	60	Estimate Operating Costs	5	8	10
60	61	Conduct Cost-Benefit Analysis	10	15	20
61	62	Prepare Cost-Benefit Report	10	15	20
61	63	Prepare Investment Schedule	5	8	10
62	64	Prepare Section for Final Report	0	0	1
63	64	Prepare Final Report	5	10	15
64	65	Print Final Report	5	10	15

Source: Lopez and Wellborn (1966).

6.5 THE TRANSPORTATION PROBLEM

Transportation problems are a class of cost minimization problems that may be formulated as follows: A known quantity of a particular commodity is available at each of m origins and is demanded at each of n destinations. Given a table of origin-destination unit shipping costs, determine the shipping schedule that minimizes total shipment costs, such that supplies at origins are not exceeded and demands at destinations are satisfied. Commonly it is assumed, without loss of generality, that the total quantity supplied is equal to the total quantity demanded.

6.5.1 THE LINEAR PROGRAMMING FORMULATION

Mathematically, the transportation problem may be stated as follows: Find a set of $f(i, j) \geqq 0$ such that $z = \sum_i \sum_j c(i, j)f(i, j)$ is minimized, subject to the $m + n$ constraints

$$\sum_j f(i, j) = a(i) \quad a(i) > 0 \qquad i = 1, \ldots, m$$

$$\sum_i f(i, j) = b(j) \quad b(j) > 0 \qquad j = 1, \ldots, n$$

$$\sum_i a(i) = \sum_j b(j)$$

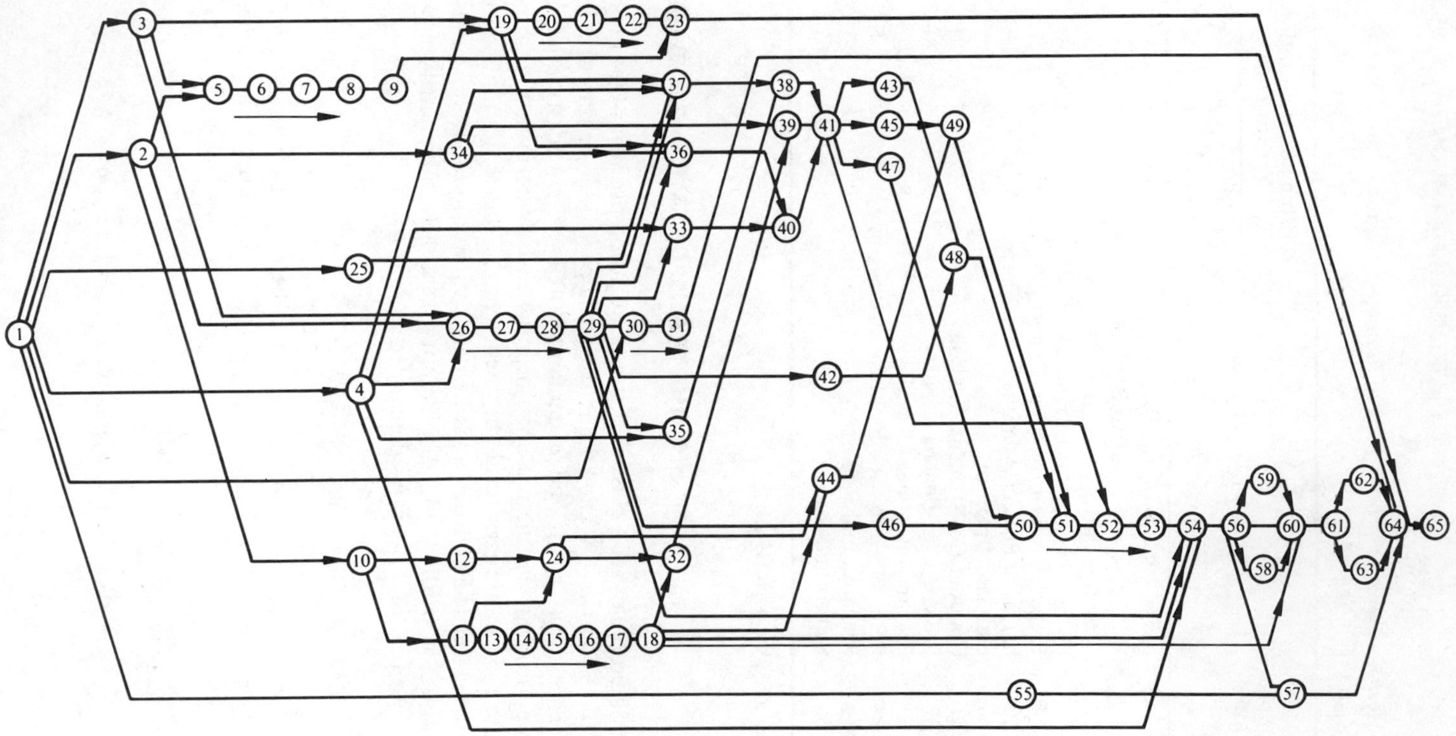

Source: Table 6.11

Figure 6.13. PERT Network: San Antonio, Chile

where

$f(i, j)$ = quantity of commodity shipped from origin i to destination j;
$c(i, j)$ = cost of shipping a unit of the commodity from origin i to destination j;
$a(i)$ = supply of commodity at origin i;
$b(j)$ = demand for commodity at destination j;
z = total shipment costs

Thus, in matrix form, we have

$$\text{minimize:} \quad z = \mathbf{c}'\mathbf{x} \tag{6.11}$$

$$\text{subject to:} \quad \mathbf{A}\mathbf{x} = \mathbf{b} \tag{6.12}$$

and

$$\mathbf{x} \geqq \mathbf{0} \tag{6.13}$$

where

$$\underset{mn\times 1}{\mathbf{x}} = \begin{bmatrix} f(1,1) \\ f(1,2) \\ \vdots \\ f(1,n) \\ f(2,1) \\ \vdots \\ f(2,n) \\ \vdots \\ f(m,n) \end{bmatrix} \qquad \underset{(m+n)\times 1}{\mathbf{b}} = \begin{bmatrix} a(1) \\ a(2) \\ \vdots \\ a(m) \\ b(1) \\ \vdots \\ b(n) \end{bmatrix} \qquad \underset{mn\times 1}{\mathbf{c}} = \begin{bmatrix} c(1,1) \\ c(1,2) \\ \vdots \\ c(1,n) \\ c(2,1) \\ \vdots \\ c(2,n) \\ \vdots \\ c(m,n) \end{bmatrix}$$

and

$$\mathbf{A} = \begin{bmatrix} \mathbf{1}_n' & \mathbf{0} & \cdots & \mathbf{0} \\ \mathbf{0} & \mathbf{1}_n' & \cdots & \mathbf{0} \\ \vdots & \vdots & \ddots & \vdots \\ \mathbf{0} & \mathbf{0} & \cdots & \mathbf{1}_n' \\ \mathbf{I}_n & \mathbf{I}_n & \cdots & \mathbf{I}_n \end{bmatrix}$$

where $\mathbf{1}_n'$ is an n-element row vector of ones, and $\mathbf{I}_n$ is an identity matrix of order n.

Transportation problems originally were formulated and solved as linear programming problems. A sizeable body of literature describing their application to military and business problem-solving attests their importance. Recent efforts to treat transportation problems as network flow problems have demonstrated that the latter formulation leads to an algorithm that is generally more efficient than the traditional simplex solution method of linear programming. Such an algorithm is the primal-dual network algorithm developed by Ford and Fulkerson (1962).

6.5.2 DUALITY AND COMPLEMENTARY SLACKNESS

Associated with every *primal* transportation problem of minimizing total shipping costs, $z = \sum_i \sum_j c(i, j) f(i, j)$, is a *dual* pricing problem of maximizing the sum of the total value of the shipment at all origins, $\sum_i u(i)a(i)$, and at all destinations, $\sum_j v(j)b(j)$. The dual variable $u(i)$ denotes the commodity's unit price at origin i. The dual variable $v(j)$ denotes the commodity's unit price at destination j. To complete the statement of the dual problem, we introduce the constraints

$$u(i) + v(j) \leqq c(i, j) \left\} \begin{array}{l} i = 1, \ldots, m \\ j = 1, \ldots, n \end{array} \right.$$

Summarizing the primal-dual relationship, we have then:

Primal

$$\left.\begin{array}{ll} \text{minimize:} & z = \sum_i \sum_j c(i, j) f(i, j) \\ \text{subject to:} & \sum_j f(i, j) = a(i) \\ & \sum_i f(i, j) = b(j) \\ & \sum_i a(i) = \sum_j b(j) \\ & f(i, j) \geqq 0 \\ & a(i) > 0 \\ & b(j) > 0 \end{array}\right\} \quad \begin{array}{l} i = 1, \ldots, m \\ j = 1, \ldots, n \end{array}$$

Dual

$$\left.\begin{array}{ll} \text{maximize:} & Z = \sum_i u(i)a(i) + \sum_j v(j)b(j) \\ \text{subject to:} & u(i) + v(j) \leqq c(i, j) \\ & u(i), v(j) \quad \text{unrestricted in sign} \\ & a(i) > 0 \\ & b(j) > 0 \end{array}\right\} \quad \begin{array}{l} i = 1, \ldots, m \\ j = 1, \ldots, n \end{array}$$

In the preceding chapter, we established the equality of the optimal solutions to the primal and dual problems (when an optimal solution exists).

Thus for the specific optimal values of $\bar{f}(i, j)$ in the primal, and the corresponding optimal values for $\bar{u}(i, j)$ and $\bar{v}(i, j)$ in the dual, we have the equality

$$\sum_i \sum_j c(i, j)\bar{f}(i, j) = \sum_i \bar{u}(i)a(i) + \sum_j \bar{v}(j)b(j)$$

Since the constraints hold in an optimal solution,

$$a(i) = \sum_j \bar{f}(i, j) \qquad b(j) = \sum_i \bar{f}(i, j)$$

hence,

$$\sum_i \sum_j c(i, j)\bar{f}(i, j) = \sum_i \bar{u}(i) \sum_j \bar{f}(i, j) + \sum_j \bar{v}(j) \sum_i \bar{f}(i, j)$$

and

$$\sum_i \sum_j \{c(i, j) - [\bar{u}(i) + \bar{v}(i)]\}\bar{f}(i, j) = 0$$

Notice that if $\bar{f}(i, j) > 0$, then $\bar{u}(i) + \bar{v}(j) = c(i, j)$, and if $\bar{u}(i) + \bar{v}(j) < c(i, j)$, then $\bar{f}(i, j) = 0$. These relationships are the *complementary slackness conditions*. They provide the fundamental rationale for the primal-dual network algorithm described below.

6.5.3 THE TRANSPORTATION PROBLEM AS A NETWORK PROBLEM

Consider the network statement of the transportation problem in Figure 6.14. We represent the origins by a set of m nodes and the destinations by a set

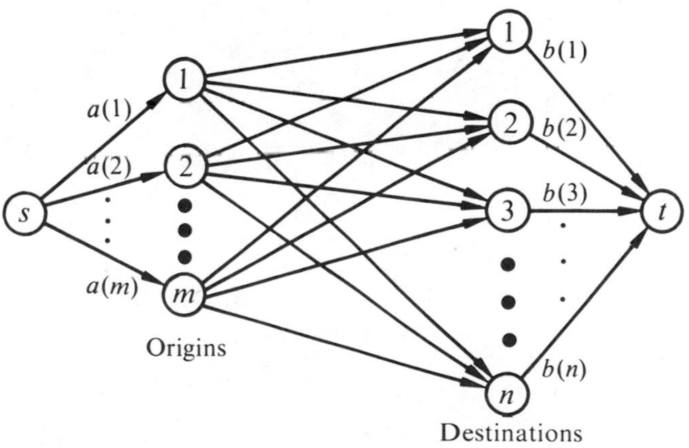

Figure 6.14. Network for the Transportation Problem

of n nodes. Each origin node is connected to every destination node and receives an arc from the source. The destination nodes are connected to the sink. Notice that all arcs are directed arcs. Those connecting the source to the origin nodes have a capacity equal to the supply at each origin; those connecting the destination nodes to the sink have a capacity equal to the demand at each destination; finally, those connecting origin nodes to destination nodes either have no capacity restrictions (that is, an infinite capacity) or have zero capacity. The complementary slackness conditions define the former as arcs for which $u(i) + v(j) = c(i, j)$ and the latter as arcs for which $u(i) + v(j) < c(i, j)$.

6.5.4 THE PRIMAL-DUAL NETWORK ALGORITHM

The primal-dual network algorithm begins with a particular feasible solution for the dual and proceeds to seek a feasible solution for the primal by solving a series of maximal flow problems over a sequence of modified networks. At each iteration, the primal constraints and the complementary slackness conditions are satisfied. After each iteration, the dual solution is improved, and the existing network is then modified to reflect this change. When the primal constraints are satisfied as strict equalities, the algorithm terminates, and a feasible solution to the primal emerges. The method of constructing this feasible solution ensures that it too is optimal.

Algorithm.

1. Set $v(j) = 0$ for all $j = 1, \ldots, n$. Set $u(i) = \min_j c(i, j)$ for all $i = 1, \ldots, m$. Define the following network:

$$\begin{aligned} k(s, i) &= a(i) \\ k(i, j) &= \infty \qquad \text{for } (i, j) \text{ with } u(i) + v(j) = c(i, j) \\ k(i, j) &= 0 \qquad \text{for } (i, j) \text{ with } u(i) + v(j) < c(i, j) \\ k(j, t) &= b(j) \end{aligned}$$

2. Using the maximal flow labeling algorithm, maximize the flow over the current network. If the maximal flow $z = \sum_i a(i)$, terminate the algorithm; the solution is optimal. If $z < \sum_i a(i)$, define sets I and J to be, respectively, the collections of all labeled origin and destination nodes at the termination of the maximal flow algorithm.
3. Set

$$\begin{aligned} u'(i) &= u(i) + \delta \qquad \text{for } i \text{ in } I \\ &= u(i) \qquad \text{for } i \text{ in } \bar{I} \\ v'(j) &= v(j) - \delta \qquad \text{for } j \text{ in } J \\ &= v(j) \qquad \text{for } j \text{ in } \bar{J} \end{aligned}$$

where

$$\delta = \min_{\substack{i \text{ in } I \\ j \text{ in } \bar{J}}} \{c(i, j) - [u(i) + v(j)]\}$$

4. Modify the current network by setting

$$k(i, j) = \infty \qquad \text{for } (i, j) \text{ with } u'(i) + v'(j) = c(i, j)$$
$$k(i, j) = 0 \qquad \text{for } (i, j) \text{ with } u'(i) + v'(j) < c(i, j)$$

Go to Step 2.

The primal-dual network algorithm terminates in a finite number of steps and, upon termination, yields an optimal solution for both the primal and the dual problems. This may be shown by noting that

$$\begin{aligned}\sum_i u'(i)a(i) + \sum_j v'(j)b(j) &= \sum_{i \text{ in } I} [u(i) + \delta]a(i) + \sum_{i \text{ in } \bar{I}} u(i)a(i) \\ &\quad + \sum_{j \text{ in } J} [v(j) - \delta]b(j) + \sum_{j \text{ in } \bar{J}} v(j)b(j) \\ &= \sum_i u(i)a(i) + \sum_j v(j)b(j) \\ &\quad + \delta\left[\sum_{i \text{ in } I} a(i) - \sum_{j \text{ in } J} b(j)\right]\end{aligned}$$

But $\delta > 0$ and $\sum_{i \text{ in } I} a(i) > \sum_{j \text{ in } J} b(j)$ until the end of the algorithm. Hence the new value of the dual increases at each iteration. Since this increasing value is bounded from above [that is, it cannot exceed $\sum_i \sum_j c(i, j) f(i, j)$], the algorithm is finite. Moreover, since the feasible primal solution that emerges at the end of the algorithm satisfies both the primal constraints and the complementary slackness conditions, this feasible solution also must be optimal.

Example. The primal-dual network algorithm will now be applied to the following simple example. A commodity is available at three origins and is demanded at four destinations according to the supply-demand schedule exhibited in Table 6.12.

Associated with the above supply-demand schedule is the unit shipping cost matrix $\mathbf{C} = [c(i, j)]$, shown in Table 6.13.

Begin the algorithm with an initial feasible solution to the dual problem. Let $u(i) = \min_j c(i, j)$ and $v(j) = 0$, for $i = 1, 2, 3$ and $j = 1, 2, 3, 4$. Thus $u(1) = 2$, $u(2) = u(3) = 4$, and $v(1) = v(2) = v(3) = v(4) = 0$. Construct the initial network (arcs with zero capacity have been omitted) as shown in Figure 6.15.

Now find the maximal flow over this capacited network. Applying the labeling algorithm three times yields a maximal flow of eight units, distributed

Table 6.12. Supply-Demand Schedule

i \ j		Destination 1	2	3	4	$a(i)$
Origin	1	$f(1,1)$	$f(1,2)$	$f(1,3)$	$f(1,4)$	5
	2	$f(2,1)$	$f(2,2)$	$f(2,3)$	$f(2,4)$	5
	3	$f(3,1)$	$f(3,2)$	$f(3,3)$	$f(3,4)$	5
	$b(j)$	1	6	2	6	15

Table 6.13. Unit Shipping Cost Matrix

i \ j		Destination 1	2	3	4
Origin	1	5	4	3	2
	2	10	8	4	7
	3	9	9	8	4

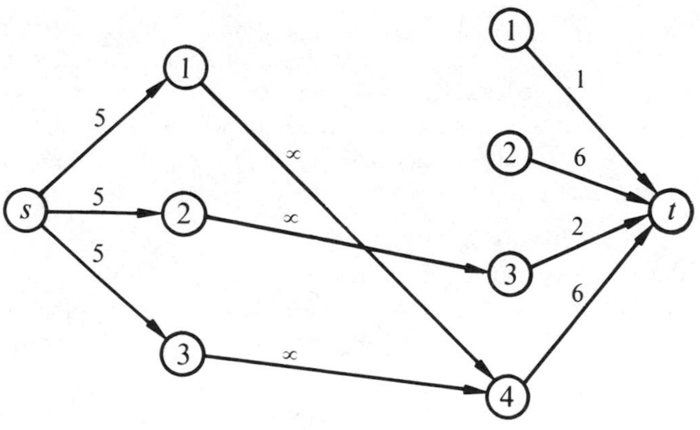

Figure 6.15. Initial Network for the Primal-Dual Network Algorithm

as in Figure 6.16(a). To find the appropriate δ for Step 3 of the algorithm, construct a dual variable matrix $\mathbf{U} + \mathbf{V}$, consisting of elements $u(i) + v(j)$, as shown in Table 6.14. On it, identify the labeled and unlabeled nodes. Then subtract the submatrix of $\mathbf{U} + \mathbf{V}$, consisting of elements with i in I and j in $\bar{J}$, from the corresponding submatrix of unit shipping costs, and

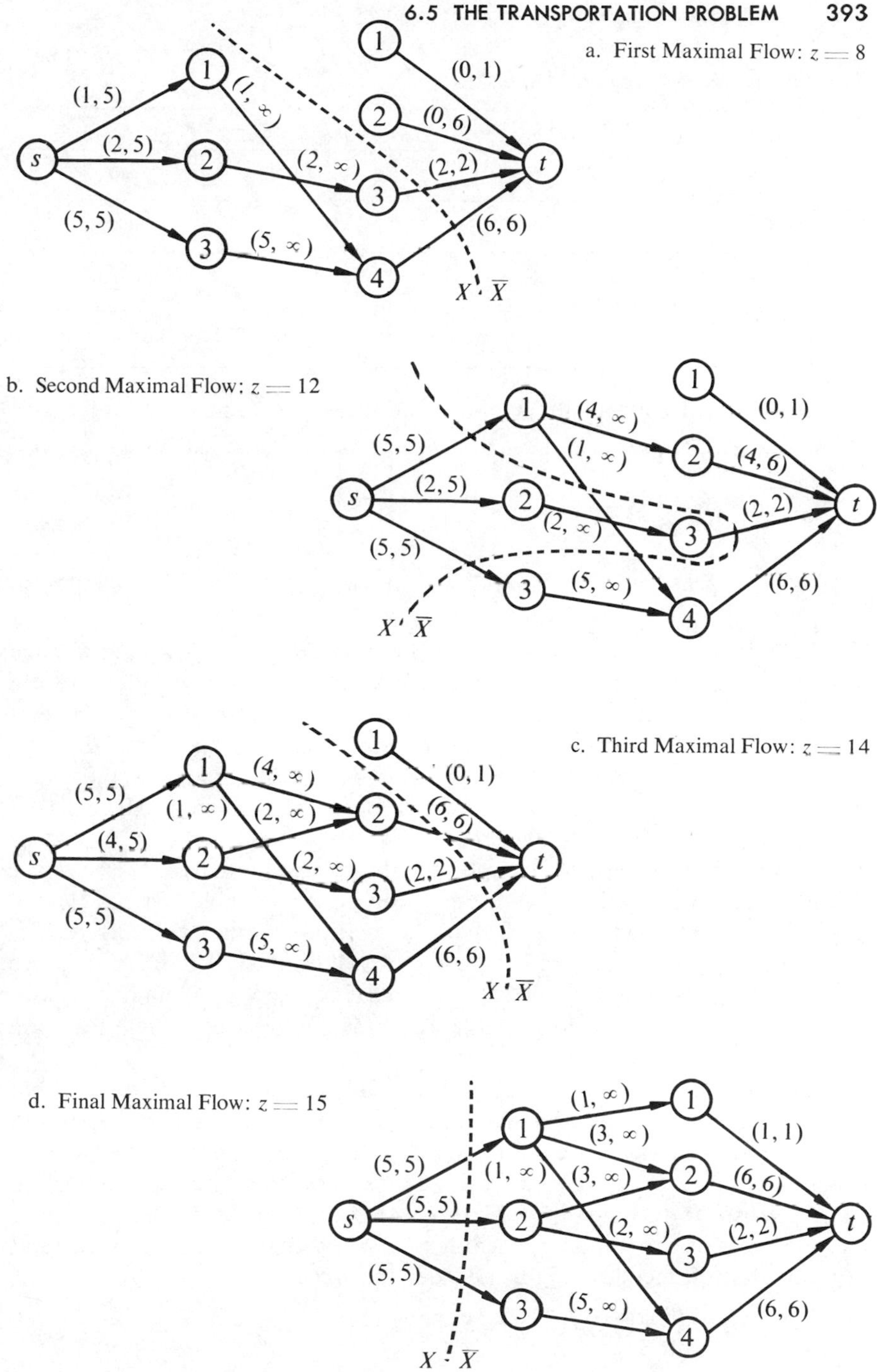

Figure 6.16. Maximal Flow Labeling Sequence

Table 6.14. Dual Variable Matrix

			$\bar{J}$		J	
		$v(j)$	0	0	0	0
	$u(i)$	$i \backslash j$	1	2	3	4
I	2	1	2	2	2	2
I	4	2	4	4	4	4
I	4	3	4	4	4	4

set δ equal to the minimal element in the resulting submatrix:

$$\begin{bmatrix} 5 & 4 \\ 10 & 8 \\ 9 & 9 \end{bmatrix} - \begin{bmatrix} 2 & 2 \\ 4 & 4 \\ 4 & 4 \end{bmatrix} = \begin{bmatrix} 3 & \textcircled{2} \\ 6 & 4 \\ 5 & 5 \end{bmatrix}$$

Having found a $\delta = 2$, form a new dual variable matrix $\mathbf{U}' + \mathbf{V}'$ (Table 6.15) by adding δ to $u(i)$ with i in I and subtracting δ from $v(j)$ with j in J. This operation does not affect the previous maximal flow result, since we still retain the same arcs in the network [that is, what we added to the $u(i)$ of the labeled nodes in I, we subtracted from the $v(j)$ of the labeled nodes in J]. However, the operation does bring another arc into the network, since now the equality $c(i, j) = u(i) + v(j)$ holds for one more arc, that is, arc (1, 2). In this way, we have increased the maximal flow that may be sent from source to sink.

For the remaining elements in the new dual variable matrix $\mathbf{U}' + \mathbf{V}'$ use the corresponding elements of the previous dual variable matrix $\mathbf{U} + \mathbf{V}$ (Table 6.14). Following Step 4 of the algorithm, modify the current network to reflect the changes in the dual variable matrix [that is, introduce arc (1, 2) into the network] and solve the maximal flow problem once again. The result is a maximal flow of 12 units, distributed according to Figure 6.16(b).

Repeated application of the algorithm leads to the sequence of maximal flow solutions and dual variable matrices presented in Figures 6.16(c) and 6.16(d), and Tables 6.15(b) and 6.15(c). The optimal primal solution consists of the flows $f(i, j)$ in Figure 6.16(d). The optimal dual solution is the set of prices $u(i)$ and $v(j)$ in Table 6.15(c). As a check, we may compute the total cost of the shipping schedule and verify that it is equal to the total value of the shipment at origins and destinations:

$$\sum_i \sum_j c(i, j)\bar{f}(i, j) = 5 + 12 + 2 + 24 + 8 + 20$$

$$= 71$$

$$\sum_i \bar{u}(i)a(i) + \sum_j \bar{v}(j)b(j) = 25 + 45 + 35 + 0 - 6 - 10 - 18$$

$$= 71$$

Table 6.15. Dual Variable Matrices

			$\bar{J}$		J	$\bar{J}$
		$v(j)$	0	0	−2	−2
	$u(i)$	i \ j	1	2	3	4
$\bar{I}$	4	1	4	4	2	2
I	6	2	6	6	4	4
$\bar{I}$	6	3	6	6	4	4

a. Second Matrix

			$\bar{J}$		J	
		$v(j)$	0	0	−4	−2
	$u(i)$	i \ j	1	2	3	4
I	4	1	4	4	0	2
	8	2	8	8	4	6
	6	3	6	6	2	4

b. Third Matrix

	$v(i)$	0	−1	−5	−3
$u(i)$	i \ j	1	2	3	4
5	1	5	4	0	2
9	2	9	8	4	6
7	3	7	6	2	4

c. Final Matrix

6.5.5 APPLICATION: A RESIDENTIAL ALLOCATION MODEL

For an application of the transportation problem, let us consider a more complex version of the assignment model described in Subsection 6.2.4 [Herbert and Stevens (1960)]. Imagine a concentric city of 10 zones and a household population divided into three income groups: low, medium, and high. Assume that each household group, after examining the available housing stock in the 10 zones, and after consulting its budget, decides that it is willing to bid the rents listed in Table 6.16 for a residence in each of the alternative locations.

Table 6.16. Rent Bid (in Dollars Per Day Per Housing Unit)

Zone

Income Group	1	2	3	4	5	6	7	8	9	10
A. High	6	1	1	2	4	3	5	7	6	9
B. Medium	1	3	1	8	7	4	5	2	2	1
C. Low	7	5	5	4	3	2	1	1	2	1

Assume, further, that the supply and demand for housing is as follows:

Supply

Zone	1	2	3	4	5	6	7	8	9	10
Housing Units	20	150	100	90	70	65	50	40	25	10

Demand

Income Group	High	Medium	Low
Households	120	350	150

Find the allocation of households to housing units that minimizes aggregate rent paid, subject to the constraint that all households are assigned to a housing unit.

The minimum aggregate rent solution may be found by applying the primal-dual network algorithm. After solving for the maximal flows of four modified networks, we obtain the allocation presented in Table 6.17. The aggregate rent for this allocation is $1,290.

Table 6.17. Minimum Aggregate Rent Allocation ($z = \$1,290$)

Zone

Income Group	1	2	3	4	5	6	7	8	9	10	Total
A. High		30		90							120
B. Medium	20	120	100			35		40	25	10	350
C. Low					70	30	50				150
Total	20	150	100	90	70	65	50	40	25	10	620

To find the maximum aggregate rent allocation, we need to maximize the primal problem and minimize the dual problem. Hence we modify the primal-dual network algorithm, as follows:

1. Set $v(j) = 0$ for all $j = 1, \ldots, n$. Set $u(i) = \max_j c(i, j)$ for all $i = 1, \ldots, m$. Define the following network:

$$k(s, i) = a(i)$$
$$k(i, j) = \infty \qquad \text{for } (i, j) \text{ with } u(i) + v(j) = c(i, j)$$
$$k(i, j) = 0 \qquad \text{for } (i, j) \text{ with } u(i) + v(j) > c(i, j)$$
$$k(j, t) = b(j)$$

2. Using the maximal flow labeling algorithm, maximize the flow over the current network. If the maximal flow $z = \sum_i a(i)$, terminate the algorithm; the solution is optimal. If $z < \sum_i a(i)$, define sets I and J to be, respectively, the collections of all labeled origin and destination nodes at the termination of the maximal flow algorithm.
3. Set

$$\begin{aligned} u'(i) &= u(i) + \delta & &\text{for } i \text{ in } I \\ &= u(i) & &\text{for } i \text{ in } \bar{I} \\ v'(j) &= v(j) - \delta & &\text{for } j \text{ in } J \\ &= v(j) & &\text{for } j \text{ in } \bar{J} \end{aligned}$$

where

$$\delta = \max_{\substack{i \text{ in } I \\ j \text{ in } \bar{J}}} \{c(i, j) - [u(i) + v(j)]\}$$

4. Modify the current network by setting

$$k(i, j) = \infty \qquad \text{for } (i, j) \text{ with } u'(i) + v'(j) = c(i, j)$$
$$k(i, j) = 0 \qquad \text{for } (i, j) \text{ with } u'(i) + v'(j) > c(i, j)$$

Go to Step 2.

Table 6.18. Maximum Aggregate Rent Allocation (z=*$3,410*)

	Zone										
Income Group	1	2	3	4	5	6	7	8	9	10	Total
A. High	20						25	40	25	10	120
B. Medium		100		90	70	65	25				350
C. Low		50	100								150
Total	20	150	100	90	70	65	50	40	25	10	620

Application of this algorithm to the data yields the allocation described in Table 6.18. The aggregate rent for this allocation is $3,410.

What are the locational implications of a change in the composition, but not the size, of the total population? Assume the following compositional change:

Income Group	High	Medium	Low
Households	90	210	320

The minimum aggregate rent allocation for this population of households yields an aggregate total of $1,240. This total differs only slightly from the previous minimum rent solution. However, the allocation is significantly different. (See Table 6.19.)

Table 6.19. Minimum Aggregate Rent Allocation for Changed Population Composition ($z = \$1,240$)

	Zone										
Income Group	1	2	3	4	5	6	7	8	9	10	Total
A. High		90									90
B. Medium	20	60	100						20	10	210
C. Low				90	70	65	50	40	5		320
Total	20	150	100	90	70	65	50	40	25	10	602

We may wish to contrast the locational implications of a change in the composition of the population, but not the total, with the locational implications of a change in the total, but not the composition; for example, assume that the composition remains proportionally constant, but that the total household population increases by 20 percent. Thus we have to locate the following household population:

Income Group	High	Medium	Low
Households	144	420	180

The minimum aggregate rent solution appears in Table 6.20. A finding of major significance is that under this scheme (a 20 percent increase in demand and a constant supply), 124 middle income households are not allocated. They, therefore, bear the brunt of the housing shortage.

Table 6.20. Minimum Aggregate Rent Allocation for Changed Population Total (z=$1,182)

	Zone										
Income Group	1	2	3	4	5	6	7	8	9	10	Total
A. High		54		90							144
B. Medium	20	96	100			5		40	25	10	296
C. Low					70	60	50				180
Total	20	150	100	90	70	65	50	40	25	10	620

EXERCISES

1. (a) Find the associated number, the relative distance, and the accessibility index of each place in the Ljubljana Metropolitan Region's road network.

(b) Find the network's degree of connectivity, its dispersion, and its diameter.

(c) Compare and contrast your results with those found for the Sao Paulo network in Subsection 6.1.2.

2. The network algorithms for the maximal flow problem and the shortest route problem dealt with directed networks. Modify these algorithms so that they can be applied to undirected networks, and illustrate their use with a numerical example.

3. Given the dollar fare schedule below, use the shortest route algorithm to find the cheapest round-trip air fare from San Francisco to New York and back, for a person willing to stop-over as many times as is necessary.

	To				
From	S.F.	Oak.	Chi.	Phil.	N.Y.
San Francisco		15	105	145	180
Oakland	15		90	135	155
Chicago	105	90		40	70
Philadelphia	145		40		20
New York	180	155	70		

4. Formulate the shortest route problem as a transportation problem, and use the primal-dual network algorithm to find the shortest route for the network in Figure 6.7.

5. The assignment of traffic to the Ljubljana Metropolitan Region's road network that was carried out in Subsection 6.3.3 was founded on several restrictive assumptions. Relax some of these assumptions and trace through their consequences on travel volumes:

(a) Assume that a half of the commuters have no access to a car and therefore are "captive" bus commuters. Apply the diversion curve formula only to the remaining half.

(b) Introduce the deterring effect of the lack of parking spaces in the central areas into the traffic assignment procedure by adding longer terminal times to trips made by car into the five city communes (that is, communes 9 through 13). Assume an additional terminal time of five minutes for trips by car into these communes.

(c) Introduce a trip origin and trip destination dependence in the diversion curve formula by using different values for the exponents. In particular, use the following four-fold classification of trips and their respective values of the exponent:

		Destination of Trip	
		Central Area	Suburban Area
Origin of Trip	Central Area (Communes 9–13)	2	3
	Suburban Area	4	5

(d) Suggest how a capacity constraint function might be used to decrease speeds over roads when volume increases.

6. During the past decade, large-scale comprehensive transportation studies have been started in most of the major metropolitan areas of the nation. Their size, measured in terms of scope, budget, and number of employees, has created significant management problems. The need to coordinate a vast number of interrelated tasks has led on several occasions to the adoption of critical path methods [Creighton (1963)].

The input data presented in the table below identify the major components of a hypothetical transportation study and list the optimistic, most likely, and pessimistic estimates of the duration of each activity. Using these data find:

(a) the expected project duration time and its variance; and

(b) the probability of completing the project ahead of the scheduled one year.

Activity	Immediately Preceding Activities	Activity Duration Time Estimates (in Weeks)		
		Optimistic	Most Likely	Pessimistic
1. Initial study design	none	8	12	16
2. Home interview survey	1	22	25	40
3. Land use inventory	1	14	20	26
4. Employment inventory	1	6	8	10

Activity	Immediately Preceding Activities	Activity Duration Time Estimates (in Weeks)		
		Optimistic	Most Likely	Pessimistic
5. Roadside interviews	1	10	12	14
6. Parking inventory	1	3	4	5
7. Highway network inventory	1	8	10	18
8. Truck and taxi survey	1	4	5	6
9. Transit survey	1	3	7	11
10. Design of regional growth models	1	10	12	14
11. Design of land use models	1	10	15	20
12. Design of traffic models	1	8	10	12
13. Calibration, testing, and refinement of the regional growth models	2,4,10	1	3	5
14. Calibration, testing, and refinement of the land use models	2,3,4,7,9,11	1	4	7
15. Calibration, testing, and refinement of the traffic estimation models	2,3,4,5,7,8,9,12	4	5	6
16. Regional growth forecasts	13	1	2	3
17. Land use forcasts	6,14,16	1	2	3
18. Traffic forecasts	15,16,17	2	3	4
19. Evaluation of the land use forecast	18	1	2	3
20. Evaluation of the traffic forecast	18	1	1	1
21. Land development plan	19,20	3	7	11
22. Transportation plan	19,20	4	5	6
23. Financing study	21,22	1	2	3
24. Final report	23	2	4	12

7. Find the expected duration time of the San Antonio Urban Development Plan Project described in Subsection 6.4.6. Identify the three different critical paths. Next, assume that each of the project activities will be completed according to the optimistic time schedule. What will the total project duration time be then? Finally, assume that an unexpected budget increase permits an expansion of the staff. What activities should receive additional staff support in order to shorten the expected duration time of the project?

8. The linear programming formulation of the critical path problem is time-oriented only; it does not consider cost-time tradeoffs. If we allow activities to be expedited at extra cost, then $t(i, j)$, the expected duration time for each activity, is no longer a constant, but becomes a variable in the linear programming formulation.

Consider the following simple linear cost-time relationship:

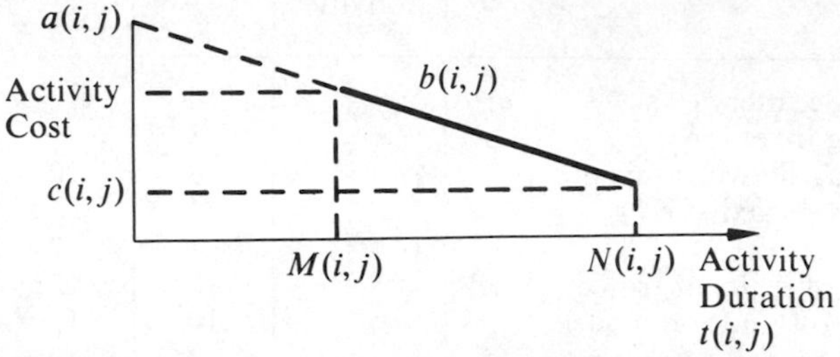

The relationship may be expressed algebraically as

$$c(i, j) = a(i, j) - b(i, j)t(i, j)$$

where $a(i, j)$ is the intercept, $b(i, j)$ is the slope, and

$$M(i, j) \leqq t(i, j) \leqq N(i, j)$$

where $M(i, j)$ is the minimum possible activity duration time (that is, the "crash" time) and $N(i, j)$ is the normal activity duration time.

Total costs for the above formulation may be expressed, as follows:

$$\text{Total costs} = \sum_i \sum_j [a(i, j) - b(i, j)t(i, j)]$$

The objective is to minimize total project costs, or equivalently, to maximize

$$z = \sum_i \sum_j b(i, j)t(i, j)$$

Formulate the cost-time critical path problem as a linear programming problem, and illustrate its application with a simple numerical example.

9. Find the maximum aggregate rent allocations that correspond to the minimum aggregate rent allocations in Tables 6.18 and 6.19.

10. The personnel assignment problem is one of assigning people to jobs in an optimal manner. Imagine a set of m personnel categories with $a(i)$ individuals available in category i and a set of n job types with $b(j)$ individuals required in job type j. An individual can be assigned to any job but can work on only one job. Assume that the ith individual working at the jth job has an efficiency measured by a nonnegative integer $e(i, j)$. Further, assume that the number of jobs to be filled is equal to the number of individuals that are in the m personnel categories. Let $f(i, j)$ denote the number of individuals from category i that are assigned to job type j. The personnel assignment problem is to find the assignment that maximizes total efficiency:

$$z = \sum_i \sum_j e(i, j) f(i, j)$$

Formulate the personnel assignment problem as a transportation problem, and illustrate its solution with the numerical example presented below. The first table provides data on the supply of and demand for workers in the two personnel categories and three job types, respectively. The second presents an evaluation of how workers in each personnel category perform at each of the three possible job types.

Find the optimal allocation of workers to jobs.

Supply-Demand Schedule for Employees

i \ j		Job Type 1	2	3	$a(i)$
Personnel	1	$f(1, 1)$	$f(1, 2)$	$f(1, 3)$	10
Category	2	$f(2, 1)$	$f(2, 2)$	$f(2, 3)$	10
	$b(j)$	4	10	6	20 employees

Efficiency Ratings

i \ j		Job Type 1	2	3
Personnel	1	3	5	12
Category	2	11	5	4

REFERENCES AND SELECTED READINGS

THEORY

Busacker, R. G. and T. L. Saaty. *Finite Graphs and Networks: An Introduction with Applications.* New York: McGraw-Hill, 1965.

Ford, L. R., Jr. and D. R. Fulkerson. *Flows in Networks.* Princeton, N. J.: Princeton University Press, 1962.

Hadley, G. *Linear Programming*, (Ch. 10, pp. 331-378). Reading, Mass.: Addison-Wesley, 1962.

Kelley, J. E., Jr. "Critical Path Planning and Scheduling: Mathematical Basis," *Operations Research*, IX: 11, 1961, 296–320.

Malcolm, D. G., J. H. Roseboom, C. E. Clark, and W. Fazar. "Applications of a Technique for R & D Program Evaluation," *Operations Research*, VII, 1959, 646–669.

APPLICATION: THE STRUCTURE OF TRANSPORTATION NETWORKS

Garrison, W. L. "Connectivity of the Interstate Highway System," *Papers and Proceedings of the Regional Science Association*, **VI**, 1960, 122–137.

Gauthier, H. L. "Transportation and the Growth of the Sao Paulo Economy," *Journal of Regional Science*, **VIII** : 1, 1968, 77–94.

Kansky, K. J. *Structure of Transportation Networks: Relationships between Network Geometry and Regional Characteristics.* Chicago: Department of Geography, University of Chicago, 1963.

APPLICATION: TRAFFIC ASSIGNMENT

Bureau of Public Roads. *Traffic Assignment Manual.* Washington, D. C.: U. S. Government Printing Office, 1964.

Overgaard, K. R. *Traffic Estimation in Urban Transportation Planning.* Copenhagen: The Danish Academy of Technical Sciences, 1966.

APPLICATION: CRITICAL PATH METHODS AND PERT ANALYSIS

Creighton, R. L. "PERTing a Transportation Study," *Highway Research Record*, **XXXVIII**, 1963, 55–77.

Lopez, W. and C. Wellborn. "The Application of PERT to a Series of Planning Studies in Chile," unpublished paper, Department of City and Regional Planning, University of California, Berkeley, California, 1966.

APPLICATION: A RESIDENTIAL ALLOCATION MODEL

Harris, B. "Linear Programming and the Projection of Land Uses," *P. J. Paper No. 20*, Philadelphia: Penn-Jersey Transportation Study, 1962.

Herbert, J. D. and B. H. Stevens. "A Model for the Distribution of Residential Activity in Urban Areas," *Journal of Regional Science*, II, 1960, 21–36.

seven characteristic roots and characteristic vectors

Several important problems in urban and regional analysis call for the solution of the following set of simultaneous linear equations:

$$\mathbf{Ax} = \lambda \mathbf{x} \tag{7.1}$$

where $\mathbf{A}$ is a known square matrix, $\mathbf{x}$ is a column vector of unknowns, and λ is an unknown scalar. Equation (7.1) expresses the *characteristic value problem,* in which we seek values for λ and $\mathbf{x}$ such that when $\mathbf{x}$ is multiplied by $\mathbf{A}$, the product is proportional to $\mathbf{x}$ itself.

7.1 CHARACTERISTIC ROOTS AND CHARACTERISTIC VECTORS OF A SQUARE MATRIX

To solve (7.1) for λ and $\mathbf{x}$, we first note that (7.1) may be expressed as the following homogeneous equation system:

$$(\mathbf{A} - \lambda\mathbf{I})\mathbf{x} = \mathbf{0} \tag{7.2}$$

where $\mathbf{I}$ is the identity matrix of the same order as $\mathbf{A}$. Since (7.2) is a homogeneous equation system, a nontrivial solution (that is, $\mathbf{x} \neq \mathbf{0}$) exists only if the determinant of the *characteristic matrix* $(\mathbf{A} - \lambda\mathbf{I})$ is zero:

$$|\mathbf{A} - \lambda\mathbf{I}| = 0 \tag{7.3}$$

Equation (7.3) is called the *characteristic equation* of the matrix $\mathbf{A}$ and may be expanded in powers of λ, as follows:

$$|\mathbf{A} - \lambda\mathbf{I}| = b_n\lambda^n + b_{n-1}\lambda^{n-1} + \cdots + b_1\lambda + b_0 = 0 \qquad (7.4)$$

7.1.1 CHARACTERISTIC ROOTS

The roots of the polynomial expression in (7.4), that is, the values of λ that satisfy it, are called the *characteristic roots* of **A** and may be denoted by $\lambda_1, \lambda_2, \ldots, \lambda_n$. These roots need not all be different from one another, and some of them may be equal to zero. A characteristic root which is repeated r times is said to have a *multiplicity* of r.

Example. As an illustration of the calculation of the characteristic roots of a matrix, consider the following square matrix of order two:

$$\mathbf{A} = \begin{bmatrix} \frac{1}{2} & \frac{1}{4} \\ \frac{1}{2} & \frac{3}{4} \end{bmatrix}$$

The matrix is nonsingular and therefore possesses two characteristic roots, λ_1 and λ_2, say. To find them, we expand the characteristic equation

$$\begin{vmatrix} \frac{1}{2} - \lambda & \frac{1}{4} \\ \frac{1}{2} & \frac{3}{4} - \lambda \end{vmatrix} = (\tfrac{1}{2} - \lambda)(\tfrac{3}{4} - \lambda) - \tfrac{1}{4}(\tfrac{1}{2})$$

$$= \lambda^2 - \tfrac{5}{4}\lambda + \tfrac{1}{4} = 0$$

and obtain the characteristic roots by factoring:

$$(\lambda - 1)(\lambda - \tfrac{1}{4}) = 0$$

$$\lambda_1 = 1$$

$$\lambda_2 = \tfrac{1}{4}$$

To solve quadratic characteristic equations that cannot be factored conveniently, we may use the familiar solution from scalar algebra:

$$x = \frac{-b \pm \sqrt{b^2 - 4ac}}{2a} \qquad (7.5)$$

for equations expressed in the form

$$ax^2 + bx + c = 0$$

Thus, returning to our numerical example, we find

$$\lambda = \frac{5/4 \pm \sqrt{(25/16) - 4(1)(1/4)}}{2(1)}$$

$$= \frac{5/4 \pm 3/4}{2} = 1 \text{ or } \frac{1}{4}$$

The order in which one selects the characteristic roots is arbitrary. In general, we shall always select the largest characteristic root first and the rest in decreasing order of magnitude. The largest characteristic root is often called the *dominant characteristic root.*

7.1.2 CHARACTERISTIC VECTORS

Associated with every characteristic root, λ_i, of a square matrix, **A**, is a column vector, $\mathbf{x}_i$, say, called a *characteristic vector* of **A**, that satisfies the relationship

$$\mathbf{A}\mathbf{x}_i = \lambda_i \mathbf{x}_i$$

or

$$(\mathbf{A} - \lambda_i \mathbf{I})\mathbf{x}_i = \mathbf{0} \tag{7.6}$$

Since the rank of the characteristic matrix is less than m and is equal to the rank of the augmented characteristic matrix $(\mathbf{A} - \lambda_i \mathbf{I} \mid \mathbf{0})$, it follows that $\mathbf{x}_i$ can take on an infinity of values. However, the elements of all such solution vectors are proportional to one another. We may obtain a unique solution vector, called the *normalized characteristic vector*, $\mathbf{v}_i$, say, by imposing the condition that the vector be of unit length:

$$\mathbf{v}_i'\mathbf{v}_i = 1$$

Example. To illustrate the derivation of the characteristic vectors of a matrix, consider, once again, the matrix

$$\mathbf{A} = \begin{bmatrix} \dfrac{1}{2} & \dfrac{1}{4} \\[2ex] \dfrac{1}{2} & \dfrac{3}{4} \end{bmatrix}$$

We have already established that the characteristic roots of this matrix are, respectively,

$$\lambda_1 = 1$$
$$\lambda_2 = \tfrac{1}{4}$$

To find a characteristic vector associated with the dominant characteristic root λ_1, we solve the homogeneous equation system

$$\begin{bmatrix} \frac{1}{2} - 1 & \frac{1}{4} \\ \frac{1}{2} & \frac{3}{4} - 1 \end{bmatrix} \begin{bmatrix} x_1 \\ x_2 \end{bmatrix} = \begin{bmatrix} 0 \\ 0 \end{bmatrix}$$

or

$$-\tfrac{1}{2}x_1 + \tfrac{1}{4}x_2 = 0$$
$$\tfrac{1}{2}x_1 - \tfrac{1}{4}x_2 = 0$$

Observe that the above two equations are linearly dependent and that the rank of the characteristic matrix $(\mathbf{A} - \lambda_1\mathbf{I})$ is unity. Therefore, the solution of the equations consists of the single vector

$$\mathbf{x}_1 = k_1 \begin{bmatrix} 1 \\ 2 \end{bmatrix}$$

where k_1 is an arbitrary constant.

To obtain the normalized characteristic vector, $\mathbf{v}_1$, we set

$$k_1 = \frac{1}{\sqrt{1^2 + 2^2}} = \frac{1}{\sqrt{5}} = \frac{\sqrt{5}}{5}$$

and find

$$\mathbf{v}_1 = \frac{\sqrt{5}}{5} \begin{bmatrix} 1 \\ 2 \end{bmatrix} = \begin{bmatrix} \dfrac{\sqrt{5}}{5} \\ \dfrac{2\sqrt{5}}{5} \end{bmatrix}$$

In an analogous manner, we may establish that the normalized characteristic vector associated with the second characteristic root, λ_2, is

$$\mathbf{v}_2 = \frac{\sqrt{2}}{2} \begin{bmatrix} 1 \\ -1 \end{bmatrix} = \begin{bmatrix} \dfrac{\sqrt{2}}{2} \\ -\dfrac{\sqrt{2}}{2} \end{bmatrix}$$

To verify the above solutions for the characteristic roots and characteristic vectors of $\mathbf{A}$, we substitute the appropriate solution values into (7.1). Thus,

$$\mathbf{A}\mathbf{x}_1 = \begin{bmatrix} \dfrac{1}{2} & \dfrac{1}{4} \\ \dfrac{1}{2} & \dfrac{3}{4} \end{bmatrix} k_1 \begin{bmatrix} 1 \\ 2 \end{bmatrix} = 1 \cdot k_1 \begin{bmatrix} 1 \\ 2 \end{bmatrix} = \lambda_1 \mathbf{x}_1$$

and

$$\mathbf{A}\mathbf{x}_2 = \begin{bmatrix} \dfrac{1}{2} & \dfrac{1}{4} \\ \dfrac{1}{2} & \dfrac{3}{4} \end{bmatrix} k_2 \begin{bmatrix} 1 \\ -1 \end{bmatrix} = \frac{1}{4} \cdot k_2 \begin{bmatrix} 1 \\ -1 \end{bmatrix} = \lambda_2 \mathbf{x}_2$$

The characteristic vectors of a square matrix may be collected to form a square matrix, $\mathbf{M}$, say, called the *modal matrix*. The modal matrix of $\mathbf{A}$ in our numerical example is

$$\mathbf{M} = [\mathbf{x}_1 \quad \mathbf{x}_2] = \begin{bmatrix} k_1 & k_2 \\ 2k_1 & -k_2 \end{bmatrix}$$

Because each characteristic vector is unique only to a scale factor, an infinite number of modal matrices may be associated with a particular matrix. However, we may impose a unit-length constraint on the characteristic vectors, to define a unique modal matrix, **N**, say, called the *normalized modal matrix*. For example, the normalized modal matrix of

$$\mathbf{A} = \begin{bmatrix} \frac{1}{2} & \frac{1}{4} \\ \frac{1}{2} & \frac{3}{4} \end{bmatrix}$$

is

$$\mathbf{N} = [\mathbf{v}_1 \quad \mathbf{v}_2] = \begin{bmatrix} \frac{\sqrt{5}}{5} & \frac{\sqrt{2}}{2} \\ \frac{2\sqrt{5}}{5} & -\frac{\sqrt{2}}{2} \end{bmatrix}$$

Another matrix which will be useful in later discussions is the diagonal matrix that is formed by arraying the characteristic roots of a given square matrix along its principal diagonal. Such a matrix is called the *spectral matrix*, and we shall denote it by Λ. Thus,

$$\Lambda = \begin{bmatrix} \lambda_1 & 0 & \cdots & 0 \\ 0 & \lambda_2 & \cdots & 0 \\ \vdots & \vdots & \ddots & \vdots \\ 0 & 0 & \cdots & \lambda_n \end{bmatrix}$$

and in our numerical example,

$$\Lambda = \begin{bmatrix} 1 & 0 \\ 0 & \frac{1}{4} \end{bmatrix}$$

7.1.3 PROPERTIES OF CHARACTERISTIC ROOTS AND CHARACTERISTIC VECTORS

Characteristic roots and characteristic vectors possess many properties and relationships that often are useful in analyses of linear equation systems. Several of the more important ones are stated, without proof, in this section and are illustrated with the second-order matrix of our earlier numerical example.

1. *The characteristic roots of a matrix and its transpose are the same.*

$$\begin{vmatrix} \frac{1}{2} - \lambda & \frac{1}{2} \\ \frac{1}{4} & \frac{3}{4} - \lambda \end{vmatrix} = (\tfrac{1}{2} - \lambda)(\tfrac{3}{4} - \lambda) - \tfrac{1}{2}(\tfrac{1}{4})$$

$$= \begin{vmatrix} \frac{1}{2} - \lambda & \frac{1}{4} \\ \frac{1}{2} & \frac{3}{4} - \lambda \end{vmatrix}$$

2. *If a matrix is multiplied by a scalar constant, its characteristic roots are multiplied by the same constant, but its characteristic vectors remain unchanged.*

$$\begin{vmatrix} \frac{1}{2}c - \alpha & \frac{1}{4}c \\ \frac{1}{2}c & \frac{3}{4}c - \alpha \end{vmatrix} = (\tfrac{1}{2}c - \alpha)(\tfrac{3}{4}c - \alpha) - c^2(\tfrac{1}{2})(\tfrac{1}{4})$$

$$= \alpha^2 - \tfrac{5}{4}c\alpha + \tfrac{1}{4}c^2$$

$$= 0$$

and

$$\alpha_1 = 1c = c\lambda_1$$

$$\alpha_2 = \tfrac{1}{4}c = c\lambda_2$$

Also,

$$\begin{bmatrix} \frac{1}{2}c & \frac{1}{4}c \\ \frac{1}{2}c & \frac{3}{4}c \end{bmatrix} k_1 \begin{bmatrix} 1 \\ 2 \end{bmatrix} = 1 \cdot ck_1 \begin{bmatrix} 1 \\ 2 \end{bmatrix} = \alpha_1 \mathbf{x}_1$$

and

$$\begin{bmatrix} \frac{1}{2}c & \frac{1}{4}c \\ \frac{1}{2}c & \frac{3}{4}c \end{bmatrix} k_2 \begin{bmatrix} 1 \\ -1 \end{bmatrix} = \tfrac{1}{4} \cdot ck_2 \begin{bmatrix} 1 \\ -1 \end{bmatrix} = \alpha_2 \mathbf{x}_2$$

3. *The sum of the characteristic roots of a matrix is equal to its trace,* that is,

$$\text{tr}(A) = \sum_{i=1}^{m} a_{ii} = \lambda_1 + \lambda_2 + \cdots + \lambda_m = \sum_{j=1}^{m} \lambda_j$$

$$\text{tr}\begin{bmatrix} \frac{1}{2} & \frac{1}{4} \\ \frac{1}{2} & \frac{3}{4} \end{bmatrix} = \frac{1}{2} + \frac{3}{4} = 1\frac{1}{4} = \lambda_1 + \lambda_2$$

4. *The product of the characteristic roots of a matrix is equal to its determinant,* that is,

$$|\mathbf{A}| = \lambda_1 \cdot \lambda_2 \cdots \lambda_m = \prod_{j=1}^{m} \lambda_j$$

$$\begin{vmatrix} \frac{1}{2} & \frac{1}{4} \\ \frac{1}{2} & \frac{3}{4} \end{vmatrix} = \frac{1}{2}\left(\frac{3}{4}\right) - \frac{1}{4}\left(\frac{1}{2}\right) = 1\left(\frac{1}{4}\right) = \lambda_1 \cdot \lambda_2$$

5. *The characteristic roots of a matrix and its inverse are inverses of each other. Both matrices, however, have the same characteristic vectors.*

$$|\mathbf{A}^{-1} - \lambda\mathbf{I}| = \begin{vmatrix} 3 - \beta & -1 \\ -2 & 2 - \beta \end{vmatrix}$$

$$= (3 - \beta)(2 - \beta) - 1(2) = \beta^2 - 5\beta + 4 = 0$$

and

$$(\beta - 4)(\beta - 1) = 0$$

Hence,

$$\beta_1 = 1 = \frac{1}{\lambda_1}$$

$$\beta_2 = 4 = \frac{1}{\lambda_2}$$

Also,

$$\begin{bmatrix} 3 & -1 \\ -2 & 2 \end{bmatrix} k_1 \begin{bmatrix} 1 \\ 2 \end{bmatrix} = 1 \cdot k_1 \begin{bmatrix} 1 \\ 2 \end{bmatrix} = \beta_1 \mathbf{x}_1$$

and

$$\begin{bmatrix} 3 & -1 \\ -2 & 2 \end{bmatrix} k_2 \begin{bmatrix} 1 \\ -1 \end{bmatrix} = 4 \cdot k_2 \begin{bmatrix} 1 \\ -1 \end{bmatrix} = \beta_2 \mathbf{x}_2$$

6. *The characteristic roots of a triangular or diagonal matrix are the elements in the principal diagonal.*

$$\begin{vmatrix} \frac{1}{2} - \lambda & \frac{1}{4} \\ 0 & \frac{3}{4} - \lambda \end{vmatrix} = (\tfrac{1}{2} - \lambda)(\tfrac{3}{4} - \lambda) - \tfrac{1}{4}(0)$$

$$= \lambda^2 - \tfrac{5}{4}\lambda + \tfrac{3}{8} = 0$$

and

$$(\lambda - \tfrac{3}{4})(\lambda - \tfrac{1}{2}) = 0$$

Hence,

$$\lambda_1 = \tfrac{3}{4}$$

$$\lambda_2 = \tfrac{1}{2}$$

7.2 DIAGONALIZATION AND OTHER MATRIX TRANSFORMATIONS

When two square matrices, **A** and **B**, say, are related by an equation of the type

$$\mathbf{B} = \mathbf{TAT}^{-1}$$

where **T** is a nonsingular square matrix, they are then said to be connected by a *transformation.* Such transformations often are very useful in urban and regional analysis, and we shall therefore consider a few of the more important ones in this section.

7.2.1 DIAGONALIZATION

Earlier, we defined the mth-order modal matrix **M** as a matrix consisting of the m characteristic vectors of a matrix **A**. Thus the characteristic vectors $\mathbf{x}_1, \mathbf{x}_2, \ldots, \mathbf{x}_m$, defining the modal matrix, must satisfy the equations

$$\mathbf{Ax}_1 = \lambda_1 \mathbf{x}_1, \quad \mathbf{Ax}_2 = \lambda_2 \mathbf{x}_2, \quad \ldots, \quad \mathbf{Ax}_m = \lambda_m \mathbf{x}_m$$

where $\lambda_1, \lambda_2, \ldots, \lambda_m$ are the characteristic roots of **A**. And if we premultiply the modal matrix by **A**,

$$\begin{aligned}\mathbf{AM} &= \mathbf{A}[\mathbf{x}_1 \quad \mathbf{x}_2 \cdots \mathbf{x}_m] \\ &= [\mathbf{Ax}_1 \quad \mathbf{Ax}_2 \cdots \mathbf{Ax}_m] \\ &= [\lambda_1\mathbf{x}_1 \quad \lambda_2\mathbf{x}_2 \cdots \lambda_m\mathbf{x}_m]\end{aligned}$$

Recalling that

$$\Lambda = \begin{bmatrix} \lambda_1 & 0 & \cdots & 0 \\ 0 & \lambda_2 & \cdots & 0 \\ \vdots & \vdots & \ddots & \vdots \\ 0 & 0 & \cdots & \lambda_m \end{bmatrix}$$

we conclude that

$$\mathbf{AM} = \mathbf{M}\Lambda \tag{7.7}$$

and assuming that the columns of **M** are linearly independent, we may premultiply both sides of (7.7) by the inverse of **M** to derive the fundamental relation

$$\mathbf{M}^{-1}\mathbf{AM} = \Lambda \tag{7.8}$$

Alternatively, postmultiplying both sides of (7.7) by the inverse of **M**, we obtain the equally important result

$$\mathbf{A} = \mathbf{M}\Lambda\mathbf{M}^{-1} \tag{7.9}$$

Equation (7.8) expresses the *diagonalization* of the matrix **A**, or the *transformation* of **A** into a diagonal matrix. It defines an important relationship between a matrix, its modal matrix, and its spectral matrix. We shall find this relationship particularly useful in our discussion of principal axes in the next chapter.

Note that (7.9) provides a useful method for deriving powers of **A**, once **M** and $\mathbf{M}^{-1}$ have been obtained, since only the powers of the diagonals in the matrix Λ are required. For example,

$$\begin{aligned}\mathbf{A}^2 &= (\mathbf{M}\Lambda\mathbf{M}^{-1})(\mathbf{M}\Lambda\mathbf{M}^{-1}) \\ &= \mathbf{M}\Lambda^2\mathbf{M}^{-1}\end{aligned}$$

and, in general,

$$\mathbf{A}^p = \mathbf{M}\Lambda^p\mathbf{M}^{-1} \tag{7.10}$$

for any integer p, including (if it exists)

$$(\mathbf{A}^{-1})^p = \mathbf{A}^{-p} = \mathbf{M}\Lambda^{-p}\mathbf{M}^{-1}$$

Any square matrix of order m that has m linearly independent characteristic vectors may be diagonalized. Two different sufficient, but not necessary, conditions for a matrix to have m linearly independent characteristic vectors are: (a) that the matrix have m distinctly different characteristic roots, or (b) that the matrix be symmetric. If either of these two conditions is met, the matrix will have m linearly independent characteristic vectors and, therefore, can be diagonalized. A matrix of order m that has multiple characteristic roots can also be diagonalized, however, if the rank of $(\mathbf{A}-\lambda_i\mathbf{I})$ is equal to $m - r_i$, for all $i = 1, 2, \ldots, s$, where $\lambda_1, \lambda_2, \ldots, \lambda_s$ have multiplicities $r_1, r_2, \ldots, r_s$, respectively. The case of m distinct roots, therefore, is the special case when $r_i = 1$ for all i.

Example. We may illustrate the diagonalization of a matrix by referring, once again, to the numerical example of Section 7.2. For that second-order matrix, we obtained the two characteristic roots $\lambda_1 = 1$ and $\lambda_2 = \frac{1}{4}$, and the modal matrix

$$\mathbf{M} = \begin{bmatrix} k_1 & k_2 \\ 2k_1 & -k_2 \end{bmatrix}$$

Thus, for $k_1 = k_2 = 1$, say, we have that

$$\mathbf{M}^{-1}\mathbf{A}\mathbf{M} = \begin{bmatrix} \frac{1}{3} & \frac{1}{3} \\ \frac{2}{3} & -\frac{1}{3} \end{bmatrix} \begin{bmatrix} \frac{1}{2} & \frac{1}{4} \\ \frac{1}{2} & \frac{3}{4} \end{bmatrix} \begin{bmatrix} 1 & 1 \\ 2 & -1 \end{bmatrix} = \begin{bmatrix} 1 & 0 \\ 0 & \frac{1}{4} \end{bmatrix} = \mathbf{\Lambda}$$

or, alternatively,

$$\mathbf{A} = \begin{bmatrix} \frac{1}{2} & \frac{1}{4} \\ \frac{1}{2} & \frac{3}{4} \end{bmatrix} = \begin{bmatrix} 1 & 1 \\ 2 & -1 \end{bmatrix} \begin{bmatrix} 1 & 0 \\ 0 & \frac{1}{4} \end{bmatrix} \begin{bmatrix} \frac{1}{3} & \frac{1}{3} \\ \frac{2}{3} & -\frac{1}{3} \end{bmatrix} = \mathbf{M}\mathbf{\Lambda}\mathbf{M}^{-1}$$

7.2.2 APPLICATION: ESTIMATION OF GROWTH MATRICES BY TEMPORAL DECONSOLIDATION

A common constraint in interregional population analysis and forecasting is the absence of reliable data concerning the behavior of the fundamental components of population change, particularly in- and out-migration. Frequently, data on births, deaths, and migration are available for an *n-unit time interval,* and it is desired to estimate the corresponding data for an "average" *single-unit time interval.* Let us define this estimation problem as *estimation by temporal deconsolidation.*

The problem of deconsolidating a growth matrix, $\mathbf{G}$, say, which defines a growth regime during an n-unit time interval into the corresponding "average" growth matrix for a single-unit time interval is equivalent to the problem of finding a matrix $\mathbf{P}$ such that

$$\mathbf{P}^n = \mathbf{G}$$

A convenient solution method is to find a diagonalization of $\mathbf{G}$ such that

$$\mathbf{G} = \mathbf{M}\mathbf{\Lambda}\mathbf{M}^{-1}$$

as in (7.10).

Since the temporal deconsolidation problem is to find $\mathbf{G}^{1/n}$, we may use (7.10) to establish the relationship

$$\mathbf{G}^{1/n} = \mathbf{M}\mathbf{\Lambda}^{1/n}\mathbf{M}^{-1}$$

For a $\mathbf{G}$ with distinct characteristic roots, a solution for $\mathbf{\Lambda}$ is a diagonal matrix with nonzero entries equal to the characteristic roots of the determinental equation

$$|\mathbf{G} - \lambda\mathbf{I}| = 0$$

and the columns of $\mathbf{M}$ are characteristic vectors that correspond to these characteristic roots. A unique solution for $\mathbf{M}$ does not exist; however, any solution will do the job.

At this point, the two-region growth process of (1.19) may serve to clarify the discussion. Recall the growth matrix $\mathbf{G}$ in (1.40):

$$\mathbf{G} = \begin{bmatrix} 1.0899 & 0.0298 \\ 0.1380 & 1.1451 \end{bmatrix}$$

The two characteristic roots of this matrix are $\lambda_1 = 1.1873$ and $\lambda_2 = 1.0477$. Hence,

$$\mathbf{\Lambda} = \begin{bmatrix} 1.1873 & 0 \\ 0 & 1.0477 \end{bmatrix}$$

$$\mathbf{M} = \mathbf{N} = \begin{bmatrix} 0.2925 & -0.5767 \\ 0.9563 & 0.8170 \end{bmatrix}$$

and

$$\mathbf{M}^{-1} = \mathbf{N}^{-1} = \begin{bmatrix} 1.0335 & 0.7296 \\ -1.2098 & 0.3701 \end{bmatrix}$$

To check our arithmetic, the reader should compute $\mathbf{M}\mathbf{\Lambda}\mathbf{M}^{-1}$ and confirm that the result is indeed the matrix $\mathbf{G}$.

With the diagonalization of $\mathbf{G}$, we now are in a position to find $\mathbf{G}^{1/10}$, say. The first step is to derive $\mathbf{\Lambda}^{1/10}$. Since $\mathbf{\Lambda}$ is a diagonal matrix, we only need to find the tenth roots of its nonzero elements:

$$\mathbf{\Lambda}^{1/10} = \begin{bmatrix} 1.0173 & 0 \\ 0 & 1.0047 \end{bmatrix}$$

Recalling (7.10), we have

$$\begin{aligned} \mathbf{P} = \mathbf{G}^{1/10} &= \mathbf{M}\mathbf{\Lambda}^{1/10}\mathbf{M}^{-1} \\ &= \begin{bmatrix} 0.2925 & -0.5767 \\ 0.9563 & 0.8170 \end{bmatrix} \begin{bmatrix} 1.0173 & 0 \\ 0 & 1.0047 \end{bmatrix} \begin{bmatrix} 1.0335 & 0.7296 \\ -1.2098 & 0.3701 \end{bmatrix} \\ &= \begin{bmatrix} 1.0085 & 0.0027 \\ 0.0125 & 1.0135 \end{bmatrix} \end{aligned}$$

By applying the one-year growth operator, **P**, to the interregional distribution in 1950, **w**(1950), we can derive an estimate of the 1951 interregional distribution, **w**(1951):

$$\begin{bmatrix} 11054 \\ 142133 \end{bmatrix} = \begin{bmatrix} 1.0085 & 0.0027 \\ 0.0125 & 1.0135 \end{bmatrix} \begin{bmatrix} 10586 \\ 140111 \end{bmatrix}$$

The off-diagonal elements of **P** allow us to estimate annual interregional flows, and by subtracting unity from the column sums we have an estimate of the rate of natural increase in each region. If we assume that the ratio between the number of births and the number of deaths that existed for the 10-year period also holds for each year, we may decompose the natural increase figure into total births and total deaths.

7.2.3 CONGRUENCE AND SIMILARITY TRANSFORMATIONS

Diagonalization is only one of several kinds of matrix transformations that may arise. In addition, we may identify the *congruence transformation* defined by the equation

$$\mathbf{B} = \mathbf{T}'\mathbf{A}\mathbf{T} \tag{7.11}$$

and the *similarity transformation* denoted by

$$\mathbf{B} = \mathbf{T}^{-1}\mathbf{A}\mathbf{T} \tag{7.12}$$

In both equations, **A**, **B**, and **T** are square matrices of the same order. In (7.11), the matrices **A** and **B** are said to be *congruent*. In (7.12), the same two matrices are said to be *similar*.

If the transformation matrix is an orthogonal matrix, its inverse is equal to its transpose, Thus an *orthogonal similarity transformation* is also a congruence transformation, and

$$\mathbf{B} = \mathbf{T}^{-1}\mathbf{A}\mathbf{T} = \mathbf{T}'\mathbf{A}\mathbf{T} \tag{7.13}$$

The matrices **A** and **B** in (7.13) are said to be *orthogonally similar*.

An important property concerning the characteristic roots and characteristic vectors of similar matrices may now be easily established. First, we recall that the characteristic roots and characteristic vectors of the matrix **A** satisfy the equation

$$\mathbf{A}\mathbf{x} = \lambda\mathbf{x} \tag{7.14}$$

Next, we premultiply both sides of (7.14) by $\mathbf{T}^{-1}$ to find

$$\mathbf{T}^{-1}\mathbf{A}\mathbf{x} = \lambda\mathbf{T}^{-1}\mathbf{x}$$

Inserting $\mathbf{T}\mathbf{T}^{-1}$ between **A** and **x** on the left-hand side of the equation yields

$$\mathbf{T}^{-1}\mathbf{A}\mathbf{T}\mathbf{T}^{-1}\mathbf{x} = \lambda\mathbf{T}^{-1}\mathbf{x} \tag{7.15}$$

Finally, if we let

$$\mathbf{y} = \mathbf{T}^{-1}\mathbf{x} \tag{7.16}$$

and

$$\mathbf{B} = \mathbf{T}^{-1}\mathbf{A}\mathbf{T} \tag{7.17}$$

then (7.15) becomes

$$\mathbf{B}\mathbf{y} = \lambda\mathbf{y} \tag{7.18}$$

Equations (7.14) and (7.18) have the same form and the same characteristic roots. Furthermore, the characteristic vectors of **B** are related to the characteristic vectors of **A** by (7.16).

7.3 SYMMETRIC AND NONNEGATIVE SQUARE MATRICES

In this section, we will consider two special classes of square matrices that are frequently encountered in urban and regional analysis and that warrant special consideration because they possess certain special properties. They are symmetric matrices and nonnegative matrices.

7.3.1 SYMMETRIC MATRICES

A fundamental property of symmetric matrices with real rather than complex-valued elements is the fact that all of the characteristic roots of such matrices are themselves real-valued. It follows, therefore, that all of their characteristic vectors are also real-valued. Moreover, when a characteristic root of a symmetric matrix has multiplicity r, there always will be r linearly independent characteristic vectors associated with it. Therefore, a symmetric matrix of order m always has m linearly independent characteristic vectors. Finally, it can be easily established that characteristic vectors corresponding to distinct characteristic roots of a symmetric matrix are orthogonal to one another. Thus the modal matrix **M** will have mutually orthogonal column vectors. We simply observe that for two different characteristic roots λ_i and λ_j of the matrix **A**, and their associated characteristic vectors $\mathbf{x}_i$ and $\mathbf{x}_j$, we have the following relationships:

$$\mathbf{x}_j'\mathbf{A}\mathbf{x}_i = \mathbf{x}_j'\lambda_i\mathbf{x}_i = \lambda_i\mathbf{x}_j'\mathbf{x}_i \tag{7.19}$$

$$\mathbf{x}_i'\mathbf{A}\mathbf{x}_j = \mathbf{x}_i'\lambda_j\mathbf{x}_j = \lambda_j\mathbf{x}_i'\mathbf{x}_j \tag{7.20}$$

Transposing (7.19) and noting that $\mathbf{A}' = \mathbf{A}$, we obtain

$$\mathbf{x}_i'\mathbf{A}\mathbf{x}_j = \lambda_i\mathbf{x}_i'\mathbf{x}_j$$

and, by (7.20),

$$= \lambda_j\mathbf{x}_i'\mathbf{x}_j$$

Thus,

$$\lambda_i\mathbf{x}_i'\mathbf{x}_j = \lambda_j\mathbf{x}_i'\mathbf{x}_j$$

$$(\lambda_i - \lambda_j)\mathbf{x}_i'\mathbf{x}_j = 0$$

and, since $\lambda_i \neq \lambda_j$,

$$\mathbf{x}_i'\mathbf{x}_j = 0$$

We conclude, therefore, that the characteristic vectors associated with two different characteristic roots of the matrix **A** are orthogonal.

Example. Let us illustrate the above properties with the symmetric matrix

$$\mathbf{A} = \begin{bmatrix} 2 & 1 \\ 1 & 2 \end{bmatrix}$$

The characteristic equation of **A** is

$$\begin{vmatrix} 2-\lambda & 1 \\ 1 & 2-\lambda \end{vmatrix} = \lambda^2 - 4\lambda + 3 = (\lambda - 3)(\lambda - 1) = 0$$

Thus the characteristic roots are

$$\lambda_1 = 3 \qquad \lambda_2 = 1$$

and the corresponding characteristic vectors are

$$\mathbf{x}_1 = k_1 \begin{bmatrix} 1 \\ 1 \end{bmatrix} \qquad \mathbf{x}_2 = k_2 \begin{bmatrix} 1 \\ -1 \end{bmatrix}$$

The modal matrix **M** is

$$\mathbf{M} = \begin{bmatrix} k_1 & k_2 \\ k_1 & -k_2 \end{bmatrix}$$

and we observe that its columns are orthogonal, that is,

$$\mathbf{x}_1'\mathbf{x}_2 = [k_1 \quad k_1] \begin{bmatrix} k_2 \\ -k_2 \end{bmatrix} = 0$$

We may normalize the characteristic vectors of such a symmetric matrix to form a normalized modal matrix. Since the normalized modal matrix of such a symmetric matrix is orthogonal, we shall denote it by **Q**, instead of by **N**, in order to distinguish it from normalized modal matrices which, in general, are not orthogonal. The orthogonal matrix **Q** for our example is

$$\mathbf{Q} = [\mathbf{v}_1 \quad \mathbf{v}_2] = \begin{bmatrix} \dfrac{\sqrt{2}}{2} & \dfrac{\sqrt{2}}{2} \\ \dfrac{\sqrt{2}}{2} & \dfrac{-\sqrt{2}}{2} \end{bmatrix}$$

Because a symmetric matrix of order m always has m linearly independent characteristic vectors, it always can be diagonalized by a similarity transformation. If such a transformation is carried out with the orthogonal matrix **Q**, then

$$\mathbf{Q}^{-1}\mathbf{A}\mathbf{Q} = \mathbf{Q}'\mathbf{A}\mathbf{Q} = \mathbf{\Lambda} \tag{7.21}$$

For the above numerical example, therefore, we have that

$$\begin{bmatrix} \frac{\sqrt{2}}{2} & \frac{\sqrt{2}}{2} \\ \frac{\sqrt{2}}{2} & \frac{-\sqrt{2}}{2} \end{bmatrix} \begin{bmatrix} 2 & 1 \\ 1 & 2 \end{bmatrix} \begin{bmatrix} \frac{\sqrt{2}}{2} & \frac{\sqrt{2}}{2} \\ \frac{\sqrt{2}}{2} & \frac{-\sqrt{2}}{2} \end{bmatrix} = \begin{bmatrix} 3 & 0 \\ 0 & 1 \end{bmatrix}$$

7.3.2 NONNEGATIVE MATRICES

We shall now consider a few useful properties of another special class of square matrices: *nonnegative matrices.* A matrix, $\mathbf{A}$, is said to be a *nonnegative matrix* if its every element is nonnegative, that is, if $a_{ij} \geqq 0$. If every $a_{ij} > 0$, then we call $\mathbf{A}$ a *positive matrix.* We shall also need to distinguish between *decomposable* (reducible) and *indecomposable* (irreducible) nonnegative square matrices. A nonnegative square matrix is said to be *decomposable* if a similarity transformation, carried out with a permutation matrix $\mathbf{P}$,[1] can transform it to the form

$$\mathbf{A} = \left[\begin{array}{c|c} \mathbf{A}_{11} & \mathbf{A}_{12} \\ \hline \mathbf{0} & \mathbf{A}_{22} \end{array}\right] \tag{7.22}$$

where $\mathbf{A}_{11}$ and $\mathbf{A}_{22}$ are square matrices and $\mathbf{0}$ is the zero matrix. A matrix that cannot be so transformed is said to be *indecomposable.*

Examples.

(i) Let us illustrate decomposable and indecomposable matrices with a few numerical examples. First, consider the matrix

$$\mathbf{A} = \begin{bmatrix} 1 & 3 & 4 \\ 0 & 2 & 0 \\ 4 & 3 & 5 \end{bmatrix}$$

By using the appropriate elementary matrix and its transpose (which is also its inverse), we can interchange the second and third rows and the second and third columns. Thus,

$$\mathbf{PA} = \begin{bmatrix} 1 & 0 & 0 \\ 0 & 0 & 1 \\ 0 & 1 & 0 \end{bmatrix} \begin{bmatrix} 1 & 3 & 4 \\ 0 & 2 & 0 \\ 4 & 3 & 5 \end{bmatrix} = \begin{bmatrix} 1 & 3 & 4 \\ 4 & 3 & 5 \\ 0 & 2 & 0 \end{bmatrix}$$

[1] A permutation matrix is a matrix with only a single nonzero element of unity in each row and column.

and

$$\mathbf{PAP'} = \mathbf{PAP}^{-1} = \begin{bmatrix} 1 & 3 & 4 \\ 4 & 3 & 5 \\ 0 & 2 & 0 \end{bmatrix} \begin{bmatrix} 1 & 0 & 0 \\ 0 & 0 & 1 \\ 0 & 1 & 0 \end{bmatrix} = \begin{bmatrix} 1 & 4 & 3 \\ 4 & 5 & 3 \\ 0 & 0 & 2 \end{bmatrix}$$

We now partition **PAP′** as follows:

$$\mathbf{PAP'} = \mathbf{PAP}^{-1} = \left[\begin{array}{cc|c} 1 & 4 & 3 \\ 4 & 5 & 3 \\ \hline 0 & 0 & 2 \end{array}\right] = \left[\begin{array}{c|c} \mathbf{A}_{11} & \mathbf{A}_{12} \\ \hline \mathbf{0} & \mathbf{A}_{22} \end{array}\right]$$

and observe that we have transformed **A** into the form defined by (7.22). Hence **A** is decomposable. Notice, however, that $\mathbf{A}_{11}$ and $\mathbf{A}_{22}$ are both indecomposable.

(ii) Next consider the matrix

$$\mathbf{B} = \begin{bmatrix} 0 & 1 & 3 \\ 2 & 5 & 3 \\ 6 & 4 & 1 \end{bmatrix}$$

We can interchange Rows 1 and 3 so that the zero is brought down to the lower left-hand corner, as follows:

$$\mathbf{PB} = \begin{bmatrix} 0 & 0 & 1 \\ 0 & 1 & 0 \\ 1 & 0 & 0 \end{bmatrix} \begin{bmatrix} 0 & 1 & 3 \\ 2 & 5 & 3 \\ 6 & 4 & 1 \end{bmatrix} = \begin{bmatrix} 6 & 4 & 1 \\ 2 & 5 & 3 \\ 0 & 1 & 3 \end{bmatrix}$$

but then we have to interchange Columns 1 and 3, which transfers the zero to the lower right-hand corner:

$$\mathbf{PBP'} = \mathbf{PBP}^{-1} = \begin{bmatrix} 6 & 4 & 1 \\ 2 & 5 & 3 \\ 0 & 1 & 3 \end{bmatrix} \begin{bmatrix} 0 & 0 & 1 \\ 0 & 1 & 0 \\ 1 & 0 & 0 \end{bmatrix} = \begin{bmatrix} 1 & 4 & 6 \\ 3 & 5 & 2 \\ 3 & 1 & 0 \end{bmatrix}$$

We cannot transform the matrix **B** into the form specified by (7.22); therefore, **B** is indecomposable.

Nonnegative indecomposable square matrices have a fundamental property that is very useful in urban and regional analysis. This property is commonly referred to as the *Perron-Frobenius theorem,* in honor of the two mathematicians who first established it. In essence, the Perron-Frobenius theorem states that any nonnegative indecomposable square matrix has a unique characteristic root, λ_1, say, that is real, positive, and not less in absolute value than any other characteristic root. Moreover, one can associate with this *dominant* characteristic root a characteristic vector, $\mathbf{x}_1$, say, that has only positive elements, that is, $\mathbf{x}_1 > 0$. If this matrix also is *primitive*,[2] then λ_1 is *larger* in absolute value than any other characteristic root of the square matrix.

7.4 APPLICATION: ANALYSIS OF STABLE GROWTH

Consider the behavior, over time, of the following matrix multiplication process:

$$\begin{aligned}
\mathbf{u}(t+1) &= \mathbf{A}\mathbf{u}(t) \\
\mathbf{u}(t+2) &= \mathbf{A}\mathbf{u}(t+1) = \mathbf{A}[\mathbf{A}\mathbf{u}(t)] = \mathbf{A}^2\mathbf{u}(t) \\
&\vdots \\
\mathbf{u}(t+n) &= \mathbf{A}\mathbf{u}(t+n-1) = \cdots = \mathbf{A}^n\mathbf{u}(t)
\end{aligned} \tag{7.23}$$

where, for example,

$$\mathbf{A} = \begin{bmatrix} \frac{1}{2} & \frac{1}{4} \\ \frac{1}{2} & \frac{3}{4} \end{bmatrix} \qquad \mathbf{u}(t) = \begin{bmatrix} 24 \\ 24 \end{bmatrix}$$

If we carry out this multiplication process for $n = 1, 2,$ and 3, we obtain the following sequence of results:

$$\begin{bmatrix} 18 \\ 30 \end{bmatrix} = \begin{bmatrix} \frac{1}{2} & \frac{1}{4} \\ \frac{1}{2} & \frac{3}{4} \end{bmatrix} \begin{bmatrix} 24 \\ 24 \end{bmatrix}$$

$$\begin{bmatrix} 16\frac{1}{2} \\ 31\frac{1}{2} \end{bmatrix} = \begin{bmatrix} \frac{1}{2} & \frac{1}{4} \\ \frac{1}{2} & \frac{3}{4} \end{bmatrix} \begin{bmatrix} 18 \\ 30 \end{bmatrix} = \begin{bmatrix} \frac{3}{8} & \frac{5}{16} \\ \frac{5}{8} & \frac{11}{16} \end{bmatrix} \begin{bmatrix} 24 \\ 24 \end{bmatrix}$$

$$\begin{bmatrix} 16\frac{1}{8} \\ 31\frac{7}{8} \end{bmatrix} = \begin{bmatrix} \frac{1}{2} & \frac{1}{4} \\ \frac{1}{2} & \frac{3}{4} \end{bmatrix} \begin{bmatrix} 16\frac{1}{2} \\ 31\frac{1}{2} \end{bmatrix} = \begin{bmatrix} \frac{11}{32} & \frac{21}{64} \\ \frac{21}{32} & \frac{43}{64} \end{bmatrix} \begin{bmatrix} 24 \\ 24 \end{bmatrix}$$

And, in general, for any given value of n, we may establish that[3]

$$\begin{bmatrix} 16 + 8\left(\frac{1}{4}\right)^n \\ 32 - 8\left(\frac{1}{4}\right)^n \end{bmatrix} = \begin{bmatrix} \frac{1}{3} + \frac{2}{3}\left(\frac{1}{4}\right)^n & \frac{1}{3} - \frac{1}{3}\left(\frac{1}{4}\right)^n \\ \frac{2}{3} - \frac{2}{3}\left(\frac{1}{4}\right)^n & \frac{2}{3} + \frac{1}{3}\left(\frac{1}{4}\right)^n \end{bmatrix} \begin{bmatrix} 24 \\ 24 \end{bmatrix} \tag{7.24}$$

[2] The square matrix $\mathbf{A}$ is said to be *primitive* if there exists an s such that $\mathbf{A}^s > 0$. Otherwise, $\mathbf{A}$ is said to be *imprimitive*. Note that primitivity implies indecomposability, but that the reverse is not necessarily true.

[3] The derivation of this general expression is not presented until (7.31). For the present, however, the reader may verify that it does indeed produce the numerical results that we have obtained with $n = 1, 2,$ and 3.

Observe now what happens when n gets very large, that is, as $n \to \infty$. All terms involving the fraction $\frac{1}{4}$ become very small, that is, $(\frac{1}{4})^n \to 0$, and we are left with the result:

$$\begin{bmatrix} 16 \\ 32 \end{bmatrix} = \begin{bmatrix} \frac{1}{3} & \frac{1}{3} \\ \frac{2}{3} & \frac{2}{3} \end{bmatrix} \begin{bmatrix} 24 \\ 24 \end{bmatrix} \tag{7.25}$$

This is the dynamic equilibrium condition, which our multiplication process is approaching over time. Upon attaining this equilibrium situation, which we shall define as the *stable state,* the vector **u** and the matrix $\mathbf{A}^n$ remain constant forever after. From that point on, the process may be said to be growing at its *stable growth rate* (which, in this numerical example, is zero), and the vector **u** may be said to have assumed its *stable distribution* [which in this example is $(\frac{1}{3}, \frac{2}{3})$]. Furthermore, it easily may be seen from (7.24) that the *stable growth rate* and the *stable distribution* are independent of the initial values in the vector $\mathbf{u}(t)$. That is, any vector $\mathbf{u}(t)$, if continually multiplied by this particular matrix **A**, in the manner defined by (7.23), will ultimately grow at a stable rate of zero and assume a stable distribution of $(\frac{1}{3}, \frac{2}{3})$. Since, in this particular example, the stable rate of growth is zero, the stable vector will always be (16, 32) for any $\mathbf{u}(t)$ which has two elements that are nonnegative and that sum to 48. Thus, for example,

$$\begin{bmatrix} 14 \\ 34 \end{bmatrix} = \begin{bmatrix} \frac{1}{2} & \frac{1}{4} \\ \frac{1}{2} & \frac{3}{4} \end{bmatrix} \begin{bmatrix} 8 \\ 40 \end{bmatrix}$$

$$\begin{bmatrix} 15\frac{1}{2} \\ 32\frac{1}{2} \end{bmatrix} = \begin{bmatrix} \frac{1}{2} & \frac{1}{4} \\ \frac{1}{2} & \frac{3}{4} \end{bmatrix} \begin{bmatrix} 14 \\ 34 \end{bmatrix} = \begin{bmatrix} \frac{3}{8} & \frac{5}{16} \\ \frac{5}{8} & \frac{11}{16} \end{bmatrix} \begin{bmatrix} 8 \\ 40 \end{bmatrix}$$

$$\begin{bmatrix} 15\frac{7}{8} \\ 32\frac{1}{8} \end{bmatrix} = \begin{bmatrix} \frac{1}{2} & \frac{1}{4} \\ \frac{1}{2} & \frac{3}{4} \end{bmatrix} \begin{bmatrix} 15\frac{1}{2} \\ 32\frac{1}{2} \end{bmatrix} = \begin{bmatrix} \frac{11}{32} & \frac{21}{64} \\ \frac{21}{32} & \frac{43}{64} \end{bmatrix} \begin{bmatrix} 8 \\ 40 \end{bmatrix}$$

$$\vdots$$

$$\begin{bmatrix} 16 \\ 32 \end{bmatrix} = \begin{bmatrix} \frac{1}{2} & \frac{1}{4} \\ \frac{1}{2} & \frac{3}{4} \end{bmatrix} \begin{bmatrix} 16 \\ 32 \end{bmatrix} = \begin{bmatrix} \frac{1}{3} & \frac{1}{3} \\ \frac{2}{3} & \frac{2}{3} \end{bmatrix} \begin{bmatrix} 8 \\ 40 \end{bmatrix}$$

The columns of the above growth matrix sum to unity. This is why the sum of the elements of $\mathbf{u}(t)$ always remains constant, or *stationary,* throughout the multiplication sequence. Stable growth rates and stable distributions also may arise in nonstationary situations. For example, if the first of the above two vectors were multiplied by the matrix

$$\mathbf{A} = \begin{bmatrix} 1 & \frac{1}{4} \\ \frac{1}{2} & \frac{3}{4} \end{bmatrix}$$

then, proceeding according to (7.23), we would obtain the following sequence:

$$\begin{bmatrix} 30 \\ 30 \end{bmatrix} = \begin{bmatrix} 1 & \frac{1}{4} \\ \frac{1}{2} & \frac{3}{4} \end{bmatrix} \begin{bmatrix} 24 \\ 24 \end{bmatrix}$$

$$\begin{bmatrix} 37\frac{1}{2} \\ 37\frac{1}{2} \end{bmatrix} = \begin{bmatrix} 1 & \frac{1}{4} \\ \frac{1}{2} & \frac{3}{4} \end{bmatrix} \begin{bmatrix} 30 \\ 30 \end{bmatrix} = \begin{bmatrix} \frac{9}{8} & \frac{7}{16} \\ \frac{7}{8} & \frac{11}{16} \end{bmatrix} \begin{bmatrix} 24 \\ 24 \end{bmatrix}$$

$$\begin{bmatrix} 46\frac{7}{8} \\ 46\frac{7}{8} \end{bmatrix} = \begin{bmatrix} 1 & \frac{1}{4} \\ \frac{1}{2} & \frac{3}{4} \end{bmatrix} \begin{bmatrix} 37\frac{1}{2} \\ 37\frac{1}{2} \end{bmatrix} = \begin{bmatrix} \frac{43}{32} & \frac{39}{64} \\ \frac{39}{32} & \frac{47}{64} \end{bmatrix} \begin{bmatrix} 24 \\ 24 \end{bmatrix}$$

and conclude that the vector $\mathbf{u}$ always will have the stable proportional distribution $(\frac{1}{2}, \frac{1}{2})$ and a stable growth rate of $\frac{1}{4}$. The reader should confirm that the same stable growth rate and stable distribution result from any other initial vector $\mathbf{u}(t)$.

7.4.1 THE DOMINANT CHARACTERISTIC ROOT AND STABLE GROWTH

Let us now reconsider the question of stability from a more general point of view. Assume that the matrix $\mathbf{A}$ in (7.23) is nonnegative, primitive, indecomposable, and has distinct characteristic roots. We then may diagonalize it as follows:

$$\mathbf{A} = \mathbf{M\Lambda M}^{-1} \tag{7.26}$$

Noting that

$$\mathbf{A}^2 = (\mathbf{M\Lambda M}^{-1})(\mathbf{M\Lambda M}^{-1}) = \mathbf{M\Lambda}^2\mathbf{M}^{-1}$$

and that

$$\mathbf{A}^n = \mathbf{M\Lambda}^n\mathbf{M}^{-1} \tag{7.27}$$

we may substitute (7.27) into (7.23) to find

$$\mathbf{u}(t+n) = \mathbf{A}^n\mathbf{u}(t) = \mathbf{M\Lambda}^n\mathbf{M}^{-1}\mathbf{u}(t) \tag{7.28}$$

Recalling that $\mathbf{M}$ is the modal matrix of $\mathbf{A}$, and denoting $\mathbf{M}^{-1}\mathbf{u}(t)$ by $\mathbf{y}$, we conclude that

$$\mathbf{u}(t+n) = \mathbf{M\Lambda}^n\mathbf{y} = [\mathbf{x}_1 \quad \mathbf{x}_2 \cdots \mathbf{x}_m] \begin{bmatrix} \lambda_1{}^n & 0 & \cdots & 0 \\ 0 & \lambda_2{}^n & \cdots & 0 \\ \vdots & \vdots & \ddots & \vdots \\ 0 & 0 & \cdots & \lambda_m{}^n \end{bmatrix} \begin{bmatrix} y_1 \\ y_2 \\ \vdots \\ y_m \end{bmatrix}$$

$$= [\mathbf{x}_1 \quad \mathbf{x}_2 \cdots \mathbf{x}_m] \begin{bmatrix} \lambda_1{}^n y_1 \\ \lambda_2{}^n y_2 \\ \vdots \\ \lambda_m{}^n y_m \end{bmatrix}$$

$$= \lambda_1{}^n y_1 \mathbf{x}_1 + \lambda_2{}^n y_2 \mathbf{x}_2 + \cdots + \lambda_m{}^n y_m \mathbf{x}_m$$

$$= \lambda_1{}^n \left[y_1\mathbf{x}_1 + \left(\frac{\lambda_2}{\lambda_1}\right)^n y_2\mathbf{x}_2 + \cdots + \left(\frac{\lambda_m}{\lambda_1}\right)^n y_m\mathbf{x}_m \right] \tag{7.29}$$

Since **A** is a nonnegative, primitive, and indecomposable matrix, we may draw on the Perron-Frobenius theorem to establish that it has a characteristic root that is real, positive, and larger in absolute value than any of its other characteristic roots. Denoting this root by λ_1, we have, as n increases without bound,

$$\lim_{n\to\infty} \frac{u_i(t+n+1)}{u_i(t+n)} = \lim_{n\to\infty} \frac{\lambda_1^{n+1}\left[y_1x_{i1} + \left(\frac{\lambda_2}{\lambda_1}\right)^{n+1} y_2x_{i2} + \cdots\right]}{\lambda_1^{n}\left[y_1x_{i1} + \left(\frac{\lambda_2}{\lambda_1}\right)^{n} y_2x_{i2} + \cdots\right]} = \lambda_1 \qquad (7.30)$$

hence, ultimately,

$$\mathbf{u}(t+n+1) = \lambda_1\mathbf{u}(t+n)$$

Thus we conclude that the multiplication process expressed by (7.23) approaches a limit, which we have defined as the *stable state*, where the elements of the vector **u** assume an unchanging proportional relationship to one another and all increase at the same constant rate. The constant *stable rate of growth* is equal to the dominant characteristic root of the matrix **A** minus unity, and the unchanging proportional relationship between the elements of the stable state vector, that is, the *stable distribution*, is defined by the associated characteristic vector with its elements scaled so as to sum to unity.

Example. To clarify the above discussion, let us return to the first numerical example of the previous section, where

$$\mathbf{A} = \begin{bmatrix} \frac{1}{2} & \frac{1}{4} \\ \frac{1}{2} & \frac{3}{4} \end{bmatrix} \qquad \mathbf{u}(t) = \begin{bmatrix} 24 \\ 24 \end{bmatrix}$$

The spectral and modal matrices for this particular **A** were computed earlier, and were found to have the following values:

$$\mathbf{\Lambda} = \begin{bmatrix} 1 & 0 \\ 0 & \frac{1}{4} \end{bmatrix} \qquad \mathbf{M} = \begin{bmatrix} k_1 & k_2 \\ 2k_1 & -k_2 \end{bmatrix}$$

Without loss of generality, we may set $k_1 = k_2 = 1$ in the modal matrix and obtain the following diagonalization of **A**:

$$\mathbf{A} = \begin{bmatrix} 1 & 1 \\ 2 & -1 \end{bmatrix} \begin{bmatrix} 1 & 0 \\ 0 & \frac{1}{4} \end{bmatrix} \begin{bmatrix} \frac{1}{3} & \frac{1}{3} \\ \frac{2}{3} & -\frac{1}{3} \end{bmatrix}$$

whence

$$\mathbf{A}^n = \begin{bmatrix} 1 & 1 \\ 2 & -1 \end{bmatrix} \begin{bmatrix} (1)^n & 0 \\ 0 & (\frac{1}{4})^n \end{bmatrix} \begin{bmatrix} \frac{1}{3} & \frac{1}{3} \\ \frac{2}{3} & -\frac{1}{3} \end{bmatrix}$$

$$= \begin{bmatrix} \frac{1}{3} + \frac{2}{3}(\frac{1}{4})^n & \frac{1}{3} - \frac{1}{3}(\frac{1}{4})^n \\ \frac{2}{3} - \frac{2}{3}(\frac{1}{4})^n & \frac{2}{3} + \frac{1}{3}(\frac{1}{4})^n \end{bmatrix} \qquad (7.31)$$

a result we used to derive (7.24). Note that the dominant characteristic root is unity and that the elements of the associated characteristic vector have the proportional relationship $(\frac{1}{3}, \frac{2}{3})$.

7.4.2 AN ITERATIVE SOLUTION ALGORITHM

The determination of the characteristic roots and characteristic vectors of large matrices is a process that requires a great deal of calculation and, therefore, is almost always carried out by digital computers. The procedure we have been using on matrices of order two, however, is not an efficient computational algorithm for larger matrices. Hence computer programs generally use numerical iterative methods to perform such computations. In particular, our proof of the convergence of an arbitrary vector to the stable distribution, in the above paragraphs, suggests a convenient method which is suitable for practical use with matrices of larger orders.

Let us approximate the unknown characteristic vector $\mathbf{x}_1$, which is associated with the dominant characteristic root λ_1 of $\mathbf{A}$, by some trial characteristic vector, $\mathbf{u}(t)$, say. We can obtain an improved approximation, $\mathbf{u}(t+1)$, as follows:

$$\mathbf{u}(t+1) = \mathbf{A}\mathbf{u}(t) \tag{7.32}$$

Next, we compute a column vector, $\boldsymbol{\alpha}(1)$, say, with elements that are the quotients of the corresponding elements of $\mathbf{u}(t+1)$ and $\mathbf{u}(t)$. That is,

$$\boldsymbol{\alpha}(1) = \begin{bmatrix} \dfrac{u_1(t+1)}{u_1(t)} \\ \dfrac{u_2(t+1)}{u_2(t)} \\ \vdots \\ \dfrac{u_m(t+1)}{u_m(t)} \end{bmatrix} \tag{7.33}$$

The vector $\boldsymbol{\alpha}(1)$ is our first approximation of the vector $\boldsymbol{\lambda}_1$, which has every element equal to the dominant characteristic root λ_1:

$$\boldsymbol{\lambda}_1 = \begin{bmatrix} \lambda_1 \\ \lambda_1 \\ \vdots \\ \lambda_1 \end{bmatrix} \tag{7.34}$$

The above computational sequence is now repeated with $\mathbf{u}(t+1)$ taking the place of $\mathbf{u}(t)$ in (7.32) and (7.33), and the whole iterative process is carried out as many times as is necessary to obtain the desired degree of accuracy in the values of λ_1 and $\mathbf{x}_1$. The reader should confirm that when the algorithm is terminated, for some $n = s$, say, the elements of $\boldsymbol{\alpha}(s)$ are the estimates of λ_1 (or one may use their average value, for example), and the vector $\mathbf{u}(t+s)$ is an estimate of the corresponding characteristic vector, $\mathbf{x}_1$ (Exercise 1).

To avoid unusually large or small numbers in the trial characteristic vectors, we generally normalize each trial vector before multiplying it by the matrix $\mathbf{A}$ in (7.32).[4]

Example. We may demonstrate the above iterative algorithm with the numerical example used earlier. Let

$$\mathbf{u}(t) = \begin{bmatrix} 24 \\ 24 \end{bmatrix}$$

Then

$$\mathbf{u}(t+1) = \mathbf{A}\mathbf{u}(t) = \begin{bmatrix} \frac{1}{2} & \frac{1}{4} \\ \frac{1}{2} & \frac{3}{4} \end{bmatrix} \begin{bmatrix} 24 \\ 24 \end{bmatrix} = \begin{bmatrix} 18 \\ 30 \end{bmatrix}$$

$$\boldsymbol{\alpha}(1) = \begin{bmatrix} \frac{18}{24} \\ \frac{30}{24} \end{bmatrix} = \begin{bmatrix} 0.7500 \\ 1.2500 \end{bmatrix}$$

and we have that

$$\mathbf{u}(t+2) = \begin{bmatrix} 16\frac{1}{2} \\ 31\frac{1}{2} \end{bmatrix} \qquad \boldsymbol{\alpha}(2) = \begin{bmatrix} \frac{16\frac{1}{2}}{18} \\ \frac{31\frac{1}{2}}{30} \end{bmatrix} = \begin{bmatrix} 0.9167 \\ 1.0500 \end{bmatrix}$$

$$\mathbf{u}(t+3) = \begin{bmatrix} 16\frac{1}{8} \\ 31\frac{7}{8} \end{bmatrix} \qquad \boldsymbol{\alpha}(3) = \begin{bmatrix} \frac{16\frac{1}{8}}{16\frac{1}{2}} \\ \frac{31\frac{7}{8}}{31\frac{1}{2}} \end{bmatrix} = \begin{bmatrix} 0.9773 \\ 1.0119 \end{bmatrix}$$

$$\vdots \qquad\qquad\qquad \vdots$$

$$\mathbf{u}(t+s) = \begin{bmatrix} 16 \\ 32 \end{bmatrix} \qquad \boldsymbol{\alpha}(s) = \begin{bmatrix} \frac{16}{16} \\ \frac{32}{32} \end{bmatrix} = \begin{bmatrix} 1 \\ 1 \end{bmatrix}$$

[4] The iterative solution algorithm also may be used to find the second largest characteristic root and vector. One simply factorizes out the dominant root and obtains the largest characteristic root of the remaining matrix. Operationally we proceed according to the following theorem: Let the dominant characteristic root of $\mathbf{A}$ be λ_1, say, and let $\mathbf{v}_1$ be the characteristic vector associated with λ_1 such that $\mathbf{v}_1'\mathbf{v}_1 = \lambda_1$; then the second largest characteristic root of $\mathbf{A}$ is the dominant characteristic root of $\mathbf{A} - \mathbf{v}_1\mathbf{v}_1'$. Continuing on in this manner, we can obtain the third, fourth, ..., and mth largest characteristic roots of $\mathbf{A}$ (Exercise 1).

7.4.3 APPLICATION: STABLE GROWTH IN THE MATRIX MODEL OF INTERREGIONAL POPULATION GROWTH AND DISTRIBUTION

In Section 1.5 we outlined three matrix models of population growth and distribution. For each model, we defined an appropriate matrix **G** which, when applied to the population vector $\mathbf{w}(t)$, advanced it to the population vector of the subsequent time period, $\mathbf{w}(t + 1)$. Thus, as we saw in (1.19), an unchanging regime of growth generates the following population projection over time:

$$\mathbf{w}(t + n) = \mathbf{G}\mathbf{w}(t + n - 1) = \mathbf{G}^n\mathbf{w}(t) \tag{7.35}$$

Equation (7.35) has the same form as (7.23). Furthermore, the matrix **G** for the simple two-region population system of (1.40) is positive and nonsingular. Hence, the Perron-Frobenius theorem and the above results, concerning the stability properties of the multiplication process of (7.23), may be applied to that particular population model. We conclude that the population system of (1.40), if subjected to the unchanging schedule of fertility, mortality, and mobility that is defined by the growth matrix in that equation, ultimately will increase at a constant *stable growth rate*, $\lambda_1 - 1$, say, and will assume an unchanging *stable distribution*, $\mathbf{x}_1$, say. Moreover, this stable growth rate is equal to the dominant characteristic root of the growth matrix **G** minus unity, and the corresponding characteristic vector, with its elements scaled to sum to unity, is the stable distribution of the total population.

We may derive the stable growth rate and stable distribution for the population system in (1.40) by solving the characteristic equation,

$$|\mathbf{G} - \lambda\mathbf{I}| = \begin{vmatrix} 1.0899 - \lambda & 0.0298 \\ 0.1380 & 1.1451 - \lambda \end{vmatrix} = 0 \tag{7.36}$$

to find the dominant characteristic root $\lambda_1 = 1.1873$ and, corresponding to this dominant characteristic root, the characteristic vector

$$\mathbf{x}_1 = \begin{bmatrix} 0.2342 \\ 0.7658 \end{bmatrix} \tag{7.37}$$

Thus we conclude that if current (that is, 1950–1960) rates of fertility, mortality, and mobility do not change, then California ultimately will contain approximately 23 percent of the national population, which will be increasing by about $18\frac{3}{4}$ percent every decade. This "horizon-year" projection is a kind of "speedometer" reading of where this particular demographic system is headed if the schedule of growth does not change. We recognize, of course, that the growth regime of this system will not remain constant; nevertheless, such indicators may be used to monitor and chart the direction of change of this system over time. Table 7.1 compares these stable state conditions with conditions that existed in 1950 and 1960, respectively.

The growth matrices in the cohort survival population models defined by (1.22) and (1.25) are square and nonnegative. However, they are decomposable. But their particular structure is such that they always have a nonnegative characteristic root that is real and larger in absolute value than any other characteristic root. Furthermore, it is possible to associate with this dominant characteristic root a characteristic vector that has only positive elements. Using the iterative solution algorithm described in 7.4.2, we obtain, for the **G** in Figure 1.1, the stable growth rate and the stable distribution presented in Table 7.2 below. The stable state solution for the **G** in Figure 1.2 is left as an exercise for the reader (Exercise 4).

Table 7.1. Past and Asymptotic Interregional Population Distributions for California and the Rest of the United States

Region	1950	1960	Stable State
California's Share	0.0702	0.0885	0.2342
10-Year Growth Rate	—	0.4843	0.1873
Rest of the U.S.'s Share	0.9298	0.9115	0.7658
10-Year Growth Rate	—	0.1555	0.1873
Total	1.0000	1.0000	1.0000
National 10-Year Growth Rate	—	0.1786	0.1873

Source: Calculated using the data in Table 1.4.

Table 7.2. Past and Asymptotic Age Distributions: The United States

Age Group	1950 Distribution	1960 Distribution	Stable Age Distribution
0– 9	0.2196	0.1949	0.2175
10–19	0.1643	0.1442	0.1835
20–29	0.1220	0.1574	0.1552
30–39	0.1325	0.1511	0.1307
40–49	0.1266	0.1279	0.1095
50–59	0.1015	0.1029	0.0870
60–69	0.0754	0.0734	0.0638
70–79	0.0453	0.0369	0.0394
80+	0.0127	0.0113	0.0135
10-Year Growth Rate:		0.1516	0.1784

Source: Calculated using the data in Figure 1.1.

7.4.4 APPLICATION: STABLE GROWTH IN THE SPATIAL ACTIVITY ALLOCATION MODEL

In Section 1.6 we described a general spatial activity allocation model that may be used to project the growth and distribution of employment and population in an urban region. The dynamic behavior of this model was summarized in (1.68), which expressed the following relationship between population and total employment over time:

$$\mathbf{w}(t + 1) = \mathbf{Me}(t + 1) = \mathbf{MSe}(t)$$

Thus if, as in the population model, we assume that the growth and distribution matrices remain constant, we have that

$$\mathbf{w}(t + n) = \mathbf{Me}(t + n) = \mathbf{MS}^n\mathbf{e}(t) \tag{7.38}$$

and the model assumes a form similar to (7.23). Hence the stability properties of the nonnegative matrix **S** may be invoked to identify the stable growth rate and stable distribution of employment and population in the urban region being analyzed. For example, returning once again to the data for the Ljubljana Metropolitan Region in Subsection 1.6.3, we may establish that the dominant characteristic root, λ_1, say, of the growth matrix **S** in Figure 1.5 is equal to 1.0615, and that the associated characteristic vector, $\mathbf{x}_1$, say, when scaled to sum to unity, is

$$\mathbf{x}_1 = \begin{bmatrix} 0.0680 \\ 0.0226 \\ 0.0084 \\ 0.0053 \\ 0.0314 \\ 0.0088 \\ 0.0161 \\ 0.0072 \\ 0.0597 \\ 0.0418 \\ 0.0710 \\ 0.0724 \\ 0.0651 \\ 0.0076 \\ 0.0107 \\ 0.5040 \end{bmatrix} \tag{7.39}$$

We may interpret these results as follows: If all the parameters of the system and its behavior were to remain forever as they are now, the Ljubljana Metropolitan Region's employment ultimately would increase by about six percent every five years, and the proportional distribution of that employment would remain in the form described by the vector $\mathbf{x}_1$ in (7.39). The corresponding "horizon-year" population would increase at the same rate and would assume the stable proportional distribution described by the vector $\mathbf{y}$, where

$$\mathbf{y} = \mathbf{M}\mathbf{x}_1 \tag{7.40}$$

This stable population distribution is set out in Column 6 of Table 7.3, which summarizes the changes in the Ljubljana Metropolitan Region's employment and population spatial distributions over time. The derivation of the corresponding results for the Garin-Lowry model, described in Subsection 2.8.2, is left as an exercise for the reader (Exercise 5).

Table 7.3. Proportional Distribution of Employment and Population in the Ljubljana Metropolitan Region and the Rest of Slovenia: 1963, 1968, and at Stability

Commune	Employment			Population		
	1. 1963 $\mathbf{e}(1963)$	2. 1968 $\mathbf{e}(1968)$	3. At Stability $\mathbf{e}(\infty)$	4. 1963 $\mathbf{Me}(1963)$	5. 1968 $\mathbf{Me}(1968)$	6. At Stability $\mathbf{Me}(\infty)$
1. Kranj	0.0636	0.0643	0.0680	0.0304	0.0307	0.0333
2. Skofja Loka	0.0187	0.0189	0.0226	0.0154	0.0156	0.0192
3. Trzic	0.0188	0.0181	0.0084	0.0070	0.0068	0.0035
4. Cerknica	0.0117	0.0110	0.0053	0.0086	0.0081	0.0041
5. Domzale	0.0326	0.0324	0.0314	0.0175	0.0176	0.0191
6. Grosuplje	0.0055	0.0057	0.0088	0.0140	0.0143	0.0222
7. Kamnik	0.0225	0.0220	0.0161	0.0126	0.0123	0.0099
8. Litija	0.0086	0.0083	0.0072	0.0103	0.0100	0.0107
9. Lj.-Bezigrad	0.0251	0.0301	0.0597	0.0211	0.0234	0.0435
10. Lj.-Center	0.0428	0.0360	0.0418	0.0263	0.0251	0.0376
11. Lj.-Moste-Polje	0.0269	0.0321	0.0710	0.0215	0.0239	0.0493
12. Lj.-Siska	0.0553	0.0546	0.0724	0.0293	0.0287	0.0395
13. Lj.-Vic-Rudnik	0.0217	0.0274	0.0651	0.0343	0.0384	0.0802
14. Logatec	0.0100	0.0098	0.0076	0.0067	0.0066	0.0054
15. Vrhnika	0.0103	0.0102	0.0107	0.0078	0.0078	0.0090
Subtotal (L.M.R.)	0.3740	0.3809	0.4960	0.2628	0.2695	0.3865
16. Rest of Slovenia	0.6260	0.6191	0.5040	0.7372	0.7305	0.6135
Total (Slovenia)	1.0000	1.0000	1.0000	1.0000	1.0000	1.0000

Source: Calculated using the data in Figure 1.5 and Tables 1.11 and 1.12. Programmed by Chyi Kang Lu.

7.4.5 APPLICATION: STABLE GROWTH IN THE CLOSED DYNAMIC INPUT-OUTPUT MODEL

The closed dynamic input-output model of Subsection 1.7.3 was defined by the equation

$$\mathbf{x}(t) = \mathbf{A}\mathbf{x}(t) + \mathbf{B}[\mathbf{x}(t+1) - \mathbf{x}(t)] \tag{7.41}$$

The form of (7.41) differs fundamentally from that of (7.23). Hence, to analyze the stability properties of this model, we must modify slightly the approach we used in the above paragraphs. First, we rewrite (7.41) as follows:

$$(\mathbf{I} - \mathbf{A})\mathbf{x}(t) = \mathbf{B}[\mathbf{x}(t+1) - \mathbf{x}(t)]$$
$$\mathbf{x}(t) = (\mathbf{I} - \mathbf{A})^{-1}\mathbf{B}[\mathbf{x}(t+1) - \mathbf{x}(t)]$$
$$\mathbf{B}\mathbf{x}(t) = \mathbf{B}(\mathbf{I} - \mathbf{A})^{-1}\mathbf{B}[\mathbf{x}(t+1) - \mathbf{x}(t)]$$

and, recalling (1.85), we have that

$$\mathbf{s}(t) = \mathbf{B}(\mathbf{I} - \mathbf{A})^{-1}[\mathbf{s}(t+1) - \mathbf{s}(t)]$$

Finally, denoting $\mathbf{B}(\mathbf{I} - \mathbf{A})^{-1}$ by the matrix $\mathbf{C}$, we have that

$$\mathbf{s}(t) = \mathbf{C}[\mathbf{s}(t+1) - \mathbf{s}(t)] \tag{7.42}$$

It may seem tempting, at this point, to rewrite (7.42) as

$$\mathbf{s}(t+1) = \mathbf{C}^{-1}[\mathbf{s}(t) + \mathbf{C}\mathbf{s}(t)] = \mathbf{C}^{-1}(\mathbf{I} + \mathbf{C})\mathbf{s}(t) = \mathbf{G}\mathbf{s}(t) \tag{7.43}$$

and to proceed as in the population and spatial allocation models. However, this would bring us up against two potential problems:

1. $\mathbf{C}^{-1}$ commonly does not exist in practical applications, since we often find that $|\mathbf{C}| = 0$; and
2. $\mathbf{G}$ is not a nonnegative matrix.

Thus we must adopt the following argument. The matrix $\mathbf{C}$ is a nonnegative matrix, since it is a product of two nonnegative matrices:[5] $\mathbf{B}$ and $(\mathbf{I} - \mathbf{A})^{-1}$. Hence, if it is primitive, $\mathbf{C}$ has a dominant characteristic root that is real and positive. Corresponding to this root, there exists a characteristic vector with only positive elements. Therefore, for the economy described by (7.41) to achieve a stable state without excess capacity (sometimes called *balanced growth*), its capital stocks must increase at a constant ratio, σ, say, such that

$$\mathbf{s}(t+1) = \sigma\mathbf{s}(t)$$

[5] The matrix $\mathbf{B}$ is nonnegative by definition. The matrix $(\mathbf{I} - \mathbf{A})^{-1} = \mathbf{I} + \mathbf{A} + \mathbf{A}^2 + \cdots$, and since $\mathbf{A}$ is nonnegative by definition, we conclude that $(\mathbf{I} - \mathbf{A})^{-1}$ also is nonnegative.

or

$$\big[\mathbf{s}(t+1) - \mathbf{s}(t)\big] = (\sigma - 1)\mathbf{s}(t) \tag{7.44}$$

Substituting (7.44) into (7.42), we have

$$\mathbf{s}(t) = \mathbf{C}\big[\mathbf{s}(t+1) - \mathbf{s}(t)\big] = (\sigma - 1)\mathbf{C}\mathbf{s}(t)$$

or

$$\mathbf{C}\mathbf{s}(t) = \left(\frac{1}{\sigma - 1}\right)\mathbf{s}(t) = \lambda_1 \mathbf{s}(t) \tag{7.45}$$

and the stable growth rate of the economy therefore is $\sigma - 1 = 1/\lambda_1$, where λ_1 is the dominant characteristic root of the nonnegative matrix **C**. Any distribution of stocks, $\mathbf{s}(t)$, that is proportional to the corresponding characteristic vector, $\mathbf{x}_1$, say, will continue to increase at the stable growth rate of $1/\lambda_1$, and it can be shown that, in the long run, no other initial distribution can grow as rapidly. Moreover, all other feasible growth rates for the economy are smaller than the stable growth rate.

Let us illustrate the above discussion with the simple closed dynamic input-output example presented in Subsection 1.7.3. There we had the following matrices and initial stocks:

$$\mathbf{B} = \begin{bmatrix} \frac{1}{10} & \frac{3}{50} & \frac{4}{25} \\ \frac{3}{100} & \frac{2}{25} & 0 \\ \frac{1}{10} & 0 & 0 \end{bmatrix} \qquad \mathbf{s}(t) = \mathbf{B}\mathbf{x}(t) = \begin{bmatrix} 70 \\ 30 \\ 20 \end{bmatrix}$$

$$(\mathbf{I} - \mathbf{A})^{-1} = \begin{bmatrix} \frac{155}{72} & \frac{95}{72} & \frac{35}{72} \\ \frac{85}{36} & \frac{145}{36} & \frac{25}{36} \\ \frac{5}{3} & \frac{5}{3} & \frac{5}{3} \end{bmatrix}$$

$$\mathbf{C} = \mathbf{B}(\mathbf{I} - \mathbf{A})^{-1} = \begin{bmatrix} \frac{449}{720} & \frac{461}{720} & \frac{257}{720} \\ \frac{73}{288} & \frac{521}{1440} & \frac{101}{1440} \\ \frac{31}{144} & \frac{19}{144} & \frac{7}{144} \end{bmatrix}$$

The dominant characteristic root of **C** is equal to unity, and the corresponding characteristic vector, with its elements scaled to sum to unity, is

$$\mathbf{x}_1 = \begin{bmatrix} \frac{7}{12} \\ \frac{1}{4} \\ \frac{1}{6} \end{bmatrix}$$

Since $1/\lambda_1 = 1$, and the initial distribution of stocks, $\mathbf{s}(t)$, is proportional to $\mathbf{x}_1$, the economy is in its stable state, and its vector of stocks will double every time period.

7.4.6 APPLICATION: STABLE GROWTH AND THE ESTIMATION OF BASIC DEMOGRAPHIC MEASURES FROM INCOMPLETE DATA

In most less developed countries of the world today, population analysis presents special problems. Demographic data in these countries often are unavailable and, when available, are generally inaccurate, because of inadequate and incomplete registration of births and deaths and because of the frequent misreporting of ages in population censuses. At the same time, the need for accurate population data in such countries is urgent, for without this information it is virtually impossible to formulate intelligent plans for social and economic development.

To assist less developed countries in their quest for better methods of estimating demographic measures from incomplete data, the United Nations recently published a manual on this subject [United Nations (1967)]. In this section, we shall describe a much simplified version of one of the techniques presented there. The method draws on the theory of stable populations and the property that a population subjected to constant mortality and fertility schedules, and undisturbed by migration, ultimately assumes a stable distribution that grows at a constant stable rate of growth.

Given a stable population distribution and its stable rate of growth, it is possible to project the population distribution of the subsequent time period by multiplying each population subtotal in the distribution by the stable growth rate. And given two consecutive age distributions, one can obtain the survivorship proportions that will survive the first age distribution to the second by means of simple division.

To illustrate the U.N. estimation method, consider the census-reported age distribution for Brazil in 1950 that appears in Table 7.4. According to that census, 8,370,880 people were in the 0–4-year age group in 1950. Assuming stability and a stable growth rate equal to 0.1225, we estimate

Table 7.4. Stable Population Estimates of Survivorship Rates Based on the Age Distribution of the Population of Brazil as Reported in the Census of 1950 and a Five-Year Growth Rate of $\lambda_1 - 1 = 0.1225$

Age Group	Reported 1950 Population $\bar{\mathbf{w}}$	$\lambda_1\bar{\mathbf{w}}$	${}_{k+5}\bar{S}_k$	Adjusted 1950 Population (in Thousands) $\mathbf{w}$	$\lambda_1\mathbf{w}$ (in Thousands)	${}_{k+5}S_k$
0- 4	8,370,880	9,396,312.80	0.9408	8,800	9,878.00	0.9248
5- 9	7,015,527	7,874,929.06	1.0094	7,250	8,138.12	0.9599
10–14	6,308,567	7,081,366.46	0.9790	6,200	6,959.50	0.9596
15–19	5,502,315	6,176,348.59	1.0182	5,300	5,949.25	0.9742
20–24	4,991,139	5,602,553.53	0.9293	4,600	5,163.50	0.9639
25–29	4,132,271	4,638,474.20	0.8709	3,950	4,433.88	0.9591
30–34	3,205,885	3,598,605.91	1.0785	3,375	3,788.44	0.9313
35–39	3,080,167	3,457,487.46	0.8750	2,800	3,143.00	0.9521
40–44	2,400,946	2,695,061.88	0.9184	2,375	2,665.94	0.9216
45–49	1,964,413	2,205,053.59	0.9087	1,950	2,188.88	0.9210
50–54	1,590,188	1,784,986.03	0.7483	1,600	1,796.00	0.8594
55–59	1,060,126	1,189,991.44	0.9990	1,225	1,375.06	0.8247
60–64	943,454	1,059,027.12	0.6044	900	1,010.25	0.8107
65–69	508,014	570,245.72	0.7950	650	729.62	0.7771
70–74	359,811	403,887.85	1.2294	450	505.12	0.6236
75–79	394,062	442,334.60		250	280.62	0.6735
80+				150	168.38	
Total	51,827,765*		0.9412	51,825		0.9319

* Does not include 116,632 persons whose age was unknown.
Source: Brazilian Census of 1950.

the survivors of this age group in 1955 to be the 1950 population in the 5–9-year age group increased by 12.25 percent:

$$\begin{aligned} w_5(1955) &= \lambda_1 w_5(1950) \\ &= 1.1225(7{,}015{,}527) \\ &= 7{,}874{,}929.06 \end{aligned}$$

Hence

$${}_5S_0 = \frac{w_5(1955)}{w_0(1950)} = \frac{7{,}874{,}929.06}{8{,}370{,}880} = 0.9408$$

In many less developed countries, the age distributions reported in the censuses reflect the considerable influence of age misreporting. This is particularly evident in published distributions by single years of age. These are often conspicuously distorted by "age heaping"—the tendency for people

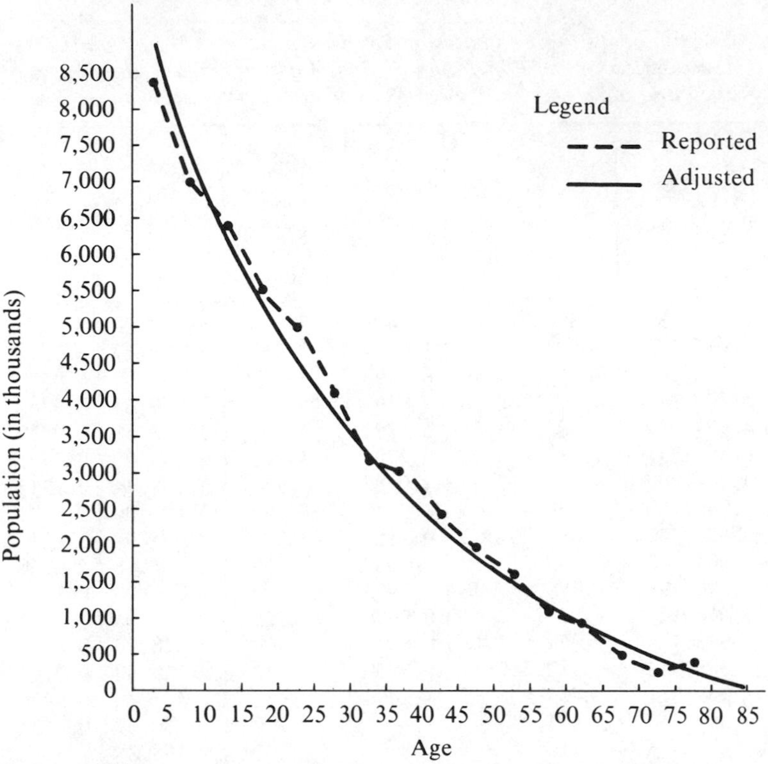

Source: Table 7.4

Figure 7.1. Total Population of Brazil by Age in 1950: Reported and Adjusted

to report a nearby age ending in zero or five, for example, rather than the correct age. Consequently, the application of the U.N. estimation method to census reported age distributions is likely to produce unrealistic results, such as the estimated survivorship probabilities set out in Column 3 of Table 7.4. Hence, we need to adjust the data before carrying out the estimation procedure. A rough attempt to do this is presented in Figure 7.1, where a hand-fitted polynomial has been applied to the data. The adjusted 1950 population distribution appears in Table 7.4, and the corresponding revised estimates of the survivorship probabilities are set out in the final column of that table.

The consolidation procedures described in Subsection 1.5.4 may be used to aggregate the 16 survivorship probabilities in Table 7.4 into a single survivorship proportion, s, say. We conclude that the fertility rate is $\lambda_1 - s = 1.1225 - 0.9319 = 0.1906$.

EXERCISES

1. Find the two characteristic roots and characteristic vectors of the population growth matrix in (2.41), (a) by factoring, (b) by the formula in (7.5), and (c) by the iterative algorithm described in Subsection 7.4.2 and in Footnote 4. Show that the iterative algorithm ultimately yields the dominant characteristic root and characteristic vector to any desired degree of accuracy. Interpret the meaning of the dominant characteristic root you have found and its associated characteristic vector.

2. Fit the two-region components-of-change population growth model defined in (1.18) to the data in Tables 1.5, 1.7, and 1.8. Deconsolidate the resulting five-year population growth matrix into the corresponding one-year growth matrix, and compare it with the California–Rest of the United States growth matrix obtained in Subsection 7.2.2.

3. Find the dominant root and characteristic vector of the following population growth matrix:

$$\mathbf{G} = \begin{bmatrix} 0 & 0 & 6 \\ \frac{1}{2} & 0 & 0 \\ 0 & \frac{1}{3} & 0 \end{bmatrix}$$

Let

$$\mathbf{w}(t) = \begin{bmatrix} 6 \\ 2 \\ 2 \end{bmatrix}$$

and assume that $\mathbf{G}$ remains constant; find $\mathbf{w}(t+1)$, $\mathbf{w}(t+2)$, and $\mathbf{w}(t+3)$. What is the pattern that emerges? Why is there no stable growth in the sense described in Section 7.4? Next, let

$$\mathbf{w}(t) = \begin{bmatrix} 6 \\ 3 \\ 1 \end{bmatrix}$$

and once again find $\mathbf{w}(t+1)$, $\mathbf{w}(t+2)$, and $\mathbf{w}(t+3)$. Why is there stable growth now?

4. Find the stable rate of growth and the stable distribution associated with the multiregional growth process described in Figure 1.2. Why is this stable growth rate different from the corresponding rate found for the growth process in Figure 1.1?

5. Find the stable rate of growth and the stable employment and population distributions associated with the spatial activity allocation model for the Ljubljana Metropolitan Region described in Subsection 2.8.2, Footnote 8.

6. Use the single-region population growth matrix set out in Figure 1.3 to project the 1961 female population of Yugoslavia forward to 1966. Next, find the five-year growth rate and assume that the Yugoslavian female age distribution in 1961 was stable. Given the female age distribution in Table 1.5 and the five-year growth rate you have derived from the projection, estimate the survivorship probabilities using the U.N. method described in Subsection 7.4.6. Replace the survivorship probabilities in Figure 1.3 with your estimates, and find the stable rate of growth of this revised version of the "true" population growth matrix. Compare your results with the "true" stable rate of growth by also obtaining the dominant characteristic root of the original population growth matrix in Figure 1.3.

7. Prove that the dominant characteristic root of a consolidated dynamic closed input-output model is equal to the dominant characteristic root of the corresponding unconsolidated model, if the consolidated model has been perfectly aggregated. Illustrate your results with the numerical example for Islandia by consolidating the Agriculture and Manufacturing sectors and demonstrating that the stable rate of growth of unity is preserved by such a consolidation.

Generalize your results to include matrix population growth models, and again use the numerical example for Islandia to illustrate your arguments.

8. For a solution to an input-output model to make sense, the vector of total output must be nonnegative for any nonnegative final demand vector; that is, $\mathbf{x} \geqq \mathbf{0}$ if $\mathbf{y} \geqq \mathbf{0}$. This will always occur if $(\mathbf{I} - \mathbf{A})^{-1}$ is nonnegative. Prove that $(\mathbf{I} - \mathbf{A})^{-1}$ will always be nonnegative if the dominant characteristic root of $\mathbf{A}$ is less than unity. (Hint: Recall that $(\mathbf{I} - \mathbf{A})^{-1} = \mathbf{I} + \mathbf{A} + \mathbf{A}^2 \ldots$ Now diagonalize both sides of the equation,

$$\mathbf{T}^{-1}(\mathbf{I} - \mathbf{A})^{-1}\mathbf{T} = \mathbf{I} + \mathbf{\Lambda} + \mathbf{\Lambda}^2 + \cdots$$

and consider the sum of the elements of the diagonal matrices on the right-hand side of the equation:

$$1 + \lambda_i + \lambda_i^2 + \cdots$$

Under what conditions will that sum converge?)

9. What is the stable rate of growth and stable distribution of the population control model defined in (2.28)?

10. The equation

$$ax(t) + bx(t-1) + cx(t-2) = 0 \qquad (t = 2, 3, \ldots)$$

is known as a *second-order homogeneous linear difference equation with constant coefficients*. Given two initial conditions, say $x(0) = K_1$ and $x(1) = K_2$, it may be solved as a system of two *first-order* difference equations. This is done as follows: Let $y(t) = x(t-1)$ for $t = 1, 2, \ldots$. Then our second-order equation may be expressed as the following system of two equations:

$$x(t) = -\frac{b}{a}x(t-1) - \frac{c}{a}y(t-1)$$

and

$$y(t) = x(t-1) \qquad (t = 2, 3, \ldots)$$

Next, let

$$\mathbf{z}(t) = \begin{bmatrix} x(t) \\ y(t) \end{bmatrix}$$

then

$$z(t) = Az(t-1) \qquad (t = 2, 3, \ldots)$$

where

$$A = \begin{bmatrix} -\frac{b}{a} & -\frac{c}{a} \\ 1 & 0 \end{bmatrix} \quad \text{and} \quad z(1) = \begin{bmatrix} K_2 \\ K_1 \end{bmatrix}$$

But recalling (7.23), we note that

$$z(t) = A^{t-1}z(1) \qquad (t = 2, 3, \ldots)$$

and, recalling (7.10), we observe that

$$A^{t-1} = M\Lambda^{t-1}M^{-1}$$

Hence

$$z(t) = M\Lambda^{t-1}M^{-1}z(1)$$

and, since the first element of $z(t)$ is $x(t)$, we have obtained our solution.

Consider the following modified version of the simple national income model presented in Exercise 10 of Chapter 2 [Samuelson (1939)]:

$$Y_t = C_t + I_t$$

$$C_t = cY_{t-1}$$

and

$$I_t = b(Y_{t-1} - Y_{t-2})$$

where Y_t, C_t, and I_t, respectively, denote income, consumption, and investment at time t; c is the marginal propensity to consume; and b is the *accelerator coefficient*. Express Y_t as a function of Y_{t-1} and Y_{t-2}. Assume that $c = 1$ and $b = 2$, and let the initial conditions be $Y_0 = 3$ and $Y_1 = 5$. Show that $Y_t = 2(2)^t + 1$.

REFERENCES AND SELECTED READINGS

THEORY

Almon, C., Jr. *Matrix Methods in Economics.* Reading, Mass.: Addison-Wesley, 1967.

Gantmacher, F. R. *The Theory of Matrices,* I and II. New York: Chelsea, 1959.

Gere, J. M. and W. Weaver, Jr. *Matrix Algebra for Engineers.* Princeton, N. J.: D. van Nostrand, 1965.

Hadley, G. *Linear Algebra.* Reading, Mass.: Addison-Wesley, 1961.

Lancaster, P. *Theory of Matrices.* New York: Academic Press, 1969.

Schneider, H. and G. P. Barker. *Matrices and Linear Algebra.* New York: Holt, Rinehart, & Winston, 1968.

Searle, S. R. *Matrix Algebra for the Biological Sciences.* New York: John Wiley & Sons, 1966.

APPLICATION: ANALYSIS OF STABLE GROWTH

Ara, K. "The Aggregation Problem in Input-Output Analysis," *Econometrica*, **XXVII**, 1959, 257–262.

Debreu, G. and I. M. Herstein. "Nonnegative Square Matrices," *Econometrica*, 1953, 597–607.

Dorfman, R., P. Samuelson, and R. Solow. *Linear Programming and Economic Analysis*. New York: McGraw-Hill, 1958.

El-Badry, M. A. "Some Demographic Measurements for Egypt Based on the Stability of Census Age Distributions," *Milbank Memorial Fund Quarterly*, **XXXIII** : 3, 1955, 268–305.

Keyfitz, N. *Introduction to the Mathematics of Population*. Reading, Mass.: Addison-Wesley. 1968.

Lopez, A. *Problems in Stable Population Theory*. Princeton, N. J.: Office of Population Research, 1961.

Morishima, M. *Equilibrium, Stability, and Growth*. Oxford: Clarendon Press, 1964.

Rogers, A. *Matrix Analysis of Interregional Population Growth and Distribution*. Berkeley, Calif.: University of California Press, 1968.

——— "A Note on the Garin-Lowry Model," *Journal of the American Institute of Planners*, **XXXII** : 6, 1966, 365–366.

Samuelson, P. A. "Interactions Between the Multiplier Analysis and the Principle of Acceleration," *Review of Economic Statistics*, **XXI**, 1939, 75–78.

United Nations, Department of Social Affairs. *Methods of Estimating Basic Demographic Measures from Incomplete Data*. New York, ST/SOA/Ser.A/42, 1967.

eight rotation of coordinate axes and factor analysis

Special problems in urban and regional analysis occasionally require that a set of points, originally defined with respect to a particular coordinate system, be expressed in terms of another coordinate system. Such coordinate transformations may be conveniently treated as rotations in *m*-dimensional space. In particular, by connecting each point to the origin of the coordinate system, we may treat the points as a set of vectors, and analyze the transformation problem as one of axis rotation for these vectors.

8.1 ROTATION OF AXES FOR VECTORS AND MATRICES

Consider, for example, the problem of axis rotation for the simple two-dimensional system illustrated in Figure 8.1. The point P may be defined by the coordinates X_1 and X_2 in the x_1-x_2 coordinate system, or by the coordinates Y_1 and Y_2 in the y_1-y_2 coordinate system. Thus the vector, **V**, say, connecting this point to the origin, may be expressed either by its projection on the first system or by its projection on the second system. That is, the column vectors

$$\mathbf{x} = \begin{bmatrix} X_1 \\ X_2 \end{bmatrix} \qquad \mathbf{y} = \begin{bmatrix} Y_1 \\ Y_2 \end{bmatrix} \tag{8.1}$$

are alternative representations of the same vector in two-dimensional space. And the problem of axis rotation becomes one of defining a *rotation matrix*,

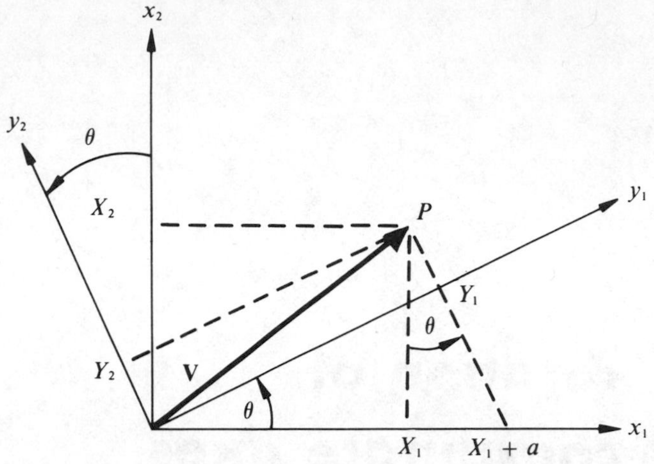

Figure 8.1. Rotation of Axes for Vectors

L, say, such that

$$\mathbf{y} = \mathbf{L}\mathbf{x} \tag{8.2}$$

8.1.1 ROTATION OF AXES FOR VECTORS

The most convenient way of describing the relative position of one coordinate system with respect to another, each having the same origin, is by means of the cosine of the angle between the two sets of axes. The cosine of this angle is called the *direction cosine* and may be denoted by l_{ij}, where the j refers to an axis of the original system and the i denotes an axis of the new system. Thus, for example, we shall denote the direction cosines of the y_1 axis with respect to the x_1 and x_2 axes as l_{11} and l_{12}, respectively.

Direction cosines may be used in Figure 8.1 to relate the coordinates of the point P on the x_1-x_2 axes to its coordinates on the y_1-y_2 axes, as follows[1]:

$$\begin{aligned} Y_1 &= l_{11}X_1 + l_{12}X_2 \\ Y_2 &= l_{21}X_1 + l_{22}X_2 \end{aligned} \tag{8.3}$$

or, in matrix form,

$$\mathbf{y} = \mathbf{L}\mathbf{x} \tag{8.4}$$

[1] The equations in (8.3) may be derived by means of simple trigonometric relationships. First we note, in Figure 8.1, the two relationships

$$\cos\theta = \frac{Y_1}{X_1 + a} \qquad \tan\theta = \frac{a}{X_2}$$

Thus,

$$Y_1 = \cos\theta \cdot X_1 + \cos\theta \cdot a \qquad \text{and} \quad a = \tan\theta \cdot X_2 = \frac{\sin\theta}{\cos\theta} \cdot X_2$$

where **x** and **y** are the vectors defined in (8.1) and

$$\mathbf{L} = \begin{bmatrix} l_{11} & l_{12} \\ l_{21} & l_{22} \end{bmatrix} = \begin{bmatrix} \cos\theta & \cos(90^\circ - \theta) \\ \cos(90^\circ + \theta) & \cos\theta \end{bmatrix} \tag{8.5}$$

$$= \begin{bmatrix} \cos\theta & \sin\theta \\ -\sin\theta & \cos\theta \end{bmatrix} \tag{8.6}$$

Example. To illustrate the computation and use of the rotation matrix, suppose that the coordinates of the vector **V** in the x_1-x_2 coordinate system are

$$\mathbf{x} = \begin{bmatrix} X_1 \\ X_2 \end{bmatrix} = \begin{bmatrix} 3 \\ 5 \end{bmatrix}$$

and assume that the angle of rotation, θ, say, is such that[2]

$$\tan\theta = \frac{3}{4}$$

Then it follows that

$$\sin\theta = \frac{3}{5} \qquad \cos\theta = \frac{4}{5}$$

and

$$\mathbf{L} = \begin{bmatrix} \frac{4}{5} & \frac{3}{5} \\ -\frac{3}{5} & \frac{4}{5} \end{bmatrix} \tag{8.7}$$

Hence, the vector **V** may be expressed in the y_1-y_2 coordinate system as

$$\mathbf{y} = \mathbf{Lx} = \begin{bmatrix} \frac{4}{5} & \frac{3}{5} \\ -\frac{3}{5} & \frac{4}{5} \end{bmatrix} \begin{bmatrix} 3 \\ 5 \end{bmatrix} = \begin{bmatrix} 5\frac{2}{5} \\ 2\frac{1}{5} \end{bmatrix}$$

By simple substitution,

$$Y_1 = \cos\theta \cdot X_1 + \sin\theta \cdot X_2$$

and, since $\sin\theta = \cos(90^\circ - \theta)$,

$$Y_1 = \cos\theta \cdot X_1 + \cos(90^\circ - \theta) \cdot X_2 = l_{11}X_1 + l_{12}X_2$$

An analogous argument may be used to establish that

$$Y_2 = -\sin\theta \cdot X_1 + \cos\theta \cdot X_2 = \cos(90^\circ + \theta) \cdot X_1 + \cos\theta \cdot X_2$$
$$= l_{21}X_1 + l_{22}X_2$$

[2] The angle with such a tangent is the smallest angle of a 3–4–5 right triangle and is equal to 36°52′.

8.1.2 PROPERTIES OF THE ROTATION MATRIX

It easily may be established that the row vectors of the rotation matrix **L** are orthonormal, that is,

$$\sum_{k=1}^{m} l_{ik}l_{jk} = 1 \quad \text{if} \quad i = j \qquad (i, j = 1, 2, \ldots, m)$$
$$= 0 \quad \text{if} \quad i \neq j$$

Therefore, **L** is an orthogonal matrix and possesses the following properties:

$$\mathbf{LL}' = \mathbf{L}'\mathbf{L} = \mathbf{I} \tag{8.8}$$

$$\mathbf{L}^{-1} = \mathbf{L}' \tag{8.9}$$

$$|\mathbf{L}| = 1 \tag{8.10}$$

Equation (8.8) expresses the fact that both the rows *and* the columns of an orthogonal matrix are orthogonal and of unit length. Equation (8.9) follows from (8.8) in that the inverse of an orthogonal matrix is equal to its transpose. Finally, (8.10) states that the determinant of an orthogonal matrix is always equal to unity.

Example. We may illustrate the above properties with the rotation matrix in (8.7). First, the row vectors of that matrix are orthogonal:

$$\tfrac{4}{5}(-\tfrac{3}{5}) + \tfrac{3}{5}(\tfrac{4}{5}) = 0$$

Second, each row vector of the matrix is of unit length:

$$(\tfrac{4}{5})^2 + (\tfrac{3}{5})^2 = 1$$
$$(-\tfrac{3}{5})^2 + (\tfrac{4}{5})^2 = 1$$

Hence,

$$\mathbf{LL}' = \begin{bmatrix} \frac{4}{5} & \frac{3}{5} \\ -\frac{3}{5} & \frac{4}{5} \end{bmatrix} \begin{bmatrix} \frac{4}{5} & -\frac{3}{5} \\ \frac{3}{5} & \frac{4}{5} \end{bmatrix} = \begin{bmatrix} 1 & 0 \\ 0 & 1 \end{bmatrix} = \mathbf{I}$$

Finally, the determinant of the matrix is equal to unity:

$$\tfrac{4}{5}(\tfrac{4}{5}) - (-\tfrac{3}{5})(\tfrac{3}{5}) = 1$$

Since the determinant of a rotation matrix always exists, we always may define the inverse of **L** and, therefore, may express the vector **x** in terms of **y**, as follows:

$$\mathbf{x} = \mathbf{L}^{-1}\mathbf{y} = \mathbf{L}'\mathbf{y} \tag{8.11}$$

Furthermore, successive rotations of axes may be carried out by applying the product matrix of the appropriate rotation matrices to the original vector of coordinates. For example, if

$$\mathbf{y} = \mathbf{Lx}$$

and

$$\mathbf{z} = \mathbf{My}$$

then

$$\mathbf{z} = \mathbf{My} = \mathbf{MLx} = \mathbf{Nx}$$

It easily can be established that the product matrix $\mathbf{N}$ is an orthogonal rotation matrix and that it therefore possesses the properties described in (8.8), (8.9), and (8.10).

8.1.3 ROTATION OF AXES FOR MATRICES

The concept of axis rotation can be extended to matrices. The two points P_1 and P_2 may be defined by the coordinate pairs (X_{11}, X_{21}) and (X_{12}, X_{22}) in the x_1-x_2 coordinate system or by the coordinate pairs (Y_{11}, Y_{21}) and (Y_{12}, Y_{22}) in the y_1-y_2 coordinate system. Thus the two vectors, $\mathbf{V}_1$ and $\mathbf{V}_2$, say, that connect these points to the origin, may be expressed either by their projections on the x_1-x_2 coordinate system or by their projections on the y_1-y_2 coordinate system. That is, the column vectors

$$\mathbf{x}_1 = \begin{bmatrix} X_{11} \\ X_{21} \end{bmatrix} \qquad \mathbf{x}_2 = \begin{bmatrix} X_{12} \\ X_{22} \end{bmatrix}$$

and

$$\mathbf{y}_1 = \begin{bmatrix} Y_{11} \\ Y_{21} \end{bmatrix} \qquad \mathbf{y}_2 = \begin{bmatrix} Y_{12} \\ Y_{22} \end{bmatrix}$$

are alternative representations of the same two vectors in two-dimensional space.

Now let us define a matrix, $\mathbf{S}_x$, say, which is a function of the vectors $\mathbf{x}_1$ and $\mathbf{x}_2$, and denote by $\mathbf{S}_y$ the matrix that is obtained when the same function is applied to the vectors $\mathbf{y}_1$ and $\mathbf{y}_2$. Thus, symbolically,

$$\mathbf{S}_x = f(\mathbf{x}_1, \mathbf{x}_2) \qquad \mathbf{S}_y = f(\mathbf{y}_1, \mathbf{y}_2)$$

and the problem of axis rotation for matrices may be defined as the problem of obtaining $\mathbf{S}_y$, given $\mathbf{S}_x$ and the rotation of matrix $\mathbf{L}$ that carries out the transformation

$$\mathbf{y}_1 = \mathbf{Lx}_1 \quad \text{and} \quad \mathbf{y}_2 = \mathbf{Lx}_2 \tag{8.12}$$

In this chapter we shall be concerned with the rotation of axes for sample covariance matrices. Hence we will be focusing on matrices $\mathbf{S}_x$ that are defined as follows:

$$\mathbf{S}_x = \begin{bmatrix} s_{x_1}^2 & s_{x_1x_2} \\ s_{x_2x_1} & s_{x_2}^2 \end{bmatrix} = \frac{1}{n}(\mathbf{X} - \bar{\mathbf{X}})(\mathbf{X} - \bar{\mathbf{X}})' \tag{8.13}$$

and

$$\mathbf{S}_y = \begin{bmatrix} s_{y_1}^2 & s_{y_1y_2} \\ s_{y_2y_1} & s_{y_2}^2 \end{bmatrix} = \frac{1}{n}(\mathbf{Y} - \overline{\mathbf{Y}})(\mathbf{Y} - \overline{\mathbf{Y}})' \tag{8.14}$$

where

$$\mathbf{X} = [\mathbf{x}_1 \quad \mathbf{x}_2] \qquad \overline{\mathbf{X}} = [\overline{\mathbf{x}} \quad \overline{\mathbf{x}}] \qquad \overline{\mathbf{x}} = \frac{1}{2}(\mathbf{x}_1 + \mathbf{x}_2)$$

$$\mathbf{Y} = [\mathbf{y}_1 \quad \mathbf{y}_2] \qquad \overline{\mathbf{Y}} = [\overline{\mathbf{y}} \quad \overline{\mathbf{y}}] \qquad \overline{\mathbf{y}} = \frac{1}{2}(\mathbf{y}_1 + \mathbf{y}_2)$$

But

$$\mathbf{Y} = [\mathbf{y}_1 \quad \mathbf{y}_2] = [\mathbf{L}\mathbf{x}_1 \quad \mathbf{L}\mathbf{x}_2] = \mathbf{L}[\mathbf{x}_1 \quad \mathbf{x}_2] = \mathbf{L}\mathbf{X} \tag{8.15}$$

and

$$\overline{\mathbf{Y}} = [\overline{\mathbf{y}} \quad \overline{\mathbf{y}}] = [\mathbf{L}\overline{\mathbf{x}} \quad \mathbf{L}\overline{\mathbf{x}}] = \mathbf{L}[\overline{\mathbf{x}} \quad \overline{\mathbf{x}}] = \mathbf{L}\overline{\mathbf{X}} \tag{8.16}$$

Hence,

$$\begin{aligned} \mathbf{S}_y &= \frac{1}{n}(\mathbf{Y} - \overline{\mathbf{Y}})(\mathbf{Y} - \overline{\mathbf{Y}})' \\ &= \frac{1}{n}(\mathbf{L}\mathbf{X} - \mathbf{L}\overline{\mathbf{X}})(\mathbf{L}\mathbf{X} - \mathbf{L}\overline{\mathbf{X}})' \qquad \text{by (8.15) and (8.16)} \\ &= \frac{1}{n}[\mathbf{L}(\mathbf{X} - \overline{\mathbf{X}})][\mathbf{L}(\mathbf{X} - \overline{\mathbf{X}})]' \\ &= \frac{1}{n}\mathbf{L}(\mathbf{X} - \overline{\mathbf{X}})(\mathbf{X} - \overline{\mathbf{X}})'\mathbf{L}' \\ &= \mathbf{L}\left[\frac{1}{n}(\mathbf{X} - \overline{\mathbf{X}})(\mathbf{X} - \overline{\mathbf{X}})'\right]\mathbf{L}' \\ &= \mathbf{L}\mathbf{S}_x\mathbf{L}' \end{aligned} \tag{8.17}$$

Observe that, as in the case of axis rotation for vectors, we may reverse the transformation:

$$\mathbf{S}_x = \mathbf{L}^{-1}\mathbf{S}_y\mathbf{L} = \mathbf{L}'\mathbf{S}_y\mathbf{L} \tag{8.18}$$

Example. To clarify the above arguments, let us turn to the following simple two-dimensional numerical example. Suppose that the coordinates of $\mathbf{V}_1$ and $\mathbf{V}_2$ in the x_1-x_2 coordinate system are

$$\mathbf{x}_1 = \begin{bmatrix} 3 \\ 5 \end{bmatrix} \qquad \mathbf{x}_2 = \begin{bmatrix} 5 \\ 7 \end{bmatrix}$$

respectively, or

$$\mathbf{X} = [\mathbf{x}_1 \quad \mathbf{x}_2] = \begin{bmatrix} 3 & 5 \\ 5 & 7 \end{bmatrix}$$

Furthermore, assume that the x_1-x_2 coordinate system is once again to be rotated through an angle θ such that

$$\tan\theta = \frac{3}{4}$$

Then, as we saw in our earlier example,

$$\mathbf{L} = \begin{bmatrix} \cos\theta & \sin\theta \\ -\sin\theta & \cos\theta \end{bmatrix} = \begin{bmatrix} \frac{4}{5} & \frac{3}{5} \\ -\frac{3}{5} & \frac{4}{5} \end{bmatrix}$$

and, therefore,

$$\mathbf{y}_1 = \mathbf{L}\mathbf{x}_1 = \begin{bmatrix} \frac{4}{5} & \frac{3}{5} \\ -\frac{3}{5} & \frac{4}{5} \end{bmatrix} \begin{bmatrix} 3 \\ 5 \end{bmatrix} = \begin{bmatrix} 5\frac{2}{5} \\ 2\frac{1}{5} \end{bmatrix}$$

$$\mathbf{y}_2 = \mathbf{L}\mathbf{x}_2 = \begin{bmatrix} \frac{4}{5} & \frac{3}{5} \\ -\frac{3}{5} & \frac{4}{5} \end{bmatrix} \begin{bmatrix} 5 \\ 7 \end{bmatrix} = \begin{bmatrix} 8\frac{1}{5} \\ 2\frac{3}{5} \end{bmatrix}$$

or

$$\mathbf{Y} = [\mathbf{y}_1 \quad \mathbf{y}_2] = \mathbf{L}\mathbf{X} = \mathbf{L}[\mathbf{x}_1 \quad \mathbf{x}_2]$$

$$= \begin{bmatrix} \frac{4}{5} & \frac{3}{5} \\ -\frac{3}{5} & \frac{4}{5} \end{bmatrix} \begin{bmatrix} 3 & 5 \\ 5 & 7 \end{bmatrix} = \begin{bmatrix} 5\frac{2}{5} & 8\frac{1}{5} \\ 2\frac{1}{5} & 2\frac{3}{5} \end{bmatrix}$$

We have, then, the relationships shown in Figure 8.2. The components of the vectors $\mathbf{x}_1$ and $\mathbf{x}_2$ are the projections of $\mathbf{V}_1$ and $\mathbf{V}_2$ on the x_1-x_2 coordinate axes, while the elements of $\mathbf{y}_1$ and $\mathbf{y}_2$ describe their projections

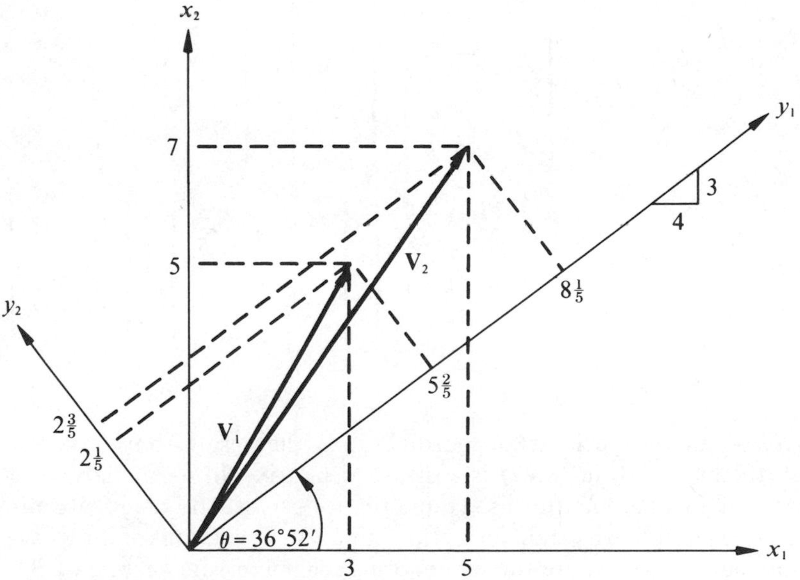

Figure 8.2. Rotation of Axes for Matrices

on the y_1-y_2 coordinate axes. Furthermore, observe that

$$\mathbf{S}_x = \frac{1}{n}(\mathbf{X} - \bar{\mathbf{X}})(\mathbf{X} - \bar{\mathbf{X}})'$$

$$= \frac{1}{2}\begin{bmatrix} -1 & 1 \\ -1 & 1 \end{bmatrix}\begin{bmatrix} -1 & -1 \\ 1 & 1 \end{bmatrix} = \begin{bmatrix} 1 & 1 \\ 1 & 1 \end{bmatrix}$$

$$\mathbf{S}_y = \frac{1}{2}\begin{bmatrix} -\frac{7}{5} & \frac{7}{5} \\ -\frac{1}{5} & \frac{1}{5} \end{bmatrix}\begin{bmatrix} -\frac{7}{5} & -\frac{1}{5} \\ \frac{7}{5} & \frac{1}{5} \end{bmatrix} = \begin{bmatrix} \frac{49}{25} & \frac{7}{25} \\ \frac{7}{25} & \frac{1}{25} \end{bmatrix}$$

and

$$\mathbf{S}_y = \mathbf{L}\mathbf{S}_x\mathbf{L}'$$

$$= \begin{bmatrix} \frac{4}{5} & \frac{3}{5} \\ -\frac{3}{5} & \frac{4}{5} \end{bmatrix}\begin{bmatrix} 1 & 1 \\ 1 & 1 \end{bmatrix}\begin{bmatrix} \frac{4}{5} & -\frac{3}{5} \\ \frac{3}{5} & \frac{4}{5} \end{bmatrix} = \begin{bmatrix} \frac{49}{25} & \frac{7}{25} \\ \frac{7}{25} & \frac{1}{25} \end{bmatrix}$$

Also note that

$$\mathbf{x}_1 = \mathbf{L}'\mathbf{y}_1 = \begin{bmatrix} \frac{4}{5} & -\frac{3}{5} \\ \frac{3}{5} & \frac{4}{5} \end{bmatrix}\begin{bmatrix} 5\frac{2}{5} \\ 2\frac{1}{5} \end{bmatrix} = \begin{bmatrix} 3 \\ 5 \end{bmatrix}$$

$$\mathbf{x}_2 = \mathbf{L}'\mathbf{y}_2 = \begin{bmatrix} \frac{4}{5} & -\frac{3}{5} \\ \frac{3}{5} & \frac{4}{5} \end{bmatrix}\begin{bmatrix} 8\frac{1}{5} \\ 2\frac{3}{5} \end{bmatrix} = \begin{bmatrix} 5 \\ 7 \end{bmatrix}$$

and

$$\mathbf{S}_x = \mathbf{L}'\mathbf{S}_y\mathbf{L} = \begin{bmatrix} \frac{4}{5} & -\frac{3}{5} \\ \frac{3}{5} & \frac{4}{5} \end{bmatrix}\begin{bmatrix} \frac{49}{25} & \frac{7}{25} \\ \frac{7}{25} & \frac{1}{25} \end{bmatrix}\begin{bmatrix} \frac{4}{5} & \frac{3}{5} \\ -\frac{3}{5} & \frac{4}{5} \end{bmatrix} = \begin{bmatrix} 1 & 1 \\ 1 & 1 \end{bmatrix}$$

8.1.4 PRINCIPAL AXES

Principal axes are the special set of coordinate axes that result from a rotation in which the matrix $\mathbf{S}_y$ in (8.17) is a diagonal matrix. In particular, since the matrix $\mathbf{S}_x$ in that equation is symmetric, we can usually diagonalize it by an orthogonal similarity transformation in which the columns of the transformation matrix, $\mathbf{Q}$, say, are the orthonormal characteristic vectors of $\mathbf{S}_x$. Therefore, comparing (7.13) with (8.17), we observe that the rotation matrix for obtaining the principal axes is the transpose of the matrix $\mathbf{Q}$. Furthermore, since the rows of the rotation matrix may be interpreted as the direction cosines for the axes, we have the result that the direction cosines for the principal axes are the orthonormal characteristic vectors of the matrix $\mathbf{S}_x$. Thus, if $p_1, p_2, \ldots, p_m$ denote the principal axes to which an original coordinate system $x_1, x_2, \ldots, x_m$ is rotated, then

$$\mathbf{p}_1 = \begin{bmatrix} p_{11} \\ p_{21} \\ \vdots \\ p_{m1} \end{bmatrix} = \mathbf{Q}'\mathbf{x}_1 \qquad \mathbf{p}_2 = \begin{bmatrix} p_{12} \\ p_{22} \\ \vdots \\ p_{m2} \end{bmatrix} = \mathbf{Q}'\mathbf{x}_2 \tag{8.19}$$

and

$$\Lambda = \mathbf{Q}'\mathbf{S}_x\mathbf{Q} \tag{8.20}$$

The vectors $\mathbf{p}_1$ and $\mathbf{p}_2$ describe the projections of the vectors $\mathbf{x}_1$ and $\mathbf{x}_2$ on the principal axes, Λ is the spectral matrix for $\mathbf{S}_x$, and $\mathbf{Q}$ consists of the set of orthonormal characteristic vectors of $\mathbf{S}_x$.

Example. To illustrate the above theoretical results, let us turn once again to the numerical example in Figure 8.2. We begin by deriving the characteristic roots and vectors of $\mathbf{S}_x$ and then construct the matrices Λ and $\mathbf{Q}$. Thus,

$$\mathbf{S}_x = \begin{bmatrix} 1 & 1 \\ 1 & 1 \end{bmatrix} \qquad \Lambda = \begin{bmatrix} 2 & 0 \\ 0 & 0 \end{bmatrix} \qquad \mathbf{Q} = \begin{bmatrix} \frac{\sqrt{2}}{2} & -\frac{\sqrt{2}}{2} \\ \frac{\sqrt{2}}{2} & \frac{\sqrt{2}}{2} \end{bmatrix}$$

and

$$\mathbf{p}_1 = \mathbf{Q}'\mathbf{x}_1 = \begin{bmatrix} \frac{\sqrt{2}}{2} & \frac{\sqrt{2}}{2} \\ -\frac{\sqrt{2}}{2} & \frac{\sqrt{2}}{2} \end{bmatrix} \begin{bmatrix} 3 \\ 5 \end{bmatrix} = \begin{bmatrix} 4\sqrt{2} \\ \sqrt{2} \end{bmatrix}$$

$$\mathbf{p}_2 = \mathbf{Q}'\mathbf{x}_2 = \begin{bmatrix} \frac{\sqrt{2}}{2} & \frac{\sqrt{2}}{2} \\ -\frac{\sqrt{2}}{2} & \frac{\sqrt{2}}{2} \end{bmatrix} \begin{bmatrix} 5 \\ 7 \end{bmatrix} = \begin{bmatrix} 6\sqrt{2} \\ \sqrt{2} \end{bmatrix}$$

As a check on our arithmetic, we compute

$$\Lambda = \mathbf{Q}'\mathbf{S}_x\mathbf{Q} = \begin{bmatrix} \frac{\sqrt{2}}{2} & \frac{\sqrt{2}}{2} \\ -\frac{\sqrt{2}}{2} & \frac{\sqrt{2}}{2} \end{bmatrix} \begin{bmatrix} 1 & 1 \\ 1 & 1 \end{bmatrix} \begin{bmatrix} \frac{\sqrt{2}}{2} & -\frac{\sqrt{2}}{2} \\ \frac{\sqrt{2}}{2} & \frac{\sqrt{2}}{2} \end{bmatrix}$$

$$= \begin{bmatrix} 2 & 0 \\ 0 & 0 \end{bmatrix}.$$

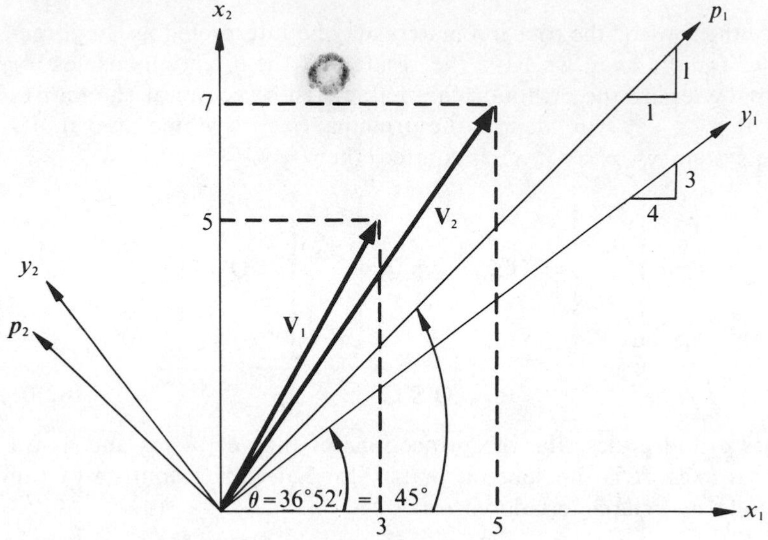

Figure 8.3. Rotation to Principal Axes

Observe that

$$\mathbf{Q}' = \begin{bmatrix} \cos\theta & \sin\theta \\ -\sin\theta & \cos\theta \end{bmatrix} = \begin{bmatrix} \frac{\sqrt{2}}{2} & \frac{\sqrt{2}}{2} \\ -\frac{\sqrt{2}}{2} & \frac{\sqrt{2}}{2} \end{bmatrix}$$

hence $\cos\theta = \sqrt{2}/2 = 1/\sqrt{2}$; we conclude, therefore, that the matrix $\mathbf{Q}'$ rotates the original x_1-x_2 coordinate axes through an angle of 45°.[3] Figure 8.3 illustrates the relative position of the principal axes p_1 and p_2 with respect to the x_1-x_2 and y_1-y_2 coordinate axes of Figure 8.2.

8.2 PRINCIPAL AXES AND THE CONCEPT OF REDUCED DIMENSIONALITY: GEOMETRICAL INTERPRETATION

Imagine two points, P_1 and P_2, say, with coordinates

$$\mathbf{x}_1 = \begin{bmatrix} X_{11} \\ X_{21} \end{bmatrix} = \begin{bmatrix} 4 \\ 4 \end{bmatrix} \qquad \mathbf{x}_2 = \begin{bmatrix} X_{12} \\ X_{22} \end{bmatrix} = \begin{bmatrix} 6 \\ 6 \end{bmatrix}$$

[3] Notice that the $\mathbf{Q}$ matrix, in this example, differs slightly from the one obtained in the numerical example of Subsection 7.3.1 in that the arbitrary constant, k_2, now is set equal to the reciprocal of the *negative* value of the length of $\mathbf{x}_2$. This modification is necessary in our current problem context, because without it we would have the inconsistency that $\sin\theta = -\sin\theta$. *To avoid such inconsistencies, we shall henceforth always choose the sign for k_i that makes q_{ii} positive.*

The centroid of this pair of points is the point (5, 5) and may be denoted by

$$\bar{\mathbf{x}} = \tfrac{1}{2}(\mathbf{x}_1 + \mathbf{x}_2) = \begin{bmatrix} 5 \\ 5 \end{bmatrix}$$

If we rotate the x_1 axis through the angle of 45° to the position y_1 and, at the same time, rotate the x_2 axis so that it maintains its orthogonal relationship with x_1, we obtain a y_1-y_2 coordinate system in which the coordinates of both points along the y_2 axis are zero, as in Figure 8.4. That is,

$$\mathbf{y}_1 = \begin{bmatrix} Y_{11} \\ Y_{21} \end{bmatrix} = \begin{bmatrix} \cos\theta & \sin\theta \\ -\sin\theta & \cos\theta \end{bmatrix} \begin{bmatrix} X_{11} \\ X_{21} \end{bmatrix}$$

$$= \begin{bmatrix} \frac{\sqrt{2}}{2} & \frac{\sqrt{2}}{2} \\ -\frac{\sqrt{2}}{2} & \frac{\sqrt{2}}{2} \end{bmatrix} \begin{bmatrix} 4 \\ 4 \end{bmatrix} = \begin{bmatrix} 4\sqrt{2} \\ 0 \end{bmatrix}$$

$$\mathbf{y}_2 = \begin{bmatrix} Y_{12} \\ Y_{22} \end{bmatrix} = \begin{bmatrix} \cos\theta & \sin\theta \\ -\sin\theta & \cos\theta \end{bmatrix} \begin{bmatrix} X_{12} \\ X_{22} \end{bmatrix}$$

$$= \begin{bmatrix} \frac{\sqrt{2}}{2} & \frac{\sqrt{2}}{2} \\ -\frac{\sqrt{2}}{2} & \frac{\sqrt{2}}{2} \end{bmatrix} \begin{bmatrix} 6 \\ 6 \end{bmatrix} = \begin{bmatrix} 6\sqrt{2} \\ 0 \end{bmatrix}$$

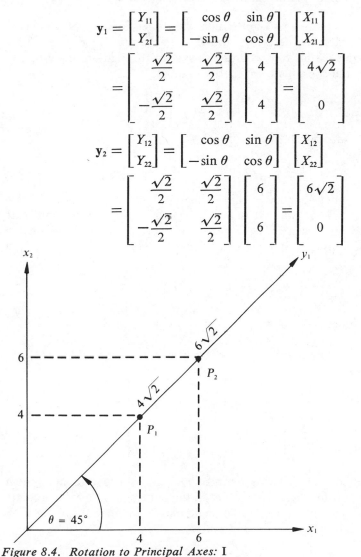

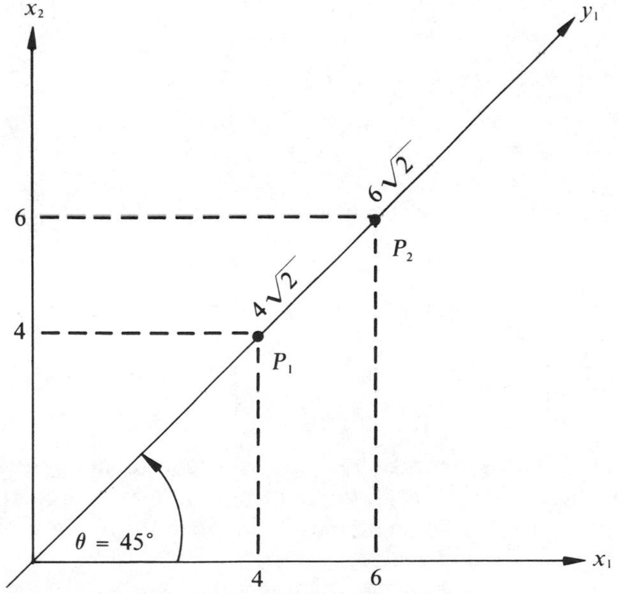

Figure 8.4. Rotation to Principal Axes: I

The net result of this rotation is that the two points, which formerly were identified by two coordinates, now can be located with one coordinate. *Thus, by an appropriate rotation of the coordinate axes, we have reduced the dimensionality of our data from two to one.* Points P_1 and P_2, which were located in two-dimensional space and referenced with respect to two coordinate axes, now can be located in the same space using only one coordinate axis.

8.2.1 AXIS ROTATION AND REDUCED DIMENSIONALITY

Generally, rotation alone will not reduce the dimensionality of a data set in the geometrical sense described above. For example, in Figure 8.3 we saw that rotation of the x_1-x_2 coordinate system through an angle of 45° will transform the coordinates of the two points

$$\mathbf{x}_1 = \begin{bmatrix} 3 \\ 5 \end{bmatrix} \qquad \mathbf{x}_2 = \begin{bmatrix} 5 \\ 7 \end{bmatrix}$$

into

$$\mathbf{y}_1 = \mathbf{p}_1 = \begin{bmatrix} 4\sqrt{2} \\ \sqrt{2} \end{bmatrix} \qquad \mathbf{y}_2 = \mathbf{p}_2 = \begin{bmatrix} 6\sqrt{2} \\ \sqrt{2} \end{bmatrix}$$

To reduce the dimensionality of this particular data set, therefore, we also need to *translate the origin,* that is, move the origin of the p_1-p_2 coordinate system to a position such that the new coordinate axes pass through the centroid of the scatter of observations. Thus we need to *translate* the origin to the point

$$\bar{\mathbf{x}} = \tfrac{1}{2}(\mathbf{x}_1 + \mathbf{x}_2) = \begin{bmatrix} 4 \\ 6 \end{bmatrix}$$

and then *rotate* the x_1-x_2 coordinate axes through an angle of 45° (Figure 8.5).

We begin by expressing the coordinates in deviation form, that is,

$$\mathbf{x}_1 - \bar{\mathbf{x}} = \begin{bmatrix} X_{11} - \bar{X}_1 \\ X_{21} - \bar{X}_2 \end{bmatrix} = \begin{bmatrix} 3 - 4 \\ 5 - 6 \end{bmatrix} = \begin{bmatrix} -1 \\ -1 \end{bmatrix}$$

and

$$\mathbf{x}_2 - \bar{\mathbf{x}} = \begin{bmatrix} X_{12} - \bar{X}_1 \\ X_{22} - \bar{X}_2 \end{bmatrix} = \begin{bmatrix} 5 - 4 \\ 7 - 6 \end{bmatrix} = \begin{bmatrix} 1 \\ 1 \end{bmatrix}$$

This has the effect of translating the origin of the x_1-x_2 coordinate system to the centroid of the observations, that is, the point (4, 6). Next, we rotate the x_1-x_2 coordinate axes through the angle of 45° by premultiplying both of the above vectors by the rotation matrix

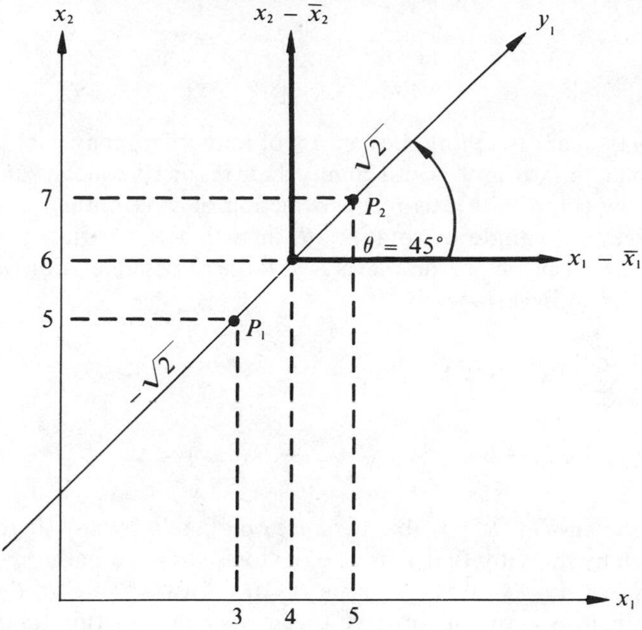

Figure 8.5. Rotation to Principal Axes: II

$$\mathbf{Q}' = \begin{bmatrix} \frac{\sqrt{2}}{2} & \frac{\sqrt{2}}{2} \\ -\frac{\sqrt{2}}{2} & \frac{\sqrt{2}}{2} \end{bmatrix}$$

Thus

$$\mathbf{y}_1 = \begin{bmatrix} Y_{11} \\ Y_{21} \end{bmatrix} = \mathbf{Q}'(\mathbf{x}_1 - \bar{\mathbf{x}}) = \begin{bmatrix} \cos\theta & \sin\theta \\ -\sin\theta & \cos\theta \end{bmatrix} \begin{bmatrix} X_{11} - \bar{X}_1 \\ X_{21} - \bar{X}_2 \end{bmatrix}$$

$$= \begin{bmatrix} \frac{\sqrt{2}}{2} & \frac{\sqrt{2}}{2} \\ -\frac{\sqrt{2}}{2} & \frac{\sqrt{2}}{2} \end{bmatrix} \begin{bmatrix} -1 \\ -1 \end{bmatrix} = \begin{bmatrix} -\sqrt{2} \\ 0 \end{bmatrix}$$

and

$$\mathbf{y}_2 = \begin{bmatrix} Y_{12} \\ Y_{22} \end{bmatrix} = \mathbf{Q}'(\mathbf{x}_2 - \bar{\mathbf{x}}) = \begin{bmatrix} \cos\theta & \sin\theta \\ -\sin\theta & \cos\theta \end{bmatrix} \begin{bmatrix} X_{12} - \bar{X}_1 \\ X_{22} - \bar{X}_2 \end{bmatrix}$$

$$= \begin{bmatrix} \frac{\sqrt{2}}{2} & \frac{\sqrt{2}}{2} \\ -\frac{\sqrt{2}}{2} & \frac{\sqrt{2}}{2} \end{bmatrix} \begin{bmatrix} 1 \\ 1 \end{bmatrix} = \begin{bmatrix} \sqrt{2} \\ 0 \end{bmatrix}$$

or

$$\mathbf{Y} = [\mathbf{y}_1 \quad \mathbf{y}_2] = \mathbf{Q}'(\mathbf{X} - \bar{\mathbf{X}}) \tag{8.21}$$

where

$$\mathbf{X} = [\mathbf{x}_1 \quad \mathbf{x}_2] \qquad \text{and} \quad \bar{\mathbf{X}} = [\bar{\mathbf{x}} \quad \bar{\mathbf{x}}]$$

A more formal way of approaching the concept of reduced dimensionality is to consider the total variation of points about their respective means and to orient the first new coordinate axis in the direction of maximum variation. That is, we seek that angle of rotation, θ, such that the variance of the points about their mean on the new axis is as large as possible. For the example in Figure 8.4, this variance is

$$s_{y_1}^2 = \frac{1}{2} \sum_{j=1}^{2} (Y_{1j} - \bar{Y}_1)^2$$

$$= \frac{1}{2} [(4\sqrt{2} - 5\sqrt{2})^2 + (6\sqrt{2} - 5\sqrt{2})^2] = 2$$

That this indeed is the maximum possible variance obtainable by any single new axis may be seen by showing that it is also the total variance in the system. To show this, we simply sum the variances of the two points in the original x_1-x_2 coordinate system and observe that $s_{y_1}^2$ is equal to this total:

$$s_{x_1}^2 = \frac{1}{2} \sum_{j=1}^{2} (X_{1j} - \bar{X}_1)^2 = \frac{1}{2} [(4 - 5)^2 + (6 - 5)^2] = 1$$

$$s_{x_2}^2 = \frac{1}{2} \sum_{j=1}^{2} (X_{2j} - \bar{X}_2)^2 = \frac{1}{2} [(4 - 5)^2 + (6 - 5)^2] = 1$$

and

$$s_{x_1}^2 + s_{x_2}^2 = 1 + 1 = 2 = s_{y_1}^2$$

Since the total variation among the points is always invariant under a rigid orthogonal rotation of the axes, we conclude that the total variance of the points P_1 and P_2 has been completely "accounted" for by the single new coordinate axis y_1. And since there is no residual variation to account for, we do not need a second coordinate axis.

Let us now complicate matters somewhat by introducing two more points, P_3 and P_4, say, with coordinates

$$\mathbf{x}_3 = \begin{bmatrix} X_{13} \\ X_{23} \end{bmatrix} = \begin{bmatrix} 2 \\ 4 \end{bmatrix} \qquad \mathbf{x}_4 = \begin{bmatrix} X_{14} \\ X_{24} \end{bmatrix} = \begin{bmatrix} 4 \\ 2 \end{bmatrix}$$

into the example in Figure 8.4. The total variance is now

$$s_{x_1}^2 = \frac{1}{4} \sum_{j=1}^{4} (X_{1j} - \bar{X}_1)^2$$

$$= \frac{1}{4} [(4 - 4)^2 + (6 - 4)^2 + (2 - 4)^2 + (4 - 4)^2] = 2$$

$$s_{x_2}^2 = \frac{1}{4}\sum_{j=1}^{4}(X_{2j} - \bar{X}_2)^2$$

$$= \frac{1}{4}[(4-4)^2 + (6-4)^2 + (4-4)^2 + (2-4)^2] = 2$$

and

$$s_{x_1}^2 + s_{x_2}^2 = 2 + 2 = 4$$

If we now rotate the x_1-x_2 coordinate axes through the angle of 45°, as in Figure 8.6, and compute the coordinates of the four points along the new y_1-y_2 coordinate axes, we obtain, in addition to the previously computed vectors $\mathbf{y}_1$ and $\mathbf{y}_2$, the vectors

$$\mathbf{y}_3 = \mathbf{p}_3 = \mathbf{Q}'\mathbf{x}_3 = \begin{bmatrix} 3\sqrt{2} \\ \sqrt{2} \end{bmatrix} \qquad \mathbf{y}_4 = \mathbf{p}_4 = \mathbf{Q}'\mathbf{x}_4 = \begin{bmatrix} 3\sqrt{2} \\ -\sqrt{2} \end{bmatrix}$$

The total variation "accounted" for by the single new coordinate axis y_1 now is less than the total variance in the system; that is,

$$s_{y_1}^2 = \frac{1}{4}\sum_{j=1}^{4}(Y_{1j} - \bar{Y}_1)^2$$

$$= \frac{1}{4}[(4\sqrt{2} - 4\sqrt{2})^2 + (6\sqrt{2} - 4\sqrt{2})^2$$

$$+ (3\sqrt{2} - 4\sqrt{2})^2 + (3\sqrt{2} - 4\sqrt{2})^2] = 3$$

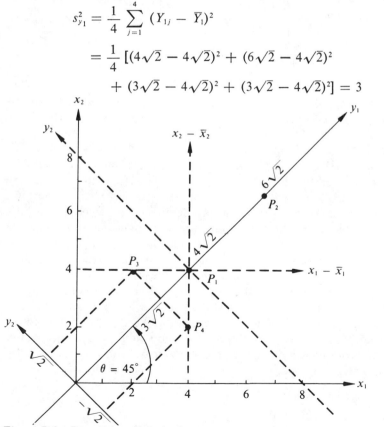

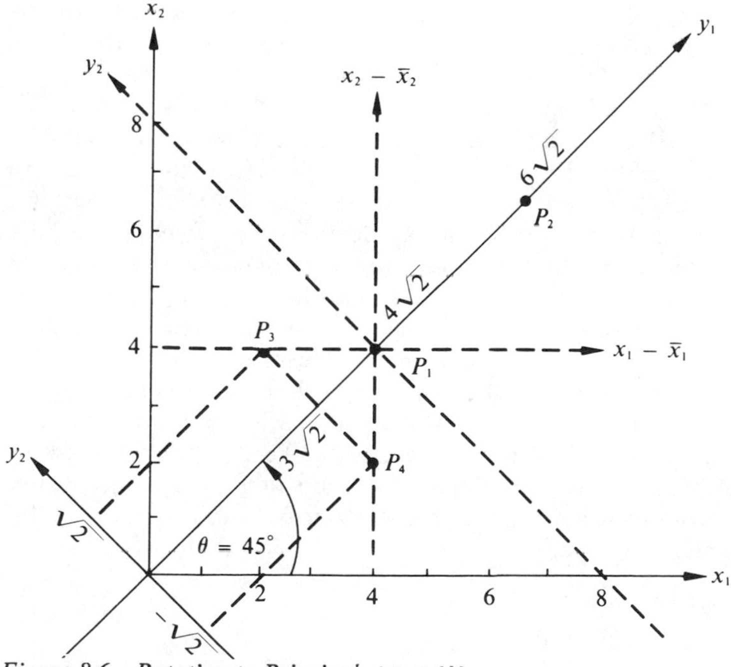

Figure 8.6. Rotation to Principal Axes: III

and as much as possible of the residual variance of $4 - 3 = 1$ is accounted for by the second new coordinate axis, y_2. That is,

$$s_{y_2}^2 = \frac{1}{4} \sum_{j=1}^{4} (Y_{2j} - \bar{Y}_2)^2$$

$$= \frac{1}{4} [(0 - 0)^2 + (0 - 0)^2 + (\sqrt{2} - 0)^2 + (-\sqrt{2} - 0)^2] = 1$$

Note that to be consistent with our earlier geometrical interpretation of reduced dimensionality, we need to translate the origin of the x_1-x_2 coordinate system to the centroid of the scatter of observations before rotating these same axes through the angle of 45° (see the dotted lines in Figure 8.6). Then by (8.21), we have that

$$\mathbf{Y} = \mathbf{Q}'(\mathbf{X} - \bar{\mathbf{X}})$$

$$= \begin{bmatrix} \frac{\sqrt{2}}{2} & \frac{\sqrt{2}}{2} \\ -\frac{\sqrt{2}}{2} & \frac{\sqrt{2}}{2} \end{bmatrix} \left[\begin{pmatrix} 4 & 6 & 2 & 4 \\ 4 & 6 & 4 & 2 \end{pmatrix} - \begin{pmatrix} 4 & 4 & 4 & 4 \\ 4 & 4 & 4 & 4 \end{pmatrix} \right]$$

$$= \begin{bmatrix} 0 & 2\sqrt{2} & -\sqrt{2} & -\sqrt{2} \\ 0 & 0 & \sqrt{2} & -\sqrt{2} \end{bmatrix}$$

In the preceding discussion, we have seen how rotation of a set of coordinate axes has resulted in a more parsimonious description of the data, in a very special sense. That is, the new coordinate axes have the property that each one sequentially accounts for as much of the total variation in the system as possible. Thus the y_1 axis, in the case of only the two points P_1 and P_2, accounted for the entire variance in the system and, in the case of the four points P_1, P_2, P_3, and P_4, accounted for 75 percent of the total variance. If, in the latter case, we conclude that this percentage is sufficiently accurate for practical purposes, then we could ignore the coordinates of the four points on the second axis and thereby obtain a reduction of dimensionality from two to one. In an analogous way, it may be possible in a problem involving a space of m dimensions to "collapse" the system into a subspace of $r < m$ dimensions with only a slight sacrifice in accuracy. It remains to be shown, however, how the rotation angle θ is determined and that the new axes in fact are *principal axes.* To do this, we need to formalize the above discussion of dimensional reduction. We shall continue to treat the two-dimensional space, but the extension to a space of m dimensions is straightforward.

8.2.2 DETERMINING THE ROTATION MATRIX

We begin by using (8.2) to express the coordinates along the first new coordinate axis, y_1, as a linear function of the coordinates along axes x_1 and x_2:

$$Y_{1i} = q_{11}X_{1i} + q_{21}X_{2i} = \mathbf{q}_1'\mathbf{x}_i \tag{8.22}$$

Next, we observe that the sample mean along the y_1 axis is

$$\begin{aligned} \bar{Y}_1 &= \frac{1}{n}\sum_{i=1}^{n} Y_{1i} \\ &= \frac{1}{n}\sum_{i=1}^{n} \mathbf{q}_1'\mathbf{x}_i \end{aligned} \tag{8.23}$$

and that the sample variance along the same axis is

$$\begin{aligned} s_{y_1}^2 &= \frac{1}{n}\sum_{i=1}^{n} (Y_{1i} - \bar{Y}_1)^2 \\ &= \frac{1}{n}\sum_{i=1}^{n} \left(\mathbf{q}_1'\mathbf{x}_i - \frac{1}{n}\sum_{i=1}^{n} \mathbf{q}_1'\mathbf{x}_i\right)^2 \\ &= \frac{1}{n}\sum_{i=1}^{n} [\mathbf{q}_1'(\mathbf{x}_i - \bar{\mathbf{x}})]^2 \end{aligned}$$

where

$$\bar{\mathbf{x}} = \frac{1}{n}\sum_{i=1}^{n} \mathbf{x}_i$$

Hence,

$$s_{y_1}^2 = \frac{1}{n}\sum_{i=1}^{n} \mathbf{q}_1'(\mathbf{x}_i - \bar{\mathbf{x}})(\mathbf{x}_i - \bar{\mathbf{x}})'\mathbf{q}_1 = \mathbf{q}_1'\mathbf{S}_x\mathbf{q}_1 \tag{8.24}$$

where $\mathbf{S}_x$ is the sample covariance matrix

$$\mathbf{S}_x = \begin{bmatrix} s_{x_1}^2 & s_{x_1x_2} \\ s_{x_2x_1} & s_{x_2}^2 \end{bmatrix}$$

We now wish to determine the position of the new axis, y_1, such that it passes through the direction of maximum variance in the scatter of points. To find the angle of rotation, θ, that will move the x_1 axis to such a position, we differentiate (8.24) with respect to $\mathbf{q}_1$, while including the constraint that the coordinates of $\mathbf{q}_1$ are normalized to unit length. We therefore introduce a Lagrangean multiplier, λ_1, say, and obtain

$$\frac{\partial}{\partial \mathbf{q}_1}[s_{y_1}^2 + \lambda_1(1 - \mathbf{q}_1'\mathbf{q}_1)] = \frac{\partial}{\partial \mathbf{q}_1}[\mathbf{q}_1'\mathbf{S}_x\mathbf{q}_1 + \lambda_1(1 - \mathbf{q}_1'\mathbf{q}_1)]$$
$$= 2(\mathbf{S}_x - \lambda_1\mathbf{I})\mathbf{q}_1 \qquad (8.25)$$

The vector $\mathbf{q}_1$ must therefore satisfy the set of simultaneous linear equations

$$(\mathbf{S}_x - \lambda_1\mathbf{I})\mathbf{q}_1 = \mathbf{0} \qquad (8.26)$$

and we have seen in Chapter 7 that for a nontrivial solution we must have

$$|\mathbf{S}_x - \lambda_1\mathbf{I}| = 0 \qquad (8.27)$$

Hence λ_1 is a characteristic root of the sample covariance matrix $\mathbf{S}_x$ and $\mathbf{q}_1$ is its associated normalized characteristic vector. To determine which of the roots should be used, we premultiply (8.26) by $\mathbf{q}_1'$ and, since $\mathbf{q}_1'\mathbf{q}_1 = 1$, we find that

$$\lambda_1 = \mathbf{q}_1'\mathbf{S}_x\mathbf{q}_1 = s_{y_1}^2 \qquad (8.28)$$

Since the coefficient vector $\mathbf{q}_1$ was selected to maximize this variance, we conclude that λ_1 must be the largest characteristic root of the sample covariance matrix $\mathbf{S}_x$; the direction cosines of the first principal axis are therefore the elements of the normalized characteristic vector associated with this root.

Examples.

(i) Returning now to our example in Figure 8.4, we first compute the sample covariance matrix

$$\mathbf{S}_x = \begin{bmatrix} 1 & 1 \\ 1 & 1 \end{bmatrix}$$

Since the rank of $\mathbf{S}_x$ is unity, it has only one nonzero characteristic root. Thus,

$$\begin{vmatrix} 1-\lambda & 1 \\ 1 & 1-\lambda \end{vmatrix} = (1-\lambda)^2 - 1 = \lambda^2 - 2\lambda = \lambda(\lambda - 2)$$

and setting

$$\lambda(\lambda - 2) = 0$$

we find

$$\lambda_1 = 2$$

Associated with this characteristic root is the normalized characteristic vector

$$\mathbf{q}_1 = \begin{bmatrix} \dfrac{\sqrt{2}}{2} \\ \dfrac{\sqrt{2}}{2} \end{bmatrix}$$

Hence our new coordinate axis, y_1, is obtained by rotating x_1 through precisely the angle we have been using, that is, $\theta = 45°$. This rotation exhausts the total variance to be accounted for: $s_{x_1}^2 + s_{x_2}^2 = 1 + 1 = 2 = s_{y_1}^2$.

(ii) Turning now to the numerical example in Figure 8.6, we derive the sample covariance matrix

$$\mathbf{S}_x = \begin{bmatrix} 2 & 1 \\ 1 & 2 \end{bmatrix}$$

The rank of $\mathbf{S}_x$ is two. Therefore, it has two nonzero characteristic roots:

$$\begin{vmatrix} 2-\lambda & 1 \\ 1 & 2-\lambda \end{vmatrix} = (2-\lambda)^2 - 1 = \lambda^2 - 4\lambda + 3 = (\lambda - 1)(\lambda - 3)$$

and setting

$$(\lambda - 1)(\lambda - 3) = 0$$

we have, in descending order of magnitude, the two characteristic roots

$$\lambda_1 = 3$$
$$\lambda_2 = 1$$

Associated with the largest root is the normalized characteristic vector

$$\mathbf{q}_1 = \begin{bmatrix} \dfrac{\sqrt{2}}{2} \\ \dfrac{\sqrt{2}}{2} \end{bmatrix}$$

Hence, once again we rotate x_1 through the angle of 45° to establish the position of coordinate axis y_1.

In the above example, the new coordinate axis, y_1, accounts for only three-fourths of the total variance in the system. Therefore, to account for the residual variation, we must introduce a second coordinate axis, y_2, orthogonal to the first, such that it accounts for as much as possible of the variance unaccounted for by y_1. That is, we seek to maximize

$$s_{y_2}^2 = \mathbf{q}_2'\mathbf{S}_x\mathbf{q}_2 \tag{8.29}$$

subject to the constraints

$$\mathbf{q}_2'\mathbf{q}_2 = 1 \tag{8.30}$$

$$\mathbf{q}_1'\mathbf{q}_2 = 0 \tag{8.31}$$

Equation (8.30) is merely the normalization constraint, and (8.31) ensures that the y_2 axis will be orthogonal to the y_1 axis.

Proceeding as before, we introduce the Lagrangean multipliers λ_2 and u, and differentiate (8.29) with respect to $\mathbf{q}_2$ to find

$$\frac{\partial}{\partial \mathbf{q}_2}[\mathbf{q}_2'\mathbf{S}_x\mathbf{q}_2 + \lambda_2(1 - \mathbf{q}_2'\mathbf{q}_2) + u\mathbf{q}_1'\mathbf{q}_2] = 2(\mathbf{S}_x - \lambda_2\mathbf{I})\mathbf{q}_2 + u\mathbf{q}_1 \tag{8.32}$$

Setting the right-hand side of (8.32) equal to the zero vector and premultiplying by $\mathbf{q}_1'$, we have, as a consequence of the normalization and orthogonalization constraints, that

$$2\mathbf{q}_1'\mathbf{S}_x\mathbf{q}_2 + u = 0 \tag{8.33}$$

Similarly, premultiplying (8.26) by $\mathbf{q}_2'$ results in

$$\mathbf{q}_2'\mathbf{S}_x\mathbf{q}_1 = 0 \tag{8.34}$$

Hence $u = 0$, and the second coefficient vector must satisfy

$$(\mathbf{S}_x - \lambda_2\mathbf{I})\mathbf{q}_2 = 0 \tag{8.35}$$

It follows that λ_2 is the second largest characteristic root of $\mathbf{S}_x$ and that $\mathbf{q}_2$ is the associated normalized characteristic vector.

Example. Turning once more to the numerical example in Figure 8.6, we recall that the second characteristic root of $\mathbf{S}_x$ was unity. With this characteristic root, we can associate the normalized characteristic vector

$$\mathbf{q}_2 = \begin{bmatrix} -\frac{\sqrt{2}}{2} \\ \frac{\sqrt{2}}{2} \end{bmatrix}$$

Hence our y_2 axis is perpendicular to the y_1 axis and accounts for the remaining one-fourth of the variation in the system. Note that our rotation matrix, as before, is

$$\mathbf{Q}' = [\mathbf{q}_1 \quad \mathbf{q}_2]' = \begin{bmatrix} \frac{\sqrt{2}}{2} & \frac{\sqrt{2}}{2} \\ -\frac{\sqrt{2}}{2} & \frac{\sqrt{2}}{2} \end{bmatrix}$$

and observe that

$$\mathbf{Q}'\mathbf{S}_x\mathbf{Q} = \Lambda = \begin{bmatrix} 3 & 0 \\ 0 & 1 \end{bmatrix}$$

which is precisely the definition of principal axes given in (8.20).

Let us now summarize the results of this section. The geometric interpretation of the problem of reducing the dimensionality of a scatter of points in a two-dimensional space has been described as the translation of the original coordinate axes to the centroid of the observations and the rigid rotation of these coordinate axes into an orientation corresponding to the maximum variance in the sample of points. This has been shown to be equivalent to a rotation carried out by a rotation matrix with rows that are the orthonormal characteristic vectors associated with the characteristic roots, *arranged in descending order of magnitude*, of the sample covariance matrix. The descending order ensures that the first new coordinate axis lies in the direction of maximum variance, the second in the direction of maximum residual variance, and so on. Thus the new axes are selected in decreasing order of importance, and a reduction of dimensionality may be achieved by selecting those first few axes that together account for a sufficiently large portion of the total sample variance.

The extension of the results of this section to m-dimensional space is straightforward. However, because it is difficult to visualize a space of more than three dimensions, it is simpler to carry out such an extension algebraically. Such an interpretation of the concept of reduced dimensionality is commonly called *principal components analysis* and is described in the next section.

8.3 PRINCIPAL AXES AND THE CONCEPT OF REDUCED DIMENSIONALITY: PRINCIPAL COMPONENTS INTERPRETATION

The essence of most multivariate statistical methods for reducing the dimensionality of a multivariate sample of observations, is to determine a smaller number of linear combinations of the original variables which, in some sense, retain most of the information carried by the original variables. Although the number of variables is reduced, it should be understood that this is not accomplished by discarding some of the original variables. Rather, it is through the elimination of redundant information, contributed by highly correlated variables, that a smaller set of "synthetic" variables can account for approximately the same degree of variation. For whereas the original variables may be highly correlated, the synthetically created variables are constructed so as to be uncorrelated with each other.

8.3.1 PRINCIPAL COMPONENTS

Principal components analysis is a formal method for extracting those linear combinations of a set of variables, called *principal components*, that are orthogonal to each other and that successively account for the largest portion of the residual sample variance. More precisely, the variance of the first principal component is the largest of all components, that of the second is next largest, and so on, until all of the total variance in the sample is partitioned among the uncorrelated principal components.

Most principal components analyses begin with a two-way table that sets out the values or scores of n observations taken on m variables:

$$\underset{m\times n}{\mathbf{X}} = m \text{ variables} \quad \begin{matrix} \\ \mathbf{X}_1 \\ \mathbf{X}_2 \\ \vdots \\ \mathbf{X}_m \end{matrix} \overset{n \text{ observations}}{\begin{matrix} \mathbf{x}_1 & \mathbf{x}_2 & \cdots & \mathbf{x}_n \\ \left[\begin{matrix} X_{11} \\ X_{21} \\ \vdots \\ X_{m1} \end{matrix}\right. & \begin{matrix} X_{12} \\ X_{22} \\ \vdots \\ X_{m2} \end{matrix} & \begin{matrix} \cdots \\ \cdots \\ \\ \cdots \end{matrix} & \left.\begin{matrix} X_{1n} \\ X_{2n} \\ \vdots \\ X_{mn} \end{matrix}\right] \end{matrix}} \tag{8.36}$$

where X_{ij} denotes the value of the jth observation on the ith variable, $\mathbf{X}_i$ denotes the vector of scores of the n observations on the ith variable, and $\mathbf{x}_j$ denotes the vector of scores of the jth observation on the m variables. No assumption needs to be made about the probability distribution of the population from which the sample is drawn, except when statistical tests of significance are desired. Furthermore, in an effort to standardize observations measured in widely different units (for example, inches, miles, pounds, years), each observation commonly is transformed into a *standard score* by subtracting from it its sample mean and dividing this difference by its sample standard deviation, namely,

$$Z_{ij} = \frac{X_{ij} - \bar{X}_i}{s_{x_i}} \tag{8.37}$$

The principal components that are obtained in each case are generally *not the same,* and the results of the analysis, therefore, depend on the fundamental units of measurement.

The first principal component of the data presented in (8.36) is the linear combination of the original m variables:

$$\begin{aligned} Y_{1i} &= q_{11}X_{1i} + q_{21}X_{2i} + \cdots + q_{m1}X_{mi} \\ &= \mathbf{q}_1'\mathbf{x}_i \qquad (i = 1, 2, \ldots, n) \end{aligned} \tag{8.38}$$

with a sample variance

$$\begin{aligned} s_{y_1}^2 &= \sum_{i=1}^{m} \sum_{k=1}^{m} q_{i1}q_{k1}s_{x_ix_k} \qquad (s_{x_ix_i} = s_{x_i}^2) \\ &= \mathbf{q}_1'\mathbf{S}_x\mathbf{q}_1 \end{aligned} \tag{8.39}$$

that is a maximum, subject to the normalization constraint

$$\mathbf{q}_1'\mathbf{q}_1 = 1 \tag{8.40}$$

Analogously, the jth principal component is defined as the linear combination of the original m variables:

$$\begin{aligned} Y_{ji} &= q_{1j}X_{1i} + q_{2j}X_{2i} + \cdots + q_{mj}X_{mi} \\ &= \mathbf{q}_j'\mathbf{x}_i \qquad (i = 1, 2, \ldots, n) \end{aligned} \tag{8.41}$$

with a sample variance

$$s_{y_j}^2 = \mathbf{q}_j'\mathbf{S}_x\mathbf{q}_j \tag{8.42}$$

that is a maximum, subject to the constraints

$$\mathbf{q}_j'\mathbf{q}_j = 1 \tag{8.43}$$

$$\mathbf{q}_i'\mathbf{q}_j = 0 \qquad (i = 1, 2, \ldots, j-1) \tag{8.44}$$

The first constraint is the normalization constraint, and the second requires that the jth component be orthogonal to the previously defined $j - 1$ principal components. A consequence of the orthogonality restriction is the invariance of the total variation under the linear transformation. That is, the variances of the principal components sum to the total variance of the original variables.

To determine the coefficients of $\mathbf{q}_1$ in (8.38), we introduce the normalization constraint of (8.40) by means of a Lagrangean multiplier, λ_1, say, and then differentiate (8.39) with respect to $\mathbf{q}_1$:

$$\begin{aligned} \frac{\partial}{\partial \mathbf{q}_1}[s_{y_1}^2 + \lambda_1(1 - \mathbf{q}_1'\mathbf{q}_1)] &= \frac{\partial}{\partial \mathbf{q}_1}[\mathbf{q}_1'\mathbf{S}_x\mathbf{q}_1 + \lambda_1(1 - \mathbf{q}_1'\mathbf{q}_1)] \\ &= 2(\mathbf{S}_x - \lambda_1\mathbf{I})\mathbf{q}_1 \end{aligned} \tag{8.45}$$

But (8.45) is precisely the same result as (8.24)! Hence the first principal component, Y_1, is the linear combination of the original variables, with coefficients q_{i1} that are the elements of the normalized characteristic vector associated with the largest characteristic root, λ_1, of the sample covariance matrix $\mathbf{S}_x$. Furthermore, by (8.26) we may interpret λ_1 as the sample variance of the first principal component, Y_1, and the importance of Y_1 as a more parsimonious descriptor of the system represented by the original data may be measured by

$$\alpha_1 = \frac{\lambda_1}{s_{x_1}^2 + s_{x_2}^2 + \cdots + s_{x_m}^2} = \frac{\lambda_1}{\mathrm{tr}(\mathbf{S}_x)} \tag{8.46}$$

where $\mathrm{tr}(\mathbf{S}_x)$ is the trace of $\mathbf{S}_x$, and α_1 is the proportion of the total variance that is accounted for by the first principal component.

By a similar argument, we may show that the jth principal component, Y_j, is a linear combination of the original variables, with coefficients q_{ij} that are the elements of the normalized characteristic vector associated with the jth largest characteristic root, λ_j, of the sample covariance matrix $\mathbf{S}_x$. Because

$$\mathbf{q}_j'\mathbf{q}_j = 1 \quad \text{and} \quad \mathbf{q}_i'\mathbf{q}_j = 0 \qquad (i = 1, 2, \ldots, j-1)$$

we may interpret λ_j as the sample variance of Y_j and measure the importance of the jth principal component by

$$\alpha_j = \frac{\lambda_j}{\mathrm{tr}(\mathbf{S}_x)} \tag{8.47}$$

We can always obtain the principal component that accounts for the maximum proportion of the total variance in our sample of observations. If this proportion is very large, we may decide that, for all practical purposes, we have sufficiently reduced the dimensionality of our data, and proceed to describe our data in terms of this newly created variable. However, if, for example, the first principal component accounts for less than half of the total variation, we may decide that a second principal component, which accounts for the maximum proportion of the residual variation, should be defined. If the two principal components together account for a sufficiently large proportion of the total variation, we may conclude that a two-dimensional representation of our data is satisfactory. Otherwise, we may continue to extract additional principal components until we are satisfied that enough of the total variation in the sample has been accounted for by our "synthetic" variables.

Example. To illustrate, once more, the computation of principal components, let us turn to our numerical example of Figure 8.6 and the sample covariance matrix

$$\mathbf{S}_x = \begin{bmatrix} 2 & 1 \\ 1 & 2 \end{bmatrix}$$

In the previous section we found that the following two linear combinations of the two original variables (or coordinate axes) successively accounted for the maximum proportion of the total sample variance:

$$\begin{aligned} Y_{1i} &= \frac{\sqrt{2}}{2} X_{1i} + \frac{\sqrt{2}}{2} X_{2i} \\ Y_{2i} &= -\frac{\sqrt{2}}{2} X_{1i} + \frac{\sqrt{2}}{2} X_{2i} \end{aligned} \tag{8.48}$$

Thus, for example, the third observation

$$\mathbf{x}_3 = \begin{bmatrix} X_{13} \\ X_{23} \end{bmatrix} = \begin{bmatrix} 2 \\ 4 \end{bmatrix}$$

was found to have principal component scores

$$\mathbf{y}_3 = \begin{bmatrix} Y_{13} \\ Y_{23} \end{bmatrix} = \begin{bmatrix} 3\sqrt{2} \\ \sqrt{2} \end{bmatrix}$$

The first principal component, Y_1, accounted for 75 percent of the total variance; the second principal component accounted for the remaining 25 percent.

Now let us consider the same sample of observations,

$$\mathbf{X} = \begin{bmatrix} 4 & 6 & 2 & 4 \\ 4 & 6 & 4 & 2 \end{bmatrix}$$

and extract the principal components from the sample correlation matrix, $\mathbf{R}$, rather than from the sample covariance matrix, $\mathbf{S}_x$. We note that the matrix of standardized observations is

$$\mathbf{Z} = \begin{bmatrix} 0 & \sqrt{2} & -\sqrt{2} & 0 \\ 0 & \sqrt{2} & 0 & -\sqrt{2} \end{bmatrix}$$

and recall that

$$\mathbf{R} = \begin{bmatrix} r_{x1x1} & r_{x1x2} \\ r_{x2x1} & r_{x2x2} \end{bmatrix} = \frac{1}{n}\mathbf{ZZ}'$$

$$= \frac{1}{4}\begin{bmatrix} 0 & \sqrt{2} & -\sqrt{2} & 0 \\ 0 & \sqrt{2} & 0 & -\sqrt{2} \end{bmatrix} \begin{bmatrix} 0 & 0 \\ \sqrt{2} & \sqrt{2} \\ -\sqrt{2} & 0 \\ 0 & -\sqrt{2} \end{bmatrix}$$

$$= \begin{bmatrix} 1 & \frac{1}{2} \\ \frac{1}{2} & 1 \end{bmatrix}$$

The characteristic roots of $\mathbf{R}$ are

$$\lambda_1 = 1\tfrac{1}{2}$$
$$\lambda_2 = \tfrac{1}{2}$$

Thus,

$$\mathbf{L} = \mathbf{Q}' = \begin{bmatrix} \frac{\sqrt{2}}{2} & \frac{\sqrt{2}}{2} \\ -\frac{\sqrt{2}}{2} & \frac{\sqrt{2}}{2} \end{bmatrix}$$

$$\theta = 45°$$

and the matrix of principal component scores is

$$\mathbf{Y} = \mathbf{Q}'\mathbf{Z}$$

$$= \begin{bmatrix} \frac{\sqrt{2}}{2} & \frac{\sqrt{2}}{2} \\ -\frac{\sqrt{2}}{2} & \frac{\sqrt{2}}{2} \end{bmatrix} \begin{bmatrix} 0 & \sqrt{2} & -\sqrt{2} & 0 \\ 0 & \sqrt{2} & 0 & -\sqrt{2} \end{bmatrix}$$

$$= \begin{bmatrix} 0 & 2 & -1 & -1 \\ 0 & 0 & 1 & -1 \end{bmatrix}$$

In this particular example, the principal components extracted from the sample correlation matrix are identical to those extracted from the sample covariance matrix. *However, as we noted earlier, this is not generally true.*

8.3.2 PRINCIPAL COMPONENTS ANALYSIS

Let us now summarize, in matrix form, our exposition of the principal components interpretation of reduced dimensionality. Because principal components extracted from sample covariance matrices are not invariant under a change of the measurement scales used, we shall henceforth deal with standardized variates,

$$Z_{ij} = \frac{X_{ij} - \bar{X}_i}{s_{x_i}}$$

and their sample covariance matrix,

$$\begin{aligned} \mathbf{S}_z &= \frac{1}{n}(\mathbf{Z} - \bar{\mathbf{Z}})(\mathbf{Z} - \bar{\mathbf{Z}})' \\ &= \frac{1}{n}(\mathbf{Z} - \mathbf{0})(\mathbf{Z} - \mathbf{0})' \\ &= \frac{1}{n}\mathbf{Z}\mathbf{Z}' = \mathbf{R} \end{aligned} \tag{8.49}$$

where $\mathbf{R}$ denotes the sample correlation matrix.

Applying (8.41) for each of $j = 1, 2, \ldots, p$ principal components extracted from the sample correlation matrix, we have that

$$\underset{p\times 1}{\mathbf{y}} = \underset{p\times m}{\mathbf{Q}'}\ \underset{m\times 1}{\mathbf{z}} \tag{8.50}$$

where

$$\underset{p\times m}{\mathbf{Q}'}\ \underset{m\times m}{\mathbf{R}}\ \underset{m\times p}{\mathbf{Q}} = \underset{p\times p}{\Lambda} \qquad (p \leqq m) \tag{8.51}$$

and

$$\underset{m\times m}{\mathbf{R}} = \underset{m\times p}{\mathbf{Q}}\ \underset{p\times p}{\Lambda}\ \underset{p\times m}{\mathbf{Q}'} \tag{8.52}$$

The rows of the rotation matrix $\mathbf{Q}'$, as before, are the orthonormal characteristic vectors associated with the characteristic roots of the sample correlation matrix $\mathbf{R}$. However, in (8.51), we have deleted characteristic roots that are zero from the diagonal matrix Λ. Hence the order of Λ may be less than m and will be denoted by p, which always will be equal to the rank of $\mathbf{R}$.

It is generally desirable for principal components to have unit variances as well as zero means. Hence, in most applications, the $\mathbf{y}$ in (8.50) is standardized as follows:

$$\mathbf{f} = \Lambda^{-1/2}\mathbf{y} = \Lambda^{-1/2}\mathbf{Q}'\mathbf{z}$$

or, more compactly,

$$\underset{p\times 1}{\mathbf{f}} = \underset{p\times m}{\mathbf{L}}\ \underset{m\times 1}{\mathbf{z}} \tag{8.53}$$

where

$$\mathbf{L} = \boldsymbol{\Lambda}^{-1/2}\mathbf{Q}' \tag{8.54}$$

Thus,

$$\begin{bmatrix} F_1 \\ F_2 \\ \vdots \\ F_p \end{bmatrix} = \begin{bmatrix} l_{11} & l_{12} & \cdots & l_{1m} \\ l_{21} & l_{22} & \cdots & l_{2m} \\ \vdots & \vdots & & \vdots \\ l_{p1} & l_{p2} & \cdots & l_{pm} \end{bmatrix} \begin{bmatrix} Z_1 \\ Z_2 \\ \vdots \\ Z_m \end{bmatrix}$$

and, applying this rotation to all of the n observations, we have that

$$\underset{p\times n}{\mathbf{F}} = \underset{p\times m}{\mathbf{L}}\ \underset{m\times n}{\mathbf{Z}} \tag{8.55}$$

where

$$\mathbf{F} = \begin{bmatrix} F_{11} & F_{12} & \cdots & F_{1n} \\ F_{21} & F_{22} & \cdots & F_{2n} \\ \vdots & \vdots & & \vdots \\ F_{p1} & F_{p2} & \cdots & F_{pn} \end{bmatrix} \qquad \mathbf{Z} = \begin{bmatrix} Z_{11} & Z_{12} & \cdots & Z_{1n} \\ Z_{21} & Z_{22} & \cdots & Z_{2n} \\ \vdots & \vdots & & \vdots \\ Z_{m1} & Z_{m2} & \cdots & Z_{mn} \end{bmatrix}$$

Equation (8.53) expresses the p principal components as linear functions of the m variables, and (8.55) expresses the "scores" of the n observations on the p principal components as the same linear functions of the scores of these n observations on the original m variables. Frequently, however, we are interested in the inverse functional relationship. That is, we wish to express the m variables as linear functions of the p principal components. To establish this relationship, we premultiply both sides of (8.53) by $\mathbf{Q}\boldsymbol{\Lambda}^{1/2}$ to find

$$\mathbf{Q}\boldsymbol{\Lambda}^{1/2}\mathbf{f} = \mathbf{Q}\boldsymbol{\Lambda}^{1/2}\mathbf{L}\mathbf{z} = \mathbf{Q}\boldsymbol{\Lambda}^{1/2}\boldsymbol{\Lambda}^{-1/2}\mathbf{Q}'\mathbf{z} = \mathbf{Q}\mathbf{Q}'\mathbf{z} = \mathbf{z}$$

or

$$\mathbf{z} = \underset{m\times p}{\mathbf{A}}\ \underset{p\times 1}{\mathbf{f}} \tag{8.56}$$

where

$$\mathbf{A} = \mathbf{Q}\boldsymbol{\Lambda}^{1/2} \tag{8.57}$$

Applying (8.56) to each of the n variables, we also have that

$$\underset{m\times n}{\mathbf{Z}} = \underset{m\times p}{\mathbf{A}}\ \underset{p\times n}{\mathbf{F}} \tag{8.58}$$

Equation (8.56) defines the fundamental model of principal components analysis. It states that each variable, Z_j, say, can be expressed as the following linear combination of p uncorrelated principal components:

$$Z_j = a_{j1}F_1 + a_{j2}F_2 + \cdots + a_{jp}F_p \tag{8.59}$$

Note that

$$\mathbf{AA}' = \mathbf{Q}\mathbf{\Lambda}^{1/2}\mathbf{\Lambda}^{1/2}\mathbf{Q}' = \mathbf{Q\Lambda Q}' = \mathbf{R} \tag{8.60}$$

by (8.52), and that

$$\mathbf{A}'\mathbf{A} = \mathbf{\Lambda}^{1/2}\mathbf{Q}'\mathbf{Q}\mathbf{\Lambda}^{1/2} = \mathbf{\Lambda} \tag{8.61}$$

Equation (8.60) expresses a "factorization" of the correlation matrix into the product of **A** and its transpose. As we shall see in Section 8.5, this is also the purpose of *factor analysis*. However, whereas in principal components analysis this factorization is unique, in factor analysis an infinity of equally valid factorizations are possible.[4]

The matrix **A** in (8.56) is sometimes referred to as the "factor loading" matrix, and its elements may be interpreted as correlation coefficients that define the degree of association between the variables and the principal components. That is, a_{ij} is the coefficient of correlation between variable i and principal component j. This can easily be seen by noting that because both the variable and the principal component scores have been standardized so as to yield zero means and unit variances, we can express the correlation between the ith variable and jth principal component as

$$r_{Z_iF_j} = \frac{1}{n}\sum_{k=1}^{n} Z_{ik}F_{jk} \tag{8.62}$$

and the matrix of such correlation coefficients by

$$\begin{aligned}
\mathbf{R}_{ZF} &= \frac{1}{n}\mathbf{ZF}' \\
&= \frac{1}{n}\mathbf{Z}(\mathbf{Z}'\mathbf{L}') \qquad \text{by (8.55)} \\
&= \left(\frac{1}{n}\mathbf{ZZ}'\right)\mathbf{L}' \\
&= \mathbf{RL}' \qquad \text{by (8.49)} \\
&= \mathbf{RQ}\mathbf{\Lambda}^{-1/2} \qquad \text{by (8.54)} \\
&= \mathbf{Q\Lambda Q}'\mathbf{Q}\mathbf{\Lambda}^{-1/2} \qquad \text{by (8.52)} \\
&= \mathbf{Q}\mathbf{\Lambda}^{1/2}
\end{aligned}$$

Hence, recalling (8.57), we have that

$$\mathbf{R}_{ZF} = \mathbf{A} \tag{8.63}$$

[4] This distinction is frequently overlooked by urban and regional analysts, who go on to rotate the results of a principal components analysis in an effort to obtain the simplest subject-matter interpretation of the components. While in such instances the relationship in (8.60) continues to hold true, the rotated principal components no longer have the maximum-variance property.

In the above paragraphs, we have extracted principal components from sample covariance or correlation matrices. If we now were willing to assume that such samples had been drawn from a multinormal population with a covariance matrix that had a specific covariance structure, then we could derive several large-sample distributional properties of the principal component coefficients and characteristic roots. These asymptotic properties would permit us to construct certain tests of hypotheses regarding the population component structure. Since the mathematics of this branch of principal components analysis is well beyond the level of this text, however, we shall not discuss this topic here, but refer the interested reader to more advanced texts on the subject, such as Lawley and Maxwell (1963) and Morrison (1967).

Example. To illustrate the above discussion of principal components analysis, let us return to our numerical example of Figure 8.6. We have seen that for these four observations

$$\mathbf{R} = \begin{bmatrix} 1 & \frac{1}{2} \\ \frac{1}{2} & 1 \end{bmatrix} \qquad \Lambda = \begin{bmatrix} 1\frac{1}{2} & 0 \\ 0 & \frac{1}{2} \end{bmatrix}$$

and

$$\mathbf{Q}' = \begin{bmatrix} \frac{\sqrt{2}}{2} & \frac{\sqrt{2}}{2} \\ -\frac{\sqrt{2}}{2} & \frac{\sqrt{2}}{2} \end{bmatrix}$$

Thus,

$$\mathbf{Q}'\mathbf{R}\mathbf{Q} = \begin{bmatrix} \frac{\sqrt{2}}{2} & \frac{\sqrt{2}}{2} \\ -\frac{\sqrt{2}}{2} & \frac{\sqrt{2}}{2} \end{bmatrix} \begin{bmatrix} 1 & \frac{1}{2} \\ \frac{1}{2} & 1 \end{bmatrix} \begin{bmatrix} \frac{\sqrt{2}}{2} & -\frac{\sqrt{2}}{2} \\ \frac{\sqrt{2}}{2} & \frac{\sqrt{2}}{2} \end{bmatrix}$$

$$= \begin{bmatrix} 1\frac{1}{2} & 0 \\ 0 & \frac{1}{2} \end{bmatrix} = \Lambda$$

$$\mathbf{R} = \mathbf{Q}\Lambda\mathbf{Q}' = \begin{bmatrix} \frac{\sqrt{2}}{2} & -\frac{\sqrt{2}}{2} \\ \frac{\sqrt{2}}{2} & \frac{\sqrt{2}}{2} \end{bmatrix} \begin{bmatrix} 1\frac{1}{2} & 0 \\ 0 & \frac{1}{2} \end{bmatrix} \begin{bmatrix} \frac{\sqrt{2}}{2} & \frac{\sqrt{2}}{2} \\ -\frac{\sqrt{2}}{2} & \frac{\sqrt{2}}{2} \end{bmatrix}$$

$$= \begin{bmatrix} 1 & \frac{1}{2} \\ \frac{1}{2} & 1 \end{bmatrix}$$

and

$$\mathbf{A} = \mathbf{Q}\Lambda^{1/2} = \begin{bmatrix} \frac{\sqrt{2}}{2} & -\frac{\sqrt{2}}{2} \\ \frac{\sqrt{2}}{2} & \frac{\sqrt{2}}{2} \end{bmatrix} \begin{bmatrix} \sqrt{\frac{3}{2}} & 0 \\ 0 & \sqrt{\frac{1}{2}} \end{bmatrix} = \begin{bmatrix} \frac{\sqrt{3}}{2} & -\frac{1}{2} \\ \frac{\sqrt{3}}{2} & \frac{1}{2} \end{bmatrix}$$

We may interpret the first principal component by noting that it has an equal and positive correlation of $\sqrt{3}/2$ with each of the two variables: X_1 and X_2. Similarly, the second principal component may be interpreted by observing that it is negatively correlated with variable X_1 and positively correlated with X_2, the correlation in each case being equal to $\frac{1}{2}$.

The principal components model, therefore, is

$$\begin{aligned} Z_1 &= \frac{\sqrt{3}}{2} F_1 - \frac{1}{2} F_2 \\ Z_2 &= \frac{\sqrt{3}}{2} F_1 + \frac{1}{2} F_2 \end{aligned} \tag{8.64}$$

As a check on our computation of **A**, we note that

$$\mathbf{AA}' = \begin{bmatrix} \frac{\sqrt{3}}{2} & -\frac{1}{2} \\ \frac{\sqrt{3}}{2} & \frac{1}{2} \end{bmatrix} \begin{bmatrix} \frac{\sqrt{3}}{2} & \frac{\sqrt{3}}{2} \\ -\frac{1}{2} & \frac{1}{2} \end{bmatrix} = \begin{bmatrix} 1 & \frac{1}{2} \\ \frac{1}{2} & 1 \end{bmatrix} = \mathbf{R}$$

and

$$\mathbf{A}'\mathbf{A} = \begin{bmatrix} \frac{\sqrt{3}}{2} & \frac{\sqrt{3}}{2} \\ -\frac{1}{2} & \frac{1}{2} \end{bmatrix} \begin{bmatrix} \frac{\sqrt{3}}{2} & -\frac{1}{2} \\ \frac{\sqrt{3}}{2} & \frac{1}{2} \end{bmatrix} = \begin{bmatrix} 1\frac{1}{2} & 0 \\ 0 & \frac{1}{2} \end{bmatrix} = \Lambda$$

Finally, we can obtain the scores of the four observations on the two principal components by computing

$$\mathbf{L} = \Lambda^{-1/2}\mathbf{Q}' = \begin{bmatrix} \sqrt{\frac{2}{3}} & 0 \\ 0 & \sqrt{2} \end{bmatrix} \begin{bmatrix} \frac{\sqrt{2}}{2} & \frac{\sqrt{2}}{2} \\ -\frac{\sqrt{2}}{2} & \frac{\sqrt{2}}{2} \end{bmatrix} = \begin{bmatrix} \frac{\sqrt{3}}{3} & \frac{\sqrt{3}}{3} \\ -1 & 1 \end{bmatrix}$$

and recalling that

$$\mathbf{F} = \mathbf{LZ}$$

Thus,

$$\mathbf{F} = \begin{bmatrix} \frac{\sqrt{3}}{3} & \frac{\sqrt{3}}{3} \\ -1 & 1 \end{bmatrix} \begin{bmatrix} 0 & \sqrt{2} & -\sqrt{2} & 0 \\ 0 & \sqrt{2} & 0 & -\sqrt{2} \end{bmatrix}$$

$$= \begin{bmatrix} 0 & \frac{2\sqrt{6}}{3} & -\frac{2\sqrt{6}}{3} & -\frac{2\sqrt{6}}{3} \\ 0 & 0 & \sqrt{2} & -\sqrt{2} \end{bmatrix}$$

Note that $\mathbf{Z} = \mathbf{AF}$.

8.4 APPLICATION: DIMENSIONAL ANALYSIS, DATA REDUCTION, AND CLASSIFICATION PROBLEMS

Classification is a fundamental concern of any science. Order is imposed on phenomena by means of a classification that groups various objects into categories, not of identical objects, but of objects that seem to behave alike. The process of ordering is thus an empirical activity involving trial and error. Moreover, the particular arrangement of objects into groups is predicated on attributes that are judged to be particularly relevant in terms of the kind of problem that is being studied.

The development of high-speed electronic computers and of multivariate statistical techniques has had a profound impact on the methods of classification that are being used in many scientific fields. For the first time, it is possible to consider large numbers of attributes in classifying phenomena, and in order to reduce the number of such descriptors, some form of dimensional reduction is commonly used. These new classification procedures generally fall under the category of *numerical taxonomy*, and their general characteristics are outlined below.

8.4.1 NUMERICAL TAXONOMY

The purpose of numerical taxonomy is to group objects into categories that are similar with respect to a set of prespecified criteria. Typically, such analyses begin with an attempt to reduce the dimensionality of the problem by means of a technique such as principal components analysis. This is followed by a transformation of an $m \times n$ matrix of variable scores into a $p \times n$ matrix of principal component scores. Since p will almost always be chosen to be less than m, a reduction in the dimensionality of the problem will have been achieved, though generally at the cost of some loss of information. Using the matrix of principal component scores, one may define a *similarity matrix* which shows the degree of similarity that exists between pairs of observations. The nature of similarity is, of course, a fundamental problem in numerical taxonomy and is generally defined so as to reflect similarity in structure (rather than, say, common ancestry). Finally, a grouping procedure is applied to the similarity matrix in order to identify those observations that are to be placed into the same category.

One way of representing similarity is by means of distance statistics in a multidimensional space, where each observation is plotted with its scores as coordinates. Those that are located close to each other are assumed to be more similar than those located further apart. Thus we may view similar objects as clusters of points in multidimensional space.

On a single dimension, the similarity of observations can be measured according to the distances that separate them. In two-dimensional space, distances still can serve as indicators of similarity and, using orthogonal axes, the distance between any two points, X_1 and X_2, say, can be found by the Pythagorean theorem. Thus, for example, if

$$\mathbf{x}_1 = \begin{bmatrix} X_{11} \\ X_{21} \end{bmatrix} \qquad \mathbf{x}_2 = \begin{bmatrix} X_{12} \\ X_{22} \end{bmatrix}$$

then the distance separating them is

$$\begin{aligned} d_{12} &= \sqrt{(X_{11} - X_{12})^2 + (X_{21} - X_{22})^2} \\ &= [(X_{11} - X_{12})^2 + (X_{21} - X_{22})^2]^{1/2} \end{aligned} \tag{8.65}$$

Generalizing (8.65) for a space of p dimensions, we have that

$$\begin{aligned} d_{12} &= \left[\sum_{i=1}^{p} \sum_{j=2}^{p} (X_{i1} - X_{i2})\,(X_{j1} - X_{j2}) \right]^{1/2} \\ &= [(\mathbf{x}_1 - \mathbf{x}_2)'\,(\mathbf{x}_1 - \mathbf{x}_2)]^{1/2} \end{aligned} \tag{8.66}$$

For example, in Figure 8.4 we can easily confirm by visual analysis that the distance between the two points P_1 and P_2 is

$$\begin{aligned} d_{12} &= [(4 - 6)^2 + (4 - 6)^2]^{1/2} \\ &= \sqrt{8} = 2\sqrt{2} \end{aligned}$$

Example. Consider, for example, the problem of classifying a sample of 10 rectangles. Assume that for each of the 10 rectangles, the following measurements have been obtained: width, height, width plus height, twice width plus height, and width plus twice height. These data, and the associated sample means, variances, and standard deviations, appear in Table 8.1. Figure 8.7 illustrates the positions of the 10 observations in the two-dimensional variable subspace of width and height.

Table 8.1. Measurements on a Sample of 10 Rectangles

Variable	Observation										Mean	Variance	Standard Deviation
	1	2	3	4	5	6	7	8	9	10			
1. W (width in inches)	2	4	4	4	5	5	5	5	7	9	5.0	3.2	1.789
2. H (height in inches)	5	2	4	6	3	5	6	9	5	5	5.0	3.2	1.789
3. $W + H$	7	6	8	10	8	10	11	14	12	14	10.0	7.0	2.646
4. $2W + H$	9	10	12	14	13	15	16	19	19	23	15.0	17.2	4.147
5. $W + 2H$	12	8	12	16	11	15	17	23	17	19	15.0	17.2	4.147

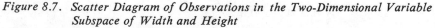

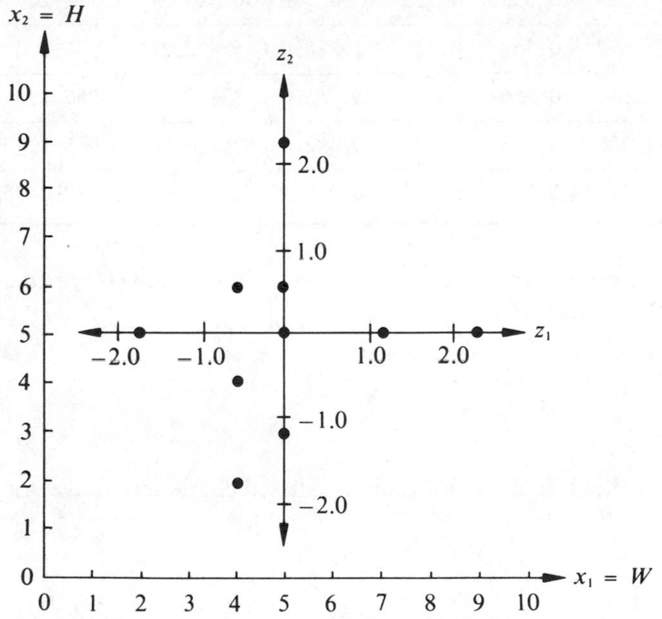

Figure 8.7. Scatter Diagram of Observations in the Two-Dimensional Variable Subspace of Width and Height

Before carrying out a similarity analysis and a grouping of the rectangles into homogeneous classes, it is useful to attempt to achieve a reduction in dimensionality with principal components analysis. Thus we begin by standardizing the data, and obtain the matrix **Z** that appears in Table 8.2

and is illustrated in Figure 8.7. Next, we compute the sample correlation matrix

$$\mathbf{R} = \frac{1}{10}\mathbf{Z}\mathbf{Z}' = \begin{bmatrix} 1.000 & 0.094 & 0.740 & 0.903 & 0.512 \\ 0.094 & 1.000 & 0.740 & 0.512 & 0.903 \\ 0.740 & 0.740 & 1.000 & 0.957 & 0.957 \\ 0.903 & 0.512 & 0.957 & 1.000 & 0.831 \\ 0.512 & 0.903 & 0.957 & 0.831 & 1.000 \end{bmatrix} \tag{8.67}$$

Table 8.2. The **Z** *Matrix of Standardized Variable Scores*

	Observation									
Variable	1	2	3	4	5	6	7	8	9	10
1.	−1.677	−0.559	−0.559	−0.559	0	0	0	0	1.118	2.236
2.	0	−1.677	−0.559	0.559	−1.118	0	0.559	2.236	0	0
3.	−1.134	−1.512	−0.756	0	−0.756	0	0.378	1.512	0.756	1.512
4.	−1.447	−1.206	−0.723	−0.241	−0.482	0	0.241	0.965	0.965	1.929
5.	−0.723	−1.688	−0.723	0.241	−0.965	0	0.482	1.929	0.482	0.965

The rank of the sample correlation matrix in (8.67) is two. Hence there are only two nonzero characteristic roots:

$$\lambda_1 = 3.925$$

and

$$\lambda_2 = 1.075$$

Thus, after deleting the zero roots and their associated characteristic vectors, we have that

$$\underset{2\times5}{\mathbf{Q}'}\ \underset{5\times5}{\mathbf{R}}\ \underset{5\times2}{\mathbf{Q}} = \underset{2\times2}{\mathbf{\Lambda}}$$

where

$$\underset{5\times2}{\mathbf{Q}} = \begin{bmatrix} 0.374 & -0.649 \\ 0.374 & 0.649 \\ 0.505 & 0 \\ 0.483 & -0.280 \\ 0.483 & 0.280 \end{bmatrix} \qquad \underset{2\times2}{\mathbf{\Lambda}} = \begin{bmatrix} 3.925 & 0 \\ 0 & 1.075 \end{bmatrix}$$

Therefore, we find that

$$\underset{2\times5}{\mathbf{L}} = \underset{2\times2}{\Lambda^{-1/2}}\underset{2\times5}{\mathbf{Q}'}$$

$$= \begin{bmatrix} \frac{1}{\sqrt{3.925}} & 0 \\ 0 & \frac{1}{\sqrt{1.075}} \end{bmatrix} \begin{bmatrix} 0.374 & 0.374 & 0.505 & 0.483 & 0.483 \\ -0.649 & 0.649 & 0 & -0.280 & 0.280 \end{bmatrix}$$

$$= \begin{bmatrix} 0.189 & 0.189 & 0.255 & 0.244 & 0.244 \\ -0.626 & 0.626 & 0 & -0.270 & 0.270 \end{bmatrix} \tag{8.68}$$

Hence, recalling (8.55), we obtain the following principal component scores:

$$\underset{2\times10}{\mathbf{F}} = \underset{2\times5}{\mathbf{L}}\ \underset{5\times10}{\mathbf{Z}}$$

$$= \begin{bmatrix} -1.134 & -1.512 & -0.756 & 0 & -0.756 & 0 & 0.378 & 1.512 & 0.756 & 1.512 \\ 1.245 & -0.830 & 0 & 0.830 & -0.830 & 0 & 0.415 & 1.660 & -0.830 & -1.660 \end{bmatrix} \tag{8.69}$$

A plot of the above principal component scores is presented in Figure 8.8. Note the projection of the original z_1-z_2 coordinate axes in the principal component space, and observe that these two coordinate systems do not lie in the same plane.

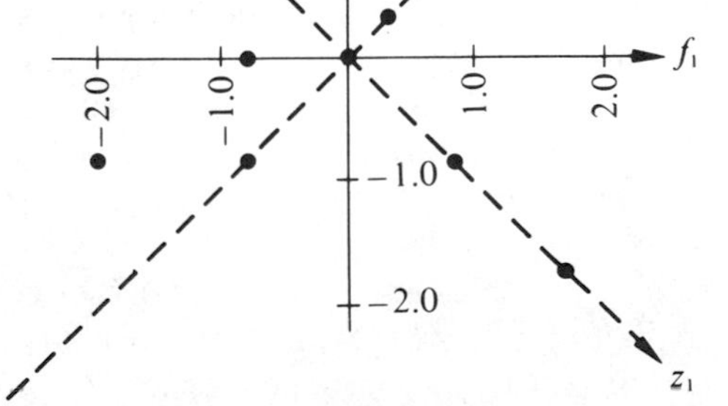

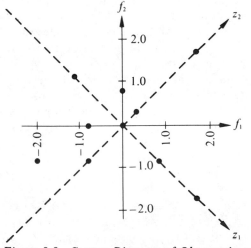

Figure 8.8. Scatter Diagram of Observations in the Two-Dimensional Principal Component Space

The above operations have reduced the dimensionality of the classification problem from five to two. In the process, the 5×10 data matrix in Table 8.1 has been transformed into the 2×10 matrix of principal component scores in (8.69). The first principal component accounts for $3.925/5.0 = 0.785 \times 100$ percent of the total sample variance, and the second accounts for the remaining $1.075/5.0 = 0.215 \times 100$ percent. Hence, no information has been lost in this particular transformation, but such instances are rare in practical applications of the technique.

In order to interpret the two principal components, we must find the principal component loading matrix, **A**. Thus we may use (8.57) to obtain

$$\underset{5\times 2}{\mathbf{A}} = \underset{5\times 2}{\mathbf{Q}}\ \underset{2\times 2}{\Lambda^{1/2}} = \begin{bmatrix} 0.374 & -0.649 \\ 0.374 & 0.649 \\ 0.505 & 0 \\ 0.483 & -0.280 \\ 0.483 & 0.280 \end{bmatrix} \begin{bmatrix} \sqrt{3.925} & 0 \\ 0 & \sqrt{1.075} \end{bmatrix}$$

$$= \begin{bmatrix} 0.740 & -0.673 \\ 0.740 & 0.673 \\ 1.000 & 0 \\ 0.957 & -0.290 \\ 0.957 & 0.290 \end{bmatrix} \tag{8.70}$$

The first column of the **A** matrix contains the correlations of the five variables with the first principal component. These indicate that this component measures "bigness," since it is positively and strongly correlated with all of the five variables measuring "size." Thus rectangles that are large in area should score positively on this component, whereas small rectangles should have negative scores on it.

The second principal component is positively correlated with height, but it is negatively correlated with width. Hence it may be appropriately labeled as a "width versus height" component and interpreted as an indicator of "shape." Thus, short and fat rectangles should have negative scores on this component, whereas tall and thin rectangles should have positive scores on it. This can be verified easily with our sample of 10 rectangles. Note that the two squares have zero scores on the "shape" component.

The relationships between the five variables and the two principal components are clearly illustrated in Figure 8.9, where the five variables are plotted as observations in the two-dimensional component space.

Finally, as a check on our computations, note that

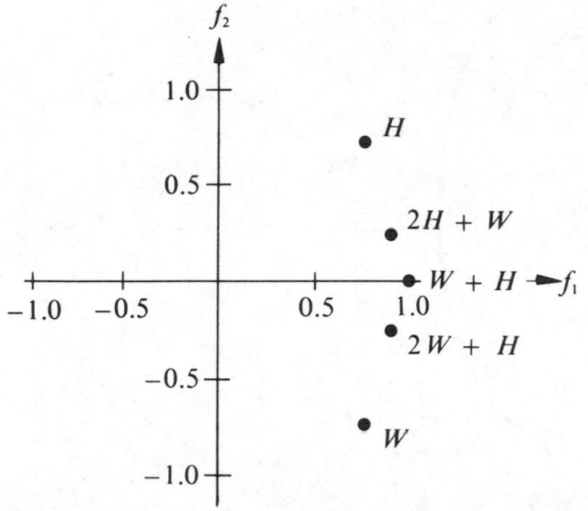

Figure 8.9. Variables in the Principal Component Space

$$\underset{5\times2}{\mathbf{A}}\ \underset{2\times5}{\mathbf{A}'} = \underset{5\times5}{\mathbf{R}}$$

and

$$\underset{2\times5}{\mathbf{A}'}\ \underset{5\times2}{\mathbf{A}} = \underset{2\times2}{\mathbf{\Lambda}}$$

Having reduced the dimensionality of our problem, and having computed the principal component scores of the 10 observations, we can now apply alternative grouping procedures to classify these 10 rectangles into meaningful categories. For example, identifying these rectangles by their observation number, we may wish to cross-classify them by size and shape, as in Table 8.3 and Figure 8.10(a). Or we may wish to collapse one of these two dimensions and deal only with the marginal totals of size or shape. These two groupings are illustrated in Figures 8.10(b) and 8.10(c). Alternatively, we can compute the matrix of distance statistics for all pairs of observations, and group the rectangles using this index as a measure of their similarity. This problem is left as an exercise for the reader (Exercise 3).

Table 8.3. A Cross-Classification of 10 Rectangles by Size and Shape

Shape \ Size	Small	Medium	Large	Shape Only
Thin	#1	#4	##7,8	##1,4,7,8
Square	#3	#6	—	##3,6
Fat	##2,5	—	##9,10	##2,5,9,10
Size Only	##1,2,3,5	##4,6	##7,8,9,10	

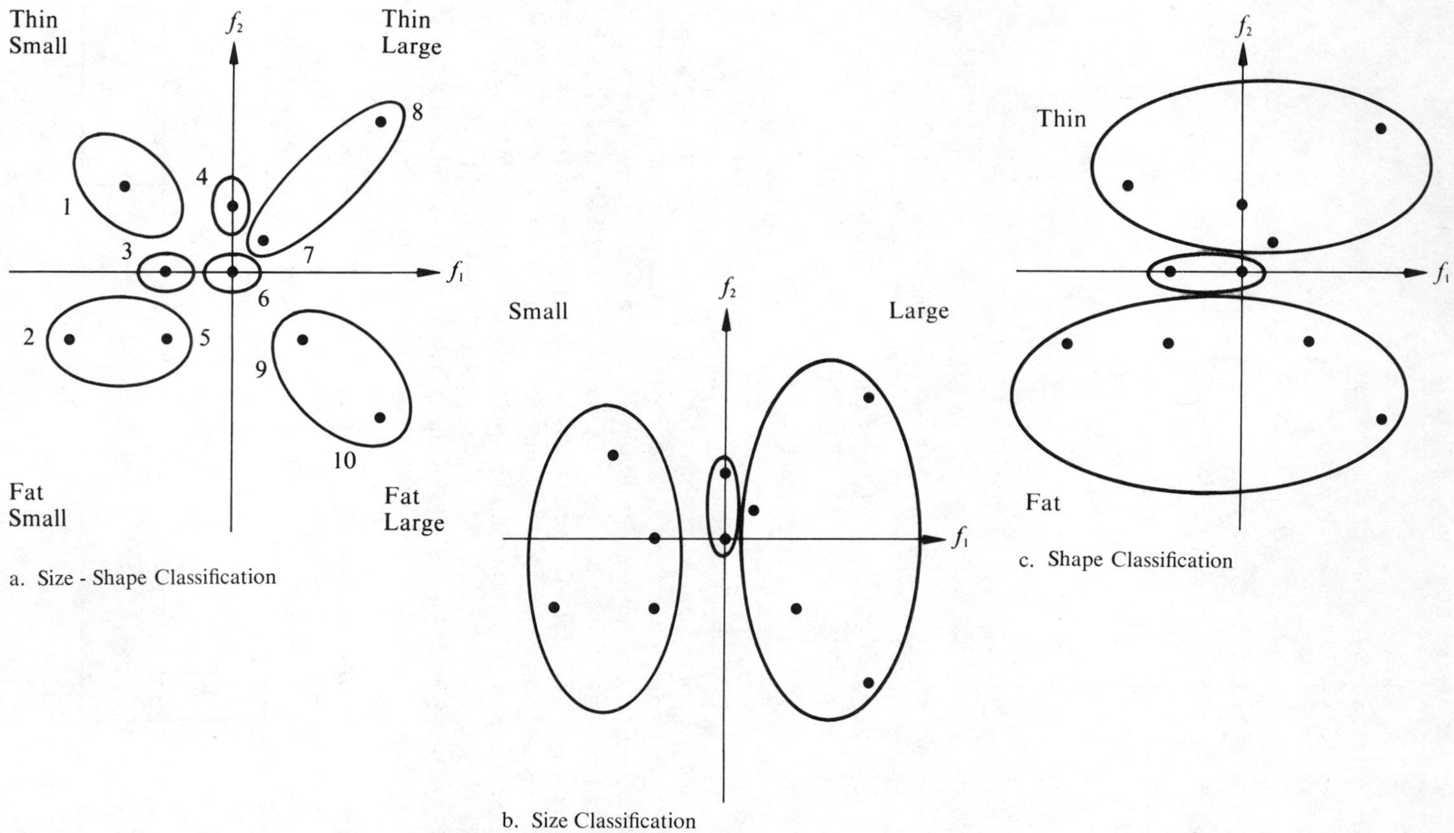

Figure 8.10. Alternative Groupings of the 10 Rectangles

8.4.2 APPLICATION: A REGIONALIZATION OF CALIFORNIA'S 19 STANDARD ECONOMIC AREAS

Regionalization is the process of classifying and grouping small areal units into larger aggregations called regions. Historically, approaches to regionalization have emphasized *homogeneity*, *nodality*, or *policy-orientation*. These emphases, respectively, seek aggregations that tend to be uniform with respect to a set of characteristics, that polarize around some important growth pole or urban center, or that reflect administrative or political coherence. In the following paragraphs, we will be focusing on the first class of regionalization procedures, although it is possible to approach the second class with similar techniques (Exercise 6).

Recall that in Section 3.7 we introduced a division of the State of California into 19 State Economic Areas (SEA's). Of these, 10 were metropolitan areas (SMSA's), and nine were nonmetropolitan areas (non-SMSA's). Assume that for these SEA's we have the data presented in Table 8.4, and consider the problem of aggregating these 19 areas into a smaller number of regions that are uniform with respect to the characteristics measured by the six variables in the table.

The six particular variables that have been selected are highly intercorrelated with one another (Figure 8.11); hence most of them identify the same underlying characteristics in the 19 SEA's. That is, the variables are redundant. Thus, before grouping the 19 SEA's into larger aggregates, it is desirable to eliminate this redundancy by a principal components analysis.

We begin by extracting the characteristic vectors of the sample correlation matrix to find

$$\begin{array}{lll} \lambda_1 = 5.422 & \lambda_2 = 0.555 & \lambda_3 = 0.020 \\ \lambda_4 = 0.003 & \lambda_5 = \lambda_6 = 0.000 & \end{array} \tag{8.71}$$

The first principal component accounts for $5.422/6.0 = 0.904 \times 100$ percent of the total sample variance, and we conclude that this is sufficient

$$\mathbf{R} = \begin{bmatrix} 1.000 & 0.994 & 0.998 & 0.995 & 0.647 & 0.979 \\ 0.994 & 1.000 & 0.999 & 0.997 & 0.642 & 0.992 \\ 0.998 & 0.999 & 1.000 & 0.997 & 0.648 & 0.988 \\ 0.995 & 0.997 & 0.997 & 1.000 & 0.619 & 0.994 \\ 0.647 & 0.642 & 0.648 & 0.619 & 1.000 & 0.594 \\ 0.979 & 0.992 & 0.988 & 0.994 & 0.594 & 1.000 \end{bmatrix}$$

Source: Calculated using the data in Table 8.4. Computed by Caj Falcke.

Figure 8.11. Sample Correlation Matrix for Six Variables on 19 Standard Economic Areas in California

Table 8.4. Interregional Distribution of California's Population, Labor Force Eligibles, and Employment, and Geographical Differentials in Per Capita Wages and Salaries

Variable: / State Economic Areas	1. Population (1950)	2. Population (1960)	3. Labor Force Eligibles (1955)	4. Average Monthly Employment (1955)	5. Average Annual Per Capita Wages and Salaries (1955)	6. Value Added by Manufacture (1958)
SMSA's						
A. S.F.-Oakland	2,240,767	2,783,359	1,629,132	683,474	1,747	2,070,563
B. San Jose	290,547	642,315	267,713	87,440	1,225	631,557
C. Sacramento	277,140	502,778	236,863	67,099	1,569	246,901
D. Stockton	200,750	249,989	142,282	39,651	1,140	147,680
E. Fresno	276,515	365,945	190,353	57,988	1,040	131,055
F. L.A.-Long Beach	4,367,911	6,742,696	3,585,361	1,720,218	1,671	7,044,686
G. San Diego	556,808	1,033,011	530,544	141,124	1,530	605,526
H. San Bernardino	451,688	809,782	381,053	100,502	1,187	319,642
J. Bakersfield	228,309	291,984	159,115	45,266	1,233	59,833
K. Santa Barbara	98,220	168,962	69,829	21,502	999	31,371
Non-SMSA's						
1. Northern Coast	129,654	187,508	102,339	42,324	1,385	163,698
2. North Central Coast	150,008	213,265	110,616	27,035	935	73,091
3. South Central Coast	262,819	379,010	197,817	45,804	1,106	93,082
4. Sacramento Valley	202,604	269,621	142,030	32,720	1,044	83,122
5. No. San Joaquin Valley	197,011	247,740	133,559	32,254	928	100,433
6. So. San Joaquin Valley	232,996	258,825	142,280	28,192	766	45,805
7. Ventura	114,647	199,138	94,085	23,626	1,192	55,505
8. Imperial Valley	62,975	72,105	42,818	9,839	973	13,686
9. Sierra	244,854	299,171	162,479	48,217	1,138	122,340

Source: Table 3.12 and Economic Development Agency, *California Statistical Abstract, 1963*. Sacramento, California: State of California, Documents Section, 1963.

for our regionalization purposes. Hence we proceed to reduce the dimensionality of the problem from six to one, by obtaining the characteristic vector that is associated with λ_1, as follows:

$$\mathbf{R}\mathbf{q}_1 = \lambda_1 \mathbf{q}_1 \tag{8.72}$$

Consequently,

$$\mathbf{q}_1 = \underset{6\times 1}{\mathbf{Q}} = \begin{bmatrix} 0.426 \\ 0.427 \\ 0.428 \\ 0.426 \\ 0.304 \\ 0.423 \end{bmatrix} \tag{8.73}$$

and

$$\underset{6\times 1}{\mathbf{A}} = \underset{6\times 1}{\mathbf{Q}}\ \underset{1\times 1}{\Lambda^{1/2}} = \mathbf{q}_1\sqrt{\lambda_1} = \begin{bmatrix} 0.993 \\ 0.995 \\ 0.996 \\ 0.993 \\ 0.707 \\ 0.984 \end{bmatrix} \tag{8.74}$$

As a check on our computations, we note that

$$\underset{1\times 6}{\mathbf{A}'}\ \underset{6\times 1}{\mathbf{A}} = \underset{1\times 1}{\Lambda} = \lambda_1 = 5.422 \tag{8.75}$$

However, because only the first principal component has been used, $\mathbf{AA}'$ does not exactly reproduce $\mathbf{R}$. That is,

$$\mathbf{AA}' \neq \mathbf{R} \tag{8.76}$$

The first principal component is highly correlated with all six variables which measure population and economic "size." Hence it may be interpreted as a dimension that measures the demographic and economic scale of each SEA. A high score on this dimension, therefore, indicates that the particular SEA has a large population and a high level of economic activity. Thus we would expect most SMSA's to have a higher score on this component than most non-SMSA's. That this indeed is the case can be verified by computing the rotation matrix,

$$\begin{aligned} \underset{1\times 6}{\mathbf{L}} &= \underset{1\times 1}{\Lambda^{-1/2}}\underset{1\times 6}{\mathbf{Q}'} = \frac{1}{\sqrt{\lambda_1}}\mathbf{q}'_1 \\ &= [0.183 \quad 0.184 \quad 0.184 \quad 0.183 \quad 0.130 \quad 0.181] \end{aligned} \tag{8.77}$$

and the vector of component scores,

$$\underset{1\times 19}{\mathbf{F}} = \underset{1\times 6}{\mathbf{L}}\ \underset{6\times 19}{\mathbf{Z}}$$

$$\begin{aligned} = [1.488 \quad & -0.136 \quad -0.044 \quad -0.349 \quad -0.353 \quad 3.812 \\ 0.193 \quad & -0.110 \quad -0.296 \quad -0.486 \quad -0.253 \quad -0.486 \\ -0.330 \quad & -0.405 \quad -0.466 \quad -0.546 \quad -0.373 \quad -0.530 \\ -0.330] & \end{aligned} \tag{8.78}$$

The 19 SEA's are ranked along the single dimension of demographic-economic scale in Figure 8.12. Notice that the three largest metropolitan areas: Los Angeles-Long Beach, San Francisco-Oakland, and San Diego, are the only observations with a positive component score, and observe that except for a few small SMSA's, the first principal component divides the 19 SEA's into metropolitan and nonmetropolitan clusters.

The problem of deriving uniform regions is a classic problem in geography. Although the fundamental ideas appeared over thirty years ago in a seminal paper by Kendall (1939), they could not be put into general use until large-scale, high-speed digital computers became easily available. Most of the recent contributions in this area have come from geographers and, in particular, from Berry (1961, 1968).

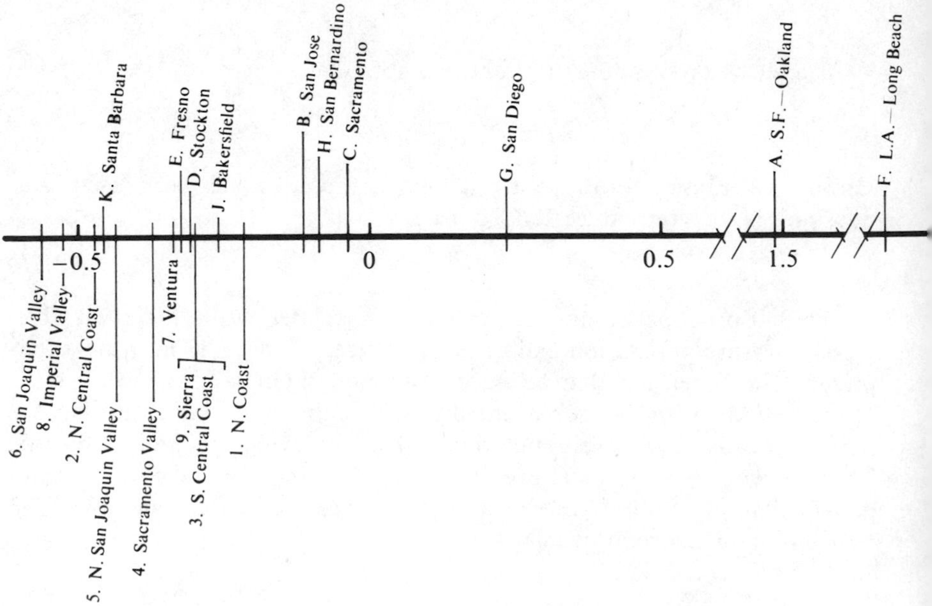

Source: Equation (8.78).

Figure 8.12. Plot of 19 Standard Economic Areas along the First Principal Component

8.5 APPLICATION: FACTOR ANALYSIS

Factor analysis is a branch of statistical theory which strives to account for the underlying structure of covariance or correlation matrices by means of a small number of hypothetical variates called *factors*. While this, to some extent, is also the purpose of principal components analysis, the latter is merely an orthogonal transformation of coordinate axes rather than the result of a model of covariance or correlation structure.

In principal components analysis, we work from the data toward the definition of a set of statistical artifacts, called principal components, which partition the total sample variance into successively smaller portions. In factor analysis, however, we work in the opposite direction, in that we first hypothesize a linear model and then see if such a model satisfactorily accounts for the observed covariance or correlation. Moreover, whereas principal components analysis focuses on the accounting of total sample *variance*, factor analysis is primarily concerned with an accounting of the sample *covariances* or *correlations*. Finally, the principal components model must be linear and additive, because it stems from a rigid rotation of the coordinate axes. The factor analysis model, however, is *assumed* to be linear, and this property, therefore, is as much a part of the hypothesis to be tested as is the proposition that exactly p factors adequately account for the sample covariances or correlations.

8.5.1 THE FACTOR ANALYSIS MODEL

Earlier in this chapter, we saw that the object of principal components analysis is to represent a variable in standardized form, Z_i, say, as a linear function of a set of uncorrelated principal components also in standardized form, F_k, say, such that each component accounts for a successively smaller portion of the total sample variance. The principal components model was expressed as

$$Z_i = a_{i1}F_1 + a_{i2}F_2 + \cdots + a_{ip}F_p \quad (i = 1, 2, \ldots, m) \tag{8.79}$$

or

$$\underset{m\times 1}{\mathbf{z}} = \underset{m\times p}{\mathbf{A}}\ \underset{p\times 1}{\mathbf{f}} \tag{8.80}$$

and

$$\underset{m\times n}{\mathbf{Z}} = \underset{m\times p}{\mathbf{A}}\ \underset{p\times n}{\mathbf{F}} \tag{8.81}$$

In contrast to the principal components approach, with its focus on maximal contribution toward the total sample variance, factor analysis seeks to maximally reproduce the covariances or correlations between variables by means of the factor model

$$Z_i = a_{i1}F_1 + a_{i2}F_2 + \cdots + a_{ip}F_p + \varepsilon_i \qquad (i = 1, 2, \ldots, m) \tag{8.82}$$

The coefficients of the factors are commonly referred to as *factor loadings*, and, as in principal components analysis, they represent the correlations between the respective variables and factors.

Expressing (8.82) in matrix form, we have that

$$\mathbf{z} = \mathbf{Af} + \boldsymbol{\varepsilon} \tag{8.83}$$

and, for $j = 1, 2, \ldots, n$ observations, that

$$\underset{m\times n}{\mathbf{Z}} = \underset{m\times p}{\mathbf{A}} \; \underset{p\times n}{\mathbf{F}} + \underset{m\times n}{\mathbf{E}} \tag{8.84}$$

Each of the m observed standardized variables in (8.82) is described as a linear function of $p \leqq m$ standardized *common factors*, F_k, and an error term ε_i. The common factors account for the covariances or correlations among the variables, while each error term accounts for the variance left unaccounted for by the factors. The error terms are assumed to be independent of each other and independent of the p common factors. We shall also assume that the latter are uncorrelated, but this is not a necessary assumption, and the reader may consult Harman (1967) or Lawley and Maxwell (1963) for a discussion of *oblique* rather than *orthogonal* factor analysis.

The factor analysis model in (8.82) strongly resembles the linear multiple regression model described in Chapter 3. Thus it may be instructive to contrast them here. As in regression, a *dependent* variable, Z_i, is expressed as a linear function of a set of *independent* variables, F_k, and, as before, the partial regression coefficients, a_{ij}, define the amount of change in the dependent variable that results from a unit change in an independent variable. Finally, as in regression, an error term is part of the model.

The principal difference between the factor analysis model and the multiple linear regression model is that in the latter one knows the values of both the dependent and the independent variables, but in factor analysis one knows the values of only the dependent variable, Z_i. Thus the equations in (8.82) cannot be directly verified, since the m variables are expressed as linear functions of p unobservable factors and m unobservable error terms. However, the equations do permit tests of hypotheses to be carried out regarding the variances, covariances, and correlations of the Z's.

Because the factors in the factor model are uncorrelated and standardized to zero mean and unit variance, it follows that the variance of the ith standardized variable can be expressed as

$$\begin{aligned} s_i^2 = 1 &= \sum_{k=1}^{p} a_{ik}^2 \left(\frac{\sum_{j=1}^{n} F_{kj}^2}{n} \right) + \operatorname{Var}(\varepsilon_i) \\ &= a_{i1}^2 + a_{i2}^2 + \cdots + a_{ip}^2 + \operatorname{Var}(\varepsilon_i) \end{aligned} \tag{8.85}$$

and the covariance of the ith and kth standardized variables as

$$s_{ik} = a_{i1}a_{k1} + a_{i2}a_{k2} + \cdots + a_{ip}a_{kp} \tag{8.86}$$

Each term on the right-hand side of (8.85) represents the portion of the unit variance of Z_i that is accounted for by the respective factor. For example, a_{i1}^2 is the portion of the variance of Z_i that is ascribable to factor F_1. It follows, then, that the total "explanatory" contribution of factor F_k may be measured by

$$V_k = \sum_{i=1}^{m} a_{ik}^2 \tag{8.87}$$

and the total contribution of all p common factors, therefore, is

$$V = \sum_{k=1}^{p} V_k \tag{8.88}$$

An indication of the degree of "explanation" provided by the particular factor model is given by the ratio V/m, which represents the proportion of the total sample variance that is accounted for by the set of p common factors.

Equations (8.85) and (8.86) can be expressed compactly in matrix form as

$$\mathbf{S}_z = \mathbf{AA}' + \mathbf{G} \tag{8.89}$$

where $\mathbf{G}$ is a diagonal matrix with elements $g_i = \mathrm{Var}(\varepsilon_i)$ along the principal diagonal, and where the diagonal elements of $\mathbf{AA}'$,

$$s_i^2 - g_i = 1 - g_i = \sum_{j=1}^{p} a_{ij}^2 = h_i^2 \tag{8.90}$$

say, are called the *communalities* of the variables.

Since the variables in the factor model are in standardized form, the sample covariance matrix is also the correlation matrix. Hence the variances and covariances on the left-hand side of equations (8.85), (8.86), (8.89), and (8.90) may be replaced by correlations. Thus we have the equivalent equations

$$r_{ii} = 1 = a_{i1}^2 + a_{i2}^2 + \cdots + a_{ip}^2 + \mathrm{Var}(\varepsilon_i) \tag{8.91}$$

$$r_{ik} = a_{i1}a_{k1} + a_{i2}a_{k2} + \cdots + a_{ip}a_{kp} \tag{8.92}$$

$$\mathbf{R} = \mathbf{AA}' + \mathbf{G} \tag{8.93}$$

and

$$r_{ii} - g_i = 1 - g_i = \sum_{j=1}^{p} a_{ij}^2 = h_i^2 \tag{8.94}$$

8.5.2 THE COMMUNALITY PROBLEM AND THE PRINCIPAL FACTOR SOLUTION

The fundamental problem in factor analysis is the fitting of the factor model defined in (8.82) to observed data. In practice, the factor loading matrix **A** is never known and must be estimated from the sample of observations. The diagonal elements of **G** are then determined by (8.93).

If the *reproduced correlation matrix,*

$$\mathbf{R}_0 = \mathbf{A}\mathbf{A}' \tag{8.95}$$

provides an adequate fit to the *reduced correlation matrix,*

$$\mathbf{R}_r = \mathbf{R} - \mathbf{G} \tag{8.96}$$

then we conclude that the factor model provides a satisfactory accounting of the structure of the sample correlation matrix. Otherwise, we reject the model.

Several alternative factor solution methods are available. The more popular ones are described in great detail by Harman (1967). However, we shall consider only the principal factor solution, which consists of the application of the method of principal axes to the reduced correlation matrix $\mathbf{R}_r$. From an algebraic point of view, this is equivalent to choosing factors in decreasing order of their contribution to the total communality. That is, the first common factor contributes the greatest total to the communalities of the variables, the second common factor, independent of the first, contributes the second greatest total to the communalities, and so on until the total communality is accounted for by the set of common factors.

For the reproduced correlation matrix $\mathbf{R}_0$ to provide an approximate fit to the reduced correlation matrix $\mathbf{R}_r$, the diagonal elements must also be reproduced accurately. If unities appear in the diagonal of $\mathbf{R}_r$, then $\mathbf{R}_r = \mathbf{R}$ and a factor model with no error terms is the result. This is the special case of a principal components model. However, if communalities are placed in the diagonal of $\mathbf{R}_r$, then $\mathbf{R}_r = \mathbf{R} - \mathbf{G}$, and $p \leqq m$ common factors will reproduce $\mathbf{R}_r$. We conclude, therefore, that the communalities determine what portions of the unit variances of the m variables are to be accounted for by the common factors and what portions are to be ascribed to error. Hence the crux of the principal factor solution method lies in the specification of the communalities.

It can be shown [Harman (1967)] that the number of common factors in a factor model is equal to the rank of the reduced correlation matrix, and the rank of this matrix depends on the values of the communalities placed in its principal diagonal. But these values determine the portion of the total variance that is to be factored! Herein lies the circularity and, hence, the communality problem: either the rank of the reduced correlation matrix or its diagonal values must be known in order to obtain a principal factor solution.

The problem of determining the communalities is one of selecting their values in a way such that the smallest number of factors satisfactorily reproduce the observed correlations between the variables. A commonly used procedure for obtaining these values is the following one. Initial communality estimates are placed in the principal diagonal of the sample correlation matrix in order to transform it into the reduced correlation matrix $\mathbf{R}_r$. This is followed by a principal factor (that is, principal axes) solution, from which the first $p \leq m$ factors are retained for further analysis and the rest are neglected.[5] Next, the sums of squares of the factor loadings occurring in these p factors are used as revised estimates of the communalities and another principal factor solution is obtained. This process is repeated until the communality estimates converge. (Although there is no proof that this iterative process will converge, in practice it almost always does.)

Several alternative initial estimates for the communalities have been proposed, but none of them has been shown to be clearly superior to the rest. Frequently, the initial estimates are all unities or the highest correlation coefficients in each column of the sample correlation matrix. The use of the squared multiple correlation of each variable with the remaining ones also has been popular, because it can be shown to be the lower bound of the associated communality.

The iterative process for determining communalities assumes that p factors exist and that they account for as much as possible of the total sample variance. And these communalities yield values for the error variances by virtue of the constraint in (8.93). However, as has been pointed out by Kendall (1957), we have not, by a combination of assumption and iteration, determined the "true" error variances such as might arise in practice. We have only estimated what they would be if there indeed were only p factors and if the error variances were as small as possible.

Example. The simplest case of factor analysis occurs when only one common factor appears in the factor model. For example, in our discussion of the regionalization problem involving California's 19 Standard Economic Areas, we saw that a single principal component accounted for over 90 percent of the total sample variance attributable to the six variables:

1. Population (1950)
2. Population (1960)
3. Labor force eligibles (1955)
4. Average monthly employment (1955)
5. Average annual per capita wages and salaries (1955)
6. Value added by manufacture (1958)

[5] No simple rule for when to stop factoring has been discovered. A standard rule of thumb is that only those factors that are associated with characteristic roots greater than or equal to unity should be retained.

Hence it is reasonable to adopt the following factor analysis model:

$$Z_i = a_{i1}F_1 + \varepsilon_i \qquad (i = 1, 2, \ldots, 6) \tag{8.97}$$

or

$$\underset{6\times 19}{\mathbf{Z}} = \underset{6\times 1}{\mathbf{A}}\ \underset{1\times 19}{\mathbf{F}} + \underset{6\times 19}{\mathbf{E}} \tag{8.98}$$

Using the principal components solution of Subsection 8.4.3 as the initial factorization, we recall (8.74) and obtain the following revised estimates of the six communalities:

$$\begin{matrix} h_1^2 = 0.986 & h_2^2 = 0.990 & h_3^2 = 0.992 \\ h_4^2 = 0.986 & h_5^2 = 0.500 & h_6^2 = 0.968 \end{matrix} \tag{8.99}$$

Next, we factor the "first-round" reduced correlation matrix,

$$\mathbf{R}_r = \begin{bmatrix} 0.986 & 0.994 & 0.998 & 0.995 & 0.647 & 0.979 \\ 0.994 & 0.990 & 0.999 & 0.997 & 0.642 & 0.992 \\ 0.998 & 0.999 & 0.992 & 0.997 & 0.648 & 0.988 \\ 0.995 & 0.997 & 0.997 & 0.986 & 0.619 & 0.994 \\ 0.647 & 0.642 & 0.648 & 0.619 & 0.500 & 0.594 \\ 0.979 & 0.992 & 0.988 & 0.994 & 0.594 & 0.968 \end{bmatrix} \tag{8.100}$$

and obtain the following "second-round" results:

$$\lambda_1 = 5.366 \qquad \mathbf{A} = \begin{bmatrix} 0.996 \\ 0.999 \\ 1.000 \\ 0.996 \\ 0.644 \\ 0.984 \end{bmatrix}$$

$$\begin{matrix} h_1^2 = 0.992 & h_2^2 = 0.998 & h_3^2 = 1.000 \\ h_4^2 = 0.992 & h_5^2 = 0.415 & h_6^2 = 0.968 \end{matrix} \tag{8.101}$$

Continuing in this manner, we ultimately converge to the following communality estimates:

$$\begin{matrix} h_1^2 = 0.960 & h_2^2 = 1.000 & h_3^2 = 1.000 \\ h_4^2 = 0.994 & h_5^2 = 0.399 & h_6^2 = 0.968 \end{matrix} \tag{8.102}$$

and the factor loading matrix

$$\underset{6\times 1}{\mathbf{A}} = \begin{bmatrix} 0.998 \\ 1.000 \\ 1.000 \\ 0.997 \\ 0.632 \\ 0.984 \end{bmatrix} \tag{8.103}$$

The residual matrix $\mathbf{R}_r - \mathbf{AA}'$ appears to be sufficiently close to the null matrix for the factor model not to be rejected.

8.5.3 FACTOR ROTATION

A given correlation matrix can be factored in an infinite number of ways. That is, if we postmultiply the factor loading matrix $\mathbf{A}$ by any conformable orthogonal matrix, $\mathbf{T}$, say, the representation of (8.93) becomes

$$\begin{aligned} \mathbf{R} &= \mathbf{AT}(\mathbf{AT})' + \mathbf{G} \\ &= \mathbf{ATT}'\mathbf{A}' + \mathbf{G} \\ &= \mathbf{AA}' + \mathbf{G} \end{aligned} \tag{8.104}$$

and although the elements of the rotated factor loading matrix differ from those of the original loading matrix, their ability to reproduce the reduced correlation matrix $\mathbf{R}_r$ is unchanged. Hence the question of a "preferred" or "more meaningful" solution always exists and can be answered only on the basis of prespecified criteria.

One such specification is the choice to represent an original set of variables in terms of factors that are determined in sequence, such that each factor accounts for the maximum proportion of the total residual variance at each successive stage. Such a solution, we have already seen, is afforded by a principal factor solution. Once this particular solution has been found, however, it is sometimes desirable to seek a solution that is more easily interpretable in the subject-matter nature of the responses. This search may be carried out subjectively, using a graphical approach, or objectively, using analytical approaches such as the Varimax procedure described by Harman (1967). In most instances, an attempt is made to simplify the structure of each factor by a rotation that forces as many of the column elements of the factor loading matrix as possible to either unity or zero. This simplifies the interpretation of each factor and, in the process, often leads to more meaningful results.

Example. To illustrate factor rotation, we must turn to our principal components solution of the taxonomy problem involving rectangles, because the example involving California regions yielded only a single factor and, therefore, a unique factorization.

Recall the plot of the five variables in the two-dimensional component space that appears in Figure 8.9, and consider a rigid clockwise rotation of the principal component axes through an angle of $\theta = -45°$. This can be carried out by postmultiplying the principal component loading matrix **A** by

$$\mathbf{T} = \begin{bmatrix} \frac{\sqrt{2}}{2} & \frac{\sqrt{2}}{2} \\ -\frac{\sqrt{2}}{2} & \frac{\sqrt{2}}{2} \end{bmatrix}$$

We have, then, the rotated principal component loading matrix

$$\mathbf{AT} = \begin{bmatrix} 0.740 & -0.673 \\ 0.740 & 0.673 \\ 1.000 & 0 \\ 0.957 & -0.290 \\ 0.957 & 0.290 \end{bmatrix} \begin{bmatrix} \frac{\sqrt{2}}{2} & \frac{\sqrt{2}}{2} \\ -\frac{\sqrt{2}}{2} & \frac{\sqrt{2}}{2} \end{bmatrix} = \begin{bmatrix} 0.999 & 0.047 \\ 0.047 & 0.999 \\ 0.707 & 0.707 \\ 0.882 & 0.471 \\ 0.471 & 0.882 \end{bmatrix} \quad (8.105)$$

Observe that the rotated principal components are no longer interpretable as "size" and "shape," but are now very definitely the dimensions "width" and "height." Note, also, that the two characteristic roots associated with the rotated principal components are no longer $\lambda_1 = 3.925$ and $\lambda_2 = 1.075$, but are now $\lambda_1 = \lambda_2 = 2.500$. Thus our rotation has indeed simplified the structure of the two principal components and in the process has provided us with an intuitively more satisfying solution. This rotation also happens to be the Varimax rotation.

8.5.4 FACTOR SCORES

While many applications of factor analysis are concerned only with the resolution of a set of variables in terms of a set of common factors, occasionally it is also desirable to obtain estimates of the scores of the observations on the set of theoretical factors.

For a given set of observations on the m variates Z_i, we cannot estimate the values of the p factors F_k and of the m residuals ε_i, since there are many more hypothetical variates than observed ones. However, if the true values of the observations on the F_k were known, we could, as in linear regression, choose their estimates $\hat{F}_k$ in such a way as to minimize, for each value of k, the sum of squares

$$\sum_{j=1}^{m} (F_{kj} - \hat{F}_{kj})^2 \tag{8.106}$$

where

$$\hat{F}_k = \beta_{k1}Z_1 + \beta_{k2}Z_2 + \cdots + \beta_{km}Z_m \qquad (k = 1, 2, \ldots, p)$$

The coefficients of the linear regression could be derived using the covariances between the F_k and the Z_i, and the sample variance-covariance matrix of the Z_i. Although we may use the sample correlation matrix $\mathbf{R}$ for the latter, the former cannot be obtained in the usual way. However, reasonable estimates are provided by elements of

$$\mathbf{a}_i' = [a_{1i} \quad a_{2i} \cdots a_{mi}]$$

the ith row of the transpose of the factor loading matrix.

We may, therefore, estimate the F_k by

$$\hat{F}_k = \mathbf{a}_i'\mathbf{R}^{-1}\mathbf{z}_j \qquad (k = 1, 2, \ldots, p) \tag{8.107}$$

where $\mathbf{z}_j$ is the column vector of standardized scores associated with the jth observation. Harman (1967) calls this the *complete estimation method* of obtaining factor scores.

We may express (8.107) in matrix form as

$$\underset{p\times 1}{\hat{\mathbf{f}}} = \underset{p\times m}{\mathbf{A}'} \ \underset{m\times m}{\mathbf{R}^{-1}} \ \underset{m\times 1}{\mathbf{z}_j} \tag{8.108}$$

or, for all n observations, as

$$\underset{p\times n}{\hat{\mathbf{F}}} = \underset{p\times m}{\mathbf{A}'} \ \underset{m\times m}{\mathbf{R}^{-1}} \ \underset{m\times n}{\mathbf{Z}} \tag{8.109}$$

Example. To illustrate the calculation of factor scores, let us apply (8.109) to our regionalization problem involving California's 19 SEA's:

$$\begin{aligned}\underset{1\times 19}{\hat{\mathbf{F}}} &= \underset{1\times 6}{\mathbf{A}'}\underset{6\times 6}{\mathbf{R}^{-1}}\underset{6\times 19}{\mathbf{Z}} \\ &= [1.269 \ -0.877 \ -0.333 \ -0.528 \ -0.263 \quad 3.812 \quad 0.434 \\ &\qquad 0.231 \ -0.261 \ -0.241 \ -0.505 \ -0.256 \ -0.166 \\ &\qquad -0.384 \ -0.421 \ -0.424 \ -0.282 \\ &\qquad -0.330 \ -0.475]\end{aligned} \tag{8.110}$$

8.5.5 APPLICATION: THE FUNDAMENTAL DIMENSIONS OF URBAN LAND DEVELOPMENT

Patterns of urban growth and the basic forces that influence their development over time have been the focus of many research efforts over the past twenty years. In particular, research carried out at the University of North

Carolina's Center for Urban and Regional Studies has taken on such an orientation during the past decade [Chapin and Weiss (1962), (1965)]. These studies have viewed the land development pattern of a city, at any moment in time, as the physical resultant of the historical accumulation of a sequence of private and public decisions and actions of individuals and groups. This approach has led to the definition of two classes of decisions: *primary* and *secondary*. Primary decisions are a class of major preconditioning actions, such as the location decision of a new highway or the extension of water and sewerage facilities into an area. These set into motion a myriad of minor secondary decisions, such as the decision to build a home at a particular site, and thereby produce the aggregate land development pattern of an urban area.

In this section, we describe the results of a factorization of a set of variables that measure certain key features of land development, into a smaller subset of fundamental dimensions which underlie them. The data used for this analysis were collected by the U.N.C.'s Center for Urban and Regional Studies during various studies of factors influencing land development. The operational definitions of the variables and the analyses carried out on them are described elsewhere [for example, Chapin and Weiss (1962)] and are therefore omitted here.

Briefly, the city of Greensboro, North Carolina, was gridded into 3,980 squares, 1,000 feet on a side. These cells constituted the basic units of observation and analysis. The "high-value corner" of Greensboro was selected as the origin of a coordinate system, and a unique pair of coordinates was assigned to each cell. After variables describing locational and areal measures were defined, various multiple regression analyses were performed in an attempt to assess the relative importance of each variable as a predictor of a set of dependent variables.

The reduced correlation matrix in Figure 8.13 is a by-product of the above-described analyses. A total of 23 variables and their respective intercorrelations are presented, and the highest correlation coefficient among those associated with each variable is taken to be that variable's communality estimate. The data set consists of a composite of 1926, 1948, and 1960 variables, arranged in the following order:

- X_1 Total land in urban use, 1960
- X_2 Dwelling density, 1960
- X_3 Residential land in urban use, 1960
- X_4 Marginal land not in urban use, 1948
- X_5 Travel distance to nearest major street element, 1960 (tenths of a mile)

X_6 Availability of sewerage, 1948
X_7 Distance to elementary school, 1960 (tenths of a mile)
X_8 Zoning protection, 1948
X_9 Assessed value, 1948
X_{10} Accessibility to work areas, 1960
X_{11} Nonwhite areas, 1948
X_{12} Blighted areas, 1948
X_{13} Total travel distance to high value corner, 1960 (tenths of a mile)
X_{14} Mixed uses, 1960
X_{15} Distance to playground or recreation area, 1948 (tenths of a mile)
X_{16} Distance to shopping area, 1948 (tenths of a mile)
X_{17} Residential amenity, 1960
X_{18} Residential amenity, raw scores, 1960 (000–300)
X_{19} Travel time from radial highway, 1960 (tenths of a minute)
X_{20} Total travel time from high value corner, 1960 (tenths of a minute)
X_{21} Change in total travel time from high value corner, 1948–60 (tenths of minute)
X_{22} Total marginal land, 1926
X_{23} Accessibility to work areas, graphic method raw scores (00–27)

The factorization of the 23×23 reduced correlation matrix in Figure 8.11 produces 23 factors with characteristic roots that range from a high of 9.266 to a low of -0.230. Only five of these, however, are greater than unity, and a Varimax rotation of these was carried out. Table 8.5 presents the Varimax rotated factor pattern.

The first factor, which accounts for 33.3 percent of the total common factor variance, is very definitely an *accessibility* factor. The high factor loadings consistently exhibit the dimension of accessibility, both in travel time and distance, to various urban functions. A subset of medium loadings, by such variables as *total land in urban use* and *availability of sewerage*, are consistent with the interpretation of this factor in that high values on the variables of this subset are associated with high values on accessibility.

The second factor contains no single high factor loading but instead exhibits many medium-sized loadings on variables such as *total land in urban use*, *dwelling density*, *availability of sewerage*, *zoning protection*, *assessed value*, *nonwhite areas*, and *blighted areas*. Thus it appears to be measuring the degree of *urbanism* present in each cell. The urbanism factor accounts for 22.0 percent of the total common factor variance.

Finally, the third, fourth, and fifth factors are *doublet* factors, and their interpretation is straightforward. Doublet factors are defined by the very strong loadings of two variables, other loadings being essentially zero.

0.7952	0.6079	0.7952	−0.3377	−0.3843	0.6551	−0.5128	0.5679	0.5908	0.6387	0.3136	0.3571
0.6079	0.6079	0.6033	−0.2395	−0.3099	0.5700	−0.4160	0.4747	0.5725	0.5380	0.4265	0.4611
0.7952	0.6033	0.7952	−0.2985	−0.3191	0.5372	−0.4467	0.5163	0.4890	0.5315	0.2786	0.3352
−0.3377	−0.2395	−0.2985	0.8515	0.2076	−0.1960	0.2411	−0.1670	−0.1747	−0.1233	−0.1060	−0.1251
−0.3843	−0.3099	−0.3191	0.2076	0.7351	−0.2915	0.2920	−0.2429	−0.2557	−0.3450	−0.1394	−0.1858
0.6551	0.5700	0.5372	−0.1960	−0.2915	0.8194	−0.4496	0.8194	0.6779	0.6748	0.3902	0.4362
−0.5128	−0.4160	−0.4467	0.2411	0.2920	−0.4496	0.5500	−0.3793	−0.3390	−0.5500	−0.2212	−0.2625
0.5679	0.4747	0.5163	−0.1670	−0.2429	0.8194·	−0.3793	0.8194	0.5595	0.5881	0.3650	0.3563
0.5908	0.5725	0.4890	−0.1747	−0.2557	0.6779	−0.3390	0.5595	0.6779	0.5470	0.2672	0.3460
0.6387	0.5380	0.5315	−0.1233	−0.3450	0.6748	0.5500	0.5881	0.5470	0.9395	0.3351	0.3798
0.3136	0.4265	0.2786	−0.1060	−0.1394	0.3902	−0.2212	0.3650	0.2672	0.3351	0.6112	0.6112
0.3571	0.4611	0.3352	−0.1251	−0.1858	0.4362	−0.2625	0.3563	0.3460	0.3798	0.6112	0.6112
−0.6222	−0.5462	−0.5122	0.1591	0.4873	−0.6461	0.5296	−0.5580	−0.5429	−0.9395	−0.3413	−0.3844
0.6087	0.5446	0.3632	−0.1956	−0.3155	0.4706	−0.3409	0.3321	0.4959	0.4442	0.2786	0.3351
−0.6151	−0.4752	−0.5065	0.1609	0.3042	−0.5832	0.5214	−0.4843	−0.4518	−0.8944	−0.2823	−0.3245
−0.5515	−0.4435	−0.4749	0.0874	0.2186	−0.5158	0.4906	−0.4441	−0.4061	−0.8191	−0.2428	−0.2929
0.1995	0.0329	0.1672	0.0064	0.1045	0.1487	−0.0990	0.1352	0.1477	0.1157	−0.0789	−0.0673
0.1849	0.0118	0.1475	0.0024	0.1234	0.1339	−0.0654	0.1282	0.1297	0.0806	−0.1023	−0.0933
−0.3387	−0.3004	−0.3042	0.2586	0.7351	−0.2284	0.1958	−0.1618	−0.2111	−0.2038	−0.1368	−0.1804
−0.6019	−0.5312	−0.4878	0.1917	0.4558	−0.6330	0.4603	−0.5380	−0.5507	−0.8083	−0.3186	−0.3610
−0.0370	−0.0127	−0.0130	0.0788	0.0562	−0.0085	0.0206	−0.0333	−0.0033	0.0527	−0.0315	−0.0326
−0.1411	−0.1324	−0.1801	0.8515	0.1445	−0.0087	0.1144	0.0174	−0.0841	0.0203	−0.0443	−0.0689
0.6740	0.5617	0.5282	−0.1729	−0.3309	0.7766	−0.5443	0.6657	0.5868	0.8469	0.3613	0.4024

Source: Center for Urban and Regional Studies, University of North Carolina at Chapel Hill.

Figure 8.13. Correlation Matrix of Variables Measuring Factors Influencing Land Development

−0.6222	0.6087	−0.6151	−0.5515	0.1995	0.1849	−0.3387	−0.6019	−0.0370	−0.1411	0.6740
−0.5462	0.5446	−0.4752	−0.4435	0.0329	0.0118	−0.3004	−0.5312	−0.0127	−0.1324	0.5617
−0.5122	0.3632	−0.5065	−0.4749	0.1672	0.1475	−0.3042	−0.4878	−0.0130	−0.1801	0.5282
0.1591	−0.1956	0.1609	0.0874	0.0064	0.0024	0.2586	0.1917	0.0788	0.8515	−0.1729
0.4873	−0.3155	0.3042	0.2186	0.1045	0.1234	0.7351	0.4558	0.0562	0.1445	−0.3309
−0.6461	0.4706	−0.5832	−0.5158	0.1487	0.1339	−0.2284	−0.6330	−0.0085	−0.0087	0.7766
−0.5296	−0.3409	0.5214	0.4906	−0.0990	−0.0654	0.1958	0.4603	0.0206	0.1144	−0.5443
−0.5580	0.3321	−0.4843	−0.4441	0.1352	0.1282	−0.1618	−0.5380	−0.0333	0.0174	0.6657
−0.5429	0.4959	−0.4518	−0.4061	0.1477	0.1297	−0.2111	−0.5507	−0.0033	−0.0841	0.5868
−0.9395	0.4442	−0.8944	−0.8191	0.1157	0.0806	−0.2038	−0.8083	0.0527	0.0203	0.8469
−0.3413	0.2786	−0.2823	−0.2428	−0.0789	−0.1023	−0.1368	−0.3186	−0.0315	−0.0443	0.3613
−0.3844	0.3351	−0.3245	−0.2929	−0.0673	−0.0933	−0.1804	−0.3610	−0.0326	−0.0689	0.4024
0.9395	−0.4572	0.8388	0.7224	−0.0468	−0.0038	0.3468	0.8503	0.0229	0.0261	−0.8191
−0.4572	0.6087	−0.4227	−0.3571	0.0525	0.3994	−0.2944	−0.4504	−0.0398	−0.0889	0.4944
0.8388	−0.4227	0.8944	0.8262	−0.1009	−0.0839	0.1670	0.7052	−0.0224	0.0199	−0.7586
0.7224	−0.3571	0.8262	0.8262	−0.1373	−0.1175	0.1431	0.6459	−0.1765	−0.0367	−0.6492
−0.0468	0.0525	−0.1009	−0.1373	0.9839	0.9839	0.0882	−0.1035	−0.1238	0.0543	0.1033
−0.0038	0.3994	−0.0839	−0.1175	0.9839	0.9839	0.0982	−0.0744	−0.1340	0.0527	0.0664
0.3468	−0.2944	0.1670	0.1431	0.0882	0.0982	0.7351	0.4244	0.0685	0.2060	−0.2029
0.8503	−0.4504	0.7052	0.6459	−0.1035	−0.0744	0.4244	0.8503	0.3537	0.0585	−0.7365
0.0229	−0.0398	−0.0224	−0.1765	−0.1238	−0.1340	0.0685	0.3537	0.3537	0.0537	0.0336
0.0261	−0.0889	0.0199	−0.0367	0.0543	0.0527	0.2060	0.0585	0.0537	0.8515	−0.0072
−0.8191	0.4944	−0.7586	−0.6492	0.1033	0.0664	−0.2029	−0.7365	0.0336	−0.0072	0.8469

Source: Center for Urban and Regional Studies, University of North Carolina at Chapel Hill.

Figure 8.13. Correlation Matrix of Variables Measuring Factors Influencing Land Development (*Continued*).

Table 8.5 Principal Factor Pattern for 23 Land Development Variables

Variable	Common Factors				
	1 Acc.	2 Urb.	3 R.A.	4 M.L.	5 A.M.T.
X_1	0.529	0.535	0.206	−0.213	−0.244
X_2	0.370	0.613	0.017	−0.136	−0.194
X_3	0.429	0.496	0.165	−0.245	−0.188
X_4	−0.102	−0.133	−0.010	0.898	0.125
X_5	−0.290	−0.115	0.129	0.078	0.764
X_6	0.509	0.677	0.125	−0.011	−0.084
X_7	−0.527	−0.263	−0.052	0.163	0.106
X_8	0.427	0.637	0.120	0.008	−0.031
X_9	0.392	0.573	0.148	−0.064	−0.136
X_{10}	0.916	0.320	0.013	0.026	−0.058
X_{11}	0.110	0.641	−0.152	−0.002	−0.010
X_{12}	0.156	0.650	−0.137	−0.023	−0.054
X_{13}	−0.859	−0.310	0.051	−0.009	0.253
X_{14}	0.309	0.458	0.232	−0.085	−0.278
X_{15}	−0.897	−0.222	−0.016	0.042	0.017
X_{16}	−0.845	−0.185	−0.041	−0.005	−0.053
X_{17}	0.109	−0.025	0.954	0.022	0.050
X_{18}	0.055	0.009	0.998	0.023	0.011
X_{19}	−0.142	−0.124	0.096	0.141	0.804
X_{20}	−0.705	−0.338	−0.059	0.008	0.387
X_{21}	0.074	−0.035	−0.161	0.024	0.235
X_{22}	0.027	−0.016	0.043	0.910	0.095
X_{23}	0.744	0.488	0.035	−0.010	−0.069
Percent of Total Common Factor Variance Accounted for by Factor					
	33.3	22.0	12.4	10.3	10.1

Source: Calculated using the data in Figure 8.13. Computed by Michael Fajans.

They, of course, are interpreted with reference to their respective doublet variables, which in this case measure:

(a) *residential amenity;*
(b) *marginal land; and*
(c) *accessibility to major thoroughfares.*

Together, these three factors account for 32.8 percent of the residual common factor variance. Thus our five-factor solution accounts for 88.1 percent of the total common factor variance.

Having resolved a set of 23 variables linearly in terms of five factors, it would be logical to follow through with a calculation of the scores of each of the 3,980 cells on these five factors. This would reduce a 23 $\times$ 3,980 data matrix (that is, the values of each of 3,980 cells on 23 variables) to a 5 $\times$ 3,980 matrix (that is, the scores of each of 3,980 cells on five factors). Putting it in another way, five maps of the city, each graphically showing every cell's score on each of the factors, could do the job of 23 maps, each showing every cell's value on each of the variables.

From such information, one could derive many interesting generalizations by comparing the factor scores of particular categories of cells. For example, a sample of cells drawn from slum areas might exhibit very high scores on the *accessibility* factor and possibly low scores on the *residential amenity* factor. A selection of cells from industrial areas would probably produce high scores on the *accessibility to major thoroughfares* factor and low scores on the *marginal land* factor.

EXERCISES

1. Recall that the first principal component extracted from the correlation matrix of the numerical example illustrated in Figure 8.6,

$$\mathbf{R} = \begin{bmatrix} 1 & \frac{1}{2} \\ \frac{1}{2} & 1 \end{bmatrix}$$

accounted for $\lambda_1/m = \frac{3}{2}/2 = \frac{3}{4}$ of the total sample variance and was defined as the following linear combination of the original standardized variables:

$$F_1 = \frac{1}{\sqrt{3}}[Z_1 + Z_2]$$

(a) Extract the first principal component from the correlation matrix

$$\mathbf{R} = \begin{bmatrix} 1 & \frac{1}{2} & \frac{1}{2} \\ \frac{1}{2} & 1 & \frac{1}{2} \\ \frac{1}{2} & \frac{1}{2} & 1 \end{bmatrix}$$

Show that it accounts for $\lambda_1/m = 2/3$ of the total sample variance and is defined as

$$F_1 = \frac{1}{\sqrt{6}}[Z_1 + Z_2 + Z_3]$$

Show that the remaining two characteristic roots are both equal to $\frac{1}{2}$ and that, therefore, each of them accounts for an equal proportion of the residual variance.

(b) Extract the first principal component from the correlation matrix

$$\mathbf{R} = \begin{bmatrix} 1 & r \\ r & 1 \end{bmatrix}$$

Show that it accounts for $\lambda_1/m = [1 + (m - 1)r]/m$ of the total sample variance and is defined as

$$F_1 = \frac{1}{\sqrt{m[1 + (m - 1)r]}} [Z_1 + Z_2]$$

Show that the second characteristic root is equal to $1 - r$.

(c) Extract the first principal component from the correlation matrix

$$\mathbf{R} = \begin{bmatrix} 1 & r & r \\ r & 1 & r \\ r & r & 1 \end{bmatrix}$$

Show that it accounts for $\lambda_1/m = [1 + (m - 1)r]/m$ of the total sample variance and is defined as

$$F_1 = \frac{1}{\sqrt{m[1 + (m - 1)r]}} [Z_1 + Z_2 + Z_3]$$

Show that the remaining two characteristic roots are both equal to $1 - r$ and that, therefore, each of them accounts for an equal proportion of the residual variance.

(d) Discuss your results, and generalize them to the case where m is any positive integer.

2. Extract the principal components from the correlation matrix

$$\mathbf{R} = \begin{bmatrix} 1 & \frac{4}{5} & \frac{3}{5} & \frac{3}{5} \\ \frac{4}{5} & 1 & \frac{24}{25} & 0 \\ \frac{3}{5} & \frac{24}{25} & 1 & -\frac{7}{25} \\ \frac{3}{5} & 0 & -\frac{7}{25} & 1 \end{bmatrix}$$

and show that the first principal component accounts for 65 percent of the total sample variance.

Express the variables in terms of the components, and interpret the components in terms of the four variables; for example, which variables define the first principal component?

3. In Subsection 8.4.1, the 10 rectangles were visually grouped into the 3×3 classification system that appears in Table 8.3. Repeat this classification of the rectangles by developing a grouping algorithm that operates on the matrix of distance statistics for all pairs of observations. That is, use the Euclidean distance between the observations as a measure of their similarity, and group the rectangles into categories according to their degree of similarity. [The paper by Lankford (1969) is a particularly useful reference for this problem.]

4. Add the following data to Table 8.4, and extract and interpret the first two principal components that are present in the eight variables:

State Economic Area	Land in Farms in Acres (1959)	Total Land Area in Acres (1959)
SMSA's		
A. S.F.-Oakland	1,391,577	2,120,320
B. San Jose	529,489	833,280
C. Sacramento	546,988	629,120
D. Stockton	901,760	924,893
E. Fresno	2,286,381	3,816,960
F. L.A.-Long Beach	824,700	3,098,880
G. San Diego	833,778	2,723,200
H. San Bernardino	1,729,969	17,473,280
J. Bakersfield	3,566,553	5,217,280
K. Santa Barbara	937,523	1,752,320
Non-SMSA's		
1. Northern Coast	2,134,630	5,976,960
2. No. Central Coast	1,059,959	1,495,680
3. So. Central Coast	4,159,638	5,424,000
4. Sacramento Valley	4,298,874	6,007,680
5. No. San Joaquin Valley	1,816,899	2,228,480
6. So. San Joaquin Valley	2,908,171	5,361,280
7. Ventura	449,265	1,184,640
8. Imperial Valley	497,802	2,741,760
9. Sierra	5,990,859	31,219,840

Compute principal component scores and group the 19 SEA's into homogeneous areas. Finally, use the reproduced communalities as revised communality estimates, iterate until they converge, and carry out a factor analysis of the same data. Discuss and contrast both sets of solutions.

5. Carry out a principal components analysis of the mortality data presented in Tables 3.5 and 3.6. Combine the male and female patterns of mortality to obtain 24 observations, and consider the 19 age groups as variables. Interpret the principal components, and group the 24 observations into homogeneous categories.

6. The discussion in this chapter of principal components analysis and factor analysis has focused on the underlying relationships that are present in a set of correlated variables. This form of analysis is referred to as R-mode analysis. An alternative formulation, known as Q-mode analysis, is one in which the mathematical operations are identical to those used in R-mode analysis, but the correlation matrix that is factored is different [Gower (1966)]. Instead of factoring the $m \times m$ correlation matrix that describes the relationships between the m variables, we factor the $n \times n$ correlation matrix that describes the relationships between the n observations.

Consider, for example, the 19 × 19 matrix of migration flows that appears in Figure 3.7. An *R*-mode analysis of this matrix would treat the origins (rows) as variables and the destinations (columns) as observations. The correlation matrix, in this case, would indicate the similarity of the origins with regard to the destinations of their out-migrants, and a principal components or a factor analysis of this matrix would reveal similar information. Thus, after obtaining the principal component or factor scores, one could group areas that were homogeneous with respect to the destinations of their out-migrants.

A *Q*-mode analysis of the migration matrix, on the other hand, would treat destinations as variables and origins as observations. What would the correlations in the correlation matrix indicate in this case?

Factor analyze the migration data in Figure 3.7, using first the *R*-mode and then the *Q*-mode analysis. Compute factor scores and group SEA's according to:

(a) similarity of destinations of out-migrant flows, and

(b) similarity of origins of in-migrant flows.

Delete the diagonal elements of the migration matrix prior to computing the correlation matrix, and use unities as the first estimates of communalities. Iterate until the communality estimates converge. Discuss and interpret your results.

7. Use principal components analysis to identify the basic structural dimensions of the 1940 and 1950 regional highway networks around Sao Paulo, as described in Table 6.1. Then group the 15 nodes into clusters that display similar patterns or profiles of connectivity.

8. Regression on principal components rather than on the original variables has been recommended as a useful technique in exploratory statistical research [Massy (1965)]. Extract the first principal component from the correlation matrix associated with the six independent variables in Tables 3.3 and 3.4. Compute the component scores of the observations and regress housing expenditures on this principal component. Is there a significant difference between the expenditure patterns of single-family residents and apartment dwellers? Is there a significant increase in the r^2 if the second principal component is introduced into the regression model? Discuss and interpret your results.

9. Write a short essay comparing linear regression and factor analysis models. Contrast their characteristics, purposes, and limitations. Illustrate your arguments with the data on Greensboro's land development pattern that appear in Subsection 8.5.5.

10. Note that significant differences exist between the initial communality estimates in Figure 8.13 and those reproduced by the factor pattern in Table 8.5. Insert the reproduced communalities into the diagonal of the correlation matrix in Figure 8.13, and refactor this matrix. Continue this "round-by-round" process until the communality estimates converge. Contrast the final factor pattern with the one in Table 8.5. Are the factors the same in both cases?

REFERENCES AND SELECTED READINGS

THEORY

Anderson, T. W. *Introduction to Multivariate Statistical Analysis.* New York: John Wiley & Sons, 1958.

Gere, J. M. and W. Weaver, Jr. *Matrix Algebra for Engineers*. Princeton, N. J.: D. van Nostrand, 1965.

Gower, J. C. "Some Distance Properties of Latent Root and Vector Methods Used in Multivariate Analysis," *Biometrika*, **LIII**: 3, 1966, 325–338.

Kendall, M. G. *A Course in Multivariate Analysis*. New York: Hafner, 1957.

Morrison, D. F. *Multivariate Statistical Methods*. New York: McGraw-Hill, 1967.

APPLICATION: REGIONALIZATION

Berry, B. J. L. "Basic Patterns of Economic Development," in *Atlas of Economic Development*, by N. Ginsburg. Chicago: The University of Chicago Press, Part VII, pp. 110–119, 1961.

——— "A Synthesis of Formal and Functional Regions Using a General Field Theory of Spatial Behavior," in *Spatial Analysis: A Reader in Statistical Geography*, ed. by B. J. L. Berry and D. F. Marble. Englewood Cliffs, N. J.: Prentice-Hall, 1968, pp. 419–428.

Kendall, M. G. "The Geographical Distribution of Crop Productivity in England," *Journal of the Royal Statistical Society*, **CII**, 1939, 21–48.

Lankford, P. M. "Regionalization: Theory and Alternative Algorithms," *Geographical Analysis*, **I**: 2, 1969, 196–212.

Massy, W. F. "Principal Components Regression in Exploratory Statistical Research," *Journal of the American Statistical Association*, **LX**: 309, 1965, 234–256.

Moser, C. A. and W. Scott. *British Towns*. Edinburgh and London: Oliver and Boyd, 1961.

Schmid, C. F. and K. Tagashira. "Ecological and Demographic Indices: A Methodological Analysis," *Demography*, **II**, 1965, 194–211.

APPLICATION: FACTOR ANALYSIS

Almendinger, V. V. "The Application of Factor Analysis to Municipal Finance," in *1400 Governments*, by R. C. Wood. Garden City, N.Y.: Doubleday, Anchor Books Edition, 1964, pp. 235–253.

Armstrong, J. S. "Derivation of Theory by Means of Factor Analysis or Tom Swift and His Electric Factor Analysis Machine," *The American Statistician*, **XXI**: 6, 1967, 17–21.

Chapin, F. S., Jr. and S. F. Weiss. *Factors Influencing Land Development*. Chapel Hill, N.C.: Center for Urban and Regional Studies, University of North Carolina, 1962.

——— *Some Input Refinements for a Residential Model*. Chapel Hill, N.C.: Center for Urban and Regional Studies, University of North Carolina, 1965.

Harman, H. H. *Modern Factor Analysis*, 2d. Ed. Chicago: University of Chicago Press, 1967.

Lawley, D. N. and A. E. Maxwell. *Factor Analysis as a Statistical Method*. London: Butterworths, 1963.

Index

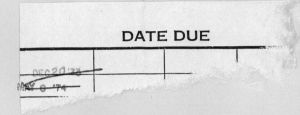